Law and the
Life Insurance Contract

THE IRWIN SERIES IN INSURANCE

EDITORS

EDISON L. BOWERS
The Ohio State University

DAVIS W. GREGG
The American College of Life Underwriters

JANICE E. GREIDER, LL.B., F.L.M.I., C.L.U.
Associate Counsel, State Farm Life Insurance Company

and

WILLIAM T. BEADLES, D.B.A., C.L.U.
Professor of Insurance, Illinois Wesleyan University

LAW AND THE LIFE INSURANCE CONTRACT

1960 · RICHARD D. IRWIN, INC.
Homewood, Illinois

First Printing, September, 1960

Library of Congress Catalogue Card No. 60-15919

PRINTED IN THE UNITED STATES OF AMERICA

To
Morris G. Fuller, C.L.U.

Preface

THIS BOOK grew out of the need for an up-to-date presentation of the law of the life insurance contract in terms that would be understandable to the person whose principal interest is life insurance generally, rather than the law. To that end, we have avoided, as much as possible, the language of law and lawyers and have made a definite effort to explain legal concepts in simple, everyday English. For the sake of precision, however, and also to acquaint the reader with some of the language of the law, we have incorporated many legal expressions parenthetically. We hope this will have meaning to the reader who has some legal background and that at the same time our nonlegal explanations will convey to the nonlawyer some of the connotations the legal terms have acquired through many years of use.

In spite of this emphasis upon simple language, some legal terms and phrases have been used again and again. This is because words such as waiver and estoppel, consideration, constructive delivery, etc., have an integral place in life insurance as well as in the law. Thus the person contemplating a career in life insurance will need to make them a part of his working vocabulary even though he does not intend to become a lawyer, just as he must have a working acquaintance with such concepts as reserves, net premiums, and loadings, although he does not intend to become an actuary.

Most of the illustrations have been taken from the law itself—the cases. When we speak of waiver, we show how the concept has been used in an actual case. When we discuss the problem of possible testamentary disposition, we show how it has actually arisen and how it has been resolved. The student is thus given a first-hand introduction to legal thinking and legal tradition.

The book is organized on a chronological basis in order to follow the different stages in the life of the contract. Legal solutions differ by reason of the way a problem arises, when it arises, and last, but never least, the jurisdiction in which it arises. We hope that some of this ever-changing, evolving pattern will be suggested by our combination of explanation, illustration, and repetition as the contract is formed and tested, as it operates during the lifetime of the insured, and at last as the benefit is paid.

We have had the most generous co-operation of so many people that it is truly impossible to mention everyone by name. We thank them all, but particularly Dr. Davis W. Gregg, President of the American College of Life Underwriters, Dr. Edison Bowers, Chairman of the Department of Economics, The Ohio State University, and Mr. Werner Lederer, Associate Educational Director of the Life Office Management Association, all of whom carefully reviewed the book while it was in preparation and helped with many valuable suggestions. Special thanks go to Mr. Paul L. Wise, Assistant Counsel of The Fidelity Mutual Life Insurance Company, who reviewed the manuscript from the point of view of a life insurance lawyer and made numerous and most helpful suggestions.

At State Farm Life Insurance Company we have had the constant encouragement and assistance of many different people. We especially thank Mr. George R. Davies, Vice President and Counsel, for his continued interest and advice, as well as Mr. Walter G. Nelson, Assistant Counsel, Mr. James Spellman, Actuary, and many others, specifically including the splendid secretarial staff, Mrs. Margaret Williamson, Mrs. Ida Cade, Mrs. Evelyn Williams, and Mrs. Luann Huth.

JANICE E. GREIDER
WILLIAM T. BEADLES

BLOOMINGTON, ILLINOIS
July, 1960

Table of Contents

APPENDIXES

INDEXES

PART I

Introduction

CHAPTER I

Insurance and Law

Insurance Affected with a Public Interest

Size and Importance of the Industry. More than 70 per cent of the people of this country own some form of life insurance. They pay more than $15 billion annually in premiums to life insurance companies, whose combined assets are now in excess of $100 billion. A business of such size, with personal significance for so many people, obviously constitutes one of the most important private financial institutions in the country.

This size and importance are recognized by both courts and legislatures, which say that insurance is, for that reason, a business "affected with a public interest." This means that it is so significant and of such importance to so many people that it is in the public interest to make sure the great power exercised by insurance companies is not abused. The safekeeping of policyholders' funds; qualified, ethical agents; adequate margins of safety; contracts which safeguard policyholders' rights—all these and almost every other aspect of the insurance business have been acknowledged as proper subjects for regulation. To this end proposed new insurance measures are introduced into the state legislatures every year and enacted into law in an almost steady stream.

Regulatory Legislation. Regulatory laws of this kind are said to be enacted under the "police power," which is a basic term in the language of government signifying the essence of the governing power. By virtue of the police power, the conduct of individuals and the ways in which property may be used are subject to regulation whenever it seems necessary for the public good. Insurance has many times been held to be a proper subject for regulation and control under the police power. For this reason regulatory statutes comprise a large segment of insurance law.

3

Law and the Life Insurance Contract

Some insurance laws relate specifically to the life insurance contract. Thus, in one sense, the law of the life insurance contract is a part of insurance law although it is not, in any sense, limited to it. Statutes must always be read and interpreted in the light of a broad base of general law, and in this case the "broad base" relates to the general law of contracts.

A study of life insurance contract law is further broadened by the fact that one must have some understanding of insurance itself. The life insurance contract is first and most significantly an insurance device. For this reason, a general understanding of the principles underlying insurance is equally as essential in considering the life insurance contract as an acquaintance with specific legal principles.

Fundamentally, the law of the life insurance contract rests upon principles that were developed in connection with contracts in general long before the life insurance contract had its beginning. In many respects it follows the same paths and is governed by these general rules and principles just as if it were any other kind of contract. Nevertheless, the special purposes of the contract, the social and economic aspects of the insurance business, and the highly specialized nature of the relationship of the insurance company on the one hand, and the individual insured on the other, have resulted in the development of a very large body of law specifically related to the life insurance contract alone. In this body of law generally recognized principles of contract law have been greatly modified, tempered in some instances, highly developed in others, all in the interest of policyholders and beneficiaries.

At the same time our study cannot be confined to contract and insurance law. Insurance companies are corporate in organization and thus transact their business through agents. For this reason the law of the life insurance contract is strongly affected by the law of agency. Rights under a life insurance policy constitute a kind of property. Therefore, the law of property often is involved. Lastly, forming the life insurance contract is an intricate and important business, and the minds of many people have been busy devising new approaches to it. For this reason the law of the life insurance contract has traveled at times and for short distances also with the law of *torts*. (This is simply the field of law which is concerned with actionable civil wrongs, compensable in damages.)

In a beginning study it is enough to have some acquaintance with the major areas of law to which the law of the life insurance contract is related. One needs some understanding of the idea of law itself and some notion of how our courts are organized and the way they operate.

This chapter is a brief survey of what law is and where it is found, how our courts are organized, and some of the basic procedures that are involved in instituting and trying a case at law.

LAW AND WHERE IT IS FOUND

What Law Is

In the general sense, law is a system of principles and rules of human conduct which are in the nature of commandments and comprise a definite and enforceable standard of conduct. A law is a specific rule or requirement (a *statute*, the lawyer says) laid down by a legislative body. However, in the general sense "law" is much more than a mere collection or even a system of individual statutes. It includes the broad general philosophies and principles of constitutional law, specific agreements embodied in treaties between nations, decisions of state and federal courts, and general principles of custom and public policy.

How Law Is Classified

Public and Private Law. For purposes of discussion or study, law may be variously classified. It is sometimes divided into public and private law. In that sense, public law is law which deals with the state in one way or another. Thus it would include such areas as constitutional law, administrative law, criminal law. Private law, on the other hand, relates to the rights and duties of one individual with respect to another. Contract law, the law of torts, and the law of domestic relations are examples of private law.

Substantive and Adjective Law. Another common classification divides the law into substantive and adjective law. Substantive law goes to the substance of a question and thus includes the law of rights and obligations. Adjective law, on the other hand, describes the ways in which these rights and obligations can be enforced. Figuratively, adjective law modifies the substantive law as an adjective does a noun. In other words, adjective law is the law of procedure—the way one proceeds to enforce his rights by judicial process.

Where Law Is Found

Numerous Sources. It is often necessary to consult a number of sources before one can determine the applicable law on any given subject. Constitutions must be examined, as well as the statutes enacted by the various legislatures and reports of decisions of the courts. Often, too, treaties between nations, executive orders and proclamations, as well as administrative regulations, have an important bearing on the question under consideration.

The constitutions and statutes of the federal government and the governments of the various states are separately compiled and published, as are the reports of appellate courts. As a matter of fact, the student of almost any phase of the law will find numerous references to reports of court decisions, which are ordinarily expressed in a standard form. For instance, in the case of *United States* v. *South-Eastern Underwriters Association* (64 Sup. Ct. 1162), the citation simply means that the case will be found in Volume 64 of the United States Supreme Court decisions, at page 1162.

Lawyers also make frequent use of various treatises on the law such as *Williston on Contracts, Vance on Insurance, Bogert on Trusts,* and of "Restatements of the Law" prepared by the American Law Institute, to name only a very few of the general references available. A study of any part of the law requires some acquaintance with these different sources of the law and a knowledge of the relationship which each bears to the others.

THE CONSTITUTIONS

What a Constitution Is

As we think of it in this country, a constitution is a written expression of the broad general principles which form the legal foundation of our government. By contrast with statutes, which are subject to relatively frequent changes, a constitution tends to be permanent rather than temporary in form, general rather than specific.

A Twofold Purpose. A constitution has a twofold purpose. On the one hand, it describes the structure of the government, defines the extent of its powers, and outlines the principles on which it is to operate. On the other, it establishes a system of safeguards and guarantees of such basic human rights as freedom of speech, freedom of worship, and the other great freedoms enumerated in the federal Constitution (the Bill of Rights).

The Federal Constitution

The Supreme Law of the Land. In the United States there are two kinds of constitutions to be considered—the constitutions of the various individual states and the Constitution of the United States. In areas involving powers delegated to the federal government, the federal Constitution is the supreme law of the land. In other areas the constitution of the state in which the problem arises will ordinarily govern. Many questions are of such a nature, however, that it is extremely difficult to say whether they are subject to powers delegated to the federal government. The power of the states to regulate the insurance business, for example, has been before the courts again and again.

Historical Background. In theory the governing power (sovereignty) rests in the people. Historically this power was first exercised individually and separately in this country by the original thirteen colonies, which had well-defined existences as political units before we had a federal government of any kind. When representatives of these colonies met together to frame a constitution for a proposed central government, the authority of that government was, of necessity, to consist entirely of delegated powers. This idea is summarized in Article X (the Bill of Rights) of the federal Constitution, which reads as follows:

The powers not delegated to the United States by the Constitution, nor prohibited by it to the States, are reserved to the States respectively, or to the people.

Adopted by the People. Nevertheless the federal Constitution was adopted by the people, not the colonies. Thus, our federal government is more than a mere confederation of sovereign states, although it operates with respect to the individual states in some ways. More important is the fact that it operates directly on the people themselves within those areas of governing power delegated to it.

Government of Delegated Powers. The governing power was and is in the people, and in many ways it is exercised for and by them through their state governments. The fact that the powers of the federal government are delegated powers has meaning primarily with respect to interpreting the federal Constitution and the laws adopted under it. With respect to the powers themselves, once it has been established that a power is properly exercisable by the federal government, the acts of that government take precedence over the acts of any state or subdivision.

The federal Constitution, the laws of the United States which are enacted under its provisions, and all treaties made under the authority of the United States are declared by the federal Constitution to be the "supreme law of the land." A law which violates a provision of a constitution, either of the state or federal government, is unconstitutional and void. A court decision which violates a constitutionally guaranteed right will be overruled. The act of an administrative officer, if unconstitutional, will be ineffective. It does not matter whether the constitution is that of a state or the federal government. But if the provisions of a state constitution and the Constitution of the United States are in conflict, the Constitution of the United States takes precedence.

State Constitutions

Limitations of Power. State constitutions perform the same functions for the state that the federal Constitution performs for the federal government. That is to say, they outline the broad general principles on which the government will be run and spell out the limitations and guarantees of fundamental human rights. It is basic in constitutional law, however, that a state constitution does not grant those rights; it simply expresses them. The rights are inherent and exist whether there is a constitution or not. Thus, the state constitution has been called the "mandate of a sovereign people to its servants and representatives."

Basic also in constitutional law is the concept that while the federal Constitution enumerates delegated powers, a state constitution is a limitation of powers. Powers not so limited are intrinsically lodged in the people. An act of the state legislature is constitutional if the constitutions, federal or state, do not prohibit it. On the other hand, an act of the federal Congress rests on and must be supported by some affirmative provision of the federal Constitution.

Supreme Law of the State. The governing power is in the people, exercised by vote. State constitutions express the powers of the state government and limit the ways they can be exercised. They also define and guarantee the rights and liberties of the individual. Under the federal Constitution some of the powers that would otherwise be exercisable by the states were given up and delegated to the federal government. In those areas the federal Constitution and the laws and treaties enacted and effected under it constitute the supreme law of the land. In all other areas, the state constitution constitutes the supreme law of the state.

Constitutions are of fundamental importance in the consideration of any legal problem. Laws enacted by legislatures or the Congress must be in accord with the powers of those bodies as defined in the constitutions or they will be declared unconstitutional and void. Court decisions must be consistent with constitutional provisions or they will be overruled. The Constitution of the United States, the constitutions of the various individual states—each operative in its respective sphere—taken together provide the broad, fundamental principles on which our government is based. To the student of insurance law, however, the most important single question in this constitutional area relates to the business of insurance: Should it be regulated by the state or by the federal government?

INSURANCE AND THE COMMERCE CLAUSE

Why There Is a Question

Federal and State Laws. Within their respective jurisdictions, both the federal Congress and the state legislatures enact laws known as statutes. Statutes are more temporary in nature than the provisions found in constitutions, and they are ordinarily expressed in more specific terms, as rules and standards of conduct. In areas of powers granted to the federal government, the Congress of the United States enacts the necessary laws. In areas that are primarily the concern of the individual states, the legislatures of the respective states enact the legislation. If it is not clear whether Congress or the state legislatures have the power to legislate in a given area, the question will be referred to the courts for the necessary decision. One of the areas in which this question has arisen again and again is that of commerce between and within the various states.

The Commerce Clause. The federal government was granted the power to regulate interstate commerce by the "commerce clause" in the federal Constitution. This is clearly stated in Article I, Section 8, which reads, in part:

Section 8. The Congress shall have Power . . . To regulate Commerce with foreign Nations, and among the several States, and with the Indian Tribes; . . .

Thus there is no question but that commerce "among the several States" is to be regulated by the federal government. The most prevalent question is whether a given type of transaction constitutes interstate commerce. Insurance has presented this question to the courts at intervals for the past hundred years.

Historical Background. The early life insurance companies were regulated by the states in which they were organized. This regulation was concerned primarily with taxation and the exercise of the corporate powers of the company. As the companies began operating in states other than those in which they were organized, however, the question arose as to whether the transaction of an insurance business across state lines constituted interstate commerce. If it did, the companies were automatically subject to federal regulation. If it did not constitute such commerce, the individual states had the right to continue to regulate the companies as they had been doing.

Insurance Cases

Paul v. *Virginia.* In 1868, the United States Supreme Court considered this question in the landmark case of *Paul* v. *Virginia.*[1] This case arose when an insurance agent named Paul refused to comply with certain statutory requirements imposed by the state of Virginia. In reaching its decision that Virginia had the right to regulate the business of insurance, the court stated quite simply: "Issuing a policy of insurance is not a transaction of commerce."

---

[1] 8 Wall. 168 (1868).

The Deer Lodge Case. Other insurance cases followed. In each of them the court made it clear that insurance was not commerce. Obviously, then, it was not interstate commerce and obviously also, it was not subject to federal regulation. The last important case following this reasoning was *New York Life Insurance Co.* v. *Deer Lodge County,*[2] decided in 1913. After the *Deer Lodge* case, there seemed little question but that insurance was subject to regulation by the individual states.

The South-Eastern Underwriters Decision. In 1944, in the case of *United States* v. *South-Eastern Underwriters Association,*[3] the United States Supreme Court reversed this unbroken line of decisions, creating one of the most tremendous upheavals in the history of insurance in this country. Insurance *is* commerce, the court declared, in a four to three decision. It is common knowledge that much insurance business is conducted across state lines. Obviously, therefore, it is interstate commerce and thus subject to federal regulation. A century of regulatory legislation on the state level hung in the balance.

Public Law 15

Why Necessary? It must be remembered at this point that insurance is "affected with a public interest," and there was no regulatory legislation on the federal statute books. Almost immediately, therefore, Congress enacted Public Law 15, which suspended the exercise of regulatory power on the part of Congress as long as state regulation was effective. In Public Law 15, Congress said, in effect, that although it had the power to regulate the insurance business, it would not exercise that power unless the individual states demonstrated that they were unable to regulate it effectively. At the present time, the statutes relating to the life insurance contract are state statutes.

Which State Statutes Govern. It should be noted, however, that the state in which the life insurance company was organized is not the only state whose laws are important in connection with the terms and operation of the life insurance contract. Complying with those laws is only the beginning. For each state has complete authority with respect to matters affecting the welfare of its citizens. Each state, therefore, has the right (and every state in one way or another has exercised that right) to specify the provisions which must be included in a life insurance contract issued or "issued for delivery" in that particular state. Thus, the people who prepare the life insurance contract are concerned with the insurance statutes of every state in which their company does business. They are also concerned with administrative rules and regulations issued by the various state insurance departments.

---

[2] 231 U.S. 495 (1913).

[3] 64 Sup. Ct. 1162, 322 U.S. 533, 88 L. Ed. 1440 (1944).

Administrative Rules and Regulations

Delegation of Rule-Making Power. Theoretically our governments, both state and federal, are based upon a clear-cut separation of powers. Under this theory laws are made only by the legislative branches. A rule set down by an administrative officer, therefore, purporting to have the effect of law, would ordinarily be a nullity.

The increasing complexities of modern business have indirectly brought about a relaxation of this strict separation-of-powers approach. Highly technical businesses require technical knowledge for the preparation of regulatory legislation. Obviously, the legislators cannot have a technical knowledge of every business that must be regulated. For this reason they have adopted the practice in many instances of enacting regulatory laws in general terms only. They then authorize the administrative officer who will have the duty of administering the law to "fill in the details" by means of administrative rules and regulations which have the force and effect of law. This delegation of rule-making power to administrative officers has been consistently upheld by the courts as constitutional as long as the rules are subject to judicial review, are within the scope of delegated power, and are surrounded by other similar safeguards.

Insurance Rules and Regulations. Today, most state insurance commissioners have some power to implement the provisions of the insurance laws of their particular states by rules and regulations. Often such rules and regulations constitute a major part of the regulatory law with which the life insurance business is concerned.

Court Decisions

Case Law. When a question concerning the life insurance contract reaches a court for decision, the statutory or constitutional law will be applied if there is any such law on the subject. If there is no applicable constitutional or statutory law, the courts which follow the common law system (and that includes most of the courts in the United States) search previous court decisions for what are called *precedents.* Any previous decision by that same court on the same question will be considered a precedent and will be followed unless there is strong reason to depart from it.

Stare Decisis. In deciding a question in accordance with precedent, a court is applying what is known as the doctrine of *stare decisis.* This does not mean that every time a question arises it will be decided in exactly the same way. It does mean that later decisions will follow earlier ones unless the courts have strong reason for approaching the question differently.

Common Law. Sometimes there is no applicable statutory law and there have been no previous court decisions on the question. In such cases the court will decide the question before it in accordance with what is called the common law. The common law is a term that is variously defined, but in this sense it means a body of general rules, principles, and maxims which have been developed or followed by courts in English-speaking countries over many hundreds of years.

Authorities differ as to whether there is a common law for every jurisdiction or one general, all-enveloping concept that takes in all the common law jurisdictions. However, the meaning of the common law for any particular jurisdiction is defined by the courts of that jurisdiction. In deciding a case in accordance with the common law, therefore, the court is making what is called "case law" and establishing a precedent that will in turn be followed in later cases involving essentially similar facts.

THE COMMON LAW

Definitions

The Common Law System. It is difficult to define the term "common law" because it means so many different things. In one sense, as we have noted, it distinguishes the system of law followed by English-speaking nations from that followed by countries in other parts of the world. It is especially used in this sense to contrast with legal systems based upon and developed from the Roman law. England, Canada, and most of the states in the United States are common law jurisdictions in this sense of the term. By contrast, France, Spain, Italy, and a few states in the United States derive their legal systems in part at least from the Roman law.

Perhaps the most distinguishing characteristic of the civil law (law derived from the Roman law) is that it attempts to bring together all the general principles of law and to organize them into a relatively complete code. Court decisions then are made only with reference to principles actually written down. In common law jurisdictions there is no attempt to write down all the principles that may be used, although such principles are often enacted into statute or expressed as case law.

As Case Law. In another sense, the term "common law" is used to distinguish case law from statutory or legislative law. In that sense the common law of a jurisdiction is made up of the decisions of courts, as contrasted with legislative enactments or written constitutions.

As General Principles. In yet another sense the common law means a kind of heritage of general principles and concepts involving customs, public policy, and basic ideas of justice which are followed as a matter of legal philosophy by courts of common law jurisdictions. The traditions of the common law were brought to this country by the early settlers from England. There it had its origin in such an early period of history that its beginnings cannot be accurately established. Local courts were in existence, however, in the days of the early Saxons.

After the Norman Conquest of England in the year 1066, the Norman kings began to send their personal delegates through the country to represent them locally in various matters, and in the twelfth century this practice developed into a regular system of itinerant courts. Eventually, these courts replaced the local courts, and the law of the "King's Courts" became the law common to everyone, nobleman or commoner, hence the common law.

EQUITY

How Courts of Equity Arose

Inadequacy of the Common Law. In the early days of the common law the person seeking justice applied for a royal order (*writ*) which authorized the judge to hear his case. During the thirteenth century these writs became highly formalized, but in order to take a problem to court, one had to fit his case into one of the writs that were available. Often this was not possible.

Decisions by the Chancellor. In cases where there was no remedy at law, special appeals were made to the King himself. He in turn would refer these questions to his special advisor, the Chancellor. By the fifteenth century, in cases where the remedy at law was not adequate, the Chancellor was issuing special decrees. The remedies thus sought were obtained "in chancery," and such remedies were known as *equitable* remedies.

Equity and the Law

The equity courts thus arose out of the inadequacy of the ordinary legal remedy. Historically, therefore, remedies available in equity courts have always been considered extraordinary in nature. For instance, the legal remedy for breach of contract is money damages. However, if money damages are inadequate, one may seek a remedy in equity known as *specific performance*. This, if granted, requires that the contract be carried out as promised. Other remedies available at equity and often used in connection with the life insurance contract are reformation of a contract in case of error and cancellation (*rescission*) of a contract because of fraud or misrepresentation of a material fact.

Jury Trial. Ordinarily in a court of law questions of fact are determined by a jury; questions of law by the judge. Thus, if a case involves a dispute as to what actually happened or what was actually said or done by either of the parties, the jury will hear the evidence and make the decision. This is called a "finding of fact." The judge, however, makes the rulings with respect to the legal effect of the facts so "found." In a court of equity the judge himself has the power to decide every question, whether of law or fact, which comes before the court. The right to a jury trial, therefore, which is constitutionally guaranteed, does not apply in courts of equity. The equity court may submit a question of fact to a jury for decision, if that procedure seems advisable, but as a general rule the finding of the jury in an equity case is advisory only.

In Our Courts. The distinction between courts of law and equity was preserved in the court systems of the United States until relatively recently. At the present time, it has been abolished by statute in most of the states. A single system of law, with a single court and a single system of procedure (*pleading* is the word often used), is now ordinarily the rule. Equitable remedies, however, continue to be distinguished from those available at law, and there has been no change in the basic principles of equity. Both legal and equitable remedies are often available in the same suit, and in cases where there is a conflict, the principles of equity will govern.

Some glimpse of the operation of this merging may be gained from the following excerpt from the case of *Connecticut General Life Insurance Company* v. *The Candimat Company,*[4] a 1949 case brought in the United States District Court for the District of Maryland. In this case the insurance company brought an action to cancel two policies of life insurance on the grounds that the insured misrepresented material facts in the applications. The defendants requested a jury trial, but the court held that the issues were equitable rather than legal and that there was no right to a jury trial. This, in part, is how the court discussed the question:

> . . . It is very well known that the Federal rules of civil procedure while generally merging law and equity cases for procedural matters, were not intended to destroy the distinction between law and equity with respect to the matter of jury trials. In a typical case for equitable relief, such as the instant case, there was no right to a jury trial. On the contrary it is well established both by Federal and Maryland law and judicial decision that in equity cases, where there is no adequate remedy at law, there is no right to a jury trial at common law or by statute.

OUR COURT SYSTEMS

Because of the dual nature of our state and federal governments, we have two general court systems. There is a system of state courts in each of the individual states and an over-all system of federal courts. In

---

[4] 83 F. Supp. 1 (D.C. Md., 1949).

matters over which they have complete authority—i.e., in areas where the governing powers have not been delegated to the federal government —the decisions of the state courts are final. In other areas appeals may be taken to the United States Supreme Court. Many questions can be tried in either a state or federal court as the parties may prefer.[5]

The Federal Courts

Established by Federal Law. The federal courts are provided for in the federal Constitution and established by laws enacted by Congress under its authority. They have been established on three levels—district courts on the first level, appellate courts on the intermediate level, and the United States Supreme Court at the top of the hierarchy. Most cases involving subjects over which federal courts have jurisdiction are brought first in the United States district courts. Next they may be appealed to one of the eleven Circuit Courts of Appeal. Lastly they may be appealed to the United States Supreme Court for a final decision.

The United States Supreme Court. The Supreme Court of the United States consists of nine judges and is basically an appellate court. This means that most of the cases it hears come to it on appeal from a lower court. Some cases, however, may be taken directly to the Supreme Court. These include cases arising under the United States Constitution, federal laws, or treaties, cases affecting foreign ambassadors, ministers, and consuls, and controversies between two or more states.

The State Courts

Courts of Original Jurisdiction. The courts of some of the states reflect the same type of three-level organization which is followed in the federal courts. Other states do not have courts on the intermediate appellate level. However, every state has a number of courts of original jurisdiction in which suits may be brought. Some of these courts, such as the justice of the peace courts, municipal courts, county courts, probate courts, and the like, are termed courts of limited jurisdiction because the kinds of cases they are authorized to decide are limited. For example, probate courts handle questions relating to wills and estates exclusively. Other courts, known variously as chancery courts, circuit courts, district courts, and sometimes superior courts, are major trial courts, courts of original jurisdiction it is true, but handling all kinds of civil and criminal cases.

Appellate and Supreme Courts. Intermediate courts, often termed appellate courts, are available in about half the states for appeals from the decisions of the courts of original jurisdiction. Lastly, each

---

[5] See further discussion of this point, p. 16.

state has a supreme court whose decision is final with respect to interpretation of the state constitution and cases brought under state and local laws. Appeals may be taken from the state supreme courts to the United States Supreme Court, however, on any question involving the federal Constitution or federal laws and treaties.

Courts and Their Jurisdictions

In a system involving so many different courts, it is obvious that there must be some rather definite rules for determining which cases are properly handled by each of the various courts. These rules are called *rules of jurisdiction.*

Jurisdiction in General. A court has jurisdiction in a given case if the constitutional or statutory provisions which establish the court give it the right or power to decide cases involving that particular subject matter, parties of that particular description, or both. In those areas the court has the power to hear cases and to make decisions which can be enforced.

Ordinarily, cases in which a court has jurisdiction are defined as those involving certain types of subjects or persons or questions arising in a certain geographical area, but often the amount in controversy will be a governing factor also. For example, justice of the peace courts do not ordinarily have jurisdiction in cases involving more than a very limited amount of money. On the other hand, the United States district courts do not have jurisdiction in some kinds of cases unless the amount involved is in excess of $10,000.

Jurisdiction over the Person. It is not enough that the statute or constitution provide that the court has jurisdiction over a certain type of case. Jurisdiction over the person being sued must also be obtained by compliance with certain constitutional requirements. Legal papers (*summons*) must be issued by the court and must be served upon the defendant, usually personally, but in some cases by publication. In any case, jurisdiction must be obtained in such a manner that the court has actually asserted its power over the person being sued, regularly and by "due process of law."

Where Jurisdictions Overlap. Often more than one court will have jurisdiction in a given kind of case. This is particularly true in insurance cases which frequently involve citizens of different states and thus present what is known as "diversity of citizenship." For this reason, many cases involving the life insurance contract can be brought either in a local state court or in a United States district court, which is expressly given jurisdiction in cases involving diversity of citizenship. Often a case is brought in the local court and removed to the district court. In either case, a summons will be served on the defendant in the regular manner and by "due process of law."

The Applicable Law

Conflict of Laws. Our discussion thus far might seem to imply that state courts apply the law of their respective states and the federal courts apply the law of the federal government. Obviously, however, there are many cases where the laws of more than one jurisdiction are involved. This is very often true with respect to cases involving the life insurance contract. A life insurance contract must meet all the requirements of the state where the insured has legal residence (his *domicile* in legal terminology) at the time it is issued and delivered. Often the insured will have lived in one state when he received the policy and another state at the time of death, while the beneficiary may bring a court action in still another state. In such cases the laws of several jurisdictions may be involved in questions of rights and obligations as well as questions of interpretation and of procedure. Certain basic principles have been worked out, which are used by courts in deciding questions of this kind. Brought together, these principles constitute a study known as the "Conflict of Laws," presenting still another field of law which is involved in the law of the life insurance contract.

Common Law and the Federal Courts. As we have pointed out, if there is no statute or constitutional provision on a given question, the court will ordinarily apply previous case law on the subject. As a general rule, this means the case law as developed by the courts of the state. This practice is followed by the federal courts because of a specific provision in the statute which created them. There it was provided that in cases involving diversity of citizenship, the federal court would apply the law of the state in which the court was sitting. This was very clear as far as it went, but law, as we have seen, is a word susceptible to many definitions. The question of exactly what law to apply soon became important.

Swift v. *Tyson.* In 1842 in the case of *Swift* v. *Tyson,*[6] the United States Supreme Court decided that the word "law" as used in the statute creating the courts meant statutory and not case law. For almost a hundred years thereafter, the federal courts conscientiously applied the statutory law of the state in which they were sitting, but if there were no applicable statutory laws, they applied their own version of the common law. In this way there was built up a federal common law which was often advantageous to insurance companies.

Erie Railroad Company v. *Tompkins.*[7] By the doctrine of *stare decisis,*

---

[6] 16 Pet. 1 (1842).
[7] 304 U.S. 64 (1938).

the *Swift* v. *Tyson* decision was followed in the federal courts until 1938. Then, in the case of *Erie Railroad Company* v. *Tompkins,* the United States Supreme Court overruled the former decision on this point and held that both the statutory and case law of the state in question must be applied by the federal courts.

HOW A CASE IS TRIED

The rules for bringing a court action are a part of what is known as procedural law. Requirements vary as to jurisdictions and the different kinds of courts. They are very simple in some courts and for some types of actions, and very technical in others. The following discussion is in general terms because of the wide variations in terminology and practices from one jurisdiction to another.

The Case Begins

A Complaint Is Filed. Ordinarily a case begins when the person suing (the *plaintiff*) files a *complaint* or *declaration*. This is simply a formal statement of his cause of action. For example, in a contract case he will set forth the provisions of the contract, state (*allege*) those respects in which the person he is suing (the *defendant*) has failed to perform his promise, and state the amount of damages he seeks. Cases for equitable relief are ordinarily brought in much the same way except that instead of declaring the amount of damages in dollars and cents, the plaintiff states the kind of relief he wishes.

The Defendant Answers. The defendant answers the complaint in a formal statement, usually termed an answer, in which he sets forth a denial or an excuse or otherwise explains the facts alleged by the plaintiff. He may admit what the plaintiff says but contend on his part that his actions still do not constitute an actionable wrong. He may deny the contentions of the plaintiff. He may admit the facts but show that his own actions are excusable under the law. Regardless of the nature of his defense, however, he files an answer.

An Issue Is Reached. If the defendant denies that the plaintiff has a case or if he denies that the facts are as stated, an issue is presented as to the truth or falsity of the various statements. The case is then ready for a trial. If the defendant admits the contentions and pleads an excuse which, if proved, would be sufficient as a matter of law, then the plaintiff must file a reply denying the facts on which the defendant seeks to be excused or denying that it is, as a matter of law, a valid excuse. In either case, an issue will have been presented and the case will be ready for the court.

How Cases Are Decided

In a Court of Law. In a court of law, as we have said, questions of fact are submitted to a jury for decision; questions of law are decided by the judge. However, in arriving at its decision the jury will be instructed by the judge, who is guided by the applicable statutory, constitutional, and case law. This entire process will be governed by rules of procedure which are also the result of many years of legal development. One cannot begin to list or even to indicate all the many concepts which have their application in this process. A few of them, however, are mentioned again and again in cases one may study in connection with any area of the law, and some idea of what they mean and how they are used is essential to any understanding of the law.

Presumptions. One of the most useful devices in the development of the law has been the concept of presumptions. In deciding a case at law, as in any other question, there must be some place to start. In law we start with a presumption. For example, a person is presumed to be capable of making a valid, binding contract. In any case involving a question with respect to the contractual capacity of one of the parties, therefore, the law starts with the presumption that he has the capacity. The person challenging this always has the privilege of showing that the person whose capacity is challenged does not have contractual capacity by reason of age, mental incompetence, etc. But the presumption with respect to any individual is that he does have contractual capacity. In the absence of evidence to the contrary, the presumption will stand.

The Prima Facie Case. Another important concept is that of the *prima facie* case. A prima facie case is simply a set of facts which, in the absence of evidence to dispute them, entitles one to the relief he is suing for. If, for example, he sets forth the provisions of a contract and failure on the part of the defendant to carry out the terms of the contract, he has presented a prima facie case of breach of contract. It is then the defendant's responsibility to show that it was not a valid contract, that he was excused from performing, that the plaintiff made it impossible for him to perform, or any of a number of perfectly acceptable excuses for non-performance. But if he does not show an excuse or deny the facts as stated by the plaintiff, the latter has set out a prima facie case and the decision will be in his favor.

Burden of Proof. A third concept of importance in this area is the idea known as the burden of proof. This simply means that in every case, one party or the other has the responsibility of establishing the truth of the statements he has made or the position he has taken. There are two schools of thought on this question, and it becomes highly technical almost as soon as it is introduced. In its simplest form, however, it means that if you have two people making opposing contentions, one will have the burden of proving the truth of his statements and if he fails, he loses the case. The fact is that we often have situations where there is some evidence on both sides. In order to establish a reasonably orderly way of deciding such questions, the burden of proof idea has been developed.

✿   ✿   ✿   ✿   ✿

AN ILLUSTRATIVE INSURANCE CASE

It has been the purpose of this chapter to outline in very broad, general terms, the scope of law in general in order to "set the scene," so to speak, for a discussion of the law of the life insurance contract. The law of any subject is found in many places—constitutional provisions, statutory enactments, administrative rules and regulations. To see the law at work, however, it is necessary to read the cases. One must see the difficult fact questions, the variations of policy wording, the ever-present attempt to develop and apply general principles. As an example, illustrating the application of some of the principles we have discussed in this chapter, the following case is presented in the actual words of the court, though not in its entirety.

GULF LIFE INSURANCE COMPANY v. MOORE [8]

(Georgia Court of Appeals)

. . . The defendant in error,[9] Mrs. Jean S. Moore, herein referred to as the plaintiff, brought suit against the Gulf Life Insurance Company in the Superior Court of Bartow County as beneficiary of a life insurance policy issued to her husband. The policy contained a clause providing for indemnity upon the death of the insured

> as the result of bodily injury caused solely by external, violent and accidental means, as evidenced by a visible contusion or wound on the exterior of the body . . . and that such death occurred within ninety days after the date of occurrence of such injury and as a direct result thereof independently and exclusively of all other causes.

[8] 60 S.E. 2d 547 (Ga. App., 1950).

[9] "Defendant in error." The defendant is the person against whom the suit is brought. However, after a case has been decided in the trial court, the losing party may appeal. One way he may do this is by requesting (*suing out*) a *writ of error*, which is a formal document requiring the lower court to send up the record for review with respect to alleged errors in the trial of the case. The person taking this action is called the *plaintiff in error* even though he may have been the defendant when the case was first tried. To avoid the confusion this practice sometimes causes, many courts elect to retain the original terminology throughout the history of any given case. In this case, the insurance company appealed and thus was the *plaintiff in error*, although it was the defendant originally. Thus the court correctly refers to Mrs. Moore as the *defendant in error* but adds that she will be referred to as the plaintiff throughout the remainder of the opinion.

The petition [10] alleged that the insured, Benjamin Moore, met his death as a result of an accidental gun shot wound. The defendant [11] contended that he was intentionally shot and killed. Upon the trial of the case the jury was authorized to find facts [12] substantially as follows: That the deceased was not acquainted with the man who shot him, Jim Baynes, and had never had any dealings with him; that the deceased, his brother, Baynes, a witness for the plaintiff by the name of Tom Brown, and certain other persons had congregated at a drinking place known as The Rock on the night in question; that Baynes was apparently not drunk; that about an hour before the shooting he had struck up an acquaintance with the witness Brown, had acted in a peculiar manner, had quarreled with him but later came back, shook hands, and said, "now, me and you are friends"; that Baynes had been cursing and arguing without provocation; that the witness had been with the deceased at his home from about sundown until the two men went down to The Rock and that Baynes had had no arguments with them at that time; that about an hour or more after Moore and Baynes had their argument and reconciliation, the deceased and his brother were standing in the Rock Service Station not more than two feet from each other and Moore was standing near the door with his back to them when Baynes suddenly drew his gun and fired, killing Benjamin Moore; that Baynes then backed out the door with the gun in his hand, went into the yard, and fired several additional shots there, apparently at nothing in particular; that the plaintiff's husband died as a result of the gunshot wounds; and that, according to his brother's testimony, "Bennie was just harmless and standing there and Jim just pulled out a pistol and shot him."

✿   ✿   ✿   ✿   ✿

The jury returned a verdict [13] in favor of the plaintiff and the defendant filed its motion for a new trial [14] on the general grounds,[15] which was later amended by adding two special grounds. The judgment of the trial court overruling this motion [16] is assigned as error.[17]

[10] "Petition." This is the legal document filed by the plaintiff to initiate the action in the first place. In other jurisdictions it is variously termed a "complaint" or "declaration," as mentioned *supra*, page 18.

[11] "Defendant." Note that the court is consistently using the terminology of the trial court. Here the insurance company is meant.

[12] "Authorized to find facts." It is the special province of the jury to "find" or determine the facts. To say that the jury was "authorized to find facts" is to imply that these facts were "found" in accordance with the law as expressed in the judge's instructions.

[13] "Verdict." This is the formal finding or decision of a jury reported to and accepted by the court. Until it is accepted by the court it is only a "finding."

[14] "Motion for a new trial." A motion is an application for relief of some specific kind. A new trial is simply a retrial of the same case as if it had never been tried before.

[15] "General grounds." The "grounds" of an action constitute the foundation of the case; the basic facts.

[16] "Overruling this motion." The trial court denied the motion for a new trial.

[17] "Assigned as error." The defendant contends that the decision of the trial judge was wrong as a matter of law and "assigns it as error."

TOWNSEND, J.[18] (After stating the foregoing facts): 1. Special ground 2 of the amended motion for a new trial assigns error on the charge of the court[19] that if the jury found certain facts the defendant would be entitled to recover "if you also further find that at the time Jim Baynes was sane." It is contended that the last quoted phrase is inapplicable in that it had the effect of causing the jury to believe that there was any issue as to the sanity or insanity of Baynes, to believe that the defendant would be liable if Baynes was insane, and that it nullified [20] the effect of that part of the charge, which was otherwise correct.

(At this point the court found that the charge was not in error, and continued as follows.)

. . . To determine whether or not the verdict was authorized by the evidence, however, it is necessary to go farther than this and to determine whether the death was in fact accidental so as to bring it within the terms of the policy, which contained a further exclusionary clause to the effect that the policy shall become null and void if the insured's death results from the intentional act or acts of any person or persons.

To make out a *prima facie* case,[21] the plaintiff must show proof of the policy, proof of death, and further proof that the death occurred from accident or accidental means as defined in the policy. See *Riggins* v. *Equitable Life Assurance Society of the United States,* 64 Ga. App. 834 *et seq.* at page 835, and cases there cited. The burden of proof [22] that the death came about as a result of violent, external and accidental means is on the plaintiff, and remains with her throughout the trial. *Schneider* v. *Metropolitan Life Ins. Co.,* 62 Ga. App. 148; *New York Life Insurance Co.* v. *Ittner,* 59 Ga. App. 89. But this rule is also subject to the provision that where a case has been made out under the terms of the policy, and such policy contains an excepting clause, where the insurance company relies upon the excepting clause in order to establish its non-liability it must prove this contention by a preponderance of the evidence,[23] and, where the evidence is circumstantial, it must be such as to "preponderate to that theory rather than to any other reasonable hypothesis." *Matthews* v. *Gulf Life Insurance Co.,* 64 Ga. App. 112 (2).

The plaintiff here made out a *prima facie* case by facts which authorized the jury to conclude that the deceased and his assailant were unknown to one another; that while the deceased was standing quietly beside his brother the assailant suddenly drew out a gun and shot him; that there was in the same room another person with whom he had quarreled earlier that evening and toward whom he had acted in an irrational manner, and that the assailant then went out into the night and continued to fire the gun. This testimony

---

[18] "J." "Justice" or "Judge."

[19] "Charge of the court." This means the instructions the judge gave the jury with respect to the law of the case.

[20] "Nullified." Made of no effect whatever.

[21] *"Prima facie" case.* A case which, if uncontradicted, would entitle the party presenting it to prevail. See previous discussion, page 19.

[22] "Burden of proof." The responsibility of presenting sufficient evidence to show that the facts one alleges are true. See previous discussion, page 19.

[23] "Preponderance of the evidence." In general terms, this phrase means evidence of the greater value; evidence having a strong power to convince.

together with the testimony of Baynes' wife that her husband, two months previously, had asked her to have him locked up because he was going to kill her, his apparent attempt to do so at that time, and his general course of conduct, was sufficient to warrant a conclusion that Baynes was irrational and not responsible for his actions. It was sufficient to indicate, *prima facie*, that there could have been no reasonable explanation for a desire on his part to injure the deceased. It was sufficient to show violent and external injury from which death resulted.

The burden of proving that the shooting was intentional then shifted to the defendant. It attempted to carry this burden by means of the testimony of the killer himself, but Baynes testified that he shot in self-defense after having been badly beaten and injured by the deceased, which testimony was refuted by two eyewitnesses. Baynes never admitted that he intended to kill Moore. Even had he done so, the jury, under the circumstances, might have discarded his entire testimony as having been discredited. The defendant then introduced two witnesses to prove that two hours after the shooting the assailant did appear in a beaten and bloody condition. The jury might have taken this as corroborative testimony of a fight prior to the shooting, in which case the plaintiff's witnesses would have been impeached,[24] but it is apparent that they reconciled the testimony instead by determining that Baynes in some manner or other sustained the injuries (self-inflicted or otherwise) after he shot the insured and ran away from the dance hall. Thus, the defendant failed to establish its contentions to the satisfaction of the jury by a preponderance of the evidence.

This case closely resembles on its facts the case of *Pan-American Life Insurance Co.* v. *Bagley,* 55 Ga. App. 610, both as to the fact that the accidental death and exclusionary clauses are identical (both omitting the words "sane or insane") and the fact that there also the assailant entered a lunchroom adjacent to a dance hall in which were located a number of persons, and shot and killed one of the men standing by the counter. In passing upon this case the court stated:

> To make the defense good [that the injury was intentionally inflicted] it was necessary that the evidence show that the shooting of Bagley was intentional. Whether the jury concluded that the assassin's conduct indicated that he was incapable of forming an intent, or whether they thought that Bagley was attempting to take the gun away from the assassin and was accidentally and unintentionally shot in the scuffle, we cannot say. However, we do think that the jury was warranted in concluding from the evidence that the insured's death resulted from "bodily injury inflicted by the insured himself or intentionally by another person."

Evidence that the assassin may have been "incapable of forming an intent" in the case of *Pan-American Life Insurance Co.* v. *Bagley, supra* rested entirely upon the circumstances of the shooting. The circumstances in the instant case as to the killing are equally bewildering so far as a rational explanation of the conduct of the assailant is concerned. There is additional evidence of insanity from the testimony of Baynes' wife. Evidence of a state of mind over a reasonable period both before and after the transaction in question is admissible as bearing upon the issue of mental competency. *Pantone* v. *Pantone,* 206 Ga. 305 *et seq.* at page 311. Although such testi-

---

[24] "Impeached." In the law of evidence, a witness is "impeached" when evidence is introduced to show that his testimony cannot be believed.

mony would not itself be sufficient to authorize a finding that Baynes was insane, since an unsuccessful attempt to have a person adjudicated insane raises a presumption that such person is not *non compos mentis* (See *Morse* v. *Caldwell,* 55 Ga. App. 804 (1-b)), it was nevertheless a circumstance which the jury was authorized to consider in determining whether the defendant had by a preponderance of the evidence established its defense that the death was the intentional act of another person. It was their conclusion that this burden had not been carried.

The trial court did not err in overruling the motion for a new trial as amended.[25]

---

[25] It should be borne in mind that this entire opinion was written by the appellate court after reviewing the record of the case as it was tried in the trial court. The trial judge overruled an amended motion for a new trial. After reviewing the case, the appellate court upheld the trial court in this decision and permitted the decision in favor of the plaintiff to stand.

CHAPTER **II**

What
a Contract
Is

IN BROAD general terms, a life insurance contract is simply a legally enforceable agreement between an applicant and an insurance company. Ordinarily, it is set forth in a life insurance policy, but this is not essential. If the actions of the parties and the documents exchanged otherwise satisfy the legal requirements for the formation of a contract, an insurance contract may be held to be effective even though no policy has been issued.

On the other hand, it is possible also that even though a policy has been issued and delivered, the company may not be obligated under it. This is true in any situation where one or more of the basic legal requirements for the formation of a contract have not been met. There are also some factors, such as misrepresentation and fraud in the application, which go to the essential validity of the contract.

In considering the life insurance contract, therefore, it is important to distinguish between the contract itself and the life insurance policy in which the agreement is expressed. Ordinarily the two are synonymous, but not always. It is essential, too, to bear in mind the general legal requirements which govern the formation and validity of *informal* contracts, of which the life insurance contract is an outstanding example. Thus, before the law of the life insurance contract can have much meaning, it is necessary to have some acquaintance with the basic principles of the law of contracts generally. The purpose of this chapter is to discuss some of the more important of these principles, with an emphasis upon those with which the life insurance contract is most concerned.

CONTRACTS ARE "MANY AND VARIOUS"

The Contract Defined

A Contract Is a Promise. A contract has been defined as a "promise or set of promises, for breach of which the law gives a remedy, or the performance of which the law in some way recognizes as a duty." [1] Fundamentally, there must be a promise or, in some cases several promises, of such a nature as to create a legal duty of performance on the part of the promisor.

The life insurance contract illustrates this definition clearly. One after another, life insurance policies read, "The A. B. C. Life Insurance Company agrees to pay . . . "; "The X. Y. Z. Life Insurance Company agrees to pay . . ."; and so on. "Agrees to pay . . . " are promissory words. No one doubts that they create a legal duty of performance on the part of the life insurance company. Court decisions have enforced that duty again and again.

The life insurance contract has often been called, from the policyholder's point of view, a "bundle of rights." From the company's point of view, the contract is a "bundle of promises" which create those rights on the part of the policyholder.

Promises by One or Both Parties

By Both Parties. Promises are sometimes made by both parties to a contract. In that case it is a *bilateral* (having promises on "two sides") contract, and one promise is said to be "consideration" [2] for the other. In other contracts there will be a promise or promises by one party only, i.e. on only one side of the contract. In a contract of this latter kind, the party to whom the promise is made (*the promisee*) already will have performed an act or acts requested by the person making the promise (*the promisor*). These contracts are called *unilateral* (having promises on one side only) contracts, and the act or acts requested by the promisor are consideration for the promise or promises he makes.

Life Insurance Contracts Are Unilateral

The Policyholder Makes No Promises. Unilateral contracts were recognized and given legal effect at a much earlier date than bilateral contracts and they are still of much greater interest to the student of life insurance. Search as you may, you will find no place in the modern life insurance contract where either the policyholder or the beneficiary actually promises to do or to pay anything. The contract can be kept alive only if premiums are paid as they fall due, but the insured does not

---

[1] *Williston on Contracts* (Baker, Voorhis & Co., Inc., 1957), Vol. I, p. 1.

[2] For explanation and discussion of this term, see page 34.

promise to pay them. If he does not pay, certain clearly defined results will follow, but he cannot be sued by the company for breach of contract.

The Company Makes the Promises. On the other hand, the life insurance company makes a legally enforceable promise to pay the amount of insurance specified, upon receipt of proof of the death of the insured. Many other promises are included in various parts of the contract, which the insurance company may or may not be required to carry out (the lawyer says *perform*), depending upon whether specified conditions are or are not met. However, when these conditions have been met, if the company does not perform its promises the policyholder or the beneficiary can sue for breach of contract. This means that the life insurance contract has legally enforceable promises made by the company but none on the part of the policyholder. It is thus one of the most important modern-day examples of the unilateral contract.

HOW PROMISES ARE MADE ENFORCEABLE

Formal and Informal Contracts

Formal Contracts. The mere fact that promises are made does not, of course, mean that they are legally enforceable. However, if people intend to make a contract, there are two main ways in which a promise can be made legally enforceable. One way concerns the form of the instrument in which the promise is expressed. Promises under seal and negotiable instruments have legal effect as binding contracts because of special formalities which are complied with in the transactions out of which they arise. Promises of this kind are binding because of their form and for that reason are called *formal* contracts.

Other contracts—and the life insurance contract is an excellent example—create legal duties because the parties have met requirements which go to the nature rather than the form of the transaction. Contracts of this kind are called *informal*, i.e. *not* formal contracts. By far the majority of present-day contracts are informal contracts.

Informal Contracts. An informal contract, defined in terms of legal requirements, is an agreement between competent parties expressing definite assent to the terms of a promise or promises and supported by legally adequate consideration. Somewhat less important, because in a sense they are implied, are the requirements that the agreement must be in a form required by law and that it not be declared ineffective (*void*) by special statute or rule of common law.

A large body of law has been developed in connection with each of these requirements and much of it applies to the life insurance contract. The remainder of this chapter will be devoted to a discussion of the various elements of the informal contract, with special respect to the law as it has been applied to the life insurance contract.

THE AGREEMENT

The informal contract is first of all an agreement. This means that two or more persons must have shown by words or actions that they have assented to the terms of a promise or promises proposed by one, called the *offeror,* and accepted by the other (the *offeree*). (The lawyer says there must be "a manifestation of mutual assent to the terms of the promise or promises concerned.")

Agreements Are Not Necessarily Contracts. A contract is often defined as "an agreement enforceable by law." In fact that is the way we defined a life insurance contract at the outset of this chapter. To say that it must be enforceable by law, however, implies that there may be other agreements which are not so enforceable. This is true. "Agreement" is a broad term and includes such things as executed sales and gifts as well as many kinds of promises of such a nature that they cannot be enforced by court action. A contract, therefore, is a special kind of agreement—one that the law will enforce.

Mutual Assent

Must Be Manifested. Lawyers use the phrase "manifestation of mutual assent" to make it clear that the law does not presume to ascertain the actual state of minds of the parties. Instead, it concerns itself with their discernible words and actions. This idea is sometimes obscured by language to the effect that a contract requires a "meeting of the minds." However, in many cases it would be impossible to ascertain the actual state of minds of the contracting parties. As a matter of law, the state of minds that actually controls is that which is evidenced by the words and actions of the parties to the agreement.

How Assent Is Shown. As a general rule, mutual assent is evidenced by the making of an offer or proposal by one party and the acceptance of it by the other. The person who makes the offer is the offeror; the person to whom it is made is the offeree.

The Offer

Definition. Defined in its simplest outlines, an offer is a proposal which, if accepted according to its terms, will create a binding contract.[3] Ordinarily an offer is in the form of a promise which will become enforceable when the person to whom it is made performs the act (for

---

[3] Literally an agreement which is not binding is not a contract. The term "binding contract" is often used, however, for purposes of emphasis and it is used for that purpose here.

a unilateral contract) or makes the promise or promises requested by the offeror (for a bilateral contract). Thus an offer is always conditional in the sense that acceptance in accordance with its terms is a condition which must be met before the offer will become a binding promise. However, an offer may also be so expressed as to remain subject to further conditions after acceptance. This is especially true of the life insurance contract, in which the promises become enforceable only when the other conditions set forth in the policy have been met.

In a Bilateral Contract. If the offer is so worded that another promise is requested in exchange, and if the promise is so given, a bilateral contract will be formed. Here the completed contract will consist of promises on both sides. The promises of the one party serve as consideration for the promise or promises of the other.

In a Unilateral Contract. If the offer is so worded as to request the performance of an act or acts on the part of the offeree in exchange for the promise or promises in the offer, the contract, when formed, will be unilateral. In other words, the completed contract will consist of promises by one party only while the other party, having performed the act, will not be bound to any further performance.

The Offer in Life Insurance. The requirements that there be an offer and that it be accepted apply just as clearly to the life insurance contract as to any other contract. Traditionally the applicant has been considered as making the offer when he completes the application for life insurance and pays the initial premium. The company is said to accept that offer when it issues, or issues and delivers, the policy. The use of the conditional binding receipt has modified the offer-and-acceptance process.[4] Nevertheless it is basic that there will be an offer and an acceptance in the formation of the life insurance contract.

Requirements of a Valid Offer

It Must Be Definite. Perhaps the most basic requirement of a legally sufficient offer is that it must be definite. When accepted, it must create a contract which, if necessary, can be given exact meaning by a court of law. As a general rule if an offer is so indefinite that the promise cannot be clearly ascertained it is not a legally sufficient offer.

It Must Be Communicated. It seems obvious that an offer must come to the attention of the one to whom it is addressed before it can be accepted. However, it is not enough that knowledge of the offer be obtained by accident. It is basic in the law of contracts that one may choose the person or persons with whom he is willing to contract. For this reason communication of an offer for contractual purposes requires that the offeror intentionally and actually bring the offer to the notice

---

[4] See detailed discussion of this point *infra*, p. 85.

of a person or persons with whom he wishes or would be willing to contract. Thus, if the offer is sent by mail it must be received by the offeree. If it is published, as in the offer of a reward, the person who performs the act requested must actually have seen the offer and must have performed the act in reliance upon or relation to it.

Duration of the Offer

May Be Specified by the Offeror. The offeror, if he wishes, may specify the length of time he will hold the offer open. If he does this, the offer will automatically terminate at the expiration of the stated period without further action on his part. Any attempt on the part of the offeree to accept after such expiration will be ineffective since one of the specific conditions stated in the offer—that it be accepted within the time specified—will not have been met.

Reasonable Length of Time. If the offer contains no mention of an expiration date, it is presumed to remain open for a reasonable length of time. What constitutes a "reasonable length of time" is a question of fact [5] which depends on many different things—the type of contract, the customs of the business, etc. It may be a very short time in contracts where circumstances change rapidly or a much longer time in connection with offers of rewards, for example.

May Be Withdrawn. Unless the offer has been made under seal or for a consideration,[6] the offeror has the privilege of withdrawing it at any time he wishes prior to acceptance. This is true even if he has said that he will hold it open for a specific length of time. At one time it was thought not to be legally necessary that notice of withdrawal be given the offeree if the latter had knowledge of actions on the part of the offeror which reasonably implied withdrawal. Today, however, it is generally considered to be necessary to notify the offeree of the withdrawal of an offer. A seasonable acceptance will otherwise be legally effective. After an offer has been accepted, of course, it cannot be withdrawn.

Termination by Death or Insanity of the Offeror. An offer may be terminated for reasons other than withdrawal or revocation by the offeror. For example, death of the offeror prior to acceptance terminates the offer, and death of the offeree, assuming that there was only one, ordinarily precludes the possibility of acceptance.

At one time the insanity of either the offeror or offeree was considered to have the same legal effect as death. More recently the legal capacity of insane persons to create a binding contract under some cir-

---

[5] If the question reaches a court of law, this, like all questions of fact, will ordinarily be decided by the jury.

[6] In which case it is an option.

cumstances has been increasingly recognized. The known insanity of either the offeror or offeree is generally held to terminate an offer. However, if the insanity is not known, the person's legal capacity to complete the contract is a question of fact to be decided in the light of all the pertinent circumstances of the particular case.

The Offeree

Two Parties Are Required. It is a legal impossibility for a person to contract with himself even in different representative capacities. The concept of offer and acceptance, therefore, assumes that in addition to an offeror who makes the offer or proposal, there must also be an offeree to whom the offer is made and who, on his part, evidences his assent by accepting the offer.

The Offeree Has Three Choices. The offeree may, if he wishes, reject the offer. If he does this the offer terminates immediately, and that particular offer cannot be revived even if the offeree wishes later to accept it in absolute accordance with its original terms. As a second choice, he may reject the offer as it stands but explain that he would be willing to contract if some of the terms were different. In other words, he may reject the original offer and make a counter-offer.

It should perhaps be noted that the offeree need not state in absolute terms that he rejects the offer. Any words or actions which are not in themselves definite rejections but which reasonably imply that the offeree does not intend to accept will be given their reasonable effect and considered to be rejections. An attempt to substitute new terms or modify the original offer, for example, will be considered a rejection of the old offer and the making of a counter-offer. This is especially applicable in the case of an answer purporting to accept the offer "on condition that . . . ." This, in legal effect, is a rejection. The offeree has clearly indicated that he is not willing to contract on the terms of the offer.

As a third choice the offeror may accept the offer in accordance with its terms and thus complete the agreement.

Acceptance

What Constitutes An Acceptance. Any words or actions on the part of the offeree indicating assent to the offer as made by the offeror will constitute acceptance. The simple statement "I accept" is sufficient if made with reference to the offer and if the offer is of such a nature as to request a promise in return. Performance of the act requested in an offer for a unilateral contract is a legally sufficient acceptance.

It is highly important, however, that the action be taken or the promise made with reference to the offer. It must be remembered that an agreement means a manifestation of mutual assent. Thus, even if each of two persons sent identical offers to the other, and the offers were received simultaneously, no agreement would result. Each promise must be made with reference to the other or the assent will not be mutual.

Who May Accept. Only the person or persons to whom the offer is made can accept it in the legal sense of the word. An offer need not be directed only to one person, however. It may be made to a very large group acting as an entity, as in the case of a corporation, for example. Or it may be directed to any member of a large group. Regardless of the number of persons who may be eligible to accept, however, some one person must manifest his assent to the offer in accordance with its terms or there will be no agreement. For this reason silence on the part of an offeree will not, as a general rule, be construed to be an acceptance although in some instances prior conduct may make it clear that such silence is to be so construed.

Acceptance Must Be . . .

. . . *Positive.* An acceptance must be sufficiently positive to indicate a clear assent to the exact terms proposed by the offeror. If an act is requested, precisely that act must be performed. If a promise is asked then that promise and no other must be given. Acceptance must be within the time specified by the offeror or within a reasonable time if none is specified.

. . . *Unconditional.* Acceptance must be unconditional. As we have previously pointed out, any attempt to impose new conditions in a purported acceptance will be construed as the making of a counter-offer. In effect the offeree has rejected the original offer and substituted an offer of his own.

. . . *Intentional.* It is sometimes said that the offeree must have an intent to accept. However, the actual intent of the parties is ordinarily not important if there is an adequate manifestation of assent. A secret intent not to be bound, for example, is of no significance if the person's actions or words are such as to justify a reasonable person in believing that the other has actually promised to do or refrain from doing something for a valuable consideration. In other words, a "meeting of the minds" in the sense that both parties must actually have the same thing in mind is not required.

However, a person's subjective state of mind *is* important if it is ascertainable from his overt acts. For example, if an offer is obviously made as a joke, one cannot accept it and complete a binding agreement. The offer is ineffective, not so much because there was no "meeting of the minds" as because there was not a manifestation of assent in the sense that a reasonable person would take action in reliance upon it.

Communication of the Acceptance

Not Always Necessary. In order to have a manifestation of mutual assent it would seem that acceptance, like the offer, should be communicated. There are, however, some instances in which acceptance does not have to be brought to the actual knowledge of the offeror. For example, in an offer for a unilateral contract the performance of an act is usually contemplated as acceptance and consideration for the promise offered.[7] In such cases, if the offeror does not specifically request that he be notified of the completion of the act, it is generally held that performance of the act is all that is necessary to complete a binding agreement.

Method of Communication. An offer for a bilateral contract contemplates acceptance in the form of a return promise. Even here, acceptance does not have to be communicated in fact if the offeree replies using a means of communication designated by the offeror. Thus, if the offeror requests acceptance by mail, the mailing of the letter of acceptance is sufficient to complete the contract even though the letter is never received. The mail service, in legal terms, is considered to be the "agent" of the offeror. Mailing the acceptance, therefore, is considered the same as delivering it to the offeror's agent. In legal effect, it is equivalent to delivering it to the offeror himself.

If an answer by telegram is requested, the delivery of a message of acceptance to the telegraph company will be sufficient to complete acceptance. In that case the telegraph company is considered to be the agent of the offeror. However, if a telegram is requested and the offeree decides to reply by mail, the mail service is considered to be the agent of the offeree. The letter, therefore, must actually reach the offeror in this case before a binding agreement will have been completed.

If the offeror does not specify any particular means of communication, he is presumed to expect the offeree to reply by the same method he has used in communicating the offer. If the offeror writes a letter, the offeree may reply by letter and the acceptance is considered to have been communicated, in the legal sense of the word, the instant the letter is mailed. In any case, if the offeree actually makes his acceptance known to the offeror it will be held to have been effectively communicated.

The Counter-Offer

As we have suggested, any attempt by the offeree to accept only

---

[7] In some unilateral contracts the act is performed by the offeror and acceptance, to create a binding agreement, is in the form of a promise on the part of the offeree. Here any question concerning communication of the acceptance is answered in accordance with the same principles that apply to the acceptance of an offer contemplating a bilateral contract.

a part of the original offer or to change any of its conditions is in legal effect a counter-offer. Often, however, the offeree may intentionally reject the original offer and make a counter-offer. In any of these cases the original offer lapses and the original offeree becomes in effect an offeror. The counter-offer is then subject to acceptance or rejection by the other party as was the original offer.

The Agreement

Effective Date. Assuming that the other requirements are satisfied, the agreement is generally considered to be complete and to become effective at the moment there is an overt act manifesting assent to the offer. In some instances, the parties may plan to reduce their agreement to writing and not to be bound until this has been done and the contract signed. Alternatively, they may enter into a binding oral agreement to execute a written contract. When there is a question as to whether the oral agreement is effective as a contract under circumstances of this kind, the person alleging the existence of a binding contract has the burden of proving his contention.

However, the mere fact that the parties plan to put their contract in writing does not necessarily preclude their having completed a binding oral contract. If they have, in fact, made the necessary promises to each other orally, the fact that they plan to reduce the contract to writing does not change the legal effect of their mutual promises. Unless that kind of contract is required by law to be in writing, the oral promises of the parties may be held to have constituted an effective contract.

WHAT CONSIDERATION MEANS

Applies to Informal Contracts Only

Promises under seal (i.e. formal contracts) were recognized and enforced at common law long before the law of the informal contract and the accompanying concept of consideration were developed. Later it was sometimes said, and it is occasionally so suggested even now, that with respect to formal contracts the seal "imports consideration." As a matter of fact, the formal contract was effective by reason of its form alone long before the idea of consideration was born. Historically, therefore, the doctrine of consideration was not applicable to formal contracts, although it is significant to note that the use of the seal has now been abolished by statute in many of the states.

With respect to the informal contract, it is fundamental that there must be a legally sufficient consideration for the promise or promises sought to be enforced. This simply means that the person who seeks to enforce the promise of another must himself have given something of value for it. He may have given another promise, a sum of money, or something else of value. He may have performed an act or refrained from doing something he was legally entitled to do. In some way he must have promised or given something the promisor requested. In brief, consideration is the price requested and paid for a promise.

When Is Consideration "Legally Sufficient"?

The Law Takes a Broad View. As a general principle, the law does not inquire into the monetary adequacy of the consideration agreed upon and given in exchange for a promise. If it is established that there was consideration and if it was what the promisor requested, the courts will not substitute their own judgment as to its value for that of the parties to the contract. In fact, the classic statement is to the effect that under such circumstances even a "pepper corn" will be considered legally sufficient. After all, adequacy and value are subjective concepts. Something which may have great value to one person may have little or no value to another. In the absence of fraud, the courts take the position that the parties presumably knew what they were doing and particularly that the promisor knew what he was requesting in return for his promise.

One Exception. There is one exception to this general principle that if there is consideration the courts will not ordinarily inquire into its adequacy. That is found in cases which involve a promise to pay in money a larger sum for a smaller. If the smaller sum represents more than its nominal value, as with a rare or otherwise valuable coin, for instance, a promise to pay it will be sufficient consideration for a promise to pay a larger sum at the same time and place. If there is no such unique value, a promise to pay a small sum in money will not be a legally sufficient consideration for a promise to pay a larger sum at the same time and place.

How It Is Determined. There are two generally accepted theories by which to determine the sufficiency of consideration. One idea, which is perhaps the more generally accepted approach, is that consideration is any act or promise requested and received by the promisor in exchange for the promise. This, it will be noted, is the definition previously given. The other is the "promissory estoppel" approach, which holds that anything that has induced another to act will be sufficient to estop the promisor from denying that he is bound by his promise. This is the so-called "justifiable reliance" theory which operates on the principle that it is wrongful to permit a promisor not to be bound by a promise if he has induced the promisee to take action in reliance on it. Under this theory any benefit to the promisor or detriment to the promisee will be deemed sufficient consideration to support a promise.

"Benefit" and *"Detriment"* *Are Legal Terms.* The words "benefit" and "detriment" must be interpreted in their legal sense. For example, a detriment in the legal sense of the word need not necessarily be to the promisee's actual disadvantage. The classic illustration of this point is the case where an uncle promises his nephew a sum of money on the latter's twenty-first birthday if the nephew refrains from smoking until that date. Here the consideration for the uncle's promise, abstention from smoking on the part of the nephew, is not in fact physically detrimental to the nephew. However, in legal theory, the voluntary foregoing of an undeniable right is a detriment. In this sense there is a detriment to the nephew (promisee) and thus a legally sufficient consideration for the promise of the uncle. It should be noted that abstention from smoking is also the action requested and received in exchange for the promise by the promisor (uncle). This example meets both tests with respect to consideration.

A Promise for a Promise. Generally speaking, mutual promises constitute sufficient consideration for each other. In other words, in a bilateral contract, each promise is consideration for the other since it is "the thing requested and received in exchange" for the promise of the other party to the contract.

Conditional Promises. Even a conditional promise will be sufficient consideration for another promise or an act if it otherwise meets the tests outlined above. It will be recalled, for example, that an offer is always conditional in that it specifies the conditions of acceptance. The promise in an offer may, however, continue to be conditional even after acceptance. That is, it may bind the promisor to act or to refrain from acting only if a certain thing shall or shall not happen. Thus a promise to pay an insurance benefit, even after the promise becomes binding in a contractual sense, may continue to be conditional in the sense that payment will be made only if the loss insured against shall occur. If this is the promise requested and given in exchange for the payment of the premium, it is sufficient consideration for the act even though the condition may not, in fact, ever be fulfilled.

COMPETENT PARTIES

As a Contractual Requirement

Effect of Lack of Competency. Consideration as a requirement in connection with the informal contract is absolute. Without it there is said to be a "failure of consideration" and therefore no contract. The requirement that the agreement be between competent parties, however, is somewhat less definite. For example, in some instances the incompetency of one or both parties to an agreement will result in what is known, not too logically, as a "void" contract [8]—that is, no contract at all. In others, the contract is held to be "voidable," which means that the incompetent party may, if he wishes, "avoid" it—that is, declare it ineffective. In still other circumstances, the parties may be bound regardless of their usually limited legal capacity to contract.

Who Is Competent?

Generally speaking, any person is presumed to be capable of entering into a valid and binding contract. Minors, married women, insane persons, intoxicated persons, convicts, and aliens, however, all either have or at some time in the past have had limited contractual capacity. At the present time, the incapacity of most of these persons is evidenced more by their freedom to disaffirm an otherwise valid contract into which they have entered than an incapacity to make a contract in the first place.

The Power to Disaffirm. The fact that some people have the power to disaffirm (in legal terms, "avoid") a contract, after having made it, is of the utmost importance to anyone who contemplates making a contract with a person of limited contractual capacity. In simple terms it means that the competent party to the contract will be bound while the other party has the privilege of deciding whether it will be to his advantage or not to carry out the contract.

Married Women

At Common Law. At common law a married woman was legally incapable of entering into a binding contract. A purported contract with her was void, not voidable. This rule has been almost completely modified or removed in most states today, but it is still important as historical background. Statutes which remove the disability must be read with the knowledge of the common law rule they change before they become very intelligible.

Insane Persons

If a party to a contract is insane, the validity of his contract varies with the circumstances. If he has been declared legally insane and a conservator has been appointed, then contracts he makes thereafter in his own name are void. If no conservator has been appointed, the courts generally take the view that the insane person may affirm or disaffirm

---

[8] Although this phrase is helpful in some situations and is frequently used, a "void contract" is by its own terms an impossibility. A contract, by definition, is a binding agreement. A void contract, therefore, is a nullity and the term is used more by habit than anything resembling logic. A voidable contract, on the other hand, is a contract that can be disaffirmed, but it is effective until disaffirmed. Thus it imposes legal duties upon the promisor or promisors until such time as someone, having the right to do so, takes the necessary action to disaffirm it.

the contract upon regaining his sanity. After his death, his personal representative or his heirs may exercise the right to disaffirm.

Aliens

Enemy Aliens. Friendly aliens are fully competent to enter into contracts, including life insurance contracts, with persons or companies in the United States, but a rather complicated situation arises in insurance contracts when the insured becomes an enemy alien by reason of the declaration of war. There have been court decisions that the policy is completely terminated under these conditions. However, the majority line of decisions holds that the insurance is suspended for the duration of the war and that an offer to pay the premiums due after the war has ended serves to revive the contract.

The United States Supreme Court, on the other hand, has taken the position that if the contract has not been performed at the time war is declared, the inability of the insured to pay the premiums, due to the fact that he is an alien enemy, serves to extinguish all contractual rights. Nevertheless, to the extent that the insured has acquired rights in the policy on the basis of surrender values, those values constitute a debt owed to him by the insurer, a debt which is suspended for the duration of the war.

Minors

Who Is a Minor? At common law a minor, sometimes referred to as an infant, was any person under the age of twenty-one. This rule has been modified by statute in many states so that the contractual capacity of a person twenty years of age, for example, will depend entirely upon the law of the state in which he makes his legal home (in legal terms, his *domicile*).

Validity of the Contracts of a Minor. At one time contracts entered into by a minor were classified as void, voidable, or valid, depending upon whether they were harmful, uncertain, or beneficial in their effect upon the minor. This placed upon the courts the responsibility of determining whether the contract was in fact harmful or beneficial. As a general rule today, a few kinds of contracts made by a minor are valid; all others are voidable but not void. This means that with respect to most of his contracts, the minor himself can decide whether it is beneficial to him or not and thus whether he wishes to be bound. The other party, however, assuming his contractual capacity is unimpaired, is bound by the agreement unless and until the minor decides to disaffirm it.

Disaffirmance

What It Means. When a minor disaffirms a contract, he simply declares that thereafter he will not be bound by the terms of the contract. He is free to disaffirm most of his contracts at any time during his minority and within a reasonable time after he has attained the age of majority. However, he cannot disaffirm a contract conveying real property until he has reached the age of majority and then he must disaffirm it within a reasonable time. If he has not disaffirmed a contract after the expiration of a reasonable time after he has reached the age of majority, he will be held to be bound by its terms. In other words, his failure to disaffirm is held the equivalent of *ratification* (actual acknowledgment that he is willing to be bound by the terms of the contract).

As a general rule, disaffirmance of a contract on the grounds of infancy requires the return of the consideration if the minor still has it in his possession. If, during his infancy and prior to disaffirmance, the minor has spent the money, he can still avoid the contract and recover what he parted with, without restoring the other party to the status he had prior to the making of the contract. There is much conflicting law on this point and the applications of the basic principles have varied widely from jurisdiction to jurisdiction.

It is important to note that a minor may also disaffirm any release which he may have signed in connection with settlement of a claim against anyone, including insurance companies. This fact has made the settlement of life insurance policies payable to minors one of the more constant problems in connection with the payment of claims.

Who Has the Right. The minor's privilege of avoiding a contract he thinks detrimental to his interests is accorded him as a protection from unscrupulous persons who might otherwise seek to take advantage of him. For this reason the privilege is almost absolute. It applies to anyone who has not yet attained the age of majority, regardless of how nearly of age he may be, regardless also of the fact that he may be engaging in business for himself or otherwise have assumed the responsibilities of adulthood.

Contracts of a Minor

Some Are Binding. There are some kinds of contracts which a minor may not disaffirm. Agreements in fulfillment of a legal duty, for example, will be held to be binding. Thus, the execution of a release of a mortgage, if the obligation has been legally satisfied, cannot afterwards be disaffirmed. So, also, such agreements as marriage, enlistment, and apprenticeship are held to be binding on a minor.

"Necessaries." It is sometimes said that a minor is liable under his contracts for "necessaries," but this is not entirely true. He is liable for the reasonable value of "necessaries" furnished him or his family, but this is not always the contract price. The term "necessaries" also requires elaboration.

Probably the earliest definition of "necessaries" was given by Lord Coke, when he said that an infant may bind himself to pay for his "meat, drink, apparel, necessaries physic, and other such necessaries, and likewise for his good teaching or instruction, whereby he may profit himself afterward." The term "necessaries" is much broader than the word "necessity," for it includes not only necessities but also other things which may be reasonably necessary for the minor's maintenance, with proper regard for his social position and financial status. Ordinarily articles of luxury are not included, but the fact that an article is expensive does not keep it from being a "necessary" if the infant is in actual need of it. Significantly, for our present purposes, life insurance has been held not to be a "necessary." Thus, special statutory permission is required before a minor can enter into a contract for life insurance under which he may execute binding releases and otherwise exercise his rights on the same basis as if he were an adult.

Life Insurance Contracts. Ordinarily a minor may disaffirm a contract of life insurance just as he may any other contract he has made. Upon such disaffirmance he may recover all of the premiums which he has paid for the insurance and thus be in the position of having had the insurance protection during the period of minority without cost.[9] Many states, however, have statutes which permit minors of a certain age and over to enter into life insurance contracts which bind them as well as the insurer. One typical statute of this kind provides as follows:

> Any minor of the age of fifteen years or more may, notwithstanding such minority, contract for life, health and accident insurance on his own life for his own benefit or for the benefit of his father, mother, husband, wife, child, brother or sister, and may exercise all such contractual rights and powers with respect to any such contract of insurance as might be exercised by a person of full legal age, and may exercise with like effect all rights and privileges under such contract, including the surrender of his interest therein and the giving of a valid discharge for any benefit accruing or money payable thereunder. Such minor shall not, by reason of his minority, be entitled to rescind, avoid, or repudiate such contract, or any exercise of a right or privilege thereunder.[10]

Where there is a statute of this kind, a life insurance contract made by a minor of the required age may not thereafter be repudiated or disaffirmed on the ground of legal incompetency due to minority. Such

---

[9] This summarizes the majority rule.

[10] Illinois Revised Statutes, Chap. 73, Art. XIV, Sec. 854 (1959).

statutes often restrict the life to be insured by the minor and limit the persons who may be named as beneficiary.

Corporations

The contractual capacity of a corporation is strictly determined by the provisions of its charter and the statutes of the state under whose laws it was organized (its *domiciliary* state). A corporation cannot have powers that are broader than those granted in its charter or the laws under which it is created. A corporation does, however, have implied and incidental powers when and if they are necessary in the performance of the powers specifically granted.

Life Insurance Companies. The charter or certificate of authority of a life insurance company usually states in general terms that the company shall have the power to transact a life insurance business. Implied is the power to issue contracts of life insurance as well as the other contracts incident to the doing of a life insurance business. However, this applies only to the state in which the company was organized. In order to qualify to do business in any other state the company must formally apply to the proper official of the state in question for permission to do an insurance business in that state. If it meets the necessary requirements of that particular state it will be granted a certificate of authority to do business there.

With respect to the contractual capacity of an insurance company, there are two basic requirements. First, the company must have been empowered, under its charter and the laws under which it was formed, to issue contracts of insurance. Secondly, it must have been authorized to do an insurance business—i.e. issue contracts of insurance—in the state where the contract becomes effective or the state of residence of the insured.

Contracts with Nonlicensed Insurers

The legal effect of a contract of insurance made with a nonlicensed insurer depends primarily upon the statutory law of the state in which the contract is completed or the insured resides. Statutes in some states declare such contracts to be void, creating no rights. In other states there are no applicable statutes. In these jurisdictions the tendency is to uphold the rights of the insured who has entered into the contract in good faith and without knowledge of the legal incompetency of the insurer.

In still a third group of states there are laws which simply provide for a penalty upon the insurer which does business in the state without being licensed. The prevailing opinion in these states is that a contract made with an unlicensed company is valid and enforceable by both parties.

A FORM REQUIRED BY LAW

Contracts in Writing

As a general rule, a contract is valid whether it is in writing or not. Contracts of importance, however, should be expressed in writing for the convenience of the parties, if for no other reason. A written contract helps to guard against memory lapses as well as actual wrongdoing, and it is much simpler to establish the terms of a written agreement if one or more of the parties should die or become legally incompetent before the contract is carried out.

Some Contracts Must Be in Writing. Some contracts are required by law to be in writing. Conveyances of land and negotiable instruments are examples. Special laws may require other kinds of contracts to be written in certain instances. The most important general group of contracts requiring written expression is found in the Statute of Frauds.

The Statute of Frauds

The Statute of Frauds was originally enacted in England in 1677, expressing as its stated purpose the "prevention of many fraudulent practices. . . ." Hence, its name. It has since been enacted in most of the states of the United States. In its most usual form it provides not that the contracts it specifically lists must be in writing but rather that they shall be unenforceable if they are not.

How It Operates. In connection with the Statute of Frauds, one must make again the fine distinction between a requirement for the formation of a contract and a legal requirement going to the heart of the agreement but still not affecting its validity. Competent parties, it will be recalled, constitute one of the requisites for the formation of a contract. Strictly speaking, the competency of the parties relates not so much to the formation of a contract as to the power of the party in question to avoid it after it has been formed. Similarly, the Statute of Frauds, in the form in which it is now most commonly enacted, does not actually concern the validity of the contract itself. In its most usual form, the statute enumerates five classes of contracts and provides that "no action shall be brought" on such agreements unless the agreement is in writing or is evidenced by some note or memorandum signed by the party to be charged. Thus it concerns the matter of proof rather than validity.

Note also that even when a contract is within the Statute of Frauds— that is to say, one of those enumerated in the statute—the contract itself does not have to be in writing. Ordinarily a written note or memorandum evidencing the promise is all that is required.

What the Statute Covers. The Statute of Frauds applies to agreements of the following kinds:

1. A promise by an executor or administrator to pay a claim against the estate out of his own funds.
2. A promise to be responsible legally for the debt or default of another.
3. A promise made in consideration of marriage.
4. An agreement to sell or a sale of any interest in real property.
5. An agreement that cannot be performed within one year after the contract is made.

Life Contract Not Generally Included. An oral contract of life insurance has sometimes been challenged on the grounds that it cannot be proved, by reason of the fifth class of agreements listed above of the Statute of Frauds. Indeed many life insurance contracts remain in effect and are not performed for many, many years. Nevertheless any life insurance contract, contingent as it is upon the death of the insured, *could be performed* within one year after the contract is made. In fact many life insurance contracts are so performed. In any case, that is the test. An agreement that *can be performed within one year,* whether or not it is so performed, is not within the Statute of Frauds as it is ordinarily enacted. Thus proof of an oral contract of life insurance is not ordinarily precluded by the Statute of Frauds.[11]

Other Special Statutes. If the legislatures of the various states believe that the life insurance contract should be in writing it is necessary for them to enact special legislation to that effect. Georgia, for example, has a statute requiring insurance contracts to be in writing. New York has accomplished this purpose with respect to life insurance contracts by special wording of the Statute of Frauds. However, in the absence of such legislation, the life insurance contract does not have to be written. Even laws setting forth required provisions have been held not to invalidate oral contracts of insurance but merely to require that such contracts be interpreted as if they included the terms set forth in the law.

---

[11] An important exception to this is found in the New York Personal Property Law, Art. 3, Sec. 31, which reads in part as follows:
"Section 31. Agreements required to be in writing
    "Every agreement, promise or undertaking is void, unless it or some note or memorandum thereof be in writing, and subscribed by the party to be charged therewith, or by his lawful agent, if such agreement, promise or undertaking;
    "1. By its terms is not to be performed within one year from the making thereof or the performance of which is not to be completed before the end of a lifetime; . . ."
By its special wording, therefore, the Statute of Frauds as enacted by The New York Legislature applies to contracts of life insurance.

To summarize—oral contracts of insurance are valid under the common law and the Statute of Frauds is not applicable. Although it is doubtful that a valid oral life insurance contract could be established as a matter of practice under the laws of most of the states, there are many instances where such a contract has been held to be in effect even though a written policy was never issued.

The Parol Evidence Rule

The parol evidence rule, as generally stated, simply provides that if a contract has been reduced to writing it will be assumed that the preceding oral agreement, if there was one, was merged into the written contract. Thereafter parol (oral) testimony will not be admitted to modify or contradict the terms of the written agreement.

Applies to the Life Insurance Contract. In the absence of a specific statute requiring it, the life insurance contract does not have to be in writing. Nevertheless most life insurance contracts are written, and as written contracts they are subject to the parol evidence rule. This means that if the facts of a specific case are not in conformity with the policy provisions as written, oral testimony cannot ordinarily be admitted to contradict the provisions of the policy.

Exceptions. The rule that oral testimony may not be used to vary or contradict the terms of a written contract, once the parties have reduced their agreement to writing, is subject to a number of well-defined exceptions. Thus it does not prohibit oral testimony showing that no contract was ever formed or that, if completed, the contract has been performed. Note in this connection the language of the court in the case of *Obartuch* v. *Security Mutual Life Insurance Company* [12] as follows:

> There is no question but that the general rule precludes the introduction of parol testimony for the purpose of contradicting, changing or adding to the terms incorporated into and made a part of a written contract. 56 A.L.R. 13. The same authority, however, recognizes an exception to the rule in cases where a written contract is procured by fraud. On page 87 of the same volume, it is said:
>
> > . . . And where a life insurance policy is contested on the ground of fraud, parol testimony tending to show the circumstances, statements, and representations which led up to, and induced, the making of the instrument, is not inadmissible on the ground that it tends to vary the terms of the written application for insurance and the written medical examination signed by the insured . . .
>
> * * *
>
> In a case such as the instant one, where the defense of fraud is invoked, in that the named insured never knowingly made application for insurance and where a person other than the named insured was substituted for the medical examination, we are of the opinion that the Parol Evidence Rule can not be

---

[12] 114 F.2d 873 (C.C.A. Ill., 1940).

invoked to preclude the medical examiner from giving testimony as to the facts and circumstances connected with and surrounding the parties at the time of such examination. The purpose of such testimony is not to vary or contradict a contract, but to show that the alleged contract never came into existence.

Oral testimony may also be admitted in the following cases:

1. *Where the Contract Is Incomplete.* If the face of the written agreement shows that something remained to be done or another provision was to be incorporated, parol evidence can be used to show those provisions on which the parties had orally agreed but which they failed to incorporate into the written agreement.

2. *Where There Is Fraud, Accident, or Mistake.* If by reason of fraud, accident, or mistake, some portion of the instrument was omitted, oral testimony may be used to show the provision or provisions so omitted.

3. *Where There Is Ambiguity.* Oral evidence is also permitted in cases of ambiguity if such ambiguity is evident on the face of the contract. This exception is sometimes stated in terms of *"patent"* and *"latent"* ambiguities. Thus, it is said that parol evidence can be used to explain an obvious (*patent*) ambiguity but not a hidden (*latent*) ambiguity. In the latter case it would be necessary to introduce oral testimony to prove that there was any ambiguity at all, and that is not permitted.

4. *Where the Terms or Expressions Used Have Technical Meanings.* Where words used in a contract have a special trade meaning or a specialized meaning by reason of the locality in which the contract was drawn up, parol evidence can be used to explain that meaning.

NOT AGAINST PUBLIC POLICY

It will be recalled that the last-named requirement for a valid contract was that it not be illegal and that there be no statute or rule of common law declaring it void or against public policy. The term "public policy" is frequently used in a discussion of contract law but it is very difficult to define. One rather standard definition summarizes it as

. . . the community common sense and common conscience extended and applied throughout the state to matters of public morals, public health, public safety, public welfare, and the like; it is that general and well-settled public opinion relating to man's plain, palpable duty to his fellow men having due regard to all the circumstances of each particular relation and situation.[13]

Illegal Contracts

If the formation or performance of the contract is a crime or an actionable, civil wrong (a *tort*) or if it is against public policy, the con-

---

[13] *Black's Law Dictionary* (West Publishing Company, 1933), p. 1374.

tract is said to be illegal. Contracts to use bribery or other unlawful means to influence the legislative or judicial processes of the government, for example, are illegal.

Their Effect. Ordinarily, the law will not aid either party to an illegal contract. If the contract has not been performed, neither party can compel performance or obtain damages. If the contract has been performed, neither can sue the other for damages.

Sometimes a particular type of contract will be declared against public policy as a means of protecting one of the parties to such a contract. Thus, as a part of the general regulatory laws of a state, statutes are sometimes enacted with respect to the validity of life insurance contracts issued by life insurance companies not authorized to do an insurance business in that particular state. Because such laws have as their purpose the protection of the citizens of the state, they often do not declare the contract void and unenforceable but instead permit the insured to bring suit against the company at fault.

Wagering Contracts

In the earliest days of the common law, wagers were not prohibited. Later, laws were enacted declaring certain kinds of wagers to be against public policy, and statutes to this effect are now in force in most of the states. In this connection it is common to distinguish between contracts which involve the exchange of more or less equivalent values, which are known as *commutative* agreements, and those in which one of the parties may recover a great deal more in value than that with which he has parted. Contracts of the latter type are known as *aleatory* contracts and include wagering contracts as well as contracts of insurance.

Life Insurance Contracts

In the Public Interest. It is commonly accepted today that insurance contracts are in the interests of society. If issued with proper safeguards, therefore, there is no question of their validity. This question has not always been so settled, however. It is obvious that a life insurance contract, binding as it does, one party to pay to the other a sum of money on the happening of an event presumably not within the control of either, bears more than a passing resemblance to a wagering contract. It is obvious also that an unscrupulous person standing to gain from the destruction of an insured piece of property or a life might feel a strong temptation under some circumstances to implement the whims of chance in his own favor. Thus life insurance contracts issued indiscriminately pose a double threat to the public welfare. To the evils attendant on gambling of any kind are added the possible creation of a motive for murder in the minds of the unscrupulous.

Insurable Interest. These problems are resolved by the concept of insurable interest. According to this idea, a person who has an insurable interest in the subject of the insurance is thought to have a motive for preserving the property or life rather than destroying it. An insurable interest is defined as a financial or otherwise undeniable interest in the preservation of the subject of the insurance—a building or contents in fire insurance, the life insured in life insurance. Such a person will also have a risk of genuine loss in the event of the destruction of the property or life.

Persons having an insurable interest in the subject of the insurance, who join together through the facilities of an insurance company to share their individual risks of loss, are not creating a chance of unlawful gain but only protecting themselves against a risk already in existence. Each person agrees, in effect, to share a small portion of every loss suffered by anyone in the group in exchange for the assumption by the group of his own individual risk of loss. These people then are exchanging risk for certainty, exactly the opposite of a wager.[14]

Not a Wagering Contract. It is precisely this exchange of risk for certainty ("transfer of risk") idea that distinguishes the contract of insurance from the wagering contract. In a true wager there is no risk until the wager is made. The wager, in other words, creates the risk. In insurance the contract removes the risk and truly exchanges risk for certainty. Thus, the only contract of insurance that is against public policy is a contract issued to someone without an insurable interest. Ordinarily such contracts are declared by statute to be void.

❋ ❋ ❋ ❋ ❋

AN ILLUSTRATIVE CASE

The discussion in this chapter has, of necessity, been in general terms. Legal principles have been discussed generally, as have been the statutes to which we have referred. In every case it must be borne in mind that court holdings and statutes alike may vary from state to state even though they may be quite similar in their over-all meaning. The following case has been selected, not only because it illustrates many of the points we have touched upon in connection with the basic principles of contract law, but also because it illustrates an important individual modification of one of the traditional provisions of the Statute of Frauds, as enacted by the legislature of the State of New York.[15]

---

[14] See more complete discussion of this point *infra*, page 107.

[15] See footnote 11, p. 43, *supra*.

GOLDBERG, ADMX., Respondent v. *COLONIAL LIFE INS. CO. OF AMERICA, Appellant* [16]

(New York Supreme Court, Appellate Division, Second Judicial Department.)

MURPHY, J.: Respondent, a widow, seeks to recover $10,000 from appellant under an alleged contract of life insurance of which she is beneficiary. In her first cause she alleges an agreement made April 29, 1953, between her husband and the appellant. These are the allegations: Her husband went to the office of one Max L. Weil, general agent of the appellant, to purchase a life insurance policy, and, after considerable negotiation, he agreed to purchase and Weil agreed to sell a straight life policy in the sum of $10,000; her husband signed an application, was examined by appellant's doctor, who indicated to her husband and to the general agent that her husband's physical condition was satisfactory; the general agent accepted a check in the amount of $425.20 made to appellant's order as the first year's premium and this check was deposited to the credit of appellant. Finally it is alleged, on information and belief, that thereafter and upon receipt by the appellant of the signed application, the prepaid premium and the physician's report appellant "duly issued the said life insurance policy on its books."

Respondent's husband died on May 18, 1953, nineteen days after he had applied for the aforesaid insurance. Appellant had never issued a policy to the deceased and refuses to pay the proceeds due under the alleged contract.

In her second cause of action, respondent seeks to recover on the ground of estoppel [17] based upon the allegation that appellant's general agent assured her husband that a contract had been created. A third cause of action has been dismissed and need not be discussed herein as no appeal has been taken from that dismissal.

The only conceivable contract with the appellant, alleged in the first cause, is one between the husband and the general agent. The additional allegations as to the making of a written application to the appellant are insufficient to show the existence of any other contract. There could be no agreement with the company until it accepted the application for insurance. (*Schultz & Co.* v. *Camden Fire Ins. Assn.,* 304 N.Y. 143, 147; *More* v. *N.Y.B. F. Ins. Co.,* 130 N.Y. 537; *Corning* v. *Prudential Insurance Co. of America,* 248 App. Div. 187, affd. 273 N.Y. 668.) Acceptance by the appellant had to be manifested by some appropriate act and such manifestation communicated to the applicant. (*White* v. *Corlies,* 46 N.Y. 467.) Of course, the ordinary means of acceptance would be delivery of a policy to the insured. In any event, however, there had to be a notification to the insured of such acceptance by the insurer. A notation by appellant on its books would not be a binding acceptance any more than would be the words of a man speaking to himself. Until acceptance was communicated to him, the applicant was free to with-

---

[16] A.D. 2d, 134 N.Y.S. 2d 865 (1954).

[17] Estoppel. This is a legal concept which can be illustrated more easily than it can be defined. Thus, if A. has, by his words or actions, led B. erroneously to believe that a set of facts is true, and if B. has taken such action in reliance upon this belief that it would be unjust to permit A. to plead the truth, A. will be estopped to deny (that is, legally precluded from denying) that the facts were as he said they were. This concept is discussed in greater detail in Chapter IX, *infra.*

draw his application and no mutually binding contract could be said to have been entered into. (*Goldstein* v. *New York Life Insurance Co.*, 176 App. Div. 813, 816, affd. 227 N.Y. 575; *Topken, Loring & Schwartz, Inc.* v. *Schwartz*, 249 N.Y. 206.)

As to the alleged contract with the general agent, the Statute of Frauds (Personal Property Law, Section 31, subd. 1) provides that every agreement is void unless there is a note or memorandum in writing and subscribed by the party to be charged if its performance "is not to be completed before the end of a lifetime." A life insurance contract clearly comes within the scope of this provision. Respondent argues to the contrary, contending that the provision was enacted to prevent assertion of claims against the estate of a decedent and that therefore it was intended to restrict application of the provision to contracts relating to the lifetime of a promisor. Even under such narrow interpretation a life insurance policy would require a writing because the insured is a promisor of premiums. In any event, it is now beyond dispute that the provision means exactly what it says, namely, "a lifetime." As stated in *Meltzer* v. *Koenigsberg* (302 N.Y. 523, 525):

> The Statute of Frauds requires that an agreement be in writing if by its terms performance is "not to be completed before the end of a lifetime" (Personal Property Law, Section 31, subd. 1). Had the legislature intended the "lifetime" referred to to be the lifetime of the promisor, the party to be charged, or the lifetime of any particular person, it could easily and readily have so provided.

Subdivision 7 of rule 107, Rules of Civil Practice, provides for dismissal on motion on the ground that the case is founded on a contract which is unenforceable under the Statute of Frauds. The rule provides that the motion may be made "on the complaint and an affidavit stating facts tending to show" the unenforceability. In support of its motion and in accordance with the rule, appellant submitted an affidavit of its assistant secretary in which he states that there was no writing other than the application of the deceased husband and his check. There is no affidavit by respondent in opposition to this statement. Obviously neither the check of the deceased husband, which was merely deposited, the aforesaid notation on the books of the corporation, nor the application signed by the deceased, singly or collectively, constitute a written memorandum of a contract signed by the party to be charged. There is no allegation in the amended complaint or showing in opposition to the motion to dismiss to the contrary. It was held in *N. E. D. Holding Co.* v. *McKinley*, (246 N.Y. 40, 44) and *Crabtree* v. *Elizabeth Arden Sales Corp.*, (305 N.Y. 48, 54, 57) that a memorandum signed by the party to be charged must contain the substance of the agreement to avoid the application of the Statute of Frauds. There is no such memorandum present in the case before us.

The first cause of action must be dismissed.

The second cause of action realleges the contents of the first cause and in addition it is alleged that appellant is estopped from asserting that no contract of insurance was made because the general agent Weil told the deceased to consider himself insured for the principal amount. It is also further alleged that up to the time of the husband's death, nineteen days after the foregoing assurance, appellant had not rejected the insurance, whereas if it had rejected the insurance, the husband would have been able to place the insurance elsewhere.

This second cause is insufficient. The representation of Weil to the deceased that he was to consider himself insured adds nothing to the allegation in the first cause, which is to the effect that the general agent entered into an oral contract. This apparently was a mutual mistake of law with respect to the efficacy of an oral contract. Estoppel cannot be invoked where each of the parties had equal means of knowledge of the unenforceability of the contract. (*New York Life Ins. Co. v. Rees*, 19 F. 2d 781, 784.)

Whatever different result might ensue if fraud or intentional misrepresentation had been alleged, or rescission or reformation sought, a contract void for lack of writing cannot be regarded as valid merely because the parties believed that it was valid at the time they entered into it. The fact that the appellant did not reject the application adds nothing whatever to this claim of estoppel as set forth in the second cause.

In consequence the second cause of action should be dismissed.

The order denying the motion to dismiss, insofar as appealed from, should be modified on the law by striking from the second ordering paragraph the word "denied" and by substituting therefor the word "granted," and by striking therefrom the third ordering paragraph. As so modified, the order should be affirmed, with $10 costs and disbursements to appellant.

ADEL, SCHMIDT and BELDOCK, JJ., concur.

CHAPTER **III**

The Meaning
of
Agency

A CORPORATION is a group of persons authorized by law to transact a business of a specified kind under its corporate name. The corporation itself is an abstract legal concept, a *legal entity*, the lawyer says. Its business is always transacted by a natural person or persons acting for the corporation, an idea which is sometimes summarized by the statement that corporations must, by their very nature, transact all their business through agents.

Because the modern life insurance company is corporate in its form of organization, it too must transact its business through agents, sometimes the field underwriter, sometimes the officers in the home or other administrative office. From the company's point of view, therefore, the story of a life insurance contract, from the first step in the application process to the final closing of the file, is a story of actions taken and words spoken by many different kinds of agents. For this reason, the purpose of this chapter is to discuss the more significant principles of agency law as they apply to life insurance and to show how they operate to affect the undertakings of a life insurance company under its life insurance contracts.

DEFINITION AND NATURE OF AGENCY

Definition

What Agency Is. Whenever one person has the power to represent and act for another, or for a corporation, in the creation or modification of contracts between the person represented and others, the relationship between the person representing and the person represented is that of agency. The person representing and acting for the other is an agent; the person represented is the principal.

With few exceptions, an agent may be appointed to perform any act which the principal himself could do. This excludes crimes or acts contrary to public policy. There are also a few perfectly lawful acts, such as voting or making a will, which must be done personally or not at all. Nevertheless, as a general rule, anything that one can do for himself he can do through an agent.

Who Is an Agent? Ordinarily an agent is called an agent. However, principles of agency law often apply in situations where no one is either called or thought of as an agent. One of the most difficult aspects of agency law is that it often applies in situations which on the surface do not seem to involve any agent-principal relationship whatsoever.

For example, in the case of *Morrison* v. *The Mutual Life Insurance Company of New York*,[1] the beneficiary of a life insurance contract visited the San Francisco office of the insurer and discussed her problem with two of the "head men," according to her testimony. In a subsequent action on the policy, the company maintained that the men she talked to did not have the power to modify a company contract. Nevertheless, on the facts as developed in the trial, the court held that the men concerned were "in responsible charge" of the office and had apparent if not actual authority to clarify her rights under the contract and bind the company. Thus the general principles of agency law were applied even though the company maintained that the men the woman talked to were not its agents. The facts of the case governed, not the terminology the parties chose to use.

Agents and Employees

Agency Relates to Contracts. It is not necessary that the agent be authorized to negotiate and complete a binding contract. Indeed, in its broadest sense the law of agency applies to persons acting in a strictly employee capacity, who have no contractual authority whatever. However, in a truer sense, and in the sense in which the word will be used here, agency means a relationship having to do with the creation or modification of contracts by one person in the name of and for another whom he is entitled to represent.

Differs from Employer-Employee Relationship. In this sense the relationship of an agent and the person he represents differs from that of an employee and his employer in both nature and scope. An agent represents his principal and acts not only *for* him but *in his place.* The employee merely works *for* the employer. The employee performs

---

[1] 15 Cal. 2d 579, 103 P.2d 963 (1940).

his duties according to the employer's directions and instructions, but he cannot commit the employer in any contractual way.

In the case we have previously mentioned, let us assume that the beneficiary first met the receptionist in the office she visited. The receptionist would have been an employee. She would have worked for the agency but without authority to change or modify company contracts in any way. No words or actions on her part could have changed the company's liability under the contract in question. What the "head men" said, however, was held binding on the company.

Agents and Independent Contractors

Responsibility of the Independent Contractor. The employee performs his duties according to the directions of the employer. At the other end of the scale, as far as instructions are concerned, is the independent contractor. His situation also is different from that of the agent. An independent contractor is a person who contracts with another to perform a service but with almost complete freedom as to methods and details of the work to be performed. The independent contractor is responsible only for the end result.

Since the same person may be an agent with respect to some actions and an independent contractor with respect to others, it is often difficult to say as a matter of law whether a specific action on the part of an independent contractor was taken in his capacity as an independent contractor or as an agent. A principal, however, is responsible for the acts of his agent within the scope of the latter's authority. The independent contractor is responsible for his own acts. For many reasons, therefore, it is often highly important to distinguish between the independent contractor and an agent.

How the Problem Is Solved. Perhaps the most important single factor to be considered in distinguishing between the acts of an independent contractor and those of an agent is the matter of control. Ordinarily the independent contractor is almost completely free from the control of the person for whom the service is to be performed. He is responsible only for the end result. By contrast, the principal has complete and continuing control over the agent even though he may not always choose to exercise it. Thus it is reasonable for a man to be responsible as a matter of law for the actions of his agent and not for those of an independent contractor who may happen to be performing work for him.

Nature of the Agency Relationship

Essentially a Matter of Power. The essence of the agency relationship is power. An agent has the power to bring about or modify contractual relationships between his principal, whom he represents, and third persons with whom the contracts are made. In legal effect the agent is substituted *for* the principal in these transactions. Any action he takes in connection with the business of his principal has exactly the same legal effect as if it had been done by the principal.

No one is an agent unless he has this power to affect the contractual relations of his principal. Also, if he has this power he is an agent, as far as the law is concerned, regardless of the title he may have. For example, the field underwriter of the life insurance company is an agent of the company as a matter of law. However, the home office officer or employee who approves risks also has the power to affect the legal relationships of the company and represents it in many ways. He, too, is an agent in the legal sense of the word.

Power Distinguished from Authority. Although power is sometimes confused with authority, it is a far broader term. An agent is *authorized* by his principal, expressly or by implication, to do certain things. However, by reason of circumstances, he may have the *power* to bind the principal in many other ways. For this reason agency law is not at all limited to situations where the agent has been actually authorized to do what he did. It encompasses all the many situations where he may reasonably *seem* to have the authority he professes to exercise. In these latter cases the agent is said to have the *power* though not the *authority* to bind his principal.

Other Characteristics of Agency

It Is a Fiduciary Relationship. Certain people, such as trustees, guardians, executors, etc., have positions involving such a high degree of trust and confidence that the law exacts of them a higher standard of conduct than is required in the usual course of business. These people are said to be *fiduciaries,* that is, persons who bear toward others a relationship of trust and confidence. An agent is a fiduciary with respect to his principal and the business with which he is concerned. He has a duty to act primarily for the benefit of the principal and to deal fairly with him in every way.

It Implies Control. Another characteristic of the agency relationship is the right of the principal to control the conduct of the agent. This right of control is continuous as far as the duties of the agency are concerned, and its presence or absence often determines whether a given relationship is or is not that of agency.

WHO MAY BE AN AGENT?

Qualifications Generally

Contractual Capacity. In legal effect, the act of an agent is the act of his principal. For this reason it is not necessary that the agent himself have contractual capacity. It is the principal's capacity that governs. Thus a contract completed by a minor agent for a principal of legal age cannot be avoided on the ground that the agent was a minor.

The modern life insurance company and its agents clearly illustrate the fact that the agent does not have to have the necessary contractual capacity in his own right. Under presently existing laws, few individuals could or would care to qualify to issue contracts of legal reserve life insurance as insurers. However, such contracts are completed by individuals acting as agents for corporate insurers every day.

Partnerships and Corporations. It is customary to think and speak of agents as individuals. However, partnerships and corporations may also act as agents. The general rules of agency law apply whether the agent is an individual, a partnership, or a corporation.

Statutory Requirements. In the case of real estate agents, brokers, insurance agents, and others whose activities involve the general public, the various states have imposed certain statutory restrictions in the public interest. Before they may be appointed to represent others in these capacities, agents must meet these statutory requirements.

Agents in Life Insurance

The Field Underwriter. Life insurance agents are among those whose activities involve the general public, and for that reason they must meet statutory requirements in almost every state. Usually the agent takes an examination given by the Department of Insurance of the state where he will represent the company, and he must otherwise satisfy the Department that he is generally fitted for such a position of public trust. The agent also has a contract with the company, which defines his authority and responsibility and sets forth the agreement of the parties with respect to commissions and other details of the relationship.

The Agent Represents the Company. Generally speaking, there is little question but that the life agent represents the company. However, the company has the right to limit and define the authority of the agent. Thus one of the most important chapters in the history of life insurance law deals with the question of whom the agent represents in completing the application for insurance. It has been decided, almost beyond question, that in filling out the application for the signature of the applicant the agent is acting for the insurance company, but this has not always been true.

A Policy Provision. If we assume that the underwriter is the agent of the company in completing the application for the applicant's signature, there are some very definite legal consequences which flow from this relationship. The agent's knowledge will be presumed to be the knowledge of the company, and the company will be responsible for any

fraud or mistakes of the agent. In an early effort to avoid some of these
consequences, the companies inserted in their policies a provision to the
effect that the agent in completing the application should be regarded
as the agent of the applicant or insured and not that of the company.

In decisions involving these policy provisions, the courts consistently
held that they were ineffective to change the representative capacity
of the agent. For example, one court said:

> It would be a stretch of legal principles to hold that a person dealing
> with an agent, apparently clothed with authority to act for his principal in
> the matter in hand, could be affected by notice, given after the negotiations
> were completed, that the party with whom he had dealt should be deemed
> transformed from the agent of one party into the agent of the other.[2]

Provision in the Application. Companies then began inserting a
provision in the application to the effect that the agent, in completing
the form, was acting as the agent of the applicant. This served as notice
to the applicant at the outset (which a provision in the policy did not
do). Nevertheless the majority of courts held that the provision was
invalid. In one case [3] the court said:

> This is but a form of words to attempt to create on paper an agency
> which in fact never existed. It is an attempt of the company, not to restrict
> the powers of its own agent, but an effort to do away with that relationship
> altogether by mere words, and to make him in the same manner the agent of
> the assured, when in fact such relation never existed.

Although case law differs from state to state, the majority holding is
that the agency relationship between the insurer and the life underwriter
cannot actually be changed by statements to the contrary either in the
application or in the policy. This is only another way of saying that the
facts of the individual case will govern.

Agency Is a Matter of Fact. It must consistently be borne in mind
that what the parties *say* they meant is not important if what they *did*
shows a different intent. Thus an insurance company cannot make the
life underwriter the agent of the applicant simply by saying he is, if the
facts show that he represents no one but the company. However, there is
nothing to keep the applicant himself from authorizing the life underwriter to represent him for certain purposes. If he does this, the underwriter will, for those purposes, be the agent of the applicant and subsequent insured.

For example, in a relatively recent case,[4] a beneficiary sued for
the $5,000 death benefit under a life insurance policy issued to her son.
The contestable period had not elapsed, and the company defended on

---

[2] *Kausal v. Minnesota Farmers' Mut. Insurance Association,* 31 Minn. 17 (1883).

[3] *Continental Insurance Co. v. Pearce,* 39 Kan. 396 (1888).

[4] *Indovina v. Metropolitan Life Insurance Co.,* 334 Pa. 167, 5 A.2d 556 (1939).

the grounds that material facts concerning the applicant's health were misrepresented in the application for the policy. The beneficiary maintained that the false statements were not made by the applicant but were inserted in the application by the agent.

The evidence showed that at the time of application the applicant told the doctor that the agent knew all the details and he, the doctor, could get the information he needed from him. On this evidence and the other facts of the case, the court held that the insured, in legal effect, had made the field underwriter his agent for the purpose of giving this medical history. The misrepresentations of the agent were the misrepresentations of the principal, but in this case the principal was the applicant.

Thus the company cannot by a mere statement, either in the policy or in the application form, convert its own agent into an agent of the insured. However, the applicant is free to appoint anyone he chooses to act as his agent, and in this case he chose the agent of the company. Again, the facts of the case governed.

Insurance Brokers

In the legal sense, an insurance broker is a person who is in business to obtain insurance for anyone who requests him to do so. For that reason he represents and is the agent of the applicant and insured, at least for the purpose of placing the insurance. In life insurance, however, the term brokerage business is often used to denote any policies issued upon applications submitted by persons who are not regular members of the company's agency force.

Because state licensing laws and the practices of the various companies differ so widely, it is impossible to discuss the subject briefly in any but the most general terms. Nevertheless, as we have seen, even the regularly licensed life agent may represent the applicant for some purposes and the insurance company for others. In brokerage business, there is a better than even chance that this will be true. The important thing, therefore, is to make a clear distinction between insurance and legal terminology. Most questions involving brokers can then be resolved by a careful examination and analysis of the facts and the application of general principles of agency law to the individual case.

WHO MAY BE A PRINCIPAL?

Generally

Contractual Capacity. As a general rule any person who has the capacity to make a contract may appoint an agent to make one for him. It will be remembered that every person is presumed to have this capacity in the absence of a contrary showing. However, persons who do not have the capacity to make a contract cannot cure that incapacity by appointing someone with contractual capacity to act as their agent and make a contract for them.

Thus an adult appointed by a minor cannot make a binding contract for the minor. Similarly if a life insurance company is not authorized to do a life insurance business in a given state, the qualifications of its agents are ineffective to make up for that lack of authority.

Principals and Life Insurance

Both Parties May Act through Agents. The life insurance company as a corporate entity must transact its business through agents. As a general rule the applicant is an individual acting for himself alone. Nevertheless there is nothing to prevent the applicant from authorizing another to act for him, as we have seen, and if the applicant is itself a corporation, as is true in many third-party ownership cases (where insurance on the life of someone other than the applicant is applied for), it *must be* represented by an agent. Thus many life insurance transactions involve agency relationships on both sides. The agent for the company deals with an agent for the applicant or the insured, and the basic rules of agency law apply in either case.

HOW AGENCY IS CREATED

Between Principal and Agent

By Mutual Consent. There are always three parties in an agency relationship, the principal, the agent, and the third party, with whom the contract is made. Between the principal and the agent, the agency relationship is created by mutual consent and not otherwise. It may be established by express agreement, as in the case of an agency contract, or it may be implied from a prior course of dealing. If there is consideration for the agreement, it is contractual. However, consideration is not necessary. An agreement may be sufficient to establish an agency relationship even though it is not a binding contract.

The principal's consent need not precede the transaction or transactions in question. Instead, he may adopt the actions as his own after they have been performed. In that case there is said to be an agency by ratification.

Agency by Ratification

What It Is. Sometimes an agent who is authorized to act in one line of business makes a contract in the name of his principal in an entirely different business. When this happens, or in any case where there is no actual authority to do what was done, the contract will not ordinarily bind the purported principal. If, by his own actions, the principal has led the third person to believe that the agent was authorized to do what he did, there may be agency by estoppel, which will be discussed later. However, if the contract so made proves advantageous, the person in whose name (but without whose consent) it was made may adopt it as his own by ratifying it. Ratification may be defined as the intentional adoption on the part of one person of the acts of another, taken purportedly as his agent but without authority. The relationship it establishes is agency by ratification.

When Ratification Is Effective. When one person as principal ratifies the acts of another as agent, the ratification reverts back and becomes effective as of the date of the performance of the act or actions being ratified. For this reason ratification is not effective if the principal could not have authorized the act at the time it took place. For example, a corporation cannot ratify the contracts of its promoters made before the date of incorporation, because the corporation was not in existence at the time the contracts were made. The purported agent must also have had the capacity to perform the act at the time it was performed. In other words, ratification cannot make a transaction valid if it was invalid at the time it took place.

Requirements for Ratification

A Purported Agency. One of the first requirements for ratification is that the agent must have assumed to act on behalf of the principal. The agent must have held himself out as an agent, and the third party must have thought he was dealing with an agent. Without a purported agency, ratification is impossible. Generally speaking, any acts which may be authorized beforehand may be ratified afterwards.

The Intended Principal Must Ratify. No one except the person intended as principal may ratify the act. Thus if agent Jones makes a contract in the name of Harold Brown, John Smith cannot ratify the action for his own benefit. The contract can be ratified by Brown and then assigned to Smith if the parties wish to do this, but it is legally impossible for Smith to ratify it.

Must Have Full Knowledge. The principal must have full knowledge of all the facts surrounding the transaction. If at the time of ratification he did not know all the facts, he may later, upon learning the truth, cancel (*avoid* is the legal term) the ratification.

Must Ratify Entirely. The principal must intend to ratify the act, have the power to do so, and ratify it in its entirety. He cannot select the parts of the transaction that he likes, ratify them, and deny responsibility for the others. In fact, if he ratifies any part of the transaction, as a matter of law he ratifies it all.

Form of Ratification

No Particular Form Required. If a special kind of authorization (a writing, for example) would have been required to authorize the act in the first place, ratification must be in that form also. Otherwise any conduct indicating approval of the act is sufficient to constitute an effective ratification. Thus ratification may consist of express words, spoken or written, or it may be implied from conduct on the part of the principal that clearly indicates that he ratifies the actions of the purported agent and accepts them as his own.

Implied Ratification. Acceptance or retention of the benefits or proceeds of the agent's activities often constitutes ratification of those activities. For example, acceptance by the company of the premium for a life insurance contract, with full knowledge of an agent's misconduct in accepting the application, may constitute ratification of the agent's action. The underlying principle is that one may not accept the benefits of a transaction while refusing to assume the responsibility it entails.

Effect of Silence. Silence alone does not indicate ratification. However, a principal will ordinarily be held to have ratified the agent's act if, with full knowledge of the facts, he fails to repudiate it within a reasonable length of time.

How Ratification Works

Applies to Either Party. Like every other aspect of agency, ratification operates with respect to either party to a contract. Thus in the life insurance field it applies to the insured as well as the insurer. In fact, some agency principles, especially those which operate without the volition of the parties, can be illustrated more clearly in connection with the insured than the insurer.

The following case has been selected for discussion because it illustrates the principle of agency by ratification. At the same time, because it involves a broker, it illustrates the point made above that a broker is more likely to represent the insured than is an agent.

In this case [5] a licensed broker, named Kantoff, negotiated a $50,000 policy for the Sedlak Motor Sales Inc., on the life of Sedlak, and made an unauthorized premium payment of $1,529 when the latter neglected to do so. When Kantoff sued for reimbursement in that amount a clear-cut question of agency was raised. Sedlak had refused to reimburse Kantoff on the grounds that the latter was an agent for the insurance

---

[5] *Kantoff v. Sedlak Motor Sales, Inc.,* 130 N.E. (2d) 289 (Ill. App., 1955).

company. He contended that under accepted rules of agency law Kantoff could not act for him and also for the company without the consent of both parties. In other words, Sedlak took the position that Kantoff was not his agent.

The court decided the case as follows:

> . . . Defendants (Sedlak Motor Sales, Inc.) urge that plaintiff (Kantoff) could not be their agent since he was also the agent for the insurance company, and this they claim violated the rule of law that an agent's duty of loyalty prevents him from acting for adverse parties without the consent of both. We think, however, that this rule is not applicable because, as the court properly found, defendants, with knowledge of plaintiff's agency with the insurance company, authorized him to represent them in obtaining insurance. *Adams* v. *Larson*, 279 Ill. 268, 277-8.
>
> We think, further, that, even if we assume that payment of the premium was beyond the scope of the authorized agency, defendants ratified this act and thereby incurred liability for the amount paid on their behalf. The reasons for this conclusion are as follows: Sedlak's acceptance of the policy made him liable for the premium. *Equitable Life Assurance Society* v. *Mueller,* 99 Ill. App. 460. After several unsuccessful attempts to see Sedlak with respect to the premium, plaintiff paid the premium during the grace period in order to protect his principal by preventing the policy from lapsing. Defendants knew plaintiff paid the premium because they received no premium notice from the company but they did receive a bill from plaintiff on his own stationery. With this knowledge they retained the policy even until the trial. They therefore had the protection of the policy (*Nalty* v. *Federal Casualty Co.* 245 Ill. App. 180, 183) and the inference is they intended to have that benefit, for the earlier policy which Sedlak rejected was returned at once. Furthermore, they at no time disclaimed plaintiff's authority to pay the premium. Under these circumstances we conclude that payment, even if unauthorized, was ratified and bound defendants, who accepted the benefits, to reimburse. *Cobb* v. *Sparr,* 153 Ill. App. 92, 99. As between principal and agent the conduct of the principal will be liberally interpreted in favor of ratification. *Holmes* v. *Morris,* 341 Ill. 351, 358.

Agency with Respect to Third Parties

As far as the principal and the agent are concerned, the ways in which an agency relationship may be created are relatively clear-cut. With respect to third parties, however, there are other ways in which the relationship may be established. In life insurance the most significant of these ways is creation of agency by *estoppel.*

Agency by Estoppel

What It Is. Agency by estoppel is more easily explained than defined. As we have said, it sometimes happens that an individual may appear to be an agent even though he has no actual authority to represent the person he claims to represent. Perhaps he has no authority at all, or perhaps the authority he has is limited in ways not known to the persons with whom he deals. In cases like these, if the action taken is advantageous to him, the purported principal may wish to ratify it and thus create an agency by ratification. On the other hand, if the action taken is not to the advantage of the purported principal, he may nevertheless have conducted himself in such a way that a reasonable man would be justified in believing that the purported agent had the authority he presumed to have. In that case, the principal may be forbidden as a matter of law (*estopped* is the legal term) to deny that the purported agent was his agent in fact.[6]

Let us assume that John Jones, without objecting, permits Bill Smith to hold himself out as his agent. Assume further that you make a contract with Bill as John's agent, believing that he is authorized to represent John. If John's conduct has been responsible for your mistake, he may be estopped to deny that Bill was in fact his agent with the authority a man of reasonable business judgment would have assumed him to have.

Estoppel Operates against the Principal. An estoppel always operates against the principal. For this reason it is absolutely essential that the principal, by his own conduct, shall have been responsible for misleading the person who seeks to establish the agency. Nothing the agent does or says will be sufficient. For one thing, no one is entitled to presume that an agency exists. Thus there must be some insignia of agency, some "holding out" of agency by the acts of the principal. It is also necessary that the third party shall actually have relied upon the appearance of agency which the principal has permitted to exist. One cannot, knowing the truth, maintain that he has been misled.

Estoppel in Life Insurance. Agency by estoppel is a frequent concept in connection with the formation and operation of the life insurance contract. One court [7] states it thus:

> As in the case of other agencies, an insurance company will be estopped to deny that a certain person is its agent or possesses the authority he assumes to exercise where the insurance company knowingly causes or permits him so to act as to justify a third person of ordinarily careful and prudent business habits to believe that he possesses the authority exercised.

Thus a life insurance company might terminate an agency and yet permit the agent to retain some or all of the credentials, documents, etc., he had used. Or the company might otherwise make it possible for third persons to be misled with respect to the existence or extent of

---

[6] The student will recall the term *estoppel* from Chapter II and the illustration given in footnote 17, p. 48. The concept is used again and again in law and for that reason is discussed at some length in Chapter IX, *infra*.

[7] *Pagni* v. *New York Life Insurance Co.,* 173 Wash. 322, 23 P. (2d) 6, 93 A.L.R. 1325 (1933).

the agency. For this reason, many life insurance companies are scrupulously particular concerning the surrender of all insignia of agency at the termination of an agency contract.

Ratification Distinguished from Estoppel

Important between Principal and Agent. As far as third persons are concerned, it makes very little difference whether the agency relationship is held to exist by reason of ratification or estoppel. In either case the principal will be bound and the third party protected. Between the principal and the agent, however, the distinction is very important.

Ratification Benefits the Agent. An estoppel operates only for the benefit of the third person. The agent presumably knew that he was not the agent of the principal and cannot be benefited by estoppel. Ratification, however, actually establishes the agency relationship. Thus it guarantees the agent his compensation and any other benefits to which he may be entitled.

Estoppel Benefits the Third Party. In agency by estoppel the principal is denied the right to rely on the true situation in order that justice may be achieved. Thus if A's conduct has caused B to contract with C, believing in good faith that C is A's agent, A will not be permitted to deny that C was his agent. But this estoppel is for B's benefit.

Liability. As a general rule, agency by estoppel operates between the principal and the third party. Ratification operates between the principal and the agent, establishing the agency after the action has been taken instead of before. Liability as the result of ratification is liability resulting from intentional acts of the principal. Liability as the result of estoppel is liability in spite of what the principal intended.

AUTHORITY

Generally

Power and Authority. Basically, the power the agent has to create or modify the contractual relationships of the principal arises out of the authority the principal gives the agent. As a practical matter, however, the agent's power may be and often is a great deal broader than the authority actually granted him.

The power of the agent to bind the principal combines three general kinds of authority. First, there is express authority. That is the authority actually given the agent by the principal and which the principal intends to give. The statement in the life underwriter's contract that he is authorized to solicit applications for life insurance and to collect the initial premiums is a clear example of express authority to perform those acts.

Second, the agent has incidental or implied authority. That is authority which is not expressly granted but which must be exercised if the express authority is to mean anything as a practical matter. An agent is said to have implied authority to transact the business of the principal in accordance with the general customs of the business. The fact that the principal may not actually be acquainted with such customs does not alter the rule.

Third, there is apparent authority. That is the authority the actions of the principal may lead innocent third parties to believe the agent has. Apparent authority includes all the authority that a person of ordinary prudence, acquainted with the customs and nature of the business, would be justified in assuming that the agent had. Apparent authority is quite apart from and often in conflict with the principal's actual intentions.

Apparent Authority and Estoppel. Apparent authority and estoppel operate together. Apparent authority is an appearance of authority which will justify a third person in assuming that the agent has actually been granted the authority he presumes to exercise. Estoppel is the legal principle which operates to prevent such a principal from denying that the agent had the authority the third person who dealt with him in good faith believed he had. Thus, estoppel does not mean that the agent's authority is established as a matter of fact or of law. It only means that the principal is forbidden to deny it as far as the wronged third person is concerned.

Apparent authority must rest upon and grow out of the actions or words of the principal. Statements of the agent are never enough to establish apparent authority or work an estoppel. However, third persons are justified in assuming that an agent has power and authority equal to the scope of his duties and equal to that ordinarily conferred upon agents of that particular kind. They are also justified in relying upon a course of dealing with the principal in which he has seemed to acquiesce in the actions of the agent in question.

The doctrine of apparent authority does not include acts which are not performed in the usual manner in accomplishing what the agent is employed to do. Nor is the principal bound if the third party knows of the limitations on the agent's authority. Lastly, the third party has the burden of proving that the facts were such as to justify him in believing that the agent was acting within his authority.

Authority for Certain Actions

Express Authority to Contract. Since agency in its truest sense relates to the formation or modification of contractual relationships, it might be supposed that an agent always has the power to complete a binding contract on behalf of his principal. This is not true. The agent always has the power to affect the contractual relationships of his principal, but he does not necessarily have the power to complete the contract. For instance, the field underwriter in life insurance works with the life contract in some of its most crucial stages, but he never has the express authority to complete a contract of life insurance except conditionally, when he issues a conditional binding receipt, or by delivery of the completed policy.

Implied and Apparent Authority to Contract. Unless the principal and agent agree otherwise, authority to make a contract is implied if the agent has the authority to carry out a transaction which involves the making of a contract incidentally, or if it is reasonably necessary in performing the main duty of the agency. Authority to make a contract may be implied from a custom of the business, and there may be apparent authority if the principal has held the agent out as possessing that power.

Customs of the Insurance Business. Since the authority to make a contract may be implied from a custom of the business, it is of special importance to note the respects in which the customs of the life insurance business differ from those of insurance generally. For example, the fire insurance agent usually has the authority to complete a binding contract of fire insurance. After underwriting review by the company the contract can be cancelled, if necessary. In life insurance the contract is not cancellable, and the agent is not authorized to complete the contract. Thus the customs of the life insurance business differ markedly from the customs of other lines in the insurance business with which most people are familiar. It is highly important that this difference be made clear to any persons with whom the life agent may deal; otherwise situations of apparent authority to complete a life insurance contract can easily develop. In this day of growing companion line businesses, where one agent may handle several lines of insurance for associated companies, such a distinction is of even greater importance.

Express Authority to Receive Payments. If the agent has the express authority to receive payments, payment to him is in legal effect payment to the principal. The full significance of this statement is not apparent until one realizes that, although the agent has a duty to deal with his principal in good faith, there is no effective guarantee that he will do so. Thus, if receiving payments is within the scope of the agent's authority, a third person who pays a debt to the creditor's agent will be protected even though the creditor himself never receives the money.

Implied Authority to Receive Payments. Authority to receive payments will be implied if the collection or receipt of money is incidental to the agency transaction or is ordinarily considered necessary in carrying out the main authority expressly conferred. An agent authorized to receive payment of a principal sum, for example, has the implied authority to receive interest payments on it.

The life insurance agent is ordinarily expressly authorized to receive payment of the initial premium. Succeeding premiums are ordinarily payable at an administrative office as provided by the policy. A course of conduct in which payment to the agent is permitted without objection could easily create a situation of apparent authority to accept the payment of renewal premiums as well.

Authority to Appoint Sub-Agents. Where personal trust or confidence is reposed in an agent, he cannot as a general rule delegate to someone else the authority granted him. However, there are several instances in which an agent has the power and the right to delegate his authority by the appointment of a sub-agent. If the principal has expressly given him the right to appoint a sub-agent, he can do so. Also, if there is no contrary agreement, he may appoint a sub-agent if his position would ordinarily include that authority. Once appointed, the sub-agent is the agent of the principal and not the employee of the agent.

The Scope of the Agent's Authority

No Presumption of Agency. It will be recalled that the law establishes certain starting points, called presumptions, in various areas. There is no presumption of agency, however. The fact that John Doe tells you that he is an agent for the Ajax Life Insurance Company does not justify you in believing that he is. You must have facts of some kind, some identification furnished by the company, an established place of business with the company name displayed, a course of dealing with him as agent of the company. One cannot merely assume that the agency relationship exists.

Limitations of Authority. The principal has the right to limit the authority of the agent in any way and as much as he may wish. Such limitations, even if secret, will be binding as far as the agent and the principal are concerned. However, they are not binding on a third party if he does not know of their existence. Thus limitations of the agent's authority must be communicated to the persons who may rely on the agency or they will not be effective with respect to such third parties. Nevertheless, if the violation of secret limitations is so flagrant as to arouse the suspicion of a reasonable person, a third party is not entitled to rely upon the fact that he was not actually informed of the limitations. In such cases he is put on notice by the unreasonable aspects of the situation and must ascertain the facts.

Limitations and the Life Insurance Agent. The life insurance company has the same right to limit the authority of the field underwriter that any other principal has to limit the authority of its agents. The limitations must be made known to the persons with whom the field underwriters deal and must not deny any settled rule of law. Generally speaking, such limitations will be considered to have been communicated to the insured, whether he actually learns of them or not, if they are set forth in the policy. As a general rule, he is presumed to read the contract even if he does not actually do so. However, limitations communicated in this manner are binding upon the insured only with respect to transactions that take place after the delivery of the policy.

To make such limitations effective with respect to transactions which take place prior to the delivery of the policy, they are often included in the application form. It is generally held that the insured is charged with notice of any valid limitations set forth in the application even though he may not actually have read them. It is his duty to read the application.

Unenforceable Limitations

Making the Agent the Agent of the Insured. We have previously mentioned the attempt on the part of many companies in the early days to make the underwriter the agent of the insured by including an appropriate provision, first in the policy, and then later in the application. By the great weight of authority, the courts have held that provisions of this kind are unenforceable.

Notice to the Agent. One limitation frequently included in applications for life insurance concerns a basic principle of agency law that notice to the agent is notice to the principal. It is quite generally held that this principle cannot be completely negated. One frequently used modification purports to limit such effective notice to statements contained in or endorsed on the application. The court decisions are in conflict as to whether such provisions are valid.

A landmark case holding that this type of provision is valid is that of *New York Life Insurance Co.* v. *Fletcher*,[8] decided by the Supreme Court of the United States in 1886. There the court said:

> Here the power of the agent was limited, and notice of such limitation given by being embodied in the application, which the assured was required to make and sign, and which, as we have stated, he must be presumed to have read. He is, therefore, bound by its statements.

The leading case holding that such provisions are not valid is the case of *Sternaman* v. *Metropolitan Life Insurance Company*,[9] a New York Court of Appeals case decided in 1902. There the court said:

[8] 117 U.S. 519, 6 S. Ct. 837, 29 L. Ed. 934 (1886).
[9] 170 N.Y. 13, 62 N.E. 763, 57 L.R.A. 318, 88 Am. St. Rep. 625 (1902).

The facts sought to be proved were contained in the oral statements made to the medical examiner, but assuming that recorded statements only were meant, the result would be an agreement that the company might perpetrate a fraud upon the insured by issuing a policy and accepting premiums thereon, knowing all the time that the contract was void, or voidable at its election. The law does not permit this, for it declares that the company is estopped from taking advantage of such a contract, because it would be against equity and opposed to public policy.

Cases on this question are so various that it is difficult to say that one line or the other represents the majority opinion. The numerical weight of authority, however, seems to be on the side of the *Fletcher* case, which upheld the limitation preventing the knowledge of the agent from being the knowledge of the principal unless the information in question is contained in the application.

KINDS OF AGENTS

How Agents Are Classified

Traditionally. Agents are traditionally classified according to the extent of their authority. Thus a special agent is one who has the authority to complete a special business transaction and nothing more. A general agent has the authority to transact all the business of the principal in connection with a specific subject matter or all the business at a certain location. Those persons who are authorized to transact all the business of a principal, of whatever kind, are said to be universal agents.

Classifications in Insurance

Terms Have Different Meanings. In the field of insurance the same terms are used as in general agency usage, but often with quite different meanings. As a result the terminology is often quite confusing. Not only do the meanings differ from those of the traditional agency terminology, but they also vary from one kind of insurance to another. Special agents for fire insurance companies, for example, usually have general powers, yet the powers of a life insurance general agent are limited.

The General Agent. A general agent in life insurance is ordinarily a person who represents his company within a certain geographical area. Regardless of his title, however, a general agent in life insurance is only a special agent in the usual sense of the term since he does not have the authority to complete a life insurance contract with the applicant.

Officers. The executive officers of the company are often said to be special agents since they have only the authority granted them by the charter or articles of association and the bylaws of the corporation. However, in the general conduct of the business the officers exercise all the powers of the corporation. Thus they should be considered general agents, as the term is ordinarily used.

Special Agents. A special agent is one who has the authority to perform some special act or acts. Solicitors, attorneys, medical examiners are all special agents of the life insurance company which they represent. The local agent is also a special agent because of the limitations on his authority.

It should never be assumed that limited authority means limited effectiveness. For example, the medical examiner's authority is narrowly restricted, but within this special area he nevertheless has the power to bind the company by his acts and by his knowledge concerning one of the most important factors of insurability—the physical condition of the applicant. Knowledge of the medical examiner with respect to diseases or prior treatment of the applicant, not disclosed on the application, is often imputed to the company and prevents it, by estoppel, from asserting an otherwise effective defense based on misrepresentation of material facts.

LEGAL EFFECTS OF AGENCY

Generally

The Acts of the Agent Are the Acts of the Principal. It is basic in agency law that the actions of the agent within the scope of his authority are the actions of the principal. (In this connection one often sees the Latin *"qui facit per alium, facit per se,"* which means "he who acts through others, acts through himself.") By virtue of the agency relationship the principal can be in many places at the same time, perform many different actions, complete many contracts. At times the agent can do for the principal, things the latter does not have the skill to do for himself. The attorney, for example, represents his client as the latter's agent and uses his legal skills in the client's behalf.

The Contract Is the Contract of the Principal. When an agent completes a contract on behalf of his principal it is exactly the same as if the principal had completed it by and for himself. In the eyes of the law it *is* the contract of the principal. He is entitled to all the benefits and is charged with all the duties and responsibilities connected with it.

In Life Insurance. In the typical agency transaction, where the life underwriter solicits applications for life insurance, accepts the first premium, and often arranges for the medical examination, he initiates a series of actions which culminate in an effective and binding contract of life insurance. That contract is a contract between the applicant, now the insured, on the one hand, and the company on the other, and the actions of the various company agents have, in legal effect, been the actions of the company.

It will be recalled also that money accepted by the agent on the principal's behalf, if it is within his authority to accept it, has exactly the same effect as if the payment had been made to the principal. Here the phrase "within his authority" is of the utmost importance. For example, it is customary for the life underwriter to have the authority to collect the first premium in connection with the application for a life insurance policy but not subsequent premiums, and a notice to that effect is ordinarily included in the policy. Ordinarily subsequent premiums must be paid direct to the home office or other designated location and not to the soliciting agent.

Suppose that, under a policy including this limitation, a renewal premium is paid to and accepted by the agent. Suppose further that this takes place immediately prior to the expiration of the grace period but that the payment does not actually reach the administrative office shown on the premium notice until after the grace period has expired. Meanwhile the insured has died. Under these circumstances, is the insurance company bound by this payment, assuming that it was made to a soliciting but not a general agent of the company?

It is situations of this kind that make the principles of agency so important, not only in the origin of the contract of insurance, but throughout its life. In fact the "life" of the contract often literally depends upon the authority of the agent whose actions are concerned. In the case outlined above, if the insurance company was bound by payment to its agent—that is, if payment to the agent was payment to the principal—the insurance policy was in effect at the date of the insured's death. If the company was not so bound, the policy was not in effect.

In a case [10] presenting this precise question, the court noted the applicable provisions in the policy, as follows:

> The first premium only may be paid to agent. All subsequent premiums are due and payable in advance at the Home Office of the Company without notice. However, they may be paid to an authorized agent of the Company on or before the date when due, but only in exchange for a receipt signed by the President, Vice-President, Secretary or Assistant Secretary, and countersigned by such agent.

Thus the policy restricted the payment of all premiums, except the first, to an authorized agent in exchange for an official receipt, and excluded the authority of the soliciting agent. Acceptance of any premium after the first was beyond the scope of the agent's authority, and that fact was made clear to the insured in the policy. Acceptance of subsequent premiums by the agent was not within the scope of his au-

---

[10] *Kansas City Life Insurance Co.* v. *Root,* 238 Ala. 412, 191 So. 219 (1939).

thority, either actual or apparent, and payment to him was not payment to the company.

The insured had the right to entrust the money to anyone he wished, but the person so entrusted would be *his* agent for that purpose. When the payment reached the company's premium collection office the premium would be paid, but not before. In the case in question, the insured paid the premium to the soliciting agent of the company, but the latter was not an agent of the company to receive renewal premiums. In accepting the premium he acted as the agent for the insured. The court concluded as follows:

> . . . but when she made said Pope her agent to remit it to the defendant, she assumed the risk of his failure to send it in and, while this may be what is termed "a hard case," we must heed the admonition of the great and lamented Chief Justice Stone, "Let not hard cases make shipwreck of the law."

Problems in Agency

It is unfortunate that much of the law of agency has been developed out of instances in which the agency relationship has either not existed or where it has been misunderstood in its nature and scope by one or another of the parties concerned. As a result, the emphasis in a discussion of the law of agency is very often on the responsibility of the principal in cases in which he did not want responsibility, on liabilities when he wanted only the benefits, on the disadvantages of the agency relationship to the virtual exclusion of the benefits. As with most human relationships, if things go smoothly the question of legal rights and responsibilities rarely arises. It is only when something goes wrong that the parties go to court for a clarification of their respective rights, duties, and responsibilities.

The following discussion relates primarily to those principles that govern when questions arise among the principal, the agent, and third parties who may be involved. However, it should be borne in mind that by far the majority of agency transactions operate to the mutual advantage of principal and agent and never reach the courts.

Liabilities of the Agent. The agent who has violated any of his duties to his principal is subject to being sued for damages. He is personally liable for any damages resulting from his fraudulent, malicious, or negligent acts. Even though he is acting as an agent, he is as responsible for his own torts (actionable wrongs) as he would be if the agency did not exist.

The Agent's Duties. The agent has the duty of proper conduct, the duty to act with reasonable care, and to act within his authority. It will be remembered that he is a fiduciary and bound to exercise the utmost good faith and loyalty towards his principal. He must not act adversely

to the interests of the principal, either to his own advantage or by
serving as agent for another third party whose interests are adverse to
those of the principal. Because of this duty of loyalty and good faith
he may not obtain any secret profit or advantage from the agency
relationship or furnish anyone else with information which might result
in actions adverse to the interests of the principal.

Liabilities of the Principal. It is a general rule of law that everyone
has a duty to conduct his affairs, whether through his own efforts or
those of his agents, in such a way as not to injure others. If he does not
do so, and if injury results to others, he may be responsible in damages.
Thus the principal is liable for all statements made by the agent in the
course of transacting his business even though they may be wrongful
(*tortious* is the legal term) and even though he has not authorized or
even known of the misconduct. He is liable for the frauds and misrepresentations of the agent within the scope of the latter's authority,
and he is chargeable with, and bound by, any knowledge or notice acquired by the agent within the scope of his authority. (Incidentally, the
principal is not liable for the statements or actions of the agent if they
are beyond the scope of the latter's authority.)

Knowledge of the Agent. Generally speaking, the knowledge of the
agent concerning matters related to the business of his principal is the
knowledge of the principal. As previously pointed out, life companies
frequently seek to limit the knowledge by which they will be bound, to
written statements contained in the application. Court decisions are
divided with respect to whether such limitations are valid. Thus there is a
strong line of cases which take the position that such limitations are not
valid, and consequently they apply to life insurance companies the same
rule applied to any other principal.

Illustrative of court opinions which apply the general principle
without modification is the case of *Mickle* v. *Dixie Security Life Insurance Co.*,[11] a South Carolina case decided in 1949. Here the company's
defense was based on the contention that the answers to the questions in
the application were fraudulent and that the insured was not in sound
health on the date the policy was issued. The principal question related
to alcoholism on the part of the insured and the fact that the soliciting
agent, an old friend, was personally acquainted with the habits of the
insured.

The court noted that no questions relating to alcoholism were included in the application and that it was therefore "for the jury to pass
upon the question of fraud and materiality." The opinion continued:

[11] 57 S.E.2d 73 (S. Car., 1949).

However, aside from this, it can reasonably be inferred that the appellant's local insurance agent, Mr. Anderson, was, through close association, fully aware that the insured sometimes drank to excess. He drank with him, knew he had been treated several times for alcoholism, and knew its probable effect upon the state of his health.

It has been uniformly held in this State that the knowledge of an agent acquired within the scope of his agency is imputable to his principal, and, if an insurance company, at the inception of the contract of insurance, has knowledge of facts which render the policy void at its option, and the company delivers the policy as a valid policy, it is estopped to assert such grounds of forfeiture. . .

Upon a consideration of the evidence in this record, it may reasonably be inferred that if alcoholism be a disease, and that it adversely affected the health of the insured, then appellant's local agent was fully conversant with the situation, and such knowledge is imputable to his principal.

TERMINATION OF THE AGENCY RELATIONSHIP

Once an agency is proved to have existed, it will be presumed to have continued unless something definite is shown to indicate its termination. An agency can be terminated only by action or agreement of the principal and the agent or by operation of law.

Termination

By Action of the Parties. The agency is terminated if the principal discharges the agent or if the agent renounces the agency. If the agent's actions are wrongful he may still abandon the agency, but he will be responsible to the principal in damages.

By Operation of the Contract. The agency contract may give either the principal or the agent, or both, the right to cancel the agency at will. It may also provide that the agency shall continue for a certain length of time and then automatically terminate, or that it shall continue until a certain objective has been accomplished. In either of these cases the agency will terminate at the completion of the time or objective named.

By Operation of Law. Ordinarily, the mere revocation of the agent's authority does not affect the rights of a third party who deals with the agent afterwards in good faith. However, at common law, unless the agency was coupled with an interest, the death of the principal automatically terminated the agency even though the third party or parties were ignorant of the fact. This rule is followed by most of the courts today. Death of the agent also terminates the agency, as would loss of a license or failure to qualify for one.

Bankruptcy of the principal terminates the authority of the agent although insolvency alone does not. Bankruptcy of the agent has the same effect if the state of his credit affects the interests of the principal to such an extent that if he had known the facts he would have revoked the agent's authority.

The outbreak of war does not necessarily terminate the agency relationship, but if it makes the agent an enemy alien of the country of the principal's residence, the agency will be terminated.

Effect of Termination

Generally. When the authority of the agent is terminated he loses all right to act for the principal. He has then only the duty to account to the principal.

Notice. If the agency is revoked by the principal the revocation is not effective until the agent is notified. Notice must also be given to third persons. Otherwise the agent's power, though not his authority, to bind his principal continues.

✿ ✿ ✿ ✿ ✿

ILLUSTRATIVE CASE

The following case has been selected because it illustrates so many of the facets of the authority of a life insurance agent and the responsibilities the company is sometimes held to have. It is printed here almost in its entirety in order that the student may follow the reasoning of the court in applying many of the principles which have been touched upon in this chapter.

SCOTT v. CONTINENTAL ASSURANCE CO.[12]

(Ohio Supreme Court. Appeal from Court of Appeals, Hamilton County.)

WEYGANDT, C. J.: This controversy involves the fraudulent misconduct of an individual named Russell who was a duly licensed agent of the defendant insurance company and sold the plaintiff his two policies. . . .

There is no dispute concerning the provisions of the two policies to the effect that all premiums were payable either at the defendant company's home office in Chicago or to a duly authorized agent. However, the plaintiff insists that the defendant consistently disregarded the terms of its own policies for a period of 14 years and thereby established a course of dealing which now estops it from asserting that its duly licensed agent was without authority to accept the various payments made by the plaintiff. The plaintiff relies on the fact that as early as 1932 he had purchased several policies from the defendant company through its agent Russell and for 14 years thereafter had made every payment to Russell either in cash or by check. In each instance the premium was accepted by the defendant company and credited to the plaintiff's policies. This procedure continued until 1946 when the company sent the plaintiff a card telling him to make his checks payable to it, and he did so. However, it was in 1940 while the old procedure was still in operation that agent Russell suggested the idea of the so-called special

---

[12] 150 N.E.2d 38 (Ohio, 1958).

premium deposit fund to be used whenever the plaintiff might default in meeting a policy premium. The plaintiff accepted the offer and gave agent Russell two checks for the total sum of $5,436.70, as requested by Russell. In return, Russell gave the plaintiff two receipts on printed forms containing the name of the defendant company and having the appearance of being genuine. But the defendant insists that they are in fact not genuine; that they contain the signature of an individual not a company officer; and that Russell did not remit the money to his company as he had done regularly with the previous policy premiums.

In its opinion the Court of Appeals concluded that "the unfortunate circumstance in this case is that Scott misplaced his confidence in Russell." That, of course, is true, but it is not the only unfortunate circumstance. Another obviously is that the defendant company, too, misplaced its confidence in Russell when it employed him as its agent, and it was this employment and authority that made it possible for Russell to defraud both the company and the plaintiff Scott. Hence, it was the company and not Scott who started the chain of circumstances which eventually enabled Russell to perpetrate the fraud.

But, as previously observed, the defendant insists that Scott should have complied with the provisions of his policies by making his payments to the defendant company instead of to Russell, although it concedes that Russell was authorized to receive payment of the first premium on each policy. And it insists, too, that the two receipts received by Scott are fraudulent although on printed forms containing the name of the company and having the appearance of genuineness. But, in any event, the fact that Russell was in possession of the printed forms—spurious or genuine—was not the fault of Scott, and for a total period of 14 years the company consistently condoned Scott's practice of making all payments to its agent Russell. Under these circumstances can the company now be heard to insist that Russell was a mere soliciting agent without apparent authority to accept payments intended for the company?

The trial court answered this question in the negative, and this court so holds.

The defendant, as did the Court of Appeals, relies on the decision of this court in the case of *John Hancock Mutual Life Insurance Co.* v. *Luzio*, 128 Ohio St. 616, 176 N.E. 446. In the fifth paragraph of the syllabus it was held:

> 5. An applicant for life insurance should exercise towards the company the same good faith which he may rightfully demand from it; the relationship demands fair dealing. If it should be proven that the insured and the soliciting agent connived for the purpose of defrauding the company, there can be no recovery.

This illustrates the contrast between that case and the instant one. There the insured and the agent attempted to conceal from the company the facts concerning the insured's condition of health. Here there is no evidence that the insured attempted to conceal anything from the company during the entire period of 14 years during which Scott made all his payments to agent Russell.

The defendant relies, too, as did the Court of Appeals on the decision of this court in the case of *Union Central Life Ins. Co.* v. *Hook*, 62 Ohio St., 256, 56 N.E. 906, in which the agent and the insured, without the knowledge of the company, entered into a parol agreement to waive payment of an annual premium. In the instant case there is no contention that Scott did not pay his premiums when due or that the premiums were not paid in a manner known and condoned by the company for a period of 14 years. Furthermore, in his opinion in the *Hook* case, DAVIS, J., said:

> We do not decide that there might not be an estoppel by conduct. . . . But that case does not arise here.

Scott made his payments for the so-called premium deposit fund in precisely the same manner as the premium payments for a period of 14 years, and it is the view of this court that under the circumstances of this case the company is estopped from avoiding liability for any payments so made.

The judgment of the Court of Appeals is reversed and that of the Court of Common Pleas is affirmed.

PART II

Formation, Construction, and Validity of the Contract

CHAPTER **IV**

The Life Insurance
Contract
Is Formed

THE STUDY OF ANY contract of insurance automatically brings together two highly specialized subjects—contract law and insurance itself. In the case of the life insurance contract the combination is especially complex because the business of life insurance is complex. Without discussing life insurance in any exhaustive sense, it is the purpose of this chapter to show how basic principles of general contract law are utilized in the formation of the life insurance contract in such a way as to make the insurance principle effective.

LIFE INSURANCE AND THE CONTRACT

How Insurance Works

Socially and economically, insurance is a means of risk distribution. By its use an individual can transfer his own risk of loss to a group of many individuals having similar risks, in such a way that a relatively small, regular contribution from each member to a common fund makes it possible for losses actually suffered to be paid in full.

Characteristics of Life Insurance

Not on an Indemnity Basis. In nearly every line of insurance except life, losses are payable on an indemnity basis. This means that at the time the loss occurs and claim is made, the claimant must prove his loss in terms of dollars and cents. Then he is reimbursed (*indemnified*) in the amount of his actual loss, within the limits established in the contract.

In life insurance, the indemnity principle rarely applies. The value insured, human life, is not ordinarily considered measurable in money, (although the "life value" concept of Dr. S. S. Huebner provides an excellent workable approach and is often used in risk appraisal to avoid overinsurance).

Generally speaking, however, life insurance is not concerned with loss measurement except at the time the contract is formed and then only in broad, general terms. Within those broad limits the life insurance company makes insuring agreements with individuals, under each of which the company promises to pay a definite amount of money (in legal terms, a *sum certain*) on the occurrence of the event (death) insured against. The promises of the company are subject to a number of conditions, the most important of which is the payment of premiums at regular intervals by the policyholder. By contrast with the indemnity principle followed in many other lines of insurance, however, if the life insurance policy is on a premium paying basis when the event insured against occurs, the full amount is payable.

Uncertainty in Life Insurance. Life insurance also differs from other kinds of insurance with respect to uncertainty and the event insured against. Under most insurance agreements the event insured against may or may not happen. By contrast, there is no uncertainty as to whether the event insured against under a whole life policy will happen; it will. The only uncertainty relates to when it will occur. If the life which is the subject of the insurance is to be truly "insurable," uncertainty in this sense of the word must exist at the time the contract is made.

As a basic principle of life insurance, each life to be insured must be insurable in this sense, and all lives insured under generally similar terms must, at the time the contract is made, be comparable as a group with respect to the probabilities of death. If these things are true, then uncertainty with respect to the death of the individual insured is replaced with statistical certainty with respect to deaths among the group, and losses can be shared on an insurance basis. It is the life insurance contract which expresses and puts into effect the complexities of promises, rights, and financial details to make this possible.

The Role of the Contract

The life insurance contract performs a dual role. Individually, the contracts define the rights of the policyholder on the one hand and the commitments of the company on the other. Collectively, however, the contracts must operate in such a way that premiums paid under them individually will be adequate collectively to meet the claims as they arise, as well as the expenses and other commitments of the company.

A Part of the Structure of the Business. The life insurance contract is more than just a "promise or set of promises" on the part of the life insurance company; it is a vital part of the very structure of the business. It is the mortar, so to speak, that holds the bricks of the association together. Thus it is not enough that the individual contract meet the requirements for the formation of a valid, enforceable agreement. The contracts of any life insurance company must operate collectively in such a way that premiums under them individually will be adequate to meet the commitments the company assumes under them.

Implicit in the formation of every life insurance contract, therefore, is the requirement that the life to be insured be "insurable." This simply means that every insured must be so selected that the risk of death assumed by the company under that particular contract will be comparable with all the risks assumed under all contracts insuring persons of the same age and sex, under the same plan, and for the same premium.

The Idea of Insurability

Strictly speaking, the idea of insurability has little to do with contract law. However, it is fundamental that one has the right to choose both the subject of a proposed contract and the person or persons with whom he is willing to do business. The selection of risks by a life insurance company, in legal effect, is nothing more than this. In third-party ownership cases, the selection of risks relates only to the subject of the insurance, that is, the life to be insured. In the more typical case, risk selection also relates to the person with whom the company is willing to do business.

Risk Appraisal and Life Insurance. Risk appraisal is common to all lines of insurance. Life insurance, however, involves an especially complicating factor not usually present in other lines. In the absence of fraud or material misrepresentation, the life contract, once formed, is not cancellable by the company. For this reason, risk selection in life insurance, by contrast with practices in most other lines of insurance, must precede the actual completion of the contract. As a result, the various steps in the formation of the contract often present legal problems which are not involved in contracts generally or even in contracts of many other kinds of insurance.

Life Agent's Authority. One major difference relates to the authority of the agent. The process of risk appraisal before completion of the contract necessitates some limitations of the authority of the life agent which are not required in other lines of insurance. Selection of risks in a life insurance company is of fundamental importance to the over-all success of the company. As a result, life insurance companies, with virtually no exceptions, reserve to specially trained personnel in policy issuing offices the authority to make this selection.

Thus, unlike most agents, even agents in other fields of insurance, the life insurance agent does not have the authority to make a contract on behalf of the company or to pass upon the insurability of an applicant. He has the authority to solicit applications, to deliver policies, and to collect the initial premium. He is not authorized to complete an unconditionally binding contract with anyone, although it should be noted that there is a wide difference between what an agent is authorized to do and what he may have the power, by reason of words or actions, to accomplish. The decision as to whether a contract shall be entered into, in connection with any application for life insurance, is made in policy issuing offices only.

WHEN AN OFFER IS MADE

Preliminary Negotiations

Distinguished from Offers. Contracts are often completed only after extensive negotiations. It is highly important, therefore, to distinguish between an act which is only part of the preliminary negotiations and an act which constitutes a genuine offer. The latter, it will be remembered, "is a proposal which, if accepted according to its terms, will create a binding contract." [1] Often, one party expresses his willingness to enter into an agreement but seems rather to be inviting an offer or suggesting the terms of a possible future bargain than making an actual offer. The distinguishing point is the matter of intent, of which one noted authority says: "The only general test which can be submitted as a guide is an inquiry whether the facts show that some performance was promised in positive terms in return for some thing requested."[2]

Importance of Selection of Risks. No matter who makes the offer, or when it is made, the process of selecting the persons with whom the company is willing to contract must precede the actual formation of the contract if the life insurance principle is to be made to work. Regardless of what this process is called—underwriting, risk appraisal, selection of risks—it underlies the entire structure of the life insurance business.

Who Must Be Insurable. Insurability is not required of every person with whom the company is willing to contract. Where one person applies for a policy on the life of another (third-party ownership cases), insurability of the applicant is of no importance. However, the life to be insured must, in every case, meet the requirements of insurability adopted by the company. If the contract is made with a third party, the life to be insured must be insurable in accordance with the requirements

---

[1] See Chapter II, page 28.

[2] *Williston on Contracts* (Baker, Voorhis & Co., Inc., 1957), Vol. I, p. 65.

of the company, and the person with whom the contract is made must have an insurable interest in that life. Both determinations are made in the issuing office and not by the agent.

Sometimes the Applicant Merely "Invites" an Offer

When He Does Not Prepay the First Premium. It would be relatively simple to follow the steps in the formation of a life insurance contract if the person with whom the company is willing to contract were first selected on the basis of his insurability and the technicalities of making an offer followed in a second clear-cut step. This is virtually what happens in those cases where an application is completed and forwarded, without premium payment, to the issuing office. In such cases, if the person whose life is to be insured is found to be insurable under the company's standard practices, a policy of life insurance is issued and forwarded to the agent for delivery and collection of the first premium. Usually the agent is specifically instructed not to deliver the policy except "during the lifetime and continued insurability" of the proposed insured.

This type of situation presents the simplest illustration of offer and acceptance in the formation of the life insurance contract. Here the applicant completes the application, thus giving the information the company requests in order that his insurability may be appraised. He states the type of policy he wishes, elects a method of premium payment, designates a beneficiary, and otherwise specifies the details of the contract in which he is interested. He does not, however, pay the premium, the act by which he would have signified his assent to the proposed agreement.

In its issuing office, the company reviews the application, together with other materials, including an inspection report and medical examiner's report if one is required. On the basis of this information, the insurability of the proposed insured is appraised, and if it is found to be within the company's standards of selection, the company issues a policy. Ordinarily the policy is to be delivered only during the lifetime and continued insurability of the proposed insured.

Nevertheless, the issuance of a policy, even though in complete accordance with the terms of the application, still does not complete a binding contract. Nor does its delivery. An essential action on the part of the applicant remains to be performed: payment of the premium. Thus the application, under these circumstances, is only an "invitation" to deal, or a request for an offer. The company makes the offer when it issues a policy and sends it to the agent for delivery as instructed.

If delivery cannot be made, and the premium paid during the lifetime and continued insurability of the applicant, the agent must return the policy to the issuing office. Even if such delivery can be made, the applicant is nevertheless free to accept or reject. He rejects the offer by simply saying that he does not want the policy or by any actions which clearly convey that meaning. He accepts by performing the act requested, payment of the initial premium, and a binding contract is made.

Delivery of the Policy. In this discussion we have frequently mentioned delivery of the policy. This is because most companies include in their application forms a provision which declares that the insurance shall not take effect until the policy has been delivered. This does not mean that delivery is a legal requirement, however. On the contrary, the provision is a condition, which may be included in the agreement, or omitted, as the parties may choose. If included, it is a valid condition precedent and will be enforced, but it can be waived by the company just as can any other condition of the agreement.

Disadvantages of this Procedure

Often, under the procedure just outlined, a considerable period of time elapses between the completion of the application and the agent's opportunity to deliver the policy. Clearly there is no coverage during this time, because there is no contract. Nevertheless, the sudden and accidental death of the proposed insured during this period points up this lack of coverage in a dramatic and tragically negative way. At best, it leaves the beneficiaries with a sense of vague injustice. At worst, it is almost impossible to explain the lack of coverage to an insuring public conditioned to practices in fire and casualty insurance where the applicant is "insured" when the agent takes his application and issues a binder. Unfortunately, it is not nearly so clearly understood that the fire policy, unlike the life insurance contract, is subject to cancellation later if the risk does not meet the requirements of the company.

From the agent's point of view, the lapse of time between the application and delivery of the policy is also a disadvantage. Often the agent must "sell" the applicant twice—once when he takes his application and again when he delivers the policy. Often, also, it is more difficult, and sometimes impossible, to make the sale the second time.

For these reasons, life companies early began experimenting with some method of bringing life insurance more closely in line with practices in the fire and casualty fields. No concession could be made with respect to selection of risks in the issuing office, however. Consequently some way had to be devised by which the agent could offer earlier coverage, subject to a final decision in the issuing office. This was accomplished with varying degrees of success by the use of what has come to be known as the "binding receipt," "conditional receipt," or "conditional binding receipt."

The Conditional Binding Receipt

A conditional binding receipt is a receipt for the amount of cash paid to the agent in connection with an application for life insurance. Its special significance in the formation of the life insurance contract arises out of its wording, which provides that insurance shall be deemed to take effect as of a date prior to delivery of the policy (sometimes the date of the receipt, sometimes the date of the medical examination) on condition that the application is approved (in some receipts) or that the applicant is found to be an insurable risk as of the stated date.

Why There Is a Problem. The exact wording of the many receipts that have been and are being used by life insurance companies varies, and court interpretations vary even more. In general terms, the purpose of the receipt is to make insurance effective at an earlier date than would ordinarily be true and yet not relinquish the company's right to determine the insurability of the proposed insured at the issuing office. The companies preserved this right by making insurability a condition which must be met before liability is incurred. At the same time, however, they introduced another condition into the process of forming the contract and opened the door to some of the most highly technical legal problems in the law of the life insurance contract.

Conditions. Because of the importance of conditions in this area of life insurance law, it is perhaps appropriate to take a moment for a somewhat more complete discussion of this subject. A promise, in general terms, is an undertaking that something shall or shall not happen in the future. It does not have to be absolute. It may be an undertaking that something shall or shall not happen in the future if something else shall happen or not happen. In this case the promise is said to be subject to a condition precedent. The promise will not become binding unless the condition happens. A condition, therefore, is an event or happening which determines whether a promisor shall or shall not be bound on his promise.

There are two major kinds of conditions. One is the *condition precedent,* which must happen or be performed before a promisor has the duty to perform his promise. It precedes the duty to perform; hence its name. The other is a *condition subsequent,* which, if it happens, takes away rights already vested or established.[3] Applied to conditional binding receipt cases, it makes a great deal of difference whether the condition of insurability or approval is a condition precedent or a condition subsequent.

---

[3] For instance, assume that John Williams owes Frank Brown $500. He promises to pay it on a specified date, with the further condition that the indebtedness will be canceled if he should die prior to the date agreed upon. John's death in this case is a condition subsequent, the happening of which will terminate Frank's right to repayment of the money.

The "Approval" Form. At one time perhaps the majority of conditional binding receipts purported to make insurance effective immediately on condition that the application was subsequently approved. This obviously gave the applicant very little more in the way of protection than he would have had if he had merely applied and waited until delivery of the policy before he paid the premium. Nevertheless most of the early court decisions upheld this requirement as a valid condition precedent. In such cases, the death of the proposed insured after the application date, but before approval, was not covered.

Other courts took the position that under this type of receipt the applicant was, in effect, paying for coverage for a period in which he actually had no insurance. It seemed inequitable to these courts to permit a life insurance company to collect the premium and then retain virtually the same rights with respect to acceptance or rejection of the risk it would have had if no premium had been paid. The tendency, therefore, was to find ambiguities in the receipt and the application and to interpret them most favorably to the insured.

Illustrative of this approach is the leading case of *Gaunt v. John Hancock Mutual Life Insurance Company*,[4] in which the court said:

> . . . An underwriter might so understand the phrase, when read in its context, but the application was not to be submitted to underwriters; it was to go to persons utterly unacquainted with the niceties of life insurance, who would read it colloquially. It is the understanding of such persons that counts; and not one in a hundred would suppose that he would be covered, not "as of the date of completion of Part B," as the defendant promised, but only as of the date of approval. Had that been what the defendant meant, certainly it was easy to say so; and had it in addition meant to make the policy retroactive for some purposes, certainly it was easy to say that too. To demand that persons wholly unfamiliar with insurance shall spell all this out in the very teeth of the language used, is unpardonable. It does indeed some violence to the words not to make actual "approval" always a condition, and to substitute a prospective approval, however inevitable, when the insured has died before approval. But it does greater violence to make the insurance "in force" only from the date of "approval"; for the ordinary applicant who has paid his first premium and has successfully passed his physical examination, would not by the remotest chance understand the clause as leaving him uncovered until the insurer at its leisure approved the risk; he would assume that he was getting immediate coverage for his money. . . . A man must indeed read what he signs, and he is charged, if he does not; but insurers who seek to impose upon words of common speech an esoteric significance intelligible only to their craft, must bear the burden of any resulting confusion.

In a number of cases the conditional binding receipt conditioned upon "approval" has been interpreted as establishing insurance immediately (*interim* insurance the courts sometimes call it), subject to a finding of insurability. For this reason, and because insurability of the

---

[4] 160 F.2d 599 (C.C.A. Conn., 1947).

proposed insured is the only condition essential to their purposes, many companies condition their receipts on insurability itself. Under receipts of this kind, insurance becomes effective as of the date of the receipt (or of the medical, if later), on condition that the proposed insured is found to be an acceptable risk for the plan, amount, and for the premium rate applied for. In such cases, if the proposed insured dies prior to the date the policy is issued, he will have been insured, assuming that any required medical examination has been completed and the condition of insurability fulfilled.

The Company Makes a Conditional Offer

A special set of circumstances is presented, legally, where the initial premium amount is collected by the agent at the time the application is completed and the agent issues a conditional binding receipt. Traditionally, the application, if accompanied by premium payment, is considered an offer on the part of the applicant. Without the conditional binding receipt, however, there is no particular reason why the applicant should pay the premium at the time of making application. The conditional binding receipt gives the agent an opportunity to persuade him to do so. In effect, the agent is authorized to make an offer on the part of the company to make the insurance effective as of a date earlier than would ordinarily be true, on condition that the proposed insured is found to be insurable as of the date of the receipt or of the medical examination, as provided by the terms of the receipt. The applicant accepts this offer by performing the act requested—paying the premium —and thereby transforms it into a binding conditional promise.

In this case, as in our first instance, the company is making the offer. Here, however, the offer is subject to a condition, and the time sequence is quite different. Both the offer, on condition, and the acceptance, by paying the premium amount, take place as of the same date. Thus the application is completed, the initial premium is remitted, and the conditional binding receipt is issued, all on the same date.

The Legal Effect. Where the first premium accompanies the application and a conditional binding receipt is issued, an agreement of some sort is obviously completed. Is this agreement subject to a condition precedent, in which case the condition must be met before insurance becomes effective? Or does the agreement put insurance into effect temporarily, subject to a condition subsequent, in which case disapproval of the application cancels the temporary insurance but does not absolve the company of liability if the insured dies in the meanwhile?

There is no question but that a company may, by the express terms of its receipt, bind itself in such a way that insurance becomes immediately effective, subject to termination if the proposed insured is found to be uninsurable. A few companies do exactly this by using what is termed a "binding" receipt.[5] Most companies, however, use only a conditional receipt, which suspends the effectiveness of the insurance until such time as they have had the opportunity to determine the insurability of the proposed insured. Nevertheless, they still run the risk of having a condition, intended to be a condition precedent, interpreted in favor of the insured and held to be a condition subsequent, if there is any ambiguity in the application and receipt, read together.

The majority of life insurance companies today use the "insurability" type of receipt. Here the insurance ordinarily is made effective as of the date of the receipt (or the medical). Under it, even though insurance is not effective unless the proposed insured is found to be insurable, death within the intervening period will not necessarily affect the risk appraisal procedures. If any required medical has been completed and if all other requirements have been fulfilled by the applicant, the company can still determine whether or not the condition has been fulfilled, after the death of the proposed insured, if necessary. In such cases, if the condition is met, insurance becomes effective as of the date specified in the receipt. The death of the insured after that date, even though prior to the date the policy is issued, will be covered.

This interpretation is followed by the majority of the courts, and under it no insurance is effective until the finding of insurability. However, a minority of the courts take the position that the finding of insurability is a condition subsequent. Under this view, insurance becomes effective as of the date of the agreement and may be terminated upon the finding that the proposed insured is not insurable. The company is on the risk, however, until notice of rejection has been given.

In legal theory, the intention of the parties governs in this situation, as is true of any contractual proceedings. This intent is to be found in the wording of the documents concerned, and if that wording is clear, the intent will be given effect. However, if the receipt and the application produce an ambiguity of any kind, and ambiguities are more frequently found in the "approval" type of receipts, the wording will be interpreted (construed, the courts will say) in favor of the proposed insured and against the insurance company, because the latter drafted the instrument. This, incidentally, is a standard rule of interpretation.

The minority line of decisions, holding that the condition is a condition subsequent, is illustrated in the case of *Ransom* v. *Penn. Mutual Life Insurance Co.*,[6] decided in 1954. The decision in that case reads, in part, as follows:

---

[5] Both Manufacturers Life of Toronto, Canada, and Western and Southern Life of Cincinnati, Ohio, have had several years of experience with unconditional binding receipts.

[6] 274 P.2d 633 (Cal., 1954).

We must determine whether a contract of insurance arose immediately upon receipt by defendant of the completed application with the premium payment, subject to the right of defendant to terminate the agreement if it subsequently concluded that Ransom was not acceptable, or whether, as defendant contends, its satisfaction as to Ransom's acceptability for insurance was a condition precedent to the existence of any contract.

The courts in several jurisdictions have construed clauses similar to the one involved here. A number of decisions have held, in accordance with defendant's view, that no contract of insurance exists until the insurer has been satisfied as to an applicant's acceptability, and that the provision that the insurance shall be in force from the date of the application means that, if and when the company is satisfied, the contract shall be considered to relate back and take effect as of that date. . . .

On the other hand a number of courts have held that the provision to the effect that the insurance shall be in force from the date of the application if the premium is paid gives rise to a contract of insurance immediately upon receipt of the application and payment of the premium, and that the proviso that the company shall be satisfied that the insured was acceptable at the date of the application creates only a right to terminate the contract if the company becomes dissatisfied with the risk before a policy is issued. . . .

✿　✿　✿　✿　✿

We are of the view that a contract of insurance arose upon defendant's receipt of the completed application and the first premium payment. The clause quoted above is subject to the interpretation that the applicant is offered a choice of either paying his first premium when he signs the application, in which event "the insurance shall be in force . . . from the date . . . of the application," or of paying upon receipt of the policy, in which event "no insurance shall be in force until . . . the policy is delivered." The understanding of an ordinary person is the standard which must be used in construing the contract, and such a person upon reading the application would believe that he would secure the benefit of immediate coverage by paying the premium in advance of delivery of the policy. There is an obvious advantage to the company in obtaining payment of the premium when the application is made, and it would be unconscionable to permit the company, after using language to induce payment of the premium at that time, to escape the obligation which an ordinary applicant would reasonably believe had been undertaken by the insurer. Moreover, defendant drafted the clause, and had it wished to make clear that its satisfaction was a condition precedent to a contract, it could easily have done so by using unequivocal terms. While some of the language tends to support the company's position, it does no more than produce an ambiguity, and the ambiguity must be resolved against the defendant.

Nevertheless, this is the minority rule. The majority rule upholds the condition as a valid condition precedent, as illustrated in the case of *Mofrad* v. *New York Life Insurance Company*,[7] decided by the United States Court of Appeals for the Tenth Circuit, in May, 1953. The applicable portions of that decision are as follows:

---

[7] 206 F.2d 491 (C.A. Utah, 1953).

. . . Appellants contend that under the terms of the agreement considered in relation to Part 3 of the application, the only reasonable construction is that the company assumed the risk of insuring Mofrad from the date of the application under a so-called "binder receipt"; that otherwise the agreement is ambiguous; that the purpose of such agreement was to give the applicant the impression that the company had insured him from the date thereof upon payment of the full amount of the premium.

But, "a contract of insurance rests upon and is controlled by the same principles of law applicable to any other contract. What the contracting parties intended, mutually agreed to, and their minds met upon, is the measure of their obligations." *Bowen* v. *Prudential Life Ins. Co.,* 178 Mich. 63, 144 N.W. 543, 51 L.R.A. (N.S.) 587, as cited in *New York Life Ins. Co.* v. *Gist,* 63 F. 2d 732. And if the intentions of the parties are clear from an examination of the contractual documents, this court will not rewrite the contract. *Bennett* v. *The Preferred Acc. Ins. Co. of New York,* 192 F. 2d 748 (10 Cir., 1951); *New York Life Ins. Co.* v. *Gist, supra.*

The language of the application and of the receipt is definite and clear; the application bears the signature of the Applicant and it must be presumed that he read the agreement and was aware of its contractual import. Certainly there is nothing in the evidence to indicate that he was misled.

And there are no provisions in the agreement which would lead to a conclusion that an interim contract was intended by the parties. There are other clearly prescribed conditions within the agreement than the payment of the premium and delivery of the receipt to the applicant, which lead only to the conclusion that the applicant, was merely applying for a contract of insurance which could be consummated only upon the fulfillment of the conditions set out in the application. And where a policy application contains such conditions precedent, performance thereof is a prerequisite to the taking effect of insurance coverage. *Hurt* v. *New York Life Ins. Co.,* 51 F. 2d 936 (10 Cir., 1931).

✿   ✿   ✿   ✿   ✿

We must conclude that the applicant failed to meet the required conditions precedent to the consummation of an insurance contract, and the judgment of the trial court is affirmed.

Sometimes the Applicant Makes the Offer

Where He Prepays the Initial Premium. As a general rule, if the agent collects the initial premium amount at the time the application is completed, he issues a conditional binding receipt. If, for some reason, no conditional binding receipt is issued even though the premium is paid, the effective offer is made by the applicant.

By submitting the premium with his application, the applicant makes it clear that he intends to enter into a contractual relationship with the insurance company. Completing the application, therefore, is no longer merely a part of the preliminary negotiations; it is a bona fide offer. The company, in issuing a policy in exact accord with the terms of the application, accepts the offer. This does not necessarily mean that insurance becomes immediately effective, for the effective date of coverage may be a part of the agreement itself. However, if the company issues a policy in exact accord with the terms of the application, it accepts the offer. If it issues a different kind of contract the company rejects the applicant's offer and makes a counter-offer, which, in turn, must be accepted by the applicant.

The Counter-Offer. The counter-offer plays an important, often crucial, part in the formation of the life insurance contract. Even though the applicant has made an offer, if the company issues a policy differing from that applied for, it is, in legal effect, making a counter-offer, which has no contractual effect until it has been accepted. The death of the applicant prior to such acceptance again presents the simple, basic question: Was he insured? In cases where a counter-offer was made and the applicant died before he had accepted, the answer is simple: He was not insured.

This type of situation is illustrated in such a case as *Kronjaeger v. The Travelers Insurance Company et al.,*[8] decided by the West Virginia Supreme Court of Appeals, in October, 1942. There the court said, in part:

> Much of the argument on behalf of appellant is based upon the contention that Kronjaeger was entitled to a "binding receipt" upon his payment of the first premium for the policy applied for. This receipt, previously referred to, was attached to the application, as was the "Temporary Term Acceptance." Even if either of the slips had been filled out and given to Kronjaeger, their effect was conditional in the manner stated, and they became binding only upon issuance of the policy as applied for, or one issued in lieu thereof and accepted by appellant. The company reserved the right to accept or reject the proposition contained in the application.
>
> The application being a mere proposal to the company, it can either accept the proposal, decline it altogether or impose such conditions as to the making of the contract, as it may choose. *McCully's Admr. v. Phoenix Mutual Life Ins. Co.,* 18 W. Va. 782.
>
> See also *Mutual Life Ins. Co. v. Young,* 23 Wall 85, 23 L. ed., 152.
>
> In this case the insurance company's reply to the application was the sending of a policy, differing in essential terms from that applied for, to the Wheeling Branch Office. This amounted to a counter-proposition and there was no contract, no meeting of the minds of the parties on the new terms, without acceptance thereof by Kronjaeger. *Fidelity & Casualty Co. v. Curtis Brown Co.,* (Okla.) 232 P. 90; *Field v. Missouri State Life Ins. Co.,* (Utah) 290 P. 979; *Farmers Mutual Assn. v. Haines,* (Neb.) 223 N.W. 655; *State ex rel. Equitable Life Assurance Society v. Robertson,* (Mo.) 191 S.W. 989; *Riordan v. Equitable Life Assurance Society,* (Idaho) 175 P. 586.
>
> The fact that the company retained the amount paid by Kronjaeger as the first premium on the policy applied for does not strengthen appellant's case, in the absence of acceptance of the counter-proposition. *Cranston v. California Ins. Co.,* (Ore.) 185 P. 292.

The Company Makes the Offer. There are three possible situations as far as the offer-acceptance analysis is concerned in the formation of

---

[8] 124 W. Va. 730, 22 S.E. (2d) 689 (1942).

the life insurance contract. In the first case the applicant expresses his willingness to contract by completing the application. The company then considers the insurability of the proposed insured, and if he is found to be insurable, it issues a policy for delivery. By issuing and delivering the policy, the company makes an offer. The applicant can accept the offer, if he wishes, by paying the initial premium (performing the act requested), and the contract is formed.

The Company Makes a Conditional Offer. In the second situation, the company may authorize its agent to make a conditional offer by issuing a conditional binding receipt at the time of the application, if the applicant pays the initial premium. Here the applicant again accepts by paying the premium, and again, subject to a condition, a contract is formed. In this case the exact status of the insurance during the period between completion of the application and issuance of the policy depends upon the wording of the receipt. If that wording is sufficiently clear, the courts will give effect to it in accordance with the intent of the company and the applicant. If there is any question about its meaning, however, (if there is any *ambiguity,* as the court would put it) the court will apply standard rules of construction and interpret the wording in favor of the proposed insured.

The Applicant Makes the Offer. In the third instance the applicant pays the initial premium at the time he applies for the insurance, but no binding receipt is issued. Here the applicant is not merely inviting an offer but is himself making an offer to be insured in accordance with the practices of the company. In such cases, if the applicant is found to be insurable, the company accepts the offer when it issues and delivers the kind of policy applied for, in the amount requested.

HOW OFFER AND ACCEPTANCE WORK

Some Actual Cases

The Conditional Offer. Let us assume that an applicant, John M. Jones, completes and signs an application for a $10,000 policy with the Ajax Life Insurance Company and submits the initial premium in cash. James Brown, the agent, issues a conditional binding receipt, forwards the application to the issuing office, makes arrangements for a medical examination, and orders an inspection report.

From the previous brief review we know that Jones, by completing the application and paying the initial premium, has accepted the conditional offer of the Ajax Life Insurance Company made by agent Brown, and that insurance will become effective prior to delivery of the policy if the applicant is found to be insurable. Let us assume further that the wording of the receipt is completely clear and the condition—that the applicant be found insurable—is a true condition precedent, which must be fulfilled before insurance becomes effective.

Where the Condition Is Fulfilled. First let us take the simple case where the condition is fulfilled. Personnel in the issuing office of the company review the application, the medical examiner's report, and the inspection report, and find that Jones does, in fact, meet their risk appraisal requirements. An authorized officer then approves the issuance of a policy on the exact plan and in the same amount that Jones applied for. We will assume that he has just approved and initialed the application when the telephone rings.

It is Brown calling long distance to say that Jones was struck by a hit-and-run driver while crossing the street. Jones died in the ambulance on his way to the hospital. Was he insured?

The answer can be given only after all the facts have been ascertained and considered, and the issuing authority may want to consult the legal counsel of the company because of the many delicate questions that may be involved. However, once the facts have been ascertained, the answer will be relatively simple. For example, the conditional binding receipt may provide that insurance will take effect as of the date of the medical if the applicant is found to be insurable as of that date. In that case the determination of Jones's insurability and the decision on the part of the appropriate officer (even after the death of the insured) that a policy shall be issued will put the insurance into effect. The condition has been fulfilled, and Jones was insured as of a date prior to his death.

In this case, therefore, insurance was effective even though no policy had been issued. As a matter of fact, the major purpose of the conditional binding receipt is to cover just this type of case and to make protection effective as of the earliest possible date compatible with the technical requirements of risk selection.

Where the Condition Is Not Fulfilled. Going back to the same set of original facts, let us rewrite the subsequent events. Let us say that agent Brown mails the application and the premium check to the company, arranges for a medical examination, and orders an inspection. Let us also say that the risk appraiser reviews the documents and finds that Jones does not meet the company's requirements in accordance with its standard practices of risk selection. He has just made that notation on the application file when the telephone rings, as in our first illustration, and Brown reports the same fatal accident to Jones.

It seems clear that in this instance Jones is not insured. The condition of insurability, specified in the conditional binding receipt, has not been met. Even though no actual notice of rejection has been sent, rejection can follow the death of the applicant. However, as a practical matter, the company should be adequately prepared to support its decision with respect to the applicant's lack of insurability and to set forth the controlling wording of the conditional binding receipt in a court of law, if necessary.

In those jurisdictions where the courts have taken the view that the receipt establishes coverage subject to a condition subsequent, the decision could be different. In cases decided on this theory, the wording of the receipt has often been found to be ambiguous, but frequently these findings have been prompted by the fact that the insurance is effective on condition that the application is approved. Approval, of course, is strictly within the discretion of the insurance company. To avoid this aspect of the problem we have deliberately made our receipt one of the "insurability" type.

In any case where the applicant dies prior to notice of the action taken by the company, every step in the negotiations with the applicant should be ascertained and the terms of the conditional binding receipt carefully reviewed. Generally the applicable legal principles are simple if the facts are clear. The underwriting principles are also clear if all the necessary information is available. As a practical matter, however, all the information is very rarely available without systematic investigation, and the facts are very rarely clear. For this reason the death of the proposed insured in any case prior to issuance and delivery of the policy should be a warning signal that a legal problem may be involved, and legal counsel should be consulted before any action is taken.

DELAY IN ACTING ON THE APPLICATION

So far in this discussion of offer and acceptance we have assumed that the activities of the various people involved have been carried out with reasonable promptness. At this point let us suppose that after completing the application and collecting the initial premium the agent does not issue a conditional binding receipt and in fact takes no further action whatsoever, not even sending in the application. Let us suppose also that it is a nonmedical case and that the applicant, although in excellent health and otherwise insurable as of the date of the application, is accidentally killed some five or six weeks later.

A case of this kind obviously points up the advantages of the conditional binding receipt, both to the company and to the applicant and beneficiary. It also helps to explain the origin of a rather unique approach to life insurance which sought to establish a liability in *tort* (the field of law dealing with actionable civil wrongs exclusive of contract) where there was admittedly no liability under standard rules of contract law.

The Tort Liability Theory. The tort liability theory was never very widely approved by the courts, and it has been severely criticized by many life insurance spokesmen and lawyers. Most of the cases following this doctrine were decided between 1913 and 1931, and it seems probable that as conditional binding receipts of the insurability type became more widely used there was less occasion to reach beyond the limits of contract law and to attempt to establish liability on other grounds. Nevertheless this tort liability theory represents a significant chapter in the history of the law of the life insurance contract and cannot be ignored in any discussion of the application process in the formation of the life insurance contract.

Liability in Contract. As noted in Chapter II, mere silence on the part of the offeree does not constitute acceptance of an offer as a matter of general contract law. By the almost overwhelming weight of authority, this principle applies just as clearly in the case of offers for life insurance contracts. However, some courts have held that where the premium is paid at the time of the application, unreasonable delay in acting on the application in effect amounts to an acceptance. The theory is that retention of the premium is inconsistent with rejection.

Illustrative of this point of view is the discussion of the Michigan Supreme Court in the case of *Wadsworth* v. *New York Life Insurance Co.*[9] The case dealt with an application for ordinary life insurance on the part of a captain in the United States air force, who paid the first full premium in cash at the time of application and received a conditional binding receipt. He was lost in action in the Korean War before the application was approved. In one section the court discusses the effect of delay in consideration of the application, as follows:

Appellant contends in her second issue that a contract arose as a matter of law through defendant's unreasonable delay in acceptance or rejection of the application filed by the deceased.

It is certainly the general rule that mere silence or inaction on the part of an insurance company does not constitute assent to an application. *Insurance Co.* v. *Young's Administrator,* 90 U.S. (23 Wall.) 85; *Equitable Life Assurance Society* v. *McElroy,* 83 F. 631; *Bradley* v. *Federal Life Insurance Co.,* 295 Ill. 381 (129 N.E. 171, 15 A.L.R. 1021), Annotation 75 A.L.R. 952.

We are not, however, prepared to say that there may not be circumstances which can give rise to an exception to the rule stated in the case law cited above.

In general contract law, under circumstances which impose a duty to speak or act, the silence and inaction of an offeree can give rise to a contract by operation of law.

American Law Institute, 1 Restatement on Contracts, Section 72, says as follows:

(2) Where the offeree exercises dominion over things which are offered to him, such exercise of dominion in the absence of other circumstances

---
[9] 84 N.W. 2d 513 (Mich., 1957).

showing a contrary intention is an acceptance. If circumstances indicate that the exercise of dominion is tortious the offeror may at his option treat it as an acceptance, though the offeree manifests an intention not to accept.

12 Am. Jur., Contracts Section 40, says:

There is a legal acceptance where silence is accompanied by acts of the offeree, such as exercise of dominion over things offered to him, which warrant an inference of assent.

Michigan, it appears, is among the minority of States in holding that there is a duty on the part of the insurance company to act with reasonable promptness. In *Robinson* v. *United States Benevolent Society,* 132 Mich. 695, p. 699, this Court stated:

In insurance contracts of this character it is the duty of the company to act with reasonable promptness. Failing to reject within reasonable time, the law implies an acceptance.

See, also, Mich. L. Rev. 484.

We do not know what other facts may be shown on retrial but where, as currently shown in the record before us, substantial delay in accepting or rejecting is coupled with retention of the first and succeeding premiums, the question of whether or not there was such unreasonable delay on the part of the defendant or its agent as to imply acceptance would be a question of fact for the jury.

In most jurisdictions, as indicated in this quoted passage, mere silence or inaction on the part of an insurance company does not constitute an acceptance of the application. There is always some delay between offer and acceptance, but even if this delay is somewhat longer than usual there is ordinarily no implication of acceptance. Furthermore, if the offeror dies during this period the offer is terminated as a matter of contract law. If the applicant is the proposed insured, his death also marks the happening of the event which was to have been insured against and thus makes the contract impossible of completion from the strict insurance point of view.

The conditional binding receipt conditioned upon insurability bridges this gap as far as the proposed insured is concerned and yet preserves to the insurance company its right to appraise the risk. However, if the receipt is conditioned upon approval of the application, and many receipts have been so worded, it does not go very far toward meeting the problem. In that case, death prior to approval of the application has the same effect as if no conditional binding receipt had been used.

In cases of this kind, delay in handling the application, either by the agent or the issuing office, could easily mean the difference between payment of the face amount of the policy and the simple return of the premium. Thus it is not surprising that before the widespread use of the insurability type of conditional binding receipt, there was a rather concerted attempt to establish obligation on some basis other than contract—in this case, in tort.

What a Tort Is. Simply stated, a tort is an actionable wrong which does not arise out of contract. It is based on a duty on the part of the person to be charged, the violation of that duty through negligence, and resulting damages to the plaintiff.

Arguments for Tort Liability. Those who have advocated the tort liability doctrine take the position that the company has a duty to act with reasonable diligence. They concede that most business organizations have no comparable duty, but they maintain that because insurance is affected with a public interest and the companies operate under a franchise from the state, there is a public duty on their part to act promptly in considering an application, either accepting or rejecting it within a reasonable length of time. Failing to do this, if the applicant has submitted the initial premium and would have been an acceptable risk except for his death prior to issuance of the policy, the company is liable in damages to the amount that would have been recoverable under the policy if it had been promptly issued and in effect at the date of death.

This point of view is most ably presented in the case of *Bekken Adm'x v. The Equitable Life Assurance Society of the United States*,[10] decided by the North Dakota Supreme Court in May, 1940. The applicable portions of that decision read as follows:

Insurance is a contract, which, like other contracts, results only from an offer and an acceptance of the offer. There is a conflict in the authorities as to whether legal obligations arise only after a contract of insurance has been made, or whether in certain circumstances a legal duty arises, from the relationship created during the negotiations between an applicant for insurance and the insurance company, to act promptly upon the application, and to inform the applicant whether the offer is accepted or rejected. Generally speaking, there are two main lines of decisions dealing with these questions. According to one view, the legal relations between an applicant and the insurance company "are fundamentally the same as those between parties negotiating any other contract, and are 'purely contractual' "; that "mere delay, mere inaction by an insurance company in passing on an application does not constitute an acceptance or establish the relationship of insurer and insured," and that such delay or inaction does not constitute any breach of duty by the insurance company. *Thornton* v. *Natl. Council*, 110 W. Va. 412, 158 S.E. 507. According to this view, no duty arises unless, and until, a contract has been created; if there is no contract, there is no duty, and consequently there is no liability on the part of the insurer because of any delay or inaction on its part in passing upon the application, or in issuing or delivering the policy.

❋   ❋   ❋   ❋   ❋

The other line of decisions holds that an insurance company that has solicited and received a completed application for insurance is under a legal duty to take prompt action on the application, and give prompt notice to the

[10] 70 N.D. 122, 283 N.W. 200 (1940).

applicant of its action; and that consequently such insurance company is liable in tort for negligent delay in acting upon the application, and notifying the applicant in case the application is rejected. . . .

In our opinion this latter line of decisions announces the correct principle. These decisions recognize the facts to be what they are. They do not attempt to force the facts to fit a ready-made legal mold. They recognize the status and relationship of the parties, as they are, and measure the obligations of the parties accordingly.

It has long been recognized that "the business of insurance is quasi public in character" (32 C.J. p. 981), and that the state has the "right to regulate the conduct by corporations, domestic and foreign, of insurance as a business affected with a public interest. This includes provision for 'unearned premium fund or reserve'; then came the limitation of dividends, the publishing of accounts, valued policies, standards of policies, prescribing investments, requiring deposits of money or bonds, confining the business to corporations. . . .'"

It is competent for the state, under its police power, to determine who may engage in the business of insurance "within its boundaries, and to prescribe terms and conditions on which the business may be conducted, and generally to regulate the business and all persons engaged in it, whether as individuals, partnerships, voluntary associations, or corporations."

✿   ✿   ✿   ✿   ✿

Under such circumstances, having in view the nature of the risk against which the insured seeks protection, is there not a duty upon the insurer to act upon the application within a reasonable time? Can the insurer, having preempted the field, retain control of the situation and the applicant's funds indefinitely? Does not the very nature of the transaction impose upon the insurer a duty to act? (*Kukuska* v. *Home Mutual Hail-Tornado Ins. Co. supra.*)

The courts, in increasing number, have answered this question in the affirmative. While the precise question has not been presented to this Court, it has been presented to a trial court in this State and received an affirmative answer (*Re Coughlin*, 53 N. Dak. 188, 205 N.W. 14), and this Court has clearly indicated its approval of the doctrine that an insurance company is under a legal duty to act promptly on an application for insurance, and to notify the applicant of its acceptance or rejection. . . . We approve that doctrine as the law in this State.

Arguments against Tort Liability. Opponents of the tort liability doctrine depend upon several arguments. First and perhaps most significant is the basic principle that mere silence or inaction on the part of the offeree does not constitute an acceptance of an offer. Obviously, this is an ineffective argument in a tort case, which acknowledges in the first place that there is no liability in contract. More important are the arguments that tort liability decisions are little more than judicial legislation, and if there is an affirmative duty on the part of the life insurance companies to act with promptness, it should be legislatively declared. This position is upheld by many courts, who point out that insurers are not public utilities and must be permitted freedom to choose the persons with whom they are willing to contract.

This point of view is ably expressed in a brief consideration and rejection of the tort liability theory in the case of *Miller, Spec. Admx.* v. *Hanson et al.,*[11] decided by the South Dakota Supreme Court in March, 1943. The decision reads as follows:

Per Curiam:[12] The question presented by this appeal is whether an insurance company may be held liable in tort for negligent delay in acting upon an application for insurance. The learned trial court entered judgment for the defendant company, and thereafter an order for a new trial. Its order granting a new trial was reversed by this court for reasons which do not relate to the merits. *Miller* v. *Hanson,* (S.D.) 4 N.W. 2d 602. The present appeal is by the plaintiff from the original judgment for the insurance company.

The authorities are collected in 15 A.L.R. 1026, and 75 A.L.R. 952, and are analyzed in 3 Chicago Law Review 39. They are in conflict. The courts which have imposed liability on the theory of tort present strong social or ethical reasons for charging an insurance company with a duty to act promptly on such an application but fail to convince us that the essential legal duty so to do exists. It is elementary that an action *ex delicto*[13] is founded upon a breach of duty.

We concur in the statement of the Supreme Court of Minnesota in *Schliep* v. *Commercial Casualty Ins. Co.,* 191 Minn. 479, 254 N.W. 618, as follows:

It is apparent that if liability is here to be imposed in an action *ex delicto* this court will be compelled to engage in judicial legislation. If and when it is desired to impose upon insurers additional burdens or requirements, the same should come through the legislative department of the government and not by virtue of judge-made law.

The judgment of the trial court is affirmed.

All the judges concur.

Landmark Cases. A court in Hawaii applied the tort liability doctrine as early as 1897.[14] However, it was first applied in continental United States in 1912, in connection with an agent's delay in forwarding to the home office an application for hail insurance. Four days after the date of the application the applicant suffered a loss, and in the suit that followed, the court held that the insurance company was liable in tort for the delay of its agent. In the next year (1913), the Iowa Supreme Court, in the case of *Duffie* v. *Bankers Life Association,*[15] upheld the application of the doctrine to life insurance companies.

In the *Duffie* case the applicant's insurability was not in question, and he had submitted the initial premium at the time of the application. The agent negligently failed to forward the application to the home office, and the applicant was accidentally killed some thirty days later. The

---

[11] 8 N.W. 2d 927 (S.D., 1943).

[12] By the court. This ordinarily means an opinion written by the entire court rather than one written by only one judge.

[13] A cause of action based upon a wrong or tort.

[14] *Carter* v. *Manhattan Life Ins. Co.,* 11 Hawaii 69 (1897).

[15] 160 Iowa 19, 139 N.W. 1087 (1913).

widow, as beneficiary, filed suit under the tort theory on the grounds that had it not been for the negligence of the agent she would have been the beneficiary of a life insurance policy on the life of her husband. The Iowa Supreme Court upheld a decision in her favor, saying:

> But it is said that a certificate or policy of insurance is simply a contract like any other, as between individuals, and that there is no such thing as negligence of a party in the matter of delay in entering into a contract. This view overlooks the fact that the defendant holds and is acting under a franchise from the state. The legislative policy, in granting this, proceeds on the theory that chartering such association is in the interest of the public to the end that indemnity on specific contingencies shall be provided those who are eligible and desire it, and for their protection the state regulates, inspects, and supervises their business. Having solicited applications for insurance, and having so obtained them and received payment of the fees or premiums exacted, they are bound either to furnish the indemnity the state has authorized them to furnish or decline so to do within such reasonable time as will enable them to act intelligently and advisedly thereon, or suffer the consequences flowing from their neglect so to do.

(Incidentally, most of the cases which have followed the tort liability theory have held that the right of action is in the applicant or his personal representative and not the beneficiary, whose rights are in contract or not at all. It is notable that the *Duffie* case did not take this view.)

Other cases followed the *Duffie* decision, although the doctrine was not adopted in every case in which it was proposed. One of the earliest and most definite rejections of the doctrine was voiced in 1929 by the Supreme Court of Mississippi in the case of *Savage* v. *Prudential Life Insurance Company*.[16] There the court said:

> The fact that the insurance companies are granted a franchise to do business in this state does not and should not impose upon them the duty to consider promptly all who offer to them the risk of insuring their lives, no more than would be required of a bank to lend money promptly to all who should make application and suffer loss while the bank was negligent in determining whether or not it would accept the offer and enter into a contract.

Although the *Duffie* view became rather popular in the 1920's, this popularity seemed to diminish during the 1930's, and in the past ten or fifteen years there has been little change in the numbers of states in which the doctrine has been adopted or definitely rejected. The use of a liberal conditional binding receipt which establishes obligation as a matter of contract from the earliest possible date, on condition that the applicant is found to be insurable, has no doubt played an important part in this slowing of what once appeared to be a popular trend. Cases where liability once seemed morally, if not legally, indicated are ordinarily within this type of conditional binding receipt and are therefore

---

[16] 154 Miss. 89, 121 So. 487 (1929).

covered as a matter of contract. Nevertheless, the opportunities for litigation on this basis remain in every case where there is delay and the applicant is found not to be insurable. For this reason the tort liability theory, based on negligent delay in handling life insurance applications, cannot safely be disregarded, particularly in those jurisdictions where it has been followed in the past.

OTHER ELEMENTS OF THE CONTRACT

The informal contract, it will be recalled, has been defined as "an agreement between competent parties expressing definite assent to the terms of a promise or promises supported by legally adequate consideration." The agreement must be in a form required by law and must not be declared ineffective by any special statute or rule of common law.

The offer and acceptance process presents special problems in connection with the formation of the life insurance contract and, for that reason, it has been discussed at some length. There remain for discussion the requirements of "legally adequate" consideration, competent parties, a form required by law, and any special statutes or rules of common law which might declare a life insurance contract void.

1. Consideration

Under the informal contract, the promise or promises to be enforced must always be supported by a legally sufficient consideration. As noted, in life insurance, except in rare cases, the promises are all made by the company. What, then, is the nature of this consideration which makes an enforceable contract of what would otherwise be a mere set of promises?

A Legal Concept. The life insurance policy often reads something like this: "In consideration of the application and the initial premium, the Ajax Life Insurance Company agrees to pay . . ." Legally, however, consideration is not determined by what the parties may say it is.

In the law of contracts, consideration takes a number of different forms. It may consist of positive actions on the part of the promisee, or it may be another promise or other promises on his part, as it is in the bilateral contract. In legal terms, it is a "benefit to the promisor or detriment to the promisee" or, alternatively, the "value requested and given in exchange for the promise or promises sought to be enforced." In insurance, this "benefit" or "value" is the initial premium.

Most life insurance policies specifically state that the insurance shall not be effective until the first premium is paid, and the validity of this stipulation has uniformly been upheld. By clear implication, therefore, payment of the first premium is the "value requested and given in exchange for the promise or promises sought to be enforced" and consti-

tutes the consideration which makes those promises on the part of the
company enforceable.

2. Competent Parties

Who Is a Party? The informal contract is "an agreement between
competent parties . . . ," and the life insurance contract is an informal
contract. However, in discussing the competency of the parties it is
perhaps advisable to clarify at the outset exactly who the "parties to the
contract" are.

The Beneficiary Is Not a Party. In some ways the life insurance contract seems to involve three parties—the applicant (who becomes the
policyowner), the life insurance company, and the beneficiary. However, in the legal sense of the term, the beneficiary is not a party to the
contract—that is, he or she is not a person with whom the contract is
made. In fact, in the most usual life insurance situation it is not necessary that the beneficiary even know that an application has been completed or a policy issued. The fact that a name can usually be canceled
without one's knowledge or consent and the name of someone else substituted is even further evidence that the beneficiary has no status as a
party to the contract.

The Insured in Ownership Cases. If one bears in mind that the applicant is the only person, other than the insurance company, who is a
party to the contract in the legal sense of the term, a great deal of
possible confusion may be avoided. This definition automatically excludes the beneficiary. It also excludes the insured in third-party ownership cases.

For example, one partner may apply for, and be issued, a policy of
life insurance on the life of his partner. In such a case we have Partner
A, the applicant, who is ordinarily, though not necessarily, also the
beneficiary; Partner B, who is the insured; and the life insurance company, with whom the contract is made. A similar example is presented
where the A.B.C. Corporation applies for, and is beneficiary of, a policy
on the life of M, an officer or key employee. In this case the A.B.C.
Corporation is a party to the contract; the officer or key employee is not.

Again, a wife may apply for life insurance on the life of her husband.
In that case we would have Wife, who applies and is beneficiary;
Husband, who is the insured; and the life insurance company, with
whom the contract is made. Here Wife and the life insurance company
are parties to the contract; Husband is not.

But now let us say that Parents, X and Y, apply for and are issued a
policy of life insurance on the life of their son, Tommy. They designate
as beneficiary Z, who is named as trustee of a trust which they have
established for Tommy's benefit. In this case, both X and Y are parties

to the contract with the life insurance company, but neither Tommy, the insured, nor Z, the trustee, is such a party.

Each of these last four cases involves a contract under which the insured is not a party. The contract insures his life but it is not made with him in any sense of the word; he is merely the "vehicle for the insurance" as it is sometimes put. In insurance terms these are "ownership cases." However, the same basic rule obtains as with any other life insurance contract. The applicant or applicants are parties to the contract on the one hand; the life insurance company is a party on the other.

Consent of the Insured. On analysis, all third-party ownership cases reduce themselves to a situation where one or more persons, having an insurable interest in another, have applied for and been issued a policy of insurance on the life of that person. The insurance company is one party to the contract; one or more applicants are also parties. The insured signs the application only to signify his consent that someone else shall be issued a policy promising the payment of money, sometimes a great deal of money, at his death. The implications of such a promise are so serious that as a matter of public policy his consent is required in every case unless there is a statute expressly providing otherwise.[17]

Assured and Insured. In the past, efforts have been made in ownership cases to distinguish between the person whose life is insured and the person or persons to whom the policy is issued, by speaking of the former as the *insured*, the latter as the *assured* or *assureds*. This practice has not been too widely adopted, however, and the policies of many companies today make the difference clear by referring to the person or persons to whom the policy is issued as the "owner" or "living owner." Of course, where the person to whom the policy is issued is also the person whose life is insured, he is both the insured and the policyowner, and no problem in terminology is involved.

Competency of the Insurer. A life insurance company is considered competent to issue binding contracts of life insurance if (1) it has been authorized to do so by the terms of its charter or articles of incorporation, and (2) it has a certificate of authority issued by the state in which the contract is completed. The competency of the company, in this sense of the word, is ordinarily certified to each year by the various individual states in which it does an insurance business.

Competency of the Applicant. Only those persons who are actually parties to the contract need to have contractual capacity. Other than

---

[17] Although some of the states have enacted this requirement into statutory law, the absence of such statutes in other states does not affect the basic rule that in the absence of a statute to the contrary, a contract of insurance on the life of an adult insured, issued without his consent, is unenforceable as against public policy. See *American Jurisprudence,* Vol. 29, p. 617.

the company, therefore, it is only the applicant or applicants with whom we are concerned in discussing competency to make a binding contract. Insurability and the presence or absence of an insurable interest are important factors, but neither is concerned in the basic question of competency in the sense of contractual capacity.

In considering the matter of contractual capacity, we start with a presumption. In the absence of evidence to the contrary, every person is presumed to be competent to make a valid contract. Immediately, there are exceptions. As mentioned in Chapter II, married women, minors, insane persons, intoxicated persons, convicts, and aliens either have, or at some time in the past have had, limited capacity to make binding contracts. For example, the contracts of a married woman at common law were void. They were not voidable; they simply never had validity. Today, most of the states have statutes removing or drastically modifying this limitation.

A contract entered into by a person who has been declared legally insane and for whom a conservator has been appointed is void. If no conservator has been appointed, the contract is merely voidable. The insane person may affirm or disaffirm the contract upon regaining his sanity. Lack of contractual capacity of a possibly insane applicant for life insurance will not as a general rule present a problem in connection with a life insurance application because of the investigation and medical aspects of determining insurability. However, the problem sometimes arises in connection with annuities.

Aliens. The citizen of a country other than ours is an alien. If the countries are at war, he is an enemy alien. Ordinarily there are no restrictions upon the rights of friendly aliens to contract with persons or corporations of this country. However, once war is declared, business activities are terminated and with them the possibility of forming new contracts of insurance. The major life insurance contract problems in connection with war, therefore, have to do with the performance, after the outbreak of war, of contracts formed while the two nations were at peace. Some of these problems were indicated in Chapter II, and the subject will be discussed more specifically in a later chapter, in connection with the operation of the life insurance contract.

The Minor Applicant. As noted earlier, the contracts of an infant are binding only as long as he wishes them to be, and at common law any person is an infant until he is twenty-one years of age. This has been modified downward by statute in some states, but twenty-one remains the age of majority in most jurisdictions.

A minor has the right to disaffirm at any time any contract he has made, except a contract for the sale of land, and he may disaffirm a contract for the sale of land upon reaching his majority. Ordinarily he will be held responsible for the reasonable value of necessaries, but life insurance has been uniformly held not to be a necessary.

The general rule is that if the minor has in his possession the consideration he has received, he must return it when he avoids the contract. Then he may demand and receive back whatever he has parted with, so that the situation is again as nearly as possible what it was prior to the making of the contract. Nevertheless, if the minor no longer has the consideration he has received, or if the property has been damaged, he may still demand and receive back whatever he himself has given.

Applied to the avoidance of a life insurance contract, this rule presents some difficulties. Obviously the minor cannot return the "protection" he has received. May he then receive back all the premiums he has paid, or should he reasonably be charged for the pure insurance coverage he has had?

The decided cases on this point are in conflict. The majority hold that where an infant repudiates a contract of insurance on his life he may recover all the premiums paid by him during his minority. There is a minority line of cases which hold that the insurer may deduct the cost of the actual benefit of the insurance during the period the policy was in force.

Most of these cases arose and were decided in an entirely different economic atmosphere from that of the present day; they involved different contracts and different practices. They are significant, however, as background for understanding present-day statutes, in effect in many of the states, which remove or modify the contractual incapacity of minors. One of the best illustrations of the majority rule is the case of *Mutual Life Insurance Company of New York v. Harry Schiavone*,[18] decided by the District of Columbia Court of Appeals, in May, 1934. It reads, in part, as follows:

> On December 11, 1931, plaintiff, then 19 years old, applied to the defendant for a $25,000 insurance on his life for the benefit of his mother and sister, and for which a policy was issued December 14th. One month before the application his father, president of a Washington bank where plaintiff was employed, had died, leaving a will by which plaintiff, his mother, and sister, were equal beneficiaries of a trust fund of $100,000.
>
> His only other resources were a salary of $80 per month from the bank and an agency for an insurance company producing sundry hopes at that time and little else thereafter.
>
> The father's estate was soon found to be insolvent; the trust fund did not materialize; the bank closed; and the infant lost his employment, when the policy was seven months gone.
>
> On December 28, 1932, the plaintiff repudiated his contract and demanded return of the premium paid, which was refused, and the suit followed.

[18] 63 App. D.C. 257, 71 F.2d 980, 94 A.L.R. 962 (1934).

✿ ✿ ✿ ✿ ✿

In the District of Columbia an infant's contracts which appear upon their face to be to his prejudice are void, while his other contracts are voidable, except for necessaries furnished to him at fair prices.

And his inability to return the consideration and restore the status quo does not deprive him of his right to repudiate. . . .

Without intimating that a policy of insurance can never be a necessary for any infant, we think the facts here clearly show that this insurance was not a necessary for this infant.

It was an ordinary life policy with his mother and sister as beneficiaries, so that he must die before even they could benefit by the contract.

But there seems little contention that the insurance was a necessary, for the main reliance of the defendant is upon what it calls the equitable doctrine which it asserts was applied by the Supreme Court in *Myers* v. *Hurley Motor Co.*, 273 U.S. 18, 47 S. Ct. 277, 279, 71 L. Ed. 515, 50 A.L.R. 1181, which went up from this court.

In that case the Supreme Court held that a vendor receiving back in a damaged condition a motor car sold to an infant in a sound condition, was entitled to recoup from the infant's claim for return of the purchase price the amount of damage done to the car by the infant, up to the extent of his claim for return.

In so holding, the court, when speaking of the principle that he who seeks equity must do equity, said:

The maxim applies, at least, where there has been, as there was here, actual fraud on the part of the infant.

When an infant of mature appearance, by false and fraudulent representations as to his age, has induced another person to sell and deliver property to him, it is against natural justice to permit the infant to recover money paid for the property without first compelling him to account for the injury which his deceit has inflicted upon the other person.

But in the present case, before the defendant made the contract, it had received and considered the plaintiff's application in writing wherein he stated his age to be 19, and the difficulty of fact arises here from no fraud or misrepresentation of the infant in obtaining the contract, but from the failure of his resources thereafter.

And it is to be noted that on the facts in the *Myers* case the Supreme Court held the infant accountable for the injury to the vendor, of which there was definite evidence, while in this case there is no such showing, relief being sought instead for an alleged benefit going to the infant from the contract.

But the cost to the company of carrying the risk is shown neither in the affidavit of defense nor in the stipulation of facts, in which respect it resembles *Rice Auto Co.* v. *Spillman*, 51 App. D.C. 378, 280 F. 452.

And the protection afforded the infant by the policy has no more merit as a benefit than the rent denied for the house occupied by the infant in *Gannon* v. *Manning*, 42 App. D.C. 206.

Even if the carrying charges to the company had been shown here, to allow them would be to hold that an infant is liable not only for necessaries, but for the cost price of purchases not necessary, so that an adult could knowingly sell anything to an infant, secure in the doctrine that if he fails to gain a profit, at least he cannot lose.

For the reasons stated, the judgment is affirmed with costs.

This case illustrates the majority opinion concerning a minor's right to disaffirm a contract of life insurance and demand the return of the premiums paid during his minority. As we have said, many states have special statutes today, which remove life insurance contracts from the group of contracts which the minor has the right to disaffirm. These statutes have the effect of placing minors of a specified age on the same status as adults with respect to life insurance contracts within the limitations specified by the statutes.

3. Insurable Interest

By far the most important statutory or common law requirement in connection with the life insurance contract is the requirement of an insurable interest. This requirement is peculiar to the insurance contract, though it is not, of course, confined to life insurance. In many ways it relates to the parties to the contract. The applicant must have an insurable interest in the life or property to be insured or the contract will be void. However, it has nothing to do with contractual capacity as such, but instead goes to the very essence of insurance. The requirement thus constitutes a "special statute or rule of law" declaring that a contract issued to an applicant who does not have an insurable interest in the life or property insured is void.

Historical Background. The requirement of an insurable interest is imposed by reasons of public policy and goes back to the early eighteenth century in England. At that time life insurance contracts were not applied for and issued to the persons whose lives were to be insured. Instead they were made by third persons, and the insureds were concerned only as the subjects of the insurance. Thus the insured himself had no rights whatsoever under the contract, either as owner or beneficiary. Often he did not know the person who obtained the insurance or even that insurance had been effected on his life.

The abuses to which this arrangement might be subjected are apparent. At one time it was almost a sport to bet that public figures would or would not live for even such a short period of time as a few days. Persons in public life were thus made the subjects of life insurance contracts by people who were not even acquainted with them. Obviously this was wagering of a peculiarly vicious nature, so vicious indeed that it shocked the conscience of an eighteenth century public not too highly noted for its squeamishness.

In 1774, Parliament finally took action and enacted a law to put an end to such "a mischievous kind of gaming." The law so enacted provided, in part, as follows:

> That, from and after the passing of this Act, no insurance shall be made by any person or persons, bodies politic or corporate, on the life or lives of any person or persons, or on any other event or events whatsoever, wherein the person or persons for whose use, benefit, or on whose account such policy or

policies shall be made, shall have no interest, or by way of gaming or wagering; and that every assurance contrary to the true intent and meaning hereof shall be null and void to all intents and purposes whatsoever.[19]

This statute has not been made a part of the common law of any of the states in the United States, as many of the early English statutes have. Nevertheless, the requirement of an insurable interest as a safeguard against the possible misuse of life insurance was early adopted, independently, in the United States. Sometimes it was enacted into statutory law; sometimes it was expressed as case law, as a matter of public policy. For instance, one of the early definitions of the term was made by the United States Supreme Court in 1881, in the case of *Warnock* v. *Davis*,[20] as follows:

> It is not easy to define with precision what will in all cases constitute an insurable interest, so as to take the contract out of the class of wager policies. It may be stated generally, however, to be such an interest, arising from the relation of the party obtaining the insurance, either as creditor of or surety for the assured, or from ties of blood or marriage to him, as will justify a reasonable expectation of advantage or benefit from the continuance of his life. It is not necessary that the expectation of advantage or benefit should always be capable of pecuniary estimation; for a parent has an insurable interest in the life of his child, and a child in the life of his parent, a husband in the life of his wife, and a wife in the life of her husband. The natural affection in cases of this kind is considered as more powerful—as operating more efficaciously—to protect the life of the insured than any other consideration. But in all cases there must be a reasonable ground, founded upon the relations of the parties to each other, either pecuniary or of blood or affinity, to expect some benefit or advantage from the continuance of the life of the assured. Otherwise the contract is a mere wager, by which the party taking the policy is directly interested in the early death of the assured. Such policies have a tendency to create a desire for the event. They are, therefore, independently of any statute on the subject, condemned, as being against public policy.

Regardless of the form in which it is expressed, therefore, the presence of an insurable interest is a requirement for a valid insurance contract under the law of most of the states today.

Insurable Interest in Life Versus Property Insurance

Briefly summarized, the idea of insurable interest is not difficult to understand. One must have an expectation of gain from the continued existence of the object or persons insured, an expectation of injury from its loss. However, the exact nature of this expected benefit or possibility of loss presents another question, and it is here that one of the basic differences between property insurance and life insurance is found.

Nature of the Interest. In property insurance an expectation of

[19] 14 Geo. III, Chap. 48.
[20] 104 U.S. 775 (1882).

benefit is not sufficient to support the insurable interest requirement unless it has some foundation in a legal right. In life insurance a reason-able probability is enough. Thus the father has an insurable interest in the life of his child, a dependent sister in the life of her brother.

Amount of Interest. There is also a difference between property in-surance and life insurance with respect to how much insurance may be collected in connection with a given insurable interest. In property in-surance the insured's recovery is limited to the amount of his actual loss in dollars and cents. In life insurance there is no similar limitation as a matter of law except in the area of credit life insurance. Ordinarily a creditor's recovery is measured by the amount of the debt, plus pre-miums, less dividends, etc. In all other areas of life insurance, however, the law takes the position that the possibility of financial loss or an ex-pectation of gain is sufficient to support an insurable interest, and it does not limit the amount recoverable in any way. In risk appraisal the company is always concerned with the possibility of overinsurance. This is strictly a risk appraisal problem, however, and has nothing to do with the legal question of insurable interest.

Time at Which the Interest Must Exist. A third difference between life and property insurance, with respect to insurable interest, is found in the date at which the interest must exist. In property insurance the insurable interest must exist at the time of loss. The coverage will be valid, as a general rule, even though there was no insurable interest at the inception of the policy, if there is an insurable interest at the date of the loss. In life insurance the rule is exactly the opposite. Here an in-surable interest must exist when the contract comes into existence or it will not be a valid contract. However, it can long have vanished at the time of the loss, and the insurance will nevertheless be payable in full.

For many years, it was the law in Texas that an insurable interest must exist at the time of the loss in life insurance as well as property insurance. A beneficiary or assignee of a life insurance policy who had no such interest at the death of the insured was forbidden to receive the proceeds of the insurance, as a matter of public policy. However, in 1953, the Texas legislature passed a law declaring that the insured under a life insurance policy might designate a beneficiary or assignee in writing who would, with respect to that policy, have an insurable interest. Thus the law of Texas was brought into general conformity with what has long been recognized as the rule in other jurisdictions.

Insurable Interest in Life Insurance

The differences between property and life insurance may be sum-marized and reconciled if we bear in mind the fact that a contract of property insurance is essentially a contract of indemnity. That is to say, it is a contract designed to replace a loss actually suffered by the insured through the destruction of, or damage to, the object or thing insured.

Life insurance is not an indemnity contract although it does have indemnity aspects. Except for term policies, the modern life insurance contract is more a contract of investment than anything else. Perhaps the most valid view of the life insurance contract is that it operates in much the same way that an annuity operates, except in reverse. The insured agrees to make payments in a certain amount and at regular intervals during his lifetime, or to pay the equivalent in a shorter period, and the company promises to pay a stated sum to a beneficiary at the death of the insured. Thus it is largely a contract of investment, permitting the insured to contribute to a fund for the benefit of his dependents after his death. As such, it is viewed with the highest favor by courts and legislatures, as a matter of public policy. Nevertheless, because of the speculative aspects of the contract and the possibility that it might be misused by unscrupulous third persons for their own benefit, the doctrine of insurable interest is applied.

Applies Only to Applicant and Policyowner. The doctrine of insurable interest is designed solely to keep people with no insurable interest from effecting insurance on the lives of others. In the field of life insurance, therefore, the requirement relates more to the applicant and owner of the contract than to the qualifications of the beneficiary where it is so often discussed.

The earliest requirement of an insurable interest related specifically to contracts made with an insurance company by the beneficiary, for that was the usual form of life insurance contract. Where the insured applies for the policy, names the beneficiary, and retains the right to change the beneficiary designation when and as he wishes, the beneficiary is not generally required to have an insurable interest. Under the modern life insurance contract, therefore, the requirement is important only with respect to some person other than the insured, who can name the beneficiary, including himself if he wishes—and that person is the applicant and third-party owner of the policy.

Where the Insured Is the Applicant. Where the insured himself applies for and is issued a policy on his own life, the transaction involves little more hazard than the making of a will. It is conceivable that the persons who stand to benefit from the early death of the insured might be tempted to hasten the event by any means readily available. However, the insured, like the testator, is presumed to know his beneficiaries or devisees sufficiently well to keep that risk within reasonable bounds. Where the insured himself is the applicant and policyowner, therefore, there is no need for the requirement of an insurable interest.

This fact has been differently stated at different times. For example, it is sometimes said that every person has an unlimited insurable interest in his own life. This hardly seems arguable, in the light of our basic definition that an insurable interest is an expectation of gain from the continued existence of the life or property insured, a prospect of loss from its destruction. But it has also been stated that an insurable interest is unnecessary if the insured himself makes the contract of insurance. Either statement seems relatively correct. Perhaps it is somewhat more precise to say that when the insured is himself a party to the contract and the contract is issued on his application, there is no need to apply the doctrine of insurable interest. However, it is important to add that if the contract is effected by a person on his own life, he also has the right to name anyone he wishes as a beneficiary. In such cases it is usually said that the beneficiary does not have to have an insurable interest. In Texas, the statute simply provides that the insured may designate a beneficiary in writing who, with respect to that policy, will have an insurable interest.

Insurable Interest in Third-Party Cases

In third-party ownership cases an applicant may procure insurance on the life of someone other than himself only if he bears a relationship to that person of such a nature as to satisfy the legal requirements concerning an insurable interest. This relationship may be by blood or marriage in some instances, or it may be a business relationship of such a nature that he may reasonably expect a benefit from the continuance of the life insured or a loss upon its premature termination.

Relationships by Blood or Marriage. There is no question but that the relationship of husband and wife is sufficient to meet the requirement of insurable interest. In fact, the technical validity of the marriage has been held not actually essential if there was a good faith belief in its validity.

It is also generally considered that blood relationship of a fairly close degree is adequate to constitute an insurable interest. The relationships between parent and child, grandparent and grandchild, brother and brother, sister and brother have been considered sufficiently close to meet the requirement as far as the law is concerned. Aunt and niece or nephew, uncles or cousins do not qualify by reason of the relationship alone.

Business Relationships. There are many relationships in the business world which, if severed by the sudden death of one of the parties, could mean serious financial loss to the survivor. In any situation of this kind the person who would lose by the death of the other has an insurable interest in the life of the other to the amount of such possible loss, and he has a valid right to insure the other's life to that amount.

Thus the employer has an insurable interest in the life of the key employee, a creditor in the life of his debtor, one partner in the life of another.

In one such case [21] the court said:

> Certainly Luchs had a pecuniary interest in the life of Dillenberg on two grounds: Because he was his creditor and because he was his partner. The continuance of the partnership, and, of course, a continuance of Dillenberg's life, furnished a reasonable expectation of advantage to himself. It was in the expectation of such advantage that the partnership was formed, and, of course, for the like expectation, was continued.

Interest of a Creditor in the Life of the Debtor

Indemnity Use of Life Insurance. In only one instance is the life insurance contract primarily used for indemnity purposes. That is the case of the creditor who insures the life of his debtor for the purpose of indemnifying himself if the insured should die before repaying the loan. Here the principles of indemnity and of life insurance meet in a somewhat conflicting situation. There are several different ways in which the problem has been resolved.

What the Problem Is. There is no question but that the unsecured creditor has an insurable interest in the life of the debtor. Certainly he stands to lose if the debtor should die before the debt is paid and leave no property out of which the debt could be satisfied. The principal question is whether his interest is limited to the actual amount of the indebtedness. In a true indemnity contract it would be so limited, but as we have seen, limitation is not in accord with the view usually taken in connection with the life insurance contract.

Although each case is ordinarily decided on its own merits, a general rule has been evolved in cases where the creditor himself has applied for and paid the premiums on the policy on the life of the debtor. In such cases, if the amount of the insurance and the amount of the indebtedness are reasonably related, there is no reason to deny the creditor the benefits of the insurance he had the foresight to procure. Consequently the courts ordinarily hold him entitled to the proceeds in full. However, if the insurance is widely disproportionate to the amount of the debt, the facts themselves suggest that the transaction is in reality a wager. In these cases, the courts generally hold that the policy is void on grounds of public policy.

Parenthetically, it should be noted that when the insured himself is the applicant and policyholder and the creditor is a collateral assignee, his recovery is always limited to the amount of the debt.

---

[21] *Connecticut Mut. Life Ins. Co.* v. *Luchs,* 108 U.S. 498 (1883).

Effect of Lack of Insurable Interest

Where the Insured Applies. As we have said, the doctrine of insurable interest is not invoked if the insured himself is the applicant for the insurance. This point is illustrated in a somewhat unusual way in the case of *Nora* v. *Unity Life Insurance Company*, decided by the Louisiana Court of Appeals, Second Circuit, in July, 1954.[22] There the insured, as a joke, offered to apply for a policy on his own life on condition that the beneficiary pay the premiums. The background of facts and the insurable interest question are best presented in the words of the court, as follows:

The only serious question which appears to be involved in this case concerns the contention that this plaintiff was without any insurable interest. In this connection the circumstances surrounding the making of the application for insurance are somewhat pertinent.

On the date of the making of the application, that is, March 24, 1952, Balthazar and an agent of defendant, one E. B. Joseph, were in a saloon owned and operated by plaintiff. It appears that Joseph was complaining of the fact that he was not doing much business in the way of writing insurance, whereupon Balthazar volunteered an offer to take out a policy if Nora would pay the premium, asserting that he would "will" the policy to Nora. The offer, which may perhaps have been initiated in jest, was taken up and acted upon by all parties; the application was filled out, signed by Balthazar, certified by Joseph and the initial premium paid by plaintiff, Nora. Nora continued to pay the premiums on the policy until the death of Balthazar, which occurred something less than four months later.

Examination of the authorities convinces us that the defense of lack of insurable interest is unsound for it appears that the use of this phrase is interpreted as having application only in those instances where the insurance is procured by a party who is designated as beneficiary, without the application or the knowledge and consent of the insured.

We find the general rule to have been definitely stated in *Dolan* v. *Metropolitan Life Ins. Co.*, 123 So. 379, in which case the court declared:

There is nothing in the law of (or) public policy which would prevent an insured from taking out a life insurance policy and designating a stranger as the beneficiary, and, upon his inability to pay the premiums, permitting the beneficiary to pay them.

                *   *   *   *   *

In the instant case there is no showing of any fraud, conspiracy, nor any act in contravention of public policy nor of good morals on the part of this plaintiff. It is obvious under the facts that the insured at any time was at liberty to make a change of beneficiary without notice to plaintiff.

Because of the careful risk appraisal practices of life companies today, it is sometimes said that the matter of insurable interest, in the legal sense of the word, is largely academic. It is true that risk appraisal

---

[22] 73 So.2d 486 (La. App., 1954).

automatically eliminates most cases where insurable interest might present a question, and no policy is issued on such applications in the first place. However, if risk appraisal practices are not conscientiously followed, or if an apparent insurable interest at the date of application is not borne out by facts as they may later develop, it is legal principles rather than risk appraisal requirements by which the question is ultimately decided. For instance, it is often stated that partners have an insurable interest in the lives of each other, and ordinarily that would be borne out by the facts. Nevertheless, there have been a number of cases involving facts and court decisions to show that this is not necessarily true. For example, in one case [23] two partners were involved in a hunting accident. The victim was insured for $25,000 in favor of the other partner, and the question of insurable interest was presented. The court said, in part:

> While it is true that partners usually, and perhaps in most cases, have an insurable interest in the life of a copartner, it is the existence of circumstances which arise out of or by reason of the partnership, and not the mere existence of the partnership itself, that give rise to an insurable interest. The legal relationship of one partner to the other does not, and should not, necessarily create an insurable interest as does the relationship of husband and wife. In *Connecticut Mut. Life Ins. Co.* v. *Luchs,* 108 U.S. 498, 2 S. Ct., 949, 27 L. Ed. 800, one partner was held to have an insurable interest in the life of his copartner when he had advanced his copartner's share of capital for the business, and in *Indemnity Ins. Co. of North America* v. *Dow, supra,* a partner was held to have an insurable interest in the life of his partner when he furnished the capital and his partner furnished the technical "know-how" to operate the business. In each of these typical cases the circumstances gave rise to a reasonable ground founded upon the relations of the parties to expect pecuniary benefit or advantage from the continuance of the life of the insured. But, in *Sun Life Assur. Co. of Canada* v. *Allen,* 270 Mich. 272, 259 N.W. 281, a case in which the facts reveal some striking similarities to the facts here, it was held that "The mere existence of a legal partnership does not establish an insurable interest," and in *Powell* v. *Mutual Ben. Life Ins. Co., supra,* it was held that if two partners have no capital invested in the partnership, and neither is indebted to the other, one partner has no insurable interest in the life of the other. For an interesting case, see *Block* v. *Mylish, supra,* where a bona fide partnership existed, but the court commented that "The element of wager . . . could serve to deny the right of the partners to a reciprocal insurable interest" because under the peculiar facts of that case, and contentions of the surviving partners, "a partner's expectation of benefit or advantage could lie not in the continuance of the lives of his partners but rather in the possibility of their deaths prior to his own."

> The better rule, and the one based on sound reasoning, is that an insurable interest does not necessarily arise by virtue of the mere partner relationship alone. Therefore, the showing by appellant that he and Hankinson were partners did not of itself establish the existence in him of an insurable interest in the life of Hankinson. We must therefore look to the circumstances

[23] *Lakin* v. *Postal Life and Casualty Co.,* 316 S.W.2d 542 (Mo., 1958).

arising out of or by reason of the partnership to determine whether an insurable interest existed in this case.

Appellant's evidence conclusively establishes that Hankinson made absolutely no financial or capital contribution whatever to the alleged partnership,
and that he did not in any way obligate himself to do so; that he had no
technical knowledge, skill or ability as a worker or manager to add to the
partnership; that he did not have any experience in the type of work he was
to do or in the business of the alleged partnership; that appellant had no legal
claim for his continued services; and that Hankinson did not purchase or
acquire an interest in the business or the tools and equipment used in the
business. Also there is nothing to indicate that Hankinson brought or could
be expected to bring any business to the partnership, or that his presence as
a partner increased or favorably affected the partnership good will.

* * * * *

Therefore, we are constrained to and do conclude that appellant's evidence
affirmatively establishes that as a matter of law he had no insurable interest
in the life of Hankinson.

In Areas Other than Contract. It was pointed out in Chapter I that
the law of the life insurance contract "travels at times and for short
distances" with the law of torts. This was intended to suggest that the
tort aspects of life insurance are relatively rare, and certainly the life
insurance contract itself has only the most tenuous connection with the
subject. However, we have already shown how the law of torts has been
invaded in connection with delay in acting on life insurance applications.
Another and even more unusual application of the law of torts in connection with the life insurance contract was reached in a 1957 case in
connection with the question of insurable interest. This case, *Liberty
National Life Insurance Company* v. *Weldon*,[24] concerned the issuance
of policies on the life of a small child on the application of the child's
aunt-in-law.

The applicant in question was a registered nurse working in a
small town in Alabama. One summer afternoon in 1952, she visited her
brother-in-law and his family in a neighboring town and during her visit
gave her two-year-old niece a soft drink in a cup. The child died before
evening. An autopsy showed arsenic in the cup, in her body in sufficient
quantities to cause her death, and in the clothes both of the child and
the aunt. The woman was charged with murder, convicted, and executed.

In the course of the murder trial it was brought out that three
life insurance companies had issued policies on the applications of the
aunt, insuring in her favor the life of the two-year-old niece. One policy,
a $500 endowment at age 17, was issued December 1, 1951. Another, a
$5,000 policy, was issued in March, 1952. A third, for $1,000, was in the
hands of the agent, though not delivered, at the time the child died.

---

[24] 100 So.2d 696 (Ala., 1957).

The child's parents had not given their consent in any of these cases.

The parents brought suit against the life insurance companies under a wrongful death statute, on the theory that the companies were under a duty to use reasonable care not to issue a life insurance policy in favor of a beneficiary who had no interest in the continuation of the life of the insured, and that issuing such policies was a breach of that duty, resulting in the death of the child by murder. A verdict in their favor was appealed to the Supreme Court of Alabama, which quoted a prior decision in part as follows:

> . . . there are forcible reasons why a mere stranger should not be permitted to speculate upon the life of one whose continued existence would bring to him no expectation of possible profit or advantage . . . wager policies, or such as are procured by a person who has no interest in the subject of the insurance, are undoubtedly most pernicious in their tendencies, because in the nature of premiums upon the clandestine taking of human life. . . .
>
> The reason of the law which vitiates wager policies is the pecuniary interest which the holder has in procuring the death of the subject of insurance, thus opening a wide door by which a constant temptation is created to commit for profit the most atrocious of crimes. . . .

The court quoted a basic rule of torts, that there is a duty upon everyone to exercise reasonable care not to injure another. It then said that a life insurance company has a duty to use reasonable care not to issue a life insurance policy to someone who has no interest in the continuation of the life of the insured.

"Policies in violation of the insurable interest rule are not dangerous because they are illegal," the court said; "they are illegal because they are dangerous."

The opinion continued:

> . . . The many decisions of this court dealing with negligence as the proximate cause, when some agency has intervened and has been the immediate cause of the injury, hold the party guilty of negligence in the first instance is not responsible, unless at the time of the original negligence the act of the agency could have been reasonably foreseen. If the act of the intervening agency could have been reasonably foreseen the causal chain is not broken. But if the injury results from an independent, intervening, efficient cause, not reasonably to be anticipated, to wit, the act of a third person, the negligence shown, if any, is not the proximate cause of the injury. . . .
>
>   * * * * *
>
> We cannot agree with the defendants in their assertion that we should hold as a matter of law that the murder of the young girl was not reasonably foreseeable. This created a situation of a kind which this court and others have consistently said affords temptation to a recognizable percentage of humanity to commit murder. . . .

The jury had held that the issuance of the policies was the proximate cause of the murder of the child and awarded damages in the amount of $100,000. The reviewing court reduced this to $75,000, but even so it remained the largest wrongful death verdict ever to come before that particular court. The case, decided in 1957, illustrates perhaps more clearly than any other argument the importance of the insurable interest requirement as a matter of public policy.

WHEN THE POLICY BECOMES EFFECTIVE

Required Legal Form

If there is no statute to the contrary an oral contract of life insurance is valid. However, life insurance contracts are so comprehensive and of such importance that it is the invariable understanding that the contract itself will be expressed in a written policy which is issued by the company upon the approval of the application and then delivered to the policyholder. The next important question, therefore, is when it becomes effective.

Factors Determining Inception of the Risk

Most life insurance applications expressly provide that the insurance shall not become effective until (1) approval of the application; (2) issuance of the policy; (3) delivery of the policy; and (4) payment of the first premium during the good health of the proposed insured. Each of these conditions must be fulfilled before the insurance becomes effective, and thus they are all conditions precedent.

Conditional Binding Receipt. The terms of the most prevalent conditional binding receipt today make insurance effective on condition that the proposed insured is found to be insurable and are so worded that if that condition is met the insurance becomes effective at a date prior to issuance of the policy, usually either the date of the receipt or of the medical examination, whichever is later. The first premium is always submitted in a conditional binding receipt case or the receipt would not be given. In these cases, therefore, issuance and delivery of the policy are not conditions precedent to the effectiveness of the insurance.

However, let us assume at this point that when our applicant, John M. Jones, completed and signed his application for the $10,000 policy of ordinary life insurance with the Ajax Life Insurance Company, he did not submit the initial premium. Agent Brown, therefore, did not give him a conditional binding receipt, although he forwarded the application to the home office, made arrangements for a medical, and ordered an inspection report, just as he did in our earlier illustrative case.

If There Is No Conditional Binding Receipt. Here the application is only an invitation for an offer. Jones has made it clear that he reserves the right to decide whether he wants the insurance or not. Assume then that the home office administrative officer reviews the application and other information, including the medical and inspection reports, as in the previous illustrations. It is found that Jones meets the company's standard requirements, and the policy is issued. Issuance of the policy constitutes an offer of insurance which the agent is authorized to complete only if the policy can be delivered during the lifetime and the continued good health of the applicant. Acceptance, by performance of the act requested (payment of the initial premium), will complete the unilateral contract. This set of facts, however, brings up the question of what constitutes delivery of the policy.

What Does "Delivery" Mean?

It Has Different Meanings. A great many cases have turned on the meaning of the word *delivery*. Does it mean that the policy must actually have been conveyed to the applicant and personally placed in his hands? Obviously, if that is true, there will be many situations where the agent himself, by negligently holding the policy for several days, could deprive the insured of coverage (possibly incurring personal liability). Sudden death during that period would present a difficult case.

The cases turning on this question present different factual situations and are difficult to reconcile. Different wordings, different actions, different situations, of necessity, produce different decisions. In addition there is the fact that in every case the decision determines whether or not a beneficiary will collect on an insurance policy. Thus it is not difficult to understand that the decisions are sometime conflicting.

General Definition. Generally speaking, delivery has been accomplished, in the legal sense of the word, any time the company has parted with legal control of the policy with the intention to be bound by it as a completed instrument. Thus in a conditional binding receipt situation, the insurance provided by the policy is put into effect at a date prior to issuance of the policy, if the condition specified is met. In such cases, delivery is accomplished the moment the company relinquishes possession of the policy by mailing it to the agent, if nothing further remains to be done but the ministerial act (that is, one which involves no discretion) of seeing that the insured receives it.

Where Delivery Is Necessary. A policy provision that the policy must be delivered before it is effective is perfectly valid. In such a case, if the policy has in fact been delivered into the hands of the applicant, the requirement of delivery has, of course, been met. It is where the policy has not actually reached the insured that the decisions are in conflict.

In the Hands of the Agent. If the policy has been prepared in the issuing office and mailed to an agent for delivery but not yet delivered, the intention of the company becomes of particular importance. Let us go back to our original set of facts concerning applicant Jones at this time. Let us say again that he submitted the initial premium and that agent Brown issued a conditional binding receipt.

We have seen that if Jones meets the insurability requirements of the company, he will have been insured as of the date specified in the receipt, even though he may have been killed prior to the actual determination of his insurability. Assume at this point, however, that he was not killed. He is found to be insurable by the risk appraisers, and he is very much alive at the moment the policy is issued and when it is received by agent Brown. In this case he meets the fatal accident while Brown has possession of the policy. Brown hears of the accident, checks the policy, and again telephones the company, this time to request instructions with respect to delivery.

Here the situation with respect to insurance is not too different from the situation which obtained prior to issuance of the policy. At that time, insurance was effective by reason of the provisions of the receipt, and no further condition remained to be met. The only difference is that now Brown, the agent, has the policy. In circumstances like these, the mailing of the policy to the agent is *construed* (interpreted) as delivery. This is said to be delivery by construction, and thus "constructive delivery." In the terms of our definition, there has been a parting of possession or control, accompanied by an intention on the part of the company to be bound by the policy as a completed instrument.

The doctrine of constructive delivery has been criticized by many writers because they believe the courts have stretched it too far—so far in fact as to make a new contract for the parties. However, it should be remembered that insurance law is a blending of commercial law and the specialized principles and requirements of insurance. Insurance is a business affected with a public interest, and the legislatures and the courts are constantly at work, in individual cases and with specific legislation, to effect some kind of working relationship between individual rights and collective requirements.

Offer by Applicant. Where the offer is made by the applicant, the situation is different. Here, even though he submits the initial premium in advance, the transactions occurring on the date of the application amount to an offer only. A stipulation in the application that the insurance shall become effective only upon delivery of the policy during the lifetime and continued insurability of the proposed insured will be given effect, as expressed in the following quotation from a recent case:

> The facts of this case reveal but one offer by the applicant, Burks. That offer is contained in his written application for a policy of insurance. If there was a contract between the parties, it must, therefore, be based upon this offer

and an acceptance of it. The offer by Burks was in fact a conditional one. He offered to buy a policy of insurance upon the express condition that such policy should not be binding upon either party until issued by the company and accepted by him while in life and good health. If this offer was ever accepted by the Defendant (and the Plaintiff contends that it was accepted either by cashing of Burks' check, or by placing OK upon the application), it would give rise only to a conditional contract. Liability on such contract would, by its own terms, be conditioned upon the condition precedent stated in the applicant's own application, namely issuance of the policy and acceptance thereof by Burks while in life and good health. *Reserve Loan Life Ins. Co. v. Phillips, Admr.*, 156 Ga. 372, 378. At the time of the death of Burks, this condition precedent had not been satisfied. Thus, neither party was unconditionally bound by any agreement at that time. Certainly nothing happening subsequent to the death of Burks could create a contract where there was none. At the time of Burks' death the policy had not been issued or accepted. Where an application contains a condition precedent, that condition must be performed before the application can ripen into an agreement, binding on the parties, with rights and liabilities incident thereto.[25]

[25] *Burks* v. *Colonial Life and Accident Insurance Company*, 98 F. Supp. 140 (D.C. Ga., 1952).

CHAPTER **V**

The Applicant
Names the
Beneficiary

THE BENEFICIARY is the person named in a life insurance policy to receive the benefit payable on the death of the insured. That person is not a party to the contract as we know it today, and ordinarily cannot exercise any contractual rights prior to the death of the insured. Nevertheless, the policy is applied for and kept in force primarily for the benefit of the beneficiary. Naming the beneficiary, therefore, is one of the most important actions the applicant takes, and his right to change the designation later if he wishes, and as often as he wishes, is one of the most significant rights he acquires under the contract. The purpose of this chapter is to outline the major legal principles which govern the designation of beneficiaries and specifications for settlement incidental to the process of applying for a life insurance policy.

THE BENEFICIARY DESIGNATION AND CONTRACT RIGHTS

The beneficiary designation is just as important to the life insurance company as it is to the applicant, although perhaps in a different way. Payment to the beneficiary and a release from her fulfills the basic promise and discharges the company from any further obligations under the contract. If the provisions of the beneficiary designation are clear and unambiguous, settlement is simple. If the provisions are not clear, court procedures may be required. Often they are expensive; always they are time consuming. For this reason, it is as much to the advantage of the company as to the policyholder that the beneficiary and settlement specifications be clear and unequivocal at the outset. It is important also that they be reviewed frequently in order that they may continue to reflect the changing needs and circumstances of the policyholder throughout the lifetime of the insured.

Rights of the Applicant and Policyholder

To Name the Beneficiary. The applicant has the right at the time of
application to name the beneficiary. In the typical situation, the applicant is the proposed insured, and he names his wife as beneficiary.
However, he exercises this right as the applicant and not as the
proposed insured. If the application is made by a third party, the proposed insured has no rights whatsoever with respect to the beneficiary
designation. When he consents that insurance shall be issued on his
life and owned by someone else, he consents also that it shall be payable
as directed by the owner.

To Change the Beneficiary. The applicant indicates in the application
that he does or does not reserve the right to change the beneficiary. If
he reserves the right, and as a general rule he does, he may revoke the
designation later if he wishes and name another beneficiary. If he
does not reserve the right to make beneficiary changes, he automatically
gives the beneficiary a different kind of right (technically a *vested*[1]
right) and thereby limits in a very definite way his own freedom to
exercise the ownership rights under the policy.

Most present-day life insurance policies provide that the policyholder may, if he reserves the right to do so, change the beneficiary as
often as he wishes as long as he complies with the procedural requirements set forth in the policy. This sometimes opens the door to numerous
questions of fact, but it makes the life insurance contract an amazingly
versatile and flexible instrument. A man's family and business needs
may change gradually and at times chaotically during the course of his
lifetime, but unlike his house or his car, his life insurance policy does
not become outmoded. He may and often does need additional life insurance, but never because his policy is out of date. A few changes will
ordinarily adapt any standard modern life insurance policy to meet new
needs of the policyholder as they arise, and much of this adaptability
arises directly out of the flexibility of the beneficiary provisions.

When the Right to Change the Beneficiary Is Reserved. When the
right to change the beneficiary is reserved, the beneficiary is said to
be revocable. The rights of such a beneficiary can be terminated by the
policyholder at any time prior to the death of the insured, by revoking
the designation and naming someone else. For this reason, the revocable
beneficiary is ordinarily said to have a "mere expectancy" as far as her
rights under the policy are concerned. The policyholder may exercise
any of the ownership rights under the policy without the consent of a

---

[1] A "vested" right, in the language of the law, is a complete right, one that is
not subject to a superior right on the part of anyone else.

revocable beneficiary, including the right to effect a policy loan or surrender the contract for cash.

Generally speaking, the policyowner also has the right to assign the policy without the consent of a revocable beneficiary. However, there is a strong minority line of cases which hold that although the revocable beneficiary's rights can be terminated without her consent, this can only be accomplished by a strict compliance with the policy provisions with respect to the change of beneficiary. An assignment obviously does not comply with those requirements. States which follow this line of reasoning, therefore, take the position that the assignee's rights are subordinate to the rights of the revocable beneficiary unless the latter has joined in the assignment or otherwise signified her consent.

When the Right to Change Is Not Reserved. If the right to change the beneficiary designation is not reserved, the person named is an *irrevocable* beneficiary and has what the law terms a vested right to the benefit payable at the death of the insured. This means that she has a right of such a nature that it cannot be taken away from her without her consent. Nevertheless, the irrevocable beneficiary's vested right is subject to other possibilities of termination. For instance, the policy must be in force, either on a premium paying basis or under one of the nonforfeiture options, at the death of the insured or there will be no benefit to which anyone will have a right. However, the irrevocable beneficiary's right to any benefit that is payable at the death of the insured cannot be impaired without her consent. Thus the policyholder, after making an irrevocable beneficiary designation, cannot exercise any ownership right which might impair that beneficiary's rights, without her consent.

Tax and creditors' exemption statutes are sometimes worded in such a way as to give an advantage if the beneficiary is named irrevocably. Nevertheless, this type of beneficiary designation is not used nearly as frequently now as was once the case. The modern life insurance contract includes many rights of value that can be realized upon prior to the death of the insured. Consequently, the person who once was designated as an irrevocable beneficiary to protect his rights as a creditor or otherwise now prepares an assignment of the policy in his favor, as a better and often less controversial protection. In current financial transactions, therefore, it is ordinarily preferable to treat the policy as property and assign it, rather than to treat it as insurance and name an irrevocable beneficiary.

Rights of the Beneficiary

Historical Development. The earliest life insurance contracts were what we now think of as third-party contracts. They were made with someone other than the insured, and the latter was concerned only as the subject of the insurance. Even when contracts were, in legal effect, made with both the insured and the beneficiary, the ownership of the policy was generally considered to be in the beneficiary alone, and the insured himself had no power to alter the interest of the beneficiary.

About the turn of the century, some life insurance companies began to include in their policies a provision permitting the insured to reserve the right to change the beneficiary if he wished. At first there was some doubt as to the legality of this kind of provision. However, the question was settled affirmatively when the standard policy form legislation, enacted in New York following the Armstrong Investigation, included a change of beneficiary provision. As a result, the life insurance contract has experienced a complete change as far as ownership of the policy is concerned. As a general rule today, if the right to change the beneficiary is reserved, the applicant and policyholder is considered to be the owner of the policy, not the beneficiary.

Rights of the Revocable Beneficiary. Logically, once the ownership of the policy had shifted from the beneficiary to the insured who reserved the right to make a beneficiary change, the revocable beneficiary should have been held to have as little in the way of contract rights as the insured had possessed under the earlier policies. In fact, that is the generally accepted rule today. However, the transition was not made in one swift step. Instead, there was an intervening period during which it was generally considered that a revocable beneficiary had a qualified interest in the policy which could be terminated by the insured's action in revoking the designation. The lawyer said it was a "vested right subject to being divested." Prior to revocation of the designation, therefore, the beneficiary's consent was considered necessary before the insured could exercise any ownership rights under the policy, although he could, of course, revoke the designation and then take whatever action he wished.

Later, the courts began to formulate a more logical rule, that the right of a revocable beneficiary is a mere expectancy until the death of the insured. As a result most, though not all, of the states today hold that the policyowner does not have to have the consent of a revocable beneficiary but may, without that consent, exercise any ownership rights available under the contract. Thus he can effect a policy loan, assign the policy, and generally deal with the policy without regard to the beneficiary. This is the present rule as it is followed in most of the states today.

Rights of the Irrevocable Beneficiary. The applicant may still name the beneficiary irrevocably simply by not reserving the right to change the designation. If he does this, the beneficiary named will have a vested interest in the contract, and the owner cannot, without her consent, exercise any of the ownership rights which might impair that interest.

THE BENEFICIARY DESIGNATION

Insurable Interest

The subject of beneficiary designations closely relates to the question of insurable interest. However, it is the generally accepted rule that if the policy is taken out by the insured himself, he may name anyone he wishes as beneficiary. Thus the question of insurable interest becomes legally important only when the policy is applied for by someone other than the person whose life is insured.

This does not by any means imply that a company's issuing office will fail to inquire fully into the reasons for naming, as beneficiary, a person who has little apparent insurable connection with the applicant, even when the latter is also the proposed insured. That is the company's privilege in risk appraisal, and the practice is carried out as a matter of routine in order to avoid any possibility of a speculative situation. Generally speaking, however, there are no legal restraints concerning insurable interest if the policy is applied for and the beneficiary named by the insured himself. As a consequence, in order to concentrate on the problems of beneficiary designations themselves in this chapter, it will be presumed that the person whose life is to be insured has applied for the insurance.

How the Beneficiary Is Designated

The applicant designates the beneficiary by simply stating in the application the name or names of the persons to whom he wishes the company to pay the benefit due at his death. He may specify that it be paid to one person alone or that it be shared by several persons in proportions as he may indicate.

Contingent Beneficiaries. In the days when the policy was applied for and issued to the beneficiary, her rights under it were of such a nature that they became an asset in her estate in the event of her death prior to the death of the insured. In fact, even where the insured himself applied for and owned the policy, the beneficiary was often considered to have a vested interest subject to being divested. This created a number of practical problems. For instance, where the insured survived the beneficiary by many years, the estate of the beneficiary would have been closed long before the insurance became payable.

For that reason, about the beginning of this century, companies began including a provision in their policies which provided that if the beneficiary died before the insured, the death benefit would be payable to the estate of the insured. This eliminated the possibility that the death benefit could become payable to the estate of someone who had died many years before, and it is the general rule today.

At the same time, the new policy provision created a new contingency which might be provided against, the possibility that the first-named beneficiary might die before the insured and the death benefit become payable to the estate of the insured. Now it became possible for the insured to name a contingent beneficiary, who would have the right to receive the death benefit if the primary beneficiary did not survive the insured. And, since the contingent beneficiary might also predecease the insured, most companies today permit the insured to name a second contingent beneficiary, or as some companies term it, a final beneficiary. Settlement will be made to this person if there is no surviving primary or first contingent beneficiary at the death of the insured.

For instance, let us say that John Jones wished to name his wife, Mary, as primary beneficiary. Agent Brown suggested that he name a contingent or successor beneficiary in case she did not survive him. John considered naming his children,[2] two, four, and six years of age, but decided to name his brother, Howard, who would, he said, take care of his affairs in the event Mary did not survive him. A final beneficiary? After giving the question some consideration, John decided that if neither Mary nor Howard survived him the benefit should be payable to his estate. The application was accordingly completed to provide that Mary Jones, wife of the insured, was to be the primary beneficiary, Howard Jones, brother, was to be the contingent beneficiary, and the estate of the insured would be the final beneficiary.

The Policy Endorsement. The clarity of the beneficiary designation as it appears in the policy is something over which the applicant himself has little control except to make his wishes as clear as possible to company personnel. The company then is responsible for drafting the beneficiary designation in the policy in such a way that the wording will not be ambiguous and the wishes of the applicant will be carried out. It must always be borne in mind that the beneficiary designation written in 1960 may very well not be acted upon until the year 2000, or later. At that time, no person concerned in phrasing the original designation may be living.

The policy provision expressing the wishes of Applicant Jones will read in general very much like this:

To Mary Jones, wife of the insured, if living; otherwise to Howard Jones, brother of the insured.

---

[2] When insurance proceeds become payable to minor children, a guardian or guardians must be appointed by the court, and the investment and uses of such funds are ordinarily under the continued supervision of the court.

Under this designation, if Mary is living at the death of John, the death benefit will be payable to her. If she is not living at that time and if Howard is, the benefit will be payable to him. If neither of them is living, the benefit will be payable to the estate of the insured because of the policy provision included in most policies today, which makes the interest of any predeceased beneficiary or beneficiaries payable to the estate of the insured.

It will be noted that if Mary is living at the death of John, the death benefit will be payable to her. This is not to say it would be paid. That is one of the disadvantages of this type of beneficiary designation. In this case it is only necessary that the named beneficiary actually *survive* the insured. If she does so by any measurable length of time and then dies, the proceeds will have become payable to her but will be paid to her estate, that is to her personal representative. As a practical matter, in this case, the results would not be too different from those following her death prior to that of the insured. In the latter case the death benefit would have become payable to the insured's brother with the understanding that it would be used for the benefit of the children. If Mary survived her husband but died before receiving the money, the benefit would be paid to her personal representative, who would satisfy her debts and then pay the remaining proceeds to her heirs, or *devisees* (recipients under a will). In most instances this would be her children. Thus, in either case, the wishes of the insured would have been fulfilled.

Where there are no children, however, a sequence such as this can often result in the distribution of insurance money in ways far different from the wishes of the insured. Ordinarily payment to the personal representative of the wife means that the money will eventually be distributed among her heirs only, a result which sometimes is quite different from the wishes of the insured. Often, also, insurance money payable to an estate becomes available for payment of the debts of the decedent, whereas, if an optional mode of settlement has been elected, the insurance benefits can ordinarily be made exempt from the claims of creditors of the payee-beneficiary by means of a spendthrift trust clause.[3] Lastly, the personal representatives of a beneficiary often cannot elect an optional mode of settlement in cases of this kind, so that the distributees are automatically excluded from these highly valuable insurance services by this sequence of events. For these reasons, the election of one of the optional modes of settlement by the insured is ordinarily preferable to a beneficiary designation relating to a one-sum settlement, such as the one we have been discussing.

---

[3] For a discussion of this type of provision, see Chapter XVI, page 361.

THE OPTIONAL MODES OF SETTLEMENT

Most life insurance policies today provide valuable alternative methods of settlement, or optional methods. Thus the policyholder may direct that the death benefit be paid to the named beneficiary in one sum, as was true in the illustrative case just discussed, or he may elect to have the benefit paid in accordance with one or more of several alternative methods provided for in the policy.

For instance, the insured may elect an optional mode of settlement under which the company will retain the death benefit at a guaranteed rate of interest and make payments of that interest at regular intervals to a designated payee. The insured may specifically provide that the principal be subject to withdrawal by the payee, or that it be held and paid at the end of a stated interval to a different payee or payees. This is called the interest option.

Under another, equally standard, mode of settlement, the insured may elect that the proceeds be retained by the company and paid out in equal payments over a stated length of time. This is the fixed period option. If he wishes to specify the amount of the payment and have that sum paid at regular intervals until the proceeds are exhausted, the policyowner will elect the fixed amount option. Lastly, he may elect to have the amount payable retained by the company and paid out in equal, regular instalments for the remainder of the lifetime of the named payee. This, of course, is the life income option. Most companies offer a variation of this option for the joint lifetime of two payees, with a continuation of the payments, in the same or a smaller amount, to the survivor. This is the joint and survivor optional mode of settlement.

When the applicant elects an optional mode of settlement, his wishes are set forth in a special agreement often called a "settlement agreement," which may or may not be attached to the policy, depending upon the practices of the company concerned.[4] Regardless of what they are called, these settlement specifications are, in effect, only elaborate beneficiary designations. As in the one-sum designation, the applicant states who is to receive the benefit payable under the policy at his death. However, in the settlement agreement he also stipulates which optional method he elects and how it is to be applied. For example, he may direct that the proceeds be retained at interest, with interest payments to be made to the primary payee during her lifetime and the principal divided equally among successor payees at her death. Alternatively, he may

---

[4] Many companies follow a practice of endorsing all beneficiary changes and elections of settlement options on the policy itself. Others follow what is called the recording method by which these changes are simply recorded in the home office, and the policyholder is free to attach the evidence of such changes to his policy if he wishes.

direct that payments be made to her in a specified amount for a stated length of time or for her lifetime, depending upon his wishes. Often he will elect one option for the benefit of a given payee and grant her the right to elect an entirely different mode of settlement if she wishes to do so.

The applicant will ordinarily name a contingent or successor payee under a settlement agreement, whose rights correspond to but are ordinarily considerably more extensive than those of the contingent or successor beneficiary in a one-sum designation. The rights of the contingent beneficiary in a one-sum designation are determined as of the moment the insured dies. If at that time the first-named or primary beneficiary is living, the rights of the contingent or successor beneficiary are automatically extinguished. The primary beneficiary takes all. If she dies immediately thereafter, payment will be made to her personal representatives.

Under a settlement agreement, on the other hand, the contingent payee may also be made a successor payee. His rights are not necessarily extinguished by the death of the insured while the primary beneficiary is living. Often by the provisions of the settlement agreement such a successor payee is entitled to take any unpaid amounts or instalments remaining unpaid at the death of the primary beneficiary or payee. Thus if the primary beneficiary lives to receive all the payments provided for (or to withdraw the total proceeds, if the right of withdrawal is granted), the successor payee's rights will be terminated. However, if the primary beneficiary does not exhaust the proceeds during her lifetime, the successor payee or payees succeed, as their name suggests, to any funds remaining at her death.

Consider again our hypothetical applicant, John Jones. Suppose he wishes the death benefit under his policy paid to his wife, Mary, if she is living at his death. If she does not survive him, he wants the money to go to their children, Mike, Anne, and Jimmy, in equal shares. Assume further that although he realizes the value of the optional methods of settlement, he learns from Agent Brown that Mary can elect an optional mode of settlement if she wishes after his death. John decides, therefore, to direct that payment of the benefit be made to Mary in one sum with the understanding that she may elect an appropriate method of settlement at the time the benefit becomes payable. We would then have a one-sum beneficiary designation as follows:

To Mary Jones, wife of the insured, if living; otherwise to the children of the insured by said wife, including Michael, Anne, and James, equally or to survivor.

In this case Mary will receive the proceeds if she is living at the date of John's death. She may elect an optional mode of settlement if she wishes, but this will have no effect upon the rights of the children. Those rights were completely contingent and were terminated by the fact that at the death of the insured the primary beneficiary, Mary, survived.

Alternatively, John could himself elect an optional method of settlement and provide that the benefit be paid to Mary in instalments or held at interest with interest payments made at regular intervals to her. By naming the children as contingent or successor payees he could make it possible for any remaining payments, or any undistributed balance at Mary's death, to be continued or paid in one sum to the children. In other words, the settlement agreement could be so worded as to give the children rights that would continue after the death of the insured and become effective upon the death of the primary payee if any instalments or amounts remained unpaid at that time. The settlement agreement approach to this problem, therefore, has provided an excellent means for planning the financial future of one's family.

NAMING THE BENEFICIARY

Who May Be Named

As we have said, if a life insurance policy is applied for and issued to the proposed insured, the applicant may ordinarily name anyone he wishes as beneficiary. Insurable interest does not ordinarily present a legal problem in this case. The major legal problems relate to the matter of identity. A beneficiary designation is essentially personal in nature. Thus the person who is to receive the benefit should either be named or described sufficiently clearly that he or she can be readily identified.

For instance, if the applicant wishes to name his estate as beneficiary, the designation should read as follows:

To the executors, administrators, or assigns of the insured.

This does not actually specify by name the person to whom the proceeds shall be paid, since the personal representative of the insured cannot be known until after his death. However, it does sufficiently describe the person that he can readily be identified. Payment made to the person so described will discharge the company of its obligations under the policy.

Wife of the Insured. The applicant typically designates his wife as beneficiary, and she is so described. As a matter of law, however, her interest as beneficiary does not depend upon her relationship to the insured. Where the wife has been designated by name, divorce does not of itself terminate her interest, in the absence of a controlling statute.

The wife should be designated by her given name—"Mary Jones, wife of the insured"—not "Mrs. John Jones." Ordinarily this type of designation will carry out the wishes of the applicant, and it indicates with certainty the person to whom the proceeds are to be paid. Both the agent and the applicant should bear in mind that the courts have almost unanimously held that the words "wife of the insured" are descriptive only. Under a designation of this kind, the proceeds would be payable to "Mary Jones" at the death of the insured whether she were then the wife of Jones or not.

This reasoning was applied to the word "fiancée" in one recent case [5] which involved a beneficiary designation of this general type:

Mary Doe, fiancée, if living; otherwise to William George Doe, Father.

The insured in this instance was killed while in military service. About six months before his death, his fiancée wrote to him saying that she was going to marry another man. The insured did not change the beneficiary designation of the policy; the fiancée was married as she had said she would be; and at the insured's death the company paid the money into court, asking a decision as to the person rightfully entitled to it.

The court said:

In *Simmons* v. *Simmons*, 272 S.W.2d 913, we held that where a beneficiary is named or can otherwise be definitely identified, her designation as wife is descriptive only. The rule applies in this case to appellee. Her name as beneficiary is followed in the policy by the word "Fiancée," and it may well be that insured would not have named her beneficiary except for his engagement to her, yet the fact remains that from February, when the engagement was broken, until July 13, when he was killed, he did not change the beneficiary nor did he do all he could have reasonably done to change the beneficiary.

Thus the court held that the proceeds should be paid to the former fiancée, although it was admitted that the claim of the father (the contingent beneficiary) appealed strongly to one's sympathies. "Our function, however," the court concluded, "is to determine the legal rights of the parties, not to sit in judgment on appellee's conscience."

Designating Children

By Name. Applicants often wish to designate their children by name, as beneficiaries of their insurance. This presents a problem with respect to after-born children. Companies for that reason usually recommend a designation worded thus:

Children of the insured, including Michael, Anne, and James, equally or to survivor.

---

[5] *Scherer et ux* v. *Wahlstrom*, Texas Court of Civil Appeals, 318 S.W.2d 456 (1958).

Under a designation of this kind, later-born children will automatically be included even though the beneficiary designation is not revised.

Children Designated Irrevocably. As a general rule, children should never be named beneficiaries irrevocably. Such a designation will, in practical effect, deprive the insured of all power to exercise the ownership rights under the policy. Even with an adult, irrevocable beneficiary, the insured can exercise his ownership rights only with the consent of the beneficiary. A child, however, cannot give consent, and consent cannot be given for him. As a consequence, the insured who names a child as irrevocable beneficiary will be powerless to exercise any rights under the policy, whether he wishes to surrender the policy, effect a policy loan, or make an assignment.

Class Designations. Children are often named as a class, a practice which avoids the problem concerning later-born children. Ordinarily, the designation is presumed to take effect as of the date of death of the insured, and the term "children," therefore, includes all children then in existence, as well as those not yet born. Class designations nevertheless present legal problems, particularly if they refer only to "children" as a group. For instance, does the term include illegitimate children? Does it include stepchildren? Furthermore, such designations present numerous problems with respect to ascertaining and locating all members of the class at the time settlement is made, not to mention the delay in settlement such inquiries may entail.

Some courts have held that the term "children" includes illegitimate children; other courts have held that it does not. Generally they will be included if the intent to include them is clear, but it is ordinarily quite difficult to determine intent, and no company willingly endorses a policy with a beneficiary designation that can be clarified only by court action. Stepchildren are not ordinarily included in the term "children" but adopted children are. The term also includes legitimated children (that is, children born out of wedlock whose parents subsequently marry).

Generally speaking, if the applicant wishes to designate his children as a class, the term "children" should be used and not the term "issue" or "heirs." The word "issue" should definitely be avoided since in its true legal sense it includes all lineal descendants regardless of degree. The word "heirs" also presents problems. Originally the term denoted those persons who by law succeeded to the real property of the person who died without a will. By statute and otherwise its meaning has been extended to include persons entitled to take the personal property also. However, the use of the term will often involve problems going far afield of the law of the life insurance contract itself.

The prompt settlement of life insurance claims is in the interest of the insured, the beneficiaries, and the insurance company. Class designations may sometimes be justified by the circumstances of the individual case. Nevertheless, they should always be worded in such a way as to make possible the identification of the members of the group at a very early date and thus insure the prompt settlement of the sum payable under the policy.

Per Stirpes Designations. Occasionally an insured will want to designate his wife, for example, as primary beneficiary with his children named as successor beneficiaries, *per stirpes.* This is a technical term used because two words can thus do the work of several, but it has a very simple definition. Let us say Robert Black wishes to designate his wife, Sara, as primary beneficiary of his policy and their children as successor beneficiaries. Their children are grown, several with children of their own. One son is in military service in the Pacific, and the other children are living in various parts of the world. Mr. Black wants his insurance distributed equitably, and he fully realizes that he himself may survive one or more of his children. If he does, he would like the orphaned grandchildren to take the share their father or mother would have taken if he or she had lived. By requesting a designation of the children, per stirpes, he achieves that result.

The term "per stirpes" simply means "by the branch." Under a designation of this kind, the insured's children take if they survive him. If one of them dies before he does, however, that child's children take, by representation, the share their parent would otherwise have received. Let us say that Mr. Black has four children, Robert, Jr., John, Sally, and Diane. Each of them is married and has one or more children, at the time Mr. Black effects the beneficiary designation. One type of per stirpes designation in a case of this kind would read as follows:

> To Sara Black, wife of the insured, if living; otherwise in equal shares to the children of the insured by said wife who are living and per stirpes to the lawful children who are living of any children of the insured by said wife who shall have died.

If, at Mr. Black's death, Mrs. Black is not living but the four children are, the benefit will be shared by the four of them, equally. However, let us say that only Robert, Jr., John, and Sally are living. In that case, assuming that Diane left two children, Jane and Roger, the benefit will still be divided into four shares, and the fourth share, Diane's, will be paid to the legally appointed guardian of Jane and Roger, assuming that they are minors.

Guardians Should Not Be Designated. Parents sometimes wish to name as beneficiaries, persons whom they wish to be, or have designated under their wills as, guardians of their minor children in the event of the parents' deaths during the children's minority. Even when they have named a guardian in their will, however, there is no certainty that that person will be living at the time of their death or, if living, that he or she will be appointed as guardian or be able to qualify.

The solution to this problem is simply to name the children as beneficiaries. Any benefit becoming payable during the minority of a beneficiary would be paid only to the legally appointed guardian of his or her property in any event.

Business Insurance Designations

In business insurance it is frequently convenient or advisable to designate a business firm as the beneficiary of the policy. Here the basic principles of beneficiary designations generally apply, but in addition there are a few special problems which arise out of the particular form of organization under which the firm is actually conducting its business.

For instance, it is not unusual for a man to be conducting, under a trade name such as the John Smith Company, a business which has never been incorporated. In that case the man and the company are one and the same. If, therefore, a policy of life insurance on the life of John Smith is endorsed with a beneficiary designation naming the firm as beneficiary, the legal effect will be exactly the same as if he had directed that the benefit be paid to his estate.

In a partnership, the traditional view is that it is the people who have legal significance and not the name under which they may be doing business. Thus, if the business is to be named as beneficiary of a life insurance policy, the names of the partners themselves must be used. Let us say that the partnership does business as Smith and Company. If it is, in fact, a partnership, and if Smith and Jones are the partners, the designation will ordinarily read as follows:

Smith and Jones, a partnership composed of John Smith and Thomas Jones.

By contrast, a corporation is a legal entity, authorized by law to carry on a business of a specified nature and permitted to sue and be sued in its corporate name. For this reason it can and should be designated as the beneficiary of a life insurance policy by its corporate name. One form of such an endorsement would read as follows:

The A.B.C. Company of Chicago, Illinois, an Illinois corporation, its successors or assigns.

It should be noted that this designation contains its own contingent beneficiary—the corporation's "successors or assigns." For this reason, when a designation of this kind is used, no other contingent beneficiary should be named.

INSURANCE AND TRUSTS

Making the death benefit under a life insurance policy payable to a trustee presents a number of legal problems. This is because a trustee is named in a trust agreement which, unless it is irrevocable by its terms, can be changed or terminated by the parties to the agreement any time they wish. The insurance company has no control whatsoever over such changes, yet it is required to carry out its contract, often by paying a large sum of money to a person who may or may not be in existence at the date of settlement, or who, if living, may not be qualified in such a way as to be entitled to receive the money. If life insurance companies seem reluctant to permit trustees, particularly testamentary trustees, to be named as beneficiaries, the reason lies in the fact that so much uncertainty is involved.

What a Trust Is. Generally speaking, a trust is established by an agreement, with or without consideration, by which one person transfers property to another, on condition that the latter hold and use this property for the benefit of yet another person. The person who transfers the property is called the *grantor* or *trustor* (also sometimes the *settlor* or *creator*). The person to whom the property is transferred is called the *trustee;* and the person for whose benefit the arrangement is made is called the *cestui que trust* (literally, "he who has the right"), or the *beneficiary* of the trust. The wishes of the grantor concerning the administration of the trust, investment practices, payment of income, and eventual disposition of the property are set forth in the instrument by which the trust is created (the *Trust Agreement* or *Deed of Trust*).

Generally speaking, this kind of arrangement is called an *inter vivos* trust. This is nothing more than a trust that is established between living persons (*inter vivos*), which is meant to take effect during the lifetime of the grantor. Let us say that Robert Black, Sr., at the time of his retirement, has an estate in excess of $100,000, made up of real property, bonds, common stocks. Capably managed this property will produce a comfortable income; without skilled management it can rapidly depreciate in value. At the time of his retirement, therefore, he decides to convey it to the Allen National Bank and Trust Company, to be held in trust for his own benefit and that of Mrs. Black. He executes a written instrument, reciting that he is conveying certain described property to the bank, in trust, setting forth the purposes of the trust, the persons to be benefited, and how the trust is to be administered.

Exactly this same arrangement can be made with respect to insurance if Mr. Black has a sufficient insurance program and wishes to create an insurance trust. In that case he would also execute an appropriate trust agreement, but he would make the trustee the beneficiary of the insurance and deliver the policies to him instead of deeds, bonds, and stock certificates. If only the life insurance policies are conveyed to the trustee, it is said to be an *unfunded* insurance trust. If Mr. Black also conveys money or property out of which premiums on the life insurance are to be paid, it is said to be a *funded* insurance trust. In either case, if the trust is created by an instrument intended to take effect during the lifetime of the grantor, it is an *inter vivos* insurance trust.

It is also possible to create a trust which is not to take effect until the grantor's death. In that case the instrument by which the trust is created is, in effect, a will, and it must be executed in accordance with the requirements relating to wills or it will not be given legal effect. A trust of this kind is called a *testamentary* trust, that is, a trust created by the last will and testament of the insured.

From one point of view, a life insurance trust will not ordinarily become effective, in any practical sense, until the death of the insured. Thus it was a perfectly natural development for the life insurance trust to be challenged as an attempted testamentary disposition of property which must be executed as a will or be held to be inoperative.

This point is hardly open to serious question today. The weight of opinion is clearly to the effect that a life insurance trust is not a testamentary trust. The reasons for this holding are set forth in the case of *Bose* v. *Meury*.[6] There the insured named the Montclair Trust Company beneficiary under several policies of insurance on his own life and deposited them with the trust company under a trust agreement which authorized the trustee to pay the income of the proceeds to the grantor's wife for life, with remainder to be paid to the children. He reserved the right to add to or withdraw policies and to revoke the trust. At his death, his estate was insolvent, and the trust was challenged on the grounds (1) that the gift in trust was incomplete because of the reserved right to withdraw policies and to revoke the trust; and (2) that the trust was testamentary. The discussion of the court is an excellent summary of the role of insurance in a trust situation and it is quoted here in part. Incidentally, the word *res* simply means the trust property.

     . . . Whatever merit there may be to the points, were the *res* in trust the property of the trustor, they are beside the question where, as here, the *res* is the proceeds of insurance on the life of the trustor which never were his property. The proceeds are the fulfillment of promises by the insurance company to the Montclair Trust Company, trustee, to pay the stipulated sums, upon the death of the insured. The insured paid the consideration for the promises and he had the right, under the terms of the policies, to change the promises at will, but when the day came—the insured's death—the obligations of the insurance company were due to the Montclair Trust Company, trustee.

[6] 112 N.J. Eq. 62, 163 Atl. 276 (1932).

Its source of title was the promise in the policies, not the trust agreement. The trust agreement is no more than a declaration of trust by the trustee that it would hold the proceeds of the policies for the benefit of the insured's wife and children, and whether it had physical possession of the policies or whether there was a stripping of interest by the "donor" or that the trust deed was testamentary, is wholly immaterial. . . .

Trusts and the Life Insurance Company. Neither the *inter vivos* nor the testamentary trust actually concerns the life insurance company. The company is not a party to the trust and has no responsibility for determining its validity. It does, however, have a basic responsibility for not endorsing on an insurance policy or recording a beneficiary designation that it cannot carry out. When the applicant specifies that he wishes the proceeds paid to a trustee, therefore, the company's first duty is to find out whether there is a trust agreement in existence.

There are not too many objections to naming a trustee as beneficiary of a life insurance policy if the trust in question is an *inter vivos* trust and a trust instrument is in existence at the time the endorsement is made. A company will usually request the date of the trust and the names of the parties to the trust agreement. There is a question as to whether the company may be charged with some of the trust responsibilities, if it has had a copy of the trust agreement itself for review. For this reason company practices differ as to requests for the actual trust instrument. Nevertheless, the company must satisfy itself that there is a trust agreement in existence. All too often the man who intends to create a trust at the time he applies for life insurance never quite gets around to doing it. (If no trust were ever created, settlement would be made in accordance with the policy provision for settlement in the absence of a beneficiary designation. However, establishing that no trust was ever, in fact, created would not only delay settlement, it might also be quite difficult to accomplish, as a practical matter.)

The second part of the company's problem is that the trust agreement, although very much in effect at the time the policy is endorsed, may have been terminated long before the death of the insured. With an ordinary beneficiary designation, if the beneficiary dies before the insured, the problem is taken care of by a policy provision making the benefit payable to the estate of the insured. With the discontinuance of a trust agreement, however, the situation is different. Here the designated beneficiary is not dead. He (or she) just isn't qualified anymore. That eventuality must be taken care of, therefore, and is taken care of by the italicized portion of the following wording:

John Doe, as Trustee, or his successor or successors in trust, under trust agreement between Robert Black and John Doe, dated November 30, 1960, and supplements or amendments thereto, *if said agreement shall then be in force* and, if not, to the executors, administrators, or assigns of the insured.

It is highly advisable to add a second paragraph in such a designation absolving the company of any responsibility if the proceeds are not disposed of according to the provisions of the trust, thus:

In no event shall the Ajax Life Insurance Company be responsible for the application or disposition by the Trustee of the sum payable. The payment to and receipt by the Trustee shall be a full discharge of the liability of the Ajax Life Insurance Company for any amount paid to such Trustee.

Corporate Trustees. The designation of a corporate trustee does not generally present as many problems. The continued existence and qualification of the corporation is ordinarily more fully assured, and a trust agreement with such a trustee will ordinarily have been prepared with the advice of counsel. However, there are possible pitfalls in the designation of a corporate trustee also, and the beneficiary designation should be worded something as follows:

The A.B.C. Bank and Trust Company of Chicago, Illinois, an Illinois corporation, as trustee, or its successors in trust, under trust agreement between Robert Black and the A.B.C. Bank and Trust Company dated November 30, 1960, and supplements or amendments thereto, if said agreement shall then be in force and, if not, to the executors, administrators, or assigns of the insured.

The Testamentary Trustee. The testamentary trust presents a number of problems that are not present in the *inter vivos* trust situation. First, all the infirmities of the will situation are involved. The will is called "ambulatory" by lawyers. This means that it continues to be subject to change until the very moment of the maker's death. No will, therefore, may be said to be effective until the date of the testator's death. Even then it may be found to have been superseded, or amended, or its validity may be successfully attacked on any of a number of grounds such as incapacity of the testator, undue influence, or failure to comply with all the statutory requirements, to name only a few of the hazards in the successful probate of a will.

A trust purportedly created by an instrument subject to so many hazards is at best uncertain, and a trustee named under such a trust is a very uncertain person to designate as beneficiary under a life insurance policy. For this reason many life insurance companies either refuse altogether to name a testamentary trustee as beneficiary of a life insurance policy or hedge their requirements in very stringent terms.

Again, however, it must be remembered that the company wishes only to make payment quickly and with as little inconvenience as possible. No one can know whether the testamentary trust will ever take effect because no one knows whether the will will be admitted to probate, and even if it is, the trustee may or may not qualify. The company which permits the applicant to designate a testamentary trustee as beneficiary of the life insurance policy must, therefore, take great care to word the endorsement in such a way that these eventualities are foreseen and provided for. A beneficiary designation of the following type is thought to protect the company, but it will not save the dependents of the policyholder delay at a time when their need for ready money is ordinarily greatest.

The trustee named in the Last Will of the insured; PROVIDED, HOWEVER, that if no will of the insured has been admitted to probate within ninety (90) days after the date of death of the insured, or if the will admitted to probate within such ninety (90) days fails to name a trustee, or if the will admitted to probate within such ninety (90) days names a trustee but no trustee shall have qualified within one (1) year after the date of death of the insured, payment of said sum payable shall be made in one sum to the executors, administrators, or assigns of the insured.

The Ajax Life Insurance Company shall not be obliged to inquire into the terms of any trust affecting this policy or its sum payable and shall not be chargeable with knowledge of the terms thereof. Payment to and receipt by the trustee or payment to and receipt by the insured's executors, administrators, or assigns, as hereinabove provided, shall fully discharge all liability of the company to the extent of such payment.

Trusts versus the Optional Modes of Settlement

From this general discussion, it is apparent that the applicant may designate beneficiaries and elect settlement options for their benefit if he wishes. Alternatively, he may establish an insurance trust for the handling of the insurance money after it becomes payable. In the latter case he explains in the trust agreement how he wishes the money invested, how the trust is to be administered, and how payments are to be made to the beneficiaries of the trust.

Ordinarily a fee is charged for the trust services, and there are no guarantees either of principal or income. The optional modes of settlement offered by a life insurance company, on the other hand, are offered at no additional cost, and the safety of the principal as well as the rate of interest are guaranteed. At first glance it might seem strange that any applicant would prefer a trust. However, there are a number of situations in which the trust may be advantageous.

Generally speaking, a trust is not advisable unless the insurance benefit is of significant size. Otherwise the fee for trust services would be a definite factor, and in addition, investment possibilities are considerably restricted. Even with a relatively large insurance estate, the optional modes of settlement are often adequate for the needs and wishes of the insured. However, if the general estate is large and if it is made up of considerable property other than insurance, the insured may have established a trust for the administration of that property. In such a case he may very logically wish to include the insurance proceeds in the same trust in order to achieve a more effective integration of his estate plan.

The trustee may also exercise a great deal of discretion in the administration of the trust if the trustor wishes him to do so. Thus if the possible needs of the beneficiaries are particularly difficult to anticipate, and if they may fluctuate widely, a trust may be much the preferable way of providing for administration of the fund. For instance, there may be an invalid or semi-invalid child for whom the insured will wish to make special provision, especially for hospital care or special education. Such needs cannot be anticipated or provided for except in a very general way under any of the optional modes of settlement, for the insurer will never accept responsibility for exercising discretion in connection with any payment it makes. However, sufficient discretion can be given a trustee that additional funds may be made available for these purposes when and as the needs arise. On the other hand, an annuity is often peculiarly appropriate in this type of situation, and that can only be provided by a life insurance company.

The remarriage problem is often cited as another instance in which a trustee is ordinarily willing to exercise discretion beyond the usual scope of the life company's activities. For instance, John Doe may wish to leave his property in such a way that his wife will receive a generous income for the remainder of her life if she does not remarry. If she does, the income is to be reduced or terminated. Life insurance companies have no way of knowing when or if the widow remarries, and for that reason the majority refuse to incorporate such a clause in any settlement agreement. A trustee, however, is ordinarily in the same town, often personally acquainted with the family, and such a responsibility is not beyond the scope of his usual duties and responsibilities.

A great deal of flexibility can be achieved by the use of the optional modes of settlement. The applicant can elect to have the benefit retained at interest and give the beneficiary the right to elect a different option if and when she wishes, for instance. On the other hand, extra payments in case of illness or other emergencies of uncertain date can best be provided through the use of a trust. Lastly, the man who wants to leave his family an advisor and counselor as well as a financial plan will do well to establish a trust.

Trusts and Optional Settlements Compared. Generally speaking, there are a number of similarities between the life insurance trust and a settlement agreement under which the optional modes of settlement are elected. The beneficiary does not have possession of the property in either case, and in both cases she receives the benefits. Under a trust, the trustee holds the property in trust for the benefit of the beneficiaries of the trust and makes payments to them as specified in the trust agreement. Under the settlement options the insurer retains the sum payable and pays it out to the beneficiary in accordance with the terms of the settlement option or options elected. Under the trust, however, the trustee has the legal title to the property. By contrast, the life insurance company holds the funds in question under a debtor-creditor relationship with the beneficiary.

Several states have statutes which permit a life insurance company to act as a trustee with respect to policy proceeds which it retains. In these states the similarity of the options and the trust situation may appear at first glance to be highly significant. However, even in this situation the settlement options differ from a trust in several essential ways.

First, the property of an individual trust is ordinarily segregated from the property of other trusts and handled separately. This means separate investment and separate accounting, although the enactment of so-called "common trust" fund laws in several states permits the commingling of the funds of small trusts for investment purposes in some circumstances. Proceeds of insurance retained by the company are not segregated, however. On the contrary, they are commingled with all other funds of the company for investment purposes, and income and losses can thus be shared by the smallest unit on exactly the same terms as the largest.

A second difference is found in the matter of guarantees. In keeping with the basic philosophy of insurance, the safety of the principal is guaranteed absolutely under the optional settlements. In addition, a minimum rate of interest is also guaranteed, as well as a share of any excess interest that may be earned. The trust, on the other hand, offers no guarantees whatsoever. This is not altogether a disadvantage. The trustor may, if he wishes, free the trustee from many restrictions expressly imposed on the investment of trust funds and provide that the trust property may be invested in common stocks or other types of equities. Under these circumstances the prospects of gain, as well as loss, may be considerably enhanced, as compared with the more limited, and therefore more conservative, investment possibilities available to the life insurer.

We have already mentioned the use of discretion on the part of the trustee. Insurers ordinarily will not assume any responsibilities under optional settlements which require the exercise of discretion. Consequently, if the needs of the insured's dependents may be expected to fluctuate widely, or if a counselor actually is needed, the trust ordinarily offers the best means of meeting the problem. On the other hand, if a guaranteed income is most important the optional settlements cannot be excelled.

It is sometimes said that a trust is much more flexible than the optional settlements, and this, to some extent, is true. It should be remembered, however, that with flexibility goes also the possibility of loss. The basic guarantees, which provide the security of the settlement options, automatically restrict the flexibility of the plans. Even in insurance, one cannot have his cake and eat it.

The final and most essential difference between trusts and the settlement options lies in the availability of the annuity form of income. This may be obtained commercially only from a life insurance company. An income for life could, of course, be provided under a trust arrangement. However, the peculiar advantages of an annuity, under which principal and income are together distributed to named payees in such a manner that both will be exhausted and yet guaranteed payments will be made during the entire lifetime of the payees, are available only through the services of a life insurance company.

SOME SPECIAL PROBLEMS

The Closed Estate

Under Settlement Agreements. At one time the rights of the beneficiary were of such a nature that they were not contingent upon her living at the time of payment. It was quite possible, therefore, that the proceeds of a life insurance policy might be payable to the estate of a beneficiary several years after her death and after her estate had been closed. Inclusion in the policy of a provision terminating the right of any beneficiary at her death prior to the death of the insured and causing those rights to revert to the estate of the insured effectively took care of this problem.

With the use of settlement agreements, this same problem returned in a different form. Where a settlement plan is adopted under which the proceeds of the policy are retained by the insurance company and paid out in accordance with the directions of the insured (or of the beneficiary if the insured did not elect an optional settlement), it is standard practice to provide that amounts remaining unpaid shall be paid to the estate of one or more of the payees. Care should be taken in drafting such instruments that payment is not made to the estate of the insured or any but the last surviving beneficiary or payee. Otherwise it may be necessary in this case also to reopen a closed estate in order to carry out the terms of the instrument.

The "Common Disaster" Problem

A common disaster is any disaster "common to" several people and in which they lose their lives. The term has no implications that it commonly occurs or that there is anything commonplace about it. Any disaster which takes the lives of several people, more or less instantly, is a common disaster. If those persons include both owners and possible heirs, special problems are frequently presented concerning the inheritance of any property concerned.

These problems are peculiarly applicable in the life insurance situation. There even the fact of liability turns on the question of death. How much is often determined by how the death occurred. Questions about the fact or manner of death, therefore, not only relate to the persons having a right to receive payment, they may also determine how much, if anything, is actually payable.

As previously noted, at one time the rights of the beneficiary were considered vested from the date of the contract. In such cases the right survived the beneficiary and was enforceable by her estate regardless of the date of the death of the insured. However, when the companies began using a policy provision providing that the rights of any beneficiary who predeceased the insured reverted to the estate of the insured, the situation changed. Survival of the beneficiary then became essential to the perfection of her right. Establishing that survival in common disaster cases brought the law of the life insurance contract face to face with the problem that had faced executors and administrators for many, many years.

How Survivorship Is Established. At common law (which ordinarily means in the absence of a statute)[7] there was no presumption with respect to survivorship in a common disaster. When the question was presented in connection with survival of the beneficiary of a life insurance policy, it was decided on various bases, primarily the view the state happened to take with respect to whether the right of the beneficiary was or was not vested.

If the interest was considered vested subject to being divested, the burden of proof was on the person attempting to show that the beneficiary did not survive. Where the interest of the beneficiary was viewed as a mere expectancy, the burden would rest on the executors or administrators of the beneficiary to show that the beneficiary had, in fact, survived the insured and the mere expectancy had ripened into actuality. In either case, if there was no competent evidence concerning survivorship, the person having the burden would fail. Thus, in cases where there was no evidence as to survivorship, the results were entirely dependent upon whether the state took the view that the beneficiary's right was vested, subject to being divested, or a mere expectancy prior to the death of the insured.

---

[7] Except in those states which derive their systems of law from France and Spain, as explained in Chapter XVI, at page 345.

For some time, however, a general movement has been in progress toward bringing uniformity into the various state laws. In keeping with this trend, an act known as the Uniform Simultaneous Death Act was introduced into the legislatures of many of the states during the 1940's and enacted into law. This or similar legislation is now the law in all the states except Georgia, New Mexico, and Ohio.

As it applies to life insurance, the law reads, generally, as follows:

> Where the insured and the beneficiary in a policy of life or accident insurance have died and there is no sufficient evidence that they have died otherwise than simultaneously the proceeds of the policy shall be distributed as if the insured had survived the beneficiary.[8]

This act provides a reasonably satisfactory solution in any case where the beneficiary and the insured die under circumstances which make it impossible to tell who survived the other. Let us say, for instance, that Jim Bennett and his wife, driving home one night, fail to see or hear a fast passenger train at an unguarded crossing, and lose their lives when the train strikes their car. Let us assume further that each is the primary beneficiary of insurance on the life of the other.

If there is no reason to believe that they were killed other than instantly, and if the Uniform Simultaneous Death Act is in effect in their state, the insurance on the lives of each will be distributed as if the other had died first. Where there are contingent or successor beneficiaries, therefore, the sum payable will be paid to them in accordance with the provisions of the beneficiary designation or settlement agreement and in accordance with the wishes of the insured. Benefits payable to the insured's estate will eventually be distributed as directed in his or her will, or in accordance with the appropriate law if there is no will.

However, let us take a more complicated set of facts. Let us say that Alice was Bennett's second wife, that he had three grown children from his first marriage, and no children of the second marriage. Most of his property was tied up in business interests, and his insurance was payable to "Alice Bennett, wife of the insured, if living; otherwise to the children of the insured, equally or to survivor."

Again, if there is no reason to believe that they were killed other than instantly, and if the Uniform Simultaneous Death Act is in effect, the insurance on Bennett's life will go to his children in equal shares as he undoubtedly would have wished. But let us say that they were not killed simultaneously. Let us say that Jim was instantly killed but that Alice lived to recognize and talk to the first people on the scene, although she was dead on arrival at the hospital. Because of the acci-

---

[8] Illinois Revised Statutes, Chap. 3, Sec. 192.4 (1959).

dental death benefit, some seventy thousand dollars of life insurance was payable under her husband's life insurance policies in a lump sum. By the mere fact of her survival it was payable to her, and therefore it went to her personal representatives for final distribution, after payment of her debts, to members of her family. The children of the insured received no part of it.

Few people would criticize this disposition if the wife had lived a longer time, as much, for example, as a year or two. However, the fact that any survival, however brief, makes payment possible to her brothers and sisters, is difficult for many people to accept. The provisions Jim had made showed that he wanted his own children benefited after Alice's death, and it is highly probable that Alice would have made different arrangements herself if she had survived long enough to make a will. Thus it should be noted that the Uniform Simultaneous Death Act provides a satisfactory solution only in those few clear-cut cases where there is no sufficient evidence to show that either party survived the other.

The "Time Clause." Because in so many common disaster situations the beneficiary survives the insured only for a very short period of time, it is often wise to use what is called a time clause. This is a provision included in the beneficiary designation, which requires that the beneficiary survive the insured for a specified length of time, usually thirty or sixty days, before becoming entitled to the sum payable. It effectively takes care of most short-term survivorship problems.

A beneficiary designation of this type reads something like the following:

Alice Bennett, wife of the insured, if living on the thirtieth day after the death of the insured; otherwise equally to the children of the insured who are living on the thirtieth day after the death of the insured, if any; otherwise to the executors, administrators or assigns of the insured.

The Optional Settlements. In the practical sense, the use of any interest or instalment settlement option for the primary beneficiary serves the same purpose as a time clause, if a successor or contingent beneficiary is designated. Here a settlement agreement would be used, naming Alice Bennett, for example, as the primary beneficiary, if living, and providing that the proceeds be held under the interest option. The settlement agreement would also name the children of the insured as successor beneficiaries or payees. Their rights, unlike those of the contingent beneficiary under a one-sum designation, survive the insured. Under a settlement agreement, successor beneficiaries will take the entire proceeds in the event that the primary beneficiary does not survive the insured, but they will also have the right to succeed to any part of the proceeds not exhausted in payments to or withdrawals by the primary beneficiary. A settlement agreement, in effect, is a plan of settlement which provides different arrangements as circumstances change even after the death of the insured.

SOME INCIDENTAL RULES OF LAW

Three Basic Areas

Property interests which may extend into the future present a number of possible problems for which special rules have been devised. For instance, it is perfectly possible to draft an instrument creating successive interests in property to continue for many, many years without vesting—that is, without becoming definitely and wholly owned by anyone. However, as a matter of public policy, the law tries to keep property in the channels of commerce. To this end there has long been a rule known as the "rule against perpetuities"—which limits the time during which such successive nonvested interests can continue.

It is also possible to provide for the accumulation of income for a very long period of time. To prevent this there are various rules against accumulations. Lastly, in order to avoid problems in connection with the distribution of any person's property at his death, there has grown up a complex of rules concerning testamentary disposition—that is, wills and instruments having the general effect of wills.

Each of these subjects, as it applies to the life insurance contract and the optional methods of settlement, could provide the material for an extensive and somewhat complicated paper. Such a treatment is beyond the scope of this book. However, the student of life insurance law needs some acquaintance with the general nature of the problems and the rules that are used in connection with them. For that reason a brief discussion seems appropriate at this point.

The Rule against Perpetuities

In the absence of any rules to the contrary, it would be possible, as we have said, for the owner of property to give it away or leave it by the terms of his will in such a way that each of an endless series of people might take a limited interest in the property but no one would ever succeed to ownership in such a sense that he could sell the property and convey complete title to it. One of the easiest ways to do this would be to establish a trust for the benefit of one's children, grandchildren, great-grandchildren etc., so that the title to the trust property would never vest as long as there were additional descendants of the original owner.

The word "alienation," in the law of real property, simply means a sale in which complete title is conveyed. Before a sale in this sense can be made, however, complete title must have vested in an identifiable person or persons. Thus any device which postpones the vesting of title to property also limits or restrains its alienation. Such a limitation, if it extends into the indefinite future (that is, a restraint tending toward a perpetuity), has long been considered against public policy.

One of the most important rules developed to limit such restraints is known as the rule against perpetuities, which is most commonly stated as follows: "No interest is good unless it must vest, if at all, not later than twenty-one years after some life in being at the creation of the interest." In general terms, this means that one cannot create an interest in property which will postpone the vesting of ownership beyond a period equal to the remaining lifetime of someone then living, plus twenty-one years. If one tries to do so, the interest is void, and vesting is immediate in the person or persons otherwise entitled to take.

How the Rule Applies. It has been said that the rule against perpetuities is easy to state but difficult to apply. Certainly it is a highly technical rule in a highly technical field of law. Fortunately it is rarely applicable in life insurance itself. It applies to life insurance trusts, just as it applies to any other kind of trust. The policyholder who elects to have the insurance benefit paid to a trustee, therefore, will be concerned with the rule against perpetuities in connection with the trust agreement. Thus the interest created by the trust must be capable of vesting within the prescribed time under any circumstances, or it is void. If there is any possibility that it will not so vest, the interest is ineffective. It is no argument that it actually does vest within the prescribed time. In every case the period is measured from the time the interest is created, the date of the inter vivos trust if that is used, the death of the testator if a testamentary trust is the instrument in question.

How the rule applies to life insurance settlement agreements is quite a different matter. The only decided case on the subject is *Holmes v. John Hancock Mutual Life Insurance Co.,*[9] where the rule was held not to apply, since the proceeds of the insurance constituted a debt and not a trust. There the court said:

Each of the policies contained provisions permitting the insured to nominate and change the beneficiary to whom the proceeds of the policies should be paid and also offering to the insured "optional methods of settlement." Before his death the insured nominated his wife, the defendant Marie F. Holmes and his nephews, the defendants William R. Holmes and Morgan Dwight Holmes, as beneficiaries under each of said policies, and directed that the proceeds of the policies be left on deposit with the company, and that the interest be paid quarterly to his wife during her lifetime and after her death to his nephews "until the elder or survivor of said nephews attains

[9] 288 N.Y. 106, 41 N.E.2d 909 (1942).

the age of thirty-five," and that thereafter the principal be paid to the nephews or to the survivor. The plaintiff challenges the validity of these directions on the ground that they constitute an unlawful suspension of the power of alienation.

We may assume that if the proceeds of the policies constituted a trust fund, these directions would be void under the provisions of section 11 of the Personal Property Law (Cons. Laws, ch. 41). The insurance company does not, however, hold the proceeds of the policy as a trust fund. By the terms of the policy it has contracted to pay stipulated amounts, at stipulated times and in stipulated manner. "The obligation of the insurance company constitutes a debt from the company to . . . the beneficiary, under the policy." The stipulated payments "are not income on personal property. They constitute deferred payments which the company agreed to make to the beneficiary . . . . (*Crossman Co.* v. *Rauch*, 263 N.Y. 264, 273.)" The provisions of section 11 of the Personal Property Law have no application to such an obligation.

It is notable that New York and a few other states have special statutes on this subject. As the above quotation shows, such statutes have been held not to be applicable in the case of insurance proceeds held under optional modes of settlement. Nevertheless, the general philosophy of the law favors limitations on any devices which tend to keep property out of the channels of commerce for any extensive period of time. For this reason, life insurance companies usually follow practices which limit settlement plans under life insurance contracts to a period which accords with that of the rule against perpetuities even though as a technical matter the rule does not apply. A settlement agreement naming the wife as primary beneficiary and the children as contingent beneficiaries ordinarily fulfills the wishes of the policyholder and yet runs no risk with respect to violation of the underlying philosophy of the rule.

The Rule against Accumulations

As a general rule, if property is left by one person to another in such a way that it is to accumulate interest for the latter for a period extending too far into the future, it is held to be an illegal accumulation. One of the most famous laws defining the periods that would be permissible was the Thellusson Act, an English law passed in 1800. The Thellusson Act specified a number of alternative methods by which the permissible period could be measured, one of which was the minority of any infant living at the death of a grantor or testator, at the time the interest was created. In other words, it was permissible to leave property at interest to be accumulated for a minor beneficiary until he became twenty-one years of age.

Because this is a simple rule and very practical, a number of states, including New York, have similar laws limiting the accumulations to the minority of infant beneficiaries. As a result, most life insurance companies will not permit interest on proceeds left under the interest option to be accumulated except during the period of minority of a minor beneficiary. In fact, some companies will not permit interest to be accumulated for even this length of time.

The Question of Testamentary Disposition

Every state has a statute or statutes relating to wills, defining the requirements which such an instrument must meet before it will be given legal effect. Since life insurance is primarily concerned with a benefit which is not payable until death, a conflict between the life insurance contract and the law of wills was a very natural development. However, it was early settled that life insurance does not constitute a testamentary disposition and, therefore, is not required to be executed in accordance with the statute of wills.

The question has more frequently been raised in connection with optional settlements and thus plays a relatively important role in connection with the settlement of death benefits and the administration of supplementary contracts. Generally speaking, such settlements have been held not to be testamentary in nature, but the court decisions and the issues involved are sufficiently important to merit a separate discussion. That discussion will be found in Chapter XIV *infra*.

¤   ¤   ¤   ¤   ¤

ILLUSTRATIVE CASES

As a matter of general law, the applicant for insurance on his own life is free to name anyone he chooses as beneficiary. With respect to how the benefit is to be paid, he has two broad alternatives. He may elect to have it paid in one sum to the beneficiary of his choice, or he may elect one of the optional methods of settlement. Legally, his choice may make a great deal of difference in the rights of contingent or successor beneficiaries, usually his children.

This point is not always clearly understood and, indeed, depends upon the wording of the settlement agreement or beneficiary designation involved. However, one of the significant legal problems in connection with the naming of the beneficiary relates to this difference in the rights of the contingent beneficiaries under a one-sum beneficiary designation, as contrasted with their rights where a settlement agreement is in effect. The cases chosen for this chapter define these differences in connection with the practices of one company and thus illustrate one of the significant legal developments accompanying the increased use of the optional modes of settlement.

THE NORTHWESTERN MUTUAL LIFE INSURANCE COMPANY v. FINK, ADMX.[10]

(United States Circuit Court of Appeals, Sixth Circuit)

HICKS, C. J.: Suit by Fannie Fink, Administratrix With the Will Annexed of the Estate of Charlotte S. Wolf, appellee, against The Northwestern Mutual Life Insurance Company, appellant, to recover certain proceeds of an insurance policy upon the life of Edwin A. Wolf.

The facts are undisputed.

Edwin A. Wolf married twice. He had two children, Virginia C. Wolf and Edwin Wolf, Jr., by his first wife. His first wife died and he married Charlotte S. Wolf. She had two children, Janis and Maurice Harrison by a previous marriage. The policy was issued October 17, 1938, and it, with the application, constitutes the entire contract.

The policy was made payable immediately upon receipt of proof of death "to the direct beneficiaries and in the manner provided in the supplemental designation, attached to and made a part" of the policy. No beneficiary was named in the face of the policy but under the heading "Beneficiaries and Contingent Beneficiaries" it contained the following provision:

11. Subject to the rights of any Assignee, the Insured (1) may designate one or more Beneficiaries if none be named herein, either with or without reservation of the right to revoke such designation; and (2) may designate one or more Contingent Beneficiaries whose interest shall be as expressed in or by endorsement of the Company on, this Policy; and (3) may change any Beneficiary not irrevocably designated; and (4) may change any Contingent Beneficiary. If there be more than one Beneficiary the interest of any deceased Beneficiary, including any unpaid benefits due or to become due, shall pass to the surviving Beneficiary or Beneficiaries *unless otherwise directed by the Insured.* Upon the death of the last surviving Beneficiary the Contingent Beneficiary or Beneficiaries, if any, shall, *unless otherwise directed by the Insured,* succeed to all the interest of such Beneficiary, including any unpaid benefits due or to become due. . . . (Italics ours.)

Under the heading "Special Provisions Relating to Settlement When This Policy Becomes Payable," were the following subsections:

Deceased Beneficiary.

3. If there be more than one Beneficiary living when this Policy becomes payable the interest of any such Beneficiary thereafter deceased, including any unpaid benefits due or to become due, shall pass to the surviving Beneficiary or Beneficiaries *unless otherwise directed by the Insured,* except that under Option "C" the interest so passing shall be limited to the stipulated installments, if any, then remaining unpaid.

Rights of Contingent Beneficiary

4. *Unless otherwise directed by the designator,* the surviving Contingent Beneficiary or Beneficiaries, if any, shall, upon the death of the last surviving Beneficiary, succeed to all the interest of such Beneficiary, including any unpaid benefits due or to become due, except that under Option "C" such interest shall be limited to the stipulated installments, if any, then remaining unpaid. (Italics ours.)

[10] 118 F.2d 761 (C.C.A. Mich., 1941).

Pursuant to clause 11 above quoted the insured made the following designation of beneficiaries, to wit:

DUPLICATE
POLICY TITLE DIV.
1938 Oct 17 AM 10 09
Detroit, Mich. October 13, 1938
Insert Date

I, Edwin A. Wolf, the insured under policy No. 2451621 issued by The Northwestern Mutual Life Insurance Company, hereby designate Charlotte Wolf and Florence W. Gage, wife and sister, as direct beneficiaries under said policy, share and share alike. In the event of the death of Charlotte Wolf, such share as she would have been entitled to receive shall be payable to Virginia C. Wolf and Edwin Wolf, Jr., share and share alike, or to the survivor of them.

This designation became a part of the contract. Thus the policy stood when insured died on November 10, 1938, at approximately 12:01 A.M. His wife Charlotte S. Wolf, died twenty-two hours later.

Appellee's contention is that the right of Charlotte Wolf to one-half of the proceeds of the policy became vested in her upon the death of the insured and that appellee as her personal representative is entitled to recover such share. If this is sound the amount of the recovery under the will of Charlotte S. Wolf would be distributed to her children, Janis and Maurice Harrison.

The District Court found for appellee and upon motion entered a summary judgment in her favor. We concur in the opinion of the District Judge that there is no ambiguity in the contract but we reach a different result.

We must keep in mind at least two general rules applicable to life insurance policies as well as to all other contracts. First, the policy must be read as a whole; and second, effect must be given to the plain, ordinary and popular meaning of the language used. This is the law in Michigan (*Hall* v. *Equitable Life Assur. Soc.*, 295 Mich. 404), as elsewhere.

Charlotte Wolf was, of course, a direct beneficiary,—but a beneficiary of what? The answer is, that she had a right to receive one-half of the proceeds of the policy. But this right was not unconditional nor unlimited. Even though insured had died, her right to receive the proceeds of the policy was not perfected, because she herself died before the execution and receipt of proof of his death.

But, this to one side, her right to receive any unpaid share of the proceeds of the policy terminated with her death. This is unquestionably true because the designation of beneficiaries must be read as a whole and in the event of her death "such share as she would have been entitled to receive" became payable to the Wolf children. The insured was fully authorized under paragraph 2 of clause 11 above quoted to designate the Wolf children as contingent beneficiaries and to fix their interest. He did this in simple language, easily understood. Appellant so understood and when the policy became payable, made settlement accordingly. It is now called upon to pay again.

To adopt appellee's insistence that Charlotte Wolf became vested with the right, title and ownership of one-half of the proceeds of the policy upon the death of the insured would be to rewrite the designation of beneficiaries. We would in effect, after the name Charlotte Wolf in the last sentence, insert the words "before the death of insured." But the insured made no such limitation. The change would constitute a material alteration which we are not authorized to make.

We are not called upon to search for the insured's intention. It is clearly expressed over his own signature. If it were necessary to look for the reason for his action it could probably be found in the natural instinct to protect, first, his widow during her lifetime, and second, his own rather than his step-children (see *Northwestern Mut. Life Ins. Co.* v. *Greiner,* 115 Mich. 639), or, in the possible contingency that the interest of his widow, Charlotte, would pass to his sister, Florence, as provided in clause 11, unless he otherwise directed. The same possibility "unless otherwise directed by the insured" lurks in clause 3 above quoted.

It is urged that the court erred in directing a summary judgment. The rule involved is 56(e), Federal Rules of Civil Procedure, 28 U.S.C.A. following section 723c. Assuming that we are correct in the view we have taken, we need not consider the point. If the judgment was erroneous it should be set aside regardless of the method pursued. The question will not again arise. "The case involves only propositions of law." *Ford Steel Wheel Co.* v. *Lewellyn,* 251 U.S. 511, 516. There are no questions of fact to be retried.

The judgment is reversed and the case remanded to the District Court with directions to dismiss.

❖ ❖ ❖ ❖ ❖

ROSSETTI ET AL., Appellants v. *HILL ET AL.,* Appellees [11]

(United States Circuit Court of Appeals, Ninth Circuit)

STEPHENS, C. J.: A sum of money ($10,060.00), the face sum of a life insurance policy, including certain incidental benefits, is on deposit with the district court registry awaiting distribution to the rightful owners. In an interpleader suit, instituted by the Northwestern Mutual Life Insurance Company, the court awarded the money to Peter B. Hill, Joanne Hill and Patricia Hill Harder, who will hereinafter be referred to as the Hill Children. The Hill Children are not the children of Genevieve Borlini Hill, but are the children of insured by a former wife. Co-executors of the estate of Genevieve Borlini Hill, widow of the insured, appeared in the action, claiming the money for the estate. They appeal.

George A. Hill, Jr. (insured), died, and thirty-nine days thereafter his widow, Genevieve Borlini Hill, who was named the direct beneficiary in the insurance policy died. The Hill Children were named in the policy as contingent beneficiaries. Proof of death of the insured had been furnished the insurance company prior to Mrs. Hill's death, but she died without making an election as to whether she would take the insurance benefits in a lump sum or, in lieu thereof, to select payments through options open to her by the terms of the policy.

The Hill Children claim the insurance benefits because they believe a certain provision of the policy, together with the fact that Mrs. Hill died before the benefits had been paid over to her, convert their interest in the policy, in effect, from that of contingent beneficiaries to that of direct beneficiaries. The district court agreed that such construction was a correct one.

The pivotal provision is found in the policy under the heading "General Provisions," sub-headed "Direct and Contingent Beneficiaries." We italicize the pivotal provision.

Sec. 11. Subject to the rights of any Assignee, the Insured (1) may designate one or more Direct Beneficiaries if none be named herein, either

[11] 161 F.2d 549 (C.C.A. Cal., 1947).

with or without reservation of the right to revoke such designation; and (2) may designate one or more Contingent Beneficiaries whose interest shall be as expressed in this Policy; and (3) may change any Direct Beneficiary not irrevocably designated; and (4) may change any Contingent Beneficiary. If there be more than one Direct Beneficiary the interest of any deceased Direct Beneficiary, including any unpaid benefits due or to become due, shall pass to the surviving Direct Beneficiary or Beneficiaries unless otherwise directed by the Insured with the consent of the Company. *Upon the death of the last surviving Direct Beneficiary, the Contingent Beneficiary or Beneficiaries, if any, shall succeed to the interest of such Direct Beneficiary, including any unpaid benefits due or to become due.* If no Direct Beneficiary or Contingent Beneficiary survives the Insured the Proceeds of this Policy shall be payable to the executors, administrators or assigns of the Insured. No such designation, revocation, change or direction shall be effective unless duly made in writing and filed at the Home Office of the Company (accompanied by this Policy) prior to or at the time this Policy shall become payable, and endorsed hereon by the Company.

Appellees and the district court were of the opinion that the italicized provision of Section 11, interpreted in the light of the whole policy, means that the insurance benefits go to the children if they have not been actually delivered to the widow before her death.

The section as quoted was written into the policy at its issue during the lifetime of all concerned and as far as in issue here, it refers to the respective status of the direct beneficiary and contingent beneficiaries, and what their rights, if any, will be at the insured's death in the separate circumstances related in each provision. Thus the pivotal provision simply defines the contingent beneficiaries' right to be that if there is no direct beneficiary at insured's death to take, they take the benefits.

But the widow, the direct beneficiary, was alive when insured died, and therefore, by the terms of the policy the unqualified right to the insurance benefits vested in her at the first point of time occurring after insured's death. The reasoning in *Chartrand* v. *Porace*, 16 Colo. 19, 26 Pac. 152, and in *Kothman* v. *Minn. Odd Fellows Mut. Ben. Soc.*, 66 Minn. 88, 68 N.W. 732, is sound, as we see it. All that remained for the widow to have the benefits actually in hand, or, in lieu thereof, the right to it by installments, was to send the proof of death of insured to the insurance company, which was done, and to make and to inform the company of her election as to how she would receive the money, which was never done.

Neither the insurance company nor anyone else had the slightest claim upon the title to the money, but a burden was upon the company to hold and protect it. The widow died before she communicated her choice of how she would receive the benefits, and since she was entitled to the whole thereof, and the installment option was in lieu thereof, the total of all benefits were payable when the death prevented a choice being made.

There is nothing significant in the fact that the problem of choosing whether or not she would take the benefits in bulk or whether she would avail herself of the privileges under the option clauses open to her had not been acted upon prior to her death. In all probability her mind was not directed primarily to her finance problems. She had lost her husband, and she, herself, was to succumb in less than a month and a half thereafter.

It is argued that if any money derived from the insurance policy remains unpaid at the death of the direct beneficiary any such money goes to the contingent beneficiaries. The provision relied upon cannot be construed so as to bring about any such result. There is nothing in the policy to indicate that the direct beneficiary's rights to take the benefits were limited in any manner or that she would forfeit them if she failed to claim them or that her title was conditional upon the actual enjoyment of them.

We have seen that Mrs. Hill had a right to take all upon the insured's death. If she had actually received the full sum of the proceeds and had deposited them in bank, it could not be logically argued that they were held by her under a limited use. Certainly, had she received the benefits in hand, and had died without spending them all, the balance would not have gone to the contingent beneficiaries. Appellees do not so contend, but the point is one of consistency. If, when insured named his wife as direct beneficiary, he had intended that the phrase "including any unpaid benefits due or to become due" should mean that all of the proceeds of the policy should be paid to the contingent beneficiaries in the circumstances, it would have been consistent for him to have provided that any unpaid installments under the option plan should, upon the widow's death, be paid to the contingent beneficiaries. Instead, it is specifically provided differently in the policy—that

> . . . Beneficiaries may make such election [as to options] in lieu of payment in one sum . . . [and when so made] the interest of any contingent beneficiaries . . . shall terminate. The policy even provides that the direct beneficiary, upon electing to take under an option plan, may name her own beneficiaries to take the unpaid balance. The fact of the matter is that the "including unpaid benefits" phrase refers only to incidental benefits which are provided for in the policy.

Thus, the argument fails, that when taken by the four corners the policy reveals that insured provided insurance benefits for the wife first but that if conditions came about so that after insured's death the wife was not to enjoy them, they would go to the children.

The appellees, the Hill Children, rely heavily upon the case of *Northwestern Life Insurance Co. v. Fink* (118 Fed.2d 761). The policies of the *Fink* case and of ours are similar but not exactly alike. There is a provision in the *Fink* case that if the direct beneficiary shall die "such shares as she would have been entitled to receive shall be payable" to someone else. No provision of this kind is in the policy with which our case is concerned. In the cited case the direct beneficiary died before collecting the insurance benefit and the district court held the policy had vested in the direct beneficiary. The circuit court reversed on its construction of the quoted phrase. There was another different fact in the *Fink* case. Proof of death had not been made when the direct beneficiary died.

We make no expression as to the decision in the *Fink* case other than to say that it does not convince us that our reasoning as above set forth is erroneous or that our conclusions are wrong.

Reversed.

CHAPTER **VI**

The Policy
Is Reviewed

THE LIFE INSURANCE AGENT will usually review the life insurance policy when he first receives it to see that the settlement provisions are in accordance with the request of the applicant and that the policy is of the form and in the amount applied for. When he delivers the policy he should also spend some time with the insured explaining the outstanding features of the policy.

As a matter of fact, of all the policyholder's personal papers none is more closely related to his daily living than his life insurance policy. As his family grows, as his finances change, as his business needs vary, the policyholder's life values in his insurance program can and should keep pace. If he is as familiar with the various provisions of the policy as he should be, he will always be in a position to utilize it to its best advantage.

The purpose of this chapter is to give a rapid, general review of the basic outline of the standard ordinary life insurance policy so that the policy can be better understood and utilized as the flexible, adaptable instrument it really is.

THE POLICY IN GENERAL

The Policy as a Written Contract . . .

. . . *Expresses the Agreement.* Applying general contract law to the life insurance contract, we say that the policy is the written expression of the agreement between the applicant and the company. Pending the issuance of the policy, the contract may be evidenced by a conditional binding receipt, and in the absence of a statute to the contrary an oral agreement may be effective. Because of the comprehensive nature of the life insurance contract, however, and the length of time it often remains in force, it is almost universal practice to issue a formal printed policy in which the agreement is completely expressed.

. . . Is Subject to the Parol Evidence Rule. The issuance of a policy is so universally the custom that one can safely say that the parties from the first "contemplate that their negotiations shall be reduced to writing." Thus the life insurance contract falls squarely within the requirements of the parol evidence rule. Once the policy has been issued and delivered, oral evidence will not be permitted to vary or contradict its terms.[1]

The Life Insurance Contract Is . . .

. . . A Contract of Adhesion. As we have seen, except in rare instances, the life insurance contract is unilateral. The obligations that are legally enforceable are all on the side of the life insurance company. More important in understanding the law of the policy, however, is the fact that it is a contract of *adhesion*. This means a contract that is drafted by one party and accepted or rejected by the other without opportunity to bargain in any way with respect to its terms.

The term "adhesion" has a somewhat modified meaning as applied to the life insurance contract. Certainly the applicant has no choice with respect to the provisions of the policy other than those which express his wishes concerning the beneficiary designation and the terms of settlement. Yet it is not exactly accurate to say that the policy is drafted by the life insurance company in the sense that the latter has any wide latitude in deciding upon its terms. As a matter of fact, life insurance contract forms are the result of a combination of legislative requirements, insurance department regulations, and the requirements of insurance itself. Thus it would be more accurate to say that the contract is a contract of adhesion only in the sense that it is not the result of negotiation between the parties with respect to its terms.

. . . Construed Most Strictly against the Company. It is customary to interpret a contract of adhesion most strictly against the party which drafted the instrument. This rule is based on the assumption that, having the freedom to choose the terms he wishes, the party drafting the instrument will have adequately protected his own interests. The rule is often applied to life insurance contracts although a few courts have held that where the provision in question is required by statute and is worded as required, the standard rule of construction against the company does not apply. In matter of actual fact, the company's freedom to choose such policy provisions as it may wish is materially limited by statutes and insurance commissioner rulings.

. . . Subject to Extensive Statutory Requirements. As a part of their regulatory insurance legislation, most of the states have laws concerning

---

[1] The reader may wish to review the parol evidence rule as it applies to contracts generally, as discussed in Chapter II, page 44, *supra.*

provisions that may or may not be included in the life insurance contract. Many of these laws set forth, sometimes in detail, provisions that must be included, others that may be, and still others that may not be included in any life insurance policy issued in the state in question or to a resident of that state.

The Standard Policy Provisions Laws

Many of the states have enacted a standard policy provisions law which requires that any policy issued in the state or to a resident of the state must include certain basic provisions relating to a grace period, misstatement of age, incontestability, etc.

Compliance May Be "In Substance." The fact that a state has a standard provisions law does not mean that life insurance policies must be worded in the exact language used in the statute, although this was true of the legislation first enacted in New York after the Armstrong Investigation. It was soon found that such a requirement was much too rigid and that the same objective could be attained by "in substance" legislation, with the additional advantage of flexibility. For this reason the early legislation in New York was soon replaced by a law which required certain provisions but permitted compliance in substance rather than in the exact words of the statute. The uniform standard policy provisions law, which was subsequently enacted by many of the other states, was so worded from the first as to require only compliance in substance.

Approval of the Commissioner

Not Necessarily Required. The insurance laws of each state are administered by an officer, usually called the insurance commissioner or the director of insurance. Every insurance commissioner has some responsibility with respect to policy forms, but his authority varies from state to state. In one group of states, for example, companies are prohibited from issuing or delivering a policy until it has been approved by the commissioner. Other states require only that policy forms be filed with the insurance commissioner. In some of these states the commissioner is required to notify the company within a stated period, usually thirty days, if the policy does not comply with the statutory requirements. Still other states require the policy forms to be filed but do not specify a length of time within which notice of any disapproval must be given.

Effect of Lack of Approval. If a policy is issued without the approval of the commissioner if approval is required, or without filing if that is the requirement, it is generally held to be a valid contract and enforceable by the insured. This is understandable. The statutory requirements are for the benefit of the policyholders. To hold a policy void, for which application has been made and premiums paid in good faith, because of the company's violation of the law would obviously be unjust. However, such contracts will be construed as if they included any required provisions that are more favorable than those actually included in the policy. Usually also there is a penalty, a fine, or in some instances even the revocation of the insurer's license to do business, for issuing a policy which has not been filed or approved by the commissioner in compliance with the statutory requirements.

How to Read the Policy

Ordinarily, a life insurance policy is intended to remain effective over many, many years and to be an important part of the policyholder's financial planning. Thus, it is important that its provisions be clearly expressed, and for this reason many life insurance companies wage a kind of continuing battle against overly technical and obscure policy language. As a result most of the archaic terminology has been dispensed with in the past several years, and the language of most present-day policy forms is surprisingly simple when compared to the wide assortment of benefits and protections the policy affords.

For purposes of discussion, it helps to break down the life insurance contract into large basic units. For instance, one entire section is devoted to the beneficiary provisions and settlement specifications. For ease of reference, this can be called the "settlement section." Another section concerns the nonforfeiture provisions entirely, and we shall so refer to it. The last section contains the general provisions, including the required standard provisions and any optional provisions the company may wish to include to simplify the administration of the contract and its use by the policyholder.

Summarized, this divides the policy contract into three large sections: (1) the settlement action; (2) the nonforfeiture benefits section; (3) the general section. There remain only the face page and any additional coverages which may be added by so-called riders and endorsements. We shall start our discussion with the face page.

THE FACE PAGE

Statutory Requirements. One of the basic objectives of legislation concerning policy provisions is to make sure that the policyholder is not deceived with respect to the coverage he gets. For that reason one of the commonest statutory provisions with respect to the face page of the policy requires a brief description to be included on the face page of every policy. This requirement, statutory in at least 21 states, is obviously intended to make clear to the policyholder the kind of coverage, at least in general terms, his policy provides.

Other Provisions. In addition to the description, the face page of every policy states the name of the company, the insured, the amount of insurance, the amount of the premium, and the effective date of the policy. There is also a simple statement of the promise of the company to pay the face amount to the beneficiary immediately upon receipt at its home office of due proof of the death of the insured. The execution paragraph, including the signatures of the company officers—usually the president, secretary, and the registrar—completes this basic statement of the most important promise in the policy.

The face page thus contains a summary of the basic promise of the life insurance company and the most important condition—premium payment—related to it. In one form or another, the face page says: "The Ajax Life Insurance Company hereby insures the life of John J. Doe, Insured, for the benefit of Mary A. Doe, Beneficiary, and agrees to pay the amount of insurance immediately upon receipt of due proof of the death of the insured while this policy is in force."

The remainder of the policy, under our three large sections, is made up of provisions defining this basic promise more precisely and explaining various privileges available to the insured or owner under circumstances which have been found to arise most typically during the lifetime of the average insured.

THE SETTLEMENT SECTION

Beneficiary Designation

In its original sense, the beneficiary designation relates to a one-sum settlement and names the person or persons to whom such settlement shall be made. Successor beneficiaries may be named to receive the death benefit if the primary beneficiary does not survive the insured. Final beneficiaries are those persons named to take in the event no primary or successor beneficiaries survive the insured.

Settlement Agreements

Relate to Optional Modes of Settlement. The development and present extensive use of settlement options make up one of the best chapters in the history of the modern life insurance policy. The optional modes of settlement have brought the life insurance companies into a multitude of activities not dreamed of in the early days, and they have presented new problems in the way of conflicts with other basic laws. More than any other innovation, however, they have expanded the usefulness of the life insurance contract and extended it from a contract

once confined to the lifetime of the insured into a contractual relationship that often runs also through the lifetimes of several beneficiaries
after his death.

When optional modes of settlement are elected by the insured, it is
customary to draw up the more complicated settlement specifications
in what is called a settlement agreement or an election of optional settlement. In these specifications the beneficiaries are named in the order in
which they are to receive payments, and the optional methods of settlement applicable to each are defined and explained.

The Optional Modes of Settlement

The Interest Option. Simply stated, there are only four basic types
of settlement options, and two of these are very similar. First, the
insured may elect to have the sum payable held by the company at
interest of a stipulated rate. Interest will be paid out at regular intervals
to the named primary beneficiary during the latter's lifetime, and at her
death the principal will be paid to a successor payee or payees. The
insured may give the primary beneficiary the unlimited right to withdraw any part or all of the principal, or no withdrawal rights at all.
Often older policies contain interest guarantees that are highly valuable.
This is not generally true of policies issued more recently, but the
privilege of leaving a relatively large sum of money with a life insurance
company at a guaranteed rate of interest is always advantageous.

Payments of a Fixed Amount. Two other optional methods are closely
related but differ as to mechanics. Under one of these methods, the life
insurance company retains the proceeds and pays them out at regular
intervals in payments of a fixed amount until the total sum is exhausted.
Under the other mode, the company retains the proceeds and pays
them out over a fixed period in equal payments. The first of these
options is generally referred to as the fixed amount option; the second,
as the fixed period option.

Life Income. Under the fourth standard optional mode of settlement,
the life insurance company retains the proceeds and pays them out to
the named beneficiary in a regular income of a stated amount for the
lifetime of that beneficiary. This option provides a privilege that is almost
unique with respect to life insurance—the privilege of directing that
payments be made for the remainder of the payee's lifetime. Some companies have an option of this kind payable to joint and last survivor
payees, which involves more than one life.

Tables Necessary. To make these options understandable in any
practical sense, tables must be provided in the policy showing the
amount of payments that can be expected from each $1,000 of policy pro-
ceeds. Thus essential information about the optional settlements takes

up much of the space in the policy. Reduced to their simplest terms, however, the optional modes only provide four additional, basic services, of which the insured may avail himself for the benefit of the beneficiary. If the insured does not elect a settlement option, the beneficiary usually has that privilege at the time of settlement.

Legal Problems. The principal legal problems related to the optional modes of settlement concern the question of testamentary disposition and the possibility of violating the rule against perpetuities, or any of the laws relating to accumulations. The testamentary disposition problem is discussed at some length in Chapter XIV, and the rule against perpetuities and the rule relating to accumulations have been discussed in Chapter V, *supra*, at pages 146 and 148.

THE NONFORFEITURE PROVISIONS

The Level Premium System

The amount of premium is specified on the face of the policy. Payment of this premium is a condition precedent to the performance of the basic promise on the part of the insurance company to pay the amount of insurance, at the death of the insured, to the beneficiary he has named. However, the level premium system averages the very low cost of life insurance in the earlier years of the insured's life and the very high cost in the later years into one level premium. For this reason, the premium payable is in excess of the cost in the early years and less than cost in the later years. By paying it, the policyholder who withdraws or lapses his policy prior to death is in the position of having accumulated equities under the policy even though, as a matter of actuarial principle, the premiums are held collectively. There is no individual account for the policyholder and no legal obligation to him prior to maturity unless he lapses or surrenders the policy and relinquishes the original death benefit coverage.

In the early days of life insurance, the policyholder who lapsed his policy for nonpayment of premiums forfeited whatever equities would have been his. The nonforfeiture provisions of the policy have been developing over a long period of time. Nevertheless, they owe their name and their presence in the policy to this basic fact—that without them the policy which lapsed for nonpayment of premium meant a loss to the policyholder of all amounts he had paid over and above the actual cost of the protection he had received. As recently as 1875, this was not considered unusual or unfair.

Nonforfeiture Laws

In 1861, Massachusetts enacted the first nonforfeiture legislation, in the form of a law providing that upon lapsation of any policy, four-fifths of the "net value" must be used to purchase extended term insurance. Similar laws were passed in other states in the next few decades, but nonforfeiture legislation received its first real impetus by reason of the standard provision laws which were recommended after the Armstrong Investigation in 1905. This legislation required that in the case of lapsation of a life insurance policy which had been in effect for a minimum stated period (usually three years), the insurer must provide a cash surrender value. Alternatively, either paid-up insurance for a reduced amount or extended term insurance, or both, must be granted in an amount which could be purchased by the cash surrender value. One of these must be an automatic option.

Based on American Experience Mortality Table. These early nonforfeiture benefits, whether cash surrender value, extended term, or reduced paid-up insurance, were computed as a general rule on the American Experience Table of Mortality at a rate of interest not to exceed an amount stated in the law.

As the American Experience Mortality Table became more and more out of date and as the rate of interest earnings of all life insurance companies declined, it became evident that something must be done about the nonforfeiture laws. In 1937, a committee was appointed to study the problem, under the chairmanship of Alfred N. Guertin. This committee's recommendation led to the adoption by the National Association of Insurance Commissioners of two model statutes referred to as the "Guertin Legislation."

The Guertin Laws. The new nonforfeiture legislation included up-to-date mortality tables and otherwise modernized the nonforfeiture requirements. One of the outstanding innovations was the complete separation of the idea of nonforfeiture benefits from the idea of reserves. Under this legislation, the nonforfeiture benefits were to be calculated as specified in the policy but quite independently of the reserves.

Under the Guertin legislation, a paid-up nonforfeiture benefit is required to be provided for every policy in case of lapse for nonpayment of premiums after premiums have been paid on the policy for at least one year. A cash surrender value must be provided if the policy has been in force for three years.

The company must include tables of benefits in the policy under the nonforfeiture section of the policy and a statement of the methods used in calculating the benefits. The nonforfeiture section of the policy is thus somewhat complicated, but it assures the policyholder that if the policy should lapse, the equities will be made available either in the form of a cash surrender value or other nonforfeiture benefit, one of which is specified in the policy to go into effect on an automatic basis if no election is made.

Legal Problems. Most of the legal problems arising out of the non-forfeiture section of the policy concern efforts on the part of a beneficiary to prove that the policy was effective under one of the nonforfeiture provisions when the life insurance company has taken the position that it was not. Since extended term insurance is ordinarily more favorable than reduced paid-up insurance, much litigation has been directed toward proving that the policy was effective under the extended term provisions. Frequently litigated also is the question of the permitted liquidation of a policy loan in connection with the establishment of extended term insurance.

The nonforfeiture section of the modern life insurance policy is designed primarily for the benefit of the policyholder in the event he defaults in payment of premiums. There is no reason, however, why he may not, if he wishes, cash surrender his policy and treat the proceeds thus made available as an endowment for his own benefit.

The nonforfeiture section may also be considered with reference to the face page of the policy. The face page sets forth the obligation of the company if the policyholder continues to pay the premiums as they fall due. The nonforfeiture section sets forth the obligations of the company if the policyholder does not continue to pay the premiums as they fall due.

Later Developments. By January 1, 1948, the Guertin nonforfeiture law had either been enacted or policies conforming to it had been permitted by law in every state. As a matter of basic constitutional law, legislation can never be enacted which will impair contracts already in effect. Life insurance policies issued prior to that date, therefore, continued with their nonforfeiture sections effective as written. Only those issued thereafter were required to conform to the Guertin legislation.

1958 C.S.O. Mortality Tables. During the past few years new mortality tables have been developed which are referred to as the 1958 Commissioners' Standard Ordinary Mortality Tables. Legislation adopting these new mortality tables as the standard for mimimum nonforfeiture values had been enacted in thirty of the states as of December 7, 1959, with a mandatory operative date of January 1, 1966, in the majority of the states where the law had been enacted.

In a very few years policies will be outstanding with nonforfeiture benefits in accordance with laws which were effective prior to 1948; others with benefits based on laws effective between 1948 and 1959; and still others will have nonforfeiture benefits which are based on the 1958 C.S.O. Mortality Tables. Each policy will be lawful; each will be valid; each will be different from those with nonforfeiture benefits based on a different set of laws. By reason of the detailed legislative requirements on the subject, however, each policy will be self-determining since it will include in its own printed provisions an explanation of the nonforfeiture benefits it provides and how they are calculated. Tables showing the amounts of the benefits will also be included.

THE STANDARD PROVISIONS

The standard provisions law, which was drafted after the Armstrong Investigation, has been adopted with some modifications by considerably more than half the states. Most life insurance policies now being issued, therefore, have been drafted to comply with this legislation and include the standard provisions which it requires.

The following discussion is intended merely as a brief review of the standard provisions and an outline of the major legal problems they present in order that attention may be kept upon the policy in its general outlines.

The Introductory Language

The standard provisions laws are usually introduced with a general paragraph similar to the following:

No policy of life insurance, except as stated in subsection three, shall be delivered or issued for delivery in this state unless it contains in substance the following provision or provisions which in the opinion of the superintendent are more favorable to policyholders: . . .[2]

Comment. Note first that the law applies to all policies delivered in the state in question or issued for delivery in that state. Thus the law automatically applies to all domiciliary companies and the policies of any out-of-state company actually delivered in the state. Second, the phrase "in substance" makes it clear that the policy provision need not be expressly worded in the exact terms of the statute. Lastly, whether the policy provisions actually used are "more favorable to policyholders" than the provisions outlined in the statute is left to the opinion of the superintendent.

The Grace Period

The Statutory Provision. The statutory requirement concerning a grace period provision in the policy usually reads somewhat as follows:

A provision that the insured is entitled to a grace period either of thirty days or of one month within which the payment of any premium after the first may be made, during which period of grace the policy shall continue in full force, but if a claim arises under the policy during such period of grace

---
[2] New York Insurance Law, Sec. 155, 1.

before the overdue premiums or the deferred premiums of the current policy year, if any, are paid, the amount of such premiums, together with interest, not in excess of six per cent per annum, on any overdue premium, may be deducted from any amount payable under the policy in settlement.[3]

The Policy Provision. For purposes of comparison, let us take an actual grace period provision from an ordinary life insurance policy:

(c) *Grace Period.* A grace period of thirty-one days shall be allowed for payment of a premium in default. This policy shall continue in full force during the grace period. If the Insured dies during such period, the premium in default shall be paid from the proceeds of this policy.[4]

Comment. The grace period, like many of the other standard provisions, was first included in life insurance policies on a voluntary basis. By the time of the Armstrong Investigation most companies were including a provision of this kind in their policies. In effect, it simply gives the insured an extra period of time after the premium falls due. During that time the policy continues in force and the premium continues to be payable. If the insured should die during the grace period prior to payment of the premium, it will be payable out of the proceeds.

How Long Is the Period? Most companies permit a grace period of thirty-one days, and if the last day of grace falls on Sunday or a holiday the premium is ordinarily payable on the following business day. If the premium is not paid at the end of the period, the policy lapses.

Occasionally when a premium is past due a premium extension agreement is used for temporary accommodation. In these circumstances, the weight of authority is that the grace period may not be added to the time stipulated in the extension agreement. The extension period dates from the day the premium was due, not from the end of the grace period.

Interest Charge. Interest earnings play a large part in the business of insurance, and if premiums are paid at the end instead of the beginning of the grace period, the insurer will have lost the investment value of the premium for one month. For this reason, the statute permits the insurer to charge interest on the overdue payments, but life insurance companies rarely do this. For competitive reasons as well as the fact that such losses are not generally too significant, most companies do not make an interest charge. If the grace period is used only for emergencies, as is its purpose, the financial loss to the insurer will not be serious.

[3] This and all other statutory quotations in connection with this discussion of "The Standard Provisions" are, except where otherwise noted, to the New York Insurance Law, Sec. 155, 1 (a) through (i).

[4] This and all other policy provisions used in this chapter are quoted from *The Spectator Handy Guide,* 1958 and 1959 editions.

The Incontestable Clause

Second in many of the standard provisions laws is the requirement that the policy contain a provision making the policy incontestable after it has been in force during the lifetime of the insured for a specified length of time, not longer than two years from its date. It is doubtful that any of the other standard provisions have been responsible for more misunderstanding and misinterpretation than the incontestable clause in the life insurance policy.

Statutory Language. The section of the New York Insurance Law which requires the inclusion of an incontestable clause in all life insurance policies reads as follows:

A provision that the policy shall be incontestable after it has been in force during the lifetime of the insured for a period of two years from its date of issue, except for nonpayment of premiums and except for violation of the conditions of the policy relating to military or naval service; and at the option of the insurer, provisions relating to benefits in the event of total and permanent disability, and provisions which grant additional insurance specifically against death by accident or accidental means, may also be excepted.

A Policy Provision. A typical policy provision in compliance with this requirement would read something like this:

Incontestable Clause. After this policy has been in force during the lifetime of the Insured for a period of two years from the date of issue it shall be incontestable except for nonpayment of premiums, and except as to provisions and conditions relating to benefits in the event of total and permanent disability, and those granting additional insurance specifically against death by accidental means, contained in any supplemental agreement attached to, and made a part of, this policy.

Comment. The incontestable clause was first introduced by life insurance companies on a voluntary basis in the latter half of the 1800's. It was introduced in an effort to counteract a growing attitude of public distrust toward the entire life insurance business. This feeling was due largely to the practices of some companies of taking full advantage of the fact that even relatively unimportant misstatements in the application for life insurance, if they were not literally true, gave the companies at that time the legal right to disaffirm the contract. (This, in essence, is the doctrine of warranties, which was applied in a very literal sense by the courts in the latter half of the eighteenth and early nineteenth centuries. It will be discussed in greater detail in Chapter VIII.)

Often premiums had been paid over a long period of time and the misstatements concerned were relatively trivial, yet the company would disaffirm at the death of the insured, leaving the beneficiary in the difficult position of trying to explain an alleged misstatement about which she knew nothing. As a result, the life insurance companies were remarkably successful in disaffirming their policies, but this success, as one commentator has put it, rapidly gained for them a reputation as "the great repudiators." The use of the incontestable clause was the company's pledge to the insured and beneficiary that it would not rely on such purely technical grounds to disaffirm its contracts.

Early Use of the Clause. The first American insurance company to use a clause of this kind was the Manhattan Life Insurance Company. In 1864, this company included in its policies a provision making the policy incontestable after five years "for or on account of error, omissions and misstatements in the application except as to age."

In 1879, the Equitable Society announced that its policies were being made incontestable after three years, with a provision as follows:

> And the said Society does hereby further promise and agree that after three years from the date hereof, the only conditions which shall be binding upon the holder of this policy are that he shall pay the premiums at the times and place, and in the manner herein stipulated, and that the regulations of the society as to age, residence, travel, occupation and employments shall be observed, and that in all other respects, after the expiration of said three years, the liability of the said society under this policy shall not be disputed.

Nature of the Clause. In legal effect the incontestable clause does not deny that a policy may be invalid. It only says that after it has been in force for a specified length of time, the company cannot avail itself of the privilege of defending on that basis. Practically, it is a guarantee of good faith, a waiver of a technical defense which would otherwise have been available to the company. As to its scope, the clause has been held to have a very broad application, even to violate one of the firmest of the law's basic rules—that fraud invalidates a contract.

There has been an astonishing amount of litigation concerning the meaning and effect of the incontestable clause in the life insurance contract. However, the better reasoned cases hold that it is, in effect, a contractual limitation upon any rights the insurer might otherwise have had to avoid the contract for technical reasons going to the validity of the contract itself. Most important of these possible rights, thus limited, is the right to avoid a life insurance contract on grounds of material misrepresentation or fraud in the application for the contract.

Legal Problems. The most important legal problem arising out of the incontestable clause is the very simple but basic question: "What is a contest of the policy?" Is it any action on the part of the company whereby it seeks to defend a denial of a claim for reasons not excepted in the clause, or payment of any sum less than the face amount of the policy? This point of view has been contended in a number of cases and upheld in some. Alternatively, is a contest only such legal action as may be taken to declare the contract itself invalid and of no effect? The latter definition has, by the weight of authority, been held to express the true meaning of the word "contest," but it is not established law in every jurisdiction.

Conflicts with Other Clauses. Most of the other legal problems related to the incontestable clause are decided by the legal approach taken in connection with this basic question of what is a contest. For example, a number of cases have turned on the question of whether there is or is not a conflict between the incontestable clause and the suicide clause. In cases where the periods are of different lengths and the incontestable clause specifies the shorter period, does the defense of suicide on the part of the company constitute a "contest" of the policy in such a sense that it is precluded by the incontestable clause? The consensus is that it does not and that, by asserting the defense of suicide, the company is upholding the validity of the contract and attempting to enforce it according to its terms.

Does the misstatement of age clause conflict with the incontestable clause? The majority opinion is that it does not, but the fact that there are a number of decisions on the question bears witness that a possible conflict has been recognized and legal interpretation has been required.

Conflicts between the incontestable clause and aviation exclusion riders are more recent in point of time, but they have brought up the same basic question. Is an aviation exclusion rider effective after the policy has passed the period of contestability? As would be expected, some courts have held to a literal interpretation of the incontestable clause, stating that the insurer may not contest the claim unless the contest is based upon an exception which is stated in the clause. Others have distinguished between a contest of the validity of the policy and a contest of a claim, on the grounds that where there is an aviation exclusion, death as a result of aviation activity is a risk that was never assumed by the insurer in the first place.

The most famous court decision on the meaning of a "contest," as that word is used in the incontestable clause, was decided by Justice Benjamin Cardozo in the case of *Metropolitan Life Insurance Co.* v. *Conway.*[5] There, in some of the most frequently quoted words in life insurance contract law, he said:

The provision that a policy shall be incontestable after it has been in force during the lifetime of the insured for a period of two years is not a mandate as to coverage, a definition of the hazards to be borne by the insurer. It means only this, that within the limits of the coverage the policy shall stand,

[5] 252 N.Y. 449, 169 N.E. 642 (1930).

unaffected by any defense that it was invalid in its inception, or thereafter became invalid by reason of a condition broken. Like questions have arisen in other jurisdictions and in other courts of this state. There has been general concurrence with reference to the answer. . . .

Where there has been no assumption of the risk, there can be no liability. . . . The kind of insurance one has at the beginning, that, but no more, one retains until the end.[6]

The "Entire Contract" Provision

Statutory Language. The New York Insurance Law also requires the inclusion of:

A provision that the policy shall constitute the entire contract between the parties, or, if a copy of the application is endorsed upon or attached to the policy when issued, a provision that the policy and the application therefor shall constitute the entire contract between the parties.

Policy Provision. A typical policy provision in compliance with this requirement reads as follows:

This policy and the application, a copy of which is attached when issued, constitute the entire contract.

Comment. This provision is so universally used that the need for it is historical only. It rests upon a standard rule of contract law to the effect that contracting parties may incorporate into their contract, by reference, any document they wish. It must be in existence at the time the contract is made and the reference must be expressly made and in such a way that the document to be incorporated can be clearly identified. However, when this is done, the document so incorporated becomes an integral part of the agreement in question, and its terms are part of the terms of the contract.

In connection with the life insurance contract, this practice was peculiarly unfair. Provisions of the company's charter and bylaws, for example, could by express reference be made an effective part of a life insurance contract even though the insured had never seen them and sometimes was unaware of their existence. This statutory provision made incorporation by reference impossible in connection with the life insurance contract and confined the contract to the policy and the application, if the latter were attached. As a result, the owner of a life insurance policy has in his contract every document which relates to the privileges and benefits under his policy.

Misstatement of Age

Statutory Provision. The age of the applicant is so important that a misstatement of age of a year or two may make a significant differ-

---

[6] The incontestable clause is of such importance in the law of the life insurance contract that Chapter VIII is entirely devoted to a discussion of it.

ence in the total premiums that should have been paid. For this reason, there are frequent problems in connection with the question of the obligations of the company where the age of the insured has been misstated.

The required standard provisions law requires the policy to include a provision as follows:

> If the age of the insured has been misstated, the amount payable and every benefit accruing hereunder shall be such as the premium paid would have purchased at the correct age.

Policy Provision. An illustrative policy provision reads as follows:

> If the age of the insured has been misstated, the amount payable and every benefit accruing hereunder shall be such as the premium paid would have purchased at the correct age.

This provision assures the policyholder that all cases involving misstatements of age will be decided in a uniform manner. Without it, such problems could be resolved either by adjusting the amount of insurance or by refunding or paying the difference in premium. Since the amount of insurance is adjusted in every case, the beneficiary is precluded from "buying" more insurance than the insured was entitled to, simply by paying the difference in premium after the death of the insured.

Divisible Surplus

Statutory Provision. One of the most important abuses brought out in the Armstrong Investigation concerned the dividend practices of some of the larger life insurance companies in connection with their participating policies. As a result, one of the recommendations with respect to legislation took the form of making it mandatory for companies to ascertain and apportion divisible surplus to the various policies and policyholders at frequent intervals. The New York Statute requires:

> A provision that the insurer shall annually ascertain and apportion any divisible surplus accruing on the policy.

Policy Provision. An illustrative policy provision reads as follow:

> *Dividends.* Annual dividends such as the company may apportion shall be payable while this policy is in force, other than as extended term insurance, without condition as to the payment of any subsequent premium. . . .

The immediate effect of this provision is to deny the company discretion with respect to when divisible surplus shall be apportioned. In connection with the operation of the policy, the allocation and payment of dividends concerns premium payment primarily. For that reason the effect of this required provision will be discussed in greater detail in the chapter devoted to the payment of premiums. Nonparticipating policies do not have this provision.

Nonforfeiture Values

Statutory Requirement. We have previously discussed the importance of the nonforfeiture provisions in the modern life insurance policy. One of the standard required provisions deals with this subject directly and requires:

A provision specifying the cash surrender values and nonforfeiture options available under the policy in the event of default in a premium payment after premiums have been paid for a specified period, together with a table showing, in figures, the options so available, and also the loan values, if any, available during each of the first twenty years after the issuance of the policy. Such options shall include a cash surrender value, and shall conform with the requirements of subsection one of section two hundred eight or two hundred eight-a.

The Policy Loan Provision

Statutory Language. The policy loan provision, like the nonforfeiture provisions, grew out of the legal reserve, level premium system. The nonforfeiture values are provided to guarantee to the policyholder an equitable share of the values he has helped to accumulate. However, they are operative only in case of lapse. To extend these values to the policyholder who does not wish to lapse his policy and yet has need to use his potential cash surrender value as collateral, the policy loan was made available, first on a voluntary basis and later by statutory requirement. The New York statute is long and will be quoted here only in part, as follows:

A provision that after three full years' premiums have been paid, the insurer issuing the same will, at any time while the policy is in force, advance, on proper assignment or pledge of the policy and on the sole security thereof, at a specified rate of interest, not exceeding four and eight-tenths per centum per annum if payable in advance or the equivalent effective rate of interest if otherwise payable, a sum equal to, or at the option of the person entitled thereto less than the amount required by section two hundred eight-b under the conditions specified thereby; . . .

Policy Provision. The policy provision is also lengthy as a general rule. An illustrative provision reads, in part, as follows:

Policy Loan. At any time while this policy is in force, other than as extended term insurance, the company, upon receipt of this policy and a loan agreement satisfactory to the company, will advance to the insured on the sole security of this policy any amount which shall be within the limit of the maximum loan value, if any, less any existing indebtedness to the company on this policy. The maximum loan value shall be that amount which, with interest at the rate of five per cent per annum to the date on which the next premium is due or, if no further premiums are payable, to the next anniversary of the Policy Date, equals, as of such date, the sum of the cash surrender value and any unapplied premium deposit reserve.

Legal Problems. Legal questions concerning policy loans relate first to the question of the basic legal nature of a policy loan. Next, they concern the question of interest, and lastly the right of the company to cancel the policy if and when the amount of the loan, plus interest, equals or exceeds the amount of cash surrender value available under the policy. These questions will be discussed at some length in the chapter on policy loans.

Automatic Premium Loan. In the past, various states have enacted laws requiring companies to include in their policies a provision for an automatic premium loan. By virtue of these provisions, the companies are required, in the event of a default in premium payment, and if there is a sufficient loan value for the purpose, to establish a loan against the policy for the purpose of paying the premium that is due.

Such requirements are no longer in force under the laws of any state except Rhode Island. There, the law requires the inclusion of an automatic premium loan provision in all policies issued in or for delivery in that state. Although not required elsewhere, a great many companies include it in their policies on a purely optional basis.

The Reinstatement Clause

The Statutory Requirements. With respect to reinstatement, the New York statute requires:

A provision that the policy will be reinstated at any time within three years from the date of default, unless the cash surrender value has been exhausted by payment or unless the period of extended insurance has expired, upon the application of the insured and the production of evidence of insurability, including good health, satisfactory to the insurer and the payment of all overdue premiums and the payment or reinstatement of any other indebtedness to the insurer upon said policy with interest at a rate not exceeding six per centum per annum compounded annually.

This may be contrasted with the Illinois statute, which requires:

A provision that if in event of default in premium payments the value of the policy shall have been applied to the purchase of other insurance as provided for in this section, and if such insurance shall be in force and the original policy shall not have been surrendered to the company and cancelled, the policy may be reinstated within three years from such default, upon evidence of insurability satisfactory to the company and payment of arrears of premiums and the payment or reinstatement of any other indebtedness to the company upon said policy, with interest on said premiums and indebtedness at the rate of not exceeding six per centum per annum payable annually.[7]

[7] Ill. Revised Statutes, Chap. 73, Sec. 836(i) (1959).

It will be noted that the New York statute provides that reinstatement must be granted "unless the cash surrender value has been exhausted by payment or unless the period of extended insurance has expired. . . ." On the other hand, the Illinois statute states that the policy may be reinstated "if . . . the value of the policy shall have been applied to the purchase of other insurance . . . and if such insurance shall be in force and the original policy shall not have been surrendered to the company and cancelled . . ."

Thus, under the New York law reinstatement would be available even if there were no cash value in the policy. In that case there would be neither cash value to be exhausted nor extended insurance to expire, and the statutory exceptions would not be applicable. Under the Illinois law, reinstatement would not be compulsory unless the policy had been in force long enough to acquire nonforfeiture values prior to its lapse, values which would "have been applied to the purchase of other insurance," i.e., extended term or reduced paid-up insurance. Neither of these statutes requires reinstatement after the cash value has been paid or the policy surrendered, and neither requires reinstatement after three years from the date of default.

It is especially notable that reinstatement is not required after the cash value has been paid or the policy surrendered. The surrender of a policy is a deliberate act. Thus it must be assumed that the insured has selected surrender in preference to the options under which the privilege of reinstatement would have been available. To permit reinstatement later would be to open the door for selection against the company.

The Policy Provision. A representative policy provision of the type used today reads as follows:

If this policy lapses and a cash surrender value has not been paid, the company will reinstate it at any time within three years from the date of lapse, subject to any indebtedness to the company on this policy at the date of lapse, upon receipt of evidence of insurability, including good health, of the insured satisfactory to the company and payment of all arrears of premiums with interest at the rate of five per cent per annum on such premiums and on any such indebtedness.

Comment. This provision says, in effect, that if the policy lapses it will be reinstated any time within three years from the date of lapse. This privilege is subject to any policy loan in effect at the date of lapse and is conditioned upon evidence of insurability, including good health of the insured "satisfactory to the company." All unpaid, back premiums must be paid, plus interest, and if a policy loan was in effect at the date of lapse, it must be repaid or reinstated.

It should be pointed out that in the absence of a statute, the reinstatement of the lapsed policy would not necessarily require a special policy provision. Contracting parties are always free to modify their agreement, discontinue it, and put it back into effect as they may agree. The insurance company and the insured, therefore, may always in the absence of either a statute or policy provision, reinstate a lapsed policy on whatever conditions they may agree. To include this right as a provision in the policy itself, however, simply adds another to the valuable "bundle of rights" in the policy. It also makes it unnecessary to negotiate concerning the terms of reinstatement when a request is made.

Historical Development. The reinstatement clause came into general use in life insurance policies in this country during the last decade of the last century. Until about 1905, there were no laws requiring a company to include a reinstatement clause in the policy, but by that time many companies were voluntarily including such a clause. At the present time, more than half the states (thirty-two by actual count) have laws which require that any policy issued for delivery in their state must include a reinstatement provision.

Significant Company Practices. Two interesting variations or modifications of the usual reinstatement clause are sometimes found in practice. One is a contractual provision under which the policyholder of a lapsed policy is granted an additional period of thirty-one days within which he may reinstate without submitting evidence of insurability.[8] This is not just a matter of company practice but a contractual right. Undoubtedly there is some selection against the company. However, it is assumed that most persons exercising this right have lapsed their policies inadvertently and are still satisfactory risks, and that the administrative savings are sufficient to offset any possible adverse selection.

A second method of achieving the same result is found in the "late remittance offer" included in the formal notice of lapse which a number of companies mail to their policyholders. The "late remittance offer" is an offer of the insurer "to accept a late remittance without requiring evidence of insurability." One illustrative offer is limited to a period of thirty-one days after the expiration of the grace period and beyond that date it is no longer valid. Payment of the past-due premium must be tendered before the death of the insured. It is specifically provided that the offer to waive evidence of insurability is "a special offer and is not to be considered a precedent," that it is not an extension of the grace period, and "does not continue the protection in force."

These practices illustrate two approaches to the problem of reinstatement. One is a contractual right and the other a privilege which the insurer offers its policyholders after their policies lapse. Each has

---

[8] Massachusetts Mutual Life Insurance Company has used a contractual provision of this kind for many years.

its advantages. Under the first method the policyholder has a contractual right to reinstatement without evidence of insurability within thirty-one days after the expiration of the grace period although he may not, as a matter of fact, be aware of it. Under the second method he receives express notice, but he has no contractual right, so that the company has the right to discontinue its practice at any time. From the point of view of the policyholder, perhaps these procedures should be combined. He would then have the contractual right as well as notice upon lapse of the policy.

PROHIBITED PROVISIONS

Nature of the Prohibited Provisions

The freedom to make contracts without unreasonable restriction is one of the great basic freedoms. However, it may be limited in the interests of public policy if such restrictions seem necessary for the public good. In addition to specifying certain required provisions, therefore, the laws of most of the states also include some provisions which may not be included in life insurance policies because they are considered adverse to the public interest.

Introductory Language. The Illinois statute, for example, lists a number of prohibited provisions, introduced with the following clause:

After the effective date of this Code no policy of life insurance shall be issued or delivered in this State if it contains any of the following provisions: ...[9]

Commencement of Action

One of the more usual prohibitions refers to provisions restricting the period of time within which an action at equity or at law concerning the policy may be begun. The Illinois statute expresses this by prohibiting:

(a) A provision limiting the time within which any action at law or in equity may be commenced to less than three years after the cause of action shall accrue.

Comment. In the absence of a specific statute, a contractual limitation with respect to the time within which suit must be brought will generally be upheld. If there is no such contractual limitation, the question will be governed by the general statutes of limitations which have been enacted by most of the states to establish time limits within which suits must be brought on different kinds of specified actions.

Statutes of Limitations. The general statutes of limitations are not

[9] Note: This and all remaining references in this section to the Illinois statutes are to Ill. Revised Statutes, Chap. 73, Sec. 837(1), (1959).

ordinarily too restrictive with respect to the periods of time during which actions may be brought. Illinois, for example, requires an action on any written contract to be brought within ten years of the date the cause of action accrued. However, a delay of this length in bringing an action under a life insurance contract could mean a definite inconvenience to life insurance companies. For this reason the statutory provision quoted above permits the period to be considerably shortened by specific provision in the contract, but not to less than three years. A number of other states have provisions of this kind, specifying periods of time ranging from one to six years. The most frequently specified periods are two and three years.

Dating Back

Occasionally the applicant will wish to have the policy dated back to "save age," which simply means to obtain the benefit of a lower premium by reason of a lower age. Within reason, there should be no objection to this. On the other hand, it can result in a definite inequity if the date back is an extensive period of time. For instance, the contestable and suicide periods may present some problems by reason of a theoretical effective date on which the policy was not in fact effective. To prevent abuses resulting from such practices, many of the states have enacted statutes making it unlawful for companies to date back policies beyond a stipulated period, usually six months prior to the date of the original application for the insurance.

Statutory Language. Illustrative of this type of prohibition, the Illinois statute prohibits the inclusion of:

A provision by which the policy shall purport to be issued or take effect more than six months before the original application for the insurance was made.

"Less Value" Statutes

Statutory Language. The "less value" statutes, enacted in a number of states, present a basic question by reason of their apparent conflict with many of the other provisions of the policy, particularly aviation amendment provisions. The Illinois statute prohibits the use of:

A provision for any mode of settlement at maturity after the expiration of the contestable period of the policy of less value than the amount insured on the face of the policy plus dividend additions, if any, less any indebtedness to the company on or secured by the policy, and less any premium that may by the terms of the policy be deducted, except as permitted by clause (c) of subsection (1) of section 224.

Legal Problems. This type of statute is obviously intended to prevent the company from promising benefits on the face of the policy which are later curtailed or extinguished in the body of the policy. The practices of most companies of excluding the hazards of war and aviation under some circumstances have brought provisions to that effect into direct conflict with this type of statute. The above quotation, however, specifically provides for such exceptions in its reference to "clause (c) of subsection (1) of section 224," which relates to aviation and war hazard restrictions.

Forfeiture with Respect to Policy Loans

Statutory Language. The Illinois Insurance Code also forbids:

A provision for forfeiture of the policy for failure to repay any loan on the policy, or to pay interest on such loan, *while the total indebtedness on the policy, including interest, is less than the loan value thereof.* (Italics added.)

The italicized portion of this statute points up the type of abuse the law is directed toward preventing. It should also be noted that it thus implements the required standard provision with respect to policy loans.

Agent of the Insured

Statutory Language. It will be recalled that courts have generally held void and of no effect any attempt on the part of an insurance company to make the agent, by policy provision, the agent of the insured for the purpose of taking the application. The Illinois Insurance Code specifically enacts this into the insurance law of the state by prohibiting:

A provision to the effect that the agent soliciting the insurance is the agent of the person insured under said policy, or making the acts or representations of such agent binding upon the person so insured under said policy.

The judicial decisions with respect to this type of provision have already been discussed.

The Policy as Reviewed

The basic promise of the life insurance company is summarized on the face page of the policy. The nonforfeiture section is made up of provisions and tables concerning benefits available to the insured in the event the policy should lapse for nonpayment of premiums. The settlement section contains the specifications concerning the persons to whom the benefits payable at the death of the insured are to be paid and explanations and tables relating to the optional methods of such payment. A third general group of provisions includes the required standard provisions relating to a grace period, incontestability, reinstatement, misstatement of age, etc. At this point there remain for discussion only those additional provisions which are not necessarily required but which the company will want to include to make the policy more understandable and to facilitate its administration.

OTHER POLICY PROVISIONS

Optional Provisions

Every life insurance company develops its own company philosophy, which will be evident in the make-up of its policies as well as in the wording of the various provisions. After it has complied with the different statutory requirements, therefore, each company will include some policy provisions which are not required, such as the assignment, suicide, and automatic premium loan provisions, and others which simply make the policy more understandable, more easily administered, or more favorable to the insured. These provisions will be reviewed briefly at this point, even though a more detailed discussion will be found in other sections of this book.

Ownership Provisions

No General Pattern. There is no general pattern with respect to ownership provisions in the average life insurance policy. Most policies are issued on the application of the insured, who names a revocable beneficiary and thus has full ownership and control over the policy throughout its existence. Most companies also have ownership policies which are applied for and issued to persons other than the insured, so that the rights of the insured and the rights of the owner are not necessarily the same. In order to make quite clear who has the right to control the policy during the lifetime of the insured, companies often state specifically in the policy who is the owner and what his rights are. The following provision illustrates this type of clarification of rights:

This policy shall belong to the Owner named herein. The word Owner in this policy shall include the successor or transferee of the Owner. The rights and privileges stated in this policy may be exercised by the Owner during the lifetime of the Insured without the consent of any beneficiary. If this policy becomes payable by reason of the death of the Insured and if the Insured immediately before his death was not the Owner, then the Owner may exercise the special rights granted in the Settlement Provisions of this policy.

The Owner may transfer this policy to a new Owner only by a written instrument satisfactory to the Company. Such a transfer shall be effective only if endorsed on this policy. The effective date of an endorsed transfer shall be the date the instrument was signed but a transfer shall be subject to any payment made or action taken by the Company before this policy is endorsed.

This practice is not new. The first policy issued by the Mutual Life of New York was applied for by a wife on the life of her husband, she being both the owner and the beneficiary. However, the frequent use of ownership policies is a modern development, most widely applied in business insurance cases. A provision of this kind points up the insured's ownership as a dominant element of the policy and makes it quite clear that he has the right to initiate policy transactions and exercise any of the ownership privileges under it. The title status of the policy is readily ascertainable at all times. It should be noted, however, that the designation of an irrevocable beneficiary will limit the right of control as specified in this provision.

Permits Transfer of Ownership by Endorsement. One of the specific advantages of this type of provision is that it permits a transfer of ownership and the designation of successor owners by policy endorsement, thus making the company a party to such changes. This is not true of changes of ownership by assignment, which often create uncertainty because of the doubtful effect of the assignment instrument and the fact that the life insurance company is not a party to the assignment.

The Assignment Provision

Not Actually Required. The owner of a life insurance policy has the right to assign it as a matter of law, and a policy provision to that effect is not required. In accordance with this fact, policy provisions with respect to assignment do not generally "grant" the right to assign. Instead, they define the company's responsibilities in case the owner elects to exercise his right to assign the instrument. One such provision reads as follows:

The Owner shall have the sole right to assign this policy. The interest of any beneficiary in this policy and any settlement option elected shall be subordinate to any assignment made either before or after the beneficiary designation or settlement option election.

The Company assumes no responsibility for the validity or effect of an assignment of this policy or of any interest therein. It shall not be charged with notice of any assignment unless the assignment is in writing and filed at its Home Office.

An assignee is not an "Owner" and an assignment is not a "transfer" as these terms are used in this policy.

Eliminates Conflicts. No language is more effective in clarifying rights than the simple statement in this provision that: "The interest of any beneficiary in this policy and any settlement option elected shall be subordinate to any assignment made either before or after the beneficiary designation or settlement option election." Other wordings have been used to accomplish this same purpose. Regardless of the language, however, the effect is to clarify a conflict which has arisen many times between the interest of the named beneficiary and that of any assignee of the policy, particularly creditor-assignees. This provision makes it clear that the assignee's rights shall be superior to those of the beneficiary and eliminates the need for litigating what was once a frequent conflict.

The Suicide Clause

If the policy does not specifically exclude suicide as a risk assumed, it is generally considered to be covered by the life insurance policy. Some states specifically limit the period of time during which suicide can be excluded, and one state, Missouri, does not recognize its exclusion for any period of time whatsoever. Generally speaking, the law recognizes the possibility that insurance policies may be obtained by persons who at the time of application are planning to take their own lives. On the other hand, the protection of the dependents of persons whose lives are terminated prematurely is one of the basic objectives of life insurance, and the reason for the death of the insured is secondary, from the point of view of his dependents. At any rate, the most typical suicide provision establishes a two-year period during which suicide will not be covered and eliminates all restrictions thereafter. This is generally considered to effect a reasonable compromise between the interests of the insurance company and society, on the one hand, and the dependents of the persons who take their own lives, on the other.

Policy Provision. An illustrative policy provision reads as follows:

If within two years from the date of issue the Insured shall die by suicide, whether sane or insane, the liability of the Company shall be limited to payment in one sum of the amount of premiums paid.

At one time there was a question with respect to the insurer's liability if the policy had no suicide provision and the insured contemplated suicide at the date of application. The consensus is that this constitutes a fraud against the company and there can be no recovery under the policy, even in Missouri.

Since most modern life insurance policies contain a suicide provision, this type of question does not generally come up today. However, there are very definite questions concerning the meaning of the phrase "sane or insane" and exactly what constitutes insanity. Other sources of litigation in connection with the suicide clause concern the possibility of conflict with the incontestable clause and the effect of reinstatement upon the suicide clause, both of which subjects are discussed elsewhere.

Change of Plan

Purpose of the Provision. The parties to any contract may, by mutual consent, change their agreement to incorporate new terms or even to effect an entirely new contract. This is equally true with respect to the life insurance contract, and a "change of plan" provision is often used to make this clear.

Illustrative Policy Provision. An illustrative provision of this type reads as follows:

This policy may be changed to any plan of insurance acceptable to the Company upon payment of such cost, if any, and subject to such conditions as the Company shall determine.

CHAPTER **VII**

Waiver of Premium for Disability and Death by Accidental Means

THE VARIOUS PROVISIONS that make up a typical ordinary life insurance policy were discussed in Chapter VI. In this chapter we turn to two almost standard additional coverages offered by most of the larger life insurance companies today: waiver of premium in the event of total and permanent disability and insurance in the event of death by accidental means.

In most cases these coverages are available upon request and for an additional premium. Occasionally they are an integral part of the policy, folded in, so to speak, and the premiums for each are included in the over-all premium for the policy. In other cases they are added to the policy by means of supplementary sections or contracts, known as riders. Regardless of how they are provided, however, the wording is not materially different, and in either case they present some of the most difficult legal problems in the law of the life insurance contract. The purpose of this discussion is to give some idea of the wording and purposes of these coverages and to discuss some of the more important of the legal problems they present.

WAIVER OF PREMIUM FOR DISABILITY

Historical Background

Early Benefits. Disability benefits were first offered in connection with the life insurance contract around the beginning of the present century, in the form of a waiver of premium for disability. Disability income was added later, first in the amount of $10 per month per $1,000 of the face amount of the policy and later in increasing amounts.

Disability Income. In offering disability benefits of any kind, the life insurance companies were embarking on what was for them an uncharted sea. No longer were they dealing with the clear-cut and ascertainable loss that death ordinarily presented. Disability is a highly subjective risk, and the only statistics available on which to base their original rates related to an entirely different set of circumstances, the experience of the fraternal orders which had been in the disability business for some time. To complicate the situation further, competition soon caused the companies to expand their benefits rapidly even though they had no assurance that their rates were adequate.

By the middle 1920's, it was recognized that the premiums for disability coverage were inadequate. Before any definite steps could be taken to remedy the situation, however, the depression had struck and with it came some of the most extremely unfavorable experience ever suffered in this or any other field by the life insurance industry. So disastrous was the period that the majority of the larger companies ceased issuing disability income coverages entirely. During the past several years, a number of life insurance companies have resumed offering this coverage although under considerably more scientific terms. Nevertheless, the disability coverage which relates most closely to the life insurance itself is the waiver of premium for disability. For that reason this discussion will be confined largely to that subject, although disability income cases will be referred to at times in connection with the definition of terms and clarification of problems common to both types of coverages.

Definition of the Risk

What Is a Disability? Exactly what kind of impairment is disabling is, of course, a subjective question. A relatively minor physical problem can be disabling to one person, an extensive impairment only a challenge to another. Obviously, therefore, disability, in the sense of an insurable risk, cannot be defined generally in terms of actual physical limitation. The concept must include the idea of loss. Disability insurance, therefore, is insurance against loss by reason of disability, and that loss is defined in terms of the insured's inability to work.

Policy Wording. The disability section of most life insurance policies provides for a waiver of premium benefit in language similar to the following:

Upon receipt at its home office of due proof that the insured has become totally and permanently disabled as hereinafter defined, and subject to all the terms and conditions of this section, *the company shall waive the payment of each premium becoming due during the continuance of such disability* commencing with the premium due on or next following the date of commencement of such disability, provided, however, that no premium shall be waived, the due date of which is more than one year prior to the date of receipt by the company at its home office of written notice of claim hereunder on account of such disability. (Italics added.)

Comment. This provision establishes two major requirements. The disability must be total and it must be permanent. Exactly what constitutes "total" disability is presumably made clear in the definition which is usually worded somewhat as follows:

Total . . . disability is disability as the result of bodily injury or disease originating after the insurance under the policy and this section took effect so that the insured is and will be thereby wholly prevented from performing any work, following any occupation, or engaging in any business for remuneration or profit, . . .

The Legal Problem. Literally interpreted, benefits payable on the happening of a contingency defined in these terms would very rarely be payable. Must one be so disabled as not to be able to work at anything? If so, an almost complete paralysis would not be disabling within the terms of the coverage, since a man sufficiently gifted and with sufficient spirit could presumably work at something. On the other hand, is it sufficient that one be only so disabled that he is unable to resume his usual and ordinary occupation? In that case the surgeon with a slight hand impairment would qualify even though he might turn to other fields of medicine with equal or better financial rewards.

Thus it has been necessary from the first to interpret this definition, and it will be remembered that the language of the contract will be construed most strongly against the life insurance company. Whether an insured is totally disabled within the meaning of the definition is a question of fact, and questions of fact are ordinarily determined by the jury. However, the court instructs the jury with respect to the law.

What "Total" Disability Means. Most life companies have followed a liberal course in their claim policy, and by far the majority of court decisions take the position that total disability does not mean a state of absolute helplessness as would be true if the definition were literally applied. Instead, the term is interpreted by the majority of courts to mean a disability of such a nature as to prevent the insured from working at his customary occupation or in any other occupation for which his background and physical and mental capacity might reasonably fit him.

There have been holdings to the effect that if the insured is unable to work at his customary occupation he is totally disabled within the meaning of this provision. However, this in effect makes it an occupational coverage, and most courts recognize it as a nonoccupational coverage. Other courts have held that if the insured is able to work at any kind of work he is not disabled. However, the majority view takes the middle course, that total disability means inability to perform his usual occupation or any other occupation for which his education and training might fit him.

An excellent summary of these views is given in *Anair* v. *The Mutual Life Insurance Company of New York*,[1] where the court said:

> . . . The decisions may be divided into three groups. In the first it is held that disability exists within the meaning of the provision if the insured is unable to work in his usual occupation, thus, in effect, changing the provision to an occupational disability provision. In the second group the test is declared to be inability to work in any occupation. In the third group an intermediate position is taken. The cases in this group recognize that "total disability" is a relative and not an absolute term or concept. For this reason the cases in this latter group make total disability depend on whether it is shown that the insured is unable to work at or follow an employment or occupation for which he is qualified, mentally or physically, by age, experience, education or training. Under this construction the occupation or work of the insured is included and others similar thereto.

When Is Disability "Permanent"?

The Legal Problem. If the courts have been somewhat uncertain as to the interpretation of the term *total* with respect to disability, they have been equally divided with respect to *permanent.* The vagaries of human existence being what they are, the only truly permanent disability obviously is one which continues until the death of the insured. However, this can scarcely be what the insurers meant. Do they not include in their own policies provisions relating to the cessation of benefits upon recovery? Obviously, under these circumstances, they cannot have contemplated only disability continuing until the death of the insured. Again, therefore, there is the entering wedge of ambiguity and the necessity of interpretation by the courts.

It seems relatively certain that in the early days the companies meant a permanent disability to be one of long-term duration. How long, however, is a different question; and what of the disability from which the insured has already recovered at the time suit is brought?

The Court Decisions. A majority of the courts have held that a permanent disability is a disability lasting for an indefinitely continuous period of time. Generally speaking, therefore, if the insured has recovered at the time the suit is brought, his disability is considered not to have been permanent, and he is not entitled to benefits. Some courts have given to the term its ordinary meaning, that the disability shall

---

[1] 114 Vt. 217, 42 Atl.2d 423, 159 A.L.R. 547 (1945).

continue until the end of the insured's lifetime. However, the more reasonable point of view is summarized in *Kramer* v. *Metropolitan Life Insurance Company*,[2] where the court quoted from a prior Ohio case, as follows:

The term "permanent disability," as used in a disability insurance policy providing for payments to one who "has become totally and permanently disabled so as to be unable at any time to perform any work or engage in any business for compensation or profit," does not mean that such disability must necessarily continue for the remainder of the life of the insured, but that it shall, with reasonable probability, continue for some indefinite period of time.

The Waiting Period

Policy Wording. As a general rule the disability section of the policy defines total and permanent disability as disability which wholly prevents the insured "from performing any work, following any occupation, or engaging in any business for remuneration or profit, and which disability has continued uninterruptedly for a period of at least six months . . ."

Efforts have been made to have this six months period construed to mean that any total disability which has continued for the period named will be presumed to be permanent in the literal sense of the word. As a general rule today, however, the courts have held that it is merely a waiting period, included in the policy for the purpose of relieving the insurance company of the expense of having to consider and investigate numerous premature claims. Actual permanency, however, is a different matter.

DEATH BY ACCIDENTAL MEANS

Policy Wording

It is customary to offer, in connection with the basic life insurance policy, a coverage which provides an additional benefit in the event of death by accidental means. Like the waiver of premium for disability coverage, this is available upon request and for an additional premium. It is also made an integral part of the policy in some instances or added to it in the form of a supplementary section or rider in others. Regardless of the mechanics of its inclusion in the policy, however, it usually provides that, in addition to the death benefit under the policy, an additional death benefit will be payable . . .

. . . on receipt of due proof that the death of the insured resulted directly, and independently of all other causes, from bodily injury effected solely through external, violent, and accidental means as evidenced by a visible contusion or

[2] 144 Ohio St. 13, 56 N.E.2d 248 (1944).

wound on the exterior of the body (except in case of drowning or internal injuries revealed by an autopsy) and that such death occurred within ninety days from the date of such injury.

Although most of the phrases used in this provision have presented legal problems at one time or another, none has been the cause of greater disagreement than the term "accidental means." This concept constitutes the heart of the provision and for that reason will be discussed first.

Accidental Means

Perhaps the majority of life insurance policies which include this coverage provide that the additional benefit is payable not in the event of accidental death but in the event of death by accidental means. The latter term is readily and clearly defined by most insurance people and insurance lawyers, particularly company counsel, as death resulting from causes which themselves are accidental. In other words, both the cause and the result must have been accidental. Thus if one's car should skid on an icy pavement, crash into a stone wall, and cause one's death, it is death by accidental means. However, many deaths which are properly termed "accidental" are only the accidental result of actions which themselves are intentional and performed in the usual and generally accepted way. Courts which adhere to a strict definition of the term, therefore, hold that deaths of the latter type are not within the accidental means coverage.

Illustrative of this type of decision is the case of *Avent v. National Life and Accident Insurance Company*,[3] decided in 1954 by the Tennessee Supreme Court. The insured in that case was receiving treatment for a stiff neck. The treatment, administered while the patient lay on a table, consisted mainly in the manipulation of the insured's head and neck. At the conclusion of a treatment late in 1951, it was noted that the insured was unable to move. He was taken to a hospital immediately where surgery revealed a chipped bone in his neck. He died thirty-six hours later.

The insurance company took the position that death was the result of a voluntary and intended act and thus was not caused by accidental means. On behalf of the beneficiary it was contended that "excessive force and pressure was unintentionally and accidentally applied . . . and, as a result, a bone in the neck was accidentally broken."

The court held for the company, saying:

. . . It is not sufficient that the injury be unusual and unexpected, but the cause itself must have been unexpected and accidental. . . .

[3] Commerce Clearing House Life Cases (2d) 662 (Tenn., 1954).

The cause of the injury which resulted in the death of Avent was the aforesaid manipulation of his neck. That manipulation was not unexpected or accidental. It was intended by both Avent and the doctor. The means, therefore, producing the injury were not accidental under the rule followed in this State. That being so, the action of the court in sustaining the demurrer was correct.

The student's own probably mixed reaction with respect to whether this death should come within the coverage intended under this section of the policy will illustrate the basic problem before the courts. Does one apply the distinction with strict logic, as was done in this case, or should one take a less technical and thus more liberal approach to the question?

The Court Decisions

Generally speaking, approximately half of the states recognize a distinction between accidental death and death from accidental means. However, the distinction is so often qualified in its application to actual cases that it is generally agreed that there is a definite trend toward its abolishment. In fact the courts of some states have taken a clear-cut stand to the effect that all distinctions between the terms have been abolished in their jurisdictions.

Two Cases of Note. Two cases are perhaps referred to more frequently than most others. One is the case of *United States Mutual Accident Association* v. *Barry* [4] decided in 1889 by the United States Supreme Court. The other is *Landress* v. *Phoenix Mutual Life Insurance Company et al.,* [5] decided by the same court in 1934.

In the Barry case, the insured, a doctor, died from internal injuries after jumping from a platform four feet high. Another doctor, who had made the same jump, testified that the insured made a heavy, inert sound when he landed. The trial court was upheld by the Supreme Court in the following instructions to the jury:

In other words if a result is such as follows from ordinary means, voluntarily employed, in a not unusual or unexpected way, then, I suppose it cannot be called a result effected by accidental means . . . you must go further and inquire . . . was there or not any unexpected or unforeseen or involuntary movement of the body, from the time Dr. Barry left the platform, until he reached the ground, or in the act of alighting? . . . Did he accomplish just what he intended to do, in the way he intended to do?

However, the court went further and said:

. . . if, in the act which precedes the injury, something unforeseen, unexpected, unusual occurs which produces the injury, then the injury has resulted through accidental means.

---

[4] 131 U.S. 100, 9 Sup. Ct. 755, 33 L. Ed. 60 (1889).

[5] 291 U.S. 491, 54 S. Ct. 461, 78 L. Ed. 934, 90 A.L.R. 1382 (1934).

Instructions of this kind illustrate some of the problems that face the courts when they attempt to make and adhere to a completely valid distinction between the terms *accidental means* and *accidental results,* with respect to an actual set of facts. The Barry case is particularly notable since it has been cited as supporting authority both by courts adhering to a strict interpretation of the term "accidental means" and by those who approach the problem more liberally.

The *Landress* case was decided in 1934 and concerned the death of a golfer by sunstroke. The court held that it was not a death by accidental means, a decision definitely contrary to the weight of authority today. The case is notable, however, because of the dissenting opinion by Mr. Justice Cardozo in which he said: "The attempted distinction between accidental results and accidental means will plunge this branch of the law into a Serbonian Bog."

Many scholars and jurists have quoted Mr. Justice Cardozo's words approvingly, and the consensus as well as the trend of decisions seems to be in favor of a liberal interpretation of the term "accidental means." Nevertheless this liberality is manifested rather in the admission of individual refinements than any general move to abolish all distinctions between the terms.

For example, if the phrase "accidental means" is used in the policy, the majority of courts would not hold the insurance company liable if the injury resulted from an intentional act performed exactly as it was intended to be performed. However, very few cases present facts which can be so neatly classified. The problems arise when a factor is present which was not intended or not known.

This point is often illustrated in connection with drug dosages. Let us say that the insured intended to take a safe quantity of a certain drug and instead took an overdose. A number of courts have held such deaths to be the result of accidental means. However, if the insured took a standard and safe dose but died because of an unusual and unknown sensitivity to it, the problem is different. Ordinarily this would be termed an accidental result and would not be within the coverage of the death from accidental means section of most life insurance policies. However, some jurisdictions take a sufficiently liberal approach to the question to recognize the presence of an unknown factor as sufficient to satisfy the requirement of accidental means.

Intentional Acts with Unintended Results

Where There Is an Unintended Factor. When the act was intended and was performed in the manner intended, only the result being accidental, it is still rather more than likely that a court will hold that the death is not death by accidental means. The growing tendency, however, is to note any slight irregularity in the performance of the act, any slip so to speak, and to hold it sufficient to satisfy the accidental means requirement. Thus if the insured pushes his car and dies of over-exertion, death is an accidental result. However, if he pushes his car, slips and is injured, dying of infection or other complications, the result would be held to have been caused by accidental means. In borderline cases this difference becomes rather tenuous.

Where There Is an Unknown Factor. There is also a large group of cases in which the insured does exactly what he intended to do in the way he intended to do it, and the result nevertheless is fatal. The situation is not changed, of course, if the action is that of another with the consent of the insured. Many anesthetic cases fall into this group, where the insured has an unusual, unknown, and unascertainable sensitivity to the anesthetic and dies on the operating table. Some courts take the position that this is an accidental result and not within the accidental means coverage. Others hold that the unknown factor is so unexpected and unusual that the sequence of events constitutes accidental means.

For example, in a South Dakota case decided in 1945, the court said:

> Plaintiff's evidence in this case was that butyn, the anesthetic, was injected into the body of insured. This was external and violent means. The evidence also shows that death resulted therefrom and that such result was unexpected and unforeseen. The result was therefore accidental. From these facts the trial court had the right to infer that the means were also accidental.[6]

It is in accordance with this general theory that the majority of courts today hold that death by sunstroke is death by accidental means. Illustrative of this type of holding is the case of *Raley v. Life and Casualty Insurance Company of Tennessee,* decided in the District of Columbia Municipal Court of Appeals in 1955. This case presents such an excellent summary of the major problems involved and of the court decisions on the subject that we are quoting it with only minor cutting, at page 194 of this chapter.

The stricter point of view is illustrated in the case of *New York Life Insurance Company, Appellant v. Bruner, Appellee.*[7] In that case the Indiana Appellate Court decided in October, 1958, that the death of the insured as the result of hypersensitivity to a spinal anesthetic was not death from accidental means. The insured, who had been given a spinal anesthetic prior to surgery for the removal of his appendix, had

---

[6] *Wolfe v. Order of United Commercial Travelers of America,* 18 N.W.2d 755 (S.D., 1945). Note: This decision was later reversed by the United States Supreme Court on other grounds.

[7] 153 N.E.2d 616 (Ind. App., 1958).

a peculiar sensitivity to the drug used and died almost immediately. The court said:

> Here the act of administering the anesthetic was performed voluntarily and exactly in the manner intended, and with the insured's consent. No mischance, slip, or mishap occurred in doing this act. The means employed were intentional and not accidental. The fact that a result followed which was unusual, unexpected or unforeseen is not sufficient to establish liability under the provisions of the policies in question.

Intentional Injury Inflicted by Another

As a general rule, if the insured dies as the result of a blow struck by another without his consent, his death is considered death from accidental means. If the insured is the aggressor, this is not true. Nor is it accidental if he deliberately exposes himself to what he knows are dangerous circumstances. Some of the borderline problems in this area, however, are suggested in a recent Illinois case, *Yates* v. *Bankers Life and Casualty Company*,[8] decided by the Illinois Supreme Court in March, 1953.

In that case the insured, who had been physically impaired since the age of eight, limped into the home of the Richardson family, apparently completely by mistake and with no evident intention of doing any harm. He walked into the living room, hands extended and open, carrying no weapon, making no threats or menacing gestures. He did not answer when spoken to, but the testimony showed that he had been hard of hearing as well as partially paralyzed since childhood. Richardson pushed him, by the shoulders, out the front door where he stumbled, fell backwards, and struck the back of his head. He died as the result of a skull fracture.

The court held that death resulted from accidental means, explaining:

> It is evident, therefore, that decedent's bewildered conduct can in no way be analogized to the type of aggressive action involved in the *Cory* and *Hutton* cases, hence, those decisions may not properly be deemed determinative. Moreover, irrespective of those cases, the death of the decedent as a result of a fall under the circumstances presented in this record cannot be deemed to be the natural and probable consequence of his confused conduct in walking into Richardson's house in full view of the occupants without manifesting an evil or aggressive intention. We do not know his purpose in limping into that household, but can only surmise from the nature of his conduct therein that he did not enter pursuant to a malevolent design which could conceivably have led to his death. As in the *Barry* case, the injuries and death of Yates were caused by something unforeseen and unexpected occurring in the course of an intentional act, i.e., the backward fall from the living room to the lower level of the porch and down the step onto the cement sidewalk, where he hit the back of his head and fractured his skull. Therefore, under the concept of

_____
[8] 111 N.E.2d 516 (Ill., 1953).

"accidental means," adopted and reiterated by the Illinois court, the jury could properly have found that the death of the insured Oliver Yates was caused by accidental means, and that plaintiff, as beneficiary of the policy issued by defendant upon Yates's life, was entitled to recover thereunder.

Other Requirements

"Violent" Means and "External and Visible" Marks. Generally speaking, the courts have been rather liberal in interpreting the requirements that the means be external and violent. With respect to "violent," for example, the word is generally held to contemplate an act that is unusual, but as a requirement it is satisfied by even a very slight force. The courts have also been liberal in interpreting the requirement that the injury be evidenced by external and visible marks. Thus any objective symptoms that are discernible or perceptible will be held sufficient.

"Risks Not Assumed"

In order further to define the kind of risk the insurer intends to cover in providing the accidental means death benefit, many companies specifically name some risks they do not intend to assume. Some of the more frequently named in this connection are risks of death resulting from the inhalation of gas, bodily infirmity or disease, and death as the result of war or aviation.

Inhalation of Gas. As a general rule, if there is no exclusion in the policy with respect to death as the result of inhaling gas, such deaths will be held caused by accidental means. If the policy contains an exclusion, the provision will ordinarily be upheld. In this area, however, company practices are sometimes more liberal than the court decisions. This is because most companies have no objection, on principle, to paying the accidental means death benefit in cases where death results from the unintentional inhalation of gas. They do, however, object to paying an accidental death benefit in the case of suicide. Because it is extremely difficult to prove an intentional death in many cases, particularly those involving the inhalation of carbon monoxide, and because the burden of proof is on the company in such cases, deaths of this kind are often excepted as a "risk not assumed." As a matter of claim policy, however, this exception is often liberally interpreted if there is no reason to believe that the death was other than accidental.

War and Aviation Risks. There have been conflicting decisions with respect to deaths in battle, but in the absence of a policy exclusion, such deaths are ordinarily considered deaths by accidental means. Since many policies except or limit the basic liability of the company in cases where death results from war or aviation activities, the accidental death section also usually excepts deaths of this kind from the accidental means death benefit.

Bodily or Mental Infirmity, Illness, or Disease. One of the most frequent problems in connection with deaths by accidental means arises out of situations in which there is an admitted accident but where the insured is also suffering from a disease of a relatively serious nature which might have caused his death exclusive of the accident. Let us suppose that the insured is involved in an automobile accident, suffers injuries of an undetermined severity, and dies. In the resulting investigation it is revealed that the insured had been receiving treatment for a serious heart condition for some time. The question then presents itself: What part did the diseased heart play in this death which would presumably otherwise have resulted from accidental means?

If the injury causes a disease and death results, it is generally agreed that the accident will be considered the actual cause of the death. It is also a general rule that the fact that the insured had a bad heart at the time of the injury will not relieve the company from liability under the accidental means death section of its policy if the accident is the direct cause of death. This is true even if the policy specifically excepts death caused by disease.

If the accident would otherwise have caused the death and the disease was only remotely concerned, there is no question. However, if the injuries were relatively slight and the heart condition very serious, the fact that a slight injury preceded the heart attack will not actually convert the situation into an accidental means case.

Borrowing from the law of torts, the lawyer frequently uses the word "proximate" in this connection to indicate a cause which is either directly responsible for the injury or which initiates an unbroken chain of events, each causing the next, which leads to and logically effects the result alleged. Thus if the accident is the *proximate* cause of the death, it is ordinarily considered to be death from accidental means. If the diseased condition is the proximate cause, the death is not from accidental means. The question will therefore ordinarily go to the jury for decision.

✿ ✿ ✿ ✿ ✿

ILLUSTRATIVE CASE

The following case illustrates a great many of the problems which have been discussed in this chapter. Extensive citations have been omitted from the opinion in the interest of brevity, but otherwise the actual reasoning of the court is presented in full in order that the student may see for himself the approach taken by a court in considering questions of this kind.

RALEY, Appellant v.
LIFE & CASUALTY INS. CO. OF TENNESSEE, Appellee [9]
(District of Columbia, Municipal Court of Appeals.)

CAYTON, Ch. J.: The question on this appeal is whether an industrial accident insurance policy covered death caused by sunstroke. The action was brought by appellant as widow and beneficiary under the policy, which was written on the life of Thomas F. Hoy. It was stipulated that Mr. Hoy collapsed at an intersection in Arlington, Virginia, on a June afternoon in 1952, and was taken to a hospital where he died several hours later. It was also stipulated that the "sole and exclusive cause of the death of Thomas F. Hoy was exposure to the sun's rays, that is to say, sunstroke." An official weather report, submitted under the same stipulation, revealed that an extreme heat wave was in progress in this locality at the time of the mishap. The trial court ordered judgment for the insurance company and plaintiff brings this appeal.

The policy insured "against loss of life through accidental means" and recited, "if the insured sustains drowning or bodily injury effected solely through violent, external and accidental means, and if such drowning or bodily injury is the direct, independent and proximate cause of the death of the insured within 90 days from the date of such injury, and if such death is not caused or contributed to by disease or infirmity, the Company will on surrender of the policy pay the principal sum specified herein. . . ."

It seems clear, as the insurance company concedes, that because the policy was executed and delivered in this jurisdiction, the rights of the parties are to be decided according to District of Columbia law. . . .

Urging us to declare that under the law of this jurisdiction a policy of this kind does not cover death caused by sunstroke, appellee insurance company relies on *Landress* v. *Phoenix Mutual Life Insurance Company*, 291 U.S. 491 (1934). There the Supreme Court, in a sunstroke case, said: ". . . the carefully chosen words defining liability distinguish between the result and the external means which produces it. The insurance is not against an accidental result. The stipulated payments are to be made only if the bodily injury, though unforeseen, is effected by means which are external and accidental. . . ." The court ruled that the insurance company was not liable.

If the language just quoted must be regarded as governing all situations of this kind, the answer in this case would be plain and the beneficiary would be out of court. (We later discuss the dissenting opinion of CARDOZO, J., which has been widely quoted and generally approved.)

But the answer is not so simple, for a number of reasons. First, we must consider that four years after the *Landress* case, *supra*, came the far reaching decision in *Erie R. Co.* v. *Tompkins*, 304 U.S. 64 (1938). There the Supreme Court overruled the hundred-year-old doctrine of *Swift* v. *Tyson*, 16 Pet. 1 (1842), and held that there is no federal general common law and that Congress and the federal courts as well are without power "to declare substantive rules of common law applicable in a State whether they be local in their nature or 'general,' be they commercial law or a part of the law of torts." The court went on to rule specifically that the common law so far as it is enforced within a State is not the general common law, but the law of that State as declared by its legislature or its highest court.

---

[9] 117 A.2d 110 (D.C.C.A., 1955).

Thus whatever the effect of the *Landress* decision in the State of Tennessee where the case arose, it cannot be said to have declared general common law or to be binding on State or Federal courts generally. A large number of Federal as well as State courts have departed from the view expressed in *Landress* and expressly ruled that death by sunstroke is a death caused by accidental means and is not merely an accidental result. The decided trend of recent decisions establishes that the majority view today is that sunstroke is covered by this type of policy, and that disability or death induced by sunstroke is caused by "accidental means." . . .

Another group of cases, not dealing specifically with sunstroke, advances the general proposition that the term "accidental means" is synonymous with "accidental result" and "accidental death." . . .

We refer also to several well considered workmen's compensation cases in which the same general views have been expressed. . . .

In their brief, counsel for appellee urge that workmen's compensation cases should be disregarded. They say: "The spirit and intent of the workman's compensation law vary considerably from the principles of contract and insurance law, and to apply the reasoning of workman's compensation cases to the issue here would be error."

While we recognize that these are two different fields of insurance law, we cannot agree that for the purpose of the single question before us there is any reason in logic or common sense for applying a stricter rule in one than in the other. In both situations the same basic test applies in determining whether an "accidental means" produced the fatality.

Cases taking the contrary view are listed in the majority opinion in the *Landress* case, and in Appleman, Insurance Law and Practice, Vol. 1, Sec. 447.

We have already mentioned that in *Landress, supra,* there was a dissenting opinion by CARDOZO, J. That opinion has several times been quoted, adopted and followed by other courts, and it seems wise to quote parts of it here:

Sunstroke, though it may be a disease according to the classification of physicians, is none the less an accident in the common speech of men. . . . The suddenness of its approach and its catastrophic nature . . . have made that quality stand out when thought is uninstructed in the mysteries of science. . . . Violent it is for the same reason, and external because the train of consequences is set in motion by the rays of the sun beating down upon the body, a cause operating from without.

In my view this man died from an accident. What killed him was a heat-stroke coming suddenly and unexpectedly upon him while at work. Such a stroke is an unusual effect of a known cause, often, no doubt, threatened, but generally averted by precautions which experience, in this instance, had not taught. It was an unlooked for mishap in the course of his employment. In common language, it was a case of accidental death.

Textwriters have pointed to the dissent, not only as stating the "better" rule, but as expressing the view now adopted by a majority of courts. Vance on Insurance, 3d Ed., p. 949; Richards on Insurance, Vol. 1, Section 17, p. 59. Appleman, Insurance Law and Practice, Vol. 1, Section 447. At page 555 the author says: "The dissenting opinion of Justice Cardozo presents one of the most brilliantly reasoned opinions in the field of insurance law, and certainly the best at expressing the reasons in back of the rule adopted by the majority of jurisdictions."

In this jurisdiction there has been only one appellate decision on the subject and that made the flat declaration that death from sunstroke is an accidental injury. *Fidelity & Casualty Co. of New York v. Burris*, 61 App. D.C. 228, 59 F.2d 1042 (1932). There the deceased was engaged in manual labor on an intensely hot day. He collapsed on his way to a water barrel and was taken to a hospital where he died later that same day "from heat prostration or sunstroke." The broad language of the opinion, per GRONER, J., gives the answer to our question:

> The decision of the case turns, we think, upon the answer to two questions: *First, is death from sunstroke an accidental injury?* Second, did the sunstroke arise "out of and in the course of employment"? *Both questions should be answered in the affirmative.* (Italics supplied.)
>
> The term "accidental injury," as used in the act, means any unexpected misfortune or mischance resulting in some form of bodily injury— an injury due to accident or caused by some sudden or unexpected occurrence. Deceased admittedly was killed by sunstroke. That was the injury. It was sudden and unexpected, and hence accidental. . . .

It is true that it was a workmen's compensation case, but there was nothing in the decision limiting its application to that class of case, or indicating or even suggesting that a different result would have been reached if an industrial insurance policy were involved. Nor, as we have already said, is there any logical reason for not applying the same rule to industrial policies.

Other and much more recent decisions in this jurisdiction also point to a holding of liability in this case. It has always been the law that ambiguities are to be resolved in favor of the insured (or beneficiary) and against the insurance company which prepared the policy. That rule has recently been extended and strengthened. In *Hayes v. Home Life Ins. Co.*, 83 U.S. App. D.C. 110, 112, 168 F. 2d 152, 158 (1948), it was said that customers of insurance companies: ". . . are, in vast majority, not informed in the obscurities of insurance expertise and not equipped to understand other than plain language. If the companies were permitted to write clear clauses of liability at one point and obscure negations of liability at another, and to maintain successfully the prevalence of the latter over the former, the temptation to sell on one clause and defend on the other would be dangerous."

That decision was cited and followed as recently as this year in *Buchanan v. Massachusetts Protective Asso.*, D.C. Cir., U.S. App. D.C., 223 F.2d 609. There the court stressed the duty of an insurance company to spell out in plainest terms—terms understandable to the man in the street—any exclusionary or delimiting policy provisions, and said that the court would: "insist upon language which unambiguously conveys such an intent to the mind of an ordinary layman. Failing such unambiguous language, doubt should be resolved in favor of the insured."

With these rules to guide us, we think our course in this case is clear. We think we must rule that the collapse and death of Mr. Hoy was not only accidental in final result, but that an "accidental means" produced the fatal injury. Laying aside "insurance expertise," and laying aside also a purely technical, scientific or medical approach to the situation, it must be said that Mr. Hoy's death was caused by "violent, external and accidental means" as surely as if he had been struck down by a bolt of lightning, or by a tree or other physical object hurled against him by a strong wind.

Reversed, with instructions to enter judgment for plaintiff.

CHAPTER **VIII**

The Contract
Is Contested

Validity and Contract Law

What Validity Means. As previously discussed, certain basic requirements relating to offer, acceptance, consideration, etc., must be met before an agreement will have effect as a binding informal contract. Even when these requirements have been satisfied, however, there are other factors which, under special circumstances, affect the validity of a contract.

Some of these factors are of such fundamental importance that their presence or absence, as a matter of law, will make an attempted contract void, that is, no contract at all. For instance, a contract of life insurance issued to someone with no insurable interest in the life insured is void as a matter of law. Other factors have less serious consequences and merely give one or the other of the parties the privilege of canceling (avoiding) the contract without liability or, alternatively, of permitting it to stand in accordance with its terms. Used in this sense, the validity of a contract means its legal "sufficiency," as contrasted with mere regularity.

Factors Affecting Validity. The situation where a rule of law or a statute declares a certain kind of contract void, as a matter of public policy, has been previously discussed. However, the validity of a contract may also be affected by a mistake or mistakes of the parties, by misrepresentation, and by fraud. Although these general subjects have many subdivisions, all relate to and affect the validity of contracts under some circumstances.

The purpose of this chapter is to discuss those circumstances as they relate to contracts in general and to see some of the modifications that have been made in connection with their application to the life insurance contract in particular.

MISTAKES, MISREPRESENTATION, AND FRAUD

Mistakes . . .

. . . *Of Law.* If the parties to a contract are mistaken with respect to the legal effect of certain facts with reference to which the contract is made, they are said to have made a mistake of law. If there has been no error in connection with the facts, a mistake of law will not affect the validity of the contract.

. . . *Of Fact.* Under some circumstances a mistake of fact may be sufficiently serious to avoid a contract. However, the mistake must relate to a fact which is material, that is, a fact which enters into and forms the basis of the contract. For example, a mistake as to the existence of the thing bargained for will destroy the validity of the contract.

A mistake of fact made by only one party (a *unilateral* mistake) does not ordinarily avoid a contract. This assumes that there was no misrepresentation and that the other party did not contribute to the error in any way. In any case where fraud contributes to the mistake the contract may be avoided. There is also considerable authority to support the statement that a mistake on the part of one party to a contract, known by the other, will afford a basis for relief by reformation of the contract. The theory is that if A made a mistake and B noticed it but said nothing, it would be inequitable not to grant reformation on A's request. This rule is often relied upon in connection with actions for the reformation of the life insurance contract.

Misrepresentation

Misstatements of Fact. In general contract law, even though one party has induced the other to act by misstating a fact, the contract is ordinarily valid if the misstatement was not intended to mislead. In some kinds of relationships, however, the party misled in circumstances of this kind has the right to have the contract set aside (avoided). Contracts between persons in relationships of unusual trust and confidence, such as guardian and ward, parent and child, trustee and *cestui que trust* (the beneficiary of the trust) are included in this class.

Concealment. Generally speaking, the fact that one party did not volunteer information which the other might have liked to know does not give the second party the right to avoid the resulting contract. However, if the parties occupy a confidential relationship they have a duty to reveal information of material significance, and if it is not so volunteered, the injured party will have the right to rescind the contract.

Fraud

If either party to a contract is guilty of fraud, the contract is avoidable at the election of the other party. Fraud has never been completely defined, partly because circumstances vary from case to case, and partly also because the dividing line between being defrauded and being careless is very, very thin. In general terms fraud is any misrepresentation of a material fact, made with the knowledge that it is not true or with a reckless disregard of whether it is true or not, made with the intention that the other party will act in reliance upon the statement, where the latter is entitled to rely upon it, does so, and suffers injury as a result.

Intent. Basic in fraud is the matter of intent. The person guilty of fraud must either have known that the information was false and thus have intended to mislead the other, or he must have acted with a reckless disregard of the truth or falsity of his statement. Obviously it is impossible to determine definitely what anyone intends. However, if the objective circumstances are such as to make it clear that he knew that the information was false, or if he spoke with a reckless disregard of whether what he said was true or false, his intent to defraud will be presumed.

What a Misstatement Is. By its very nature, a misstatement of fact must relate either to the present or the past. With respect to the future, the only misrepresentation possible is a misstatement of intention, and that can constitute fraud only if a promise is made with the intent not to keep it. A misstatement of opinion or of value will not ordinarily be considered fraudulent unless it is made by an expert who has information not available to the other party and who makes the misstatement of opinion with the intention that the other will act in reliance upon it to his detriment. A misstatement of law falls in the same category.

Reliance upon the Statement. The injured person must rely upon the misstatement and must suffer damages as the result. If he knew the truth, or if he could have ascertained it merely by looking at something readily available, he cannot maintain that he was the victim of fraud. Under such circumstances he would not have been justified in relying upon the misstatement. If the truth is hidden, if the subject matter is so technical that he cannot be expected to understand it, or if means of ascertainment are not available, he may rely on the statement and, if injured, claim fraud. If there is no damage, however, there is ordinarily no actionable wrong.

How Rights May Be Lost

Under Voidable Contracts. If a contract is voidable it can be set aside by the injured party. If he does not set it aside, the contract is valid and enforceable. The injured party may also lose the right to rescind or avoid a contract if, knowing all the facts, he affirms the transaction, does not object within a reasonable time, or retains property and uses it after knowledge of the facts. These rules are of the highest importance in connection with voidable life insurance contracts.

VALIDITY AND THE LIFE INSURANCE CONTRACT

Misrepresentation

The General Rule. As previously noted, the general rule is that if one party to a contract has induced the other to act by innocently misstating a fact without intending to mislead, the validity of the contract is not affected. However, it will be recalled that in some kinds of relationships a person who enters into a contract by reason of misrepresentation, even though the misstatement is innocently made, will have the privilege of avoiding the contract when the misstatement is discovered. In relationships of unusual trust and confidence, this is the rule. Thus it is also the rule in connection with the life insurance contract, which is generally considered to be a contract of the highest good faith (*uberramae fidei*).

In Life Insurance. It will be remembered that in order for the insurance principle to function in life insurance it is necessary that the lives to be insured be selected carefully so that the actual mortality experienced will approximate that assumed under the mortality tables used. For purposes of making this selection, the insurance company requests, in the application form, detailed information from the applicant concerning the health, family history, occupation, etc., of the proposed insured. Often there is a medical examination and ordinarily a routine inspection.

In the case of nonmedical coverages the company makes its risk appraisal decision almost entirely on the basis of the representations of the applicant in the application. The assumption is that these representations are true. The applicant signs the application with the understanding that the company will rely upon them. If they are not true, the company will have been induced by misrepresentation to make a contract with a person with whom it would not have contracted if the truth had been made available. Although modified by statute in many states, the general rule is that a misstatement of a material fact, even though innocently made, will give the insurer, at its option, the right to rescind the contract.

In this connection, perhaps it should be noted that life insurance companies occupy a quasi-fiduciary relationship to their policyholders with respect to the funds collected from them and held. Thus any contract that would not have been made except for material misrepresentations in the application gives that policyholder an unfair advantage over all the other policyholders in the group. In fairness to the other policyholders, therefore, such a contract should be avoided in accordance with the right given the insurance company as a matter of basic contract law.

How Misrepresentation Is Found. Material misrepresentation in the application for a life insurance policy is most commonly discovered in connection with the payment of death benefits. As a matter of routine, any life insurance company initiates investigation into the background of medical history and other factors relating to insurability, in connection with any claim which arises during the contestable period of the policy. In the course of these investigations some instances of material misrepresentation in the application are discovered. If the misrepresentation is sufficiently serious the claim will be denied.

Sometimes material misrepresentation is discovered during the lifetime of the insured. For instance, when an application is received it is a matter of routine for the company to search its records for previous applications submitted or policies already in force on the life of the proposed insured. If the company did not do this it would have no control over the aggregate amount of insurance issued on any one life. Companies also have frequently been held to be on notice, as a matter of law, with respect to any information concerning applicants which may be in their files. Remember, in this connection, that the right to avoid a contract is lost if the injured party, knowing all the facts, affirms the transaction or fails to object within a reasonable time. Knowledge is an extremely important element in this area of contract law.

As a matter of procedure it is also important to distinguish between material misrepresentation discovered during the lifetime of the insured and that discovered after his death. The legal procedures initiated by the company are different when it is dealing with a living policyholder-insured from those utilized in connection with remedies available after the insured's death.

The Test of Materiality. Generally speaking, the test of materiality is whether the company would have taken different risk appraisal action on the application if it had known the truth about the fact or facts misrepresented. Suppose, for example, that the application question is: "What is the date of birth of the proposed insured?" The applicant answers: "September 17, 1934." As a matter of fact the date of birth is September 19, 1934. In this case there would be a misrepresentation but it would not be material to the risk. The decision of whether to contract or not to contract with that applicant would not have been different if the company had known the truth.

With respect to ill health and treatment by a physician, the answers could be equally unimportant. Suppose, for example, that the applicant records a visit to his personal physician in August, 1958, and states as his reason for the visit, "ankle sprain." As a matter of fact the condition was not technically a sprain. The distinction would not ordinarily be material to the risk. But if the proposed insured has been receiving treatment for a condition as serious as cancer or a heart impairment, the company is entitled to know it. Consequently, if questions on the application which are designed to bring out just that type of information are falsely answered, the applicant is guilty of a misstatement of a material fact. In such cases the insurance company is entitled to avoid the contract during the insured's lifetime or deny the claim at his death, if such action can be taken during the contestable period. Any question as to the company's right to take such action will, of course, be determined by the court.

Let us take, for example, an application from a man we will call George Anderson. Mr. Anderson owns a small business in a medium-sized town in a midwestern state. On June 2, 1959, he applies for $5,000 of term insurance for "mortgage protection." The company makes its routine check of previous applications and finds that it has two policies already in force on Mr. Anderson's life. One, in the amount of $3,000, was issued on September 26, 1958. The other, for $1,500, was issued on May 27, 1957. Both were on a nonmedical basis.

Two days after the new application is received at the home office a telephone call is received from agent Brown stating that Mr. Anderson has had a heart attack and is in the hospital in critical condition. Investigation discloses that he has had a serious heart problem for many years. He has been undergoing treatment with his present physician and had suffered at least one heart attack prior to the date of his earliest application for insurance with the company. However, no mention of any of this adverse health history was made on any of the applications. After a thorough inquiry into the facts, the company notifies the insured that his pending application is rejected and that the company is taking action to rescind the $3,000 policy previously issued—that is, to have it declared null and void. No action is taken with respect to the $1,500 policy.

Life insurance students will readily understand why the $1,500 policy was continued in force and why the company took steps to rescind only the $3,000 policy. "The $1,500 policy," they will explain, "was past the contestable period." But what is the contestable period, as a matter of law, and how does it operate? To understand this we must go back for a brief look at the incontestable clause in the life insurance policy.

THE INCONTESTABLE CLAUSE

The Policy Provision

The incontestable clause of the modern life insurance policy reads essentially thus: "This policy shall be incontestable after it has been in force during the lifetime of the insured for a period of two years from its date except for nonpayment of premium."

What It Means

As a Practical Matter. In the practical sense the incontestable clause simply means that after the policy has been in force for two years from its date the insurer is precluded from claiming that it is invalid as a matter of law. However, the exact meaning of the phrase, "invalid as a matter of law," has occupied some of the best legal minds for the past half century, and the question has not yet been settled.

As a Matter of Law. From the legal point of view, the incontestable clause of the life insurance contract is unique. It is not found in other kinds of contracts. In fact it is directly opposed to one of the most cherished maxims of contract law, that fraud vitiates a contract. In life insurance law, except for a very few decisions to the contrary, the maxim must be revised to read something like this: Fraud vitiates a contract unless it is a life insurance contract and the contestable period has expired.[1]

What then is so unusual about the life insurance contract that it should be required by law to include a provision directly contrary to a basic maxim of general contract law? To answer this question it is necessary to know something about the development of the life insurance contract in the light of contract law in general.

The Incontestable Clause

Why We Have It. As we have said, if the questions in the application concerning the health and insurability of the proposed insured are not answered truthfully, and if they are material to the appraisal of the risk, the life insurance company is entitled to rescind the resulting contract, or, if the insured has died, to deny the claim. There was a time, however, when the question of materiality was unimportant.

In the early insurance contracts the statements of the insured were warranties, and warranties were, and still are, quite different from representations. A representation is a statement made in connection with the formation of a contract, which tends to influence the other party's estimate in connection with the risk to be assumed. A warranty is part of the contract itself and is a statement or condition relating to a fact or action to be taken, which fact must be exactly true or which action must be taken in exactly the manner stated or the contract will be void.

During the latter half of the eighteenth and the early part of the nineteenth centuries, warranties in insurance contracts were enforced by the courts both of England and of the United States with complete technical exactness. If they were not true exactly as stated the insurer could avoid the contract. In connection with marine insurance, where

---

[1] Under The Uniform Life Insurance Act of Canada, however, a fraudulent statement gives the right to avoid the contract at any time.

the doctrine was first developed, this did not ordinarily work an unusual hardship. The contract of marine insurance was made with the insured himself, and ordinarily no extensive period of time had elapsed between its making and any litigation concerning it.

These same principles were applied to the life insurance contract with very different results. Here the contract had ordinarily continued for a number of years when its validity was first challenged. By that time, the person who had made the warranties was dead, and the beneficiary, who had had nothing to do with the negotiations for the policy, was seriously handicapped in defending against the assertions of the company with respect to the technical exactness of statements about which she knew nothing. Technically right, perhaps, the companies nevertheless found that by the latter half of the nineteenth century their readiness to litigate with respect to every deviation from the absolute truth in the application was creating an atmosphere of serious distrust.

To counteract some of this distrust the companies began voluntarily including in their policies a provision waiving their right to contest the policy after it had been in effect for a stated period of time. The first step of this nature was taken by the London Indisputable Life, an English company, which included a provision in its charter, in 1848, prohibiting itself from disputing a policy for any reason whatsoever. In the United States, the Manhattan Life Insurance Company, in 1864, introduced the incontestable clause in the form in which we usually think of it.

By the time of the Armstrong Investigation, in 1905, a majority of the companies were using an incontestable clause. The Standard Policy Law, enacted in New York following the Armstrong Investigation, included an incontestable clause and made its use mandatory. Later the Committee of Fifteen, which was appointed in the wake of the Armstrong Investigation, recommended model state legislation which also included an incontestable clause. This was subsequently enacted into law by considerably more than half the states.

Requiring an incontestable clause as a matter of law, however, did not succeed in solving the problems presented in connection with the validity of the life insurance contract generally. Unfortunately a new question arose almost immediately: What is a contest of the policy?

What Is a Contest?

It is generally agreed by lawyers and students of the life insurance contract that life insurance companies included the incontestable clause in the first place as a waiver of their right to contest the policy for misrepresentation, concealment, or fraud in the application. These are all factors which go to the essential validity of the policy. Nevertheless the wording of the clause itself casts much doubt upon this point and has probably been responsible for most of the adverse decisions which have been handed down by courts in which this question has been considered.

A very simple version of the clause was purposely quoted at the outset of this section. More frequently, the clause reads something as follows:

This policy shall be incontestable after it has been in force during the lifetime of the insured for two years from its date of issue, *except for nonpayment of premiums, and except for violation of its provisions regarding military and naval service.*

If the italicized exceptions had never been added, there would probably have been little question as to the legal effect of the clause. The word "contest" would have been accepted as meaning a challenge of the validity of the contract based on rules applicable to contracts generally. The incontestable clause would have been accepted for what it was undoubtedly intended to be, a pledge of good faith in the form of a waiver, after two years, of any legal right the company might otherwise have had to challenge the validity of the contract with respect to technical defects in its inception.

The Exceptions. Defenses based on nonpayment of premiums or violation of policy provisions regarding military and naval service have nothing to do with technical defects going to the validity of the contract. In fact, defenses of this kind assume the validity of the contract and allege a violation of its terms or failure to fulfill its conditions. To include them as exceptions to a challenge of validity, therefore, is to create a serious doubt concerning the meaning of the word "contest."

This doubt is increased by the application of a standard rule of construction to the effect that when one thing is specifically expressed in a policy provision or legal document, other similar items not so expressed are presumed to be excluded. Lawyers often state this rule in the Latin, thus: *Expressio unius est exclusio alterius.* When this is applied to the incontestable clause, the conclusion is that the company, having expressed one or two "exceptions" which are in reality defenses, should be required to except *all possible defenses* or be held to have waived them. In any case, this point of view has been taken by a number of courts. In those jurisdictions it would seem that the only way an insurer could be certain it would be permitted to rely on exceptions or exclusions expressed in its policies would be to incorporate them all into the incontestable clause itself.

Conflict with Other Policy Provisions

Since some valid defenses against liability were included as exceptions to a "contest," it seemed logical to many courts, on the grounds just indicated, that other defenses were waived. As a result the incontestable clause has been thought to conflict with many other clauses in the policy. The suicide clause, the misstatement of age clause, aviation exclusions, and any of the ordinarily accepted conditions specified in the policy have been thought to conflict with the incontestable clause and have been challenged on that basis at one time or another.

The Suicide Clause. The suicide clause of most policies provides that in case of self-destruction of the insured within one or two years, the company's obligation under the policy is limited to a return of the premiums. Is this payment of the premium only, in case of suicide within the first two years, a "contest" of the policy?

A number of the early courts held that it was. Where the suicide period was two years and the incontestable period only one year, these courts held that the company's defense, based on suicide, was barred by the incontestable clause. However, most later cases have held that the fact that the policy has become incontestable does not bar a defense of suicide if the suicide occurs within the suicide period. For example, one court stated that a defense based on suicide was just as permissible as a defense on the grounds that the insured was still alive. These cases, representing the majority opinion, simply hold that death by suicide, under a policy including a suicide clause, is a risk which was not intended to be covered until the lapse of a stated period of time. Thus, regardless of the incontestable clause, the insurer should not be held liable on a risk which the policy stipulated was not assumed.

Misstatement of Age. Because the age of the insured has such a vital relationship to the risk of death, a misstatement of age clause was commonly used by life insurance companies even before the introduction of the incontestable clause. With the growing use of the latter, however, the question arose as to whether an adjustment for misstatement of age could be made after the expiration of the contestable period.

In some of the earlier policies, misstatement of age was included in the incontestable clause itself as one of the exceptions. In such cases, the general holding has been that the incontestability of the policy does not prevent the insurer from making adjustments because of the misstatement of age. Since the latter is an exception, the incontestable clause is not operative in this area.

Even where a separate misstatement of age clause is used, the majority of the courts have reached the same conclusion, but for different reasons. For instance, in one 1939 case [2] the court held:

> No person can testify to his own age except from hearsay. No doubt many persons do not have accurate information as to their correct ages. Yet the cor-

---

[2] *Langan v. United States Life Insurance Co.*, 344 Mo. 989, 130 S.W.2d 479 (1939).

rect age of insurants is the chief corner-stone of the life insurance structure. If a person obtains insurance by stating a given age, nothing further being said on the subject in the policy, then, under the statute, it may be that the company can not question the correctness of the age stated. But is there anything in the statute which prevents a person from obtaining insurance at a stated age, qualified by a provision in the contract for adjustment according to correct age? We do not so read the statute. Nor do we know of any dictate of public policy to prevent such an age adjustment clause.

SOME MILESTONE CASES

The Monahan Case

The Facts. The case of *Monahan* v. *Metropolitan Life Insurance Company*,[3] decided in 1918 by the Illinois Supreme Court, marked one of the first important milestones in the development of the language of the incontestable clause. The case involved an incontestable clause which read as follows:

> After two years this policy shall be non-contestable except for nonpayment of premiums. . . .

Note that it made no mention of the lifetime of the insured, as is usually the case today. At that time it had not occurred to anyone that such wording was needed. If the insured died during the contestable period and there had been material misrepresentation or fraud in the application, it was not questioned that the company could deny the claim on that basis. The obligations of all parties to the contract were fixed as of the date of death, or so it was assumed. Thus even though suit were brought after the expiration of the period, the defense of misrepresentation would be available if the insured had died during the contestable period.

In the *Monahan* case the insured did die during the contestable period, there was misrepresentation in the application for the policy, and the company denied the claim. The beneficiary waited until after the expiration of the contestable period and then brought suit.

The Decision. The Illinois Supreme Court interpreted the clause literally. Since the contestable period had expired at the time of the suit, the court said, in effect, the company was precluded from defending on the basis of material misrepresentation in the application. In short, the fact that the insured died during the contestable period did not mean that a defense available at that time would continue to be available to the company even after the expiration of the period specified.

Results. According to the decision in the *Monahan* case, the insurer's only remedy in another situation presenting the same set of facts, would be to take action immediately, without waiting for the death claim to

---

[3] 283 Ill. 136, 119 N.E. 68 (1918).

be submitted, and bring suit for rescission prior to the expiration of the contestable period. In many cases this would have been inconvenient; in others, impossible.

For these reasons, steps were taken almost immediately to amend the various state statutes to permit the use of an incontestable clause including the words "during the lifetime of the insured." New York amended its standard provisions law to this effect in 1921, and Illinois adopted the same kind of law in the same year, with further provisions relating to the exception of benefits relating to disability and death by accident.

Shortly afterwards the National Convention of Insurance Commissioners recommended legislation permitting the inclusion of the "during the lifetime of the insured" phrase in the incontestable clause, and the statutes of most of the states have now been amended in this manner. As a result, when the policy includes an incontestable clause with this phrase, it is generally agreed that if the insured dies before the policy has been in force the specified period of time, the policy never becomes incontestable. Thus with an incontestable clause so worded another *Monahan* case would be impossible.

The Johnson Case

Another prominent case in which the incontestable clause was discussed is that of *Northwestern Mutual Life Insurance Company* v. *Johnson*,[4] decided by the United States Supreme Court in 1920. This case dealt with two life insurance policies, one of which had no suicide clause. One of the questions was whether a contract having no suicide clause was against public policy.

The opinion was written by Justice Holmes who said, among other things, that the suicide clause, though differently expressed, has the same kind of effect as the incontestable clause. After the expiration of the specified period, suicide is not a defense. However, he then continued to discuss the incontestable clause in the following language:

> . . . The object of the clause is plain and laudable—to create an absolute assurance of the benefit, as free as may be from any dispute of fact except the fact of death, and as soon as it reasonably can be done.

Taken out of context, this language would seem again to ignore the distinction between a dispute of the validity of the contract and a dispute of liability under it.

Metropolitan Life Insurance Company v. Conway [5]

How It Arose. This case arose, not between beneficiary and life in-

---

[4] 254 U.S. 96, 41 S. Ct. 47, 65 L. Ed. 155 (1920).

[5] 252 N.Y. 449, 169 N.E. 642 (1930).

surance company, but between life insurance company and the Superintendent of Insurance of New York. The latter had refused to approve an aviation rider which limited recovery to the payment of the reserve if the insured's death occurred under circumstances defined in the rider. He took the position that the provisions of the rider were inconsistent with the incontestable clause as required by the New York law. It was as if the Superintendent were saying to this company: "After two years from date of issue the incontestable clause prohibits you from contesting the policy. Yet you are now requesting permission to include in your policies a provision expressly declaring that if the insured should meet his death by reason of aviation activities you will not be liable for more than the reserve."

The company took the position that even though a policy became incontestable after two years, the company was nevertheless free to specify risks it was unwilling to assume at the outset and throughout the life of the contract. Thus under a policy so drafted as to provide that aviation deaths were not covered, the company in paying the reserve would, in effect, be carrying out the terms of the policy, not contesting it.

The case presented the basic question squarely. Does the word "contest," as used in the incontestable clause, mean a dispute of the policy based on circumstances or conditions giving the company the right to avoid it as a matter of law? Or does it mean any defense, on any grounds whatsoever, by which the company may be legally justified in paying less than the face amount of the policy?

The Decision. The appellate court held with the insurance company that an aviation rider was not a provision permitting the company to "contest" the policy if the insured were killed while engaged in aviation activities. The New York Court of Appeals upheld that decision in one of the most famous and classic expressions of life insurance law. The decision was written by Justice CARDOZO, later Justice of the United States Supreme Court, who said:

We agree with the Appellate Division in its holding that rider and statute in this instance are consistent and harmonious. The provision that a policy shall be incontestable after it has been in force during the lifetime of the insured for a period of two years is not a mandate as to coverage, a definition of the hazards to be borne by the insurer. It means only this, that within the limits of the coverage the policy shall stand, unaffected by any defense that it was invalid in its inception, or thereafter became invalid by reason of a condition broken. Like questions have arisen in other jurisdictions and in other courts of this state. There has been general concurrence with reference to the answer. . . .

The meaning of the statute in that regard is not changed by its exceptions. A contest is prohibited in respect of the validity of a policy, "except for non-payment of premiums and except for violation of the conditions of the policy relating to military or naval service in time of war." Section 101, Subd. 2.

Here again we must distinguish between a denial of coverage and a defense of invalidity. Provisions are not unusual that an insured entering the military or naval service shall forfeit his insurance. A condition of that order is more than a limitation of the risk. In the event of violation, the policy, at the election of the insurer, is avoided altogether, and this though the death is unrelated to the breach. No such result follows where there is a mere restriction as to coverage. The policy is still valid in respect of risks assumed.

Citing *Northwestern Mutual Life* v. *Johnson,* Cardozo continued:

> The clause there in question was not a limitation as to coverage. It was a provision for a forfeiture. . . . What was said by HOLMES, J., of the effect of the "incontestable clause," must be read in the light of the question before him. It is true, as he says, that with such a clause the death of the insured, coupled with the payment of the premiums, will sustain a recovery in the face of a forfeiting condition. It is quite another thing to say that the same facts will prevail against a refusal to assume the risk. Later cases in the Federal courts develop the distinction clearly.

Later Developments

The Bernier Case. The same question of the legality of aviation riders was presented to the Louisiana Supreme Court just two years after the *Conway* case was decided, in the case of *Bernier* v. *Pacific Mutual Life Insurance Co.*[6] In this case, the Louisiana court reached the opposite conclusion. In the course of its opinion the court said:

> The provision . . . making the contract incontestable after a stated period, means something more than that the insurer cannot then contest the validity of the policy on the ground of breach of a condition; it means that the company cannot contest its obligation to pay, on due proof of death of the insured, the amount stated on the face of the policy, except for a cause of defense that is plainly excepted from the provision making the policy incontestable.

The *Conway* case held that the incontestable clause was "not a mandate as to coverage." A few cases, illustrated by the Bernier holding, have held that it is a mandate as to coverage, that unless the cause of defense is "plainly excepted from the provision making the policy incontestable" the company cannot "contest its obligation to pay."

Other Possible Solutions

Legislation. Justice Cardozo's clear language has been a strong influence toward the view that the incontestable clause is not "a mandate as to coverage," but it has not been unanimously followed, as the *Bernier* case shows. Because of the possibility of other divergent opinions, therefore, attention has been turned toward a possible solution by way of legislation.

In one attempt to simplify the clause and clarify its meaning, the

_____
[6] 173 La. 1078, 139 So. 629 (1932).

Legal Section of the American Life Convention, in 1932, recommended wording which would have avoided the questions relating to "date of issue" and what constitutes a "contest" of the policy. Nevertheless, this wording has not been actively sponsored by the companies or the commissioners of insurance and has not been enacted into law in any state.

A later attempt was made in this direction in the late 1940's when the Joint Legislative Committee of the American Life Convention and the Life Insurance Association of America appointed a committee to draft model statutory provisions for use in connection with the revision of insurance laws in the various states. The incontestability statute recommended by this committee would have clarified the meaning of the word contest, but this wording also was never widely adopted.

Statutory Limitations of Coverage. A legislative remedy of a different nature was adopted in 1939 by the legislature of New York when it passed a law specifying exactly what limitations of coverage life insurance companies could include in their policies. This subsection of the standard policy provision law reads in part as follows:

2. No policy of life insurance delivered or issued for delivery in this state shall contain any provision which excludes or restricts liability in the event of death caused in a certain specified manner, except the following provisions, or provisions which in the opinion of the superintendent are substantially the same or more favorable to policyholders.[7]

Provisions relating to military and naval service, aviation, and suicide within two years from the policy date are specifically listed. Legislation of this kind has also been enacted in several other states.

CONCEALMENT AND FRAUD

Factors Relating to Validity

The factors most frequently involved in questions concerning the validity of the life insurance contract are misrepresentation, concealment, and fraud. For purposes of simplification, the previous discussion was devoted almost entirely to material misrepresentation in the application. With the effect of the incontestable clause clearly in mind, we turn now to the more technical factors of concealment and fraud.

Concealment and Fraud. The law with respect to concealment and fraud is closely related to material misrepresentation. Each goes to the essential validity of the contract and, if established, gives the insurer the legal right to avoid it. Specifically, however, the law is more technical both as to concealment and to fraud, and both are more difficult to establish.

---

[7] New York Insurance Law, Sec. 155, 2.

Concealment

Basis for Avoidance of the Contract. As we said earlier, the mere fact that one party does not disclose information which the other would have considered of value does not permit the latter to avoid the resulting contract, as a general rule. However, in relationships of special trust and confidence there is a duty to disclose any information that would be of value to the other party in considering whether or not he wishes to enter into the contract. Since the relationship between the life insurance company and the applicant is one of trust and confidence, there is a duty on the part of the applicant to disclose information which he knows or ought to know is material to the risk, even though no question relating to that particular subject may be included in the application.

A Form of Misrepresentation. In a sense, the failure to volunteer material information is misrepresentation by concealment. The word itself implies intent—the intentional hiding or withholding of information. The information the life insurance company considers material will ordinarily be requested by means of the detailed questions in the application. If information not so referred to is material to the risk, it is ordinarily so unusual in nature that it can hardly be assumed to have been innocently withheld. In any case, the rule is that concealment of a material fact in connection with the application for a life insurance contract will justify the life insurance company in avoiding the contract only if such information was withheld with fraudulent intent. An illustration will help in understanding how this rule applies.

✿ ✿ ✿ ✿ ✿

Illustrative Case. The following case is not reprinted in its entirety because of its length. However, the first half of the opinion and the conclusion are given in the exact words of the court because they illustrate so clearly the rule in cases of concealment and how it is applied.

DE BELLIS v. UNITED BENEFIT LIFE INSURANCE COMPANY [8]

(Pennsylvania Court of Common Pleas No. 5 at Philadelphia County.)

Kun, P. J.: On May 1, 1947, the defendant issued in the name of Rinaldo Joseph DeBellis combination life and health and accident policies, naming the plaintiffs, a brother and nephew, beneficiaries. The life was insured for $5,000, with provision for an additional payment of $5,000 in case of accidental death. On October 14, 1947, a little over five months after the policy was issued, the body of the insured was found under a railroad bridge in South Philadelphia, stabbed to death. The plaintiffs, in their affidavit as claimants, disclosed that the insured was also known as Joseph DeLuca, which also appeared in the

---

[8] 15 Commerce Clearing House Life Cases 343 (1952). Note: This case was appealed to and the decision affirmed by the Pennsylvania Supreme Court. The latter decision may be found at 372 Pa. 207, 93 A.2d 429 (1953).

death certificate. This was the first time defendant (the insurer) had any such information. The defendant on learning of the activities of the insured under the name of DeLuca, which will hereafter be referred to, refused to pay the claim. . . .

Defendant denied liability on the policy because it alleged that the insured made certain false and fraudulent representations in his application for the insurance, to wit, (1) as to his name and identity; (2) as to his habits being correct and temperate; (3) as to his occupation, and (4) as to prior medical attention or accident. . . .

At the trial, the plaintiffs produced the policy and proofs of death and rested. The defendant produced evidence which adequately proved that the insured, in 1938, had been involved in a shooting and had been shot by two men and treated at a hospital under the name Joseph DeLuca, had been charged with and convicted of a conspiracy to commit a felony and violation of the Uniform Firearms Act, and was sentenced to serve from three to six years in the Eastern State Penitentiary; that the insured was paroled in 1941, and that he was returned to the Philadelphia County Prison for violation of parole on November 15, 1941. He was thereafter transferred to the Eastern State Penitentiary in 1943, where he served until July 3, 1946, and thereafter paroled under a maximum sentence which would not expire until 1956. All this had occurred to the insured under the name of Joseph DeLuca, but he applied for the policy in suit under the name of Rinaldo Joseph DeBellis in 1947, while he was serving a sentence on parole under the name of DeLuca, which would not expire for nine years.

The principal question in the case is whether in the circumstances the insured was guilty of intentional misrepresentation sufficient to avoid the policy in concealing his true identity, and in answering "yes" to the question as to his habits being "correct and temperate." There is no case in point because, perhaps, never before has anyone ever had the temerity to procure insurance under such circumstances. On behalf of the plaintiffs it was argued that when the insured was asked his name, and he gave the name given him at birth, as he was not asked whether he had an alias or any other name, he made no misrepresentation. The law is not so naïve. The contention overlooks entirely the doctrine that in an insurance contract the utmost good faith is required of the insured because the insurer takes the risk largely on the representations of the insured. The contention also overlooks the principle that there may be misrepresentation by concealment. As stated in the early case of *Smith* v. *Columbia Insurance Co.*, 17 Pa. 253, at page 261:

> It is not sufficient for the insured to answer all the questions propounded to him. Like a witness on the stand, he is bound to tell the whole truth without waiting to be interrogated. The contract of insurance is eminently a contract of good faith.

In the later case of *Curry* v. *Sun Fire Office*, 155 Pa. 467, the principle of misrepresentation by concealment was again recognized. As stated in the syllabus, properly drawn from the opinion:

> If an applicant for insurance conceals his belief that an attempt has been made by unknown parties to set fire to his house, and his fear that the attempt might be repeated and his house burned, he is self-convicted of the concealment of a fact material to the risk, and he cannot recover on the policy.

In that case, because of subsequent explanations by the insured as to the nature of the incident referred to, it was held that the question was one for the jury. However, the principle as stated was recognized.

While these cases involved property insurance, the rule is no different in life insurance. No less a distinguished jurist than Judge Sharswood, in his charge to the jury in *LaFavour* v. *Insurance Company*, reported in 1 Phila. 558, stated that concealment of a fact material to the risk voids a contract of insurance. Judge Sharswood said:

> There is no doubt that this is the law in life policies as well as in policies of marine insurance. Good faith is required on the part of the assured. He knows, and the underwriter is not presumed to know, whatever is material, and he is not confined to the warranties contained in the policy.

. . . The doctrine is universally followed in all other jurisdictions and it has never been questioned in Pennsylvania.

It is true that ordinarily, where no question is asked of the insured and he makes no representations, he may presume that nothing more as to the risk is desired from him; but where there is something unusual about the situation which apparently increases the risk, he is bound to disclose it: 45 C. J. Section 115. Of course, not every nondisclosure will forfeit the policy, but as stated by Circuit Judge William H. Taft in the well-known case of *Penn. Mutual Life Insurance Co.* v. *Mechanics' Savings Bank and Trust Co.*, 72 Fed. 413:

> . . . It is clearly just to require that nothing but a fraudulent nondisclosure shall avoid the policy. Nor does this rule result in practical hardship to the insurer, for in every case where the undisclosed fact is palpably material to the risk the mere nondisclosure is itself strong evidence of fraudulent intention.

. . . What is the purpose of an insurer in asking for an applicant's name? It is not merely to learn the name in the abstract, but to identify the person dealt with so that inquiry may be made about him. We cannot conceive of any greater fraud on an insurance company than an applicant giving his name as "X" and failing to disclose that he is also known as "Y," when, in fact, under the name of "Y" he has a long criminal record and was actually at the time he applied for the insurance under the name of "X" serving a parole sentence under the name of "Y," which would not expire for nine years.

We think the trial judge on the evidence presented in the case, partly on the admissions in the pleadings and otherwise on uncontradicted evidence of the facts referred to without regard to other misrepresentations, should have directed a verdict for the defendant, since on this major point in the case there was no fact in dispute. The misrepresentations here, as to the applicant's name and as to his habits being "correct and temperate," were so gross the trial judge should have declared it as a matter of law.

✩   ✩   ✩   ✩   ✩

Fraud

Fraud has been defined as a material misrepresentation made by one party to a contract with the intent that the other party shall rely upon the information, where the second party has the right to rely upon it, does so rely, and suffers damage as the result. Misrepresentation may be by concealment which, if it is fraudulent, will give the life insurance company the right to avoid the policy. Actual misstatements, if intentionally made for the purpose of misleading, also constitute fraud.

Intent. The difficulty in connection with fraud is the problem of establishing intent. However if the facts are sufficiently clear, the courts will presume an intent to defraud. For example, in one Pennsylvania case [9] the applicant had had at least thirteen consultations with four different physicians in a city one hundred miles from her home within two years of the date of application. Yet she stated in her application that there had been no consultations with any physician within the past seven years. The court said:

> The consultations were clearly of such important character and of such recent occurrence as could not be forgotten, and the insured must have been fully cognizant that she hid them from the insurer by her false answer. In this connection, we said in *Evans* v. *Penn Mutual Life Ins. Co.*, 322 Pa. 547, 553:
> > The circumstances preceding and attending the making of the statements may be such that the insured must be said to have been aware of their falsity at the time, or that an inference of fraud is otherwise irresistible, as for instance where an unreported illness or disability of insured was so serious and so recent that he could not have forgotten it.

Statutory Modifications of the General Rule

The general rule is that even an innocent misstatement of a fact material to the risk will give the life insurance company the option to avoid the contract. The possibilities of abuse in connection with this rule have prompted the enactment of statutes in many of the states to clarify or modify it. For example, the Illinois Insurance Law specifically provides as follows:

> . . . No such misrepresentation or false warranty shall defeat or avoid the policy unless it shall have been made with actual intent to deceive or materially affects either the acceptance of the risk or the hazard assumed by the company.[10]

Under this statute an innocent misrepresentation which affects the acceptance of the risk will give the insurance company the right to avoid the policy, and it has been so interpreted numerous times.

Medical Examiner's Certificate. On the other hand, a number of the states have enacted legislation requiring that the misstatement be made with fraudulent intent before the company may avoid the contract. One of the more unusual types of statutes in this area of the law is found in the Iowa Insurance Code. This statute makes it necessary to prove fraud in any case where a medical examiner has certified to the soundness of the risk. The Iowa statute reads as follows:

---

[9] *Bailey* v. *The Pacific Mutual Life Ins. Co. of Calif.*, 336 Pa. 62, 6 Atl.2d 770 (1939).

[10] Illinois Revised Statutes, Chap. 73, Sec. 766 (1959).

In any case where the medical examiner, or physician acting as such, of any life insurance company or association doing business in the state shall issue a certificate of health or declare the applicant a fit subject for insurance, or so report to the company or association or its agent under the rules and regulations of such company or association, it shall be thereby estopped from setting up in defense of the action on such policy or certificate that the assured was not in the condition of health required by the policy at the time of the issuance or delivery thereof, unless the same was procured by or through the fraud or deceit of the assured.[11]

In the case of *McNabb* v. *State Farm Life Insurance Company*,[12] decided in 1953, the Iowa Supreme Court quoted the requirements that must be met by the company, in the light of the statute, as follows:

We have frequently held that to establish the affirmative defense of fraud required by this section, the proof must be clear, satisfactory, and convincing, and must show (1) a material representation of an existing fact (2) its falsity (3) scienter [13] (4) intent that it be relied upon (5) that the examining physician relied and acted thereon and (6) that the company was thereby defrauded.

In the *McNabb* case the applicant in his application denied having received medical treatment of any kind during the past five years. As a matter of fact he had been a patient in an institution for the treatment of mental disorders for several months, less than two years prior to the date of the application, and during that time had received several shock treatments. The court concluded:

Upon the entire record the court finds that the false statements quoted in this memorandum were fraudulently made, concerned material matters, that they were believed and relied upon by defendant's examining physician and the defendant and induced the issuance of the policy in suit.

FRAUDULENT IMPERSONATION

Effect of Fraud

Wording of the Incontestable Clause. The incontestable clause which is most frequently used today establishes a period of one or two years within which the life insurance company can make whatever investigations it wishes and after which the contract shall be incontestable. In spite of the general attitude of the courts with respect to fraud, it is held that a defense of fraud in connection with the application for a life insurance policy is barred after the expiration of the contestable period. By contrast, if the clause is so worded as to make the policy incontestable from date of issue, it is generally agreed that the defense of fraud will continue to be available to the insurance company.

---

[11] Code of Iowa, Sec. 511.31.

[12] 116 F. Supp. 641 (D.C. Iowa, 1953).

[13] Knowledge on the part of the person making the statement.

These views are supported on the grounds that the two-year incontestable provision gives the insurer a reasonable period of time in which to investigate and thus does not totally except a defense of fraud. However, where the policy is declared incontestable from date of issue the company has no opportunity whatever to protect itself from fraudulent applicants. For this reason, and because fraud is abhorrent to the law, fraud is considered to be an implied exception in all policies which are made incontestable from date of issue.

Exception. One of the more important exceptions to this general rule is a line of cases dealing with situations where the application for life insurance is completed by one person as the proposed insured and yet another person takes the medical examination. In such cases the prevailing rule is that the incontestable clause, regardless of wording, is *not* operative because *no contract was ever formed.*

It will be recalled that there is a definite difference between requirements for the formation of a valid contract and factors going beyond such formation and relating to the essential validity of a contract. This particular line of cases points up that distinction with force and clarifies the operation of the incontestable clause in the language of basic contract law.

✿   ✿   ✿   ✿   ✿

Illustrative Case

Because it gives an excellent review of the incontestable clause, the matter of fraud, and the basic question of the validity of a life insurance contract, we quote at length from the case of *Obartuch* v. *Security Mutual Life Insurance Company.*

OBARTUCH v. SECURITY MUTUAL LIFE INSURANCE COMPANY [14]

(United States Circuit Court of Appeals, Seventh Circuit.)

(This case began as an action to recover upon two life insurance policies, each in the amount of $10,000, issued upon the life of Frank Obartuch. The company admitted that the contestable period had elapsed but denied that payment was due because the application was either not signed by or not knowingly signed by Frank Obartuch and some person unknown to the company was fraudulently substituted for the alleged applicant at the medical examination.)

The court entered findings of fact and conclusions of law submitted by the defendant. The substance of such findings was:

1. That the policies in suit were issued upon the life of some person other

[14] 114 F.2d 873 (C.C.A. Ill., 1940).

than Frank Obartuch, which other person submitted to a medical examination by Dr. Rubens;

2. That if Frank Obartuch signed the insurance application and answers to questions of the medical examiner and amendments thereto, he did so, not knowing the contents of said documents or with the intention of obtaining insurance from the defendant;

3. That the policies were obtained by the plaintiff and her sons, without the knowledge or consent of Frank Obartuch, by the substitution with their knowledge of a person other than Frank Obartuch at the medical examination.

The substance of the court's conclusions of law was:

1. That it is contrary to public policy for any person to obtain life insurance by substituting an individual other than the named insured for medical examination, and a policy secured by such substitution is void;

2. That the incontestable clause in the policies in suit does not preclude the defense that the person examined by the defendant's medical examiner was not Frank Obartuch, but somone else who impersonated said Frank Obartuch.

3. That said policies did not constitute a valid contract with Frank Obartuch and, if valid at all, were contracts upon the life of the person examined by the defendant's medical examiner.

4. That there was never any valid contract of life insurance upon the life of Frank Obartuch because he never knowingly signed any application therefor or authorized any other person to sign an application for him. . . .

What we have said thus far comes near to disposing of the first contested issue, adversely to the plaintiff. The reason for the effort made to limit the issue to that of substitution and thereby preclude the defendant from relying upon any finding except that of substitution is discernible from a reading of the authorities relied upon by the defendant to remove the bar erected by the incontestable clause. By thus confining the issue, it is sought to escape the rationale of these authorities. We apprehend that plaintiff would concede that if Obartuch signed the application without knowledge of its contents, that is, had no intention of applying for insurance, and that some person other than he was substituted for the medical examination, (facts found by the court), that such clause would no longer be effective.

In the *Maslin* case, the court held that the defense of impersonation was not barred by the incontestable clause on the theory that no contract was made with the named insured. True, as plaintiff points out, the named insured neither signed the application nor submitted to medical examination, but the matter of substitution was stressed by the court. On page 370, it said:

. . . There cannot be the slightest doubt that the person whom an insurance company intends to make a contract with and intends to insure is the person who presents himself for physical examination. . . .
The defendant's only contract was with the man who made the application and took the examination.

In the *Ludwinska* case, a similar situation is considered. The person named as the insured was an imbecile and the application for insurance was made by her sister who also impersonated the named insured at the medical examination. The court held that if anyone was insured it was the sister and not the one named in the policy. On pages 30 and 31 (Atl.), it is said:

. . . The contract must be made by someone capable of contracting under the insurance law. Without this neither the incontestable clause

contained in the policy nor the policy itself have any life. The clause can
rise no higher than the policy; the incontestable clause cannot of itself
create the contract.

   . . . Insurance companies do not insure names. They insure lives . . .

In the *Logan* case, which referred to a statute requiring the incontestable
provision, the court, on page 292, said:

   . . . This statute certainly has reference to cases where there is a contract between the insured and the insurer. If the insured never made any
application to the association for insurance, either by making the application herself, or authorizing another to do so for her, then there never was
a contract between the insured and the insurer and the statute above
quoted could not have application at all.

In the *Harris* case, this court considered a situation where the policy was
placed for inspection in the hands of the one who applied for the policy. In
the meantime, the person died and the named beneficiary sought to recover.
It was held that no contract existed and that the incontestable clause did not
bar a defense. On page 130, of 80 F.2d, it is said: ". . . The expressions of
these courts, while not the whole basis of the decisions, tend to uphold our
view that there is no effective incontestable clause when the policy is clearly
shown never to have been accepted by the insured in his lifetime as a contract. . . ."

❖ ❖ ❖ ❖ ❖

Comment

Lack of Insurable Interest. By this same reasoning, it is held that the
incontestable clause does not bar a defense based on lack of insurable
interest. It is well established that one cannot take out a valid and enforceable policy of insurance for his own benefit on the life of a person
in which he has no insurable interest. Such a contract of insurance is
void as a matter of public policy. The contract is "void in its inception,"
and since the incontestable clause is a part of that contract, it necessarily
fails with the contract of which it is a part. In short, no contract came
into existence in the first place and the incontestable clause, therefore, is
of no avail. As quoted above from the *Ludwinska* case, ". . . the incontestable clause cannot of itself create the contract."

SOME MISCELLANEOUS PROBLEMS

Date from Which the Contestable Period Runs

What the Clause States. As a general rule, the statutes which require
the incontestable clause state that the clause shall make the policy incontestable after it has been in effect for two years from "date of issue."
Most of the policy provisions, therefore, use the same language. However, the policy date and the date on which the insurance became effective are often different, and there is a very real question as to which of
these dates is the one from which the contestable period shall be computed.

Court Decisions. The majority of courts hold that the date of issue controls if the insurance does not become effective until later. However, where the policy bears a later date than that on which the insurance became effective, the period will be held to begin on the date the insurance became effective. In this, as in other instances, the terms of the policy will be construed most favorably toward the insured and the beneficiary; hence an interpretation giving the beneficiary the benefit of incontestability at the earliest possible moment.

What Is a Contest?

As a Matter of Procedure. We have discussed at some length the meaning of the word "contest" as it is used in the incontestable clause. However, we have not said what the company must actually do in order to "contest" the contract in the procedural sense of the term. It has been pointed out that where material misrepresentation, concealment, or fraud are discovered during the lifetime of the insured, the policy can be avoided if the contestable period has not expired. The court action necessary to perfect this right has not been described. Also, under present-day wording, if the material misrepresentation (or concealment or fraud) is discovered after the death of the insured, but within the contestable period, the company is entitled to deny the claim at any time. However, this action has not been discussed in terms of legal procedures.

It is not the purpose of this book to discuss procedural law in any real detail. However, the idea of the "contest" of a policy in the procedural sense, as the word is used in the incontestable clause, is sufficiently important to receive a note of explanation.

Ordinarily, it is held to mean some affirmative or defensive action in court, in which the insurance company and the insured, or his representatives or beneficiaries are parties. The word "contest" implies litigation. Thus there must be a suit in equity to have the policy set aside or a defense to a suit at law on the policy.

It will be remembered that the death of the insured during the contestable period fixes the rights of the parties, if the incontestable clause includes the words "during the lifetime of the insured." Under these conditions the company may contest the policy at any time and deny a claim on the grounds of material misrepresentation. If these words are *not* included the company may lose this right by the expiration of the contestable period and thus does not have an adequate remedy at law. For this reason it is entitled to bring an action in equity for cancellation of the policy.

A mere denial of a claim or a notice that the company intends to rescind or repudiate the contract does not constitute a contest. Furthermore, a suit by an insurer to have a policy reformed so that it will conform to the actual agreement of the parties has been held not to be a "contest" within the meaning of the clause.

DISABILITY BENEFITS

Incontestable Clause a Prior Development

The incontestable clause was originally adopted by life companies in connection with life coverages only. At the time of the Armstrong Investigation it had already been adopted by the majority of life companies. At the time it was being introduced, however, the only disability benefits offered were in health and accident policies. For this reason the early legislation requiring the incontestable clause related only to life insurance coverage. No provisions were made for excepting disability benefits because no such benefits were offered.

In the years that followed the Armstrong Investigation, life companies began offering disability benefits in connection with life insurance although they were not permitted to except such provisions from the incontestable clause. When the question was presented to the courts the incontestable clause was generally held to apply also to the disability benefits.

Nevertheless, even in this period, some courts recognized an essential difference in the nature of the respective coverages and held that the statutory incontestable requirements for life insurance did not apply to disability benefits even though the sections providing them were in the same policy.

In 1922, the National Convention of Insurance Commissioners recommended that statutes requiring the incontestable clause be amended to permit life companies to except disability and accidental death benefits from the operation of the incontestable clause.

Legislation. This option was first offered in 1923, when the New York legislature amended the New York Insurance law to allow an exception in the incontestable clause of "provisions relating to benefits in the event of total and permanent disability and provisions which grant additional insurance specifically against death by accident." A provision of this kind has since been incorporated into the statutory law of about half the states.

Incidentally, New York has since amended this law to require that disability benefits also be made incontestable, but the requirements are separately stated from those relating to life coverage, and the period of time, three years, is different. Thus the essential difference in the nature of the two coverages has continued to be recognized.

Why Disability Benefits Are Different. The incontestable clause was voluntarily introduced by the companies, primarily as a selling device. However, it was approved by the courts and required by the legislatures in spite of the fact that it meant the incidental condoning of fraud in some instances. The unique nature of the life insurance contract was felt to justify this possibility. The fact that it runs for a long period of time makes it highly unfair to allow the insurance company, after the expiration of that time, to take advantage of purely technical defenses. A second important consideration is the fact that the party penalized in connection with the life coverage is not the guilty person, as a general rule, but the beneficiary, the very person life insurance presumes to benefit.

Neither of these reasons apply in the same degree to the disability benefits. Here the contract will not necessarily have run for any considerable length of time. Proof and witnesses, including the insured, are ordinarily available. More important, however, is the fact that the person to be penalized, if the insurer contests the disability benefits, is the contracting party himself, whose possible immunity from the consequences of his own fraud is very difficult to justify.

The Court Decisions

Generally speaking, court decisions relating to the exception of disability benefits fall into two groups. The first group relates to policies in which the incontestable clause specifies no exception. The second group involves policies containing clauses which expressly except the benefits concerned.

Where No Exception Is Made. By the weight of authority, where no exception is made in the incontestable clause, disability benefits and accidental death benefits are held subject to the provisions of the incontestable clause in the same sense as is the life coverage. After the expiration of the contestable period the policy cannot be rescinded for fraud or misrepresentation with respect to any of the benefits, and claims cannot be defended on those grounds.

Under this view the company can always show that a risk was not assumed in the first place. For instance, the company may introduce evidence to show that disability is not total or permanent. It should be recalled, however, that this distinction between "contesting" the policy on the basis of factors going to the essential validity of the contract, and showing that the risk was not assumed in the first place, is not unanimously followed.

Where Disability and Accidental Death Provisions Are Excepted. Where disability and accidental death provisions are excepted, there is some confusion. By the weight of authority such exceptions should free these benefits entirely from the operation of the clause, and prior to

1934 the cases so held. In that year, however, a United States Court, in *Ness* v. *Mutual Life Insurance Company*,[15] held that the incontestable clause applied to the accidental death and disability clauses of the policy even though an exception had been specified as to "restrictions and provisions applying to double indemnity and disability benefits as provided in sections 1 and 3."

In this case, and in two others in which it was followed, the exceptions as to "sections 1 and 3" did not include all of the sections relating to the additional benefits. Thus there was some basis for the holding that the exception created an ambiguity which must be decided in favor of the insured. However, this conclusion was later applied to a different set of facts in which there was no such ambiguity, and thus established a very difficult precedent as far as any logical application of legal principles was concerned.

Illustrative of the more liberal point of view is the holding in *Equitable Life Assurance Society of the United States* v. *Deem* [16] where the court said:

> The policy as a whole includes three separate kinds of insurance, which constitute in reality three major promises of insurance protection, life, accident and disability. It seems entirely clear that the insurer intended to avail itself of the statutory authority to make the incontestable clause inapplicable to the latter two of these risks, and thus excepted from the clause those two provisions of the policy relating to them.

And later:

> While ambiguities which fairly exist in insurance policies must be resolved in favor of the insured, it is not permissible for courts by a strained and over-refined construction of ordinary words to create an ambiguity which would not otherwise exist. . . . And while the incontestable clause is a valuable feature of life insurance and is to be liberally construed to effectuate its beneficent purpose, there is no reason to deny to the insurer the option given by statute to except from its operation the additional features of disability and double indemnity benefits, where its purpose to do so has been definitely expressed. "To make a contract incontestable after the lapse of a brief time is to confer upon its holder extraordinary privileges." We must be on our guard against turning them into weapons of oppression.

Where the incontestable clause contains an express exception, it is believed that the majority of the courts have upheld the company's right to contest the validity of the disability provisions even after the expiration of the contestable period. However, many courts have denied the companies this right. Numerous cases have arisen on this question since 1930, and the decisions are highly conflicting.

---

[15] 70 F.2d 59 (C.C.A.N.C., 1934).

[16] 91 F.2d 569 (C.C.A. W.Va., 1937).

CHAPTER IX

The Ideas
of Waiver
and Estoppel

The Doctrine of Warranty

The Incontestable Clause. The doctrine of warranty was discussed in Chapter VIII, as well as its one-time widespread use by life insurance companies as a basis for avoiding life insurance contracts, often on highly technical grounds and many years after the contracts had been made. As was noted, the incontestable clause was introduced by the companies themselves on a voluntary basis in an effort to counteract some of the growing distrust on the part of the insuring public. This clause was later made a mandatory part of the life insurance policy by legislation enacted in the majority of the states.

Other Legislation. Many legislatures also enacted laws which in effect made all statements in the application for insurance policies, in the absence of fraud, representations and not warranties. Often this legislation further provided that misrepresentations in the application could only be used against the insured if they were included in a written application and made a part of the policy by actual inclusion and attachment.

Action in the Courts. In this chapter we turn to two devices which have been and are applied by the courts in an effort to achieve much the same purpose. These devices, both highly technical, are the doctrines of waiver and estoppel. They have long been used in various areas of the law, but they have achieved what is probably their highest development in connection with suits in which the validity of life insurance policies is challenged.

WAIVER AND ESTOPPEL DEFINED

Distinct Concepts

It is sometimes said, and many court decisions would seem to bear it out, that there is little, if any, difference between waiver and estoppel. Since the concepts are related and often occur together, this sometimes seems to be true. However, there is a clear technical distinction between the two terms, and this large and very important area of the law of the life insurance contract often becomes seriously confused if one does not approach it with a full understanding of the basic meanings of the terms waiver and estoppel.

What a Waiver Is

A waiver is the intentional and voluntary giving up of a known privilege or right. The person who gives it up may expressly say that he is doing so, or his words or actions may be of such a nature as to admit of no other reasonable interpretation. In more legal language, this idea is summarized by saying that a waiver may be "express or implied."

It must also be remembered that whatever one may do for himself he may do through an agent. Thus an authorized agent may waive a privilege or power for his principal. In the case of the life insurance company, waiver is *always* by an agent since even an officer of the company is, in technical terms, acting as an agent.

Some Waivers Are Contractual. A waiver always involves intent and consent, although it may not be of such a nature as to constitute an enforceable promise or contract. In connection with the life insurance contract, one of the important waivers, the waiver of premium for disability, is enforceable as a promise. The company intentionally and voluntarily promises, for a consideration, to give up its right to enforce the premium payment condition during all periods of total and permanent disability, as described and defined. Since there is a consideration for this promise the waiver is contractual.

Some Waivers Are Not Contractual. Waiver is more frequently thought of in a less formal sense, as illustrated in the case of *Johnson* v. *Life Insurance Co. of Georgia,* a Florida case decided by the supreme court of that state in May, 1951.[1] The policy sued upon was a nonmedical policy, and the company denied liability on the grounds of breach of the condition expressed in the application requiring the insured to be in sound health at the time the policy was delivered.

A former employee of the insurer testified that he had taken the application and collected the premiums on the policy. According to his testimony, "about two months after the policy was issued" he learned

[1] 52 So.2d 813 (Fla., 1951).

that the insured had gone to a tuberculosis sanitarium, but he added that
the insured "only went there for ninety days and we thought he was all
right." Consequently the agent continued to collect the premiums, with
knowledge of the insured's tuberculous condition until he died, a little
less than a year after the application was made.

The evidence was clear that the insured was not in sound health at
the time the policy was delivered and that he had received medical treatment within two years of the date of the issuance of the policy. The evidence was also clear that the defendant's agent had actual knowledge of
the insured's tuberculous condition not later than two months after the
policy was issued, and in the face of that knowledge continued to collect
the premiums as they fell due. On the basis of this evidence the trial
court entered a decision for the beneficiary, but only for the amount of
the premiums paid. On appeal, the supreme court said:

. . . If, as contended by appellant, the admitted facts show a waiver, as a
matter of law, of the provisions of the policy here relied upon, then the trial
judge must be held in error.

No point is here made of the fact that the knowledge acquired by the
agent as to the tubercular condition of the insured, might not have been communicated to the company, and properly so, since under the circumstances
here present the knowledge of the agent is imputable to his principal whether
disclosed by him to it or not, and the company will be bound by such knowledge. . . .

At the outset, we mention the familiar and oft-quoted rule that a forfeiture
of rights under an insurance policy is not favored by the law, especially where,
as here, a forfeiture is sought after the happening of the event giving rise to
the insurer's liability. And it is equally well settled in insurance law that, when
an insurer has knowledge of the existence of facts justifying a forfeiture of the
policy, any unequivocal act which recognizes the continued existence of the
policy or which is wholly inconsistent with a forfeiture, will constitute a
waiver thereof. While, ordinarily, the insurer is not deemed to have waived
its rights unless it is shown that it has acted with the full knowledge of the
facts, the intention to waive such rights may be inferred from a deliberate
disregard of information sufficient to excite attention and call for inquiry as to
the existence of facts by reason of which a forfeiture could be declared. . . .

In the instant case, the defendant had knowledge of the fact that the
insured was suffering from tuberculosis only two months after the date of
issuance of the policy; and, from the very nature of this disease, the only
reasonable inference is that the insured was suffering therefrom on the date
of the issuance of the policy. Instead, however, of making the further inquiry
dictated by reasonable prudence, the defendant deliberately disregarded this
information, and we think it must now be held to be charged with knowledge
of the facts which such an inquiry would have disclosed, and upon which
defendant now relies as a defense to the payment of the full amount due under
the policy. . . .

The acceptance and collection of the premiums with constructive notice
of the facts here relied on as a defense is certainly an "unequivocal act which

recognizes the continued existence of the policy" and which is "wholly inconsistent with a forfeiture," under the rule hereinabove stated. . . .

The uncontroverted evidence shows, as a matter of law, a waiver by the defendant of the forfeiture provisions of the policy here relied on as a defense. It was, therefore, error to deny to plaintiff the full amount of the policy sued upon, and the judgment is reversed and the cause remanded with directions to enter judgment for such amount.

What an Estoppel Is

Legal Estoppel. There are two basic kinds of estoppels. One, known as legal estoppel, refers generally to estoppel by record or deed and dates back to the beginnings of the common law. An estoppel of this kind becomes operative whenever one has executed a deed or other solemn instrument in which he has made certain statements of fact. In such cases he will not thereafter be permitted to deny the truth of those statements. In other words, he is *estopped* by the statements he has made in the deed.

Equitable Estoppel. In life insurance contract law we are primarily concerned with the concept of equitable estoppel, or *estoppel in pais.* This principle was first used in courts of equity and has been adopted by courts of law relatively recently. Briefly, it is applied in cases where one person has, with knowledge of the truth, falsely represented or concealed a material fact from another, who does not know the truth, intending that the latter shall act on the information falsely represented or concealed, with the result that the latter does so to his injury. In such cases the person who misrepresented the facts will be estopped to deny that those facts were as he represented them to be, if to do otherwise would be to perpetrate an injury to the other. The equitable estoppel is thus used to protect rights which are equitable and just.

The application of this principle in connection with the subject of agency has been discussed. There, it will be remembered, if Brown has permitted Smith to appear to be his agent, and if Jones, misled by this apparent agency, contracts with Smith believing that he is Brown's agent, Brown will not be heard (that is, he will be *estopped*) to deny that the facts are as he permitted them to seem to be. This is known as agency by estoppel. As was pointed out in Chapter III, the purpose is not to establish an agency relationship in fact but to prevent an injustice to someone who relied upon what he thought was true to his own injury.

Equitable estoppel is used in many other areas of the law, but it is peculiarly applicable to the many conditions and prerequisites in connection with the life insurance contract. Since the life contract is a contract of the highest good faith, it is inequitable to permit its terms to be interpreted with such technical exactness that decisions may be characterized as "legally right but morally wrong." The parties do not deal with each other at arm's length, and if the conduct of the company, through its agents, is not in good faith, it may frequently be estopped to plead the truth of a situation which would otherwise constitute a valid defense.

The law with respect to equitable estoppel is particularly well summarized in the case of *Haggerty* v. *St. Louis Police Relief Association*,[2] a Missouri case decided in 1940. There the court said:

> . . . It is a general rule in this state that there can be no estoppel unless the party alleging it relies upon the representation of the other party and was induced to take some action to his injury. . . . Nor will mere silence or some act done, where the means of knowledge are equally open to both parties, estop the party doing the act or remaining silent. . . .

In our state it is settled law that an estoppel *in pais* must be based on five elements, as set out in Bigelow on Estoppel 5th Ed., p. 570, as follows:

> First. There must have been a false representation or a concealment of material facts. Second, the representation must have been made with knowledge, actual or virtual, of the facts. Third. The party to whom it was made must have been ignorant, actually or presumably, of the truth of the matter. Fourth. It must have been made with the intention, actual or virtual, that the other party should act upon it. Fifth. The other party must have been induced to act upon it.

When we apply this universally approved definition of the fundamental elements of estoppel to the facts in this case, not one of those elements is present. Estoppel is invariably based on the word or act of the party to be estopped, and not on an improvident or improper word or act of the one who seeks to invoke it. It is purely an equitable doctrine, and though measured out in both law and equity cases, it cannot rest alone on a situation solely created by the one who seeks to invoke it, otherwise it would cease to be an armor of protection to the innocent, and could be used as a weapon purposely forged to circumvent another's rights.

WAIVER AND ESTOPPEL GENERALLY

Reasons for Their Use

Besides the high good faith aspect of the contract, a second reason for the application of the principles of waiver and estoppel was the common law rule that a party to a written contract is presumed to know and to consent to its terms. This was not unreasonable in connection with contracts made at arm's length so to speak, between competent adults, and expected to be performed within a reasonably short period. In fact it was only just to assume that when a man entered into such a contract, if he had not read it, he should have done so.

Applied to the life insurance contract, however, this principle has been much criticized. The contract of life insurance is prepared by the company and acquiesced in by the applicant, who often does not have the opportunity to read it until it has gone into force. Furthermore, the

---

[2] 141 S.W.2d 174 (Mo. App., 1940).

contract is complex, containing terms such as settlement options, non-forfeiture values, dividends, reserves, etc., with which many people are completely unacquainted. To assume that the insured knows and assents to all the provisions of such an instrument is not very realistic, and holdings based on such an approach are sometimes difficult to justify. To establish an equitable balance, therefore, the concepts of waiver and estoppel have been extensively applied against insurers.

Waiver and Estoppel Often Confused

Estoppel May Serve as Consideration. Basically, waiver and estoppel are separate and distinct. Nevertheless, just as the two sides of a coin are different and yet together constitute a whole, so waiver and estoppel often occur together and constitute two sides of the same essential situation. Many waivers are inoperative without consideration, but a detriment to the promisee is valid consideration. If we review the concept of equitable estoppel, we find that it consists of conduct or permissive behavior on the part of the person estopped of such a nature that it misleads the other and causes him to suffer a detriment. This detriment, therefore, is often consideration for a waiver.

Thus if an insurance company takes such action as to indicate that a breach is waived, and if A relies upon it to such an extent that to permit the company to plead the breach thereafter would amount to a detriment to A, that detriment may be viewed as sufficient "consideration" to create a waiver. However, one may look at it from a different point of view and say that the company is estopped to plead the breach. In either case the decision will be for A, and often the cases are not too technical as to the reasons. As a result, the two concepts are often treated together and frequently viewed as virtually the same.

However, let us take the situation where an agent, without authority, is alleged to have waived a condition. Most courts hold that if the lack of authority is known to the applicant or insured, such an alleged waiver will be ineffective. With an equitable estoppel it is different. The actions even of an unauthorized agent may constitute a situation resulting in an equitable estoppel against the life insurance company. It is important, therefore, to keep the basic distinctions in mind.

Waiver Contrasted with Estoppel. Basically, a waiver is an agreement, though not necessarily a contract, and it is closely related to contract law. Estoppel relates more to torts and concerns an action of such an inequitable nature as to preclude the person estopped from availing himself of a defense which would otherwise be his. Waiver gives effect to the intention of the party alleged to have waived the right even though it may at times have implications of which he was not completely aware. An estoppel is enforced contrary to the intention of the party against whom it is invoked, and he is said to be estopped to claim rights he would otherwise have had and which he in no wise intended to relinquish.

"*Equity and Good Conscience.*" Courts of equity are much given to using the phrase "equity and good conscience." This is a good phrase to bear in mind. Although equitable estoppel is frequently applied in courts of law, it is essentially an equitable doctrine and it carries with it many of the attributes of the court of equity. An equitable estoppel ordinarily requires words or actions of such a nature that they lead the other party to rely on them in good faith and to suffer a loss as a result. The court then says in effect, and sometimes in actual words, that the person who permitted the situation to arise or was responsible for it cannot "in equity and good conscience" be heard to say that the facts were not as he represented or permitted them to seem to be.

The Parol Evidence Rule

And Equitable Estoppel. Because equitable estoppel, in effect, assumes something contrary to the intention of the party against whom it is invoked, it also frequently involves a set of facts contrary to the terms of the contract itself. It will be remembered, however, that the whole point of the parol evidence rule is to prevent the admission of evidence tending to deny or contradict the terms of a written contract.

It will be remembered also that equitable estoppels were adopted by common law courts from courts of equity, and it is perhaps obvious that the parol evidence rule is a rule of evidence which applies to actions involving juries. Thus there were no parol evidence problems in courts of equity, but a conflict with the parol evidence rule was inevitable when the concept of equitable estoppel was adopted by the common law courts.

Court Holdings. Generally speaking, if the estoppel is shown to have occurred after the contract became effective, it will be upheld. However, with respect to estoppels arising before or at the inception of the contract, there is a difference of opinion. Several courts have held that the parol evidence rule prevents the admission of evidence showing such estoppels. Others refuse to apply the doctrine in cases where the insured had in his possession but did not read the life insurance policy which included false statements inserted by the insurance agent.

A Landmark Case. One of the significant cases in the development of the doctrine of equitable estoppel in connection with the life insurance contract was the Wilkinson case.[3] That case involved a warranty in the

---

[3] *Union Mutual Life Insurance Co.* v. *Wilkinson*, 13 Wall. 222, 20 L. Ed. 617 (1872).

application, which was not true. The application was signed by the insured, all of the statements in it were warranted to be true, and it was made a part of the contract. The warranty in question concerned the age of the mother of the insured at the time of her death. Alleging the untruth of this warranted age, the life insurance company denied the claim.

Evidence was offered to show what actually took place at the time of the application. According to the testimony of witnesses, the agent asked the insured the age of her mother at her death, and the insured said she did not know. Someone else who was present volunteered an answer which was inserted in the application by the agent. It was later found to be incorrect. If admitted, this evidence would show an equitable estoppel. The question was whether oral evidence could be admitted under such circumstances and for such a purpose.

The court held that the evidence was admissible, and the finding was for the plaintiff. On appeal to the United States Supreme Court, the decision was unanimously upheld, as follows:

> It is in precisely such cases as this that courts of law in modern times have introduced the doctrine of equitable estoppels, or, as it is sometimes called, estoppels *in pais*. The principle is that where one party has by his representations or his conduct induced the other party to a transaction to give him an advantage which it would be against equity and good conscience for him to assert, he would not in a court of justice be permitted to avail himself of that advantage. And although the cases to which this principle is to be applied are not as well defined as could be wished, the general doctrine is well understood and is applied by courts of law as well as equity where the technical advantage thus obtained is set up and relied on to defeat the ends of justice or establish a dishonest claim. . . . The modern decisions fully sustain this proposition, and they seem to us founded in reason and justice, and meet our entire approval. This principle does not admit oral testimony to vary or contradict that which is in writing, but it goes upon the idea that the writing offered in evidence was not the instrument of the party whose name is signed to it; that it was procured under such circumstances by the other side as estops that side from using it or relying on its contents; not that it may be contradicted by oral testimony, but that it may be shown by such testimony that it cannot be lawfully used against the party whose name is signed to it.

This holding has been followed by the courts of almost all of the states, although in 1902 the United States Supreme Court reversed its position and refused to uphold an equitable estoppel of this kind.

Parol Evidence and Waivers. One of the most frequently recurring situations involving alleged waivers concerns the stipulation often found in the policy that it shall not take effect until the first premium is actually paid in cash and the policy delivered to the applicant. Assume that the applicant does not have the cash at the time of delivery but with the agent's acquiescence gives a promissory note for three months, and the policy is delivered. Then the insured dies before the note is paid.

The question immediately arises: Can parol evidence be introduced to show this agreement? At first it would seem that such evidence would contradict one of the terms of the contract. However, an analysis of the situation brings us to a different conclusion.

When a policy is issued, the effectiveness of the contract is often conditioned upon acceptance and prepayment of the first premium in cash. However, there is nothing to prevent the agent from removing or altering this condition if he has adequate authority. In that case he waives the condition of prepayment of the first premium. The question, therefore, concerns the making of the contract and not the terms of the contract already made. The parol evidence rule applies only to the promissory provisions of a written contract and not to circumstances involved in the making of the contract. The cases, therefore, hold that the insurance company, through an authorized agent, may waive the condition and that this waiver may be shown by oral evidence. The contract itself is not involved, for it has not been made.

Now assume that the life insurance policy is avoidable by the company because of a breach of a condition. At a later date the insurance company learns of the breach, expressly states that it is of no importance, and premiums are thereafter accepted. This type of case illustrates a subsequent waiver of a breach of condition, and it is generally agreed that it, too, can be shown by oral evidence.

SOME COMMON RULES CONCERNING WAIVERS

The Importance of Intent

It is essential to all forms of waiver that the person alleged to have waived something must have had the intention, express or implied, to do what he actually did. For that reason, we have several well-settled rules. For one thing, the unauthorized act of an agent cannot create a waiver although it may raise an estoppel. For another, acts of the insurance company which might, under some circumstances, create a waiver—acts such as furnishing forms for proof of loss—will not have that effect if the company, by notice, either in the policy or elsewhere, expressly denies that a waiver is intended. However, once a privilege or power has been waived, the waiver can never be revoked.

Many actions taken by an insurance company with knowledge of a breach of condition will be interpreted as showing an unequivocable intent to continue the contract in force. Thus it is almost unanimously held that the collection of subsequent premiums waives any known existing defense under the contract.

Some Waivers Are Forbidden

As a general rule a party to a contract may waive any privilege or power available to him under a contract. Thus the insurance company may waive the benefit of any provision of a policy even though it is a standard provision required by statute. However, there are several exceptions to this rule, particularly with respect to the insured.

Exceptions. A party to an insurance contract cannot relinquish a right conferred by any rule of law or statute in the maintenance of which the public is concerned. Thus where a statute provides that no policy shall be forfeited for nonpayment of premium unless notice of default is given by the insurance company, the insured cannot waive his privilege to receive this notice.

Nor can one waive a fact. Therefore the agreement by the insured, set forth in the policy, that the person who is really the agent of the insurance company shall be considered the agent of the insured cannot operate as a waiver of the truth, which is that the agent is the representative of the insurance company.

There are also certain rules of the common law in which public policy is so deeply concerned that parties to a contract will not be permitted to waive them. One example is the rule prohibiting the making of insurance contracts which are not supported by an insurable interest. Such an unlawful agreement cannot be made enforceable either by waiver or estoppel. According to some courts also, an agreement in the policy that the insurance company shall not be charged with knowledge acquired by the agent in the course of the company's business, or be responsible for the fraud perpetrated by such agent in the course of his employment, is inoperative. However, there are decisions to the contrary on this point.

Cannot Create Coverage by Waiver

Generally speaking our law does not impose upon a person any contractual duty unless his promise is supported by consideration or is under seal. Thus if the insurance company is not liable with respect to a given type of loss, there can be no effective waiver of that nonliability. This is illustrated most clearly, perhaps, in cases where the policy does not cover losses where the insured is beyond a specified age. Under the better view the company cannot by waiver create liability for losses occurring beyond that age, but there are a number of holdings to the contrary.

Releases

On the same principle, if one has a legal right to the payment of a sum of money by another he may release the right by agreement on consideration or under seal, but it cannot be waived. Thus if the beneficiary makes claim for both the death benefit and the accidental death benefit under a life insurance policy, payment of the death benefit is not consideration for a release of her possible rights to the accidental death benefit also. On the other hand, if there is truly a dispute as to the amount properly payable, and if the parties come to an agreement, and payment is made, it will be held effective as against later proof that a larger sum was in reality due and payable. This is an *accord and satisfaction* and has always been held to be an effective discharge of an obligation to pay a disputed sum of money.

Policy Provisions re Waivers

Limitations of the Agent's Authority. Many policies contain provisions forbidding any representative of the company to waive any terms of the contract except in a specified manner, usually by writing indorsed on the policy. The consensus is that a provision of this kind is solely for the benefit of the company, and that it, as well as any other provision of the policy, may be waived. This type of limitation, therefore, operates merely as notice to the insured of limitations on the powers of the agent under the policy. After receipt of the policy the insured is deemed to have knowledge of the limitation, and if the company does not waive it, or permit an estoppel to arise, a subsequent, attempted waiver on the part of the agent will be ineffective. It should be noted that in connection with estoppels the question is not whether the action of the agent alleged to be an estoppel is authorized but whether it was within the course of his employment.

The Duty to Act

Silence. Under the general rules of contract law, silence is not ordinarily operative to change legal responsibilities unless there are special circumstances which place one of the parties under a duty to speak. A party to the contract of life insurance, therefore, is under a duty to speak only when to remain silent would be inequitable.

For example, breach of a condition has very much the same effect as the discovery of material misrepresentation. It does not avoid the contract but only gives the company the right to avoid it, if it wishes. If the company exercises this power and does avoid the contract, it extinguishes all legal relations created by it. A duty to pay cannot thereafter be re-created without a new contract. However, if the company fails to exercise this power of avoidance and with full knowledge of the breach remains silent, what is the legal effect of this inaction?

Increasingly the courts are holding that on the happening of a breach of a condition subsequent the insurance company has only the power to disaffirm the contract and that this power must be exercised within a reasonable time after knowledge is acquired or it will be regarded as having been waived. The policy may be worded in such a way as to require the power to be exercised in a very particular way, as by instituting legal proceedings. If so, such legal proceedings must be instituted. Otherwise the privilege will be held to have been waived. It may also be extinguished by the expiration of the period fixed by statute or by the incontestable clause.

THE DOCTRINE OF ELECTION

The doctrine of election is often mentioned in connection with the over-all subject of estoppel, although it is a very special application of it. Fundamentally it involves a choice among two or more inconsistent or irreconcilable legal remedies of such a nature that having elected one course of action, the plaintiff will be estopped from pursuing any of the others thereafter.

Let us say, for example, that a life insurance company takes action to cancel a life insurance contract including provisions for the payment of disability benefits. The insured brings an action against the company for the fraudulent breach of the contract and is awarded damages. Subsequently he brings another action for disability benefits which would have accrued to him prior to the date of the previous suit had it not been for the cancellation of the contract by the company. Note that in the first instance he alleged that the contract was breached and that he was entitled to damages as a consequence. In the second suit he demanded benefits that would have been payable if the contract had not been breached. This is clearly a case of the attempted pursuit of a second course of action inconsistent with the first.

In one case presenting this set of facts, the court quoted from a prior decision as follows:

. . . If a party should invoke a remedy appropriate to a certain state of facts, and there should exist another remedy appropriate to a different state of facts, inconsistent with and repugnant to the first state of facts, his invocation of the first remedy is an election which by the bare commencement of the action will bar his right to invoke the other remedy.[4]

Applying the law to this particular set of facts, the court held that the insured was bound by his first choice of remedy and could not proceed with the second action.

[4] *McMahon* v. *McMahon*, 122 S.C. 336; 115 S.E. 293, quoted in *The Pacific Mutual Life Insurance Co. of Calif.* v. *Rhame*, 32 F. Supp. 59 (D.C. S.C., 1940).

MATERIAL MISREPRESENTATION, WAIVER, AND ESTOPPEL

Material Misrepresentation

As we have seen, the insurance company has the right, as a matter of law, to avoid a policy of life insurance if material facts have been misrepresented in the application. However, it is the life insurance agent, as a general rule, who actually writes the answers in the application from information given to him by the insured. The application is then signed by the insured who, in legal effect, thus makes the answers his own.

False Answers Inserted by Agent. Now let us suppose that in writing the answers to the application questions, the agent is given the correct answers by the proposed insured but, knowing that the application may not be accepted if the truth is given, he inserts false answers which he knows will not be questioned. May the company in this situation deny the claim after the insured's death, or rescind the policy during his lifetime, on the basis of material misrepresentation in the application?

The general rule is that the insurance company cannot rely upon the falseness of those answers to deny the claim or rescind the policy. This assumes that correct answers were given by the insured, that there was neither fraud nor collusion on his part, and that he did not know of the duplicity of the agent. The courts generally take the approach that the agent is representing the insurance company, his knowledge is imputed to the company, and the company is therefore estopped to plead the falsity of the answers. There are a few decisions to the contrary, but this general rule is decidedly the majority opinion. To protect itself, it has been said, the company "needs only to select competent and trustworthy agents."

Duty to Read the Application. Before this rule will apply it is essential that correct answers must have been given to the agent and that there be no question of fraud or duplicity on the part of the applicant. Even when this is true, however, there is a question as to whether he will be held under a duty to read the application and thus be charged with knowledge of the incorrect answers inserted in it.

Generally speaking the applicant *is* under a duty to read the application, and he will be held charged with knowledge of its contents. This is the holding of the majority of the courts although often only slight circumstances will be considered sufficient excuse for his not being aware of the falsity of the answers.

Two actual examples will illustrate this. In one case,[5] the evidence showed that the applicant gave correct information concerning the diabetic condition of her daughter (the proposed insured) to the agent,

---

[5] *Hart v. The Prudential Insurance Company of America,* 47 Cal. App. 2d 298, 117 P.2d 930 (1941).

who recorded incorrect answers which made it appear that the daughter's health was good. After her death the company denied the claim on the grounds of misrepresentation of material facts in the application. In the suit the company contended that even if the agent inserted false answers, the applicant was presumed to have knowledge of the false statements since the application was attached to the policy. The mother testified that there was no copy of the application in the policy, however, and that was the finding of the court. The holding, therefore, was against the company.

In another case [6] the applicant had suffered a severe head injury while in the service. The evidence showed that at the time the application was filled out he discussed this with the agent, who said: "Well, as long as you do not have a medical discharge they don't care about all this. As long as you have an honorable discharge and not a medical discharge you can sign this application." The head injury, therefore, was not mentioned in the application, and the company denied the claim for that reason.

Of the insured's duty to read the application under these circumstances, the court said:

> Defendant correctly states that when the insured has a copy of the application in his possession he is presumed to have read it, and to be aware of any misstatements therein even though they were not due to his own fault. . . . The rule would not apply here to charge Boggio with knowledge he did not have when he signed the application unless he could have ascertained that his statements were false in the sense that they withheld information sought to be elicited by the questions contained in the application. This was not the case. He relied on Angelino's statement that the questions did not call for information as to the injury received in the service unless it had led to medical discharge. Having had the question interpreted for him in this manner, repeated reading of the questions and answers would not have led him to believe that his service injury was material. He knew at all times that his answers were literally untrue but not that they would be deemed untrue by the company in determining whether he was an insurable risk. On the facts found the case was correctly decided.

Fraud of Applicant or Collusion with Agent. The law is clear with respect to estoppel where the agent is told the truth and writes false answers in the application. But here again there are other possibilities. For instance, consider a situation where the agent writes false answers that were agreed upon with the proposed insured; in other words, the applicant and the agent conspire to submit a fraudulent application. This is squarely within one of the important exceptions to the general rule, the agent is definitely acting outside the scope of his authority, and the company is fully justified in relying upon the material misrepresentation in the application as grounds for avoiding the contract.

[6] *Boggio* v. *California Western States Life Insurance Co.,* 239 P.2d 144 (Cal. App., 1952).

PART III

The Contract in Operation

CHAPTER X

The Policyholder Pays the Premium

IN THE LARGEST sense, the operation of any insurance company turns upon the regular collection of premiums, their investment, and the prompt payment of claims. The long-range nature of the life insurance contract and the level premium, legal reserve system make the subject of premium payment, and particularly the consequences of nonpayment, considerably more complicated with respect to the life insurance contract than in connection with other kinds of insurance. The purpose of this chapter is to outline the major problems which can arise in connection with the payment of the life insurance premium and to discuss the legal principles most frequently applied in reaching their solutions.

THE NATURE OF THE LIFE INSURANCE PREMIUM

From the Policyholder's Point of View

The more than $15 billion of life insurance premiums that are paid in this country every year are paid in amounts ranging from a few cents in some instances to several thousands of dollars in others. Often they are paid over a long period of time. Literally, therefore, nearly all premiums are paid in instalments. Legally, however, there are some very basic differences between life insurance premium payments and the instalment payments the policyholder may make on his car, refrigerator, or other household appliances.

No Promise to Pay. First and most fundamental is the fact that there is no promise to pay the premium. When a policyholder buys a car he receives something tangible at the outset, and he promises to pay the purchase price in a stated number of future instalments of a specified amount. The something tangible which he receives is consideration for his promise to pay, making it a valid and enforceable contract on which he can be sued, if necessary.

When one applies for and is issued a life insurance policy, he receives conditional promises from the life insurance company and the privilege of keeping the policy in force by paying the premiums. Courts have almost unanimously held that an unpaid insurance premium is not an indebtedness and that the payment of premiums is not an obligation in the legal sense of the word. Insurance premiums, therefore, may be considered payments, but they are payments the policyholder can discontinue any time he wishes, and the insurance company is powerless to compel him to continue. On the other hand, if he keeps the policy in force by payment of premiums, the promises on the part of the company are legally enforceable. The fact that so many policyholders continue to pay premiums on their policies year after year, without compulsion other than the nature of the contract, is a most convincing, silent tribute to the value of this privilege.

From the Company's Point of View

The Level Premium, Legal Reserve Plan. Life insurance, as we know it today, did not truly come into existence until the adoption of the level premium, legal reserve plan. This plan transformed a relatively limited kind of agreement into a *plan of insurance,* with premium payments tailored to the average person's earning power pattern and his life insurance needs. Directly in some respects, indirectly in others, the level premium, legal reserve plan permitted the development of the highly flexible contract that we know today. Under it, relatively modest premium payments at regular intervals will assure a sizeable estate for one's dependents at his death or for himself at retirement.

Funding a plan of such flexibility and unique value is not a simple matter, and it could not be accomplished at all on a basis of individual contracts unrelated to each other. In considering the payment of premiums, therefore, as in the area of risk selection, it is necessary to bear in mind that the life insurance contract is not merely an enforceable agreement between an individual and the life insurance company, it is also an insurance device.

The Legal Problem. Prior to the level premium, legal reserve plan the life insurance premium presented no special problem as a matter of law. An annual premium under a life insurance policy was very much the same, legally, as the premium for fire insurance coverage or the premium in any other policy of insurance. Payment of the premium by the insured for a given term was consideration for the carrying of the risk on the part of the insurance company for the same period. Under the legal reserve, level premium plan, however, life insurance entered the long-range era, with commitments often running into the next century, and the premium for any given year was no longer related only to the insurance protection for that year.

The level premium is possible because the legal reserve does two things: (1) As it increases from year to year it reduces the net amount at risk;[1] and (2) it puts compound interest to work for the policyholder.

Basic to the legal reserve system is the fact that all policy reserves are established by the company for the benefit of all policies. Technically, there is no such thing as an individual reserve for any one policy. In the field of legal problems, however, it is most frequently an individual policy that is in question. For that reason, we turn to the individual policy to see how it is affected by the level premium, legal reserve system.

Under the Individual Policy. In the early years, the level premium paid for a whole life or endowment policy (or any life insurance policy running more than a year, except, perhaps, a decreasing term policy) is more than sufficient to provide for both the current year's mortality needs and expenses. If a level expense portion is deducted from the gross premium, there remains a level net premium which provides for more than the policy's share of the current year's death claims. Any balance is set aside and invested to provide for the time in later years when the level net premium would not, by itself, be sufficient to provide for the policy's share of the current year's claims. This balance that is set aside creates the legal reserve, a liability of the company.

As the insured grows older, a larger amount of the net premium goes to provide for the current year's mortality and a smaller amount remains to be set aside for future policyholder claims. However, the reserve liability continues to grow since, for a while at least, additional funds are being received and interest is being earned on those funds which have previously been set aside. When an individual insured dies, the amount of that policy's proportionate segment of the company's reserves offsets a corresponding amount of the claim.

In other words, the company knows that any one insured could die in any year. Furthermore, his chances of dying in any given year increase with each year he lives. By the level premium, legal reserve method, the net amount at risk is annually reduced for each policy. This avoids any need for premium increase and permits a guaranteed level premium.

Since the legal reserve and its companion idea, the level premium,

---

[1] The net amount at risk is the difference between the benefit payable and the amount of the reserve. This difference is the amount which must be made up by the mortality portion of the net premiums received during the year.

have such technical [2] and far-reaching implications, it is not surprising that there was at first some question concerning the legal nature of this life insurance premium, which the policyholder may pay if he wishes, but which he doesn't really have to pay.

The Legal Nature of the Premium

The Early View. In one of the early life insurance cases in which this problem was considered,[3] the court took the position that each premium subsequent to the first purchased two things. First, it paid the cost of the insurance for the year in question, and second, it paid for the right to renew the insurance for another period of the same length. Although this approach was followed by a few other courts, it seems clear that it overlooks the basic level premium idea, that the contract is designed to function on a long-term basis, and the premium is related to that same basis even though it is payable annually.

The Better View. It seems most highly appropriate that one of the clearest opinions, as far as an interpretation of the legal nature of the life insurance premium is concerned, was written by an actuary-lawyer, turned judge. Mr. Justice Bradley, a student of actuarial science and practicing lawyer in Newark, had served as consulting mathematician for one of the leading life insurance companies for several years before becoming a member of the United States Supreme Court. With this background he was almost uniquely equipped to write the opinion in the case of *New York Life Insurance Co.* v. *Statham,*[4] which concerned the legal effect of the suspension of premium payments under a life insurance policy, by reason of the War between the States. For our present purposes, the important part of that decision is as follows:

We agree with the court below, that the contract is not an assurance for a single year, with a privilege of renewal from year to year by paying the annual premium, but that it is an entire contract of assurance for life, subject to discontinuance and forfeiture for non-payment of any of the stipulated premiums. Such is the form of the contract, and such is its character. It has been contended that the payment of each premium is the consideration for insurance during the next following year,—as in fire policies. But the position is untenable. It often happens that the assured pays the entire premium in advance, or in five, ten, or twenty annual instalments. Such instalments are clearly not intended as the consideration for the respective years in which they are paid; for, after they are all paid, the policy stands good for the balance of the life insured, without any further payment. Each instalment is, in fact,

---

[2] The exact relationship of premiums, mortality, and interest in any specific case is dependent upon a varying set of technical factors, which are controlled to a large extent by state insurance law and regulation.

[3] *Worthington* v. *Charter Oak Life Insurance Co.,* 41 Conn. 372, 19 Am. Rep. 495 (1874).

[4] 93 U.S. 24 (1876).

part consideration of the entire insurance for life. It is the same thing, whether the annual premiums are spread over the whole life. The value of assurance for one year of a man's life when he is young, strong, and healthy, is manifestly not the same when he is old and decrepit. There is no proper relation between the annual premium and the risk of assurance for the year in which it is paid. This idea of assurance from year to year is the suggestion of ingenious counsel. The annual premiums are an annuity, the present value of which is calculated to correspond with the present value of the amount assured, a reasonable percentage being added to the premiums to cover expenses and contingencies. The whole premiums are balanced against the whole insurance.

Thus, the basic question was whether the life insurance contract could be separated into yearly promises and yearly premiums. It seems obvious that with the level premium, legal reserve system this is impossible. To make this system work it is necessary to consider premium payments on a long-term basis. The court's interpretation in the *Statham* case, from which we have quoted, takes this long-range approach and gives it legal significance. It places both the company's promises and the insured's premium payments on a continuing basis, with the effectiveness of the promises being conditioned on the payment of premiums.

Initial and Subsequent Premiums

Adopting the interpretation of the *Statham* case, we find that the premiums under the life insurance contract must be divided into two groups. The first or initial premium constitutes the consideration for the insurance company's promise and puts the contract into force. Most insurance policies are expressly declared not to be effective unless and until the first premium is paid during the lifetime and continued insurability of the insured. At that time, by the clear implication of this wording, insurance *does become effective*, and the insurance company is bound on its promises. Thus, the first or initial premium is the consideration "requested and given in exchange" for the company's promises, the "legally adequate" consideration, which makes the life insurance contract a valid and binding agreement.

The promises of the life insurance company become effective at the time of delivery of the policy and payment of the first premium, or at an earlier date if there is a conditional binding receipt. They will continue to be effective *if* the insured continues to pay the premiums as they fall due. It is this "if" which puts the promises of the company on a conditional basis and makes the payment of succeeding premiums what the lawyer calls a *condition precedent*.

It is not always easy to distinguish between a condition and a promise, but the consequences of nonperformance in the two cases are widely different. A person who fails to perform a promise will be liable in damages for breach of contract. A person who does not perform a condition only loses the right to require the promisor to perform. Generally speaking, he has no liability. It is this freedom from liability that the policyholder has with respect to nonpayment of the premium under his life insurance contract, and it is that absence of liability for nonperformance that makes it clear that payment of the life insurance premiums as they fall due is a condition and not a promise.

The life insurance contract is termed an "aleatory" contract because the values exchanged are not necessarily equivalent. This is possible with the individual life insurance contract because the pooling of all premiums and all policy reserves permits the law of large numbers to function in such a way that dependable averages are developed. Fundamentally, therefore, life insurance contracts must be considered in groups, under which premiums will be paid in such amounts that the present value of all premiums to be paid will be equal to the present value of all death or maturity benefits to become payable. The individual contract, then, is set up in such a way that the promises of the insurance company are conditioned upon payment of the premiums as they fall due. Whether one considers the contracts individually or collectively, this dual significance must be kept in mind.

THE PAYMENT OF PREMIUMS

The Initial Premium

As we have seen, the first premium plays an essential role in the formation of the life insurance contract. Ordinarily, the policy provides that insurance will not become effective unless and until the first premium is paid. However, the policy often also contains a provision referring to the initial premium, "receipt of which is hereby acknowledged." In such cases, unless the agent is fully aware of the legal implications of his actions, it is quite possible for the insurance to be held effective as a matter of law even though the first premium has never been paid.

A Matter of Proof. Assume that a life insurance policy has been delivered, and at the time of the death of the alleged insured the policy is in his possession. What is the legal position of the company if it contends that the insurance was never actually in force because the initial premium was never paid?

The case of *Woloshin* v. *The Guardian Life Insurance Company of America*,[5] discusses this question at some length. In that case, the policy was in the possession of the insured at the time of his death, just one month after the policy was issued. The company refused to pay the death benefit, contending that the initial premium was never paid.

---

[5] 146 Pa. Super 152, 22 A.2d 54 (1941).

The question was whether possession of the policy by the beneficiary at the date of death creates a presumption of delivery and payment of the first premium of such a nature as to require that it be submitted to the jury.

The court said:

The evidence does not support the contention of defendant that the policy was delivered to Woloshin for inspection merely and that the delivery, therefore, was not absolute. The agent mailed the policy to him with a bill for the premium. No interim receipt was taken pending payment. Delivery of the policy was made on the credit of the assured and resulted in a contract between the parties conditioned only by its terms. But assuming that the question of conditional delivery were in issue, that question, clearly, was for the jury.

> The beneficiary's lawful possession of a life insurance policy after the death of the insured, and especially when, as here, there is no allegation of fraud, accident, artifice, or mistake, to impeach this possession, *prima facie* sustains the burden of proof resting on the plaintiff, by raising a strong presumption that the policy was not only manually delivered but was also *legally* [6] delivered to the insured, and puts the defendant in a position where, to avoid an adverse verdict, it must offer evidence of the conditional delivery alleged, sufficiently convincing to countervail the strong presumption of legal delivery arising from the lawful possession of the policy by the beneficiary. . . .

> . . . That case is also authority for the rule that where a policy, unconditionally delivered, contains an acknowledgment of receipt of the first premium, the presumption that payment was made is one of law and is conclusive. Without a specific acknowledgment of the initial premium, as in this case, the beneficiary's possession of the policy makes out a case, *prima facie,* though it raises no more than a rebuttable presumption of fact that the consideration was paid.

In this case, the court held that the question of payment was a question of fact, to be decided by the jury. Most cases hold similarly. Possession of a life insurance policy at the death of the insured, in the absence of fraud, creates a presumption that the initial premium was paid. This presumption is especially strong if the wording of the policy acknowledges receipt of the premium. The life insurance company is free to introduce evidence to show that the premium was not paid, if such evidence is available. However, if there is no admissible evidence, or if it is legally insufficient to overcome the presumption, the latter stands as a matter of law.

Payment Can Be Waived. An insurance company or its agent can waive payment of the first premium. Under these circumstances, also, the insurance becomes effective without the actual payment of the premium. Illustrative of such a situation is the case of *Henderson* v. *Capital*

---

[6] The reader may wish to refer to the general definition of delivery, in the legal sense of the term, Chapter IV, page 118.

Life and Health Insurance Company,[7] decided in 1942. There, a mother applied for a policy on the life of a minor child, and the policy was delivered while she was away from home. The father of the insured testified that the agent left the policy and receipt book and said that he would collect the first premium on his next visit. Before that next visit the insured had died.

Upon learning of the death, the agent went out to the house and picked up the policy and receipt book, saying that he would do everything he could to obtain the proceeds of the policy for them. However, he refused to return the policy. On suit, the lower court held that the actions of the agent constituted a waiver of the payment of the first premium, and the reviewing court upheld that decision, saying:

> . . . Under the well settled rule, the company may waive the time and method of the payment of premium. It will be observed that the policy by implication acknowledges receipt of the initial premium. It has been repeatedly held in this State that the manner and method of the payment of the initial premium may be waived and that credit may be extended for the initial premium. . . .
>
> I think the effect of the plaintiff's testimony in this case was that credit was extended for the initial premium until the agent made his next visit, but if it be construed as a promise on the part of the agent to advance the premium for the plaintiff, and to be reimbursed on his next visit, such would be evidence of waiver by the company, particularly in view of the fact that the policy contained no stipulation that it was not to be effective until the premium was paid and, as above stated, impliedly recognized the payment of the initial premium.

Subsequent Premiums

The insurance company has the right to decide how and where subsequent premiums shall be paid. It may require cash or it may accept personal checks, promissory notes, drafts, or any other kind of payment it may wish. If the premium is required to be paid at the home office, that requirement must be met. However, if the premium is paid to an agent who is not authorized to receive payment, it will nevertheless be effective if it actually reaches the home office before the grace period expires.

Time of Payment

Premiums must be paid on or before the exact date specified in the policy unless an extension of time is given by the company. It is sometimes said that "time is of the essence" in this respect, which simply means that if the premium falls due on June twentieth, payment on June twenty-first is too late. However, payment may be made at any time

---

[7] 199 S.C. 100, 18 S.E.2d 605 (1942).

prior to midnight of the due date, and if a premium is due on Sunday, payment on Monday will be sufficient.

Premium Payment Date. Companies have sometimes followed a practice of dating the policy the date of the application or the date of issue rather than the date the insurance actually becomes effective. As a result, where the insurance does not become effective until the first premium has been paid "during the lifetime and continued insurability" of the insured, we may have a situation where the first annual premium actually covers less than twelve months of insurance. For instance, the policy may be dated November 15, 1960, with the insurance becoming effective on December 20, 1960, and the next annual premium falling due November 15, 1961. Some of the problems resulting from this type of situation have been presented to the courts a sufficient number of times that several relatively standard rules have been developed.

First, where delivery of the policy is not required to put it into effect, if the insurance takes effect on payment of the first premium and the policy expressly states the date from which the premium period is to run, that date will control. Where the contract takes effect only upon delivery, however, court decisions are divided. Some cases have held that even though the policy is not effective until a later date, if a date is expressly stated for premium payment, that date must control. Other courts have held that the premium periods are to be computed from the date of delivery of the policy and payment of the first premium, regardless of the date specified in the policy for payment of the premiums.

Illustrative of decisions holding that the date specified must control is the case of *Timmer* v. *New York Life Insurance Company,*[8] decided in 1936 by the Iowa Supreme Court. There the court said, in part, as follows:

The insured had the opportunity of having the contract of insurance dated either at the time the application was signed or when the policy was issued. She chose the date of the signing of the application. She received what she requested. The undertaking on the part of the insurance company was a life contract, conditioned upon the payment by the insured of the premiums on the specified dates. The default on the part of the insured in the payment of any premium after the first, within and during the grace period of thirty-one days, after having received notice that her policy would lapse and become null and void if the premium was not paid before January 8, 1935, terminated the liability of the insurance company, and hence beneficiary is not entitled to the relief sought.

The date of delivery of the policy and payment of the first premium was held to control in the case of *Lentin* v. *Continental Assurance Co.,*[9] where the court discussed the question as follows:

[8] 222 Ia. 1193, 270 N.W. 421, 111 A.L.R. 1412 (1936).
[9] 105 N.E.2d 735 (Ill., 1952).

An examination of the many cases cited as bearing on the issue here raised leads to the following general conclusions: First, that parties to an insurance contract are competent to fix the date when the contract shall become effective, and when it appears that the parties themselves have clearly agreed upon a date upon which the policy shall take effect, that date governs concerning the payment of premiums and the expiration of the policy even though the contract contains a provision that it shall not go into effect until delivery and payment of the premium. The express agreement between the parties is deemed to remove the ambiguity in the two provisions and the date agreed upon is binding. Typical of cases falling within this category are *Shira v. New York Life Ins. Co.*, 90 Fed. 2d 953, where the insured agreed and specifically stipulated in his application that the policy should become effective on a stated date, and *Mutual Life Ins. Co. v. Hurni Packing Co.*, 263 U.S. 167, 68 L. ed. 235, wherein the applicant himself inserted in his application the date the policy was to become effective. Such cases can have no bearing on the construction of the policy being considered, for the effective date stipulated in the policy is not based on any express agreement of the parties.

Second, where the parties to an insurance contract have not expressly agreed to a definite effective date, courts have varied as to whether the date stated in the policy should prevail over the provisions of the application which state that the insurance shall not take effect until delivery, payment of the first premium, etc. One line of decisions holds that the date stipulated in the policy is the effective date, and that the provisions in the application simply impose a condition precedent to the taking effect of the insurance coverage. These cases have found no ambiguity in the provisions when read together and construe them to mean that the insurance contract shall not take effect until the conditions stated in the application are complied with, but, that when it does take effect it operates from the date stated in the insurance contract. Cases supporting this view are: *New York Life Ins. Co. v. Silverstein*, 53 Fed. 2d 986; *Travelers Ins. Co. v. Wolfe*, 78 Fed. 2d 78; *Pladwell v. Travelers' Ins. Co.*, 234 N.Y.S. 287, and *McCampbell v. New York Life Ins. Co.*, 288 Fed. 465. One of the reasons underlying the result reached is stated in the case last cited as follows: "The time when a premium is due should be definite, and that cannot be if the date upon which the first premium was in fact paid should fix the dates upon which subsequent premiums should be paid. Therefore the date mentioned in the policy for the payment of premiums governs. The date when the first premium was paid, which is almost always uncertain, and in most instances impossible of ascertainment, is immaterial." The insurance policies involved in the cases cited contained only a condition with regard to the payment of premium; it is the company's contention, however, that the same construction and reasoning applies to an insurance contract which contains a condition regarding delivery, and this view has been adopted in some jurisdictions. *Wall v. Mutual Life Ins. Co. of New York*, 228 Iowa, 119, 289 N.W. 901; *Pace v. New York Life Ins. Co.*, 219 N.C. 451, 14 S.E.2d 411; *Fawcett v. Security Benefit Ass'n*, 99 Utah 193, 104 Pac.2d 214.

The other view adopted has been that where the contract expressly provides that it shall take effect only on the condition of payment of the first premium, or of delivery, that such provision controls both as to the date upon which premiums must be paid and as to the expiration date of the policy, nothing more appearing except that the insurance company has dated the policy on a date prior to the payment of the first premium, or delivery, and has provided for the payment of subsequent premiums on the policy date. To this effect are *Shinall* v. *Prudential Ins. Co.*, 91 Colo. 194, 14 Pac.2d 183; *Stramback* v. *Fidelity Mut. Life Ins. Co. of Philadelphia*, 94 Minn. 281, 102 N.W. 731; *Halsey* v. *Amer. Cent. Life Ins. Co.*, 258 Mo. 659, 167 S.W. 951, and *Hampe* v. *Metropolitan Life Ins. Co.*, (Mo. App. 1929) 21 S.W.2d 926. The rationale of these cases is that since the premiums are payable in advance, a mere dating of the policy at a time prior to its effective date and the subsequent payment of premiums on the date of the policy's date are not sufficient to change an explicit provision in the contract that it takes effect as of a later date. To hold to the contrary would result in the insured's paying for insurance over a period during which the insurance company was under no liability to him and in which he had no insurance. This, we believe, is the better view, for to hold that the payment of the first premium, which contemplates that it be for a year's insurance, guarantees insurance for a period less than a year, is to give the insured something substantially less than what his express agreement with the company called for.

Backdating to Save Age. If the policy is backdated, at the insured's request, to give him the benefit of a lower premium, he will be held bound by his agreement. In such cases, the premium period begins to run from the date so requested, regardless of the date on which the policy was actually delivered. Because of the possible inequities in this connection, however, a number of states have laws limiting the length of time a policy can be backdated. For example, the Illinois Insurance Code [10] prohibits the issuance or delivery of any policy of life insurance in Illinois if it contains, among other things:

A provision by which the policy shall purport to be issued or take effect more than six months before the original application for the insurance was made.

Different state laws establish different limits upon this dateback privilege, but six months is the most representative period.

Grace Period. As we have noted, the insurance laws of most states require that policies issued or issued to be delivered in their states must include a grace period of a month or thirty-one days, within which the premium may be paid without default. Payment in such cases may be made at any time prior to midnight of the last day of grace. Generally speaking, also, the premium due may be paid during the grace period even though it is not so paid until after the death of the insured. There are a few holdings to the contrary, but this is by far the prevailing rule.

Extension of Time. Since the prompt payment of premiums is for the benefit of the company, it would seem that the company would have the right to waive this privilege at its discretion and to grant extensions of time for the payment of any premium, as it might wish. As a matter of fact, such extensions are not unusual.

---

[10] Ill. Revised Statutes, Chap. 73, Sec. 837(1)(b) (1959).

In the past, agreements to this effect have sometimes been held to conflict with the statutory requirement that the policy and the application contain the entire contract. However, the weight of authority is to the effect that such statutes relate only to contemporaneous or prior agreements. Thus they do not preclude any subsequent arrangements the parties may wish to make concerning an extension of time for the payment of any premium after the initial one.

Mode of Payment

The company may make whatever terms it wishes with respect to the medium in which the premium must be paid. It has the right to demand payment in cash. Alternatively it may accept promissory notes, post office money orders, personal checks, bank drafts, or it may make whatever other arrangements it may wish with the insured. Payment by personal check is the most customary method of payment today. However, payment by promissory note presents so many technical questions that the subject deserves more than a passing reference.

Payment by Promissory Note. There is no question but that an insurance company may waive the requirement that a premium be paid in cash and accept a promissory note instead, if it wishes. However, as the student will remember, waiver is a technical subject, and a promissory note is a separate legal instrument adding its own set of technical rules to those already effective in connection with the life insurance contract. As a result, most cases involving promissory notes present numerous questions both of fact and law.

Legally, the unconditional acceptance of a promissory note instead of cash, as payment of a life insurance premium, is the equivalent of payment. Thereafter, default on the part of the insured is default on the note, not the premium, and the company is powerless to take action to declare the policy forfeited. For this reason, when a company accepts a promissory note, it will ordinarily attempt to make it clear that the note does not operate as payment of the premium if the note itself is not paid when due. As a general rule, if promissory notes are contemplated, both the policy and the note or notes should contain provisions for the forfeiture of the policy on nonpayment of the notes. Provisions of this kind are uniformly held valid and enforceable.

Payment by Check

If there is no agreement to the contrary, payment of a premium by the insured's check is conditional upon the check's being honored, even though a premium receipt has been given. If the check is dishonored and a premium receipt has been given, the company has a choice of action. If it wishes to lapse the policy for nonpayment of premium it may do so, but it should act promptly, return the check, request the premium receipt, and declare the policy forfeited. If the decision is to take action with respect to the dishonored check, the privilege of lapsing the policy may be held to be waived. If the company takes no action but retains the check, the waiver will be presumed.

Illustrative Case. In *Sjoberg* v. *State Automobile Insurance Association, Des Moines, Ia.,*[11] the insurance company was sued on a $5,000 health and accident policy after the insured was killed in an automobile accident. The company contended that the policy had lapsed prior to the date of death, because of nonpayment of the last premium. The facts showed that the death occurred on August 5 and that the last quarterly renewal premium, due July 1, was paid by personal check on July 8, well within the grace period. The check was returned, however, with the notation "insufficient funds." The company did not return the check, rescind the receipt, and declare the policy canceled, as would have been its right. Instead, the local agency was requested to contact the insured and secure a bankable check or other remittance. This had not been accomplished at the date of death.

The court noted the general rule, that payment by check is conditional upon the check's being honored, if there is no agreement to the contrary, and said:

. . . There is authority, however, that if a check is unconditionally accepted as payment of the premium even though it turns out to be worthless the acceptance will prevent a forfeiture.

. . . In the case at bar the defendant on the occasion of a prior default followed strictly the terms of the policy. On the occasion in question instead of doing so it gave the insured a full receipt of the premium upon receiving his check. There was some delay in the presentation of the check for payment but when it was returned dishonored defendant did not repudiate the transaction but wrote his agents to contact insured to get "bankable check or other remittance." The agent notified the insured thereof. Neither the letter nor the conversation between defendant's agent and the insured referred to a forfeiture of the policy. Instead the whole tenor of both was to effect the collection of the check. Such negotiations indicate an intention to keep the policy in force. . . . They indicate defendant's election to rely upon the check rather than upon forfeiture and reinstatement.

Postdated Checks. Ordinarily, a postdated check is considered effective payment of a life insurance premium, as of the date of the receipt, if it is paid according to its terms, on the date it bears.

Persons to Whom Payment May Be Made

Most life insurance policies issued today contain a simple statement providing that premiums subsequent to the first shall be payable to

[11] 48 N.W.2d 452 (N.D., 1951).

the company at its home office, or to an authorized agent in exchange for an official receipt signed by the secretary of the company and countersigned by the agent. For this reason, policyholders generally have little trouble if they send their payments to the home office.

Payment to an Agent. Payment of premiums to an agent ordinarily presents no problem if the agent actually remits the premium to the company's home office. If he does not do so, a question of authority may be raised. Payment to an agent, it will be remembered, is payment to the principal, even though the agent may have only apparent authority. However, if the agent does not have actual authority to receive the premium, evidence must be submitted to show that he had such apparent authority as to justify a reasonable person in relying upon it.

Who May Pay the Premium

Ordinarily the owner of the policy pays the premiums, or they are paid by someone else at his direction and with his approval, as by his agent. Nevertheless, there are a number of instances where persons other than the insured may pay the premium without his express consent, sometimes over extensive periods of time. In such cases, questions often arise as to the legal rights of these persons as the result of their payments. The following section relates to the payment of premiums by persons other than the insured or owner of the policy.

The General Rule. Generally speaking, anyone who wants to do so may pay a life insurance premium. Life insurance companies have no duty to look behind the payments and ascertain whether or not the payors have any rights under the policies in question, and as a matter of practice, they do not. Unless the payor has some kind of interest in the policy, however, he will have no claim by reason of having paid the premiums. The general rule is this: In the absence of fraud or mistake, a person without interest in the policy who pays the premium due is a mere volunteer. He secures no rights under the policy and has no claim against those who do have rights, for the premiums so paid.

By the Beneficiary. This general rule is perhaps most frequently tested in the following representative, though hypothetical situation. Let us say that John Smith has a policy on his own life, with his wife named as a revocable beneficiary. John takes no interest in his policy *or* his wife and children, and the wife keeps the premiums paid as they fall due. Several years later, the Smith's marital troubles reach a point where there is a divorce, and John remarries. Then he wants to change the beneficiary of his life insurance.

The general rule in this situation is that payment of the premium by the beneficiary will not prevent the insured from changing the beneficiary designation in accordance with the rights outlined in the policy.

The beneficiary has the right to pay the premiums on a life insurance policy and keep it alive after the insured has discontinued the payments. However, a revocable beneficiary cannot increase or enlarge her "mere expectancy" under the policy simply by paying the premiums. Such payment continues whatever rights she does have, but she pays, subject to the conditions expressed in the policy concerning the right to change the beneficiary.

However, in cases such as the one outlined, other problems are frequently involved. For instance, the wife often has the policy and refuses to surrender it. Often also community property rights are involved. In other cases the divorce decree itself defines and clarifies the rights of the parties to the life insurance policy. Until all possibilities of this kind have been ruled out, therefore, the basic principle cannot safely be relied upon.

By the Assignee. If there is no agreement on the subject, the duty of premium payments remains with the insured, even after the policy has been assigned as collateral. If there is an agreement, the assignee is entitled to recover the amount of premiums paid. Naturally, an absolute assignee has the duty as well as the privilege of paying the premiums, since ownership has been transferred to him.

The Company's Position. The company's position with respect to the identity of the premium payor is excellently illustrated in the case of *Atlas Life Insurance Company* v. *Davis*,[12] decided in 1950. There the insured had paid the premiums by military allotment for a time and then requested that the allotment be discontinued. A department of the government paid the premiums after that, although it was without authority to do so. After the death of the insured, the company contended that the policy was not in full force and effect because payment of premiums was made without authority.

The court said:

It is undisputed that the policy was issued, and that the company received and retained all the premiums due upon said policy. The facts under the pleadings stand admitted. It is apparent, therefore, that the issue involved is whether the payment of premiums by a third party, or one other than the insured, is sufficient to maintain a policy of life insurance in force and effect. We think it was, since, from the insurer's point of view, it is immaterial who pays the premiums and payment by a third party is sufficient.

OTHER WAYS OF PAYING PREMIUMS

Premiums Paid in Advance

Most insureds wish to pay their premiums as they fall due, and many people realize that the risk of death during the premium paying

---

[12] 232 P.2d 146 (Okla., 1950).

period gives them a very slight but real advantage if they do not pay up their policies. On the other hand, many insureds are concerned that they may not be able to meet the premium payments as they fall due. This is particularly true with respect to insureds whose income is somewhat irregular. In other typical cases, an older person may wish, for example, to give a grandchild a policy on the latter's life and to provide a fund for the payment of premiums until the child is grown and able to take over that responsibility for himself. To accommodate the needs of people like these, most companies have made some provision for accepting sums equal to the discounted value of premiums payable for a specified number of years in the future. As each premium falls due, the amount necessary is withdrawn from the deposit and the remainder retained separately until the next premium paying date, when the process is repeated.

Legal Problems. Generally speaking, it is considered within the authority of a life insurance company to accept premiums paid in advance, on the theory that it is an activity reasonably related to the company's basic corporate duty. In other words, it is in the nature of an implied power, which is necessary or appropriate in connection with the express power of a life insurance company. However, when these sums are subject to withdrawal at the request of the payor it is apparent that the insurance company is providing a service which resembles that provided by banks, a fact which some of the state legislatures and officials have noted with varying results.

The two principal legal problems presented by this method of premium payment are: (1) May the payor withdraw premiums paid in advance prior to the date the respective premiums fall due; and (2) what disposition should be made of the unapplied balance of the fund remaining at the death of the insured?

Withdrawal Rights. Life companies ordinarily grant the right to withdraw the unapplied portion of the fund at the payor's discretion, subject to some limitations. Sometimes there is a limitation as to the date on which withdrawal may be made and in others only the entire amount unapplied may be withdrawn. In other cases the request is specifically made subject to deferral at the company's option. Generally speaking, some variation of this practice is permitted in every state except Wisconsin. There, a ruling of the Attorney General specifically prohibits any company doing business in that state from accepting deposits from policyholders, if they are withdrawable on demand.

Payment of Unapplied Balance. Often, of course, some funds remain in the deposit at the death of the insured. To whom should they be paid? The receipt given at the time the money is accepted may provide that the unapplied funds will be paid to the beneficiary or to the payor's estate. In most cases, the prepaid premiums are deposited by the insured. To return the remaining sum to "the payor" at the insured's death, therefore, means paying it to his executors or administrator. As a matter of convenience, if the sum is not large, it is ordinarily preferable to make it payable to the beneficiary.

Pre-Authorized Check Plan

The pre-authorized check plan is a plan for paying premiums by means of instruments termed checks, which are drawn by the company to its own order, as authorized by the policyholder, on the bank in which the latter maintains a checking account. The plan requires an authorization from the policyholder for the company to draw the check and type the policyholder's name where his signature would otherwise appear. The policyholder must also authorize the bank to accept and process the checks in the regular course of business.

A separate agreement between the bank and the life insurance company provides that the insurance company will hold the bank harmless from any liability it might otherwise incur by reason of accepting the checks. The exact provisions of this agreement vary, although recommended forms have been worked out by several interested associations.

Arguments for the Plan. Those persons who favor the pre-authorized check plan take the position that we are living in a monthly payment economy and that this plan only cooperates with policyholders who are already paying most of their bills on a monthly basis. They also point out that the plan frees the policyholder from having to remember to pay his life insurance premium, and thus he avoids the risk of inadvertently letting a policy lapse and being temporarily, or permanently, without coverage.

Arguments against the Plan. Banks and bankers have opposed the pre-authorized check plan, in some instances rather strenuously, principally on the grounds that since the policyholder is not notified each time the insurance company draws a check on his account, overdrafts are likely to occur and present problems with respect to the effectiveness of the insurance. It is the purpose of the indemnity agreements between the banks and the life insurance companies to meet, insofar as possible, these potential difficulties on which the objections are based.

Generally speaking, if the check so drawn clears through regular banking channels, the premium is paid just as effectively as if the policyholder himself had drawn the check. If for some reason the check does not clear, the bank is protected from liability by the indemnity agreement with the life insurance company, and the company, ordinarily, will take the same action it would take when any other check is returned for insufficient funds.

The Automatic Premium Loan

The automatic premium loan provision, included in the policy itself, permits the company to effect a policy loan against the cash value of the policy if the premium is not paid at the expiration of the grace period. At the present time, inclusion of this type of provision is compulsory only in Rhode Island. However, even there, inclusion of the provision on an elective basis is sufficient compliance, and on that basis it is found in the policies of most companies. In such cases, the policyholder must elect to have it operative before it will be invoked by the company. If the policyholder makes such an election, however, the provision will be invoked when necessary to prevent the lapse, for non-payment of premium, of any policy having a loan value at the time sufficient to pay the past-due premium. The company simply establishes a policy loan in an amount sufficient to pay the premium and interest on the loan to the next premium payment date and credits "premiums paid." It is customary to notify the policyholder of the transaction.

Advantages of the Automatic Premium Loan. The premium loan, if properly used, can be a decided advantage. Certainly it keeps the policy in force in the event of an inadvertent lapse, and it has the further advantages of maintaining the disability and accidental death provisions in force, as well as avoiding the trouble of reinstatement, even if the insured would be able to meet the insurability requirements. Used properly, the premium loan provision maintains the policy through periods of inadvertent lapsation, and the insured can repay the loan[13] at his convenience without loss other than the interest on the loan.

Disadvantages of the Automatic Premium Loan. Perhaps the most general criticism of the automatic premium loan is that it makes it too easy for the insured to defer payment. Used indiscriminately, it can give a false sense of security, and often the establishment of the first loan is the beginning of a process ending in lapse. The continued use of the loan inexorably exhausts the cash value, so that at the time of lapse there is only a minimal, if any, value to be applied under the standard non-forfeiture options.

Let us take, for example, a juvenile policy owned by an adult purchaser, a parent, but without a waiver of premium benefit for death of the purchaser. Assume that the ownership arrangements provide that ownership shifts to the child at the death of the purchaser and that the purchaser dies prior to the minor's age twenty-one. In such a case ownership shifts to the child, but because of his minority he

---

[13] For further discussion of this privilege, see Chapter XIII.

cannot exercise the ownership rights. Under these circumstances, if no further premiums are paid and if an automatic premium loan is in effect, the loan value of the policy will be systematically used in payment of the premium until the policy lapses. Without the automatic premium loan the cash value would ordinarily be applied to purchase extended term insurance. In the case of a child, this would often continue the policy in its face amount past the age of majority, at which time the insured could make whatever arrangements he might wish concerning insurance on his own life.

Legally, the premium loan for the payment of premiums operates in exactly the same way as any other policy loan. The policyholder is not borrowing his own money; he is effecting an advance from the company, secured by the cash value of the policy, for the single purpose of paying the premium then due.

Allotment Plans

Under the federal government allotment plan, members of the military service have the privilege of authorizing the regular deduction of sums from their pay for the purpose of paying premiums on their life insurance. These deductions are made on a monthly basis and continue to be made until the policyholder or someone on his behalf authorizes them to cease.

Salary allotment plans accomplish the same purpose in connection with private employment. There the employee authorizes the employer to withhold the amount of insurance premium from his salary and to forward it directly to the company.

Like the pre-authorized check plan, the payment of premiums in advance, and the automatic premium loan, allotment plans are merely mechanical means to assure that premiums will be paid when they fall due. Special problems sometimes arise in connection with their operation, particularly concerning the responsibilities of the various parties involved, but the basic principles with respect to payment of premiums are not changed. Premiums must still be paid when they fall due, and the responsibility is upon the policyholder to pay them, not upon the life insurance company to see that they are paid.

PREMIUM NOTICES

When Notices Are Required

The general rule is that a life insurance company has no legal responsibility to send premium notices unless there is a statute or a policy provision requiring it. Nevertheless, as a matter of practice, all companies send notices because it is good business to do so. Sending premium notices has proved to be an effective means of keeping life insurance contracts in force, particularly during their early years, and the practice, for that reason, has become routine.

Specific Agreement. If the insurance company specifically agrees to give notice of premiums due or dividends, it will, of course, be required to do so. Thus, if the policy includes a provision to that effect, the company must send the notice as specified.

Course of Conduct. If the company has consistently sent premium notices over an extended period of time, it may be precluded from discontinuing the practice without specific notice to that effect. The courts are not in complete agreement on this point, but the majority holding is that where it has been customary to give notice, a company cannot discontinue the custom without warning and then declare a forfeiture if the policyholder does not pay the premium when due. The theory is that by following such a course of conduct for a sufficient length of time that the insured has been led to rely upon it, the company is thereafter estopped from relying upon what would otherwise have been its right to declare a forfeiture.

Statutes Requiring Notice. New York, Illinois, Ohio, Kansas, and a few other states have statutes which make it unlawful for a life insurance company to declare a policy forfeited for nonpayment of premium unless premium notices have been sent. The Illinois statute is illustrative.[14] It simply states that a policy cannot be declared forfeited for nonpayment of premiums or interest within six months after default in the payment of a premium *unless* a premium notice has been mailed to the insured or assignee at least fifteen and not more than forty-five days prior to the due date of the premium. The affidavit of a company employee having the responsibility of mailing the notices, that notice was given as required and that it was duly addressed and mailed, is expressly declared to be presumptive evidence that the notice was given as required. Incidentally, however, this requirement does not apply to life policies on which the premiums are payable monthly.

The New York statute is very similar to this, as is the Kansas statute, although the latter is considerably more detailed. The Ohio statute is somewhat unusual since it applies only to foreign (out-of-state) companies and requires them to send premium notices to policyholders and assignees who reside in Ohio.

Statutory notice requirements are held to be for the benefit of the policyholder, and any attempted waiver of such notice, on the part of the insured, by application or policy provision, will be held void.

---

[14] *Illinois Revised Statutes,* Chap. 73, Sec. 846 (1959).

Dividends

In general business usage, a dividend represents an apportionment of the earnings of the enterprise, paid to the stockholders as their share of the profits. In insurance the word has a very different meaning, although there are dividends in the usual business sense, in the case of stock life insurers. In participating life insurance, however, the premium is established at such a level that the company expects to be able to operate on a smaller amount. The difference is a margin of safety. If the operations of the company are as expected, a part of the premium is returned to the policyholder at the end of specified intervals, and that refund is called a "dividend." Obviously it has nothing to do with profits, and in legal effect it is a premium abatement. For this reason, life insurance dividends are not subject to personal income tax, and they are always taken into account in figuring the "cost" or the "investment" in a life insurance policy for tax purposes.

The amount of the premium, therefore, is very definitely affected by dividends and the way in which they are paid or applied. Handling the dividends as instructed by the insured is one of the responsibilities of the company toward its policyholders, and the right to direct the application or payment of dividends is one of the many rights an applicant obtains when he is issued a participating policy.

Dividend Options. Participation in the surplus of a company has been legislatively recognized as a possible source of abuse since the days of the Armstrong Investigation, and for that reason it has been made the subject of statutory regulation by a number of the states. The Illinois statute,[15] for example, requires that the participating policy include "a provision that the policy shall participate annually in the surplus of the company beginning not later than the end of the third policy year; . . ." This statute continues:

. . . and the insured under any annual dividend policy shall have the right each year to have the dividend arising from such participation either paid in cash, or applied in reduction of premiums, or applied to the purchase of paid-up additional insurance, or be left to accumulate to the credit of the policy, with interest at such rate as may be determined from time to time by the company. . . .

Most states have statutes specifying the rights of policyholders to participate in the surplus of a life insurance company and the distribution of such surplus to the policyholders. Many of these statutes require the determination of such surplus participation at stated intervals. A few of them, notably Illinois and New York, also set forth the optional

---

[15] *Illinois Revised Statutes,* Chap. 73, Sec. 836(1)(e) (1959).

methods of application of dividends that must be provided for in the policy. Other states provide for optional methods of dividend application, although they do not spell them out in detail in the statute.

The Illinois law, quoted above, is somewhat more detailed than many, but it summarizes the practices of many companies, stating that each dividend shall be: (1) Paid in cash; (2) applied to reduce premiums; (3) applied to purchase paid-up additional insurance; *or* (4) accumulated to the credit of the policy, with interest.

A "fifth option" is sometimes included under present-day contracts, which provides that the dividend shall be applied to purchase single premium, one-year term insurance in an amount equal to the cash value of the policy. This is an entirely optional choice, however, and was used originally in connection with relatively restricted plans of insurance. Many companies also provide options which will pay up the policy or mature it as an endowment, if the policyholder so wishes.

The Illinois law further provides that if the insured does not notify the company of his election of a dividend option, the policy shall specify which of the methods shall automatically go in force. A few states specify which of the options shall be the automatic option, and unfortunately they do not all specify the same one. Thus, four states provide that if no option is elected, dividends shall be payable in cash, and two states provide that dividends shall be applied to purchase paid-up additions.

Notice Required. If dividends are to be applied to reduce premiums, it is obvious that the policyholder will not know the exact amount of premium he must pay unless and until he receives a premium notice. In such cases, the company is legally obliged to send a premium notice. Otherwise nonpayment of the premium when due cannot be held to work a forfeiture.

Insurer's Duty to Apply Dividends

It is well settled that the insurer cannot declare a life insurance policy forfeited for the nonpayment of a premium if the company has in its possession accumulated dividends sufficient to pay the premium. It is equally clear that if the dividend accumulation is not sufficient to pay the entire premium which is due and payable, a part payment is not sufficient and a forfeiture can be declared. However, a number of questions can and do arise with respect to the dividend option elected and the company's duty with respect to the application of such dividends toward the payment of premiums.

In one case,[16] the insured elected at the time that he applied for the policy to have the dividends accumulate. Later he effected a policy

---

[16] *State Mutual Life Assur. Co. of Worcester, Mass.* v. *Fleischer,* 186 F.2d 358 (C.A. Mo., 1951).

loan under a loan agreement assigning all "right, title and interest in and to said policy including all dividends, dividend accumulations and paid-up additions." The policy lapsed, and he died shortly after the expiration of the extended term insurance as computed by the company. The beneficiary sued, contending that the dividends should have been applied either to reduce the loan, increase the cash value, or to pay the premium then due. If any of these actions had been taken the policy would have been in force at the date of the death of the insured.

The court held in favor of the beneficiary, saying:

> We are of the view that dividends assigned to the insurance company as security for a loan should be applied in payment of the loan, at least where to do so will prevent the forfeiture or cancellation of the policy unless the policy specifically provides otherwise. If, however, defendant under the circumstances here disclosed was not required to apply the dividend apportioned to this policy in reduction of the loan, the plaintiff was entitled to have it applied on a quarterly portion [17] of the annual premium and thereby increase the net cash value so as to carry the policy beyond the day of death.

Funds held under a special agreement are not subject to this rule, however. Thus in *Sugarman* v. *Equitable Life Assurance Society of the United States*,[18] the court held that the proceeds of a matured policy, held at interest, were completely subject to the deposit agreement. Thus the insurance company had no authority to depart from the terms of that agreement and apply any part of the funds so held toward the payment of premiums due on another policy.

EXCUSES FOR NONPAYMENT OF PREMIUMS

Relating to the Policyholder Only

There is almost no excuse for the nonpayment of premiums which will prevent the forfeiture of a life insurance policy on that account, unless the policyholder can show that he was ready and willing to pay and that an act or acts on the part of the insurer prevented payment. Thus, physical or mental disability of the policyholder, poverty, accident, illiteracy, even disappearance, have been and are generally held not to excuse the failure to pay premiums.

A moment's reflection will show the soundness of this as a general proposition of law. Payment of premiums is a condition precedent. Performance of the company's promises is subject to this condition, and there is no right to have the promises performed unless the condition has been fulfilled. For this reason, nonpayment of premiums is a good defense in a suit against the life insurance company, and excuses for nonperformance of the condition have little bearing on the case unless they relate to

---

[17] By reason of a policy provision to that effect.

[18] 71 A.2d 148 (N.J. Sup. Ch., 1950).

conduct on the part of the promisor, in this case the life insurance company.

Relating to the Company

Waiver. The insurer is always free to waive the forfeiture conditions of the policy. Provisions requiring punctual payment of premiums, and the forfeiture of the policy if they are not so paid, are considered to be for the benefit of the insurer, and as a consequence they may be waived by it.

Probably the facts most frequently alleged to constitute a waiver (or an estoppel) are those relating to a "course of conduct" of accepting late premiums. Thus in one case [19] the court said:

> On the issue of waiver and estoppel the evidence is that for a period of six years all premiums had been paid by Mrs. Boggs to Hansen, either in cash or by her personal check, and that no one of these payments was exchanged for the company's receipt signed by the president or secretary as required in the policy. It is also in evidence that each and all of these payments were made in this manner while the insured was in default, and in many cases after the period of grace had expired. During this period of six years eighteen separate premiums became due. Fourteen of these were accepted by appellant after the period of grace had expired. In only one instance—September, 1940—the appellant demanded and received an application for reinstatement.
>
> . . . we conclude that the course of conduct in relation to the payments of premiums running over a period of six years was such that the respondents were entitled to assume that the terms of the policy need not be adhered to strictly, and that the appellant was estopped from insisting upon a strict compliance with those terms until it had given the respondents reasonable notice of its change in policy.

Refusal of Tender. The importance of the actions of the insurance company and its agents is illustrated in the case of *Harms* v. *The John Hancock Mutual Life Insurance Company.*[20] The statement of facts and the decision of the court in this case are brief and will be quoted rather than summarized, as follows:

> WICKHEM, J.: On November 22, 1944 defendant issued a policy of insurance to Bayard E. Hatch, Jr., naming plaintiff, Josephine Hatch (Harms), his mother, and Bayard Hatch, his father, as beneficiaries. The annual premium was $95.90 subsequently divided into four quarterly premiums of $25.40 each. The first premium was paid when due; the second due on February 22, 1945 was paid on March 14th of that year; the third due on May 22, 1945 was never paid. There was a thirty-one day grace period in which an insured could pay any premium after its due date, the policy to remain in force during this grace period. The grace period for the quarterly payment in question expired

---

[19] *Gleed* v. *The Lincoln National Life Insurance Company,* 65 Cal. App. 2d 213, 150 P.2d 484 (1944).

[20] 34 N.W.2d 687 (Wis., 1948).

on June 22nd and the insured died on July 3d, twelve days thereafter. Bayard Hatch died subsequent to the commencement of this action and plaintiff Josephine Hatch remarried.

The circumstances which raise the precise point involved in this case are as follows: The insurance in this case was solicited by an agent of defendant named Balistreiri who collected the first two premiums and called at plaintiff's house on June 20, 1945 to collect the last quarterly premium. This was two days before the expiration of the grace period. Defendant's agent informed Mrs. Hatch that he had come to collect her son's insurance. She told him that the son was sick and would not have a paycheck until July 5th and that she would have to pay the premium herself although she wished that the youngster would pay for his own insurance. She extracted three ten dollar bills from her pocketbook and told the agent that he might as well take it. The agent declined and said that he would hold the matter open until the 10th of July so that the boy would have a chance to pay it. As he left plaintiff said, "Well, Mr. Balistreiri, it's right here," and the agent said, "It's all right Mrs. Hatch. I will hold it open until the 10th of July."

The jury found that plaintiff Josephine Hatch offered to pay and that the agent put off the matter as above indicated.

It is contended by appellant that the agent having no authority to issue policies could not grant an extension of time for the payment of a premium. This contention misses the point and the case is governed adversely to appellant by *Baumann* v. *Metropolitan Life Ins. Co.*, 144 Wis. 206, 128 N.W. 864. The point is that the amount of the premium was offered to a collecting agent of the company who declined to take the money and under those circumstances it must be held that plaintiff was

> deterred from making such payment by conduct or statements on the part of such agent which induced in her an honest belief that a failure to then make the payment or tender would not then be relied upon by the company to work a failure or forfeiture of the policy.

General contract law recognizes what is called a tender of performance in connection with conditions, which is similar to, though not exactly the same as, the tender of payment in connection with debts. Offering to pay a life insurance premium, therefore, is the tender of performance of a condition precedent, if it is accompanied by ability and willingness to perform, and is itself not subject to a condition. Such a tender is sometimes said to be the equivalent of performance, but that is not strictly true. It is the equivalent of performance only in the sense that it establishes the liability of the promisor whose promise was subject to the condition, performance of which was tendered. Thus a refusal of a tendered premium on the part of the life insurance company will excuse the nonpayment of the premium in the sense that the company will then be precluded from declaring a forfeiture for the nonpayment.

Relating to War

War, as a possible excuse for nonpayment of premiums, presents a unique situation. Beyond the control of either the insured or the insurer, it tests legal principles perhaps more harshly than any other set of circumstances that might affect the payment of premiums. It is not surprising, therefore, that the conclusions reached by the several jurisdictions in which the question has been considered have not always been in accord.

State Court Decisions. The question, as most frequently litigated, is simple to state: What is the status of a life insurance contract at the end of a war between the respective countries of the insured and the insurer when, because of that war and for that reason alone, it has been impossible for the insured to pay the premiums?

This question was litigated extensively at the close of the War between the States, in cases which set forth the basic alternatives which are still being propounded today. Summarized, state court decisions fall generally into two groups: One group is composed of holdings that the contract is not terminated by nonpayment of premiums because of war, and the payment of premiums is only suspended; the other group holds that the contract is completely terminated by reason of nonpayment of premiums, in accordance with the provisions of the policy.

The earliest holding in point of time, a Kentucky case, was decided on the principle that cancellation of the contract for nonpayment of premiums would effect a forfeiture, which the law traditionally "abhors." Thus the decision was in the beneficiaries' favor, the court saying: "None of the parties can be presumed to have contemplated such a disabling war or to have intended by the condition of avoidance more than voluntary failure to pay, when there was a legal ability to receive the premiums." [21]

In a series of cases, the Supreme Court of Virginia developed the view that war only suspended a contract of insurance. At war's end, the contract could be resumed by payment of the back premiums. Here, again, the court took the position that payment of the premium was the performance of a condition to prevent a forfeiture. The courts of New York and New Jersey took much the same position, that the effect of war was to suspend rather than cancel the contract.

Meanwhile, the Georgia Supreme Court, in the case of *Dillard* v. *Manhattan Life Insurance Company*,[22] reached an analysis more in accord with present-day thinking, as follows:

Indeed, a contract of life insurance is, at best, nothing but an undertaking that the company will take the annual premiums paid, invest them safely, and pay to the insured the product, after deducting the expense of the business. Indeed, if every person insured lived to an average age, this would be exactly

---

[21] *New York Life Insurance Company v. Clopton,* 7 Bush. (Ky.) 179 (Summer Term, 1870).

[22] 44 Ga. 119 (July Term, 1871).

the contract, but as any individual may die at any time, the company agrees to pay what his premiums would amount to, making up its losses on him by the payments of those who live beyond the average age. The regular annual payment agreed upon under the contract is thus a condition precedent of the contract and not a condition subsequent.

The court then pointed out the basic principle that failure to perform a condition precedent does not work a forfeiture, because the right which is subject to it never vested in the first place. "A failure to perform a condition precedent is a failure to do the thing necessary to acquire the right," the court said. "Hence the conclusion is reached that the plaintiff should recover nothing."

The Federal Cases. In the most significant federal decision, a new note was added—the idea that equities were involved even though nonpayment of the premium was a failure to perform a condition precedent. In the case of *New York Life Insurance Company* v. *Statham*,[23] from which we have previously quoted,[24] the court said:

We are of opinion, therefore, first, that as the companies elected to insist upon the condition in these cases, the policies in question must be regarded as extinguished by the non-payment of the premiums, though caused by the existence of the war, and that an action will not lie for the amount insured thereon.

Secondly, that such failure being caused by a public war, without the fault of the assured, they are entitled *ex aequo et bono* [25] to recover the equitable value of the policies with interest from the close of the war.

It should be remembered at this point that by the decision of *Erie* v. *Tompkins*, the federal courts are obliged to apply the common law of the state where the question under consideration arose. For example, in cases arising under the law of Virginia, the federal courts would follow the common law as defined by that state. The decision in the *Statham* case, therefore, does not have the weight at the present time that it would have had prior to the decision in the *Erie* case.

The Versailles Treaty. The effect of World War I on life insurance contracts previously in force between nationals of enemy countries was specifically defined in the Treaty of Versailles.[26] Such contracts were not to be considered as having been dissolved by the outbreak of the war, and any amount which might, during the war, have become payable under a contract, was specifically declared to be recoverable after the war, with interest at 5 per cent from the date on which it became pay-

---

[23] 93 U.S. 24 (1876).

[24] See *supra*, page 244.

[25] "In equity and good conscience."

[26] Treaty of Versailles, Part X, Sec. V, Annex, Clause III of Annex to Sec. V, pars. 11 and 15.

able. Contracts which had lapsed because of nonpayment of premiums during the war could be surrendered for cash as of the date of lapse, or be restored within three months following the date of the treaty, upon payment of arrearages of premiums with interest at 5 per cent.

World War II. Of the numerous treaties signed at the close of World War II, none repeated the provisions of the Versailles Treaty which, in effect, merely suspended those contracts of insurance on which premiums had not been paid by reason of the war. In the early years of the war, legislation had been proposed which would have kept in force all contracts of insurance written by American companies on the lives of non-enemy persons unable to escape enemy-occupied countries, but it was not enacted. Generally speaking, therefore, American insurance companies took the position that since their contracts contained automatic nonforfeiture provisions, the most equitable course of action was to continue all contracts in force in accordance with their terms.

RECOVERY OF PREMIUMS PAID

When They Are Recoverable

Two Basic Situations. Fundamentally, the life insurance policy transfers a risk of loss from an individual to a group of insureds as of the moment the insurance takes effect. The company thus assumes the risk, and the policyholder pays the premium. Generally speaking, therefore, in any question concerning recovery of the premium paid, the basic question is: "Has the risk been assumed by the company?" Ordinarily, if it has, the premium is considered to have been earned, and the payor is not entitled to its return. On the other hand, if the risk has not been assumed by the company, the payor of the premium is ordinarily entitled to receive it back upon demand.

Where the Risk Has Been Assumed. As a general rule, if an effective contract has been entered into, the premium payor is not entitled to a return of premiums paid. Thus the mere fact that the company has reorganized without the consent of the insured, though with proper legal authority to do so, does not give the insured the right to a return of the premium paid to the reorganized company. Also, if overpayments or assessments are made voluntarily and with full knowledge of the facts, they cannot ordinarily be recovered by the payor. However, if the money is paid under a mistake of fact, or through fraud on the part of the agent, it is ordinarily recoverable.

Illustrative of payment under a mistake of fact are those cases where premiums are paid after the death of the insured. For instance, in one

Utah case [27] the wife of the insured continued to pay the premiums on his life insurance after he had disappeared while herding sheep. He apparently became lost, and although his horse returned to camp, he did not. There was an alleged agreement between the wife and the mother of the insured (the mother was the beneficiary) concerning the insured's property, and the wife paid the premiums until her husband's body was found some two years later. The case itself concerned the rights of the wife as the result of having paid the premiums voluntarily, and the court held that the mere payment of the premiums gave her no rights whatsoever as against the named beneficiary under the policy. However, the company had already refunded the amount of premium she had paid, since it was paid under a mutual mistake of fact—that is to say, their ignorance of the death of the insured.

Where the Risk Has Not Been Assumed. As a general rule the premium payor can recover any premiums paid by him if the insurance has not taken effect as a binding contract. Obviously if the application is rejected, the applicant is entitled to return of the premium. Also, if the policy issued is not in accordance with the application, the applicant may refuse to accept it and is then entitled to recover back the premium paid.

Illegal Contracts. In connection with recovery of premiums paid under illegal contracts of insurance, the decisions of the courts are not in complete accord. Generally speaking, if the contract is illegal or invalid for lack of insurable interest, for example, the premium payor can recover the premium if the parties are not *in pari delicto.* This is a frequently used Latin phrase which, roughly translated, means "in equal fault." Thus if the applicant acted in good faith, and if he had no part in the wrong, he is not ordinarily penalized by reason of the illegality of the contract and can recover the premium paid. If the parties are *in pari delicto,* however, the premium cannot be recovered. Some courts take the position also that if the contract is illegal they will leave the parties where they found them. Under this approach, the premium cannot be recovered regardless of the good faith of the payor.

*   *   *   *   *

ILLUSTRATIVE CASE

The following case has been selected for purposes of illustration because it brings together in one case the importance of prompt payment of premiums, the use of an express negation of waiver, and the possible effect of an agent's promise to pay the premium.

---

[27] *Cook v. Cook,* 174 P.2d 434 (Utah, 1946).

SPIEGEL v. METROPOLITAN LIFE INSURANCE CO., ET AL.[28]

(New York Court of Appeals.)

FULD, J.: The plaintiff, as beneficiary, brought this action against defendant Metropolitan Life Insurance Company and defendant Levy, one of the company's agents, to recover death and accidental death benefits under a policy on the life of her husband. The defendant company opposed payment on the grounds that the policy had lapsed without value because of the non-payment of a premium and that, in any event, the plaintiff was not entitled to accidental death benefits since the insured had died, not as the result of accident, but of natural causes. The plaintiff, not disputing that there was a failure to pay the premium when due, argues that the Metropolitan, by requesting payment of the next quarterly premium, waived the failure to pay the earlier premium. In addition, she seeks to hold defendant Levy on the ground that he promised to keep the insurance in force by paying the premium out of his own funds.

After hearing the evidence, the trial court dismissed the complaint as to the company and directed a verdict in favor of Levy, and the Appellate Division affirmed the resulting judgment.

Viewing the evidence, as we must, in the light most favorable to the plaintiff, it appears that in November, 1952, the agent Levy who, over a thirteen-year period, had sold the deceased several small life insurance policies, wrote the application for the policy in issue and collected the first quarterly premium of $39.75. The application was approved and a policy for approximately $7650, plus $3000 if death resulted from accidental means, was issued and delivered. The second quarterly premium fell due on February 26, 1953, and the formal notice, notifying the insured of such fact, contained this further provision:

DO NOT PERMIT YOUR POLICY TO LAPSE

EFFECT OF FAILURE TO PAY PREMIUMS—Unless the premium covered by this notice shall be paid . . . on or before the date when due (or within the 31-day grace period), the policy . . . will become forfeited and void.[29]

Although the plaintiff paid Levy the premiums due on her husband's smaller and earlier policies, she advised him, on February 24, 1953, that she did not have the money for the new policy. The plaintiff testified, however, that Levy assured her that he would "take care of" paying the premiums and would look to her for reimbursement when she obtained the money from the summer rental of her home at Long Beach. Then, toward the end of March, just a few days before the expiration of the thirty-day grace period provided for by statute (Ins. Law, § 155), the plaintiff received another notice reminding her that the premium had not been paid and that the grace period was about to run out. On the very day this was received, the plaintiff testified, she spoke to Levy and in response to her query, "didn't you tell me that you were taking care of this thing for me and not to worry, not to think about it: you were covering me?" he assertedly replied, "I told you I would take care of it, and I am taking care of it, and don't worry." And, indeed, after the policy had, in fact, lapsed, the plaintiff declared that Levy, when collecting

---

[28] 6 N.Y. 2d 91, 188 N.Y.S. 2d 486, 160 N.E.2d 40 (1959).

[29] A warning similar to this one is contained in the policy itself.

the other premiums, again assured her that he "would take care of the big one." [30]

Had the policy remained in force, the next quarterly premium would have fallen due on May 26, and during the early part of that month, Metropolitan's home office inadvertently sent a notice of premium to the insured. This notice, upon which the plaintiff relies to establish a waiver, specifically recited, as do all of the company's premium notices, that the premium should be paid only if "said policy be then in force." No premium was ever paid in response to this notice and on June 16, 1953, the insured, an electrician, died of a coronary thrombosis suffered while working in the normal course of his employment.

The plaintiff's appeal from the judgment in Metropolitan's favor may be quickly disposed of. Certainly, the due date of the premium was not extended, nor the lapsed policy reinstated, by virtue of any statements made by Levy that he would "take care" of the premium or policy. Quite apart from other considerations, it is enough to note that the policy explicitly provided that "No agent is authorized to alter or amend [it] . . . or to extend the due date of any premium." (See, e.g., Drennan v. Sun Indemnity Co., 271 N.Y. 182, 185-188; Abbott v. Prudential Ins. Co., 281 N.Y. 375, 378-381.) Equally unavailing is the claim that the sending of a premium notice constituted a waiver; the purely mechanical act falls far short of proof that the company waived, or intended to waive, the insured's failure to pay the second premium. (See Ross v. New York Life Ins. Co., 68 F.2d 727; Curtis v. Prudential Ins. Co. of America, 55 F.2d 97.) And, we would simply observe that no evidence was offered at the trial that the other policies on the insured's life could have been utilized for their loan or cash value to prevent the lapse of the policy in the suit. The complaint against the Metropolitan was, therefore, properly dismissed.

However, the evidence presented did require that the case against the defendant Levy be submitted to the jury. He had promised to pay the second quarterly premium in order to keep the policy in force. In short, if the jurors believed, as the plaintiff in effect testified, that Levy had told her not to worry about the February premium, that he would pay it and look to her for reimbursement in the future, they would have been justified in holding him liable. . . . In Landusky v. Beirne (80 App. Div. 272, affd. 178 N.Y. 551, supra), the defendant, an insurance agent, promised to obtain a "good policy in a very good company" upon the plaintiff's house in Pennsylvania. However, the defendant procured a policy from a company which had no authority to do business in Pennsylvania or New York. The property was destroyed by fire, but no insurance was ever paid. The defendant was held liable for the damage sustained, the Appellate Division writing that the plaintiff "made out a violation of the defendant's contract when he showed that the policy procured was not enforcible in New York or Pennsylvania" and that the company issuing it refused to pay. . . . And, in the Lawrence case (223 Ark. 584 Supra), the court wrote that, when an insurance agent "undertakes to procure a policy of insurance for another, the law imposes upon [him] the duty . . . to perform the obligation that he has assumed, and the agent may be held liable for any loss . . . suffered . . . attributable to the agent's failure to procure such insurance."

Although the cases cited deal with an agent's failure to obtain insurance

---

[30] It should, perhaps, be noted that Levy flatly contradicted the plaintiff's testimony.

after a promise to do so, the principle underlying the decisions applies with equal force to the situation now before us. An agent who fails to keep a policy in force after promising to do so is in no better position than one who neglects to procure a policy after agreeing to do so.

The amount of Levy's liability will, of course, depend upon whether the insured did or did not die by "accidental means." If he did not, then, Levy—if the jury concluded that he made the promise to take care of the premium due—would be liable, at most, for the face or principal amount of the policy, $7650. On the other hand, if the insured died as a result of an accident (within the meaning of the rider), then, Levy would be liable for the further sum of $3000.

The record before us is devoid of any evidence that death resulted from other than natural causes. The insured's fatal heart attack took place while he was engaged in the course of his employment as an electrician, and death was not the result of any "unusual or extraordinary happening." . . . Since this issue was tried, the trial court would have been under the necessity, in any view of the case, of dismissing so much of the plaintiff's cause of action as sought a recovery for death by accidental means. Accordingly, the issue upon the new trial will be limited to the question of Levy's liability for the face or principal amount of the policy.

The judgment dismissing the complaint against the defendant Metropolitan Life Insurance Company should be affirmed, with costs. The judgment, insofar as it affects the defendant Levy, should be reversed and a new trial granted as to his liability in connection with the basic policy in the amount of $7650, with costs to abide the event.

CHAPTER XI

The Policy as Property

As a result of the legal reserve, level premium system and the non-forfeiture policy provisions, the modern life insurance contract is more than a mere promise to pay a sum of money at the insured's death. It is also an evidence of present rights of undeniable value, of which the policyholder cannot be deprived except as the result of his own actions. Thus, in many respects, the life contract today is very similar to other evidences of present property rights, such as corporate bonds, mortgages, and certificates of stock.

The purpose of this chapter is to explore the more frequent uses of life insurance as property and to outline some of the legal principles that should be observed if the use of the policy as property is not to nullify or seriously impair its primary value as life insurance.

THE "VALUES" OF THE CONTRACT

In one of the famous cases on insurable interest, *Grigsby* v. *Russell*,[1] Mr. Justice Holmes spoke of the property characteristics of life insurance as follows: ". . . life insurance has become in our day one of the best recognized forms of investment and self-compelled saving. So far as reasonable safety permits, it is desirable to give to life policies the ordinary characteristics of property." And later in the same case: "To deny the right to sell . . . is to diminish appreciably the value of the contract in the owner's hands."

"Value in the Owner's Hands." This "value of the contract in the owner's hands" and the possibilities of dealing with it in many respects as he would any other kind of personal property have given the life insurance policy a usefulness it did not have before. Its value, both to the insured on a personal basis and in the business world, has been tre-

---

[1] 222 U.S. 149, 32 S. Ct. 58, 56 L. Ed. 133, 36 L.R.A., N.S. 642, Ann. Cas. 1913B, 863 (1911).

mendously enlarged. If the policy is on his own life, for example, the insured may cash it in, effect a loan on it, sell it, or give it away. In addition to these possibilities, if the policy is on the life of someone else, the policyholder may also dispose of it by will or leave it as an asset in his estate, to be distributed by his administrators in the same way he would any other item of his personal property.

Value as Insurance. In spite of the lifetime values, however, the value of the policy in the hands of the beneficiary after the death of the insured is ordinarily much greater than its value to the insured during his lifetime. The property aspects of the contract were developed incidentally to its avowed purpose, which is to provide a benefit of value, payable upon the death of the insured, to a named beneficiary.

Because of this basic purpose, life insurance has been the object of many protective laws which have not been enacted with respect to any other kind of property. When Justice Holmes prefaced his statement with the words, "So far as reasonable safety permits," he voiced a definite recognition of the fact that the life contract involves rights and characteristics that do not lend themselves to an indiscriminate application of the rules and principles applicable to such instruments as certificates of stock, negotiable instruments, and bonds. If the growing uses of life insurance as property are not to jeopardize its fundamental and still major purpose of family protection, the property rights which the contract evidences must be exercised with an ever-present awareness and consideration of the rights of the beneficiary.

Its Dual Values. There are no valid reasons why the life insurance contract cannot have a wide usefulness as property while yet preserving its basic value as insurance. Many of the possible conflicts between the rights of the beneficiary and those of the assignee are being avoided by a better understanding of the legal effects of the provisions of the policy and the policyholder's actions. Most helpful is the wording of many modern policies, which defines the ownership rights under the policy and the legal effects of an assignment. Thus there seems no reason to believe that these conflicts cannot eventually be resolved on a middle ground which will retain the best of the uses of life insurance as property while maintaining the policy in its fullest possible effect as insurance.

THE NATURE OF PROPERTY

What Property Is

The word *property* is popularly associated with objects of a tangible nature such as land, buildings, furniture, automobiles, and the like. Legally, however, property does not mean the objects themselves but rather the rights that inhere in them. Rights of possession, of control, of disposition (rights of *user*, the lawyer might say) are ownership rights, and ownership rights constitute property in the legal sense of the word. The person in whom ownership rights are vested is known as the owner.

Kinds of Property. If the rights of ownership inhere in land or objects permanently attached to it, such as buildings, the property is said to be *real* and one is said to own real property. If one's ownership rights concern movables, such as furniture, automobiles, jewels, valuable paintings, or such intangibles as certificates of stocks or bonds, the property is classified as *personal.* (The terms *real* and *personal* are derived from the forms of legal action which were used in the early days of the common law to enforce one's rights of ownership, and they are descriptive of the property only in that sense.)

Personal Property

There are two kinds of personal property: (1) *choses* (i.e., things) *in possession;* and (2) *choses* (i.e., things) *in action.* (It might be helpful to recall at this point the fact that for some time after the Norman Conquest, French was spoken in the courts and by the aristocracy of England. Hence the French word *chose* for what the Saxon would have called *thing.*)

"Choses." The phrase *choses in possession* refers to tangible objects which are capable of being possessed; for instance, the movables mentioned above. A chose in action, on the other hand, refers to ownership rights which are evidenced by something tangible but which evidence does not have value in or of itself. With a chose in action, one may have to take legal action to recover the value it represents. In other words, a chose in action does not have value in itself but is an evidence of a right to values. A certificate of stock is an example. The paper on which it is printed has only minimal value, but the rights which it evidences may, and sometimes do, have very great value.

It is in this connection that the legal sense of the word *property* has its clearest application, meaning not the thing itself but rather the rights which inhere in it. Thus rights of property and ownership are virtually synonymous and mean not one right but rather a collection or "bundle" of rights which one person, known as the owner, may exercise, knowing that his right to do so will be protected by law.

The Life Insurance Contract Is a Chose in Action

The Policy, an Evidence of Value. As we have seen, a life insurance contract comprises a great many rights of value which are exercisable prior to the maturity of the contract. The policyholder has the right to effect a policy loan, to withdraw or direct the disposition of dividends, to surrender the policy for cash. All are ownership rights. Thus the life insurance contract has many of the characteristics possessed by bank accounts, evidenced by the pass book; creditor interests, evidenced by mortgages, bonds, and notes; or ownership, evidenced by certificates of stock. In this respect it can be considered a chose in action and, as such, it is governed by the same laws which govern any other chose in action and may be dealt with in the same way.

Uses of the Contract as Property. Since the contract represents rights of definite value, it is sometimes advantageous to transfer those rights either for value (a sale), gratuitously (a gift), or as security for a loan (a pledge). All of these are property uses.

In case of divorce, the contract is a part of the property and a proper subject for a property settlement. In case of death, third-party ownership policies pass, with the decedent's other personal property, to his executor or representative for distribution to his heirs or *legatees* (those to whom he leaves personal property by will).

In all these situations, the life insurance contract is subject to the same laws which govern any other chose in action, but it is complicated by a value which is not usually associated with any other chose, the right to a benefit payable on the death of the insured. This right is ordinarily conferred upon someone other than the owner, the beneficiary, and by methods different from the transfer of a chose in action, since this is not a right to which the policyholder is presently entitled, although it is a right which is his to confer.

How the law of property fits in with, and must be modified by, this most basic of all rights under the life insurance contract has been the subject of a great many conflicting court decisions and hopeful policy provisions. In this chapter we will try to outline most of the major uses of the life insurance contract as property, to suggest some of the problems which may be involved in such usages, and to note the legal principles which are applied in working out solutions in these areas.

THE TRANSFER OF A CHOSE IN ACTION

Dual Nature of the Life Insurance Contract

Rights of the Beneficiary. As we have pointed out, the life insurance contract has a dual nature. Its avowed purpose is to provide a benefit at the death of the insured. Therefore, the most important right under the contract is the right of the beneficiary, which is perfected at the death of the insured. Incidentally, after the death of the insured the beneficiary may assign her rights as she may wish unless they are subject to restrictions by reason of settlement specifications endorsed on the policy.

Rights exercisable under the contract prior to the death of the insured are ownership rights of the policyholder, usually, though not always, the insured. Where the beneficiary is named irrevocably the insured's ownership rights cannot be assigned or otherwise exercised in any way that might diminish her rights. However, where the beneficiary is revocable the policyholder is ordinarily free to take whatever action he wishes with respect to the insurance contract, including the revocation of any beneficiary designation.

This complete freedom on the part of the policyholder to deal with the contract as he wishes gives him the equivalent of "title" in other lines of property. Thus he has the "title" to the life insurance policy; he is the owner in the property sense of the word.

Perhaps the most important characteristic of ownership is the right which inheres in an owner to transfer his ownership rights or any portion of them to another on almost any basis he may choose. With respect to a chose in action, transfer of title is accomplished by means of an assignment.

What an Assignment Is

A Transfer of Rights. An assignment is a transfer of some or all of the rights of ownership with respect to a chose in action, made by one person, known as the assignor, in favor of another, known as the assignee. Originally a chose in action was not transferable. Even now, unless there is a statute which declares otherwise, the assignee of a chose in action must sue in the name of the assignor. This limitation has been removed in most states by statute, however, and in the United States it is generally accepted that a chose in action can be readily assigned whether as a gift or for a consideration.

Assignments Classified

Absolute and Collateral Assignments. If the purpose of the assignment is to transfer *all* the ownership rights in question, the assignment is said to be absolute; thus an *absolute assignment.* If the assignment is given for the purpose of transferring some or all of the ownership rights to another, but only on condition that they are to return (the lawyer would say *revert*) to the assignor upon the repayment of money currently being borrowed or otherwise owed, the assignment is called a *collateral assignment.* It is made as collateral security for the repayment of the loan or loans. Thus the owner may transfer all or only a part of his ownership rights as security for a loan, with the understanding, express or implied, that the rights shall return to him at such time as he repays the loan.

Gifts. If no price is paid by the assignee, the assignment is said to be made "without consideration." In that case it is a gift. A gift has been defined as a "voluntary transfer of his property by one to another without any consideration or compensation therefor."[2] It must be a present transfer of an interest in property. If it is to take effect only in the future it is a mere promise to make a gift and is unenforceable because of lack of consideration.

These principles are often utilized in estate planning. For instance it is sometimes advisable for some of a man's life insurance on his own life to be owned by his wife. The wife may, of course, initiate an application for such insurance over her own name, and the policy will be issued to her as owner. On the other hand, if the insured wishes to make her the owner of life insurance already in force on his life he can do so by means of an absolute assignment to her without consideration, in which case the transaction constitutes a gift.

Sales. If the insured transfers all the ownership rights in the policy to another *for a consideration,* it is a sale.

ASSIGNMENTS OF THE LIFE INSURANCE CONTRACT

After Death of the Insured

At the death of the insured the rights under a life insurance contract become fixed. Thereafter the policy is no different from any other claim for a fixed amount of money, and even a policy provision *prohibiting* assignment is generally held inoperative to prevent an assignment after the insured's death.

This general rule is expressed in an illustrative case[3] as follows:

The general rule, supported by a great wealth of authority, is that general stipulations in policies, prohibiting assignment thereof except with the insurers' consent, or upon giving some notice, or like conditions, have universally been held to apply only to assignments before loss, and, accordingly, not to prevent an assignment after loss, of the claim or interest of the insured in the insurance money then due in respect to the loss.

After maturity, therefore, the life insurance contract can be assigned as freely as any other claim for a stated sum of money. It is assignments prior to maturity, made by the policyholder himself, that present problems.

Prior to Death of the Insured

Who May Assign. Generally speaking, the owner of a life insurance contract may assign whatever rights he has under the contract to whomever he may wish, unless the assignment is in the nature of a

---

[2] *Gray* v. *Barton,* 55 N.Y. 68, 14 Am. Rep. 181 (1873).

[3] *Lain* v. *Metropolitan Life Insurance Company,* 388 Ill. 576, 58 N.E.2d 587 (1944).

wager. He can assign no more rights than he has, and he cannot defeat rights of others which may be vested. Thus he cannot impair the rights of an irrevocable beneficiary, although the latter may join with him in executing a valid and effective assignment of all interests under the policy. It is also the general rule that if the owner has reserved the right to change the beneficiary designation, an assignment without the consent of the revocable beneficiary will give the assignee a prior right to the extent of his claim.

Formal Requisites for an Assignment

Ordinarily an assignment is in writing, and if it is an assignment of a chose in action, the evidence of the rights so transferred (that is, the stock certificate, bank book, insurance policy, etc.) is ordinarily delivered by manual delivery to the assignee at the time of the assignment.

A Writing. In the absence of a statute or a policy provision, it is not necessary that an assignment be in writing. In fact delivery without any writing may be sufficient to effect an equitable assignment under some circumstances. The case of *Sundstrom* v. *Sundstrom* [4] illustrates some of the possibilities growing out of this principle. In that case there were two claimants under the policy, the mother of the insured and his wife. The policy was first issued with the mother as the named beneficiary. Some time after the insured's marriage he changed the beneficiary designation to his wife. Later still, the wife sued for divorce, and the insured again changed the beneficiary back to his mother.

The case presented an especially difficult set of facts. The wife had worked and supported the insured, who had arthritis and was able to work only sporadically. Together they had paid his parents the money the latter had charged him for furnishing care prior to his marriage. When that indebtedness had been reduced to a relatively small sum, the insured changed the beneficiary to his wife and gave her the policy with words indicating that it was to be hers. Seven years later the wife was very seriously injured in an automobile accident. After a few weeks her husband closed out their joint bank account and went back to his parents, taking with him the life insurance policy. The wife sued for divorce, but before the decree became final the insured had died, after having changed the beneficiary back to his mother. On this set of facts the court held that there was an equitable assignment in favor of the wife, as follows:

We are convinced that this evidence, if believed by the trial court, fully warranted it in finding that the insured had made an equitable assignment of the policy to respondent in 1932. It is apparent that he was at that time a hopeless cripple. For four years, his wife had faithfully worked to help sup-

---

[4] 15 Wash. 2d 103, 129 P.2d 783 (1942).

port him, and had given him every attention possible. More than that, her earnings had been the principal means by which his personal, premarital debt to his parents had been reduced from five hundred eighty dollars to seventy dollars. Presumably he not only felt a deep affection for her, but also was sincerely grateful for all that she had done. In addition, he had agreed to transfer the policy to her as soon as *they* got "the folks" paid up. The language employed by him when he delivered the policy to her indicated that it was his intention then and there to invest her with full ownership of the proceeds thereof.

It is true that no formal written assignment of the policy was executed, as required by the provision of the policy hereinabove quoted. But that provision, as we have seen, is designed solely for the protection of the insurance company, and its rights are in no way involved here. Although the transaction between the insured and the respondent with reference to the transfer of the policy was simple and informal, it was only natural for a husband and wife to deal with each other in that way at a time when the relationship between them was one of affection and when there was no occasion for either of them to suspect the other of possible future double-dealing. Nor would it be expected that a wife, even if she were aware of the express requirements of the policy and were familiar with legal phraseology, would insist, under the circumstances then existing, that the terms of the transaction be reduced to writing. The evidence amply justifies the conclusion that it was the insured's intention on October 28, 1932, to transfer to respondent a present interest in the ultimate proceeds of the policy, that he delivered the policy to respondent for that purpose, and that by the form of expression which he then used he made an absolute appropriation of such proceeds to her, relinquishing further control or power of revocation with reference thereto. That being the case, the trial court had sufficient grounds for holding that the insured effected an equitable assignment of the insurance policy to the respondent.

Delivery of the Policy. As a general rule, in order to constitute a valid assignment of a life insurance contract, either the policy or a written assignment must be delivered to the assignee. However, the majority of the decisions have been to the effect that where there has been a duly executed assignment, delivery of the policy is not essential to its validity.

Notice to the Company. Generally speaking, it is not essential to the validity of an assignment that notice of it be given to the insurer. Certainly an assignment of which notice was not given would be valid as between the parties to the assignment. It is also generally held that a policy provision requiring the filing of a copy of the assignment with the insurer is for the benefit of the company and may be waived.

Nevertheless, as a practical matter the performance of the contract is very much affected by the question of notice. The company is powerless to follow the terms of an assignment of which it knows nothing, and it has no duties beyond discharging its promises to the persons who, by its records, are entitled to payment. It is a general rule of law that a debtor who pays an assignee without notice of other prior rights is discharged of liability to such other persons.

Rights of Successive Assignees. The question sometimes arises as to the priority of rights of successive assignees when notices of their rights have been given in different order from the dates of the assignments. Let us say that John Jones assigns a life insurance policy in the face amount of $50,000 to the A.B.C. Company as collateral security for amounts advanced to him. He does not deliver the policy to the assignee and later assigns it again to the First National Bank as security for a loan. The bank notifies the insurer of its assignment immediately after it is made. The A.B.C. Company gives notice only after the death of the insured but before payment has been made. There are two leading rules by which this type of situation is governed. One is known as the English rule; the other is the American rule.

According to the English rule, the assignee who first gives notice is the one entitled to the proceeds, if he had no notice of any prior assignment. Several [5] of the states have followed this rule. However, the majority rule in this country is that the assignee under the assignment first made has the preferable claim. There have been express decisions in some fourteen or fifteen [6] states following this rule. In any case presenting a question of this kind, however, the company always has the right to pay the proceeds into a court and ask the court to decide the proper payee. This legal remedy, called *interpleader,* is discussed in Chapter XVII *infra.*

Responsibility of the Company

The Policy Provision. Under most life insurance policy provisions, the company assumes no responsibility for the "validity or effect" of any assignment of the contract. The provision most commonly used also requires that notice of the assignment be given the insurer at its home office, in writing, before it may be charged with notice.

Ordinarily the assignment of a life insurance contract is something over which the company has no control. Its validity is governed almost entirely by factors with which the company is powerless to deal. The law of the state where the assignment is made; the competency of the parties to the assignment; the nature of the rights assigned and their extent; the provisions of the instrument setting forth the conditions of the assignment; even the purpose of the assignment may have an effect on the validity of the transaction. Since the company is not a party to the transaction, it is not required to assume liability for the validity of the assignment.

The responsibilities of the company are clearly set forth in the case

---

[5] California, Colorado, Connecticut, Maryland, Mississippi, Missouri, Ohio, Oklahoma, Pennsylvania, Tennessee, Vermont.

[6] Including Illinois, Indiana, Iowa, Kentucky, Massachusetts, Minnesota, New Jersey, New York, North Carolina, Oregon, Texas, Virginia, Washington, and West Virginia.

of *New York Life Insurance Company* v. *The Federal National Bank of Shawnee, Oklahoma.*[7] There the insured and the beneficiary joined in assigning his life insurance policy. The assignee borrowed the full loan value, and after the death of the insured the balance was paid to the assignee. Later the beneficiary was declared incompetent, and the guardian of her estate, the bank, sued the life insurance company to recover the face amount of the policy, alleging that the assignment was invalid because of mental incapacity of the insured at the time. On appeal, the court held the insurance company had no duty to inquire into the competency of the insured-assignor at the time of the assignment. When payment has been made in good faith to a beneficiary or assignee of record, the company cannot be required to pay a second time. Pertinent excerpts from this decision are as follows:

> No case has been cited, and our search has failed to reveal one, which has compelled an insurance company to pay a policy a second time when in good faith it has paid the amount of the policy to a new beneficiary or to an assignee, on the ground that the assignment or the change in beneficiary was void because of lack of mental capacity of the insured at the time the change was made, and that is so even though the original beneficiary did not join in the application for change of beneficiary or in the application for the assignment of the policy. The cases upon which the appellee relies to sustain its contention in this respect are not in point. . . .
>
> . . . There is yet another reason why the Bank may not prevail. That part of the policy which gave the insured the right to assign contains this provision: "The company assumes no responsibility for the validity of any assignment." This provision was a part of the contract made at a time when the parties were competent to contract, and must be given effect. There is no ambiguity or uncertainty as to the meaning of this provision. It can only mean that the Company shall not become liable by virtue of the assignment which for any reason was invalid. There was a good reason for the inclusion of such a provision. The Company had a large number of policy-holders. Many requests for the assignment of policies would be received. The Company no doubt realized that fraud, duress or undue influence might be practiced in many instances which would go to the validity of the assignment, or that assignments might be invalid for many other reasons, including impaired mental capacity or even lack of mental capacity to make the assignment. If the Company was to be charged with liability if an assignment was invalid for any of these reasons, it would of necessity be compelled to deny the right to assign, or in each instance would be compelled to carefully investigate the application before it was granted. This would place an impossible burden upon the Company. It was for these reasons that the Company in substance said to the insured: "We will give you the right to assign, but we shall not be liable if for any reason the assignment is invalid." This provision would not, of course, protect the Company in case of an irregular assignment because that would put it upon notice, or in cases in which it had knowledge of the mental condition of the insured, or in cases in which it had knowledge of facts which should put it upon inquiry. But this is not such a case.

[7] 151 F.2d 537, 162 A.L.R. 536 (C.C.A. Okla., 1945).

Assignments Intended to Secure Indebtedness

Collateral Assignments. Life insurance contracts are most commonly assigned as security for indebtedness. Ordinarily termed a collateral assignment, a transfer of this kind closely resembles a pledge as security for the payment of a debt. Ordinarily a collateral assignment transfers only a part of the ownership rights under the policy, rarely the right to designate or change the beneficiary, and the transfer is always on condition that the assignment shall be canceled and the rights so transferred shall revert to the assignor on payment of the debt.

As a general rule, there is not too much question with respect to the rights transferred under such an assignment during the lifetime of the insured. However, questions sometimes arise, and when they do they must be answered in accordance with the terms of the instrument itself and the applicable principles of property law. This is not always simple. For instance, in the case of *Greenberg* v. *Equitable Life Assurance Society of the United States*,[8] the company received from the assignees a request for the cash surrender value under two life insurance policies which had been assigned to them. Before payment had been made, the insured's attorney notified the company that the insureds had not consented to this request and that if the funds were released they would initiate an action against the company.

The United States District Court for the District of Minnesota held that the company must pay the cash surrender value to the assignees since the assignment provided that this right was granted them. The company contended that it was on notice as to a dispute, but the court said:

> . . . The unqualified right of an assignee cannot be limited by the mere assertion of a claim by the assignor which is not ultimately substantiated.

✿   ✿   ✿   ✿   ✿

> The primary purpose of the assignment privileges granted to the insured is to enable the latter to utilize that asset in business transactions as collateral or otherwise. If the unqualified right of a banking institution, for instance, to an assigned insurance policy for a loan could be thwarted by unsupported claims and contentions by an assignor as to the validity of the assignment, it must be apparent that no banking institution could assume to accept such an asset as collateral in a business transaction with the insured.

Right to Repayment of Debt Out of Death Benefit. The primary problem with respect to assignments arises out of the conflict of the rights of the assignee and those of any beneficiary or beneficiaries whose rights are not expressly made subject to the rights of the assignee or assignees. At this point, it should be noted that under most standard assignment

---

[8] 167 F. Supp. 112 (D.C. Minn., 1958).

forms, a collateral assignee may ordinarily satisfy the indebtedness out of the benefit payable at the death of the insured. A question arises, however, where the beneficiary has not joined in executing or otherwise consented to the assignment. Nevertheless, the majority rule is that the right of an assignee under a collateral assignment is superior to the rights of the beneficiary, even though the latter did not consent to the assignment. The underlying reasons for this holding are suggested in the following:

> From an every day, practical standpoint it is desirable to hold that an assignee of a policy containing a clause permitting a change of beneficiary and an assignment of the policy secures a right in the proceeds of the policy superior to the rights of the named beneficiary. If an assignee, in the absence of the consent of the beneficiary, does not obtain such right it will be practically impossible for an insured to borrow on a policy in time of need of financial aid in those cases where compliance with the form prescribed in the policy cannot be followed. No bank or individual would be likely to lend on the security of a policy where the right to enforce the reduction of the security to cash would only mature in case the insured outlived the beneficiary, and where the continued life of the policy depends upon the payment of the annual premium. As stated in the case of *Matter of Whiting* (3 Fed. Rep. 2d 440, 441): "To hold that the beneficiary of such policy has a vested interest would be tantamount to destroying the 'changed beneficiary' provisions of the policy itself." (Cf. Vance on Insurance (2d ed.), 646; 48 Yale L. J. 315.)
> That the question is a practical one is illustrated by the large number of decisions involving the issue.[9]

After the assignee has been paid the amount of his claim, the beneficiary is entitled to the remainder of the sum payable, either in a lump sum or under one of the settlement options. As a matter of practice, the company will request some evidence of the amount of the assignee's claim and then will make settlement to the assignee in a lump sum and to the beneficiary in accordance with the choice of the policyholder, or the beneficiary if the policyholder made no election.

Absolute Assignments. Often an absolute assignment is executed for the purpose of securing an indebtedness. In such cases if it can be shown that the assignment was executed as collateral security it will be treated as if it were a collateral assignment, and the rights of the assignee will be determined on that basis.

Illustrative of this type of holding is the case of *Albrent* v. *Spencer,* a Wisconsin case decided in March, 1957.[10] There the insured made an absolute assignment of policies on his life, together with stock he owned in a freight and storage corporation, as collateral security for the payment of a note on which there was approximately $140,000 due. After

---

[9] *Davis et al.* v. *Modern Industrial Bank et al.,* 275 N.Y. 405, 18 N.E.2d 639, 135 A.L.R. 1035 (1939).

[10] 81 N.W.2d 555 (Wis., 1957).

the insured's death, the assignee collected the proceeds of the policies, satisfied the indebtedness, and retained the difference allegedly amounting to approximately $90,000. The court said:

We consider that the case presents the issue of whether it is against public policy for a creditor of the insured to avail himself of an absolute assignment of a previously pledged life insurance policy issued upon the life of the debtor, which assignment is intended to end the creditor-debtor relationship, for any other purpose than enabling the creditor to realize the cash surrender value of the policy.

. . . It offends one's sense of justice that a creditor should realize more out of the proceeds of the policy than the principal and interest due on the loan for which the policy was pledged plus any expenditure of the creditor for premiums necessary to protect his security. To uphold the result reached below in the instant case would be to encourage creditors to bring pressure upon necessitous debtors to convert the rights of the creditor from that of pledgee to that of owner in order that he might gamble upon the life of the insured in the hope of realizing the difference between the amount due on the loan and the face of the policy. In the instant case it is alleged that such difference amounted to the huge sum of approximately $90,000.

While it must be conceded that the majority rule is that, where an owner of a life insurance policy has an insurable interest therein he may make a valid assignment of the policy to a third party having no such insurable interest, (29 Am. Jur., Insurance, p. 313, Sec. 357) it clearly is in the interest of public policy to engraft an exception on to such rule to cover situations such as that which confronts us here. A desirable exception and one that we are compelled to adopt is that any purported absolute assignment by a debtor to a creditor of a policy, which had previously been pledged as security to the creditor is only valid between the immediate parties to the extent of enabling the creditor to realize the cash surrender value of the policy. If the creditor after receiving such absolute assignment and the creditor-debtor relationship is terminated, continues to hold the policy for the purpose of gambling upon the life of the insured, he becomes a constructive trustee for the benefit of the estate of the deceased of any proceeds received upon the death of the insured, to the extent that such proceeds exceed the amount that would have been due such assignee if the creditor-debtor relationship had not been extinguished.

A precedent for enforcing such a constructive trust is provided by the decision of the United States supreme court in *Warnock* v. *Davis, supra.* In that case the insured assigned a policy upon his life to a trust association, which had no insurable interest, in consideration for the association agreeing to pay the premiums due on the policy, it being agreed that upon his death the association was to retain nine-tenths of the proceeds received on the policy. The insured died and the insurance company paid the amount of the face of the policy to the association and it accounted for one-tenth thereof to the widow of the insured. The court held that it was against public policy to assign a life insurance policy to one not having an insurable interest in the insured.[11] Therefore, the agreement between the insured and the association whereby the latter was to retain nine-tenths of the proceeds was void. The court then went on to state . . . :

---

[11] This statement, standing alone, does not summarize the majority rule. See statement, page 289.

It (the agreement) is one which must be treated as creating no legal right to the proceeds of the policy beyond the sums advanced upon its security; and the courts will, therefore, hold the recipient of the moneys beyond those sums to account to the representatives of the deceased. It was lawful for the association to advance to the assured the sums payable to the insurance company on the policy as they became due. It was, also, lawful for the assured to assign the policy as security for their payment. The assignment was only invalid as a transfer of the proceeds of the policy beyond what was required to refund those sums, with interest. To hold it valid for the whole proceeds would be to sanction speculative risks on human life, and encourage the evils for which wager policies are condemned.

Assignments Intended to Be Absolute

As a Gift. As a general principle, an insured may assign a life insurance policy on his own life to anyone he chooses and on any terms he may wish. If he makes such an assignment without consideration, the transaction is a gift. In most states such an assignment, in the absence of a policy provision to the contrary, operates to give the assignee much the same rights as a beneficiary would have had. Some courts have held that the assignee must have an insurable interest, but that problem arises more frequently in connection with assignments for value.

As a Sale. On general principles, an absolute assignment for value should be permitted the policyholder without question. The law takes the position that property should be freely transferable, and in many cases it is important that one be permitted to transfer his life insurance policy for value. Nevertheless there are some very strong minority cases holding that an assignee must have an insurable interest.

The Minority View. Cases requiring the assignee to have an insurable interest constitute the minority view, but they are vividly illustrated by the case of *Werenzinski* v. *Prudential Insurance Company of America*,[12] decided by the Pennsylvania Supreme Court in January, 1940. This case is best presented in the court's own words, as follows:

STERN, J.: Frank Cybuck, a man without either property or income, was occasionally employed to tend the furnace in a small apartment house belonging to plaintiff Joseph Werenzinski and he also did odd jobs around the place, sleeping in one of the rooms occupied by plaintiff's family or in the basement. He was found one evening lying in front of the boilers so horribly burned that he died immediately thereafter.

Four policies of insurance were issued by defendant on the life of Cybuck payable to his estate, but in each case the policy was assigned some months thereafter to plaintiff. At the trial of the suit brought on these policies defendant contended that plaintiff was not entitled to recover because he had no insurable interest in Cybuck's life. The learned trial judge charged the jury that the controlling question was as to who paid the premiums after the making of the assignments; if they were paid by plaintiff the policies would then represent

---

[12] 339 Pa. 83, 14 Atl.2d 279 (1940).

wagering contracts and plaintiff would be barred from recovery, but if the insured continued to pay the premiums the verdict should be for plaintiff even though admittedly he had no insurable interest in Cybuck's life. The jury found for defendant (as another jury had done on a previous trial of the case), but the court granted plaintiff a new trial solely on the ground that "the question of whether the assignments were made in good faith and not as a mere cloak or cover for the procuring of insurance by the plaintiff who was without an insurable interest should have been submitted to and passed upon by the jury." . . .

The court was in error in granting a new trial. The charge of the trial judge correctly defined the issue, and the verdict should have been upheld. There was ample evidence to warrant the conclusion, which the jury must have reached, that plaintiff, at least after becoming the assignee of the policies, paid the premiums, and if this was so the law would not permit plaintiff to recover, irrespective of any question of good faith.

There are two propositions so well established both by decision and statute that there can be no doubt in regard to them. The first is that a person may take out a policy of insurance on his own life and name as beneficiary whomsoever he pleases, regardless of whether or not such beneficiary has an insurable interest, or, having taken out a policy, he may assign it to one without an insurable interest, provided, in either event, the insured continues at all times to pay the premiums; under such circumstances no question arises of a wagering contract obnoxious to public policy: . . . The other proposition is that a person cannot take out a valid and enforceable policy of insurance for his own benefit, and pay the premiums thereon, on a life in which he has no insurable interest. . . .

A more doubtful situation, from the legal standpoint, exists when a policy of insurance taken out by one on his own life, and thus valid in its inception, is subsequently assigned by the insured to a person having no insurable interest and the assignee thereafter pays the premiums. If such assignment is merely a subterfuge, planned or contemplated when the policy was issued, to enable the assignee thereby to accomplish what he could not have done directly, namely, to obtain insurance on a life wherein he had no insurable interest, it would not be sustainable. But where the assignment is not in execution of such a pre-existing purpose to circumvent the law, but arises from subsequent happenings, may the assignee recover on the policy? There has been a wealth of discussion pro and con on this subject in judicial opinions and in textbooks, and there is a sharp division of authority. In the great majority of jurisdictions it is held that such an assignment is valid, even though the assignee pays the premiums: . . . The best arguments in support of this view are to be found in *Grigsby* v. *Russell*, 222 U.S. 149 (followed in *Midland National Bank* v. *Dakota Life Insurance Co.*, 277 U.S. 346, 350). But there are a number of states, among which Pennsylvania has consistently maintained its place, where it is held that the assignment of a policy, whether in "good faith" or not, to one who has no insurable interest and who thereafter pays the premiums is as contrary to public policy, and therefore as legally objectionable, as the original issuance of the policy to such a person would have been. This viewpoint has been maintained in Pennsylvania through a course of so many years and by such a number of repeated affirmations that, if it were now sought to change it in order to bring it into harmony with the prevailing doctrine, the appeal for that purpose would have to be directed to the legislature and not the courts. Among the multitude of cases enunciating and upholding the Pennsylvania ruling may be cited the following: . . .

As against this formidable array of authorities plaintiff relies upon two decisions of the Superior Court, *In re Estate of Vincent Szymanski, deceased,* 109 Pa. Superior Ct. 555, and *Pashuck, Administrator,* v. *Metropolitan Life Insurance Co.,* 124 Pa. Superior Ct. 406. In the former of these, an insured, being unable to continue to pay the premiums, assigned the policies to his nephew, who paid the premiums thereafter; it was held that the nephew was entitled to the proceeds of the policies. It may be said of that decision that the Act of 1921 recognizes as an insurable interest one which, in the case of persons related by blood or law, is engendered by love and affection, . . .

In the *Pashuck* case the beneficiary paid the premiums, but there was evidence that she was a creditor of the insured. The court, in a decision in her favor, mistakenly relied upon a dictum in the opinion in *First National Bank of Glen Campbell* v. *Burnside National Bank,* 314 Pa. 536, 539, that "the insured may take out insurance on his own life, and transfer the policy to whomsoever he pleases, and the transfer will ordinarily be held valid." The authorities cited in support of that statement are all cases in which the insured continued to pay the premiums, and obviously it was only to such situations that the dictum referred.

Since the instructions of the learned trial judge to the jury correctly expressed the law, the court was in error in granting a new trial. To have injected into the case the issue of "good faith," which the court below now thinks should have been done, would have been improper in the light of the well-established law of this Commonwealth.

The order granting a new trial is reversed, and the record is remitted with directions to enter judgment upon the verdict in favor of defendant.

It should be noted that the court in this case specifically stated that if the rule were to be changed, the appeal should be "directed to the legislature and not the courts." In 1951, the Pennsylvania Legislature amended the insurance law of Pennsylvania by adding the following sentence:

If a policy of life insurance has been issued in conformity with this section, no transfer of such policy or any interest thereunder shall be invalid by reason of a lack of insurable interest of the transferee in the life of the insured or the payment of premiums thereafter by the transferee.[13]

The student may find this action of special interest, not only as removing Pennsylvania from the states which follow the minority rule with respect to the requirement of an insurable interest on the part of an assignee, but also as pointing up the respective roles of courts and legislatures in defining and shaping the law of the life insurance contract.

The Majority View. The prevailing view, as conceded in the case just quoted, is that if the policy is taken out by the insured himself or by someone else who has an insurable interest in the life insured, and if the transaction is in good faith and not solely for the purpose of later assign-

[13] 40 Purdon's Pennsylvania Statutes, Sec. 512.

ing the policy to one who could not have taken it out originally, the owner can assign it to whomever he wishes. It does not matter that the assignee has no insurable interest in the life insured or that he pays the premiums. This rule is well stated by the Missouri Supreme Court in the case of *Butterworth et al.* v. *Mississippi Valley Trust Co.,*[14] decided in June, 1951. There the court said:

> There is some difference of opinion. But the prevailing view, and the greater weight of authority and the better and more soundly reasoned conclusions of the courts was tersely expressed by Mr. Justice Holmes in *Grigsby* v. *Russell*, 222 U.S. 149, 32 S. Ct. 58, 56 L. Ed. 133, wherein, ruling this precise question, he said, in part: "And cases in which a person having an interest lends himself to one without any, as a cloak to what is, in its inception a wager, have no similarity to those where an honest contract is sold in good faith." The principle of the good faith of the assignment transaction runs like a scarlet thread through the better reasoned cases. The decided trend of adjudications unquestionably is to establish the rule that an insurable interest in the insured by the assignee of a policy of life insurance is not essential to the validity of the assignment if the party to whom it was issued in good faith had an insurable interest, and if the assignment was in good faith and not made to cover up a gambling transaction. We unequivocally approve that rule.
>
> . . . Without the power of assignment life insurance contracts would lose much of their value. In a commercial age and with a commercial people, and in recognition of commercial practices, the courts are not unaware of the frequent necessity for the transfer by assignment of such contracts in the usual course of every day business. To limit the assignment of such contracts otherwise valid to those having an insurable interest, and to thus ignore the bona fides of assignments of convenience or necessity, would not only impair the value of such contracts as a plan of estate building and economic protection but would work unconscionable injury to policyholders who are no longer financially able to or who no longer desire to continue such contracts.

Assignment with Fraudulent Intent. A number of assignment cases have reached the courts because the circumstances of their making indicated that they were not made in good faith. Thus the assignee was permitted to obtain an interest he could not otherwise have gotten. The law is very strict with respect to anything that suggests trafficking in human lives, and whenever the facts of an assignment case suggest that it was in reality only a wagering contract, the assignment will not be upheld. Under such circumstances the majority of courts have held the policy valid but the assignment void for lack of insurable interest in the assignee.

Effects of the Assignment

We have discussed at some length the fact that the life insurance policy is a chose in action. It is important also that it is not a negotiable instrument. As a nonnegotiable chose in action, it cannot be transferred

---

[14] 240 S.W.2d 676 (Mo., 1951).

in such a way as to give the assignee any more rights than the assignor himself had. Ordinarily, therefore, the rights of the assignee of a life insurance policy will be lost by any violation of the terms of the policy which would have that effect upon the rights of the original policyholder.

Rights of the Beneficiary. As previously noted, the principal problem in connection with the assignment of life insurance policies arises out of the possible conflict of the rights of the assignee and the rights of the beneficiary. Where the policy is payable to the estate of the insured, it is generally held that the rights of the assignee are unquestioned. Where a beneficiary has been designated and is not revoked at the time of the assignment, and where her consent has not been given, a very definite possibility of conflict arises.

Where the beneficiary is irrevocable, she has a "vested" contingent right, and nothing and no one can deprive her of that right without her consent. Where the beneficiary is revocable, court decisions are divided. The majority hold that the assignee's right is superior to that of the beneficiary, to the amount of the debt. They reason that the owner must have intended that the assignee have adequate security, and since he could have revoked the beneficiary designation, they hold that, in effect, he did so when he executed the assignment. This rule has been stated in about half the states. However, in a few states the courts have held that the beneficiary can only be changed by following the procedure outlined in the policy, and if that has not been done, the assignee, so they hold, has no right to the proceeds.

Illustrative of this general point of view is the case of *Continental Assurance Co. v. Conroy,*[15] where the court said:

It has long been the law in New Jersey that there are two sets of interests in an insurance policy; that of the beneficiary to the proceeds of the policy if he survives the insured, and that of the insured's representatives to the proceeds of the policy if the insured outlives the beneficiary. . . . Moreover, a beneficiary is said to take a vested interest which can be defeated only by a change of beneficiary made in accordance with the procedure specified in the policy. . . . When the insured in the present case assigned his policy to the trustees he made no attempt to comply with the provisions of the policy concerning the substitution of beneficiaries. Therefore, all that was transferred to the trustees, by virtue of this assignment, was the contingent interest of the insured's representatives to the proceeds of the policy in the event that the insured outlived the beneficiary. The insured's subsequent application for the change of beneficiary in favor of the trustees included an express reservation of the right to make further changes in futuro. Such a reservation constitutes convincing evidence of an intent on the part of the insured that the insurance trust be a revocable one.

---

[15] 209 F.2d 539 (C.A. N.J., 1954).

ASSIGNMENTS IN PRACTICE

With the typical life insurance policy, a good collateral assignment should effect such a transfer of rights under the policy as to give the assignee all the security he needs and yet retain for the beneficiary the maximum possible protection consistent with the lien of the assignee. This is a delicate balancing of rights, and different procedures have been followed in an attempt to achieve it.

The earliest method, and one which is still being used, required three different transactions. Under this method, the insured first revokes the named beneficiary and designates his estate to receive the proceeds of the policy. Then he executes the assignment, assigning the desired rights to the lender, with provision that the latter is to be repaid out of the proceeds in the event of the insured's death. The insured then renames the former beneficiary, subject to the prior rights of the assignee, and reinstates the original settlement agreement if there was one, and if it is still appropriate.

This is complicated, it takes a certain amount of time, and it has an even more serious objection. The very fact that a collateral assignment is involved indicates increased financial obligations. Yet there is a period of time, while the intricacies of these transactions are being worked out, during which the proceeds of the policy are payable to the insured's estate. During that time, the statutory exemption of insurance proceeds from the insured's general creditors could easily be lost in the event of the insured's death.

A second method is to execute the assignment and change the beneficiary in the same instrument and at the same time. Because the two transactions are essentially different, the instrument must be drawn with extreme care. A change of beneficiary is effective only as provided in the policy; the assignment is effective when executed. The different times at which the two actions become effective thus make the procedure particularly technical and subject to error.

A *Policy Provision.* Although the usual policy provision absolves the company from responsibility for the validity or legal effect of any assignment of the policy, the company nevertheless must recognize any assignment of which it has notice. In case of any serious dispute under an assignment, the company would pay the proceeds into a court and ask the court to decide the question. In legal terms, it would file a bill of interpleader.

This possibility affords a protection to the company from having to pay twice. It does not protect the company from the time, expense, and delay involved in litigation, and it does not protect the beneficiary from having the proceeds reduced by court costs and fees, to say nothing of having the entire proceeds tied up until the question can be resolved.

It is generally agreed that most of the conflict resulting from assignments could be avoided if, at the time the assignment is executed, consideration were given to the beneficiary provisions of the policy. It would seem equally true that most conflicts could be avoided also if at the time the policy is drafted consideration were given to the possibility that the policy might someday be assigned. From the company's point of view this is the most effective and the most practical way to meet the problem—to specify in the policy itself what the effect will be if the policy is assigned. One company does this with the following policy provision:

> The company assumes no responsibility for the validity or effect of any assignment of this policy and no assignment will be recognized until it has been duly filed with the company. An assignment of this policy shall operate to the extent thereof to transfer the interest of any beneficiary whom the assignor has the right to change, and to render any part of the sum payable to which the assignee is entitled payable in one sum, notwithstanding any settlement agreement endorsed hereon at the time the assignment is executed.

A policy provision of this kind simplifies the assignment of the policy and clarifies the rights of everyone concerned. The assignment can be drawn up without regard to the technicalities of revoking the named beneficiary. The policy itself does that. Thus execution of the assignment accomplishes the desired result automatically. The assignee has all the protection to which he is entitled or which he should want. The beneficiary's rights are disturbed only to the extent actually required by the assignment. Lastly the insurance company knows that at the death of the insured the rights of the various parties will be readily ascertainable.

How Assignments Are Released

Since a policyholder is completely free to assign his life insurance policy, either absolutely or as collateral, he has the same freedom with respect to obtaining written evidence that the rights of the assignee have been released. Life insurance companies are only interested in having evidence of such a release before the policyholder will be permitted to resume the exercise of rights under the policy without the consent of the assignee.

As a general rule, an absolute assignment is the equivalent of a sale. If it has been used for collateral purposes, however, the assignee may wish to release his rights to the policy at such time as the indebtedness in question has been satisfied. The appropriate evidence of such a release is another absolute assignment back to the original assignor.

Effective releases under a collateral assignment may range in form all the way from a formal recital of the rights so released, signed and witnessed, to a simple statement on the letterhead of the assignee in question, to the effect that the indebtedness has been satisfied and that all rights and title to the captioned policy are thereby released. The important consideration is not the precise form of the release but its legal significance, and in any case of doubt as to the latter the advice of competent counsel should be obtained.

The American Bankers Association Form of Assignment

The ABA Form No. 10 was developed by the Bank Management Commission of the American Bankers Association, with the collaboration of the Association of Life Insurance Counsel. It is officially termed an "Assignment of Life Insurance Policy as Collateral" but it is considerably more exacting than the usual collateral assignment form. Thus it was hoped that the ABA Form would satisfy those lenders who once demanded an absolute assignment while nevertheless making clear the purpose of the assignment as collateral.

Under Part B of this form the following rights are specifically declared to pass by the assignment to the assignee and to be exercisable by him: the sole right to collect the net proceeds of the policy at the insured's death or on maturity of the policy; the sole right to surrender the policy for cash; the sole right to effect a policy loan; the sole right to receive dividends; the sole right to exercise all nonforfeiture rights.

The following rights are reserved and do not pass by the terms of the assignment: the right to collect disability benefits payable in cash; the right to designate and change the beneficiary; the right to elect an optional mode of settlement.

The assignee covenants and agrees that the balance of any sums collected, after satisfying the indebtedness, shall be paid to those persons who would have been entitled to them if there had been no assignment; that the right to surrender the policy or effect a loan will not be exercised unless and until there has been a default and notice on the part of the assignee has been mailed to the assignor; and that the policy will be forwarded to the insurance company for endorsement of any beneficiary change or settlement agreement.

Many of the problems once arising in connection with assignments have been resolved by means of policy provisions and such specific enumeration of rights as are found in this American Bankers Association Form No. 10. As the uses of the policy as property become more clearly defined it is believed that the problems once frequent will become less prevalent, and that the dual nature of the policy—as property and as insurance—will give it a double usefulness rather than an ever-present possibility for trouble.

CHAPTER XII

The Policyholder Changes the Beneficiary

NAMING THE BENEFICIARY, as we pointed out in Chapter V, is one of the most important actions the applicant takes in connection with his application for a life insurance policy. Furthermore, his right to change the designation later if he wishes, and as often as he wishes, is one of the most significant rights he acquires under the contract. The purpose of this chapter is to discuss the procedures by which this right is exercised and some of the more frequent legal problems that may result from carelessness, mistake, or imperfect knowledge of the facts in the course of these procedures.

RIGHTS UNDER THE CONTRACT

The Beneficiary's Rights

In the early days, the beneficiary was a party to the life insurance contract, and all rights under it were her rights. By the beginning of the present century this had changed. By that time, life insurance contracts were customarily made between the person whose life was insured and the insurer, for the benefit of, but not with, the beneficiary. Nevertheless, the rights of the beneficiary under these early contracts were still more extensive than is true of the beneficiary's rights under the present-day life insurance policies.

In those days it was assumed that the insured intended to part with all rights with respect to the benefit payable on his death, when he named the beneficiary. Thus her rights were considered irrevocable and absolute from that date. In fact, they were so completely vested that if she died prior to the insured, her right to receive the benefit payable upon his death was held to pass to her executor as an asset of her estate.

By the turn of the century many of the life insurance companies were beginning to include two important provisions in the life insurance policy by which the rights of the insured-policyholder were considerably enlarged and the rights of the beneficiary diminished. One of these provisions terminated the rights of the beneficiary upon her death prior to that of the insured. In that case the rights so terminated reverted to the insured. The other policy provision made it possible for the insured, at his option, to reserve the right to change the beneficiary designation *without the consent of* the beneficiary, any time he wished and as often as he wished. Both these provisions are the rule today rather than the exception.

The Insured's Rights. Under the present-day life insurance contract the rights of the insured (or a third-party owner), as owner of the policy, are all but unquestioned. The contract is made between the insured (or a third-party owner) and the insurance company, and all rights—as one company says, all "living" rights—are exercisable by the owner.

The beneficiary, in legal language, is a "third-party beneficiary," who, if revocable, has no actual rights under the contract until it has matured as a death claim. In the absence of legislation permitting it, a third-party beneficiary has no right to bring suit under the contract in her own name. However, such legislation has been enacted in most of the states, and as a general rule there is no question with respect to her right to sue in her own name for the death benefit after the death of the insured, if suit is necessary.

THE RIGHT TO CHANGE THE BENEFICIARY

The Right Is Contractual

There is no question but that the applicant has the right to designate the beneficiary at the outset, and ordinarily he indicates at that time that he does or does not wish to reserve the right to change the beneficiary. Thus from the beginning, the right to change the beneficiary is a matter of contract, and it is very generally held that the right to change the beneficiary does not exist unless it is specifically reserved at the time the contract is made.

A Power of Appointment

We have previously pointed out that the right to name the beneficiary under a life insurance contract is a unique type of right. Legally it is closely related to what has long been called a "power of appointment." This power has been defined as "a power or authority conferred by one person by deed or will upon another (called the 'donee') to appoint, that is, to select and nominate, the person or persons who are to receive and enjoy an estate or an income therefrom or from a fund, after the testator's death, or the donee's death, or after the termination of an existing right or interest." [1]

A power of appointment relates to future interests in property, as indicated in this definition, but it has another connotation also, which is sometimes overlooked in connection with the life insurance contract. That is the fact that it is a right exercisable by one who is not actually an owner by which he may say who will be an owner with respect to certain specified property. To use an example, if A, owning Blackacre, wishes to leave a life estate to his wife, B, he may also specify the person or persons who will take title after the wife's death. Often, however, he may wish to leave her a life estate *and* the right to say who is to receive the property at her death. In the latter case she is said to have a power of appointment with respect to Blackacre. She has the right to say, by will or by deed, who will take Blackacre, although she does not have the right to sell the property. A power of appointment, therefore, is ordinarily a power one person, not the owner, has to say who the persons are (to select or appoint) who will take as owners at a date specified by the donor of the power.

Applied to the life insurance contract, this becomes rather technical, but also quite valid. The owner of a life insurance policy has many ownership rights with respect to the contract, but *he does not own the death benefit*. With respect to that benefit he has only the power to appoint, just as did B with respect to Blackacre in the example given above. It is this fine distinction that makes the conflict between the rights of an assignee and a beneficiary under the life insurance contract so very technical; it is also this difference that makes a careful consideration of the legal factors of paramount importance.

In legal terms, the power to appoint the beneficiary or beneficiaries under a life insurance contract is granted at the time of the application. If reserved, the owner has the right to change the beneficiary designation as he may wish, always in accordance with the provisions of the life insurance contract itself.

If the Right Is Not Reserved

Applicants for life insurance today ordinarily reserve the right to change the beneficiary and to perform other acts which have the effect of diminishing or terminating the rights of the beneficiary. However, if the right to change the beneficiary is not reserved, the beneficiary designation is irrevocable, and the beneficiary takes a vested interest in the proceeds. This simply means that the only person who could

---

[1] *Black's Law Dictionary* (West Publishing Co., 1933), p. 1392.

have deprived her of that right has divested himself of the right to do so. (It will be remembered, however, that a provision found in most policies today terminates the right, even of an irrevocable beneficiary, upon her death prior to the death of the insured.)

If the Right Is Reserved

Where the right to change the beneficiary is reserved, the courts are not in unanimous agreement with respect to the legal nature of the beneficiary's rights. In broad general terms there are two possible views. One line of cases, the majority, takes the approach that the beneficiary has nothing by reason of her designation but a mere expectancy. By reserving the right to change the beneficiary, to surrender the policy for cash, to effect a policy loan, etc., the insured made it clear that he did not intend to make a present gift of a future interest to the beneficiary. The designation is merely an instruction to the insurance company, and the latter owes no duty to the beneficiary whatsoever.

If the right to change the beneficiary is not exercised, the beneficiary will receive the proceeds payable at the death of the insured. If the right to change is exercised, there is nothing the displaced beneficiary can do about it. Thus her right is completely subject to the wishes of the policyholder, a mere expectancy.

The other view is that the beneficiary takes a vested right, subject to the possibility of its being divested. This particular point of view is definitely in the minority, but it is held in a few states and cannot be dismissed without comment. If the beneficiary's right is considered vested subject to being divested, her right while she has it is superior in quality to that of a mere expectancy, and it takes more to divest her of it. Generally speaking, courts taking this view hold that the right can be terminated only by action in strict accordance with the provisions of the policy. Thus her right is superior to that of an assignee, if she did not join in the assignment. The insured retains the power to change the beneficiary, but he must exercise it in strict accordance with the policy provision or the beneficiary's right is unaffected.

In general terms the decisions of the courts fall into these two broad classes. However, within the groups, the decisions are not at all clear-cut. Different factual situations, the equities of the various parties, and the general indefiniteness of such terms as "mere expectancy" and "vested subject to being divested" contrive to create a confused area in which generalizations are often misleading, if they are justified at all.

How the Right Is Exercised

The general rule with respect to changing the beneficiary under a life insurance contract is very simple. The policyholder changes the beneficiary only by following the procedure prescribed by the policy. It is well settled that the insurer may prescribe or regulate the procedure by which the policyholder may change the beneficiary. In fact the procedure for changing the beneficiary is one of the conditions in the contract of insurance. Ordinarily, then, the policyholder can change the beneficiary only by that method; he cannot change it by will, for example.

The law on the question of attempted changes of beneficiary by will is summarized rather succinctly in the case of *Cook* v. *Cook,*[2] decided by the California Supreme Court, in 1941. There on this precise question the court said:

> . . . Of course, there are instances in which an insured may transfer his policy by will. Where the policy has no named beneficiary but is payable to the estate of the insured, the policy may be disposed of by will or pass by intestate succession if the insured dies intestate (14 Cal. Jur. 585; 110 Cal. App. 439). Where the named beneficiary predeceased the insured and the power is reserved to change the beneficiary, the latter thus having no vested right in the policy or proceeds, the insured may dispose of the policy by will. This is true for the reason that, under such circumstances, the mere expectancy held by the beneficiary during the life of the insured vanishes with the death of the beneficiary prior to the death of the insured; and naturally the proceeds fall into the estate of the insured and are subject to testamentary disposition. (*Supreme Council etc.* v. *Gehrenbeck,* 124 Cal. 43; *Estate of Castagnola,* 68 Cal. App. 732.) And there may be instances in which by the terms of the particular policy involved, it is transferable by will. There may be other instances, but the rule cannot have any application to the facts in the instant case. A will does not become operative until death; prior to death it is revocable at the whim of the testator, and the objects of the testator's bounty have no vested rights. In that respect it is very similar to the rights of a beneficiary under a life insurance policy in which the insured reserves the right to change the beneficiary such as we have in the instant case. However, upon death the beneficiary's right becomes vested, and that being the case, no expression in the insured's will purporting to assign his life insurance policy or change the beneficiary can be effective. At death he no longer has a policy to assign. It has passed to his heirs, if no beneficiary was designated; if a beneficiary is named it passes to such beneficiary. He cannot then change the beneficiary because the right of the named beneficiary has vested.

Thus the basic rule with respect to the right to change the beneficiary and the procedure for doing so are very simple. The principal questions are those which arise as the result of different and difficult factual situations.

The Beneficiary Provision

Most policies permit the policyholder to change the beneficiary as often as he may wish simply by filing a written request for the change at the home or other administrative office of the company, usually sub-

---

[2] 17 Cal. 2d 639, 111 P.2d 322 (1941).

mitting the policy for endorsement. Under this type of requirement the change takes effect either as of the date of the writing or of the endorsement, as specified in the policy provision. Of recent years a number of companies have been requiring only that the written request for a change of beneficiary be filed with the company. Under this, the recording method, the company does not endorse the new beneficiary designation on the policy, and unless the insured carefully keeps copies of his request with the policy the beneficiary of record can only be ascertained by consulting the files of the company itself.

The majority of companies follow the endorsement method of beneficiary change, which requires that the new beneficiary designation be actually typed on the policy itself. Obviously this is somewhat safer than the recording method, since the sequence of specifications is actually written on the policy itself. On the other hand, the recording method has seemed to prove satisfactory to those companies which have followed it.

How the Right to Change May Be Lost

The Insured May Waive It. As is true of any other right, the right to change the beneficiary, even if reserved as far as the policy is concerned, may nevertheless be waived. For instance, in the case of *Handrahan, Trustee etc.* v. *Moore, etc.*,[3] decided by the Massachusetts Supreme Judicial Court in 1955, the insured had made a property settlement with his first wife, prior to their divorce, in which he had agreed to maintain insurance in the amount of $10,000 in force on his life, with his wife named as beneficiary. A trust was established for the wife's support and the insurance policies delivered to the trustee. Later these policies became worthless and others were substituted. Later still the insured notified the trustee that he was designating his present wife as beneficiary under the policies, instead of the former wife. The court held that by reason of the property settlement the insured had waived his right to change the beneficiary, saying:

. . . As against his wife and trustee he waived his right to change the beneficiary in these two policies outstanding at the time of his death which together amount to less than $10,000. Indeed it appears that Moore had designated his first wife as the beneficiary in these two policies in 1947. He informed her in December, 1950, that she was the beneficiary in the two policies now in question. We think the inference is plain that Moore recognized his obligation to maintain insurance for her benefit and that all parties understood that the policies in question were substituted for the certificate of the group insurance which had become worthless. We think the plaintiff acting as trustee for the mother acquired an equitable interest in the policies by virtue of the contract with her father and her right to enforce the contract and

[3] 124 N.E.2d 808 (Mass., 1955).

to collect the proceeds of these policies was superior to that of the defendant second wife.

The Insured May Be Estopped. The insured may sometimes place himself in a position where he has relinquished, or where he will be denied, the power to change the beneficiary. For one thing, if he has designated someone as beneficiary for the purpose of securing an existing debt he will not be permitted to change the beneficiary until the debt has been extinguished. Secondly, if he delivered the policy to the named beneficiary with gift intent, a later beneficiary change may not be permitted. For instance, in the case noted in Chapter XI, page 279, *supra,* such a delivery, with words of gift intent, was held to be an equitable assignment, and a subsequent attempted endorsement of a change of beneficiary was held ineffective.

WHO CAN CHANGE THE BENEFICIARY

By the terms of the life insurance contract the policyholder has the right to designate the beneficiary in the first place, and it is he who reserves (or fails to do so) the right to change the beneficiary later, if he wishes. Nevertheless this does not automatically guarantee that he may change the beneficiary, as we have already seen. He may, by his own acts, have waived the right; he may have acted in such a manner that he will be estopped to make another change; or he may be incompetent as a matter of law to make any change in designation.

If He Is a Minor. We have previously discussed the situations where minors are enabled by statute to apply for and exercise contractual rights under life insurance contracts on their own lives or, in some cases, on the lives of their dependents. In any case where the contract has been effected by reason of such laws, the minor can, of course, exercise his contractual rights as if he were an adult. This includes his right to designate and to change the beneficiary designation.

But what of the case where a policy is issued to the parent on the life of a minor insured? Here the law is very clear. The contractual rights, including the power to designate the beneficiary, are exercisable only by the owner of the policy, in this case the parent. If the parent-owner should die during the minority of the child, leaving ownership in the child, the latter cannot ordinarily change the beneficiary, and the legal guardian of his estate is powerless to change it for him.

In one rather unusual illustration of a confusion of rights under a policy of this kind, the policy was applied for and issued to the mother of the insured, who had named herself as the beneficiary. After a divorce between the parents, the father was given custody of the child. He then attempted to change the beneficiary under the policy by signing the name of his son "by" himself. The court held [4] that the policy was issued to the mother and that she alone had the right to change the beneficiary. The attempted change on the part of the father was without legal effect, and payment on the part of the insurance company, to the father, was erroneously made.

If He Is Mentally Incompetent. An insane or incompetent policyholder is without the power to make an effective change of beneficiary. The test of competency in this respect is very much the same as it is with respect to the capacity of a person to make a will or execute a deed or a contract. It has been summarized by one court as follows:

> The test to be applied in determining the mental competency of deceased at the time the change in beneficiary was attempted is: Did he have sufficient mental capacity to understand the extent of his property and how he wanted to dispose of it, and who were dependent upon him.[5]

The person who would ordinarily question the mental capacity of the policyholder would, of course, be the person standing to lose by reason of the purported change—the beneficiary of record. If she questions it, the burden is on her to prove that the insured did not have the capacity to make a valid change at the time he attempted to do so.

Change by Guardian. Generally speaking the guardian of an incompetent or minor insured cannot change the beneficiary under a life insurance policy for the ward. Occasional cases have held that such a change, if supported by a court order, would be valid. Ordinarily, however, the change of beneficiary is considered a true power of appointment, and exercising it by the guardian is in the same legal category as executing a will for the ward; it cannot be done. His will, and a change of beneficiary, must be executed by the ward himself or not at all.

Responsibility of the Insurer. As a general rule the insurance company will not be responsible if it pays money to a beneficiary who was named by an incompetent insured. The rule in such a case is exactly the same as where the company pays to an assignee of record, not knowing that the assignment was made at a time when the insured was incompetent.

A number of cases have held that payment in good faith of the full amount of a life insurance policy to the last regularly designated beneficiary, without knowledge of the lack of mental capacity to make the designation under which payment was made, discharged the insurer's obligation under the policy, and that no duty rested upon the company to make inquiry into the mental status of the insured making application for a change of beneficiary.[6]

---

[4] *Carpenter* v. *Home Beneficial Life Insurance Co.,* 4 Commerce Clearing House Life Cases (2d) 520 (Tenn. C.A., 1959).

[5] *Harris* v. *Copeland,* 59 N.W.2d 70 (Mich., 1953).

[6] *New York Life Insurance Co.* v. *The Federal National Bank of Shawnee, Oklahoma,* 151 F.2d 537, 162 A.L.R. 536 (C.A.A. Okla., 1945).

However, if the policy is surrendered by an insane insured and a cash value of less than the face amount of the insurance is paid, the insurance company may nevertheless, upon the subsequent death of the insured, have to pay the beneficiary the difference between that cash value, plus any other credits such as premiums, and the face amount which would have been due. In other words, the surrender may be avoided after the insured's death by his personal representative or heirs, just as any other contractual transaction may be.

THE RULE OF "SUBSTANTIAL CONFORMITY"

It is generally held that the insurance company has the right and duty to set forth in the policy contract the method and procedure by which the policyholder may change the beneficiary, assuming that the right to do so has been reserved. It has also consistently been held that the method so set forth is an exclusive method and that the insured cannot change the beneficiary by any other method.

However, in spite of the definiteness of these holdings, there is an equally well-established exception. Thus, if the insured has done all in his power to comply with the procedure set out in the policy but has failed because of circumstances beyond his control, the change of beneficiary will be held to be effective. This is the "substantial compliance" rule. It simply means that substantial compliance with the requirements set forth in the policy will be sufficient to change the beneficiary in cases where to hold otherwise would be definitely inequitable. As might be suspected, there is a tremendous number of cases in this area, and it has been said that the individual facts of these cases weigh perhaps more heavily than in any other one area of the law of the life insurance contract.

An Equitable Principle. The "substantial conformity" holdings rest on a common principle of equity, that equity regards as done that which ought to be done. Thus the rule will be applied in cases where the beneficiary and the insured have been divorced and the beneficiary deliberately withholds the policy in order to prevent the insured from effecting a valid change of beneficiary. In such cases, if the insured has executed a request for the change, has sent it to the company, and has otherwise done everything in his power to comply with the requirements set forth in the policy, the courts will ordinarily hold that the change has been accomplished even though the new designation has not been endorsed on the policy in accordance with the requirements of the policy.

This rule was applied in one case [7] as follows:

---

[7] *Doering v. Buechler,* 146 F.2d 784 (C.C.A. Minn., 1945).

The insured's intent that the proceeds of the policy in suit should be payable to his sister, and should not be payable to his wife, was clear. In attempting to effect a change of beneficiary in substantial compliance with the terms of the policy, the insured did all that it was practicable for him to do, in view of the fact that he did not have the policy, that his wife had it, and was holding it in order to prevent a change of beneficiary. It is a reasonable inference that a demand upon her for the policy would have been futile, and we do not believe that the insured was required to sue her for its possession. We think that the right of the appellee (the sister) to the proceeds of the policy, under the facts as found by the District Court, was, in equity, superior to the claim of the appellant. The appellant was in no position to take advantage of the failure of the insured and the insurer to bring about an endorsement upon the policy of the change of beneficiary. The requirement that the policy be delivered to the Company for endorsement was not for the protection of the appellant, but was for the protection of the Company. *Royal Union Mutual Life Insurance Co.* v. *Lloyd*, 8 Cir., 254 F. 407, 410. The Company, by bringing the action in interpleader, has waived any defense it may have had to the claim of either party. *Carter* v. *Thornton*, 8 Cir., 93 F.2d 529, 532.

Change Not Endorsed Prior to Insured's Death. It not infrequently happens that an insured completes a request for a change of beneficiary and sends it, together with the policy for endorsement, to the life insurance company, but the endorsement has not been completed at the time of his death. In such cases, if everything the insured could do has been done, and if nothing remains to be done except endorsing the beneficiary change on the policy, the courts will ordinarily hold that the new beneficiary is entitled to the policy proceeds. In such cases it is generally said that the endorsement is merely a ministerial act (that is, that it does not require discretion) and that it can be, and should be, performed even after the death of the insured.

These holdings are particularly justified where the delay has been occasioned by the company or its agents in some way. In one case,[8] for instance, the court permitted reformation of a certificate of insurance (where the sisters of the insured were named as beneficiaries) to make the wife of the insured the beneficiary. This was proved to be the intent of the insured, and the court held that it was proper to permit the contract to be reformed since the error was made by the company.

However, there have been some holdings to the effect that the policy provisions must be specifically complied with. This is particularly true if the consent of the insurer is required by the terms of the policy. In every case, the court is weighing the equities. If they are in favor of strict compliance, the holding will ordinarily be to that effect; if they are in favor of substantial compliance, the holding will ordinarily be to that effect.

Intent. Proof of intention alone is not enough. The insured must

[8] *Prudential* v. *Beulah Glasgow*, 208 F.2d 908 (C.A. N.Y., 1953).

not only have evidenced his intention to change the beneficiary but he must also have taken some substantial affirmative action. Then, under the principles outlined above, the courts may hold the change to be effective even if there has not been a strict compliance with the terms of the contract concerning such changes.

Rights of the Assignee versus Rights of the Beneficiary

As we have previously pointed out, most courts hold that an assignment, even without the consent of the beneficiary, will be sufficient to give the assignee a right superior to that of the beneficiary to the extent of the indebtedness. In other words, even though the strict change of beneficiary procedure outlined in the policy has not been complied with, the rights of the assignee are superior to those of the beneficiary, to the amount of the debt. This view is often supported and justified by the statement that the formal assignment is substantially in conformity with the beneficiary change provisions of the policy and that it operates as such a change. Alternatively, it is sometimes said that the beneficiary had a mere expectancy and that the assignment destroyed it.

One minority view in this type of case is illustrated by the courts of New Jersey, and sometimes called "the New Jersey Rule." There the courts hold that if the beneficiary does not consent to the assignment the assignee receives only those rights that the insured continued to have. Thus the beneficiary's claim is superior to that of the assignee in this and a few other jurisdictions.

However, even in New Jersey this rule is subject to some modifications. These modifications are summarized in the case of *Continental Assurance Company* v. *Conroy* [9] as follows:

> The first modification of the rule relates to an assignment of his policy by the insured to the insurer as security for a loan on the policy. New Jersey has recognized the priority of such an assignment over the interests of a beneficiary, reasoning that a policy loan is a privilege reserved to the insured by the contract of insurance and a possibility of defeasance to which the beneficiary's interest had always been subject, . . . This rule enabled the Continental Assurance Company in this case to enforce Conroy's assignment to it to the extent of his outstanding debt. The rule, of course, does not affect the assignment of March 29th.
>
> The second modification of the New Jersey rule is that if an insured in attempting to change a beneficiary has done all he could to comply with the policy requirements and has substantially complied, a change will be effected, . . . As there was no attempt as of March 29th to make Howard Eastwood and the bank beneficiaries, this modification does not convert the assignment into a change of beneficiary.
>
> The third modification of the rule prevails when the policy of insurance provides by its terms that an assignment shall operate to transfer the interest

[9] 111 F. Supp. 370 (D.C. N.J., 1953).

of the beneficiary as well as that of the insured. In *Phoenix Mutual Life Ins. Co. v. Connelly, supra,* the policy provided,

> If the right to change the beneficiary has been reserved to the insured, an assignment, release or surrender of this policy or any interest therein by the insured, if of legal age, shall operate to the extent thereof to assign, release or surrender the interest of any and all beneficiaries hereunder.

The court held that this clause subjected the beneficiary interest to an additional power of defeasance. As there is no such provision in the policy in this case, this modification of the New Jersey rule also does not govern the March 29th assignment.

The fourth modification of the New Jersey rule relates to the situation which arises when the estate of the insured is the beneficiary of the policy. If there is an assignment of the policy under such circumstances, it is effective to vest in the assignee both the insured's and the beneficiary's interests, . . .

Where a controversy arises between a beneficiary and an assignee, after the death of the insured, the majority of courts hold that the assignee's rights are superior to those of the beneficiary. However, some jurisdictions hold that the beneficiary has a vested interest, which can be divested only by following exactly the procedure set forth in the policy for a change of beneficiary.

CHAPTER **XIII**

The Policyholder
"Borrows"
on His Policy

WE HAVE discussed the prematurity values under a life insurance contract at some length and noted the policyholder's freedom to treat the contract in many ways much the same as he would any other item of intangible personal property. Thus he may give the policy away, sell it, or borrow, using the policy as a pledge for repayment of the loan.

The owner of most present-day life insurance policies may also effect a policy loan under the policy loan provision of the policy. In doing this, however, he is not treating the policy as property in the general sense of the word. Instead, he is availing himself of a privilege which differs in a basic, legal way from his freedom to use the policy as collateral security for a bank loan, for example. The purpose of this chapter is to show the legal nature of this difference and to note the more important possible problems which the use of the policy loan may involve.

TWO KINDS OF "LOANS" AVAILABLE

The Collateral Assignment

We have previously discussed the collateral assignment, under which the policyholder pledges the policy as security for repayment of indebtedness. Under the collateral assignment, the policyholder transfers rights under the policy on condition that they be used only to protect the assignee against loss in case of default. It will be recalled that in such a transaction the policy is ordinarily delivered to the assignee and that the collateral assignment operates very much like a pledge of any item of personal property.

The Policy "Loan"

Under the policy loan provision of most present-day life insurance policies, the owner may request an advance [1] from the life insurance company itself. Thus he has two strings to his bow, so to speak, if he needs money on a temporary basis. He may use his policy as a pledge and borrow money from a bank on the security of the nonforfeiture values prior to his death and repayment out of the death benefit if he does not repay the debt before he dies. Alternatively, he may request and receive an advance, not to exceed the amount of the cash surrender value, directly from the life insurance company, under the policy loan provision.

The procedures by which the policyholder negotiates the "loan" in these two cases differ markedly. Although the word "loan" is used in each case, the legal nature of the transactions differ as do also their legal effects. Policy loans involve negotiations directly with the company, while the company is not a party to collateral assignments. Nevertheless, most companies become involved in collateral assignments in one way or another, as well as policy loans. Furthermore, both transactions involve the impairment of the basic purpose of the insurance—family protection—and both arise because the policyholder needs money on a temporary basis.

As a general rule, a discussion of policy loans is concerned with request loans and automatic premium loans only. The loan the policyholder negotiates at the bank is usually discussed in connection with a general treatment of assignments. In using the policy to its maximum effectiveness, however, both as property and as insurance, the policyholder should consider the relative values of a loan from the bank versus a loan from the life insurance company. For that reason, the two ways in which the policyholder can "borrow on his policy" and incidentally diminish its value as insurance, are discussed together in this chapter.

There are two kinds of policy loans, the request loan and the automatic premium loan. Either or both may be available to the policyholder, depending upon state insurance laws, the provisions of the policy itself, and the practices of the company. Both, however, must be provided for in the policy or they are ordinarily not available.

LEGAL NATURE OF THE POLICY LOAN

Origin

Because of the legal reserve, level premium system, life insurance

---

[1] See later, "An Advance, Not a Loan," p. 309.

companies accumulate and invest large sums of money under a quasi-trusteeship for the benefit of the policyholders. Except as different rights are spelled out in the policy, the only right an individual policy-holder has in these pooled funds is the right to have the amount of insurance specified in his policy paid to a named beneficiary at the death of the insured. Very early in the history of level premium insurance, it began to be recognized that the policyholder who is unable to, or does not want to continue his policy in force by premium payment, suffered a very definite loss in the forfeiture of his policy. Because he had a moral, if not legal right to a share in the fund which his own payments had helped accumulate, the nonforfeiture rights were established, first by voluntary action of the companies, and later by reason of statutory law.

It seemed obvious that some policyholders would have a need for money on a temporary basis and yet not actually want to surrender their policies. Furthermore it was definitely to the advantage of the company to discourage the surrendering of a policy for cash if some other method could be found for making funds available to the policy-holder on a temporary basis. It was only reasonable, therefore, to take steps to make some of the accumulated values available to the policy-holders on a loan basis, at least for the payment of premiums, permitting him to continue his policy in full force and effect, subject to the repayment of the loan. This the companies did, first for the purpose of paying a premium otherwise in default, and later, on a more general basis, for any purpose the policyholder might have in mind.

The Policy Loan Provision

As we have seen, the policy loan provision, like so many life insurance liberalizations, was first included in the policy on a voluntary basis. Today it is required by law to be included in the life insurance policy in every state in which the Uniform Standard Provisions Law has been enacted. Since this includes the states in which life insurance plays its most important part, it is safe to say that a provision providing for a policy loan is included in most policies which are issued today.

The automatic premium loan provision, on the other hand, is a required provision by the laws of Rhode Island only. However, if it is included in the policy it provides another in the bundle of rights to which we have so often referred.

For ease of reference, we quote again a typical policy provision providing for the policy loan:

Policy Loan. At any time while this policy is in force, during the lifetime of the insured, other than as extended term insurance, the company, upon receipt of this policy and a loan agreement satisfactory to the company, will advance to the insured on the sole security of this policy any amount which shall be within the limit of the maximum loan value, if any, less any existing indebtedness to the company on this policy. The maximum loan value shall be that amount which, with interest at the rate of five per cent per annum to the date on which the next premium is due or, if no further premiums are payable, to the next anniversary of the Policy Date, equals, as of such date, the sum of the cash surrender value and any unapplied premium deposit reserve.

Interest on the loan shall accrue from day to day at the rate of five per cent per annum and shall constitute an indebtedness to the company against this policy as and when it accrues. Interest shall be payable on each anniversary of the Policy Date subsequent to the date of loan until such loan is repaid and if such interest is not paid when due it shall be added to and form a part of the loan, and bear interest at the same rate except that, if at any time the total indebtedness to the company on this policy, including accrued interest, is equal to the then maximum loan value, the accrued interest shall be then payable.

All or any part of the loan may be repaid, with accrued interest on the amount so repaid, at any time while this policy is in force other than as extended term insurance, provided this policy has not matured as an endowment and the death of the insured has not occurred. Whenever the total indebtedness to the company on this policy is no longer within the limit of the then maximum loan value, this policy shall be void thirty-one days after the company has mailed notice to the last known address of the insured and the assignee of record, if any.

An Advance, Not a Loan

Note first that the policy provision is worded as follows: "At any time while this policy is in force, other than as extended term insurance, the company, upon receipt of this policy and a loan agreement satisfactory to the company, *will advance to the insured. . . .*" Thus the policy does not say "will loan. . . ." Nor does the statute use the word *loan.* This is in exact accordance with court rulings, perhaps the most important of which was stated by Justice Oliver Wendell Holmes, as follows: "The so-called liability of the policyholder never exists as a personal liability, it never is a debt, but is merely a deduction in account from the sum that the plaintiffs (insurance company) ultimately must pay." [2]

No Promise to Repay. The most significant reason why a policy loan is not a true loan in the legal sense of the word is the fact that the policyholder does not promise to repay it. Note again the language of the policy provision: "All or any part of the loan may be repaid, with accrued interest on the amount so repaid, at any time while this policy is in force other than as extended term insurance, provided this policy

---

[2] *Board of Assessors v. New York Life Insurance Co.*, 216 U.S. 517, 30 S. Ct. 385, 54 L. Ed. 597 (1910).

has not matured as an endowment or terminated by the death of the insured." Note that the loan may be repaid, but the provision does not say it must be. Furthermore there are several situations in which it may not be repaid. It cannot be repaid after the death of the insured,[3] for instance, but must be deducted from the death benefit. This is perhaps the most essential reason why the policy loan has been held again and again not to be an indebtedness in the legal sense of the word, and therefore not to be a charge against the estate of the policyholder at his death.

No Promise to Pay Interest. With respect to interest, the provision reads as follows:

> . . . Interest shall be payable on each anniversary of the Policy Date subsequent to the date of loan until such loan is repaid and if such interest is not paid when due it shall be added to and form a part of the loan, and bear interest at the same rate except that, if at any time the total indebtedness to the company on this policy, including accrued interest, is equal to the then maximum loan value, the accrued interest shall be then payable.

Note that here again the provision does not contemplate a personal liability on the part of the policyholder even for payment of the interest.

Not Borrowing "Own Money." The statement is sometimes erroneously made that the policyholder is really "borrowing his own money." This is not precisely true. The policyholder, as we have seen, has no accumulated funds in his own name. The pooled funds of the company are held for the benefit of all policies, and the individual policyholder has a specific share only if he wishes to surrender his policy for cash, or if he keeps it in force until his death, at which time the face amount of the policy is paid to his beneficiary. The company does not operate like a savings bank in any sense of the word.

Amount of Interest. The fact that interest is charged on these "advances" does not make them loans in the legal sense, although courts have held insurance companies to be subject to the same laws with respect to interest rates that other "lenders" are. Thus, if there is no statute permitting otherwise it has been held that only simple interest can be charged.

The Standard Provisions Law permits compound interest, and most policies provide that the interest, if unpaid, will be added to and become a part of the principal of the loan. The only reason for the provision adding accrued, unpaid interest to the principal is to bring the policy loan transaction into harmony with the computation of policy reserves. Since reserve calculations involve compound interest, individual policy loans should be calculated in the same way.

---

[3] However, under special company practice, a number of companies permit the repayment of policy loans after the death of the insured.

Provisions for Forfeiture. Lastly, the policy provision describes the disposition of the policy if the policy loan, with accrued interest, becomes equal to or in excess of the cash surrender value. In that case the policy shall be void thirty-one days after the company has mailed notice to the last known address of the insured and to the assignee of record, if any. Since the policyholder is not obligated to repay the loan, the remedy, if the loan plus interest exceeds the cash surrender value, is in the provision that the policy shall be canceled.

By statute, it is often required that the company give thirty days' notice of termination of the policy. There have been a few cases in which the courts have held that the insurance company must take exactly the same procedures that would be necessary in foreclosing on a pledged policy. These cases have been superseded, however, and there is no question at the present time that the insurer can, in accordance with its policy provision, terminate the policy upon notice to the insured.

Policy Loans Generally

A policy loan is an advance made by the company to a policyholder, secured by a pledge of the policy. Interest is charged for three principal reasons. First, no company wishes to encourage its policyholders to reduce the values under their policies by effecting these advances. If no interest were charged, or a very low rate imposed, this would undoubtedly be the effect. Second, the company is required to maintain a sufficiently flexible cash position to accommodate the requests for loans when they are made, and if the funds so held and those advanced do not earn a rate of interest comparable to that earned by other investments, it is only right that the policyholders who are benefited by the service should pay for it. Third, the company's reserves are calculated at a stipulated rate of interest. If any appreciable amount of money is out on policy loans at a significantly lower interest rate, the result will be unfairly discriminatory toward policyholders who do not effect loans on their policies.

The policy loan does not have to be repaid until such time as the insured dies or the policy values shall have been dissipated. However, this is not an unmixed blessing. If the insured dies while the loan is outstanding, it is ordinarily deducted from the sum payable and the beneficiary receives only the remainder. This not only reduces the amount available to the beneficiary but it often destroys the effectiveness of plans utilizing the settlement options for her benefit.

Characteristics of a Bank Loan

Where the policyholder borrows the money he needs from a bank and pledges the policy, under an assignment, he is personally obligated on his promise to repay the loan. The lender is entitled to payment out of the proceeds of the policy—the cash values during the policyholder's life, the death benefit after his death—but his first line of recovery is from the policyholder himself.

Most collateral assignment forms give the assignee the right to cash in the policy without the policyholder's consent in case of default in payment of the loan. All give the assignee the right to recover the amount of the unpaid debt out of the proceeds of the policy at the death of the insured. Where the total estate of the insured consists of insurance, therefore, the ultimate effects of the policy loan versus the bank loan are approximately the same. In both cases the amount of the unpaid loan is deducted from the amount payable, and the named beneficiary receives the remainder. However, let us take a case where there is other property. In one such case, for example, *In Re Estate of Schwartz,*[4] decided by the Pennsylvania Supreme Court in 1952, the insured had two policies on his life with loans on both. Suit was brought on the theory that the beneficiaries were entitled to reimbursement out of the general estate to the amount of the loans, which were deducted from the proceeds of the policies, and the trial court agreed. The opinion of the Supreme Court of Pennsylvania is given in full because of the excellent analysis of the legal nature of the policy loan and the rights of the beneficiaries under policies in which loans were in effect.

* * * * *

IN RE ESTATE OF SCHWARTZ

(Pennsylvania Supreme Court, Eastern District.)

STEARNE, J.,: The question involved is whether a "policy loan" upon a life insurance policy is a debt of such a nature as enables the designated beneficiary, upon the insured's death, to require the loan to be repaid from the insured's general estate, thus enabling the beneficiary to receive the full insurance proceeds. The court below ruled that it was such a debt and directed its repayment. This appeal follows.

George J. Schwartz, the decedent, was insured by two policies of life insurance, each in the amount of $5,000. In one policy decedent named two of his daughters beneficiaries, and in the other he designated his first wife. Neither policy reserved the right to change beneficiaries. But each policy *obligated* the company to make "loans" to the insured to the limit of its cash surrender value. "Loans" were granted in the aggregate amount of $3,466.80.

By his will the testator-insured directed his executors "to pay my funeral expenses and all my just debts as soon after my decease as may conveniently be done." It was upon the theory that the "policy loans" created a debtor-creditor relationship between the insured and insurer, that the learned court below decreed that the beneficiaries were entitled to reimbursement from the

[4] 369 Pa. 574, 87 A.2d 270 (1952).

general estate in order that they should receive the full face amounts of the policies.

In support of its ruling the court below relied upon our decision in *Wilson Estate*, 363 Pa. 546, 70 A.2d 354, wherein we decided that in an assessment of transfer inheritance tax, credit must be allowed for an indebtedness of the decedent-insured where a loan was made to him by a bank, and his life insurance policy, payable to designated beneficiaries, was pledged as collateral security. We said, p. 551:

> Decedent (settlor) merely assigned the insurance policies as collateral for his loan. As with any other collateral, when a loan is repaid the collateral is returned to the owner. Had the creditor bank used decedent-settlor's insurance collateral to liquidate its loan, the designated insurance beneficiaries could have enforced their claim against the estate of the decedent under their right of *subrogation*, to the same extent as if they had been the original creditor.

In the case now before us, contradistinguished from the facts in *Wilson Estate, supra*, the "debt" was owed to the insurance company and not to a third person with the insurance policy assigned as collateral. This raises the narrow but important question whether any sound difference exists between the fundamental natures of these transactions. More accurately: does such an insurance "loan" from the insuring company upon the policy itself create a debtor-creditor relationship?

The learned court below, and counsel at argument stated that they have been unable to find any reported case in this jurisdiction which has decided this question. Our own research has disclosed none. But courts in at least six other jurisdictions have considered the problem. They unanimously agree that a "loan" granted pursuant to a policy right does not create a debtor-creditor relationship. The nature of such a "policy loan" has recently been discussed in *Fidelity Union Trust Co.* v. *Phillips*, 5 N.J. Super. 529, 68 A.2d 574. It is said, p. 575:

> A clear distinction is drawn between a loan made by an insurance company to an insured against a life policy, and a collateral loan made by a third party secured by an assignment or pledge of the policy on the life of the borrower. The former "is not a loan in the strict technical sense, for there is no obligation of repayment on the insured, but rather an advancement on the cash value of the policy, the repayment of which will reinstate the depleted insurance without the issuance of a new policy and the submission of evidence of insurability. A 'loan' by the insurer in such circumstances does not give rise to the relationship of debtor and creditor." *David* v. *Metropolitan Life Insurance Co.*, 135 N.J.L. 106, 50 A.2d 651, 653, (Sup. Ct., 1947), affirmed 136 N.J.L. 195, 54 A.2d 731, (E. & A., 1947). Mr. Justice Holmes declared in *Board of Assessors* v. *New York Life Insurance Co.*, 216 U.S. 517, 30 S. Ct. 385, 386, 54 L. Ed. 597, 1910, "This is called a loan. It is represented by what is called a note, which contains a promise to pay the money. But as the plaintiff (insurance company) never advances more than it already is absolutely bound for under the policy, it has no interest in creating a personal liability, and therefore the contract on the face of the note goes on to provide that if the note is not paid when due, it shall be extinguished automatically by the counter-credit for what we have called the reserve value of the policy. In short, the claim of the policyholder on the one side and of the company on the other are brought into an account current by the very act that creates the latter. The so-called liability of the policyholder never exists as a personal liability, it never is a debt, but is merely a de-

duction in account from the sum that the plaintiffs ultimately must pay."
Therefore, when an insurance company advances to an insured a sum of
money against his policy, and upon the death of the insured retains the
amount required to satisfy the "loan" or advance, the beneficiary named
in the policy is not entitled to recover from the estate of the insured the
amount by which the insurance had been depleted by borrowings by the
insured upon the policy. *Wagner* v. *Thieriot*, 203 App. Div. 757, 197
N.Y.S. 560, affirmed 236 N.Y. 588, 142 N.E. 295 (Ct. App. 1923); *In re
Hayes' Will*, 252 N.Y. 148, 169 N.E. 120 (Ct. App. 1929); *In re Wald-
burger's Estate*, 78 Colo. 516, 242 P. 982, 45 A.L.R. 518, (Sup. Ct.
1926).

In the foregoing case, the insured had first borrowed from the insurance
company and later repaid such "loan" and borrowed from a bank assigning the
policy as collateral in order to obtain more favorable interest rate. The New
Jersey court decided that while a debtor-creditor relationship existed in such
latter three-party transaction, yet because of the terms of a trust agreement
executed by the insured, it was disclosed that the insured only intended the
beneficiaries to take the *net* proceeds of the policies without right of subrogation against his estate.

A portion of the language of Justice Holmes of the United States Supreme
Court relied on by the New Jersey court was also quoted with approval by
Justice Linn in *Kanatas* v. *Home Life Insurance Company of America*, 325
Pa. 93, 100, 189 A. 293, in considering whether unearned premiums should
have been applied to an outstanding loan in order to extend the insurance.

The reason why the subrogation rationale of *Wilson Estate, supra*, cannot
be applied to a "policy loan," is well stated in *Faris* v. *Faris*, 76 Ind. App. 336,
130 N.E. 444, p. 446.

With this primary fund [the insurance proceeds] for its protection, out of
which it had agreed to collect the debt, it had no rights, in lieu thereof,
against the general personal estate. Such being the case, there were no
rights to which appellant could be subrogated.

See also *Walker* v. *Penick's Ex'r.*, 122 Va. 664, 95 S.E. 428; *Allen* v.
Southard, 177 Tenn. 541, 151 S.W.2d 1072.

Substantially the same rule was adopted by this Court in *Black's Estate*,
341 Pa. 264, 19 A.2d 130. The insurance policy there included a provision
almost identical with that now under consideration, except that payment by
insurer was more accurately termed an "advance" rather than a "loan." Decedent had bequeathed his business to his son subject to payment of all his
personal and business debts. A dispute arose between the son and the widow,
as residuary, legatee, as to whether certain items were debts or obligations
payable out of the business. Concerning a cash advance to decedent from his
insurance company, we said (p. 270):

The auditor and court below held that the advance was not such a debt
as was required to be paid out of the business of decedent. With that
conclusion we are in accord, for the association could not make any claim
against the estate of the decedent. It could not have proceeded against
the decedent at the date of his death. Consequently there was no indebtedness, as clearly appears from a perusal of the agreement. The policyholder had the right to repay the advance made but he could not be
compelled to do so.

While counsel for appellees point to factual distinctions between that
case and the present one, such distinctions have no bearing on the legal principle here involved.

Legal digests and text writers appear to be equally unanimous.

Although a policy loan is termed a "loan," it differs from an ordinary commercial loan, and, in fact, is not a "loan" in the ordinary sense of the word. It is merely a deduction from the sum insurer ultimately must pay, and is more accurately described as an advance. 44 C.J.S. Insurance, sec. 337, p. 1291.

Accord: 29 Am. Jur. Insurance, sec. 463; Goldin on Insurance in Pennsylvania (2d ed.) page 631; 2 Couch on Insurance, sec. 335; Cooley's Briefs on Insurance (2d ed.) page 157.

Appellees argue that the insured's will and his testamentary scheme, considered in the light of his family circumstances, reveal that he intended his insurance beneficiaries to receive the full face amount of the policies. But the insured's *testamentary intent* is not the controlling consideration. We are obliged first to determine his *contractual* intent at the time he entered into the contracts of insurance wherein the rights of the insurance beneficiaries were created. We cannot interpret the meaning of contracts entered into on June 11, 1913, by speculating on testamentary intent adopted by insured in his testamentary scheme of April 2, 1949, nearly thirty-six years thereafter. The terms of the insurance contracts are clear and unambiguous; they give the insured an absolute right to demand at any time an advancement of any sum of money up to the reserve value of the policies. Under no discernible doctrine could it be held that the insured was incurring a *personal liability* by exercising this contractual right. The insured could, of course, have directed by his will that the "policy loans" be paid out of his general assets so that the beneficiaries would receive the face amounts of the policies. As he chose not to do this we have no power to do it for him. We cannot construe a direction to pay "debts" as applicable to an advancement of money which did not create a personal liability. As an insurance policy loan does not create a debtor-creditor relationship, the beneficiaries of these policies so encumbered are entitled only to the *net* proceeds.

Decree reversed at appellees' cost.

CHAPTER **XIV**

Life Insurance
and the
Law of Wills

A "TESTAMENTARY disposition" of property is a disposition not intended to take effect until the death of the owner. Generally speaking, documents intended to have this effect must be executed in accordance with the statute of wills of the jurisdiction concerned or they will be held ineffective as a matter of law. No one would think of raising this question today in connection with the life insurance contract itself, but other types of life insurance arrangements, particularly those involving the optional modes of settlement, have occasionally been challenged as "attempted testamentary dispositions," not executed in accordance with the statute of wills, and therefore invalid.

In the majority of cases involving this challenge, the validity of the instrument has been upheld. Nevertheless, it presents a relatively close question of law, which it is the purpose of this chapter to discuss.

"TESTAMENTARY" DISPOSITION

The Law of Wills and Testaments

To most people the term "last will and testament" is just a complicated way of referring to a person's will. A will is a document in which one specifies how his property shall be distributed after his death, and the word "testament" doesn't seem to add much, if anything. Technically, however, and historically, a will directed the disposition of *real property* (land and attached buildings), and a testament served the same purpose with respect to personal property. Thus the terms were used together to designate an instrument which directed the disposition of *all* of a person's property, both real and personal, at his death. The custom has been retained in the technical language of the law.

The law of wills and testaments has had a long and technical development. Regardless of when it is executed, a will does not take effect until the death of the person who made it (the testator). Often it is secret, or at least highly confidential, until that time. For these reasons, and because the controversies arise only after the death of the best witness, the testator, the entire subject has presented the opportunity for much confusion and at times for fraud. From an early date, therefore, there have been statutes setting forth requirements that must be met before an instrument purporting to direct the disposition of one's property after his death can be given effect. In spite of the apparent clarity of these laws, a large body of case law has been developed out of the attempt to distinguish those instruments, intended as wills, which have in fact been executed in accordance with the statute of wills and may be given legal effect as wills. The basic principle on which these statutes and court decisions rest is simply this: that any attempt to say how one's property shall be distributed *after his death* must be executed in accordance with the statute of wills of the jurisdiction concerned,[1] or it will be held invalid and ineffective. In that event the decedent will be held to have died *intestate* (i.e., without a will), and his property will be distributed according to the statute of intestate succession.

Exceptions. In spite of this relative strictness, the law has recognized, from an early date, that there may be legitimate ways to arrange the ownership of one's property so that it will shift to others of one's own choice at his death, without the necessity of a will. Holding property in joint tenancy is one example of this. One of the characteristics of joint tenancy is that at the death of one joint tenant, ownership automatically vests in the survivor or survivors. Another method is through a special kind of gift called a *gift causa mortis*. This is simply a gift in contemplation of one's own death, made when death seems imminent, but on condition that if one doesn't die as anticipated, of the illness or injury then suffered, ownership of the property in question returns (*reverts*) to the giver.

Traditionally there is a strong question as to whether contracts are ever to be considered as governed by the statute of wills in the sense that they must meet the requirements there set forth or be held invalid. Basically the statute of wills relates to the transfer of property at the death of the owner, without consideration. Certainly it doesn't relate to a sale of such property. Also the possibilities of fraud, undue influence, and other considerations which have been felt to make strict requirements necessary for wills are not as compelling in the case of

---

[1] Ordinarily, with respect to personal property, this means the law of the place where the decedent made his home at the time of his death; with respect to real property, it means the law of the place where the property is located.

contracts, where there are other requirements of sufficient solemnity to accomplish these same general purposes. It has sometimes been flatly said that the rules concerning testamentary disposition have no relation to contracts. However, there is strong authority to the contrary, and that is not a satisfactory answer to the question.

The Life Insurance Contract. The life insurance contract becomes payable on the death of the insured and thus presents a question more nearly synonymous with that in connection with wills than does the third-party donee contract[2] in other areas of the law. Nevertheless, with respect to the life insurance contract itself, its validity so far as any testamentary disposition question is concerned, seems to have been firmly settled at a relatively early date. It has been suggested that the nature of the early contracts of life insurance, which had no lifetime values and were often purchased by someone other than the insured, may have been largely responsible for this favorable holding with respect to the life insurance contract and the law of wills. In any case the question of a possible testamentary disposition in connection with the basic life insurance policy seems to have been settled many years ago.

TESTAMENTARY DISPOSITION AND THE OPTIONAL SETTLEMENTS

The Life Contract

Not a Testamentary Disposition. As we have pointed out, the validity of the life insurance contract itself, including as it does the direction for payment of money to a beneficiary at the death of the insured, has nevertheless been firmly established. It is not an attempted testamentary disposition of property and need not be executed in accordance with the requirements for the execution of a will.

The beneficiary of the life insurance contract fits into the tradition of the third-party beneficiary in contract law generally, and as stated above, there seems never to have been a very strong threat that the beneficiary designation might be held to be an attempted testamentary disposition of property. Since there was no property until the insured's death, the analogy with wills was somewhat difficult. Furthermore, since the early policies were often effected by the beneficiary herself, even if there had been lifetime values, they would have belonged to the beneficiary from the first, and again there would have been no question of testamentary disposition. The development of lifetime values, belonging to the insured, was sufficiently gradual that the possible problem

---

[2] Contracts made between two or more persons but intended to benefit another, or "third party," who is not a party to the contract, are known as third-party beneficiary contracts. If such benefit is in the nature of a gift, the third party is a third party *donee.*

had been resolved before the circumstances developed that might have given firmer grounds for challenge.

The Optional Settlements

Election by the Insured. Where the insured elects to have the proceeds held by the company and paid to the beneficiary under one of the optional methods of settlement, we have a somewhat different situation from that presented by the contract in the first place. Even here, however, the money held was never actually the property of the insured. Thus, the settlement agreement cannot be said to be a *disposition of the insured's property,* to take effect on his death.

Let us say then that he provides that the money be held for his wife, with permission to withdraw all of it if she wishes, but with the further provision that at her death the remainder shall be payable in equal sums to such of the children as shall then be living. Here the second contingency is the death of the wife, and again this cannot truly be said to be a testamentary disposition since it does not take effect at the death of the person who caused the instrument to be executed.

Even in connection with the optional settlements, therefore, the question of attempted testamentary disposition has not been raised very often, and it has been sustained in a very small number of cases. The nature of life insurance and the practices of life insurance companies, however, make it important to consider any factor which might interfere with the prompt settlement of claims and the absolute dependability of the carrying out of life insurance obligations. It is not enough that a settlement will be upheld in a court of law; the life insurance company must be in a position to guarantee to its policyholders and their beneficiaries that no question will be raised. Life insurance must mean immediate funds at the death of the insured; a lawsuit, even though unwarranted, destroys that meaning and reduces to that extent one of the essential advantages of life insurance over any other type of property arrangement. In only one area have lawsuits based on the testamentary question posed any appreciable threat, and that is the area of optional settlements where the option has been elected by the beneficiary or payee.

Election by Beneficiary. Most life insurance contracts provide that if an optional method of settlement has not been elected by the insured prior to his death, the beneficiary may herself elect to have the proceeds to which she is entitled held by the insurance company and distributed in accordance with one of the optional methods of settlement.

Let us take, as an example, John Smith, insured, whose life insurance policy in the amount of $50,000 is payable to his wife, Mary, in one sum. Mary elects to leave the proceeds with the company under the interest option, with full right of withdrawal, and requests that the supplementary contract be so drawn that any sums remaining at her death shall be payable equally among such of her children as shall be living on that date. Here, obviously, we have a different situation. Here there definitely was a sum of money to which Mary had just as complete a right as if it were her deposit in a bank. Her agreement with the life insurance company to leave it on deposit at interest, with the further provision that if she should die while any amounts remain, they should be paid in equal sums to her surviving children, is undoubtedly a disposition of her property not to take effect until her death. How does this situation differ from others in which a will, executed in complete conformity with the requirements of the statute of wills, is required to make the disposition effective?

Noninsurance cases can be cited showing that similar arrangements involving bank deposits have been held ineffective to pass an interest to the persons named to take at the death of the person making the arrangements.

Three principal cases in the last twenty years have upheld the validity of supplementary contracts in which the optional methods of settlement were elected by the payee, with directions that any funds remaining with the insurance company at the death of the primary payee be paid, not to her personal representatives, but directly to named persons. This, in technical terms, is a "gift over." The effect, of course, is to avoid the necessity of making a will. Where the distribution under the laws of intestacy would be different from that elected under the contract, however, it is quite possible that someone may challenge the arrangement on the grounds that it is void as an attempted testamentary disposition of property not executed in conformity with the statute of wills.

The Cases

The Ellis Case.[3] This case was decided in 1942 in the United States Circuit Court of Appeals, Second Circuit, and arose in New York. The wife, beneficiary of four life insurance policies on the life of her husband, elected to take the proceeds, not under one of the standard options, but under a somewhat different agreement between herself and the company, under which the income was to be paid to her during her life, with the principal payable at her death to her husband's three sisters. At her death, the sisters made claim for the payment, and the administrator of the beneficiary's estate also made claim. The company paid the money into court and asked the court to decide among the claimants. The district court held that the sisters were entitled to the money "upon the

---

[3] *The Mutual Benefit Life Insurance Company* v. *Ellis et al.,* C.C.A. N.Y., 125 F.2d 127, 138 A.L.R. 1478 (1942).

theory that the certificate was either a supplementary insurance contract or created a valid trust in their favor." The appellate court said: "We are in accord with the result of the decision but on the ground that the sisters were entitled to recover as third-party donee-beneficiaries."

The most pertinent part of the court's decision went as follows:

> The crucial question is whether the sisters acquired the right to recover the proceeds of the policies as third-party donee-beneficiaries, or whether they were precluded from this because the agreement to pay them was invalid as an ineffective attempt to dispose of property upon Mrs. Addie's death without the formality of a will. In *McCarthy* v. *Pierit,* 281 N.Y. 407, an agreement extending a bond and mortgage provided that upon the death of the mortgagee the interest was to be paid, one-half to his brother and the other half to the heirs of his deceased sister, and the principal to the same persons when the mortgage matured. A majority of the court held that the agreement constituted an attempted testamentary disposition and as such violated the Statute of Wills. The court refused to regard the agreement as giving the brother and heirs of the deceased sister any rights as third-party beneficiaries and treated the transaction as a gift which failed because the extension evidenced no intention to transfer an interest to them during the lifetime of the mortgage. . . .
>
> . . . A sufficient answer to the argument that it would violate the Statute of Wills to enforce the agreement for the sisters lies in the fact that their right to enforce is based upon a contractual obligation and not on any interest in the property of the decedent. The appellant cites no Colorado decision having any bearing on the present situation except *Smith* v. *Simmons,* 99 Colo. 227. There a bank to which certain bonds were delivered by the owner, with a letter instructing it as to the disposition of the bonds after the owner's death, was held an agent and not a trustee, and the bonds were therefore held a part of the transferor's estate, of which she had made no proper testamentary disposition. In the case at bar, however, the title to the proceeds of the policies passed to the company, leaving only contractual rights in Mrs. Addie and the sisters. The Colorado decisions are to the effect that such a right, though subject to be divested in the manner provided in the contract, is a vested right arising when the contract is made and enforceable unless and until terminated pursuant to the provisions of the instrument of settlement. . . .

For the foregoing reasons, we hold that the appellees were entitled to recover as third-party donee-beneficiaries.

Toulouse v. *New York Life Insurance Company.*[4] This case involved a twenty-year endowment policy which matured during the lifetime of the insured. At its maturity he requested that $6,000 be left with the company under option 1 and that any amount remaining with the company at his death be paid in equal shares to his four nieces and a nephew. The company issued a supplementary contract providing for settlement in accordance with his request.

There were no withdrawals, and at the death of the insured the accumulated values in the possession of the company amounted to $7,164.31. The executor of the insured's estate brought an action to

---

[4] 245 P.2d 205 (Wash., 1952).

recover that amount, contending that the part of the supplementary contract relating to distribution to the nieces and nephew was void "as an attempted testamentary disposition in violation of the statute of wills." The company, on the other hand, contended that the supplementary contract constituted a "valid third-party donee-beneficiary contract."

In considering the question the court pointed out that the right to take advantage of optional methods of settlement is a valuable one. The beneficiary acquires a vested interest in the company's performance of that portion of its contract of insurance, a right which is in the nature of a property right and would be protected.

The court referred to the case of *Mutual Benefit Life Insurance Co. v. Ellis* and pointed out that, contrary to the facts in that situation, the rights of the nieces and nephew in the supplementary contract under consideration were "derived from the original insurance contract through the exercise of Option 1."

"Appellant has cited no cases," the court continued, "and we have found none holding that supplementary insurance contracts such as the one in the present case are void, as testamentary dispositions in violation of the statute of wills."

Appellant had cited a case which involved the question of a gift, and the court discussed that case, but continued:

We are not here concerned with the law of gifts, *inter vivos* or *causa mortis;* but with the question of whether or not the supplementary insurance contract between the insurance company and Mr. Sherlock confers any rights on Mr. Sherlock's nieces and nephew named therein, to whom the company promised to pay any of the proceeds of the original insurance policy (plus accumulated interest) which might be in its possession when Mr. Sherlock died. Their rights under that contract are based upon the contractual obligation of the company to do what it agreed with Mr. Sherlock it would do. Mr. Sherlock might have defeated their rights by withdrawing all the money, but he had no right under the agreement to substitute someone else in their stead as the third-party donee-beneficiary; he could make no change in exhibit No. 5, in which the insurance company's obligations were set forth. By analogy to insurance policy cases the supplementary insurance contract gave the named nieces and nephew a vested interest (*Massachusetts Mutual Life Insurance Co. v. Bank of California,* 187 Wash. 565, 60 P.2d 675)—not in any specific property or to any amount of money, but in the performance of the contract by the insurance company.

The court concluded, with the gist of the decision as follows:

The mere fact that the death of one of the parties to a contract is designated as a contingency upon which a promise to deliver property to a third-party donee-beneficiary turns, is not alone sufficient to make such a contract a testamentary disposition and subject it to the statute of wills. *Warren v. United States,* 68 Ct. Cl. 634, certiorari denied, 281 U.S. 739, 74 L. Ed. 1154, 50 S. Ct. 346; . . . As was said in the last cited case and quoted with approval in

In re Howe's Estate, 31 Cal. 2d 395, 399, 189 P.2d 5, 1 A.L.R. 2d 1171, "their right to enforce is based upon a contractual obligation and not on any interest in the property of the decedent."

The majority opinion in this case would be comforting support to the life insurance company title department if it were not for the very strong dissenting opinion. In the dissenting view, Justice Donworth takes issue with the theory that the supplementary contract grew out of the insurance contract by reason of the election of Option 1.

It is very plain to me that this so-called supplementary contract is an entirely new contract between the parties which is not supplementary to, nor in anywise connected with option 1 of the endowment policy in so far as it purports to designate substitute payees upon Mr. Sherlock's death. There is nothing in the endowment policy relating to the payment of the proceeds to any person other than Mr. Sherlock *after the close of the endowment period.*
. . . This supplementary contract is a new contract having nothing whatever to do with life insurance. The fact that the depository of the proceeds was a life insurance company is immaterial. It might have been a bank or an individual.

The dissenting judge notes the fact that the majority opinion assumes that the interest of the nieces and nephew is a vested one, by analogy to the beneficiary under a life insurance policy where the insured has not reserved the right to change the beneficiary designation. The dissenting opinion, however, points out that the insured in this case reserved the right to destroy the rights of the nieces and nephew by withdrawing all of the funds at his discretion. "The rule is," the judge continued, "that if an insured retains the power to extinguish the rights or interest of a beneficiary, even though he cannot change his designation of the beneficiary, then the beneficiary has a mere expectancy or contingent interest."

It cannot, therefore, be maintained that even by analogy to the law of life insurance the named nieces and nephew acquired at any time prior to Mr. Sherlock's death vested rights to the balance of the fund.

* * * * *

. . . It is fundamental that a valid gift *inter vivos* can be completed by delivery to another person for the benefit of the donee. But it is equally fundamental that in such a case the donor must irrevocably divest himself of dominion and control over the subject matter of the gift. In the present case, Mr. Sherlock expressly retained control and dominion over the funds during his lifetime, and the transaction must, then, fail both as an abortive attempt to make a gift *inter vivos* as well as an abortive attempt to make a testamentary disposition of the funds.

By the decision in this case, it is held for the first time that the owner of personal property may avoid probate proceedings and the expense of administering his estate by the simple expedient of reducing his assets to cash and entering into a contract with a bank, insurance company or individual (similar

in form to the supplementary contract here involved), while still retaining
control over the money during his lifetime.

If such a revolutionary change is to be made in this state in the method
of transmitting property at death, which has heretofore been recognized as
exclusive, only the legislature should make it effective. It surely did not amend
or repeal the statute of wills by enacting the section of the insurance code
(RCW 48.23.300) which is quoted in the majority opinion.

The Hall Cases. In January, 1952, the New York Supreme Court,
sitting at special term, decided the case of *Hall* v. *Mutual Life Insurance
Company of New York*[5] and held invalid, as an attempted testamentary
disposition, a supplementary contract issued in settlement of a life insurance policy on the life of the beneficiary's father. The beneficiary
elected settlement under the interest option and named her then husband as the person to whom any sums remaining at her death were to
be paid. The power to change this supplementary beneficiary was not
reserved, although, as in the *Toulouse* case, the beneficiary could at
any time she wished withdraw all or any part of the amounts so held.

Nine years after the supplementary contract was issued the husband
and wife were separated and later divorced. The wife remarried and
died shortly afterward.

The arguments of the *Toulouse* majority and minority opinions were
utilized in this case. The husband urged that the supplementary contract
was an extension of the policy and that the use of the optional modes
of settlement had been authorized by the legislature. The wife's executors
took the view, put forth by the minority opinion in the *Toulouse* case,
that the supplementary contract was a new and independent contract
which "insures nothing; it is simply a contract for the deposit of a
fund, fully in existence, upon which interest is to be paid. Being neither a
contract nor part of a contract of insurance, the gift over is claimed
invalid as an attempt to effect a testamentary disposition without conforming to the Statute of Wills."

This view was adopted by the Special Term court, which held that
as a new and independent contract "its provision for payment over of
any unpaid balance of principal on the death of the policy beneficiary,
was an invalid testamentary disposition for failure to comply with the
requirements of the Statute of Wills (Dec. Est. Law, Section 21)."

The Second Court Decision. The New York Supreme Court, Appellate Division, summarized the situation in a second decision on this
question,[6] and stated its own point of view thus:

The mere statement of the respective contentions of the parties reveals a
battle of words and nominal distinctions stirred up by the issue. It may seem

[5] 109 N.Y. Supp. 2d 646 (1952).

[6] *Hall v. Mutual Life Insurance Co. of N.Y.*, 122 N.Y.S. 2d 239 (1953).

blunt and over simple, but the fact is that a supplementary contract partakes both of an insurance contract and an independent contract for the deposit of a fund. It is fruitless and a vain concern to try to fit, what is so obviously a transaction that bridges two categories of legal thinking, into one or the other, simply because the law and lawyers as a convenience to thinking, and to make possible communication between finite minds, have invented separate categories of thought and words to mark the separation.

It is obvious that the policy beneficiary has the right to a settlement option, only because that right was given by the policy. Nor could an insurance company grant such a contract independent of a policy. Moreover, we may take judicial notice that with changes in interest rates it is sometimes to the disadvantage of the insurance company to enter into the supplementary contract; but it loses its freedom by virtue of the insurance policy it had issued. On the other hand, it is equally true that once the insured had died, all the insurance aspects of the contract of insurance were fully terminated, at least in the actuarial and legal sense. The supplementary contract clearly provides for the continued holding, or deposit, of the fund now arisen, very much in the manner of a bank if the fund were given to the bank. But this provision obviously could not have arisen unless it were inchoate in the original insurance contract. From another aspect too, the deposit is related to the policy of insurance: There is no doubt that the insured in purchasing this policy and in paying his premiums was definitely buying optional modes of settlement. It is common knowledge that the methods of settlement are very frequently a very valuable part of the policy. That is particularly true these days, if the options arise from an older policy where the terms are likely to be more beneficial. In this case the policy was issued in 1925.

Accordingly, it would seem the more sensible view to determine the question on the basis of whether we are dealing with a social evil or hazard or a social good, and to be controlled in that view by legislative intention, if it has been expressed or may be implied.

. . . In the instant case, the supplementary contract was fully executed and accepted by both parties, the insurance company and the policy beneficiary. The trivial variance, whether the interest payments were to be made annually or quarterly and with respect to the right to withdraw principal, did not change the contract from being supplemental to the original policy of insurance. Again we are faced with the need not to confuse the word with the meaning of the word. For the purpose of binding the insurance company *without other action by the insurance company,* insured or policy beneficiary must accept the option in the unvarying terms offered in the policy. The slightest variance may avoid the company's liability—so the court held in the *Gram* case. That is fundamental law of contract. A qualified acceptance is simply a counter offer. That does not mean, and cannot possibly mean, that as to third parties, any variation in the executed supplementary contract from the terms of the policy constitutes a new contract, and not one derived from the policy. To so hold would mean that the principles and realities applied to modifications of contracts are not to be applied to contracts of life insurance.

. . . It does not merit extended discussion to prove the very high public interest in the extension of the life insurance system, as a major provision for thrift and security for individuals and families. . . . Part and parcel of this system for many decades, is the optional mode of settlement, with power to make gift over the unused principal. This is no evil to be hobbled; no course of conduct with incidence of recurring injustice to be limited by safeguards, slowing but necessary.

Perhaps the most significant factor behind this decision was the fact that by reason of the adverse holding in the Special Term Court, the New York legislature had enacted an amendment to the Personal Property Law providing that a supplementary contract, even where it provides for a gift over in the event of death is not repugnant to the Statute of Wills. Interpreting the enactment of this amendment as the most recent expression of legislative approval of exactly the kind of arrangement under attack in this case, the court concluded:

> The supplementary contract is a valid extension of the policy of insurance providing for the continued deposit of the fund for the purpose of paying interest thereon, and the gift over on the death of the policy beneficiary is not subject to the statutes governing the making of testamentary dispositions.

Legislation. Legislation along the lines enacted in New York as the result of the first adverse holding of the court in the *Hall* case has been proposed in a number of other states and enacted into law in some of them. Generally speaking, opposition has come principally from those persons who believe that by proposing legislation on the subject the life insurance industry is, in effect, conceding that there is a problem. It is their position that since so few cases are ever litigated it is really wiser to assume that the practice is valid. Those who favor legislation take the position that there can always be an adverse set of facts, where the equities are not with the persons who will take under the supplementary contract if its validity is upheld. In such cases it is quite possible that a court could, on perfectly valid grounds, reach a conclusion which would be adverse to the interests of the many thousands of persons having rights at the present time to the more than $7 billion of accumulated funds left with life insurance companies under supplementary contracts.

The difficulty of the entire question is summarized in the second *Hall* decision quoted above:

> It may seem blunt and over simple, but the fact is that a supplementary contract partakes both of an insurance contract and an independent contract for the deposit of a fund. It is fruitless and a vain concern to try to fit, what is so obviously a transaction that bridges two categories of legal thinking, into one or the other, simply because the law and lawyers as a convenience to thinking, and to make possible communication between finite minds, have invented separate categories of thought and words to mark the separation.

These cases have been discussed at some length because they anaylze the principal arguments both for and against the validity of supplementary contracts involving a gift over in the event of the death of the named beneficiary. The problem arises when the beneficiary elects the optional settlement and provides for a gift over in the event of her death prior to withdrawal or completed payments under the contract. The same problem arises when, at the maturity of an endowment or surrender of any policy for cash, the insured himself elects to have the proceeds retained under one of the optional methods of settlement and provides for a gift over in case of his death prior to settlement of the entire proceeds.

CHAPTER XV

The Policyholder
Reinstates

THE REINSTATEMENT of a life insurance contract, in general terms, is an agreement between the parties that the provisions of a lapsed policy shall again constitute an effective contract between them. This involves procedural requirements similar in some ways to the formation of the contract in the first place. In addition to these considerations, however, the reactivation of the provisions of the old contract presents many questions and conflicts that are not involved in connection with contracts which are continued in full force throughout the lifetime of the insured.

The purpose of this chapter is to outline some of the problems incidental to the reinstatement process itself and to consider the major legal problems and conflicts involved in the operation of the contract after reinstatement has been effected.

WHEN A POLICY LAPSES

A policyholder has several choices when his legal reserve life insurance policy lapses for nonpayment of premiums after it has acquired a cash value. He may apply for the cash surrender value, accept it, and the contract will be terminated. Alternatively, he may leave the cash value with the company and elect one of the other nonforfeiture benefits, either reduced paid-up, or extended term insurance. One of these latter benefits is required to be specified in the policy as the automatic nonforfeiture option. Therefore, if the policyholder makes no election, his insurance will automatically be continued either as extended term or reduced paid-up insurance, as provided by the policy.

Inadequacy of the Nonforfeiture Options. At best, the benefits under the nonforfeiture section of the policy are decidedly less advantageous than those provided while the policy is on a premium paying basis. Sections providing for disability and accidental death benefits are usually terminated at the date of lapse, and the nonforfeiture coverages themselves are limited. Extended term insurance is by its very nature impermanent, and reduced, paid-up policies always provide benefits of only a fraction of the face amount of the policy. As a consequence, when the policyholder's life insurance needs are greatest, the extended term coverage may have expired or the reduced paid-up amount may be so small as to be of little benefit.

Thus, except in those rare instances where the need for life insurance has passed, the owner of a lapsed policy should sooner or later decide whether he wants to apply for new insurance or restore the lapsed policy to a premium paying status. The latter he has a contractual right to do because of the reinstatement provision of the policy.

Reinstatement

The Policy Provision. As a general rule, the reinstatement provision states that if the policy lapses for nonpayment of premiums it will continue to be eligible for reinstatement at any time within three (or sometimes five) years from date of lapse. The insured must furnish evidence of insurability, including good health, "satisfactory to the company," and all unpaid back premiums must be paid, plus interest. If a policy loan was in effect at the date of lapse, it must be repaid or restored as a lien against the policy.

Advantages of Reinstatement. It will be immediately noted that the policyholder is not only required to furnish evidence of insurability, he is also charged all unpaid, back premiums, with interest, on exactly the same basis as he would have paid had the policy been in full effect during the period of lapse. Thus if more than a slight period of time has passed since the policy lapsed, it may be financially advisable to apply for a new policy. In any case, a new application is always an available alternative to reinstatement.

Nevertheless, if the older policy has been in effect for several years, it may include privileges of special value, particularly optional settlements which either are no longer offered or, if available, provide for less favorable interest or mortality assumptions. Prematurity rights attain significant value sooner in a reinstated policy than in one newly issued, and for business purposes this is sometimes an advantage. Ordinarily also the procedure for reinstatement is simpler than that involved in applying for a new policy. Other things being equal, therefore, there are often persuasive reasons why the policyholder may prefer to reinstate a policy already issued rather than to apply for a new one.

REQUIREMENTS FOR REINSTATEMENT

Evidence of Insurability

Why Necessary. Even though the right of reinstatement is a contractual right, it is nevertheless necessary to require evidence of insurability because of the effect of reinstatement on the insurance principle. We have previously seen that the success or failure of life insurance lies in the application of the law of large numbers to a group of insureds whose risks of death are reasonably comparable. For this reason, the insurance company must have the opportunity at the outset to select the persons with whom it is willing to contract. To put it differently, all persons included in the insured group must be selected on an impartial basis in accordance with principles of insurability.

Complete freedom to reinstate would destroy this impartial balance. It is understood that the insurability of the individual insureds will change as the contracts continue in operation. It might be argued, therefore, that to reinstate the lapsed policy after the insured has become uninsurable would place the company in no worse a position than if he had become uninsurable while maintaining his status as a premium paying policyholder. This would be true if all lapsed policies were eventually reinstated. As a matter of fact, they are not, and it is the uninsurable policyholders who ordinarily want to reinstate. Those who are still insurable are not so anxious to do so. For this reason the mortality experience of the company would be very adversely affected if reinstatement were permitted without restrictions of any kind. Evidence of insurability is required in order to prevent this kind of adverse selection.

What Insurability Means. The word "insurability" has such a definite technical meaning in life insurance that it is somewhat surprising to find that there is an extensive history of litigation over its meaning. At the present time, it seems hardly open to question that the word, as it should be used in connection with reinstatement, has exactly the same meaning, except as to age, that it had when the original application was received. Thus the company is free to consider such elements as habits, occupation, finances, etc., as well as the good health of the applicant for reinstatement just as if he were applying for a new policy of life insurance. However, this has not always been true.

Prior to 1906, the common requirement for reinstatement was expressed as "good health." After the Armstrong Investigation, however, the standard policy provision statute used the phrase "evidence of insurability" satisfactory to the company. Today the phrase "evidence of insurability" is most commonly used, often with the words "including good health" to make the requirement as clear as possible.

A Broader Term Than "Good Health." With only a few exceptions, the courts have held that "insurability" is a broader term than "good health," and thus includes other factors than those of health alone. One of the clearest expressions of this point of view is found in the case of *Kallman* v. *Equitable Life Assurance Society.*[1] In this case the policyholder met the requirements of insurability as far as health was con-

---

[1] 248 A.D. 146, 288 N.Y.S. 1032 (1936).

cerned, but reinstatement was refused because of his financial situation and the large amount of life insurance (in excess of $159,000) he was already carrying. The company's refusal was challenged in a court action a few months after the applicant had committed suicide. The court upheld the company, saying:

> The distinction between "good health" and "insurability" might be illustrated in the case of a criminal condemned to death. On the eve of his execution he might be found to be in perfect physical condition, but it could not be reasonably contended that his situation did not affect his insurability. There are numerous circumstances which affect insurability. In *Ginsberg v. Eastern Life Insurance Co. of New York*, 118 N.J. Eq. 223, 178 A. 378, affirmed 120 N.J. Eq. 110, 184 A. 348, the Court said that it is common knowledge that an insurance company will not reinstate a policy where it is known that the insured is financially insolvent and the circumstances [show] probability of suicide. . . .
>
> We are of the opinion that the language of the statute and of the policy "evidence of insurability satisfactory to the company" does not limit the inquiry upon an application for reinstatement to the good health or good physical condition of the insured. . . . Here, the insured's pecuniary circumstances coupled with his heavy over insurance, entirely out of line with his incoming financial condition, had a definite bearing upon his longevity and created a moral hazard which directly affected his insurability.

Minority Decisions. Two cases are frequently cited as authority for holding that "evidence of insurability" must be confined to evidence of "good health." One is the case of *Sussex* v. *Aetna Life Assurance Company*,[2] a Canadian case decided in 1917, and the other is *Missouri State Life Insurance Co.* v. *Hearne*,[3] a Texas case decided in 1920, in which the *Sussex* case was cited with approval. These cases are analyzed in a relatively recent case, as follows:

> In the *Sussex* case, *supra*, the policy had lapsed for nonpayment of premiums and it was provided that it might be reinstated upon payment of delinquent premiums and production of evidence of insurability. When the policy was issued insured was a commercial traveler but when he sought reinstatement he was a member of the armed forces and subject to service in World War I.
>
> The policy contained the following provision:
>
> This policy contains no restrictions regarding change of occupation, residence, travel, or service in the militia or army or navy in time of war or in time of peace;
>
> Insurer declined reinstatement except upon inclusion of certain conditions regarding military service. The trial court said: "Proof of insurability, in condition 14, means that the insured, at the time of application for reinstatement, is a proper risk for insurance *upon the basis of the original contract,* and the condition of the health of the insured is the only matter to which I can think it could apply *in this case;* and, at all events, it is the only matter to which it did in fact apply, *upon the circumstances here.*" (Italics ours.)
>
> . . . We think the learned author of the opinion in *Missouri State Life*

---

[2] 33 Dominion Law Reports 549, 38 Ontario Law Reports 365 (1917).

[3] 226 S.W. 789 (Tex. Civ. App., 1920).

Insurance Company v. *Hearne, supra,* misconstrued the opinion in *Sussex* v. *Aetna Life Insurance Company, supra,* else he would not have cited it as authority for the legal proposition he there declares.[4]

The court had held in the *Hearne* case that "insurability," when used in a life insurance contract reinstatement clause, was "no more comprehensive than good health and an insurable interest." [5]

Summary. There is some authority to support the contention that "insurability" means nothing more than good health and an insurable interest. However, the weight of authority is to the effect that it is definitely a broader term and includes all matters which would have been considered by the company on an original application, except age.

Satisfactory to the Company

Wide Range of Decisions. There have been a number of different interpretations of the meaning of the phrase "satisfactory to the company" as applied to "evidence of insurability." For instance it has been held that the "judgment and conscience" of the officers of the company are absolutely controlling [6] and it has also been held that if the insured made a reasonable compliance with the requirements as concluded by men of common sense and reason, reinstatement should be compelled.[7]

The Majority Rule. By what has come to be recognized as the majority rule, the courts will consider the practices of other insurance companies in the same situation and judge the decision of the company on that basis. This position is summarized by the court in the case of *Kennedy* v. *Occidental Life Insurance Company,*[8] as follows:

The overwhelming weight of authority is to the effect that an agreement to reinstate an insurance policy upon "satisfactory evidence" or insurability does not give the insurer the power to act arbitrarily or capriciously, but that evidence which would be satisfactory to a reasonable insurer is all that is required.

THE APPLICATION FOR REINSTATEMENT

Effect of Application

If Conditions Are Not Met. The conditions as set forth in the reinstatement provision of the policy are conditions precedent. If they are

---

[4] *Kirby* v. *The Prudential Insurance Company of America,* 239 Mo. App. 476, 191 S.W.2d 379, 162 A.L.R. 660 (1945).

[5] *Ibid.*

[6] *Conway* v. *Minnesota Mutual Life Insurance Company,* 62 Wash. 49, 112 P. 1106 (1911).

[7] *Lane* v. *New York Life Insurance Co.,* 147 S.C. 333, 145 S.E. 196 (1928).

[8] *Kennedy* v. *Occidental Life Insurance Company,* 18 Cal. 2d 627, 117 P.2d 3 (1941).

not met at the time the policyholder applies for reinstatement, therefore, the reinstatement will not become effective. If the insured dies after having applied for reinstatement but before receiving notice of declination, the beneficiary can recover only such nonforfeiture benefits as may be in effect under the lapsed policy.

If Conditions Are Met. Let us say, however, that the requirements set forth in the policy provision have been met. The policyholder has furnished evidence of insurability, including evidence of good health, and submitted his check for all back premiums with interest. This information reaches the company just before notice of the insured's accidental death. Here, it seems obvious that we have a different situation. The company has not accepted the application it is true; but it has not declined it either. And since the expressed conditions have been met, there is a clear-cut legal question as to whether the company has the right to decline after the death of the insured.

Two Main Groups of Court Decisions

Approval Not Necessary. There are two main groups of court decisions on the question of whether the company must approve an application for reinstatement of a life insurance contract. One group takes the position that if the specified conditions have been met and application has been made for reinstatement, it is of no consequence that the insured may have died before the company has had the opportunity to act upon the application.

Illustrative of this line of decisions is a Colorado case [9] in which the insured had applied for reinstatement, furnishing evidence of insurability satisfactory to the company and otherwise meeting all the requirements. Before the company had approved the application, he was killed in an automobile accident. There had been some delay in checking his answers to the application questions concerning visits to a physician. The visits proved to have concerned an infected tooth, however. The court held that reinstatement was effective, saying:

> . . . Where a policy contains a provision of this kind, where proof of insurability which is not open to valid objection as to form or substance is submitted within the authorized time, where payment of all premiums then in arrears plus interest thereon is tendered, where the insured thus fully complies with the conditions of his contract, and where his death is wholly accidental and in no way involved in his proof of insurability, the policy is reinstated and the restoration relates back to the time of the submission of the application and the tender of the premiums.

Under this line of decisions, if all conditions have been met, the reinstatement automatically becomes effective as of the date of the request

[9] *Bowie* v. *Bankers Life Co.*, 105 F.2d 806 (C.C.A. Colo., 1939).

and changes in health between that date and the date of approval by the company do not affect the situation.

Approval Is Necessary. Courts which take the position that reinstatement is itself a contract, separate and distinct from the life insurance contract, and those which view reinstatement as effecting a new contract of life insurance, both hold that the approval of the company is necessary before reinstatement can be effected. Under either of these theories the reinstated policy is held not to go into effect until the application for reinstatement has been accepted in accordance with basic principles of contract law, or until a reasonable length of time has elapsed. This means that the standard requirements of offer and acceptance are held to apply, and thus it is necessary that the offer be accepted during the lifetime of the offeror, in this case the policyholder.

As a general rule, the parties to the contract are held to have the right to specify in the policy the requirements that must be met to make a reinstatement effective. Thus if the policy itself requires that the application for reinstatement be approved by the company, that requirement will be enforced. However, in one of the more important recent cases,[10] the nature of reinstatement was held to be such that a policy requirement of this kind was invalid. This case contains such an excellent summary of the different approaches to this question that we are quoting it at some length:

> Courts are not in agreement as to the legal effect of reinstatement clauses in insurance policies. Some courts have held that an application for reinvestment of a lapsed policy constitutes an offer to enter into a new contract which must be accepted by the insurer before any contract exists between the parties. . . . Under this theory the insurer's agreement to waive the lapsing of the policy will be treated as consideration for the agreement of the insured to be bound by any new terms imposed in the application for reinstatement (*Foley* v. *New World Life Ins. Co., supra*) and no recovery may be had for any loss occurring before the insurer has accepted the application for reinstatement, either expressly or, perhaps, by allowing an unreasonable time to lapse without acting thereon. . . .
>
> We are of the opinion, however, that reinstatement under a policy such as is present in this case does not involve the formation of a new contract. By the terms of the policy the insured is given a right to reinstatement after lapse upon compliance with certain conditions. During the period in which reinstatement is possible the policy is not void but merely suspended. The right to revive the policy by reinstatement is a valuable contractual right, the consideration for which is found in the premiums paid and to be paid under the original policy, and the insurer has no arbitrary or discretionary right to refuse reinstatement if all the conditions therefor have been complied with. These views are supported by the weight of authority. . . .
>
> Applying this theory of the nature of reinstatement, we hold that the pro-

---

[10] *Kennedy* v. *Occidental Life Insurance Company,* 18 Cal. 2d 627, 117 P.2d 3 (1941).

vision in the application for reinstatement that it should not be effective until approved at the home office of the company during the lifetime of the insured cannot vary the terms of the original policy. The insured had a contractual right to be reinstated under the terms of his policy and any agreement to impose different terms is unsupported by consideration. . . .

Summary. Most commentators on this question simply say that some courts hold reinstatement to be automatic if the requirements have been met and application made prior to the date of the insured's death. Other courts hold that the application for reinstatement must be accepted by the company and that such acceptance must be accomplished during the lifetime of the insured or it will not be effective. In the case of *Kennedy* v. *Occidental Life Insurance Company*, from which we have just quoted, the court says that the weight of authority supports the view that reinstatement is a valuable contractual right and the insurer has no arbitrary or discretionary right to refuse reinstatement if all the conditions have been complied with. It is almost impossible to make a considered evaluation of this question because so many of the cases which, numerically, might support one view or the other are early cases involving different policy wording and different economic circumstances. The law of the life insurance contract is constantly changing, and the impact of financial and economic factors is nowhere more important than in this area of the effect of lapse and reinstatement. In considering trends, however, the language of *Kennedy* v. *Occidental Life Insurance Company* is undoubtedly significant as indicating a trend toward emphasizing the "contractual right" approach to reinstatement.

The Insurer Has a Reasonable Length of Time in Which to Act. A number of courts take the position that the insurance company must be permitted a reasonable length of time in which to approve or disapprove the application for reinstatement. If the insured should die during that period of time, the policy is not in effect on the reinstated basis. What constitutes a reasonable length of time is a question of fact to be decided by the jury. However, as so determined, it has varied from as little as one week to as much as fifteen months.

Unreasonable Delay. As a general rule, the courts hold that an unreasonable delay in approving or declining an application for reinstatement has the effect of waiving the insurance company's right to insist upon a forfeiture of the policy. Illustrative of this point of view is the language of the court in the case of *Froehler* v. *The North American Life Insurance Co. of Chicago*,[11] an Illinois case decided in 1940. Strictly speaking, this case involved the question of material misrepresentation in the application for reinstatement. However, the evidence showed no reason to believe that the insured knew of his impaired physical condi-

---

[11] 374 Ill. 17, 27 N.E.2d 833 (1940).

tion (a brain tumor) at the time he completed the application for reinstatement. With respect to the question of delay, the court said:

> In his original policy of insurance the deceased bought and paid for a
> right to be reinstated after default in payment of premium upon furnishing
> evidence of insurability satisfactory to the company, and the payment of all
> past-due premiums with interest. The record shows that he was solicited to
> reinstate his policy and that he furnished the company all the evidence that it
> required of his insurability. It is unnecessary for us to decide, and, therefore,
> we do not decide, whether the company might thereafter have required further
> evidence. . . .
>
> The record shows without dispute that the insured had furnished all the
> evidence he had been asked to furnish and that that evidence was entirely
> satisfactory. The jury found it was honestly given and the situation was no
> different than if the insured had been struck by lightning or hit by a truck on
> May 15, 17, or 19, 1933. The company had no contractual right to hold the
> deceased's money while it delayed for an unreasonable length of time a ful-
> fillment of the contractual right to reinstatement. Two juries have found that
> it did so, and at the same time have found that the insured, honestly and in
> good faith, complied with the terms of his contract by furnishing all the evi-
> dence of insurability required by the company.

LEGAL IMPLICATIONS OF REINSTATEMENT

By what seems to be the majority line of decisions, the application
for reinstatement is acknowledged to be different from an application for
a new policy. Reinstatement is itself a contractual right, and ordinarily
it cannot be exercised after the contract has been terminated by surrender for cash. At the time of reinstatement, therefore, the contract is
already in operation in a limited sense. The motor is still idling though
the car is not in motion. The application for reinstatement is, in a sense,
only the shifting of gears that moves the policy out of the extended term
or reduced paid-up insurance status and puts it back into operation on a
premium paying basis. The majority of courts, therefore, hold that reinstatement is not a separate contract, that the reinstated contract is not a
new contract,[12] and that the process of reinstatement is not the effecting
of a new contract but rather the exercise of a contractual right.

Because the policyholder has this contractual right to restore the
original policy to full force and effect, the status of the reinstated contract has presented a number of questions through the years. For one
thing, does the insurer have the right to impose new conditions in connection with the restored policy? For another, is the reinstated policy
contestable, assuming that the original period of contestability has expired? A third question relates to the effect of suicide of the insured

---

[12] Nevertheless, as shown later, the incontestable clause is ordinarily held to
"run anew" from the date of reinstatement. See p. 340.

after reinstatement but after the original suicide period under the policy has expired.

Addition of Conditions

Because the right of reinstatement is a contractual right, it is generally held that the insurance company cannot impose additional conditions in connection with reinstatement. This problem arises in a number of areas. Perhaps the most important is that of the war hazard clauses. Let us say, for example, that at a time when the company was issuing policies without war hazard limitations of any kind, it issued to one Joseph Conley a policy for $12,500 at age 24. Two years later the policy lapsed for nonpayment of premiums. After two more years Joe applies for reinstatement. He offers evidence of insurability, including evidence of good health, and pays the unpaid back premiums with interest. At this time the company is issuing all its policies with a war hazard rider if the applicant is between the ages of 18 and 45. Can the company reinstate Joe's policy subject to the war clause they are currently including in every new policy they issue to anyone in Joe's age group?

The answer seems very clear that the company cannot. The policyholder has a contractual right to restore his policy to premium payment status, if he furnishes evidence of insurability, including good health, and pays the unpaid back premiums, with interest. Once he has done this, the company cannot impose additional conditions that were not included in the original policy.

Illustrative of this holding is the case of *Schiel et al.* v. *New York Life Ins. Co.*,[13] which arose in Arizona and was decided in 1950 by the United States District Court, District of Arizona. In this case the insurer had permitted reinstatement of a policy on the life of a young prospective pilot but only on condition that the double indemnity provision be omitted and an aviation clause be included. The original policy was free of all conditions pertaining to legitimate occupations whether involving the armed services or not. The court said:

> . . . The Company made no claim that Schiel had become uninsurable for ordinary life purposes in the amount originally written; in fact it conceded by its conduct that he was insurable for those purposes and in that amount. It declined, however, to reinstate the ordinary life policy except upon a condition importing a concept of insurability at variance with the policy as written. This we think it might not do.

An understanding of the view taken may require some further analysis of the terms of the original policy. The clause relating to occupation has been quoted earlier. It provides that the policy is free of conditions as to residence, travel, occupation, and military and naval service, *except as to provisions and*

---

[13] 178 F.2d 729 (C.A. Ariz., 1949).

conditions relating to double indemnity, etc. . . . . In respect of the ordinary life coverage, however, the insurer had contracted that the policy was free of conditions pertaining to any legitimate occupation, whether in connection with the armed services or otherwise. The condition imposed on reinstatement of the ordinary life coverage for all practical purposes nullified the occupation clause. Under guise of reinstatement the insurer undertook to rewrite the contract in such fashion as to repudiate a risk assumed at the outset. If it could do that it could with equal facility have excluded altogether the risks of military service or travel, whereas the insured's liberty of action in all those matters was a measure of his insurability fixed and determined by the original contract. Without further laboring the point, we add only that the word 'reinstate,' as used in the policy, is entitled to be given its ordinary meaning, which is to restore to a former state or position.

This case states what is undoubtedly the general rule, that the provisions of a reinstated policy cannot be modified by new conditions imposed in connection with the reinstatement process.

Contestability of the Reinstated Policy

Most life insurance policies, as we have seen, contain a clause making them incontestable after a specified period, usually two years, from date of issue. If, as very often happens, a policy has been in force beyond this period when it lapses, what is the status of the incontestable clause after reinstatement?

There are three main groups of decisions on this point. One group takes the position that only the original contestable period is effective. After that has expired the company is powerless to contest the policy on any grounds going to the essential validity of the contract. Another group holds that a new contestable period starts after each reinstatement. A third and very minor group holds that only the original contestable period is effective with respect to the policy as a whole but reinstatement itself is a separate agreement which can be contested for fraud at any time since there is no applicable contestable period with respect to it.

Illustrative of the decisions holding that only the original contestable period is effective is the case of *Munn v. Robison et al.*, a case which arose in Arkansas and was decided in 1950.[14] In that case the company sought to deny liability under policies in the amounts of $1,000 and $6,000 respectively, on the grounds of fraud in the applications for reinstatement. The plaintiffs challenged this defense on the grounds that the incontestable clause had admittedly expired prior to the reinstatement.

With respect to reinstatement and the incontestable clause, the court said:

Among the provisions of the policy is one giving the insured the absolute right, under the facts of this case, to reinstate. John Hancock accepted and approved each application for reinstatement, which, under the Arkansas law, is

[14] *Munn v. Robison*, 92 F. Supp. 60 (D.C. Ark., 1950).

conclusive that the condition "production of evidence of insurability satis-factory to the Company" was satisfied. Thus, while the policy may have lapsed for non-payment of premiums, it was, by virtue of this provision, not a "dead" contract, because the reinstatement was made under a then existing right of the insured conferred thereby rather than a gratuitous privilege conferred by John Hancock. And, it is settled beyond dispute in Arkansas that "the rein-stated policy is not a new contract, but is the same old policy." *N.Y. Life Ins. Co. v. Dandridge*, 202 Ark. 112, 149 S.W.2d 45. As expressed in *N.Y. Life Ins. Co. v. Campbell*, 191 Ark. 54, 57, 83 S.W.2d 542:

> It necessarily follows from what we have said, and the cases cited in sup-port thereof that the reinstatement of the insured by appellant created no new contract between them, but simply revives and reinstates the original contract and all provisions thereof, and subsequently the rights and obliga-tions of the respective parties thereto must be measured thereby.

In *N.Y. Life Ins. Co. v. Dandridge, supra,* the court said:

> Most of the courts, holding a contrary view to ours, seem to base their reasons on the idea that reinstatement creates a new contract and that the incontestable clause, although barred by lapse of time, is revived and be-comes available to contest a reinstated policy for fraud. Our idea is that to so hold, something must be read into the policy that is not there, but might have well been there, had the company so desired. Such a holding changes the incontestable clause to read that "this policy shall be incon-testable after two years from its date of issue or after the date of any re-instatement thereof." It is well settled that courts do not or should not, make contracts for the parties, and the contract as written will be most strongly construed against the party writing it.

An excellent summary of the three different holdings with respect to this question and a conclusion in favor of a rerunning of the incontest-able clause after reinstatement is found in the case of *Johnson v. The Great Northern Life Insurance Company*.[15] This was a North Dakota Su-preme Court case, decided in January, 1945, and in it the court said:

> . . . Neither the statutes nor the policy under consideration contain any provision to the effect that the incontestable clause in any way limits the right to contest a reinstatement. In such circumstances there seem to be three rules which find support in the authorities. One of these is that an incontestable clause in a policy has no application whatever to a reinstatement and the re-instatement may be contested at any time. Another is that an incontestable clause will prevent a contest of a reinstatement if the time in which the original policy was contestable has expired. The third rule is that the incon-testability provision applies to the reinstatement in the same manner as it did to the original issuance of the policy, that is to say; the time within which the reinstatement may be contested is the same period thereafter as that within which the original policy might have been contested, and the grounds for such contest are limited to those which arise out of the negotiations leading to the reinstatement.
>
> The rule last stated appears to be the majority rule. . . . It is also the rule which seems to us to be best founded upon reason. We would reject the rule, first above stated, because, while not contrary to the contract or to express statute, it is contrary to legislative policy fairly to be inferred. This rule

---

[15] 73 N.D. 572, 17 N.W.2d 337 (1945).

rests also upon the conception that the reinstatement is a new contract which is contrary to our holding in *Rott* v. *Provident Life Insurance Co., supra.* The second rule completely eliminates any requirements of good faith in the negotiations for reinstatement and is contrary to our holding in *New York Life Insurance Company* v. *Hansen, supra.*

We therefore adopt the rule last stated and hold that defendant may contest its reinstatement of the instant policy only during the same period of time thereafter as was fixed for contesting the original policy, or upon grounds expressly excluded from the operation of the incontestability provision. The question then is, is fraud, upon which defendant relies in its cross complaint, expressly excluded from the operation of the incontestability provision.

The majority rule was further explained in the case of *Sellwood* v. *Equitable Life Insurance Co.,*[16] as follows:

> . . . The authorities reason that, since it is fundamental that fraud vitiates everything into which it enters . . . it cannot be supposed that the parties intended that an insured should have what Judge Learned Hand . . . characterized as "a license forever to cheat the insurer"; and that the reasons for the public policy that, absent fraud, statements by an insured in an application for insurance should be deemed to be representations and not warranties and that a limit should be set on the time within which the insurer should have the right to contest the policy for false statements of the insured in an application, apply to an application for reinstatement the same as to one for the original issuance of the policy itself. This view has been adopted by many authorities, regardless of whether the reinstatement be regarded as the continuation of the original contract of insurance or the making of a new one.
> . . . We adopt the rule that, upon reinstatement of a lapsed life insurance policy, the incontestable clause runs anew as to misrepresentations in the application for reinstatement. This rule is not only supported by the weight of authority, but also is a just and fair one.

The third and decidedly minority holding is that the contract of insurance is reinstated by separate agreement or contract of reinstatement. Because this contract is separate, the incontestable clause of the policy has no application, and misrepresentations in the negotiations with respect to reinstatement may be relied upon to avoid the reinstatement contract itself at any time.

Effect on the Suicide Clause

Where the operation of the suicide clause of a reinstated policy is concerned, the majority of the courts have held that reinstatement merely continues the original contract in force so that the original suicide period, having once expired, would not thereafter be revived by the reinstatement process.

Most of the courts reach this conclusion on the theory that reinstatement does not create a new contract but merely revives the original policy and continues it in force as from its original date. In one of the

---

[16] 42 N.W.2d 346 (Minn., 1950).

outstanding cases presenting the question,[17] Judge Learned Hand favored this theory but felt it necessary to yield to the weight of authority in his jurisdiction. Cases in his jurisdiction had favored the theory that a reinstated policy must be considered as having been reissued on the date of reinstatement. Even adopting that view, however, Judge Hand held that the suicide clause must be read as effective from the original issue date, the majority conclusion. This case is much cited and presents an excellent example of Judge Hand's approach to a legal problem. For those reasons we are quoting his decision at some length as follows:

. . . The relevant clause of the policy read as follows: "If the Insured shall within one year from the date hereof," December 6, 1926, "commit suicide . . . the liability of the Company shall be limited," etc. The policy, as required by statute (section 101, subd. 10, N.Y. Insurance Law), gave the insured three years within which he could reinstate it, "upon evidence satisfactory to the Company . . . as to the insurability of the person upon whose life this policy was issued, (Insured), and upon payment of the arrears of premiums" with interest. The defendant argued that the year within which suicide barred the right should date from the reinstatement, but the judge thought otherwise and gave judgment for the plaintiff on her motion on the pleadings. The defendant appealed.

Were we free to decide the point as *res nova*, we should say that the reinstatement of a lapsed policy is not a new contract at all, when the insured can revive it merely by satisfying the company of his insurability and by paying the arrears. Those are the conditions upon what by the lapse has become a conditional obligation; but which is still an obligation from which the insurer cannot withdraw at will, being bound to approve if he is in fact satisfied. We should not be disposed therefore to go along with *International Ins. Co. v. Mowbray*, 22 F.2d 952 (C.C.A. 7). As in other similar situations satisfaction is a question of fact, which, once proved, makes the obligation absolute. . . . The insurer's approval is only an admission of satisfaction with which the insured might dispense if the insurer refused it, when in fact satisfied; he might even compel the reissuance of the policy by specific performance. *Mutual Life Co. v. Lovejoy*, 203 Ala. 452, 456, 83 So. 591 (semble).[18] In that view of course the policy, when reinstated, remains what it was before; its terms cannot be read as though it had its inception at the time of reinstatement; and those cases which allow the insurer to contest the reinstatement for a fraud occurring after the policy has become incontestable, are only instances where the insured has never in fact fulfilled the prescribed conditions. Though he has procured an admission from the insurer, the fraud in its procurement destroys its evidential force. Cases like *Teeter v. United States Life Ins. Ass'n*, 159 N.Y. 411, 54 N.E. 72, holding that the reinstated policy again becomes incontestable when the original period has elapsed after reinstatement, may possibly accord with this view; but if so, it must be confessed it is only by a considerable wrench of the language.

---

[17] *Tatum v. Guardian Life Insurance Company*, 75 F. (2d) 476, 98 A.L.R. 341 (C.C.A. N.Y., 1935).

[18] From the French, meaning "it would seem."

However, the great weight of authority is flatly against our analysis of the situation. . . . We feel bound to yield to the preponderant opinion. But although we are therefore to consider the policy as though it had been issued anew on February 14, 1933, it by no means follows that in construing it we must read it as though it spoke throughout from that date. By its very terms the policy is "reinstated;" the parties have thus chosen a word which presupposes, not a new contract, but the revival of an old one. The insured must pay not a single premium, but all arrears; and thereafter only at the old rate, however many years have passed. All benefits—e.g., the surrender and loan value, term and paid-up insurance—go again into force as of the original date; they do not begin anew. Moreover, in the case at bar the defense of suicide was limited to one year from "the date hereof;" that is, the date upon the policy. In several cases the insurer has been held strictly to this when it varied from the date of actual inception. . . . Perhaps too the contrast between that phrase in the policy at bar and "the date of issue" in the incontestability clause, may be taken as some indication of a change of intent. Judged textually, therefore, there is very good reason for holding that the clause speaks from the original date. It is of course true that our interpretation exposes the insurer to a risk which it would otherwise escape. An insured who had let a policy lapse might at any time within three years conceive the notion of getting it reinstated and then killing himself. Nevertheless we are disposed to hold that even on the theory of a new contract, which we should not ourselves have adopted, the reinstated policy is to be referred *pro tanto* to the date of the original; at least that the insurer who prepared the instrument must bear the doubts, so far as there are any. In the only decisions in which the point has arisen this has been the result. . . .

Those cases which allow the insured to prove fraud in procuring the reinstatement though the period of incontestability has passed, do not indeed fall in so easily with the accepted view as with our own. They may nevertheless be made to fit with it. Though the new contract be a reissue of the policy as of the date of the renewal, it would force beyond all reason the meaning of the incontestability clause to say that it barred a fraud which did not even exist when the policy became incontestable. The clause is one of limitation, not a license forever to cheat the insurer; unless construed in that preposterous way it must be an exception to the general principle that the policy as reinstated speaks from its old date. It may be the only exception; at least the suicide clause is not one.

Judgment affirmed.

WAIVER AND ESTOPPEL

As we have already seen, some courts take the position that an unreasonable delay by the company in acting on an application for reinstatement will, in effect, estop the company from declaring a forfeiture of the policy. This same general result will sometimes be held effective as the result of the retention of the premium for an unreasonably long time. For example, the court in the case of *Waldner* v. *Metropolitan Life Insurance Company* [19] said:

. . . The defendant could not indefinitely hold the application for reinstatement without disapproving it, retain the money of the insured until long after

[19] 149 Kan. 287, 87 P.2d 515 (1939).

her death, and thereafter escape liability on the ground the insured had not provided satisfactory proof of insurability. In *Andrus* v. *Insurance Assn.*, 168 Mo. 151, 67 S.W. 582, it was said:

> The company must take one horn of the dilemma or the other. It cannot retain the benefits and deny the existence of the contract. If it does not wish the receipt of the premium to have the effect in law of reinstating the policy or of preventing a forfeiture, it must refuse to receive the money until the health certificate is filed and until the president and medical director act.

Attachment of Copy of Application. As a general rule, when a request for reinstatement reaches the company the policy is in the hands of the insured. For that reason, the courts have generally held that it is not necessary that a copy of the reinstatement application be attached to the policy in order for the insurer to avail itself of a defense based upon fraud or misrepresentation in the application. However, if there is an applicable statute, the holding will be different, as illustrated by the case of *Acacia Mutual Life Insurance Company* v. *Weissman.*[20]

In this case the policy was issued May 12, 1949, in the sum of $5,000. The next year the policy lapsed for nonpayment of premiums, and three months later the insured filed an application for reinstatement. On August 14, the company reinstated the policy. Premiums were paid as they fell due until the death of the insured on April 23, 1952. At that time the company sought cancellation of the policy on the ground that the answers to some of the questions in the reinstatement application were fraudulent.

The widow of the insured asked judgment for the amount of the policy, alleging first that the plaintiff company's action was barred by the incontestable clause. Secondly, she stated that the company had failed to furnish the insured, as a part of the policy, a copy of the application for reinstatement, and that it was thus estopped to deny the truth of statements made in that application. Judgment was for the widow and the company appealed.

The opinion of the court illustrates the interpretation and operation of this type of statute so clearly that it is quoted in full, as follows:

ACACIA MUTUAL LIFE INSURANCE COMPANY v. *WEISSMAN*
(Ohio Supreme Court.)

WEYGANDT, Ch. J. This court is of the view that the lower courts were correct in holding that the failure of the plaintiff company to furnish the insured a copy of the application for reinstatement estopped the company from denying the truth of the application.

Section 9389, General Code (Section 3911.04, Revised Code) reads as follows:

> Every company doing business in this state shall return with, and as part

---

[20] 128 N.E. 2d 34 (Ohio, 1955).

of any policy issued by it, to any person taking such policy, a full and complete copy of each application or other document held by it which is intended in any manner to affect the force or validity of such policy. A company which neglects so to do, so long as it is in default for such copy, shall be estopped from denying the truth of any such application or other document. In case such company neglects for 30 days after demand made therefor, to furnish such copies, it shall be forever barred from setting up as a defense to any suit on the policy, any incorrectness or want of truth of such application or other document.

The plaintiff company contends that these statutory provisions apply alone to the original application for the policy and not to the application for reinstatement. However, that is not the comprehensive language of the statute. Not only must the company furnish a complete copy of "each" application but also of any "other document" affecting the force or validity of a policy. It is not the province of the courts to read into this sweeping language a limitation that "each" means merely some applications or the original application.

While, of course, the terms of the particular statutes are controlling, it is commented generally in 44 *Corpus Juris Secundum,* 1074, Section 268, that such a statute

is applicable, not only to an application for the original policy, but also an application for the restoration or revival of a policy which has lapsed for the nonpayment of premiums, and to an application for the renewal of a policy.

The company claims further that it complied with the requirement of the statute by supplying the defendant widow with a copy of the application when a request therefor was made after the death of the insured, since the insured himself made no such demand. Again this contention finds no support in the statute. The simple, unambiguous language is that the company *"shall return with, and as part of any policy issued by it, to any person taking such policy,* a full and complete copy of each application." The company reinstated the policy on August 14, 1950. The death of the insured did not occur until April 23, 1952—more than a year and eight months later—and still the company had not furnished him a copy of the application.

Hence, it is the opinion of this court that the plaintiff company is not entitled to a cancellation of the policy. Furthermore, the lower courts were not in error in rendering a judgment for the defendant widow on her cross-petition.

Judgment affirmed.

CHAPTER **XVI**

Other Rights
by Operation
of the Law

WE HAVE ALREADY DISCUSSED the policy as property and the rights which, in the absence of a policy provision to the contrary, the policyholder is entitled to exercise solely as a result of the fact that he *owns* the policy. These are rights he has by reason of the general law of property rather than by the terms of the life insurance contract itself.

There are other people, also, who have or may obtain rights under a life insurance contract by operation of the law rather than the terms of the contract. Wives or husbands in community property states, for instance, creditors of the insured under some circumstances, trustees in bankruptcy—all, under appropriate circumstances, may assert rights under the contract which are not spelled out by the provisions of the contract itself. The purpose of this chapter is to discuss some of these rights and the circumstances under which they may be asserted and maintained.

THE LIFE INSURANCE CONTRACT AND COMMUNITY PROPERTY

The early settlers of this country, who had a major voice in the formation of the constitution of the United States and the constitutions of the earlier states of the union, brought their ideas of law to this country from England. Thus, the life insurance contract had its origin and most of its development in a legal climate based on the common law.

It must be remembered, however, that the explorers of the South and West brought their ideas of law from the countries of their origin also— in this case France and Spain. For that reason, the legal systems of Arizona, California, Idaho, Louisiana, Nevada, New Mexico, Texas, and Washington are strongly influenced by, if not actually based upon, the legal systems of France and Spain. As a result, all include a concept which is foreign to anything in the common law, the concept of community property.

What Community Property Is

The term *community property* relates to the property a man and wife acquire during their marriage. Under the community property law, husband and wife are considered to constitute a "community," and all property acquired by either of them during the marriage, except by gift or inheritance, is owned by both of them in equal shares. Property owned by either husband or wife prior to marriage is ordinarily considered his or her separate property. Property inherited or acquired by gift or devise (will) during marriage is also separately owned by the person who receives it. All other property acquired during the marriage belongs to the community and is community property. The ownership concept applies to every item of it.

The Life Insurance Contract. The impact of the community property law upon the rights under the life insurance contract is perhaps obvious. The fact that the life insurance contract developed primarily under the common law means that ownership rights are customarily interpreted in accordance with common law principles. As we have seen, numerous rights arise under the contract solely by operation of the law even in common law states. The creditors of the insured, a trustee in bankruptcy, the heirs of a third-party owner of a life insurance contract—all, under certain circumstances, acquire some or all of the rights under the contract. In a sense, however, these rights are all derived from the rights of the policyowner himself.

In community property states, the general principles of common law applying to ownership rights came into conflict with a completely different concept of ownership, that marriage itself creates rights of ownership in the policyowner's spouse. Court decisions resolved some of the problems that resulted, but often the same basic question was decided differently in different community property states. Thus, there are some areas in which the effect of the community property law on the rights under the life insurance contract differs markedly from one state to another, and other areas in which the effect has not yet been decided. Nevertheless, the administration of the contract, the exercise of the right of control, and the distribution of the proceeds of the policy may be very seriously affected by reason of the community property laws in those states which follow that system.

General Rules of Community Property Law

There are a few general rules of community property law which are helpful as starting points in considering life insurance problems. First, property is either community property or it is not, at the time it is acquired; and its status does not change throughout the marriage. Property acquired before marriage is separate property and remains separate property. Property acquired after marriage, except by gift or inheritance, is community property and remains community property.

Second, property acquired with community funds is community property. Thus, a contract of life insurance purchased with community funds constitutes community property, in which the spouse of the owner has community property rights. For example, if premiums are paid or assets are purchased out of the husband's *earnings,* the policy or other assets would be community property. Ordinarily, if both community property and separate funds are used in acquiring property, the property so acquired is owned by the husband and wife in the same proportions as the funds that were used.

Lastly, although ownership of community property is in the husband and wife equally, the right of management is in the husband, subject to some very definite limitations. For instance, the husband has the right to control or sell the property of the community, but he cannot ordinarily make a gift of it except for the benefit of the community, and he can *never* exercise his right of management to defraud the wife.

When a Life Insurance Policy Is Community Property

Basic to any discussion of community property rights in connection with the life insurance policy, is a determination of whether the policy does or does not constitute community property. In considering this question, there are two broad classes of contracts: (1) those formed prior to marriage, and (2) those entered into during marriage.

Contracts Made Prior to Marriage. Where the husband insures his life prior to his marriage, the contract is separate property at the time it is issued, and in most community property states it remains separate property even though, after marriage, premiums are paid on it out of community funds. Decisions in Louisiana, New Mexico, and Texas follow this rule. At the death of the insured, if the wife is not the beneficiary, and if any premiums have been paid out of community funds, the community is entitled to reimbursement out of the proceeds for the amount of premiums so paid.

In California and Washington, if a policy is issued prior to the marriage of the insured but premiums are paid out of community property after the marriage, the contract is owned by the husband and wife in proportions equal to the ratio of community funds to separate funds which were used in payment of premiums. The proceeds at the death of the insured are treated as part community property and part separate property in the same proportions.

Contracts Made after Marriage. Where the husband applies for and is issued a contract of life insurance on his own life during marriage, the premiums are ordinarily paid out of community funds, and the principal questions arise in connection with the designation of the beneficiary. If the policy is payable to the insured's estate and premiums have been paid out of community funds, the policy is ordinarily considered community property and the wife has a one-half interest in the proceeds. There are decisions to this effect in California, Louisiana, New Mexico, Texas, and Washington.

Where the wife is the named beneficiary and the premiums are paid out of community funds, the policy is also ordinarily considered to be community property during the lifetime of the insured, but the proceeds, when paid, are the separate property of the wife. Thus, in California, if the wife is the beneficiary, premiums paid out of community property are considered gifts to her, and the proceeds are her separate property although the policy is community property.

In California, also, if the wife is named the beneficiary of a policy on the life of her husband, the insured cannot thereafter change the designation to someone else without her consent, even if he has reserved the right to do so. If he does make a change, the wife can avoid it and claim one-half the proceeds. In Washington, if the policy is payable to the wife, and if premiums are paid out of community funds, an attempted change of beneficiary to someone other than the wife is not avoidable by her; it is void, and the wife is entitled to the entire proceeds.

In New Mexico, the proceeds of a life insurance policy are the separate property of the wife if she is the named beneficiary when it is issued. However, the policy itself is community property and subject to the management of the husband during the marriage and prior to his death.

Community Property Problems

Generally speaking, if a life insurance contract is community property, there are three distinct areas in which a community property problem is likely to arise. The question of management and control arises in connection with the exercise of prematurity rights, such as the rights to change the beneficiary and to surrender the policy for cash. Questions relating to the husband's power to make a gift arise in connection with beneficiary designations. Lastly, community property questions are particularly likely to arise in connection with the disposition of the proceeds at the death of the insured. In this discussion, therefore, we will consider first the right to change the beneficiary; second, the right to surrender the policy for cash; and third, the rights involved at the time the death benefit becomes payable.

The Right to Change the Beneficiary. Naming someone other than the wife is essentially the same as making a gift to that person. States which recognize the right of the husband to make gifts of community property hold that the husband has the right to change the beneficiary designation on a policy on his life from his wife to someone else. If they recognize no such right, then they hold that he cannot make such a change.

For example, Texas holds that the husband may make moderate gifts without the wife's consent so long as they are not in fraud of the wife's interests. Arizona courts also follow this theory, and Nevada has the same basic philosophy although the point has never actually been decided in connection with life insurance. In California, the husband cannot make a gift of more than one-half the community property without his wife's consent. A change of beneficiary from the wife to someone else is valid unless the wife objects, but she has a right to one-half of the proceeds if she gives notice of her claim prior to payment on the part of the life insurance company.

In Washington, the insured cannot name anyone other than his estate or his wife as beneficiary of a policy of life insurance on his life, if it is community property, without her consent. Such a designation is not merely voidable; it is void, and the wife is entitled to the entire proceeds. The only case that has been decided in Louisiana took the position that a change of beneficiary to the mother of the insured was within the rights of the insured. Consequently the claim of the mother was upheld as against the claim of the wife.

The Right to Surrender the Policy for Cash. Surrender of the life insurance policy for cash is a management transaction. The general community property theory, therefore, is that notwithstanding the wife's ownership of one-half of the community property, the husband has the complete right of management during the marriage except that he cannot exercise this right in fraud of the wife. There are very few case decisions on this particular point, but the statutes of most of the community property states express this basic principle.

Death of the Insured. As far as the life insurance company is concerned, the principal problem at the death of the insured arises under policies payable to someone other than the wife. In such cases, it is always possible that the wife may have an interest. The nature of this interest under the law of California is illustrated and described in the case of *Bazzell* v. *Endriss*, decided by the California District Court of Appeal, November 12, 1940.[1] There the court said:

WARD, J.: This action for declaratory relief [2] and to quiet title involves conflicting claims to the proceeds of a life insurance policy in the sum of $1,000, issued to R. C. Endriss, in which the mother of the insured was named

---

[1] 41 Cal. App. 2d 463, 107 P.2d 49 (1940).

[2] For explanation and definition of this term, see p. 378, *infra*.

as beneficiary. Endriss died on June 6, 1938, and the mother less than two months thereafter. Plaintiff, a sister of the insured, as the executrix of the mother's estate, brought this action against the insured's surviving widow who claims a half interest in the policy by reason of the fact that premiums thereon were paid with community funds and that she had not consented to a gift of the policy to the mother. The trial court found the facts to be in accordance with this contention and gave judgment for the widow, from which plaintiff prosecutes this appeal.

It is the contention of appellant that the evidence shows the insured was indebted to his mother in an amount exceeding the value of the policy, and that under such circumstances there could be no gift of the policy.

The insured and defendant were married in 1918, and the policy was issued in 1929. The widow testified that all premiums were paid from earnings of the insured's business. In *Union Mutual Life Ins. Co.* v. *Broderick*, 196 Cal. 497, 507, the court said:

> It is no doubt the settled law of this state that, where the premiums on an insurance policy issued on the life of a husband after coverture are paid entirely from community funds, the policy is a community asset, and, in view of the provisions of section 172 of the Civil Code, the husband cannot make a valid gift thereof without the written consent of the wife; and that where the husband attempts to do so, by naming a third party as beneficiary, the transaction as to the wife's share is voidable and subject to her right of revocation.

This view of the law was also held in *Mundt* v. *Connecticut Life Ins. Co.*, 35 Cal. App. (2d) 416, 421, where the court said:

> From the leading case of *New York Life Ins. Co.* v. *Bank of Italy*, 60 Cal. App. 602 [214 Pac. 61], through the many intervening cases, down to *Travelers Ins. Co.* v. *Fancher*, 219 Cal. 351 [26 Pac.(2d) 482], the only test applied to this problem has been whether the premiums (on a policy issued on the life of a husband after coverture) are paid entirely from community funds. If so, the policy becomes a community asset and the nonconsenting wife may recover an undivided one-half thereof "without regard" [as said in *Dargie* v. *Patterson*, 176 Cal. 714, 721, 169 Pac. 360] "to the amount or condition of the estate remaining in his [the husband's] hands at the time of his death," and we might add, without regard to the disproportionate size of the premium when compared with the face of the policy.

In the first cited case it was held that the change of beneficiary was made by reason of the fact that the insured was indebted to his sister, and that under such circumstances the change was made for a consideration and was not a gift. In the second case the trial court found against an indebtedness of the insured to his mother and the judgment for the widow was sustained.

In the present case the insured's mother was named at all times as the beneficiary. There is considerable evidence that the insured at various times, before and after marriage, had given certain sums of money to his mother. Bank accounts indicated also that the mother had withdrawn various amounts and delivered them to the insured for use in his business, for his hospital bills and different unexplained purposes. Appellant, the sister of the insured, testified that in April of 1937 her brother had said "I owe Mother $3,000." There was no showing that the mother had, since her husband's death, any source of income except that given her by her son, plus some indefinite amount earned by keeping a rooming house.

The court found that the naming of the mother as beneficiary constituted a voluntary gift without valuable consideration, and that at no time did the wife consent to a gift of her community interest in the policy. Reading the record in its entirety, and taking into consideration statements that prior to marriage the insured had contributed to his mother's support, and that she in turn had loaned money to establish him in business and to pay his hospital and other bills; also the fact that the widow paid the last premium during the insured's illness, and considering conflicting evidence and inferences that could be drawn from the testimony, we find ample evidence to sustain the trial court's conclusion. . . .

The judgment [3] is affirmed.

The nature of the wife's interest in the proceeds of life insurance under the law of the state of Washington is graphically illustrated in the case of *California-Western States Life Insurance Company* v. *Jarman, Admx., Respondent, Tollette, Appellant,*[4] decided by the Washington Supreme Court in 1947.

There, after an interlocutory decree [5] of divorce, the husband applied for and was issued a policy of life insurance on his own life, naming his mother as the beneficiary. On his death prior to the date the divorce decree would have become final, the company filed a bill of interpleader, which means that it paid the money into court and asked the court to decide between the rights of the wife under the Washington community property laws and the mother as the named beneficiary under the policy. The court held in favor of the wife, as follows:

Is the mother of an insured, named as his beneficiary in a life insurance policy, entitled to the proceeds of such policy, where her son paid one monthly installment of the annual premium while living separate and apart from his wife, who had obtained an interlocutory decree of divorce which did not become final because the insured died prior to the expiration of the statutory period of six months? That is the sole question, which is not an open [6] one in this state, presented in the case at bar.

In *Occidental Life Ins. Co.* v. *Powers,* 192 Wash. 475, 74 P.(2d) 27, 114 A.L.R. 531, we held that, when the premiums on life insurance are paid with community funds, the proceeds of the policy on the life of the husband constitute community property, and that the wife's interest in the community property is a vested interest, of which she cannot be deprived without consideration.

. . . In *Hanley* v. *Most,* 9 Wn.(2d) 429, 115 P.(2d) 933, we cited with approval *Occidental Life Ins. Co.* v. *Powers, supra,* and held that a life insurance policy, on which the premiums were paid out of community funds, constitutes community property, and that the husband may not, without the consent of his wife, substitute his mother and his secretary as beneficiaries of such policy. . . .

---

[3] For the widow, as stated on p. 350.

[4] Wash., 185 P.2d 494 (1947).

[5] An interlocutory decree of divorce is one that is temporary, not final.

[6] An open question is one that is not settled or determined.

All property, with certain exceptions not pertinent in the case at bar, acquired after marriage by either husband or wife, or both, is community property. Everything that is produced by either spouse, whether it be by toil or talent, is earned by the community and belongs to the community. . . .

In the absence of any evidence to the contrary, property acquired during coverture is community property. . . . In the case at bar, there is no evidence to overcome the presumption that the proceeds of the insurance policy is community property; hence, that presumption is conclusive.

. . . The right of respondent to the proceeds of the policy of insurance was not in any wise changed by the entry of the interlocutory order in the divorce action, for the reason that the marital status of the parties was not changed, and for the further reason that their respective property rights were never adjudicated. . . .

. . . We are committed to the rule that an interlocutory decree of divorce abates and becomes a nullity for all purposes on the death of one of the parties prior to the entry of the final decree (21 Wash. L. Rev. 178), and that an interlocutory divorce decree, which had not become final at the time of the death of the insured, does not prevent a divorced wife from taking the proceeds of an insurance policy as a wife for the reason that, during the term of an interlocutory decree of divorce, the marital relation exists in law as well as in practical effect. 2 Couch, Cyclopedia of Insurance Law 1278.

. . . In the case at bar, the community property, the nature and extent of which are not disclosed by the record, remained in the hands and under the management of the husband. That property included the property then in existence; the interest, accumulations, and earnings—it included all property acquired after the marriage (Rem. Rev. Stat., Section 6892 [P.P.C. Sections 434-27]) which was not, and of course cannot now ever be, dissolved by a court.

The judgment is affirmed.[7]

Termination of the Community. The husband-wife community is terminated by death, divorce, or annulment of the marriage. In some of the community property states a husband and wife cannot make an agreement which would alter the nature of their community property interests. This is the gist of statutes in effect in Arizona, Louisiana, and Texas. However, in Arizona, California, Nevada, New Mexico, and Washington, the parties may make a property settlement agreement in contemplation of divorce or separation.

In Texas, until recently, divorce ended the wife's insurable interest in the life of her husband. Accordingly, the earlier decisions held that her rights and interest in a policy on his life were terminated upon the divorce. In later decisions, however, the courts recognized a difference between the interest the wife might have in the proceeds of the policy and her right to a share of the cash surrender value.

Illustrative of this point of view is the case of *Womack* v. *Womack*,[8]

[7] For the wife.

[8] 142 Tex. 299, 172 S.W.2d 307 (1943).

decided by the Texas Supreme Court, June 16, 1943. The major portions of that decision were as follows:

SHARP, J.: Petitioner and respondent[9] were divorced in April, 1941. The divorce decree made no disposition of four life insurance policies, three insuring the life of the husband, naming the wife as beneficiary, and one insuring the life of the wife, naming the husband as beneficiary. At the time of the divorce decree the cash surrender value of the policies on the life of the husband was $1,542.84, and the cash surrender value of the policy on the life of the wife was $252.00. All of the policies were obtained during the married life of the husband and wife, and all premiums were paid from their community funds. The terms of the policies remained unchanged from the time of their issuance to the date of the divorce decree. None of the policies were assigned. The husband and wife divided the other property rights between them, but the legal question as to whether the cash surrender value of the policies constituted community property was left open for determination by the courts as if no divorce had been granted, to the end that the parties should not be prejudiced by the fact that the divorce had been granted. In the trial of this cause the husband and wife agreed to account for the amount of the cash surrender value of each policy, should same be decreed community property. The trial court held that the cash surrender value of the policies at the date of the divorce decree constituted community property, and entered judgment in favor of respondent and against petitioner for one-half of the difference between the cash surrender value of the policy upon the life of respondent and the amount of the cash surrender value of the policies upon the life of petitioner. The Court of Civil Appeals affirmed the judgment of the trial court. 168 S.W.(2d) 663. This Court granted a writ of error based upon the allegation that the opinion of the Court of Civil Appeals in this case conflicted with the opinion in the case of *Whitesell* v. *Northwestern Mutual Life Ins. Co.* (Com. App.), 221 S.W. 575.

The only question presented here for determination is whether the cash surrender value of the life insurance policies is community property.

Article 4619, Vernon's Annotated Civil Statutes, as amended in 1927, defines community property as follows:

All property acquired by either the husband or wife during marriage, except that which is the separate property of either, shall be deemed the common property of the husband and wife; and all the effects which the husband and wife possess at the time the marriage may be dissolved shall be regarded as common effects or gains, unless the contrary be satisfactorily proved.

The word "property" has been frequently defined and its meaning determined by many decisions of the courts. In the case of *Titus* v. *Terkelsen*, 18 N.E.(2d) 444, 445, 302 Mass. 84, the court, in discussing the word "property," said:

It is a word of comprehensive meaning. *Holbrook* v. *Brown*, 2 Mass. 280, 282; *Raymer* v. *Tax Commissioner*, 239 Mass. 410, 413, 132 N.E. 190. In its ordinary legal signification it "extends to every species of valuable right and interest, and includes real and personal property. . . ."

. . . It is true that in the early decisions of the courts of this country, in-

---

[9] Where a legal action is begun by a "petition" rather than a "complaint" or "declaration," the person filing the petition is called a "petitioner." The person against whom the action is brought is called a "respondent."

cluding the decisions of the courts of this State, it was held in some of them that policies of life insurance were not property. The history of Article 4619, as amended, clearly shows that the Legislature intended to give the term "community property" a broader meaning than it was originally given. Many of the modern decisions hold that a life insurance policy is property. In the case of *Grigsby* v. *Russell,* 222 U.S. 149, 56 L. Ed. 133, Mr. Justice Holmes, speaking for the Supreme Court of the United States, said:

> Life insurance has become in our days one of the best recognized forms of investment and self-compelled saving. So far as reasonable safety permits, it is desirable to give life policies the ordinary characteristics of property.

The word "property" in our bankruptcy laws is construed to include the "cash surrender value" of life insurance policies, and such property rights pass to the creditors of the insured. The courts recognize the right of the insured to pay his creditors the "cash surrender value" of his policy and retain the policy. . . . The courts of this State have held that the "cash surrender value" of a policy is property, and may be considered and treated as community property. . . .

. . . The trial court and Court of Civil Appeals correctly held that the cash surrender value of the policies was community property, and that respondent was entitled to judgment for one-half thereof.

The rule announced in the case of *Whitesell* v. *Northwestern Mutual Life Insurance Company, supra,* as well as in any other cases holding contrary to the rule announced herein, is expressly overruled.

The judgments of the trial court and Court of Civil Appeals are hereby affirmed.

In California, the rights of the wife, as beneficiary, do not cease upon divorce. Unless the husband is precluded by some legally enforceable claim on the part of the wife (an assignment, for example), he may change the beneficiary designation to whomever he wishes after the divorce. However, if community funds have been used to pay the premiums and he changes the beneficiary, the wife is entitled to reimbursement for her share of the premiums so paid.

Exoneration Statutes. In spite of the apparent technicalities of these laws, every community property state except New Mexico and Nevada has what is sometimes known as an "exoneration statute." This is simply a statute which makes payment in good faith to the beneficiary or assignee of record, and without knowledge of an adverse claim, sufficient to discharge the company of liability. Illustrative of this type of statute is the following from the California Code: [10]

Payment in accord with terms of policy or assignment: Discharge of insurer: Notice of claim to payment or interest in policy. Notwithstanding the provisions of Sections 161a and 172 of the Civil Code, when the proceeds of, or payments under, a life insurance policy become payable and the insurer makes payment thereof in accordance with the terms of the policy, or in accordance with the terms of any written assignment thereof if the policy has

[10] California Insurance Code, Sec. 10172.

been assigned, such payment shall fully discharge the insurer from all claims under such policy unless, before such payment is made, the insurer has received, at its home office, written notice by or on behalf of some other person that such other person claims to be entitled to such payment or some interest in the policy.

RIGHTS OF CREDITORS

Creditors, as they are concerned with the life insurance contract, may be divided into two large general groups. First, there is the group of creditors who are parties to or assignees or beneficiaries of the contract. Their rights are derived directly from the contract and have been discussed in Chapter XI, *supra.* Second, there is a group of creditors who have no connection with any particular life insurance contract as such, but who attempt to assert rights to the contract *as property*, in accordance with the statutory procedures open to creditors generally with respect to the property of their debtors.

Rights under the Contract

Except for those instances where the contract has been effected for wagering purposes, the creditor who has the foresight to protect himself against possible loss by reason of the death of his debtor by insuring the debtor's life in his own favor, is ordinarily held to be entitled to the proceeds in their entirety. This is true even though they may be in excess of the actual amount of the indebtedness. The collateral assignee ordinarily has a right to share in the proceeds only to the extent of the indebtedness, and if an absolute assignment has been executed for collateral purposes, it will be treated as if it were a collateral assignment. This same reasoning has also been applied to the creditor-beneficiary's rights.

These rules, discussed and illustrated in Chapter XI, are repeated here not only for purposes of review but also as a reminder that the creditor is always free to apply for and own life insurance on the life of his debtor or to request a collateral assignment, in his favor, of a policy already in effect. If he does not do so, however, the possibility of his perfecting a claim to the life insurance contract, as property, are very strictly limited. In this area, the contract's primary purpose as insurance has been and remains paramount.

Rights by Operation of the Law

Every state has its own procedures by which a creditor may sue a debtor, obtain a judgment, and then take further action to have property of the debtor sold to satisfy the judgment. These procedures differ from

one state to another, and they differ also with respect to the nature of
the property concerned. Most important to our present discussion is the
fact that some kinds of property are specified by statute to be "exempt"
from the claims of creditors, and life insurance occupies a very high position on the list. As a matter of fact, a discussion of the rights of creditors
in and to contracts of life insurance effected by debtors might more
aptly be titled "privileges of debtors." This is especially true if a third
person is named as beneficiary.

The Exemption Statutes

Why We Have Them. There is a traditional line of thinking, particularly in this country, to the effect that granting to the hopelessly insolvent
debtor the right to retain a homestead and the "tools of his trade," in the
interest of his possible rehabilitation, will prove to be a benefit to society
in the long run. Exempting life insurance proceeds from the claims of
creditors of the insured only extends this thinking to the members of the
insured's family. Proponents of generous exemption statutes thus take
the position that while a man should, perhaps, be "just before he is
generous," he should also be encouraged to make whatever reasonable
provisions may be possible for the welfare and support of his widow and
orphan children. Society itself has an interest in this type of protection.

What They Are. Every state has its own type of exemption statute,
and individual questions are, of course, governed entirely by the statutory
and other applicable law of the jurisdiction concerned. In a general consideration of the question, however, the statutory exemptions for creditors
with respect to life insurance contracts may be divided into three general
groups. First, there are a number of statutes which derive from the
original married women's statutes. These statutes enabled a married
woman to apply for and own insurance on her husband's life and, incidentally, included a provision exempting such insurance from the claims
of the husband's creditors. Second, there are a number of statutes in
effect, primarily in the western states, which establish a liberal exemption
in favor of life insurance but limit the amount of such exempt insurance
to that which is purchasable by a stated amount of premiums annually. A
third type of statute follows the lead of an early New York exemption
statute and establishes a sweeping exemption in favor of most life insurance policies effected either on the life of the insured-debtor or by
him on the life of another.

The Married Women's Statutes. We have previously mentioned that
married women, at common law, were unable to make contracts but that
this disability has been removed or modified by statute in every jurisdiction today. The first Married Women's Act was passed in New York
in 1840. It made it possible for a married woman to contract for life in-

surance on the life of her husband, naming herself as beneficiary. It also provided that the life insurance so contracted for would be free from the claims of the husband's creditors. Today this type of law, in effect in some twelve states,[11] has significance not only because it enables a married woman to apply for and own life insurance but also because it is effective as an exemption statute.

Illustrative of this type of statute is the following, from the law of Maryland: [12]

Article 45, Sec. 8. Any married woman, by herself and in her name, or in the name of any third person, with his assent, as her trustee, may insure or cause to be insured for her sole use the life of her husband for any definite period, or for the term of his natural life; and any husband may cause his own life to be insured for the sole use of his wife and may also assign any policy of insurance upon his own life to his wife for her sole use; and in case of the wife surviving her husband, the sum or net amount of such insurance becoming due and payable by the terms of the insurance shall be payable to her for her own use, free from the claims of the representatives of her husband or any of his creditors.

Exemptions Limiting the Amount by Premiums Paid. Several of the western states [13] have statutes which are very broad in scope, often including the claims of the beneficiary's creditors as well as those of the insured. However, these statutes often limit the amount of the insurance to which they apply. For instance, the California statute limits the exemption to that amount of life insurance which can be purchased with an annual premium of $500. Thus, Section 690 of the Civil Procedure Code expressly declares as "exempt from execution or attachment":

All moneys, benefits, privileges, or immunities, accruing or in any manner growing out of any life insurance, if the annual premiums paid do not exceed five hundred dollars ($500), or if they exceed that sum a like exemption shall exist which shall bear the same proportion to the moneys, benefits, privileges, and immunities so accruing or growing out of such insurance that said five hundred dollars ($500) bears to the whole annual premium paid.[14]

The New York Type of Exemption Law. What was originally Section 55-a of the New York Insurance Law has been used as a model and enacted in a number of other states. The original law read as follows:

If a policy of insurance, whether heretofore or hereafter issued, is effected by any person on his own life or on another life, in favor of a person other than himself, or, except in cases of transfer with intent to defraud creditors, if a policy of life insurance is assigned or in any way made payable to any

[11] Alabama, Arkansas, Delaware, District of Columbia, Kentucky, Maryland, Massachusetts, New Jersey, North Carolina, Ohio, Tennessee, and Vermont.

[12] *Laws of Maryland Relating to Insurance,* Art. 45, Sec. 8.

[13] In addition to California, they are Idaho, Montana, Nevada, and Utah.

[14] California Civil Procedure Code, Section 690.19.

such person, the lawful beneficiary or assignee thereof, other than the insured or the person so effecting such insurance, or his executors or administrators, shall be entitled to its proceeds and avails against the creditors and representatives of the insured and of the person effecting the same, whether or not the right to change the beneficiary is reserved or permitted, and whether or not the policy is made payable to the person whose life is insured if the beneficiary or assignee shall predecease such person; provided, that, subject to the statute of limitations, the amount of any premiums for said insurance paid with intent to defraud creditors, with interest thereon, shall enure to their benefit from the proceeds of the policy; but the company issuing the policy shall be discharged of all liability thereon by payment of its proceeds in accordance with its terms, unless before such payment the company shall have written notice, by or in behalf of a creditor, of a claim to recover for transfer made or premiums paid with intent to defraud creditors, with specification of the amount claimed.[15]

It will be noted that this exempts policies on the life of the applicant and on the life of someone other than the applicant. The exemption is available regardless of beneficiary designation, as long as someone other than the applicant is named, or his estate. Enacted in 1927, this law was in force in New York all during the depression, but it was repealed in 1939. The present exemption from claims of creditors statute will be found in Section 166.

Miscellaneous Statutes. These three general groups account for the majority of exemption statutes in effect at the present time. Nevertheless, there are numerous miscellaneous laws in effect in different states which establish exemptions in greater or lesser degrees and in different ways. Louisiana, for instance, has a law which exempts the "proceeds, avails and dividends of all life insurance" from liability for debt.[16]

Another type of law found in several states concerns life insurance which is not payable to a named beneficiary. These statutes simply declare that insurance payable to the estate of the insured will nevertheless be paid to the insured's widow and children, free from the claims of creditors of the insured.

The Prematurity Values

As we have seen, the legal reserve, level premium system resulted in the creation of certain prematurity values under the life insurance contract, which gave that instrument some of the attributes of a type of property. Nevertheless, the nature of the life insurance contract is sufficiently unique that creditors have not been very successful in reaching these values, and this is true even of policies owned by the insured and payable to him or his estate. The provisions of the contract ordinarily control. If the policyholder must take affirmative action to surrender

---

[15] New York Insurance Law, 1927, Sec. 55-a.

[16] Sec. 4105 G. S. Louisiana, 1939.

his policy for cash, the courts ordinarily take the position that he cannot be compelled to do so. Until he does take such action, therefore, the insurance company is under no duty to pay the value to him, there is no immediate right to the cash surrender value, and thus no "property" in the true sense of the word for the creditor to proceed against.

The life insurance contract is first and foremost *life insurance*, with a purpose which it is in the public interest to protect. In one relatively recent case, insurance exemption statutes (in Minnesota) were held to extend to endowment policies, as follows, even though the statutes did not expressly include them.

It is also to be noted that Sections 61.14 and 61.15 are remedial statutes enacted for the public good to effectuate the beneficent purpose of protecting a debtor's dependents by giving them a preferred status over his creditors as to the proceeds of a life insurance policy upon his life; as such, these statutes are to be given a liberal construction to accomplish their intended purpose. See *Grimestad* v. *Lofgren,* 105 Minn. 286, 291, 117 N.W. 515, 517; Annotation, 164 A.L.R. 914. Insofar as such dependents are the beneficiaries, the insurance proceeds by statutory command inure to their separate use and benefit and are exempt from seizure by such creditors. It is elementary that statutes are to be interpreted and construed in keeping with the object to be attained. Section 654.16. If we were to hold that the cash-surrender option of the insured, or any other interest of the insured under the policy prior to its maturity, is a property right which is not exempt, but is available to the insured's creditors, the protective benefits would be wiped out, and we would thereby defeat the statutory purpose.[17]

Benefits on Maturity

Life insurance benefits expressly payable to the estate of the insured are settled when the companies pay these proceeds to the executor of the insured (if there is a will) or the administrators of the insured (if there is no will). The executor or administrator has certain duties as a matter of law and one of these duties is to pay the debts of the decedent. In the absence of a statute to the contrary, life insurance proceeds paid to the insured's estate are used for this purpose exactly as are any other moneys or property.

If the proceeds are payable to a named beneficiary, the situation is different. There the rights of the beneficiary vest (belong to him absolutely) at the moment of the insured's death. The personal representatives (executors or administrators) of the insured, and hence his creditors, have no right to any part of the proceeds. It is important to note here that the theory of insurance, as the pooling of contributions out of which death benefits are paid, plays an important part in this connection. The insured has made a contract with the company to pay a benefit to the named beneficiary on his death. As consideration for the performance

---

[17] *Fox et al.* v. *Swartz et al.,* 51 N.W.2d 80 (Minn., 1952).

of that contract, he has paid premiums for a specified length of time or until his death. At his death, however, the company does not pay the insured's money to the beneficiary. It pays only the death benefit it has agreed to pay. As a general rule, therefore, death does not result in a transfer of funds in the ordinarily accepted sense of the word.

The United States as Creditor

An important exception to the previously stated rule is found in a recent pair of cases decided by the United States Supreme Court in 1958. These cases clarified the rights of the United States government to collect income tax owed by the deceased insured out of the proceeds of life insurance on his life, payable to a named beneficiary. For some time prior to that date, this question had been variously decided, sometimes favorably to the government, sometimes unfavorably. In the cases of *Commissioner* v. *Stern* [18] and *United States* v. *Bess*,[19] the United States Supreme Court clarified this question and brought some degree of order out of what had been disorder.

In both cases, the court held that the state procedures for perfecting claims against property would be given effect in favor of the United States government just as they would be for any other creditor. In one case, the policy proceeds were effectively protected by the operation of the statute of the state concerned, which was Kentucky. In this case, *Commissioner* v. *Stern*, the court held that since there was no evidence that Stern had paid premiums in fraud of creditors, the exemption statute was effective against the claims of the United States government just as it would have been with respect to any other creditor.

The other case, *United States* v. *Bess*, arose under the law of New Jersey. There the court held that a lien had attached to the cash surrender value prior to the death of the insured, and that the lien was enforceable after his death, to the amount of the cash surrender value. A dissenting opinion expressed the point of view that none of the proceeds could be reached in the hands of the beneficiary because the cash value was extinguished at the insured's death and the lien with it. Although this is the minority opinion, it is especially significant as expressing the ordinarily accepted insurance view with respect to the cash value of a life insurance policy. These two cases are highly significant because they clarified a question until then unanswered, and also because they held that the law of the state concerned applies and will be given effect in

---

[18] *Commissioner* v. *Stern*, 58-2 USTC ¶ 9594, 357 U.S. 39, 2 L. Ed. 2d 1126, 78 S. Ct. 1047 (1958), aff'g *Stern* v. *Commissioner*, 57-1 USTC ¶ 9429, 242 F.2d 322 (CA-6, 1957), rev'g 15 TCM 114.

[19] *U.S.* v. *Bess*, 58-2 USTC ¶ 9595, 357 U.S. 51, 2 L. Ed. 2d 1135, 78 S. Ct. 1054 (1958), aff'g *U.S.* v. *Bess*, 57-1 USTC ¶ 9528, 243 F.2d 675 (CA-3, 1957), aff'g 55-2 USTC ¶ 9673, 134 F. Supp. 467 (D.C. N.J., 1956) in part.

connection with federal income taxes just as would be true in connection with the claims of any other creditors.

Creditors of the Beneficiary

The creditors of the beneficiary ordinarily stand in a somewhat better position with respect to effecting a lien or otherwise satisfying their judgments out of the proceeds of life insurance. The proceeds *are* the property of the beneficiary as of the date of the death of the insured, and the insurance concept no longer cloaks the money with the idea of pooled contributions which do not "belong" to any one person. Nevertheless, the idea of preserving the insurance moneys for the purposes intended, that is, protection for a man's dependents, remains uppermost. As a consequence we have a number of statutes which exempt the proceeds of life insurance from the claims of the creditors of the beneficiary as well as the insured, and we also have the spendthrift trust provision.

The Spendthrift Trust. Under a true trust, one person, called the *trustee*, holds a property interest under an agreement with the grantor which requires him to keep or use that interest for the benefit of another person, called the *cestui que trust*. Under a spendthrift trust, the property is conveyed to a trustee under the same kind of agreement, but it is also provided that the beneficiary's interest *shall not be transferable by him (the beneficiary) and shall not be subject to the claims of his creditors as long as it is in the hands of the trustee*. This italicized provision makes it a true "spendthrift" trust—i.e. a trust designed to protect a spendthrift [20] from his own weaknesses as far as money is concerned.

In the latter half of the 1800's, there was considerable conflict as to whether the grantor of a trust could include in the trust agreement any provision of this kind, that would make the money or property of the trust free from the claims of the beneficiary's creditors. At the present time, however, such provisions are valid in all but a few states, in some by special statute, in others without. The theory is that the creditors of the beneficiary are not harmed by it. Prior to the creation of the trust they had no rights in the property; after the creation of the trust they had no rights. Thus, they are not harmed by such a provision.

This is not true, however, with respect to the creditors of the grantor himself. Before the creation of a trust, his creditors have rights which they can attach against his property. Any attempt to deprive them of those rights by creating a trust in the grantor's own favor, exempt from claims of his creditors, will be considered void as to his creditors.

In view of the strong emphasis upon protection of life insurance

---

[20] The modern use of this term does not in any sense imply that the beneficiary *is* a spendthrift.

from the claims of creditors, it was only natural that those responsible for drafting agreements providing for settlement under the optional modes of settlement would think of the spendthrift trust as a possible means of protecting the proceeds from the claims of the creditors of the beneficiary. However, since the life insurance company's relationship with the beneficiary is not one of trustee-*cestui que trust*, special statutes were required before this could be done. Such statutes have now been enacted in well over half the states.[21] There are a few differences, but in general there is a very definite similarity among the various statutes and often identical wording is used.

Illustrative of this type of statute is a provision of the Illinois Code,[22] as follows:

> Any domestic life company shall have the power to hold the proceeds of any policy issued by it under a trust or other agreement upon such terms and restrictions as to revocation by the policyholder and control by beneficiaries, and with such exemptions from the claims of creditors of beneficiaries other than the policyholder as shall have been agreed to in writing by such company and the policyholder. Upon maturity of a policy in the event the policyholder has made no such agreement, the company shall have power to hold the proceeds of the policy under an agreement with the beneficiaries. Such company shall not be required to segregate funds so held but may hold them as part of its general company assets. A foreign or alien company, when authorized by its charter or the laws of its domicile, may exercise any such powers in this State.

The student will note first that this statute confers certain powers upon the domestic life insurance company and thus cannot apply to foreign or alien companies, whose powers are granted or modified only by the state under whose laws they are organized. Nevertheless, if such foreign or alien companies are authorized by their domiciliary state laws to exercise such powers, they are given the right by this statute to exercise them in Illinois.

Secondly, the company is given the power to hold policy proceeds under an agreement which provides for exemptions from the claims of the creditors of the beneficiaries but not those of the policyholder. This means that if the policyholder is the payee, under a settlement agreement relating to funds payable on surrender for cash, for instance, or the maturity of an endowment, he cannot make an agreement with the company which will preclude his own creditors from any rights in the funds. This simply recognizes our previously mentioned point that

---

[21] Alabama, Arizona, California, Colorado, Connecticut, Delaware, District of Columbia, Idaho, Illinois, Indiana, Iowa, Kansas, Kentucky, Massachusetts, Michigan, Minnesota, Mississippi, Nebraska, New York, Ohio, Oklahoma, Oregon, Pennsylvania, Rhode Island, South Carolina, Texas, Vermont, Virginia, Washington, West Virginia, Wisconsin, and Wyoming.

[22] Illinois Revised Statutes, Chap. 73, Sec. 853 (1959).

the policyholder is in a very different position with respect to effecting a protection in his own favor from that in which he exempts the funds from the claims of creditors of the beneficiary. The money was payable to him, and when he attempts to leave it with the company for his own benefit, but exempt from the claims of his own creditors, he is depriving them of rights. The Illinois statute does not permit this.

Spendthrift provisions included in settlement agreements are drafted in many different forms. One illustrative example reads as follows:

> No payee other than the insured . . . under settlement agreement elected by the insured shall have any right in advance of actual receipt of payment from the company, to transfer, assign, alienate, encumber, anticipate, or commute any instalment or payments, or to make any change in the pro-visions elected; and, except as otherwise prescribed by law, no payment of the interest or principal shall, in advance of actual payment of the company to payee, be subject to the debts, contracts, or engagements of any payee, nor to any judicial process to levy upon or attach the same for the payment thereof.

When Premiums Are Paid Out of Embezzled Funds

Even the most cursory examination of the law makes it clear that life insurance is a highly preferred kind of property as far as the claims of creditors are concerned. For instance, insolvency alone is not enough to bar the operation of the exemption statutes, and the only general excep-tion, as far as the exemption statutes are concerned, deals with transfers in fraud of creditors.

Generally speaking, it is just as difficult to decide what constitutes fraud in this area as in any other, and the exemption statutes are very liberally interpreted. In one specific set of circumstances, however, neither the insured nor the beneficiary is protected. That is the case where embezzled funds are used to pay the premiums. The courts are in very general agreement in such cases that the person from whom the funds are embezzled has the right to follow those funds and enforce a right against the proceeds. However, they differ with respect to the amount which may be recovered.

As a general rule, the courts hold that the proceeds of life insurance on which premiums have been paid out of embezzled funds are "im-pressed with a constructive or resulting trust" in favor of the person whose money was thus wrongfully used. The same general result has been reached by saying that the wronged person is entitled to a lien against the proceeds.

The principal question arises in connection with the amount of money the wronged person may recover out of the proceeds. As a general rule, if all the premiums were paid out of wrongfully acquired funds, then all the proceeds are held to be payable to the person to whom the funds rightfully belonged. If only a part of the premiums was wrongfully acquired, then the person from whom the funds were taken has a right to a share of the proceeds of the insurance equal to the proportion of premiums so wrongfully acquired. A few decisions have held that the wronged person is entitled only to recover the premiums wrongfully appropriated.

One of the more interesting decisions in this general area is a Louisiana Supreme Court decision, *Succession of Joseph L. Onorato*,[23] decided in March, 1951. This case concerns the civil law of Louisiana which, as we have previously pointed out, has a very different historical development from that of the common law, followed by most of the states. The reader will remember that Louisiana is one of several states whose law is based on French or Spanish (in this case, French) law, rather than the English common law, which formed the background of legal thinking of the majority of the states.

In the *Onorato* case, the insured had been an agent for the collection of rents. In the course of his duties, he misappropriated more than $26,000 belonging to others, and out of this he paid more than $5,000 in premiums for insurance on his own life. In this case, the court held that the persons from whom the funds were taken had the right to recover the amount of those premiums out of the proceeds of the insurance. The way this conclusion is reached under the civil law of Louisiana and the similarity of basic principles with those of the common law are illustrated by the following excerpts from the opinion of the court:

". . . it is a natural and immutable law, that he who is the owner of a thing should always continue to have the property of it, until he has divested himself of it voluntarily, or until he be divested of it by some just and legal way . . ." I Domat's Civil Law (Strahan's tr), pp. 49, 59, 60, 62.

There flows from this natural law the doctrine recognized in the civil law that, as between the owner and the thief, one whose property has been stolen may recover it even though the thief has changed the form of the property. As stated in 10 Scott, The Digest of Justinian, 35:2:53(14), p. 268, "Where anyone steals a silver ingot belonging to me, and makes cups out of it, I can either bring suit for the theft of the ingot, or a personal one for the recovery of the property.

"The same rule applies to grapes, and their unfermented juice, and seeds; for the action for the theft of grapes, their unfermented juice, and their seeds, can be brought, as well as a personal action."

＊　＊　＊　＊　＊

Under these principles of law, in the event a thief steals money and with the funds of his theft purchases or buys insurance, the owner can recover from the proceeds of the insurance the amount of the money so taken. The title of the owner cannot be considered as inferior to that of the thief or his representative, for, as pointed out above, the thief himself has no title whatever to the property stolen.

[23] 219 La. 1, 51 So.2d 804, 24 A.L.R. 2d 656 (1951).

The courts of other states almost without exception hold that, when embezzled or stolen funds are used to purchase exempt insurance, the exemption does not deprive the owner of recourse to the proceeds from such insurance. This holding is based on what is termed the common law constructive trust theory, which, as the writer appreciates it, is that the embezzler gets legal title when he uses the funds so entrusted to him to purchase other property, but he holds the equitable title in trust for the one from whom he has embezzled or stolen the funds.

Under the doctrine of our civil law, the embezzler never gets any kind of title against the one from whom he steals, for, when he purchases with stolen funds, the title is in the one from whom he stole the funds. Whatever may be the distinction between the two doctrines, the underlying principle of each is justice, equity, and fair dealing.

. . . In our opinion, in this case the civil law doctrine should not be applied to the extent that the proceeds of exempt life insurance, when the premiums are paid or the insurance purchased with stolen funds, should be given to the owner of the property thus stolen, but he is entitled to recover the amount of the stolen funds which was used by the thief in payment of premiums or purchase of the insurance itself. By permitting this recovery, the fraud is made ineffective, equity and justice are served, and the public good and the policy of the statute creating the exemption are in no way impaired since the family and loved ones of the insured are assured of the proceeds that the misappropriated money bought.

INSURANCE AND THE BANKRUPTCY ACT

Under the federal Constitution (Article I, Section 8), Congress is authorized to "make uniform laws on the subject of bankruptcies throughout the United States." From the earliest times, however, Congress has followed the practice of giving effect in bankruptcy laws to the exemption statutes of the various states with respect to life insurance proceeds. This practice holds even though the result has been, to that extent, a departure from uniformity.

The Exemption Statutes. Of the two sections of the Federal Bankruptcy Act which are specifically concerned with this problem, Section 6 is the more important and reads, in part, as follows:

This title shall not affect the allowance to bankrupts of the exemptions which are prescribed by the laws of the United States or by the State laws in force at the time of the filing of the petition . . .

In determining whether insurance policies will or will not be included in the assets which pass to the bankruptcy trustee for the benefit of creditors, one rules out first those policies which have no cash surrender value. In those cases there is no property to which the trustee may take title. Then those policies which have a cash surrender value must be reviewed in the light of the special exemption statute or statutes of the state of the policyholder's legal residence (in legal terms, his *domicile*).

Because of the wide variations in the wording and application of the state statutes, it is impossible to discuss the question of when an insurance policy will be exempt from bankruptcy proceedings in general terms that will have any real meaning. The question always comes down to an analysis and interpretation of the particular exemption statute of the specific state in question as well as the pertinent court decisions. This is true whether the states are community property states or common law states, whether the right to change the beneficiary was reserved or not reserved, whether the amount of insurance is large or small.

The Cash Surrender Value. Another provision of the bankruptcy law gives some protection against the claims of creditors even though the policy may be payable to the estate of the insured and have a cash surrender value to which the trustee in bankruptcy takes title. This provision is found in Section 70-a of the Act, which permits a bankrupt to keep a policy, even though payable to his estate, or to other beneficiaries which may not fall within the class specifically designated under the exemption statute, if he pays an amount equal to the cash surrender value to the trustee within thirty days after the ascertainment of the amount.

Of particular importance is the fact that the title of the trustee in bankruptcy does not extend to any values under the policy except the cash surrender value. Thus, in one case,[24] where a trustee took title to a policy on a given date, in accordance with the bankruptcy law, and the insured subsequently died, it was held that the trustee was entitled only to that sum which would have been available to the bankrupt at the time of the bankruptcy as a cash asset.

Recent Developments. A case such as the *Burlingham* case, decided in 1913, may tend to suggest that this subject is of academic interest only. This possibility was definitely terminated by the decision of the United States Court of Appeals for the Fourth Circuit, handed down January 5, 1955, in the case of *Lake* v. *New York Life et al.*[25] This was a consolidation of five suits brought by a trustee in bankruptcy to recover the cash surrender values of life insurance policies under which the companies had granted policy loans amounting to some $45,000 after, but without knowledge of, the bankruptcy of the insured. In that case the companies were held liable to the trustee for the full amount of the cash surrender values of the policies even though the loans had been made without knowledge of the bankruptcy of the insured. In April, 1955, the United States Supreme Court refused to review this decision of the Circuit Court of Appeals.

As a result of this decision, every loan made by a life insurance com-

---

[24] *Burlingham* v. *Crouse*, 228 U.S. 459 (1913).

[25] 218 F.2d 394 (C.A. Md., 1955).

pany and every cash surrender value it pays subjects it to possible double liability if the policyholder is in bankruptcy at the time of the payment. Actual notice to the company is not required. For this reason, whenever a request for a loan or a cash surrender is received which involves a substantial amount of money, precautions are ordinarily taken to ascertain whether the payee is in bankruptcy or not. For example, one company has a bankruptcy search made in the district court in which the policyholder resides in every instance where the payment amounts to $10,000 or more. Other companies have different monetary limits. However, this possibility of double liability is very real, and until corrective legislation is enacted, precautions will have to be taken by the companies themselves if they are to protect themselves against it.

CHAPTER XVII

Remedies

GENERALLY SPEAKING, the parties to the life insurance contract have available to them the same remedies available to the parties to any other contract. Because some kinds of problems arise more frequently in connection with the life insurance contract, however, the remedies applicable to those problems are more frequently sought by the parties to the contract. The remedy of interpleader, for instance, is particularly valuable in resolving questions concerning the parties who are entitled to receive the proceeds of the policy. It is probably more frequently used by the life insurance company than is any other remedy. However, rescission and reformation are also used. It is the purpose of this chapter to discuss these and other remedies which have proved to be particularly valuable in solving some of the special problems which arise under the life insurance contract.

INTERPLEADER

Under the equitable remedy of interpleader, any person, corporation, or association holding money or property belonging to someone else and claimed by two or more adverse claimants, may deposit the money or property with the court and request that the claimants prove their claims. The funds or property can then be paid to the person the court decides is rightfully entitled to it. The entire question is thus settled in one court proceeding instead of the several which might be required if the claims were decided separately.

Requirements

No Remedy at Law. Basic to the right to file a bill of interpleader is the fact that there must be no adequate remedy at law by which the plaintiff may protect himself from the threat of multiple suits. The purpose of interpleader is not so much to protect from double liability as from this threat of multiple litigation.

The jurisdiction of a federal court to entertain a bill of interpleader is not dependent upon the merits of the claims of the defendants. . . . It is our opinion that a stakeholder, acting in good faith, may maintain a suit in interpleader for the purpose of ridding himself of the vexation and expense of resisting adverse claims, even though he believes that only one of them is meritorious. As the Supreme Court said in *Myers* v. *Bethlehem Corporation,* 303 U.S. 41, 51: "Lawsuits also often prove to have been groundless; but no way has been discovered of relieving a defendant from the necessity of a trial to establish the fact." [1]

Another court has said:

The fundamental basis for interpleader is to permit the holder of a fund who admits he is not the owner of it to put the fund in the hands of the court, so that claimants with substantial contentions may fight out their claims to it and so that the holder will be shielded from the danger of deciding at its peril who is rightfully entitled to the fund, as well as from the burden of defending and danger of losing separate lawsuits brought by each claimant.[2]

A Disinterested "Stakeholder." The person who seeks the remedy of interpleader must, as the quotations above indicate, be a disinterested "stakeholder." In other words, he must not have a claim of his own to the money or property in question.

Also, the claims must have a common origin and the claimants must claim the same thing. The mere fact that one may be faced with a number of lawsuits is not enough; they must all relate to claims to the same money or property.

The Federal Interpleader Act

The first Federal Interpleader Act was passed in 1917 and repealed in 1926, when a new act was enacted. In 1936, another act was passed to replace the 1926 act, and in 1948 a revision of the Judicial Code resulted in the present code section under which the remedy is available. Under this Section 1335, Title 28, U.S.C., federal courts have jurisdiction in cases involving a "certificate, policy of insurance, or other instrument of value or amount of $500 or more."

Under the Code the claimants must be legal residents of different jurisdictions. This is generally termed "diversity of citizenship." Incidentally, the remedy of interpleader is also available under the laws of most of the individual states.

A Bill in the Nature of a Bill of Interpleader. A bill in the nature of a bill of interpleader is very much the same as a bill of interpleader except that the person or corporation holding the money is not truly a disinterested stakeholder. In other words, he has some interest in the outcome although perhaps not actually a claim to the money itself.

---

[1] *Hunter* v. *Federal Life Insurance Company,* 111 F.2d 551 (C.C.A. Ark., 1940).

[2] *United Benefit Life Insurance Company* v. *Katz,* 155 F. Supp. 391 (D.C. Pa., 1957).

Interpleader and the Life Insurance Company

The remedy of interpleader is especially appropriate for the life insurance company. After years of policy transactions, beneficiary changes, assignments made and released, policy lapses and reinstatements, there are frequently questions among successive beneficiaries, beneficiaries and assignees, persons claiming by reason of property rights in community property states or oral transactions of various kinds. The bill of interpleader permits the life insurance company to pay the money due into a court and require these various claimants to "interplead" their claims. A final court decision settles the question, and the company is discharged of all further liability. If one of the claimants sues the company *before* a bill of interpleader has been filed, the company ordinarily has the right to defend by filing a cross bill of interpleader.

Illustrative Case

The case of *California-Western States Life Insurance Co. v. Jarman, Admx. Respondent, Tollette, Appellant,* discussed in Chapter XVI,[3] illustrates the use of the bill of interpleader where there were adverse claimants to the proceeds of an insurance policy under the community property laws of Washington. The following case illustrates and explains the purpose of interpleader and the procedural aspects of the remedy. It will be noted that the point at issue relates to the facility of payment clause of the policy and adverse claimants under it.

NIXON v. LIFE INSURANCE COMPANY OF VIRGINIA [4]

(District of Columbia Municipal Court of Appeals.)

Rover, Ch. J.: One Barton M. Ewers, at the time of his death, was the holder of two industrial life insurance policies with the appellee insurance company; neither policy designated a beneficiary, but each contained a so-called "facility of payment" clause reading as follows:

> The Company may make any payment provided for in this Policy, to husband or wife, or any relative by blood, or lawful beneficiary, or connection by marriage of the Insured, or to any other person who may appear to be equitably entitled to the same by reason of having incurred expense on behalf of the Insured for his or her burial, or for any other purpose; and the production by the Company of a receipt signed by any or either of said persons, or of other sufficient proof of such payment to any or either of them shall be conclusive evidence that such benefits have been paid to the person or persons entitled thereto, and that all claims under this Policy have been fully satisfied.

After the death of Ewers the policies were delivered to the company by the appellant who claimed that she was entitled to their proceeds because for

[3] See p. 351.

[4] 124 A.2d 305 (D.C. Mun., App., 1956).

some four years prior to his death, the deceased had lived at her house, she had furnished him clothing, housing and food, had assisted him in his business, all without compensation, and had paid premiums on the policies.

Annie May Ewers, the widow of the deceased, also claimed the insurance proceeds either in her individual capacity or as administratrix of decedent's estate by appointment of the Probate Court of this District.

The insurance company confronted with these conflicting demands did not avail itself of the provisions of the "facility of payment" clause, but filed a complaint for interpleader and the court authorized the company to deposit the proceeds of the policies in the registry of the court.

Both the appellant and the widow answered admitting that the policies contained the "facility of payment" clause and each set forth the basis of their respective claims as stated. The court, after opening statements of counsel, but without taking evidence, awarded the proceeds of both policies to the widow as administratrix and entered judgment accordingly. Appellant appeals from this judgment.

Appellant's contention, which we think dispositive of this case, is that the court below should not have ruled that the administratrix of the deceased-insured was entitled to the proceeds of the policies as a matter of law. Her position is that the court should have heard proof of the merits of her claim and exercised its equitable power to decide who was entitled to the disputed funds. A consideration of the nature and purpose of interpleader together with an examination of the cases, convinces us that appellant is correct in this contention.

Interpleader is a long established equitable remedy designed to avoid multiplicity of claims and circuity of action. Its foundations are in equity and where allowed the court is called upon to determine to which of the various claimants the money deposited with the court should be awarded. Where, as here, the remedy is invoked by the insurer, we think the better rule is that it is the duty of the court to pass upon the merits of the claimant's rights to the proceeds.

At this point appellee contends, as she did in the trial court, that no beneficiary having been specifically named in the policies, the proceeds must be distributed to the representative of the insured's estate. She cites authority in support of this contention but our examination discloses that much of it is distinguishable from our present case. Most of the cases cited concern policies which themselves are distinguishable in that they expressly make the proceeds payable to the administrator or executor of the insured *unless* at its option the insurance company elects to pay under the facility of payment clause. . . .

. . . Similarly, in *Ellis* v. *Metropolitan Life Ins. Co.*, Mo. App., 3 S.W.2d 397, where the insurance company interpleaded both the insured's administratrix and a woman with whom he had boarded before his death, the latter contending the deceased was indebted to her for board, lodging and washing, and the payment of premiums, the court in the exercise of its equitable powers, reversed the trial court and directed a judgment against the administratrix and in favor of the adverse claimant. It is to be noted that the court so acted even though the policy expressly named the administrator as beneficiary.

. . . This procedure is in keeping with the fundamental nature and purpose of proceedings by way of interpleader by preventing circuity of action, a course sure to result from the trial court's action relegating the appellant to an independent suit either against the administratrix or the distributees of the estate. We fail to see any valid reason why the insurance money should pass through decedent's estate, or how the orderly processes of justice would be served by such circuitous procedure. Indeed, it is manifest that such a requirement would have the effect of merely postponing for decision that which is now subject to the court's disposition in one proceeding, not to mention the additional hardship and expense to appellant who would be obliged to file suit in the same court. . . .

RESCISSION

We have written earlier, at some length, of the right of the insurance company to cancel (*avoid*) a contract of life insurance if there was fraud, material misrepresentation, or concealment in the application. This right is enforced by means of the equitable remedy of rescission, under which a court of equity may declare a contract canceled and of no legal effect whatsoever.

When Rescission Is Used

During the Lifetime of the Insured. Whenever fraud, material misrepresentation, or concealment in the application are discovered during the lifetime of the insured, *but after the expiration of the contestable period,* the company is ordinarily precluded by the incontestable clause from taking any action whatever. If it is discovered prior to expiration of the contestable period, however, the only legal remedy open to the company is to ask a court of equity to rescind the contract. The insurer cannot wait until the insured dies, for that may be beyond the contestable period, and there is no other means by which the company can have its obligations under the contract canceled.

After the Death of the Insured. If fraud, material misrepresentation, or concealment in the application are discovered after the death of the insured but prior to the expiration of the contestable period, the facts so revealed may ordinarily be used in defense of a suit by the beneficiary for the death benefit. Thus the company has an adequate remedy at law.

Let us say that John Doe, insured under life policy No. 427-B-828, dies of leukemia three months after issuance of a policy. The death certificate states that the illness was of two years' duration and investigation supports this statement. The illness was actually diagnosed some two years prior to death and the insured was informed of the diagnosis. Nevertheless, the answers to the application questions relating to his health gave no hint of ill health of any kind. The company will deny the claim for the death benefit, in accordance with its usual procedures for denial. If the beneficiary sues, the company will show that information material to the appraisal of the risk was withheld at the time of the application, and this will ordinarily constitute an effective defense to the suit.

In this connection it will be recalled that in the *Monahan* case,[5] although the insured died during the contestable period, the beneficiary waited until the expiration of that period to bring her suit. The court then held that the company was precluded by the incontestable clause from contesting the validity of the policy. Subsequently, legislation was enacted to permit the companies to include in the incontestable clause the phrase "during the lifetime of the insured." The effect of this phrase was to preserve to the company the right to defend at any time, on grounds of material misrepresentation or fraud, in any case where the insured died during the contestable period of the policy. Thus a life insurance company continues to have a remedy at law in cases involving fraud or misrepresentation, if the insured dies during the contestable period and the policy includes the phrase "during the lifetime of the insured."

Some companies consider this a somewhat dubious advantage, however. Because the company has an adequate remedy at law, it cannot go into a court of equity when the insured dies during the contestable period, even though it might be advantageous to have the question decided by the judge rather than a jury. For this reason, in addition to the policies issued prior to the *Monahan* case, policies issued since that time sometimes have incontestable clauses which do not include the phrase "during the lifetime of the insured," in order to preserve to the company the right to have the contract rescinded in equity at the death of the insured during the contestable period.

Illustrative Case

The case of *Massachusetts Mutual Life Insurance Company* v. *Goodelman*,[6] decided by the United States District Court for the Eastern District of New York, in April, 1958, illustrates how the equitable remedy of rescission is available if the phrase "during the lifetime of the insured" is not included in the incontestable clause.

MASSACHUSETTS MUTUAL LIFE INS. CO. v. GOODELMAN

(United States District Court for the Eastern District of New York.)

BRUCHHAUSEN, D. J.: The defendant moves for a dismissal of this action for the rescission of a contract of insurance upon the ground that the plaintiff has an adequate remedy at law.

It is alleged in the complaint that the plaintiff is a foreign corporation; that defendant resides in this district; that on February 27, 1956, the plaintiff issued a policy of life insurance upon the life of Leon Goodelman in the face amount of $100,000; that on or about April 22, 1957, the defendant was duly

[5] See Chapter VIII, p. 207.

[6] 160 F. Supp. 510 (D.C. N.Y., 1958).

designated as primary beneficiary thereof; that Leon Goodelman died on or about December 22, 1957; that the policy contained a provision that it would be incontestable after it had been in force for a period of two years from the date of its issue; that within the said two year period and prior to the commencement of this action, plaintiff elected to and did rescind said policy and notified defendant of said election and tendered payment of the premiums paid thereon; that such rescission was based upon false representations or concealment of facts and that the insured was not in good health and was not insurable when the policy was delivered, but on the contrary suffered from diabetes and from arteriosclerosis, associated with said diabetes and was taking insulin.

The plaintiff's action was commenced on February 20, 1958. After the expiration of the contestable period of two years, the defendant instituted an action against the plaintiff to recover the proceeds of the policy, which action is hereinafter called the second action.

The ground urged by defendant for dismissal of the instant action for rescission is that the sole issue between the parties is basically legal in nature; that the plaintiff has a complete and adequate remedy at law in that it can assert its claims of fraud and misrepresentation in the aforesaid second action and thus assure the present defendant of her right to a trial by jury of that action.

The principal issue on this motion is whether the Mutual Company had the right to resort to a court of equity with its claims for rescission or should have delayed action until the beneficiary sued on the policy and then interposed its defenses in such action. Mutual contends that if it had delayed bringing its action beyond the two year period from date of issue of the policy, it would have lost its right to defend by the operation of the incontestability clause in the contract. It reads as follows:

> Incontestability. This policy . . . shall be incontestable after it has been in force for a period of two years from its date of issue.

It is crystal clear from a mere reading of the provision that if Mutual had any remedy pertaining to the policy, such remedy must be asserted within the two year period, in this case prior to February 27, 1958. It could not be availed of beyond that time. Similar clauses have been so construed in *Mutual Life Insurance Co.* v. *Hurni Packing Co.*, 263 U.S. 167, and *Killian* v. *Metropolitan Life Insurance Co.*, 251 N.Y. 44. The beneficiary's contention that the clause is not in compliance with Section 155 of the New York Insurance Law has no merit.

Mutual was not precipitate in instituting its action for rescission. It delayed doing so until its claim was about to be outlawed by the incontestability clause. In fact, barely one week remained for it to take action or forfeit its right to do so. In a similar rescission case, *American Life Insurance Co.* v. *Stewart*, 300 U.S. 203, the plaintiff's right to resort to equity by way of claim for rescission was upheld, Mr. Justice Cardozo writing for the Court, said:

> If the policy is to become incontestable soon after the death of the insured, the insurer becomes helpless if he must wait for a move by some one else, who may prefer to remain motionless till the time for contest has gone by. . . . Accordingly an insurer, who might otherwise be condemned to loss through the mere inaction of an adversary, may assume the offensive by going into equity and there praying for cancellation.

The motion is denied.

REFORMATION

Life insurance policies are carefully checked and life company employees, on the whole, have an excellent record for accuracy. Wherever work is done, however, mistakes will sometimes be made; and a mistake in a life insurance policy is almost always serious.

Perhaps a twenty-year endowment values page was inadvertently included in a twenty-pay life policy back in 1943. Possibly a typist moved a decimal point one place to the right; perhaps figures have been reversed. In any case, there is only one thing to do, administratively speaking. The policyholder must be informed of the error; the nature of the error must be explained; permission to correct the error must be requested.

Now, let us assume that permission to correct the error is *not* granted. The policy states the value as $7,893.27 (instead of $789.33) and the policyholder intends to enforce it according to its terms. It is at this point that the lawyer thinks of the equitable remedy of reformation.

What Reformation Is

Reformation is the remedy by which a written instrument is reformed or construed in such a way as to express the true intentions of the parties, when the contract, as actually written, fails to do so. Reformation has been possible in courts of equity for many, many years, but like all equitable remedies it is *extraordinary* in nature and will be granted only for compelling reasons.

How Reformation Is Used

The purpose of reformation is not to make a new contract but to reform the one presently existing so that it will be in the form in which it should have been expressed in the first place. It is not to substitute a new contract but to make the original contract effective as intended.

Before a contract can be reformed, it must clearly be shown that, as written, it does not express the agreement of the parties, either because of mistake or fraud. If the error is the result of mistake, it must be a mutual mistake or a mistake on the part of one party, with fraud or inequitable conduct on the part of the other.

Illustrative Case

In *Flax* v. *Prudential Life Insurance Co.*,[7] decided by the United States District Court, in February, 1956, the plaintiff sought to recover $5,495.26, plus 7 per cent interest from February 19, 1955, on a policy which originally provided for a death benefit of $1,864.00, with $463

---

[7] 148 F. Supp. 720 (D.C. Cal., 1956).

as a pure endowment at the end of twenty years. The company contended that the correct amount due was $1,994.65 and that the $5,495.26 sought to be recovered was based on what the law has continued to term a "scrivener's error," meaning, of course, the error of one who wrote the contract.

The court said:

> . . . The defendant had no knowledge of the existence of the mistake until during the month of June 1954, at which time, in the course of processing an application by the plaintiff for a loan on the policy, it discovered it. The defendant immediately notified the plaintiff of the mistake and requested him to join in the reformation of the policy to rectify it, which he has refused to do.
>
> The Answer and counterclaim seek the reformation of the policy to conform with the intention just outlined.

✻ ✻ ✻ ✻ ✻

> When the policy was executed, the option exercised and the rider in controversy attached, the plaintiff was a resident of the State of New York. The policy issued to him conformed to the requirements of the laws of the State of New York. This being a diversity case, the law of New York controls in interpreting the *contractual* rights of the parties arising under the policy. The plaintiff's trial memorandum concedes this (p. 8).
>
> New York courts have held uniformly that incontestability clauses of the type inserted in this policy do *not* prevent a contest of the policy on the ground of fraud or mistake. To the contrary, these courts make these defenses available to the insurer whenever an action is instituted to enforce any of the terms of the policy. They take the view that when, either through mutual mistake or unilateral mistake by one party which is known to the other, the policy does not express the intention of the parties, reformation may be had either when an action is instituted by the insured to enforce its provisions or in a direct action brought by the insurer to make the policy speak verity.
>
> In one of the cases, an action was brought by the insurer to reform a disability policy so that it would stipulate that the disability insurance to be paid to the insured *would be $100 per month instead of $1,000*, which had been inserted through a scrivener's mistake. The policy was issued in 1926 and the action was not begun by the insurer until 1937. Notwithstanding this, the trial court granted reformation. The judgment was affirmed by the Appellate Division whose decision, in turn, was affirmed by New York's highest court, The Court of Appeals.

✻ ✻ ✻ ✻ ✻

> . . . So we come to these important considerations: (a) Was there a mistake in the execution of the rider which was attached to the policy when the insured on March 20, 1936, exercised one of the options under the policy converting it into paid-up insurance? (b) Was the mistake of a type for which relief can be granted in an action of this character?
>
> Answers to these questions require a brief consideration of the circumstances under which, generally, equity will grant relief for mistakes. From time immemorial, it has been the function of equity as administered in the federal courts to remedy what is known as "scrivener's mistakes"—mistakes

performed by the person who drafted the instrument in such a manner that it did not express what was *actually* agreed. In an early case, the Supreme Court of the United States has stated the principle and the reasons for it in this manner:

> There are certain principles of equity, applicable to this question, which, as general principles, we hold to be incontrovertible. The first is, that where an instrument is drawn and executed, which professes or is intended to carry into execution an agreement, whether in writing or by parol, previously entered into, but which, *by mistake of the draftsman, either as to fact or law, does not fulfill, or which violates, the manifest intention of the parties to the agreement, equity will correct the mistake, so as to produce conformity of the instrument to the agreement.* The reason is obvious: the execution of agreements, fairly and legally entered into, is one of the peculiar branches of equity jurisdiction; and if the instrument which is intended to execute the agreement be, from any cause, insufficient for that purpose, *the agreement remains as much unexecuted, as if one of the parties had refused, altogether, to comply with his engagement;* and a court of equity will, in the exercise of its acknowledged jurisdiction, afford relief in the one case, as well as in the other, *by compelling the delinquent party fully to perform his agreement, according to the terms of it, and to the manifest intention of the parties.* So, if the mistake exists, not in the instrument, which is intended to give effect to the agreement, but in the agreement itself, and is clearly proved to have been the result of ignorance of some material fact, a court of equity will, in general, grant relief, according to the nature of the particular case in which it is sought. (Italics added)

The principle has been followed in later cases and it is now an accepted norm of equity jurisprudence as administered in the federal courts that reformation will be granted for mistake. Even unilateral mistake may be the basis for relief when it is known to the other party to the contract.

✿　✿　✿　✿　✿

The case before us is an almost perfect illustration of the classical instance referred to in the books, that of a person looking at cheap jewelry and seeing what he, at once, recognizes as being a valuable jewel, which, by mistake, had been placed with the "paste," purchases it at a price wholly unrelated to its real value. In the circumstances, as the Restatement puts it:

> The shopkeeper is entitled to restitution because the shopkeeper did not, as A knew, *intend to bargain except with reference to cheap jewelry.*

The plaintiff is an experienced businessman and should have known that in modern business and insurance practice, a clause which would make the surrender value of a policy more than double its maturity value, without additional obligations on his part was not within its contemplation. His coverage at the inception of the policy (omitting the endowment) was $1,864, which was increased on conversion to $2,755.

✿　✿　✿　✿　✿

. . . To summarize: The plaintiff either did or did not know of the mistake. *If he did,* it appearing that the mistake *was not known* to the insurer, we have the type of unilateral mistake for which relief by way of reformation is granted. *If he did not* know the mistake, we have a case of mutual mistake for which reformation also lies. Indeed, relief may be granted by disregarding the printed words which the scrivener erroneously failed to delete.

✿　✿　✿　✿　✿

. . . Entering into business undertakings, parties *do not intend* to over-reach each other, but rather mean to make equitable and conscionable agreements.

One of California's Court of Appeals has summed up the principle in these words:

> In every contract there is an implied covenant of good faith and fair dealing.

* * * * *

. . . So, if plaintiff's present demands were allowed, he would receive something which he did not bargain or pay for,—something for nothing. The language of the Persian poet applies:

> Sue for a Debt he never did contract,
> And cannot answer—
> Oh, the sorry trade.

It would be neither good morals nor good law to sanction the application of such a policy to business relations.

On the other hand, a ruling for the defendant avoids a palpable injustice and still allows the plaintiff the full benefit of the contract *he intended* to make. Judgment will, therefore, be for the defendant.

THE DECLARATORY JUDGMENT

A declaratory judgment simply *declares* the rights of the parties to the action or sets forth the opinion of the court on a given question. It does not require the parties to do or pay anything. Thus it differs markedly from the usual court decision, and its use, particularly in the United States, is a relatively recent development in the law. Only a few states, prior to 1919, had declaratory judgment statutes and even the development of the Uniform Declaratory Judgments Act did not stimulate interest in this form of relief to any marked extent. That act was adopted in not more than about half the states. The enactment of a Federal Declaratory Judgments Act in 1934, however, seemed more effective, and there has been an increased interest in this area of the law since that date.

Nature of the Declaratory Judgment

The most important thing about the declaratory judgment is that it does not involve any procedure for carrying out the decision of the court. The judgment stands by itself as a clarification of rights or facts in a given case. Originally it was thought that the remedy would concern only questions of status or property rights and the construction of various legal instruments such as wills. Applied to the life insurance contract, this function has a great many possible applications. One of them is illustrated in the case of *Liner et al., Plaintiffs* v. *Penn. Mutual Life Insurance Company*, decided by the New York Supreme Court, Appellate Division, in October, 1955, and printed at page 380 of this chapter.

The declaratory judgment has been found advantageous in connection with disability benefits, also. For instance, where claim is made for disability benefits and the company denies liability on the grounds that the insured is not disabled within the terms of the policy, the company is often faced with a claim based on repudiation of the policy. An action for a declaratory judgment in such cases is one of the most effective ways of clarifying the rights of the parties and the status of the contract.

Another difficult problem is presented in connection with claims under which the company pays the face amount of the policy but denies the accidental death benefit. In such cases, the company pays the face amount of the policy without prejudice to the rights of the beneficiary under the accidental death section of the policy. This discharges the company with respect to the face amount of the policy but leaves its liability open with respect to the accidental death portion. It is sometimes said that payment of the face amount, in practical effect, often "finances" a law suit. If there is any real possibility that suit may be filed against the company, an immediate action for a declaratory judgment offers one way to have the facts ascertained while evidence is fresh and before witnesses have scattered.

This same advantage is occasionally offered in connection with a denial of a claim for the face amount of the policy. Even though the company is convinced of the soundness of its decision, it nevertheless remains vulnerable to a possible suit by the beneficiary until the expiration of the statute of limitations or the period of time specified in the policy. During that time, witnesses may die or become widely scattered as a matter of geography, and the ascertainment of the truth may become progressively more difficult.

An additional difficulty is encountered in some states in the form of statutory penalties imposed for wrongful and vexatious delay in settling life insurance claims. An unfavorable decision after the expiration of the period specified in these statutes means not only liability but also a statutory penalty. In such cases, an action for a declaratory judgment furnishes one method for clarifying the rights of the parties and may enable the company to support its decision by a court decision and thus avoid the statutory penalty.

Most life insurance companies do not particularly want to support a denial of a claim, per se. They do not deny the claim unless they believe denial is completely justified. Numerous factors may be involved, however, including evidence in the hands of the beneficiary or her attorney, which has never been made available to the life insurance company. In any case the declaratory judgment presents one way for the insurer to bring the question into court and thus affirm its good faith in the action it has taken.

Illustrative Case

As we have said, one of the proverbial functions of the declaratory judgment is to construe legal instruments. Applied to the life insurance contract this function may have a multitude of uses. One very advantageous application is illustrated in the case of *Liner et al. v. Penn. Mutual Life Insurance Company*, decided by the New York Supreme Court, Appellate Division, in October, 1955. It is printed here in full, not only to indicate the usefulness of the declaratory judgment but also to show the reasoning of the court in exercising this kind of authority.

LINER ET AL., Plaintiffs, Appellants v. PENN
MUTUAL LIFE INS. CO., Defendant, Respondent [8]

(New York Supreme Court, Appellate Division, Fourth Department.)

VAUGHAN, J.: These two actions require the interpretation of two policies of life insurance. The policies were taken out for educational purposes and contain double indemnity clauses. The insured having died an accidental death, the question is whether the stated amounts subject to annual withdrawal are thereby doubled. The beneficiaries seek declaratory judgments to that effect. The insurance company, on the other hand, contends that the double indemnity clauses have no other effect than to increase the principal sum of the policies, with the withdrawal privileges remaining unchanged. That was the position taken by the Supreme Court, and the beneficiaries appeal from the resulting declaratory judgments.

The first policy was issued in 1940, when the insured's son Richard was less than one year old. The policy was in the principal amount of $5,000 with double indemnity. Upon the death of the insured, the net proceeds were to be retained under Option D and interest paid to Richard for life. After reaching age 17, Richard could withdraw twice in each year "an amount equal to but not to be more nor less than the sum of $625.00." It will be noted that the principal was to be conserved until Richard was ready for college; thereafter, $1,250 could be withdrawn annually, so that the proceeds would be exhausted during a four year college course. During Richard's minority all sums due to him were to be paid to the insured's widow as trustee, and she was to exercise the right of withdrawal for him. On Richard's death the net proceeds remaining were to be paid to her in one sum. By a "supplemental agreement attached to and made a part of the policy," the company agreed to pay the double indemnity benefit "in addition to and together with the sum insured by this policy." It should be noted that the application for this policy provided that after Richard attained age 17, one-eighth of the proceeds could be withdrawn twice yearly for educational purposes. In place of the proportion (one-eighth) the policy contains a figure ($625) which is one-eighth of $5,000, and it would seem that the policy was not intended to vary the application. The numerical equivalent of the fraction employed by the insured in his application adequately expressed his primary intention and could only fail to do so in case of his extremely unlikely death by violent, external and accidental means.

Further evidence that the insured regarded $625 as the practical equiva-

[8] 145 N.Y.S. 2d 560 (A.D. 4th, 1955).

lent of one-eighth may be found in the fact that in his subsequent application
for a policy to benefit his second child Victoria, he again provided that one-
eighth of the proceeds could be withdrawn twice yearly. For the proportion,
the policy as issued again substituted the numerical equivalent. The policy
for Victoria was issued in 1942, when she was only a few months old. Payment
of the double indemnity benefit was to "be made in the same manner as and
shall be in addition to the sum insured or death benefit." The policy was substantially like that taken out for Richard, except that before Victoria attained
age 17 her mother as trustee was entitled to withdraw $500 per year. It un-
doubtedly occurred to the insured, as it would to any sensible man, that if he
were to die leaving two young children, his wife might have a difficult time.
Accordingly, he permitted a limited withdrawal before Victoria reached age
17. Thereafter, "an amount not to exceed $1,250.00 in any one year" could
be withdrawn. The withdrawal privileges were to be non-cumulative.

On July 9, 1943, the insured executed a change of beneficiary of both
policies. The beneficiary clauses of both policies are now identical. The insured
continued to elect Option D. The interest is payable to his widow as trustee
during the minority of the beneficiary. The widow may also exercise the
withdrawal privileges during the beneficiaries' minority. Before the receipt by
the company of an affidavit from a college to the effect that the beneficiary is
enrolled there, $500 may be withdrawn each year in one sum. After receipt
of such an affidavit, $1,250 may be withdrawn each year in one sum or in
multiples of $625. The withdrawal privileges are non-cumulative. Upon the
death of the primary beneficiary, the remainder shall be paid to the widow in
one sum.

The purpose of the insured throughout these transactions was to protect
his children during approximately the first twenty years of their lives and to
insure that they would receive a college education. The period during which
he desired to assist them was substantially certain and known to him; it would
not vary according as he might or might not die an accidental death. Regardless of the manner in which he might die, he wished to assist his children
through college so that they could take care of themselves. That would require
twenty years, not forty. Yet the insurance company interprets the withdrawal
privileges so that the duration of the protection period varies according to the
way in which the insured met his death. We think the desired protection
period would be the same in either case.

The insured obviously contracted for double indemnity for the reason
that a sudden death from violent, external and accidental means would deprive
him of all opportunity to make further provision for his children. He accordingly provided that in that event the principal amount of each policy should
be doubled. But the extra $5,000 must be distributed at the same time and in
the same way as the basic death benefit. The supplemental agreements use the
language "in addition to and together with" and "in the same manner as and
. . . in addition to" the basic $5,000. An article on double indemnity has
stated:

Double indemnity is a desirable supplement to the primary life insurance.
It is intended to provide double payment to the beneficiary at the time of
greatest need when the insured meets an untimely and premature death
as the result of accidental injury. (Kelly, Recent Developments in Double
Indemnity Law, 33 Corn. L. Q., 360).

The "time of greatest need" in the present case is the time immediately after
the insured's death, when his children are still dependent. It is then that he

intended them to have the benefit of the double indemnity provisions. "Double indemnity" means twice as much, not twice as long.

We conclude that the withdrawal privileges under Option D should be doubled. Nothing else would satisfy the purpose of the insured to provide for his children during a fixed period of their lives which would not vary according to the manner of his death, and nothing else would satisfy his direction set forth in the supplemental contract that the extra $5,000 be distributed "in addition to and together with" the basic death benefit.

The judgments are reversed and judgments granted to the plaintiffs declaring that $1,000 may be withdrawn each year until receipt of the affidavit mentioned in the change of beneficiary and $2,500 per year thereafter.

ANTICIPATORY BREACH

Another rather technical remedy sometimes discussed in connection with the life insurance contract is that of anticipatory breach. A breach is the legal term given to the situation where a promisor fails to perform when the time arrives for such performance. The promisee then has a right to sue at law for damages for breach of contract, although he does not ordinarily have this right prior to the time specified for performance.

The repudiation of some contracts, prior to the time specified for performance, gives the wronged party a present right to sue, if he wishes, for what is termed an "anticipatory breach." Under such circumstances, he may, of course, wait until the time for performance and sue then, or alternatively, he may treat the contract as at an end and ask to have it rescinded.

Ordinarily, if a life insurance company denies a claim for the benefit payable on death, no matter how completely justified the denial may be, the beneficiary may treat this action as a breach and sue for damages. Let us say, however, that the company becomes insolvent. It seems obvious here that the company will not pay at such time as payment falls due, because it will not be able to do so. Yet the beneficiary or the insured has no action for breach since there has not been a breach in the true, legal sense of the word until the actual time for the performance. The same general situation obtains where an insurance association refuses to accept premiums and requests that its members submit to a different plan of insurance. In one case [9] of this kind, the refusal of the association was held to be an anticipatory breach, giving the members of the association the right to sue. The New Jersey Supreme Court said:

> By the great weight of authority, when there has been a renunciation of an executory contract by one party, the other has the option of treating the contract as terminated for all purposes of performance and to maintain an action at once for damages occasioned by such repudiation without waiting the time fixed by the contract for performance, or the latter may elect to treat

---

[9] *Wartsky et al.* v. *Progressive Order of the West,* 4 Commerce Clearing House Life Cases 893 (N.J., 1940).

the contract as still binding and, when the day of performance arrives, proceed to enforce his contract as of that time. Such renunciation is not a breach of the contract unless it is treated as such by the adverse party. Upon such a repudiation of an executory agreement by one party, the other may make his choice between two courses open to him, but can neither confuse them or take both.

Where the life insurance contract includes provisions for disability benefits payable in instalments and the company denies the insured's claim for those benefits, the breach is a present one, but the right of action concerns only the benefit due at that time. Benefits to fall due in the future are not includible in the damages sought. This point has led to the use of the term "anticipatory breach" in connection with actions for damages measurable not only by the amount of the benefit presently due but by all the instalments which might become due in the future as well. It is this element of futurity which prompts the use of the anticipatory breach approach.

Nevertheless, in the law of contracts generally, the doctrine of anticipatory breach is not ordinarily held to apply if the promise involves only the payment of money. Nor does it usually apply to any contracts except those which involve mutual and interdependent obligations, and it will be recalled that the life insurance contract is unilateral in nature. The obligations under the life contract are not interdependent; they are the obligations of the company alone.

It is not surprising, therefore, that court decisions upholding the application of the doctrine of anticipatory breach in the case of the life insurance contract are in the minority.

The majority holdings are summarized in the case of *John Hancock Mutual Life Insurance Company* v. *Cohen,*[10] as follows:

> We conclude the general rule to be that the doctrine of anticipatory breach has no application to suits to enforce contracts for future payment of money only, in installments or otherwise. *Cobb* v. *Pacific Mutual, supra; Flinn* v. *Mowry, supra; Brix* v. *People's Mutual Life Ins. Co., supra; Sulyok* v. *Penzintezeti,* 111 N.Y.S. 2, 75, 82; 105 A.L.R. 460; Restatement, Contracts, §§ 316-318; 5 Williston on Contracts, 3740-3743; 12 Cal. Juris. 2d, Contracts, §§ 246-250; see also Calif. L. Rev. 216.

[10] 254 F.2d 417 (U.S.C.A. Cal., 1958).

PART IV
The File Is Closed

CHAPTER XVIII

The Benefit Is Paid

IN ONE FORM OR ANOTHER, every life insurance policy contains a promise to pay a stated sum to the beneficiary, upon receipt in the home office of due proof that the insured died while the policy was in force. Payment of this benefit is the purpose of the insurance, and the purpose of this chapter is to explore the ways in which this promise, and those related to it, are fulfilled and some of the legal problems that may be involved.

REVIEWING DEATH CLAIMS

The Conditions of the Promise

We have frequently noted that the life insurance contract is a conditional contract. The basic promise, to pay the death benefit, is conditioned on the payment of premiums as specified in the policy. The company must also receive "due proof" that the insured died and that all other conditions specified in the policy have been met.

Claim Review

The exchange of individual uncertainty for group certainty is the essence of life insurance. Thus payment of death claims as they arise carries out the purpose of the company. The aleatory nature of the contract, however, that is to say, the possibility of receiving a large payment as a death benefit after having paid a very small amount in premiums, constitutes a grave temptation to the unscrupulous to misuse the life insurance contract for fraudulent purposes. For this reason, death claims are carefully reviewed by a life insurance company.

Nevertheless, life insurance ordinarily constitutes the resource most immediately available to the widow at a time when ready funds are most seriously needed. For this reason, life insurance companies consider it an essential part of their service to pay death claims the same day completed proofs of loss are received.

Is The Benefit Payable?

Administratively, the claims examiner reviews a claim for many things. Most important, of course, is the question of whether the benefit is payable. Is the policy on a premium paying basis? Did death occur during the suicide period, and if so, is there a possibility that the insured took his own life? Is accidental death coverage involved, and did death occur under circumstances where there might be a question on this point?

The claims reviewer must be constantly alert for evidence of misrepresentation and fraud. Deaths which occur during the contestable period, therefore, are scrutinized with particular care since it is only during this period that the company can interpose the defense of material misrepresentation or fraud.

Evidence of Death. Generally speaking, a certified copy of the death certificate is accepted as satisfactory evidence that the insured is dead. Nevertheless, this does not mean that it cannot be challenged and other evidence presented to show that the certificate is incorrect. In some instances, also, the reported cause of death is open to question. The evaluation of the death certificate as competent evidence of the facts it sets forth, therefore, constitutes a separate legal question in and of itself.

To Whom Is the Benefit Payable?

Obviously, claim should be made by the beneficiary. However, in cases where the policyholder has indicated his wishes to change the beneficiary but has not completed the procedures necessary to make the change effective, determining the correct beneficiary may constitute a very definite legal problem. In this connection, it should be borne in mind that legal problems of this kind are not the rule; they are the exception. Hundreds of claims are processed and paid without question. When a legal problem is revealed, however, the claim is given individual consideration and the problem must be resolved before payment is made.

The Estate of the Insured. If the benefit is payable to the estate of the insured, the proper claimant is the administrator or executor of that estate, and the company will require evidence of the appointment. Ordinarily, in such cases, a certified copy of the Letters of Administration or comparable documents are requested.

The Trustee-Beneficiary. Policies are sometimes made payable to trustees. Here the proceeds will be claimed by the trustee, but the company will need evidence of the trustee's appointment and power to act. Certified copies of the trust agreement itself are necessary in some cases. In this, as in all cases, the important thing is to be quite certain that the person to whom payment is made is the person entitled to payment, both by the terms of the contract and the law.

Minor Beneficiaries. Some of the most difficult questions are presented in connection with minor beneficiaries. The minor's capacity to receive and give a valid receipt for the proceeds of the life insurance contract is affected by many laws and circumstances. As we have noted, many of the states have statutes which make the minor capable of effecting a binding contract of life insurance as if he were an adult, in specifically designated cases. However, these statutes must be carefully checked. For instance, the Illinois statute, quoted in Chapter II of this book, removes the disability of the minor with respect to the purchase of contracts of insurance on his own life or the lives of his wife or children. Nevertheless, it does not remove the minor's disability with respect to his right to receive and to be bound by his receipt for the proceeds of life insurance on the life of someone else.

Where a guardian has been appointed, claim should be filed by him and supported by a certified copy of the court order appointing him. It should, perhaps, be noted that this appointment is just as necessary in the case of a surviving parent who is named guardian as in connection with a nonrelative. The parent is the *guardian of the person* of the child, but except under the civil law and laws derived from it, he has no right to receive or control any part of the estate of the child. Thus payment of the proceeds of a life insurance policy naming a minor beneficiary can only be made to the guardian of the estate of the minor. No one else has the power to give an effective receipt for such payment. A number of the states have laws making it possible to pay to and receive an effective receipt from persons other than the legally appointed guardian of the estate of a minor where the amount in question is less than a stated sum. For instance, the Illinois law makes such a provision with respect to amounts not in excess of $1,000, and provides as follows:

Upon receiving an affidavit that the personal estate of a minor does not exceed one thousand dollars in value, that no guardian has been appointed for his estate, and that the affiant is a parent or a person standing *in loco parentis* to the minor, any person or corporation indebted to or holding personal estate of the minor may pay the amount of the indebtedness or deliver personal estate to the affiant. In the same manner, and upon like proof any person or corporation having the responsibility for the issuance or transfer of stocks, bonds or other personal estate may issue or transfer the stocks, bonds or other personal estate to or in the name of the affiant. Upon the payment, delivery, transfer or issuance pursuant to the affidavit, the person or corporation is released to the same extent as if the payment, delivery, transfer or issuance had been made to the legally qualified guardian of the minor and is not required to see to the application or disposition of the property.[1]

---

[1] Illinois Revised Statutes, Chap. 3, Sec. 480 (1959).

Pennsylvania has an unusual kind of law which makes it possible to name a guardian in the beneficiary designation section of a life insurance policy. This statute reads as follows:

Any person, who hereafter makes a deed or gift *inter vivos* or exercises a right under an insurance or annuity policy to designate the beneficiary to receive the proceeds of such policy, may in such deed or in the instrument creating such gift or designating such beneficiary, appoint a guardian of the estate or interest of each beneficiary named therein who shall be a minor or otherwise incompetent. Payment by an insurance company to the guardian of such beneficiary so appointed shall discharge the insurance company to the extent of such payment to the same effect as payment to an otherwise duly appointed and qualified guardian.[2]

The New York Insurance Law permits a minor of the age of eighteen years to receive and give a binding receipt for insurance proceeds in a single sum of not more than $3,000 or for periodical payments of that amount under a settlement agreement with the life insurance company. The statute reads as follows:

Any minor domiciled in this state, who shall have attained the age of eighteen years, shall be deemed competent to receive, and to give a full acquittance and discharge for a single sum or for periodical payments, not exceeding three thousand dollars in any one year, payable by a life insurance company under the maturity, death or settlement agreement provisions in effect or elected by such minor under a life insurance policy or annuity contract, provided such policy, contract or agreement shall provide for the payment or payments to such minor and provided that prior to such payment the company has not received written notice of the appointment of a duly qualified guardian of the property of such minor; but no such minor shall be deemed competent to alienate the right to such payment or payments or to anticipate the same.[3]

THE INSURED TAKES HIS LIFE

Suicide, a Legal Concept

Suicide has been defined as "the deliberate termination of one's existence, while in the possession and enjoyment of his mental faculties."[4] Mere self-destruction is not suicide, in the legal sense of the word. For this reason, the words "sane or insane," which are often included in life insurance policies, extend the meaning of suicide considerably beyond its usual legal significance.

In the Absence of a Policy Provision. Where there is no express policy provision and the policy is payable to the estate of the insured, the majority of courts have held that intentional self-destruction while sane

---

[2] Purdon's Penna. Statutes, Title 20, Decedents' and Trust Estates, Sec. 1178.

[3] New York Insurance Law, Sec. 145.

[4] *Black's Law Dictionary* (West Publishing Co., 1933), p. 1676.

is not a risk that is covered by the policy. If the policy is payable to a third person, however, recovery has been allowed. It seems the universal holding that if there is no express policy provision to the contrary, self-destruction while insane is covered by the policy exactly as any other death would be.

The Policy Provision. By far the majority of present-day life insurance policies contain a provision expressly excepting suicide from coverage for a limited period of time. Usually this period is two years, sometimes one, and it is included for the purpose of effecting an equitable compromise between two acknowledgedly incompatible interests. First there is the generally recognized purpose of life insurance, that it is to provide a sum payable at death for the benefit of the dependents of the insured. This need is just as definite if the insured commits suicide as if he is killed in an automobile accident. On the other hand, there is the fact that the procurement of life insurance for the purpose of inequitable gain by reason of suicide would definitely be unfair to the other insureds and perhaps against public policy as having a tendency to encourage the taking of one's own life. In any case, it is believed that a two-year suicide clause is sufficient to protect the company against those persons who might be tempted to make a profitable occasion of their already decided upon departure from this life.

Few people, it is thought, will procure a life insurance policy with the intention of committing suicide and then wait two years before doing so. In any case, after two years the company is willing to assume any chances of suicide as one of the normal exigencies of life.

Statutes. Some of the states have statutes expressly permitting the life insurance companies to except the risk of suicide. Usually these statutes specify a period, one year or two, for which the risk may be excepted, and after that suicide will be covered.[5] The Missouri statute on this subject is the most unusual and has serious implications for the life insurance company doing business in that state. It reads as follows:

In all suits upon policies of insurance on life hereafter issued by any company doing business in this state to a citizen of this state, it shall be no

---

[5] Specifically, seven states have statutes on the subject. They differ widely. Colorado, North Dakota, and Utah, for example, all provide that suicide after one year shall not be a defense. New York has a two-year period for legal reserve companies, while Virginia permits a provision providing for the return of premiums only in the event of suicide within two years from the policy date. The Missouri statute provides that suicide shall not be a defense unless it was contemplated by the insured at the time of application, while the Georgia statute provides simply that "Death by suicide . . . shall release the insurer from the obligation of his contract." (Colo. Rev. Stat. 1953, Sec. 72-3-23; N. Dak. Rev. Code 1943, Sec. 26-0324; Utah Code Ann., 1953, Sec. 31-22-07; N. York Consol. Laws, 1953, Chap. 28, Art. 14, Sec. 155; Va. Code, Sec. 38.1-437; Missouri Stat. Ann., 1949, Tit. 24, Sec. 376.620; Ga. Code Ann. 1953, Sec. 56-909.)

defense that the insured committed suicide, unless it shall be shown to the satisfaction of the court or jury trying the cause, that the insured contemplated suicide at the time he made his application for the policy, and any stipulation in the policy to the contrary shall be void.[6]

Practically speaking, it is almost impossible to prove the intent of the applicant when he signed the application for life insurance. The practical effect of this statute, therefore, is to prohibit any excepting of the risk of suicide from a life insurance policy issued to a citizen of Missouri.

This statute has been litigated extensively, but it has been held constitutional and has even been held to apply to a policy issued when the insured was a resident of another state but which was reinstated after he became a resident of Missouri.

Interpretation of the Suicide Provision. Policy provisions excepting death by "suicide" are generally interpreted to refer only to self-destruction of the insured while sane. When the words "sane or insane" are used, there is a conflict in the court decisions. Where the policy provides that suicide, "sane or insane" is a risk not assumed, the majority of courts have held that self-destruction while insane is a valid exclusion. However, there is a strong minority group of courts which take the position that self-destruction, if the insured is so insane as not to realize the natural consequences of his act, is not suicide "sane or insane." In these latter cases especially, the question of what constitutes a state of insanity is important.

Two Rules. Two general rules have been developed in connection with the question of what actually is meant by the word "insanity" in this connection. One rule is followed by the English courts and in this country by the courts of Massachusetts and New York. It is called the English Rule. Under this rule, if the insured understood the consequences of his act and hoped for death, it is a death within the suicide exclusion. In other words, it is suicide.

The other rule is called the American Rule. It does not differ a great deal from the English Rule. Under the American Rule, if the insured voluntarily takes action which causes his death, knowing that death will result, but with his mental faculties so badly impaired that he does not understand the moral and other consequences of his act, or if he is under the influence of an irresistible, insane impulse, it is not suicide within the exclusion.

Presumption against Suicide. At the present time the majority of suicide cases relate to questions of fact and whether the self-destruction in question was actually suicide. Because the factual situations are especially difficult to interpret, the courts have developed a very strong

---

[6] Mo. Stat. Ann., 1949, Tit. 24, Sec. 376.620.

presumption against suicide. In other words, the courts take the point of view that self-destruction is against the natural inclinations of the average person. Therefore, if the facts are susceptible to more than one interpretation the presumption is that the insured did not take his own life. Since the presumption is against suicide, the party wishing to establish that the death *was* suicide has the burden of supporting his contention with enough evidence to satisfy a court of law. In life insurance cases the party wishing to establish this—that is, the party with the burden of proof—is the life insurance company.

Illustrative Case. The following case has been selected as illustrative because it does not involve any question of the accidental death benefit. It deals solely with the question of suicide as an affirmative defense [7] on the part of the life insurance company. It is printed here in the words of the court, as follows:

ANGELUS, Respondent v. *GOVERNMENT PERSONNEL LIFE INS. CO., Appellant* [8]

(Washington Supreme Court. Appeal from Superior Court, Spokane County.)

WEAVER, J.: Plaintiff, mother of the insured, is beneficiary under an insurance policy on her son's life, issued by defendant insurance company. She brings this action on the policy, alleging that the insured died October 31, 1955, as the result of a gunshot wound.

Defendant, by affirmative defense in the nature of confession and avoidance, admits the contract of insurance that, in part, provides:

If the Insured shall commit suicide while sane or insane within two years from the date of issue hereof [April 1, 1954], the liability of the Company under this policy will be limited to the premiums that have been paid hereon and no more.

Defendant further alleges that the insured, "by his own act, took his life by shooting himself with a .45 calibre revolver," and thus committed suicide.

The insured died in Japan while on active duty with the armed forces of the United States. No testimony was taken at the trial. Counsel stipulated

. . . that the Marine Corps Investigation, and enclosures, . . . shall be all of the evidence in the above entitled action.

and

. . . that the Court is to disregard any opinions relative to whether or not the deceased died as a result of accident or suicide, which opinions were given by the investigating officer, Major Robert S. Hemstad.

The trial court did not have the advantage of seeing and listening to witnesses. It only considered the same written record that has been certified to us in its entirety. We may, therefore, determine the merits of the question raised without reference to the findings of fact entered by the trial court. *In re Black,* 47Wn. (2d) 42, 45, 287, P.2d 96 (1955).

It should be noted that we are only concerned with recovery under the

_____

[7] An affirmative defense in this connection simply means a defense which must be specifically interposed by the defendant (in this case, the company). The company then has the burden of proving its contention.

[8] 321 P.2d 545 (Wash., 1958).

terms of a *life* insurance policy. We are *not* concerned with (a) death under the terms of an accident insurance policy, nor (b) with death under the provision of a life insurance policy that provides for a recovery of double-the-face value of the policy in the event of death by accidental means, as may be defined therein.

The sole question is: Did decedent commit suicide?

Plaintiff establishes a *prima facie* case with evidence that the insured died while the policy of life insurance was in effect. Liability follows a showing of death, unless there is an affirmative showing that death was within an exception contained in the policy.

In this case, suicide is an affirmative defense. The insurance company must establish, by a preponderance of the evidence (*Selover* v. *Aetna Life Ins. Co.,* 180 Wash. 236, 38 P.2d 1059 (1934), that the wound that caused the death of the insured was intentionally self-inflicted. *New York Life Ins. Co.* v. *Newport,* 1 Wn. (2d) 511, 517, 519, 96 P.2d 449 (1939). Although not necessarily controlling, the presence or absence of motive for suicide is an element to be taken into consideration.

There is very little, if any, dispute as to the facts surrounding the death of the insured. The disagreement is over the conclusion to be drawn from these facts.

The following appears from the written statements gathered by the investigating officer:

Decedent, twenty years old at the time of his death on October 31, 1955, was attached to a Marine fighter squadron as an aircraft radar technician. He was assigned to a guard company for temporary duty, which was to terminate the day of his death.

His guard duties required that he be familiar with a .45 calibre automatic pistol. On numerous occasions, while acting as corporal of the guard, he had given instruction on the use of the automatic pistol and on safety precautions to be observed while handling it.

Throughout decedent's tour of duty with the guard, all pistols assigned to personnel on post or on duty were kept with a loaded clip inserted, but no round of ammunition was in the chamber. It was common knowledge among members of the guard that all pistols in actual physical custody of guard personnel were loaded.

Decedent is described as a happy-go-lucky individual with no known disturbing problems. He was a good worker, cheerful, and competent in his temporary additional duty assignment. One of his associates states:

"He was an exceptionally good natured marine and I never knew him to worry or sweat anything. I had known him a good while and was a very close friend of his. It always appeared to me life was just a big joke to him and I told him several times he ought to take things more seriously."

About eleven a.m. the day of his death, decedent talked with Corporal Last, who reported that he "seemed to be in a very good mood. He was especially happy because he was off guard and had liberty that night."

About five p.m. of the same day, Sergeant Nelson asked decedent "when he was coming back to work with me in fire control. He told me that he would be down in the morning and ready to go to work."

About five-thirty p.m. decedent and Corporal Tishler, with whom he was going on liberty, entered hut No. 5. Decedent talked with Corporal Ball, who stated:

". . . He was laughing and seemed to be in very good spirits as he was going on liberty and he was kidding me because I had the duty. He walked into the head [lavatory] to comb his hair and I heard him laugh and then the report of the .45."

While Corporal Tishler was combing his hair, decedent grabbed a pistol belt hanging on a peg, pulled the pistol out of the holster, "jacked a round into the chamber," put the pistol to his head, and said "here's to it," and fired the pistol. He died several hours later.

On previous occasions, decedent had been observed playing a modified version of "Russian Roulette" with a .45 calibre automatic pistol, the same type which caused his death. He would squeeze the release on the clip, allow it to slide down, then pull the slide to the rear, and release it. If the clip dropped about half an inch, the slide would not pick up a round from the clip and place it in the chamber. The clip was then locked in place, the pistol placed at his temple, and the trigger pulled. In truth, this is not "Russian Roulette," which is played with a revolver and not an automatic pistol. His safety depended upon sleight-of-hand and not chance.

He would never do it unless he was just trying to "shake someone up." He always laughed afterwards.

One witness stated that *the clip was not in the weapon* when it was recovered from the floor after the shooting. Another witness stated, when describing the weapon after the shooting,

The pistol was fully cocked with one (1) round in the chamber and three (3) rounds in the magazine *when recovered.*

This suggests the hypothesis that decedent believed he had released the clip and caused it to drop, so that the slide had not "jacked a round into the chamber" of the pistol. If this be true, he was mistaken.

In *United Benefit Life Ins. Co.* v. *Schott,* 296 Ky. 789, 796, 177 S.W.2d 581, 150 A.L.R. 1359 (1943), a case factually akin to the instant one, the court said:

The brandishing and flourishing of the weapons, in the manner described by Fields and McDowell, do not impress us as having been more than the mere blustering and swaggering of a swashbuckler. Persons intent upon committing suicide are not apt to behave in that manner.

We agree with the trial court; appellant did not establish suicide by a preponderance of the evidence.

The judgment is affirmed.[9]

DEATH AS THE RESULT OF WAR

Under most life insurance policies today, death as the result of suicide during a specified suicide period is a risk not assumed. The death benefit, therefore, is not ordinarily payable under such circumstances. The amount payable is sometimes limited also if death occurs as the result of or while the insured is in the military service of a nation at war, if the policy includes a war hazard limitation provision.

What Is War? Let us say that death occurs while the insured is in military service, engaged in actual fighting, and the policy includes a provision specifically limiting the liability of the company to a return

---

[9] Note that suicide, the "affirmative defense," was not proved. Therefore, judgment is for the plaintiff.

of premiums or the reserve under the policy if death occurs as the result of war or while the insured is in military service. If these things are true, two basic questions are presented. The first concerns the meaning of the word "war" as used in the contract. The second has to do with the meaning of the words "as the result of" or "while in military service."

The action of the United Nations armed forces in connection with the communist aggression in Korea in 1950 presented one of the more recent situations involving a real question as to what constitutes war in the contractual sense of the word. Previously, the same question had been raised in connection with deaths at Pearl Harbor. Some three thousand military and naval personnel were killed there on December 7, 1941, but in four cases on the subject it was held that a state of war, as that word was used in the war clause of life insurance policies, did not exist until war was officially declared by Congress on December 8, 1941.

In connection with the Korean conflict, court decisions varied. For instance in the case of *Beley* v. *Pennsylvania Mutual Life Insurance Company* [10] the court held that the word must be given its strict constitutional meaning. War was not actually declared by Congress; therefore, the activity in Korea was not war. A New Jersey court, considering the same question shortly afterward, held that the words must be given their "ordinary and generally accepted meaning" rather than their technical or legal meaning, and held that the Korean hostilities constituted war, in the practical or ordinarily accepted meaning of the word. This latter point of view has been followed by the majority of the appellate courts and the federal district courts in considering the question with respect to Korea.

It has been submitted [11] that a state of war results wherever armed intervention is met by armed resistance. This would include the fatalities at Pearl Harbor as well as the deaths in Korea.

Included in the question, "What is war?" is the second question: "When does war cease?" It is rather generally agreed that it does not cease when the actual shooting ends. But does it end when an armistice is signed? The consensus is that the hostilities in Korea, which began in June, 1950, constituted war in the contractual sense of the word and that war continued at least until August, 1954.

Effect of "Status" versus "Result" Wording. The wordings of the various war clauses which have been the subject of litigation have varied widely and the court decisions are often difficult to reconcile. Generally, the clauses fall into two large groups—those limiting the

---

[10] 373 Pa. 231, 95 A.2d 202, cert. denied, 346 U.S. 820 (1953).

[11] See *The Georgetown Law Journal*, Vol. 45, No. 1, p. 45: "The Legal Status of the Korean Hostilities," by A. Kenneth Pye.

amount payable if death of the insured occurs "while" he is in military service and those limiting liability if death occurs as the "result" of such service. The former is often referred to as the "status" clause since the limitation applies simply because of the status of the insured at the time of his death. The latter is a "result" clause since the limitation is effective only if the death is the result of military service.

Ordinarily, there is little question with respect to the effect of a war clause of either the status or the result type if death occurs in actual combat. War clauses have generally been held valid, and some states have laws specifically prescribing the wording that the companies may use. The war clause is ordinarily worded in such a way as to be a limitation and not a forfeiture, so it is not generally considered to be in conflict with the incontestable clause. Nevertheless, such limitations are ordinarily listed as specific exceptions in the incontestable clause itself in order to preclude any question on this point.

The principal question arises when the insured meets his death while in service but from a cause which is not related to war in the ordinarily accepted meaning of the term. This question was presented in an especially difficult form during the influenza epidemic of World War I. The war clause most commonly used at that time provided that the liability of the company would be limited in case the death of the insured occurred "while" the insured was "engaged in" military or naval service in time of war. The influenza epidemic accounted for the deaths of large numbers of persons in military service, just as it did among the civilian population. For this reason, it seemed especially difficult to justify a limitation which applied only to those who happened to be in military service when they died. As a result, the term "engaged in" was ordinarily interpreted to mean that military service must in some way have caused the death.

In World War II, the insurance companies and the courts had their World War I experience on which to draw and "status" clauses were ordinarily sufficiently free of ambiguity that they were upheld. For a summary of the different types of court decisions and as an illustration of a status clause that was upheld, the following case is printed with minor omissions of technical detail.

JORGENSON, Plaintiff, Appellant v. METROPOLITAN LIFE INSURANCE CO., Defendant, Respondent.[12]
(New Jersey Supreme Court.)

WACHENFELD, J.: This case presents the construction and validity of a life insurance policy provision exempting liability for accidental death benefit, i.e., double indemnity, where death occurs while insured is in military or naval service in time of war.

___

[12] 136 N.J.L. 148, 55 A.2d 2 (1947).

The respondent issued on August 3, 1936 two policies of life insurance on the life of Wilbur Jorgenson under which the appellant, his wife, was the beneficiary. Each policy was for the principal sum of $500 and provided double that sum would become due and payable as a result of the accidental death of the insured, but liability was limited by the following provision:

No Accidental Death Benefit will be paid if the death of the Insured is the result of self-destruction . . . or while the Insured is in military or naval service in time of war.

On October 18, 1944, the insured was a member of the United States Army in the corps of military police on duty at Bangalore, India. While on town patrol in that city, the motorcycle which he was riding became involved in an accident and he suffered a fractured skull from which he died the same date.

Upon proof of death and claim for $1,000 under each policy, the company only paid the principal sum of $500, refusing to pay the sum due for accidental death on the ground the insured was not covered since he was a member of the military forces in time of war. In an action instituted to recover the additional $500 under each policy, the Middlesex Court of Common Pleas, on a stipulation of facts, rendered judgment in favor of the respondent.

The first question presented is one of construction as to whether the provision exempting liability of the insurer applies to death from any cause while insured is in military service or merely to death due to a cause peculiar to such service. Admittedly the insured was a member of the United States armed forces, stationed in India in time of war at the time of his death. The language of the exemption clause clearly expressed the intention to establish such status as the basis of exemption from liability. *Caruso* v. *John Hancock Mutual Life Ins. Co.*, 25 N.J. Misc. 318.

It is argued that behind the apparent clarity of the clause there lurks an ambiguity which should be resolved in favor of the insured. This argument stems from decisions in other jurisdictions which indicate conflicting results have been reached in the interpretation of military or naval service exemption provisions. The phraseology of these policies is of paramount consideration in determining whether status or causation of military service is intended as the basis for exemption of liability. Where status of military service has been rejected as the basis of exemption, there has been, in most cases, a word or phrase indicating that death due to a cause peculiar to military service was intended, or at least a doubt was raised which should be resolved in favor of the insured. In this category are the cases construing the exemption of liability for death while insured is "engaged" in military service. . . .

Other cases have reached the same conclusion where the insurance clause exempted liability for death "in consequence of" military service, *Gorder* v. *Lincoln National Life Ins. Co.*, 46 N.D. 192, 180 N.W. 514, or death "resulting from military service." . . .

On the other hand, it has been held the status of the insured as a member of the armed forces was contemplated by a provision exempting liability for death "while in" the military service. *Life & Casualty Ins. Co.* v. *McLeod*, 70 Ga. App. 181, 27 S.E. (2d) 871. . . .

Certain rules for the construction of insurance contracts have been enunciated by the courts of this State. Forfeitures of insurance policies are not favored in the law and such policies will be liberally construed to uphold the contract. *Hampton* v. *Hartford Fire Ins. Co.*, 65 N.J.L. 265; *Rockmiss* v.

New Jersey Manufacturers, etc. Co., 112 N.J.L. 136. The insurer having in most cases drawn the particular policy, all doubt as to the construction of terms in an insurance policy is to be construed most strongly against the insurer and in favor of the insured. . . .

The words in an insurance policy, however, will be given their ordinary and usual meaning; and if there is no ambiguity a strained or distorted construction will not be applied. . . . As stated in *Kupfersmith* v. *Delaware Ins. Co.*, 84 N.J.L. 271, 275, and followed in *Smith* v. *Fidelity & Deposit Co.*, 98 N.J.L. 534:

> The law will not make a better contract for the parties than they themselves have seen fit to enter into, or alter it for the benefit of one party and to the detriment of the other. The judicial function of a court of law is to enforce a contract as it is written.

The terms of the instant contract are clear. The latent ambiguity found by courts of other jurisdictions in construing military service exemption clauses is not applicable here since those provisions were of different terminology. To adopt the view that military service status was not meant by this clause would do violence to the express terms of the contract and "under such circumstances would be to misconstrue the terms of a contract concerning which there is no room for construction, because the meaning is perfectly plain." *Harris* v. *American Casualty Co.*, 83 N.J.L. 641, 645.

The validity of this military service exemption clause is challenged as being contrary to public policy. It is argued such a provision tends to deter voluntary enlistment and to induce the holder of such a policy to resist involuntary service.

The purpose of such a clause is not insidious or difficult to understand. Military or naval service in time of war, whether in training or combat, is admittedly hazardous, fraught with incalculable danger. It is difficult to determine the scope of risks assumed by members of the armed forces in view of the methods of warfare, keeping in mind the possible devastation of present and future developments. An insurance company has the right to limit its liability to particular risks. If it will only assume risks which it feels can be calculated, and clearly and plainly so states, this court will not increase such liability.

No evidence has been presented showing a tendency or effect of this provision to deter enlistments; nor does the provision cause a forfeiture of the policy, but merely suspends liability of the company during the period of service, and that for only double indemnity.

Public policy has been defined by decisions of this State as "that principle of law which holds that no person can lawfully do that which has a tendency to be injurious to the public, or against the public good." *Driver* v. *Smith*, 89 N.J. Eq. 339, 358. Public policy, however, is not a circumscribed legal principle only adverted to in a particular case but, rather, underlies all judicial action. Stemming from our State and Federal Constitutions, it is also public policy to uphold the freedom of contract, but this court is reluctant to enforce the exercise of that freedom where it tends to result in injury to persons beyond the immediate parties. Hence, an agreement to surrender a personal right will not be invalidated if its effect is limited to the parties thereto . . . ; but an agreement extends beyond the scope of the immediate parties when it is caculated to interfere with the production of necessary war material, *Driver* v. *Smith*, *supra*, or to disrupt the family relationship of others,

Girard Trust Co. v. *Schmitz*, 129 N.J. Eq. 444, or to tend improperly to influence official action. *Stone* v. *William Steinen Mfg. Co.*, 133 N.J.L. 16.

The validity of clauses of this type has been uniformly upheld by other jurisdictions. The court in *Miller* v. *Illinois Bankers' Life Ass'n*, 138 Ark. 442, 212 S.W. 310, 7 A.L.R. 378, 380, succinctly explained:

> We do not think the argument is well-founded. An insurance company has the right to select the particular risks it is willing to assume, and there is no public policy against a contract of this sort exempting the insurance company, in advance, from liability for death of the insured while in the military or naval service of the government. The stipulation does not provide for a forfeiture of the policy, merely for an exemption from liability under certain circumstances and conditions. It holds out no inducements to the insured to refrain from enlistment in his country's service, and does not constitute, in any sense, an agreement not to enlist or evade the Draft Law. No authorities are cited by counsel in support of the contention, and we are unable to find any cases in which the question has been raised.

This result has subsequently been specifically approved in other jurisdictions. . . .

Having determined that the provision concerned applies to the instant case and its validity is not contrary to public policy, the respondent is not liable for double indemnity.

Judgment affirmed, but without costs.

DEATH AS THE RESULT OF AVIATION

The aviation exclusion, found in some, though not many, life insurance policies today, simply limits the amount payable if death occurs as the result of certain specified aviation activities. Ordinarily the exclusion is used in cases where there is an added risk by reason of aviation activities on the part of the proposed insured and the applicant does not wish to pay the added premium necessary to compensate for the added risk.

The increasing safety of aviation in general has been reflected in a gradual but steady liberalization of aviation restrictions, and today the exclusions used ordinarily do not apply if the insured is being transported as a passenger only. Often liberalizations of company policy apply to previously issued policies also, so that the actual handling of a claim may reflect practices more liberal than the wording of the contract itself would indicate.

Cases reaching the courts have involved many questions of policy wording and a great many cases interpret specific phrases such as "fare-paying passenger" and "regularly scheduled flight." Another type of question which has sometimes been presented relates to what are essentially war deaths occurring while the insureds are in flight. In such cases as these, if the life insurance policy does not contain a war hazard exclusion, the aviation exclusion has been held to apply only to civilian aviation.

Another class of case presenting a relatively close question involves the death of an insured who brings his plane down safely but alights on a desert or a lake, for example, and loses his life by reason of perils incident to the terrain. In one such case,[13] the insured's plane landed safely on a lake, but he was drowned trying to swim to the shore. There the court said:

Defendant contends that drowning, after a forced landing of a land-based plane in cold water, is an undisputable risk associated with aerial flight in a private plane and further that it was a risk intended to be excluded from the operation of this policy. If this argument is logical it would mean also that if a person were forced to land his private plane in a pasture, where, after safely alighting, he was gored to death by a vicious bull, an insurer would not be liable on a policy containing the clause now under consideration. Likewise, such a landing made in a public highway followed by the accidental death of the insured after alighting from his plane and resulting from being struck by a passing automobile, would be similarly excluded from such a policy.

There is no evidence in this record that the death of the insured resulted directly or indirectly from injuries sustained by him while in the airplane or in falling or descending therefrom or therewith. Furthermore, there is no evidence from which such an inference can be reasonably drawn. After leaving the plane he swam a considerable distance in cold water and drowned. The exclusion clause of the policy does not apply to this case.

DEATH BY ACCIDENTAL MEANS

In Chapter VII we discussed the underlying distinction the courts of about half the states make between accidental death and death by accidental means. We have shown some of the different factual situations which sometimes present a problem under this type of coverage, but we have not mentioned one which often arises in connection with the handling of claims. This is the problem presented in connection with death under circumstances lending themselves to interpretation either as death from accidental means *or* suicide.

In cases of this kind, the presumption against suicide often plays an important part. For instance, in one case [14] the insured died as the result of injuries suffered in connection with a dynamite explosion. The court said:

There is no need to detail the evidence at length. It may be said in resume that there was no eye witness to the explosion, that some circumstances and certain statements made by the insured immediately after it occurred point strongly to suicide but that other circumstances indicate persuasively that it was an accident, and that no motive for suicide was shown. In Colorado, death by unexplained violence is presumed to have been

[13] *McDaniel* v. *Standard Accident Insurance Co.*, 221 F.2d 171 (C.A. Ill., 1955).

[14] *Parfet* v. *Kansas City Life Insurance Co.*, 128 F.2d 361 (C.C.A. Colo., 1942).

accident, evidence establishing death by violence without explanation as to the manner in which the violence was inflicted constitutes prima facie proof that the death was accidental, *Occidental Life Ins. Co.* v. *United States Nat. Bank of Denver, Colo.*, 98 Colo. 126, 53 Pac.2d 1180; and, if under the evidence death by violence can be explained on any reasonable hypothesis other than suicide, it is the duty of the court or the jury to do so, *Prudential Ins. Co. of America* v. *Cline*, 98 Colo. 275, 57 Pac.2d 1205. Taken as a whole and fairly construed, the evidence did not conclusively establish suicide. Instead, it presented an issue for the jury.

MYSTERIOUS DISAPPEARANCE

Claims based upon the mysterious disappearance of the insured present a somewhat different problem. Here the basic question does not relate to *how* death occurred but rather to whether it did. People often disappear without explanation, leaving questions relating to property rights and responsibilities, including insurance problems, to be worked out as satisfactorily as possible. Because this is not unusual, the law has developed some basic principles and presumptions in connection with the clarification of problems relating to property, some of which are used in connection with the life insurance contract. One of the most important is the presumption of death after an absence of seven years.

The Presumption of Death. The presumption of death after an unexplained absence of seven years has been developed over the last 150 years. Prior to 1800, in the absence of evidence to the contrary, an absent person was presumed to be living even though he might be ninety or one hundred years old. As generally stated today, however, a person will be presumed to be dead (a) if he has been missing from his home or usual residence for a period of seven years; (b) if such absence has been continuous and without explanation; (c) if persons most likely to hear from him have heard nothing; and (d) if he cannot be located by diligent search and inquiry. At the present time, this presumption is recognized in almost all the states, either by statute or judicial recognition of the common law rule. However, it has been abrogated by the enactment of a uniform act [15] on the subject in three states—Wisconsin, Maryland, Tennessee.

It is generally agreed that the presumption may be rebutted. This means that the person to whose advantage it is to show that death has *not* occurred may present evidence to meet the presumption. If such evidence is not offered, the decision must be that the person is dead. If such evidence is offered, the jury decides from the facts presented whether death did or did not occur.

Unexplained Absence. Sometimes it is shown that the missing person was a fugitive from justice. The majority of courts do not hold that this

[15] The Uniform Absence as Evidence of Death and Absentees' Property Act.

showing destroys the presumption, but only that it then becomes a question for the jury to decide. Similar rules are ordinarily followed in connection with missing persons who were in serious financial or domestic troubles at the time of their disappearance.

Date of Death. Often merely establishing the *fact* of death is not enough. In connection with life insurance, for instance, the actual date of death is often important. Many life insurance policies on the lives of persons missing for extended periods of time lapse prior to the expiration of seven years. Obviously it is to the advantage of the beneficiary to prove, if possible, that the insured actually met his death sometime during the period of seven years and prior to the date the policy lapsed.

There are two rules with respect to establishing the date of death. Under the majority (or English) rule, the missing person is presumed to be dead at the end of the seven years but the exact time of death is left open to be established separately. Under the minority rule, the missing person is presumed to have died at the end of the period. Under the latter rule the person wishing to establish death prior to that time has the burden of introducing evidence to that effect. Thus in either case it is necessary to present evidence relating to the exact date of death. The principal difference relates to the amount and kind of evidence that will suffice. Under the minority rule, it is usually necessary to show that the insured was exposed to some specific peril before an earlier date of death can be established. Under the majority rule, on the other hand, evidence of character, habits, domestic relations, and other circumstances may ordinarily be presented.

In either case, the only safe procedure under a life insurance policy is for the beneficiary to continue payment of premiums until the end of the seven-year period when the question can be judicially settled. If, at that time, death is determined to have occurred prior to the end of the seven years, the overpayment of premiums may be recovered by the payor.

Uniform Act. The Uniform Absence as Evidence of Death and Absentees' Property Act, in effect in Maryland, Tennessee, and Wisconsin, was prepared some twenty years ago by the National Conference of Commissioners on Uniform State Laws. It abolishes the presumption of death after seven years' absence and provides that the issues of death and the date of death be submitted to the jury in every case.

Reappearance

One of the truly complicating aspects of this problem of mysterious disappearance, as it relates to the life insurance contract, is presented when the insured reappears after having been declared dead and after settlement of the death benefit or benefits has been made. Let us say that the Ajax Life Insurance Company paid the insurance proceeds to the beneficiary of a life insurance policy on John Doe's life after John's unexplained absence for seven years and then, two years later, John reappears. What, if any, are the rights of the company?

General Rules. The general rule is that, if the full benefit provided by the policy has been paid to the beneficiary in good faith and the insured later reappears, the amount paid may be recovered by the insurance company on the basis that it was paid under a mistake of fact. If less than the full amount provided by the policy has been paid, as in a compromise settlement, for example, it cannot be recovered. The ruling principle here is that the settlement of a doubtful claim will not be disturbed.

Company Practice. In spite of the general rule, the fact remains, of course, that the money cannot be recovered from a beneficiary who no longer has it or the equivalent in property. For this reason, and because the settlement at best is laden with uncertainty, most insurers require a bond with adequate surety when they settle any disappearance claim. If a compromise settlement is involved, the bond is imperative because the money cannot be recovered from the beneficiary.

It seems probable also that when benefits which have been paid are later recovered under these circumstances, the beneficiary is entitled to reinstatement of the policy. Thus in a suit to recover such benefits the insurance company would ordinarily offer to reinstate the policy upon payment of unpaid back premiums.

Illustrative Case

There are two aspects to this problem. One relates to the establishment of facts sufficient to justify payment of the claim in the first place. The other is concerned with the company's rights if the insured should reappear. The following case illustrates both phases of the problem and the majority rules with respect to recovery of money so paid.

PILOT LIFE INSURANCE CO. v. CUDD [16]

(South Carolina Supreme Court.)

TAYLOR, A. J.: This action was commenced in the Spartanburg County Common Pleas Court in March, 1944, by the service of summons and complaint. Plaintiff seeks to recover on the ground of alleged mistake, as alleged in the complaint, the sum of $1,013.36, paid to defendant as beneficiary under a policy on the life of her nephew and foster son, Lewis Edward Cudd, of which the sum of $1,000.00 was death benefit and $13.36 was premium refund.

Defendant answered, admitting the payment, denying mistake, and alleging that the payment was voluntary and was in the nature of a compromise settlement by plaintiff, as set forth in the answer.

[16] 208 S.C. 6, 36 S.E.2d 860 (1945).

The cause came on for trial on January 16, 1945, before Honorable William H. Grimball, presiding Circuit Judge, and a jury.

At the conclusion of all the evidence, motion was made for judgment in favor of each party. After argument his Honor directed a verdict in plaintiff's favor for $1,013.36. Later during the term, his Honor filed an order granting judgment for plaintiff accordingly, and judgment has been duly entered in favor of plaintiff thereon.

In due time defendant served notice of intention to appeal to the Supreme Court from the rulings, orders, decrees, and judgments of the presiding Judge and the cause now comes before this Court on the transcript of record and exceptions which for all practical purposes raise the following issues:

(1) Was such payment a material mistake of fact or error of judgment on the part of the company?

(2) Was such payment a voluntary one?

(3) Was such payment a compromise settlement by plaintiff?

The respondent, Pilot Life Insurance Company, issued its policy, dated April 12, 1936, for $1,000.00 on the life of Lewis Edward Cudd, naming the insured's aunt and adopted mother as beneficiary; on or about November 18, 1942, the insured sailed from Ceylon as a member of the Merchant Marine aboard the American Export Lines vessel, Swaokla; on January 16, 1943, Elizabeth Blackwell Cudd who was married to the insured in April, 1942, received the following letter from the War Shipping Administration:

WAR SHIPPING ADMINISTRATION

> 99 John Street
> New York, New York
> January 15th, 1943

Mrs. Elizabeth Cudd
111 West 16th St.
New York City

Re: SA-Lewis E. Cudd

Dear Madam:

This letter will advise you that the above-named member of the crew of the indicated vessel has been reported missing as a result of enemy action.

There was war risk insurance effective upon his life. This office is in possession of documentary evidence that you were designated as the beneficiary of this insurance. In order to facilitate the payment thereof, if and when it is determined to be due and payable, a questionaire is herewith enclosed for your completion and return to this office with the documents checked on page 5 thereof. A certified copy of an English translation should, if necessary, accompany the documents requested.

Your prompt attention to this matter will be appreciated.

> Yours very truly,
>
> (s) E. A. Bloomquist
> Chief Adjuster
> Division of Wartime Insurance

On January 21, 1943, she received the following telegram from the Navy Department:

The Navy Department deeply regrets to inform you that your husband, Lewis Edward Cudd, is missing and presumed lost following action in the performance of his duty and in the service of his country. The Coast Guard appreciates your great anxiety and will furnish you further information promptly when received. To prevent possible aid to our enemies please do not divulge the name of his ship.

Vice-Admiral R. R. Waesche, Commandant,
U. S. Coast Guard.

On February 9, 1943, the Maritime War Emergency Board issued the following Certificate of Presumptive Death:

Maritime War Emergency Board
Washington, D.C.
Certificate of Presumptive Death
Form A

I hereby certify that the Maritime War Emergency Board has found that Lewis Edward Cudd with the rating of 2nd Cook and Baker is presumed to have died on or about November 28, 1942, as a result of a cause specified in the applicable Decisions of the Maritime War Emergency Board; and that under date of February 9, 1943, the Maritime Emergency Board duly made and entered its Order declaring said person presumptively dead in accordance with the provisions of its applicable Decisions and authorized the Secretary of the Board to issue a Certificate of Presumptive Death of said person.
Dated May 8, 1943

(s) Erich Nielsen
Secretary

. . . The local agent inquired of the beneficiary whether or not she had received a Certificate of Presumptive Death and learned it was in the possession of the wife, thereupon respondent communicated with the Maritime War Emergency Board stating that it had been advised of the death of the insured and requested "a copy of the original Certificate of Presumptive Death" and received same under date of May 8, 1943, which was based on the original order of the Board dated February 9, 1943, together with their letter advising "We believe this will be sufficient for you to pay the beneficiary the amount of the policy carried by you on the deceased." As a result of this death, claims were signed and filed by the appellant. Respondent then issued its check for $1,013.36 covering the face amount of the policy plus a premium payment of $13.36 which had been paid after the date of presumptive death. This check was delivered to the beneficiary who endorsed it and received payment therefor, June 7, 1943, respondent having at the time of delivery of the check taken up the original policy.

On August 20, 1943, the U. S. Coast Guard wrote the wife, Mrs. Elizabeth Cudd; said letter being signed by Lieutenant of the Coast Guard, title "Chief, Merchant Marine Personnel Records and Welfare Section" as follows:

You are advised that this office is in receipt of an official report from the Prisoner of War Information Bureau, through the International Red Cross, that your husband, Lewis Edward Cudd, is a prisoner of War of Japan. He is interned in the Hakodate Prisoner of War Camp located on Hokkaido Island, Japan.

All prisoner of war communications are subject to censorship; it is therefore, suggested that all such communications deal only with personal matters. To facilitate clearance in the Far East, communication should be either typed or hand-printed in capital Letters and the envelope containing any communication to your husband should be addressed as follows:

Postage Free

Civilian Internee
Mr. Lewis Edward Cudd
American Civilian Internee Held by Japan in Hakodate Camp

Det. 1, Hokkaido Island, Japan
c/o Japanese Red Cross, Tokyo, Japan
Via New York, New York

On October 8, 1945, respondent received from the Maritime War Emergency Board a certificate correcting the Certificate of Presumptive Death. Thereupon respondent's agent called upon the appellant and informed her of same and asked that she refund the money and reinstate the policy, no definite answer being given, respondent wrote and asked that this be done. Later attorneys for respondent visited the beneficiary for the purpose of getting a restoration of the status which has been refused by the appellant.

That the insured is alive and back in the United States at this time is undisputed.

This case was tried as an equity case and from this there is no appeal; therefore, it will be so considered by this Court.

It is a firmly established general rule that money paid to another under the influence of a mistake of fact, that is, on the mistaken supposition of the existence of a specific fact which would entitle the other to the money, which would not have been paid if it had been known to the payor that the fact was otherwise, may be recovered, provided the payment has not caused such a change in the position of the payee that it would be unjust to require a refund. The ground on which the rule rests is that money paid through misapprehension of facts belongs, in equity and good conscience to the person who paid it.

Both parties to this action had been advised that the insured had sailed from Ceylon and that his ship and all aboard had been unheard from and were presumed lost as a result of enemy action. Both parties exhausted their sources of information and all accepted the death of the insured as a fact. The U.S. Government also thought and so certified as a result of which appellant filed her claim and accepted the payment of the policy by respondent. It is obvious that both parties accepted as a fact that the insured had died shortly after sailing from Ceylon. There is no evidence of fraud, therefore, the question resolves itself into whether or not there was a mutual mistake. Appellant contends that there was no mutual mistake but rather a mistake or error of judgment on the part of the insurer. That settlement was made under the realization of an uncertainty and that the settlement was a compromise of a doubtful liability.

All the facts available to one of the parties was available to, and known by, both and their reactions thereto were the same. The acceptance of the death of the insured as a fact was a mutual mistake of fact equally concurred in by both parties. The whole situation having arisen because of the acceptance by the parties as a fact that the insured came to his death shortly after he sailed from Ceylon, when such fact did not exist. To follow appellant's line of argument would be to allow the beneficiary to be enriched to the amount of $1,013.36 for which the essential prerequisite was the death of the insured when in fact he is still alive. A mistake of fact having existed the proposition is elementary that repayment to the insurers could be compelled: *Masonic Life Ass'n v. Crandall*, 41 N.Y.S. 497, 11 L.R.A. (N.S.) 234.

In *Riegel v. American Life Ins. Co.*, 19 L.R.A., 166, 11 L.R.A. 857, we find the reverse of the position of the parties in this case. The plaintiff-beneficiary held a policy for $6,000.00 on the life of a debtor, Leisenring, who had not been heard from for about thirteen years. The beneficiary was paying premiums on this policy in an annual amount of $153.90, which premiums were burdensome to her and an arrangement was worked out whereby she surrendered the $6,000.00 policy and accepted a new policy, paid up, for $2,500.00 and was thereupon relieved from the payment of premiums. This, of course, was based upon the assumption of fact by both parties that the insured was alive. A short time later it was discovered that Leisenring, the insured had died some time prior to the arrangements between the beneficiary and the insurer, and thereupon the beneficiary brought action against the company for recovery on the original policy of $6,000.00. The insurer there defended very much upon the grounds that appellant here contends for and filed a demurrer, contending that there was a compromise settlement based upon a doubtful fact. The Circuit Judge sustained the demurrer and dismissed the action, holding that "Where both parties treat upon the basis of the fact being doubtful, and the transaction shows that both parties took the risk of the doubt, equity will not interfere, but will leave the parties where they were." This order was reversed on appeal by the Supreme Court of Pennsylvania which said:

> The case presented on these facts was that of a contract entered into under the influence of a mutual mistake, and a claim for relief from such contract. The mistake was in relation to the fact of Leisenring's death. Both parties evidently supposed, and acted on the supposition, that he was alive, and that the annual premiums upon his life, which had become burdensome to Mrs. Riegel must be continued indefinitely, until his death should take place.

> At the time she made it (the contract of settlement) she was already relieved from the burdensome premiums, and the entire amount of the policy was honestly due her from the Company. What was the effect of the mistake upon her? Simply to take from her the difference between the two policies and give her absolutely nothing for it. . . . The Company parted with nothing. She secured nothing. The whole transaction was a mistake, and if the decree of the court below stands, the result will be to take $3,500.00 from Mrs. Riegel, and give it to the Insurance Company.

After the case was tried on its merits and the lower Court had held that the beneficiary was not entitled to relief, the Supreme Court reversed that Order and held that the original policy of $6,000.00 should be reinstated and that amount paid to the beneficiary. In discussing the right of the beneficiary to relief because the parties had proceeded upon the mistaken assumption that the insured was alive, when in fact he was dead, the Court quoted portions of its opinion on the first appeal. The Court points out that the Circuit Judge, on the hearing on the demurrer, had treated the arrangement as a compromise, but that it did not partake of a compromise because "both parties to the transaction were acting, in respect thereto, on the basis that Leisenring was alive," and the Court says, with respect to such a situation:

The general rule is that an act done or a contract made under a mistake of a material fact is voidable and relievable in equity. . . . It makes no difference in application of the principle that the subject-matter of the contract be known to both parties to be liable to a contingency which may destroy it immediately; for, if the contingency has, unknown to the parties, already happened, the contract will be avoided as founded on a mutual mistake of a matter constituting the basis of the contract. . . .

It cannot be doubted that in exchanging the old for the new policy both parties acted on the basis that Leisenring was then alive. Their every act in the transaction was predicated on that as an assumed fact. . . . If the exchange was not made on the assumption by both parties that Leisenring was then alive, the Company stultified itself by issuing a paid-up policy on the life of one who was then in his grave; and the plaintiff was guilty of extreme folly of paying $3,500.00 for exemption from a liability which, by the previous death of Leisenring, had ipso facto ceased. . . . she and the company were both at that time ignorant of the fact that the life on which the original risk was taken had previously dropped. . . . The central fact underlying the transaction, and to which every circumstance connected therewith clearly points, was the assumption by both parties that Leisenring was then in full life.

The logic of this case is inescapable and simply by reversing the position of the parties very appropriate to the case now before us.

In the case of *Duncan v. McCormick County,* 192 S.C. 216, 6 S.E.2d 265, the administratrix brought an action against McCormick County for execution fees which the deceased treasurer was entitled to but had paid into the County general fund. The County attempted to defend on the grounds that he had voluntarily paid these moneys out without compulsion and that he was estopped to demand them of the County and had waived his right to recover them. In that case it was said by this Court:

The principle that whenever one has money in his hands belonging to another which in equity and good conscience he ought to pay over to that other an action will lie to recover it, is derived from the civil law and is founded in natural justice. Perhaps a statement of this doctrine more nearly applicable to the case at bar is the following from 41 C. J., 41, 42: "When one has received money from a third person through some *mistake* or fraud by law or authority, which, but for the mistake or fraud, would have vested the right to the money in plaintiff, plaintiff may recover such money in an action for money had and received."

This principle was also recognized in *Glenn v. Shannon,* 12 S.C. 570; *Braig v. Thompson,* 19 S.C. 572.

Appellant argues strenuously and at length that what occurred in the payment of the face of the policy was voluntary and made in compromise, and, therefore, is not the subject of rescission.

That cannot be said with propriety to be voluntarily done, where a formal assent thereto is induced by mistake . . . as to facts material to control the operation of the will therein any more than where such formal assent is extorted by the application of a force which fetters and obstructs its free working. *Kenneth v. S. C. Railway Co.,* 15 Rich. L. 284; 98 Am. Dec. 382.

A compromise as shown by the principal authority, cited by appellant (*Taylor v. Insurance Company,* 196 S.C. 195, 12 S.E.2d 708) involves the essential element of a dispute or a controversy. The Taylor settlement was upheld because there was a bona fide basis for dispute between the parties as to whether the insured had committed suicide. But here there was no dispute, nor claim for double indemnity nor controversy between the parties. Both parties had substantially the same information and proceeded upon the same mistake of fact.

Appellant does not argue the question of whether or not the Court erred by impressing a trust upon "Any bonds, money or other property into which defendant had invested the moneys paid her by plaintiff," therefore, under the rules of this Court it is deemed abandoned and the Court intimates no opinion therein.

This Court is of the opinion that all exceptions should be dismissed and it is so ordered. Judgment affirmed.

BAKER, CH.J., FISHBURNE, STUKES and OXNER, J.J., concur.

TO WHOM IS THE BENEFIT PAYABLE

After it has been determined that the benefit is payable, there may nevertheless be questions as to the person or persons to whom it is to be paid. Here we have the basic problems of attempted but not completed changes of beneficiary, the beneficiary who murders the insured, the beneficiary designation which is, in effect, changed by reason of divorce, and the interposition of numerous persons whose rights are based on the law in general, as opposed to those whose rights are based entirely on the terms of the contract itself.

In this section, we will discuss only those problems which have not previously been discussed. Of these, perhaps the most important is the situation which results when the insured meets his death at the hands of the beneficiary.

The Beneficiary-Murderer

There is probably no principle better established in the law of the life insurance contract than the rule that a beneficiary of a life insurance policy who feloniously kills the insured will not be permitted to receive the proceeds. The rule is grounded in public policy. To permit a murderer to receive the insurance benefit payable upon the death of the very person he has murdered would violate one of the basic tenets of the law, which is to protect human life and discourage anything tending to encourage murder.

As this principle is actually applied in the settlement of a life insurance policy, there are two major divisions. One concerns policies applied for and issued in good faith. Under them, the murderer-beneficiary will not be permitted to receive the proceeds, but the insurance company is nevertheless not discharged from its responsibility for paying. Thus, there are a number of sometimes conflicting decisions in this area concerning the person entitled to receive the proceeds. The other subdivision concerns life insurance policies issued to persons who at the

time of application are contemplating the murder of the person whose
life is being insured.

Where the Policy Was Procured with Intent to Murder. In cases
where the beneficiary procured the policy with intent to murder the
insured, the company may be held to have no liability, on the grounds
that the policy as issued did not constitute a valid contract in the first
place. Illustrative of this kind of case and this particular type of holding
is *Colyer's Admr., Appellant v. New York Life Insurance Company,*[17]
decided by the Kentucky Court of Appeals in June, 1945. The facts of this
case are stated in the court's own words, as follows:

> On April 10, 1942, Finley Duncan brutally murdered his 20-year old
> brother-in-law, Edward Colyer, who had been making his home with Duncan
> for several years. Duncan sought to establish his innocence by saying that
> Colyer met his death in an automobile accident. He was sentenced to the
> penitentiary for his natural life. *Duncan v. Commonwealth*, 294 Ky. 783, 172
> S.W.2d 665. On March 12, 1942, through Duncan's instigation, a $10,000
> accident policy was issued on Colyer's life with Duncan and his wife as
> beneficiaries. On March 16, Duncan made application for a guarantee reserve
> life policy on Colyer, paying approximately $1,000 travel and $700 auto
> death benefits, with Duncan as beneficiary. The policy was issued the following
> April 1. . . .

On April 6, another policy was issued on Colyer's life in the amount of
$2,000 with Duncan as beneficiary. Duncan took the policies home and
put them under a mattress on April 8. On April 9, he contrived the death
of Colyer, attempting to make it appear to be an automobile accident.
He was tried and sentenced to life imprisonment.

The court differentiates other cases and states the law which controls
in this instance, as follows:

> . . . but those decisions are based upon a valid insurance contract and
> involve situations where the intent or purpose of the beneficiary to do away
> with the insured arose after the issuance of the policy. In the case at bar it
> is clearly established that there was a predetermination on the part of Duncan,
> before the policy was issued, to kill Colyer. Under such a circumstance there
> can be no recovery, either on the part of the beneficiary or the estate of the
> insured, because the contract of insurance was void from its inception. In
> fact there was no contract of insurance between Colyer and the Company.
> While this precise question seems not to have been before this Court hereto-
> fore, there is ample authority to support the statements just made. 29 Am.
> Jur., Insurance, Section 1313 and the Annotation to the case of *Smith
> v. Todd*, 155 S.C. 323, 152 S.E. 506, 70 A.L.R. 1529. One of the leading
> cases on the subject is *New York Mutual Life Ins. Co.* v. *Armstrong*, 117 U.S.
> 591, 29 L.ed. 997, 6 S.Ct. 877. That case is referred to in the American
> Jurisprudence citation and also in the Annotation in 70 A.L.R. The *Arm-
> strong* decision also holds that evidence as to the procurement of other
> policies by the beneficiary at or about the same time is admissible.

[17] 300 Ky. 189, 188 S.W. (2d) 313 (1945).

The conclusions just stated seem to us to be inescapable when it is considered that, at or about the time Duncan was negotiating with the Company relative to a policy on Colyer's life, he secured two other accidental policies on Colyer with himself as beneficiary; that he wanted a double indemnity policy; and that only two days after the policy in question was issued he brought about Colyer's death through an alleged automobile accident. As a matter of fact, reference to the case of *Duncan v. Commonwealth, supra,* will show that Duncan knocked Colyer in the head; tied his legs together; placed him on the floor back of the front seat of the car; set the car on fire; and caused it to run over a 200 foot embankment.

Under the circumstances, we think the judgment should be and it is affirmed. (For the insurance company.)

It should be added that although this presents an interesting kind of decision, this rule has not been applied in any large number of cases.

Policies Applied for and Issued in Good Faith. By far, the majority of the cases involving the murder of the insured by the beneficiary concern policies applied for and issued in good faith. Thus, there is no question concerning the liability of the company. The only question relates to the person or persons who are entitled to receive the proceeds.

In answering this question, one turns first to the applicable statutory law, if any, of the state in question. Some twelve or more states have statutes specifically relating to this question in connection with insurance proceeds, and other states have general statutes disqualifying murderers from inheriting property from the persons they have murdered. The statutes which specifically relate to the disposition of insurance proceeds sometimes provide that if the primary beneficiary murders the insured, the proceeds of the policy shall be payable to any contingent beneficiary or beneficiaries who may be named. Others make no such provision, and the general statutes, of course, do not touch upon the question.

If Only One Beneficiary Was Named. The basic law with respect to distribution of the proceeds where the beneficiary murders the insured is stated in the case of *Austin v. United States of America,*[18] where the court said:

The fact that public policy prevents the payment of the insurance benefits to the murderer does not void the insurance policy; the liability of the insurer is just the same when death is the result of murder as when it is produced by any other cause, and if there is any person who has a right to the benefits of the policy, his rights will be enforced.

Under this rule, if only one beneficiary was named and that beneficiary is disqualified from taking, the proceeds, by the terms of most life insurance policies, are payable to the estate of the insured.

---

[18] 125 F.2d 816 (C.C.A. Ill., 1942).

Where a Contingent Beneficiary Is Named. In most policies, if a contingent beneficiary is named, the designation is worded something like this:

Mary Doe, wife of the insured, if living; otherwise Sara Doe, mother of the insured.

The difficult question is presented by the fact that Mary Doe, by murdering the insured, disqualifies herself from receiving the proceeds but because she herself was alive at the time of the insured's death, the contingency on which Sara's rights depend has not happened.

If there is a governing statute which provides that if the primary beneficiary is disqualified by reason of having murdered the insured, payment should be made to the contingent beneficiary, there is no question about Sara's right under this designation. However, where there is no governing statute clarifying the question, court decisions differ. Some courts have held for the contingent beneficiary, others for the insured's personal representatives.

Thus, in one case [19] the California Supreme Court held that the general rule disqualifying the primary beneficiary from receiving the proceeds of insurance on the life of the person he had murdered should not be used to impair the rights of the contingent beneficiary. Accordingly, the court held that the contingent beneficiary should receive the proceeds.

Was It Murder?

One other important aspect of this question deals with the nature of the crime the beneficiary has actually committed. There are a number of gradations of felonious killing, not all actually termed murder. There are also a number of technical rules of evidence relating to whether one can introduce evidence of a conviction in a criminal case, into a civil case. In other words, if John Brown, insured, is killed by Anne Brown, his wife and primary beneficiary under his life insurance policy, is her acquittal in the criminal case sufficient to qualify her to receive the proceeds of the policy?

These are primarily legal questions with little place in a general discussion of the life insurance contract except that they should be noted as possible sources of trouble. Illustrative of the kind of questions that can arise, and also important as showing the application of the general principle in cases related to murder of others than the insured, is the case of *United States* v. *Kwasniewski* [20] decided by the United States District Court for the Eastern District of Michigan, June, 1950.

In the *Kwasniewski* case, the insured, Raymond C. Grzenkowicz,

---

[19] *Beck* v. *West Coast Life Insurance Company,* 241 P.2d 544 (Cal., 1952).

[20] 91 F. Supp. 847 (D.C. Mich., 1950).

died while in the military service, leaving his insurance benefits payable to his mother, Stella Yucha Kwasniewski, as principal beneficiary and Joseph Kwasniewski, his stepfather, as contingent beneficiary. After benefits had been paid from March until September, Joseph, the stepfather of the insured and the contingent beneficiary, shot and killed Stella, the mother of the insured. A bill in the nature of a bill of interpleader was filed to determine the persons, from among the brothers and sisters of the insured, his natural father, and the stepfather, to whom the benefits should be paid.

Because the killing took place under circumstances of severe emotional stress, a defense of temporary insanity was interposed, and the defendant was acquitted. Nevertheless, the circumstances of the death, sufficient for an acquittal in the criminal case, were held not sufficient to avoid the disqualification of the accused under the rule of public policy we have been discussing. The court said:

> It is a fundamental rule of common law that no man shall be permitted to profit by his own wrongful act. Courts have consistently held that a beneficiary who intentionally and feloniously kills the insured is barred from claiming insurance proceeds on the life of the insured. The same principle applies to a case involving killing of a principal beneficiary by a contingent beneficiary. . . .
>
> It is claimed on behalf of Joseph Kwasniewski that he killed the principal beneficiary during a period of temporary insanity; that such killing was not intentional and felonious; that he was acquitted of the murder charge in the criminal proceeding, and hence is not barred from claiming the insurance funds. The fact that the person who would acquire property as a result of the death of the person killed has been acquitted of the killing does not prevent the application of the rule. Restatement of the Law, Restitution, Property Acquired on Death, Sec. 187, subd. e, f.
>
> The record of the criminal proceeding in which Joseph Kwasniewski was acquitted of the murder charge is not binding upon this court. *Metropolitan Life Insurance Co. v. McDavid, et al.*, 39 F. Supp. 228. Testimony was submitted in the present case relating to the circumstances which led to the death of Stella Yucha Kwasniewski. Although the jury found in the criminal proceeding that Joseph Kwasniewski killed his wife during a period of temporary insanity which warranted acquittal of the murder charge, it cannot be said, for the purposes of the instant suit, that the killing was not intentional and felonious.

Other Problems Relating to the Identity of the Beneficiary

The Effect of Divorce. Under a Michigan statute, the wife's interest as beneficiary of a policy of life insurance on the life of her husband is automatically terminated by a divorce decree, unless the decree itself specifies to the contrary. Under a Kentucky statute, the wife's rights are automatically terminated by divorce, even though she was designated irrevocably. Missouri and Minnesota both have statutes permitting the insured husband to change the beneficiary designation after divorce, even though the designation was by its terms irrevocable. Frequently, the only way the beneficiary, in connection with policies on the lives of residents of these states, may be effectively determined is by court action.

Simultaneous Deaths. We have previously discussed the problems incident to the rights of persons, beneficiaries and insureds, who lose their lives so nearly at the same time that it is impossible to say with certainty which of them has survived the other. The remedy of inter-pleader is often used to clarify this problem.

Incomplete Changes of Beneficiary. Another important area where questions often arise concerns policies where the policyholder has initi-ated the procedures necessary for changing the beneficiary designation but has been unable, for one reason or another, to complete the change. The effect upon the rights of the various persons concerned are different depending upon the state in which the problem arises. In some states, as discussed in Chapter XII, the courts have taken a strict approach to the question; in others, they have viewed it more liberally. However, in any case in which there is a doubt, the company will ordinarily pay the proceeds into court and ask the court to make the determination.

Unfortunately, there is always some expense involved in connection with interpleader, and this expense, as a general rule, is payable, in part or in its entirety, out of the proceeds of the policy. Thus, the funds which actually reach the payee or payees are ordinarily somewhat diminished by reason of the interpleader action. For this reason, and also because any court action means delay in performing a service that is ordinarily performed promptly, life insurance companies have good reason not to initiate any interpleader action unless it is actually necessary. Never-theless, the use of the remedy is sometimes open to misunderstanding.

❖ ❖ ❖ ❖ ❖

ILLUSTRATIVE CASE

The following case is included for its value in clearing some of the questions which sometimes arise in connection with the company's use of the remedy.

DEMMER, Appellant v. *AMERICAN NATIONAL INS. CO., ET AL.,*
Appellees [21]

(Texas Court of Civil Appeals.)

POPE, A. J.: Appellant instituted this suit for recovery of all the proceeds under a life insurance policy. The appellee American National Insurance Company has never denied owing the amount of the policy, tendered the funds into court, and interpleaded certain claimants and heirs of the insured,

[21] 263 S.W.2d 795 (Texas Civ. App., 1953).

to determine to whom the money should be paid. The trial court awarded the proceeds of the policy to appellant, who has appealed from that part of the trial court's judgment which denied appellant's claim for attorney's fees and twelve per cent penalty, under Section 3.62, Insurance Code, Vernon's Ann. Civ. Stats., and also that part of the judgment which granted appellee's claim for an attorney's fee in its interpleader suit.

Minnie Barth, the insured, died on July 12, 1952. The policy named Fannie Barth as the beneficiary, but she predeceased the insured, having died on November 22, 1951. No other beneficiary was ever named. The record discloses several facts which justify the insurer's delay in paying the policy. Appellant, by affidavit, asserted that she was entitled to the proceeds as a creditor, since she had paid the premiums for eight years. Since the policy was in force for about twenty-one years, appellant's demand on its face disclosed that she was not entitled to all the proceeds. The insurer also received a claim to the policy proceeds from Theodore Barth, who was represented by counsel. Moreover, appellant asserted in her affidavit and demand, that there were only two heirs, herself and Theodore Barth, but investigation by the insurance company showed that there were six heirs, one of whom was a minor.

Faced with competing claimants, the insurer acknowledged owing the policy proceeds, and expressed a willingness to make payment by a check payable jointly to the heirs. The insurer later stated that it would make payment upon being furnished with a release. Appellant refused payment on such terms and submitted a second affidavit, which stated that she had paid the premiums for twenty-one years, rather than eight years as stated in her former affidavit. Appellant then filed suit and named Theodore Barth as one of the defendants, apparently because she acknowledged that he, like herself, claimed the funds. Theodore Barth filed a disclaimer, but he did so by assigning any interest in the policy he might have, "to the other interested parties, the heirs of said Fannie Barth, deceased." After Theodore Barth had scattered his claim, whatever it was, among those other heirs, appellant sued all of them. The insurer answered and impleaded all the heirs, all of whom made default except appellant.

Appellee has never refused to pay its policy, but was entitled to determine the true and lawful claimants before payment. When it was faced with claimants, disputing and in conflict with each other, there was no duty on the part of the insurer to act as judge and jury. It tendered the money into court and left for the court the matter of determining who, among the claimants, should receive it. The court correctly denied appellant a judgment for penalty and attorney's fees, and correctly allowed appellee its attorney's fee as interpleader. *Franklin Life Ins. Co. v. Greer*, Tex. Civ. App. 219 S.W.2d 137; *Whittet v. Reliance Life Insurance Co. of Pittsburgh*, Tex. Civ. App. 213 S.W.2d 164.

The judgment is affirmed.

Appendixes

A. Regular Life Application Form

REGULAR LIFE APPLICATION—Page One

Adult Juvenile Pur suppl for WPP Change of Plan Added Benefits

Dated on_____

at_____

Signature of Agent
as Witness

| AJAX LIFE INSURANCE COMPANY |

Personal Signature of Applicant
(If Juvenile application, the Purchaser shall sign own name above as Applicant)

In submitting this application to the _____ Life Insurance Company of _____ for insurance as herein specified, it is hereby represented for that purpose that all statements, answers, representations and agreements in this application, consisting of Application and Medical History (as well as a supplementary Application and Medical History on life of Purchaser, if Waiver of Premium for Purchaser [WPP] is being applied for), are true and complete, and correctly recorded; and that no material circumstance or information has been withheld or omitted concerning the past and present state of health, habits of life and occupation of the Proposed Insured (or Insureds).

It is understood and agreed that no one except the president, a vice-president, the secretary, or an assistant secretary has the power on behalf of the company to make, modify, or discharge contracts, or to waive any of the company's rights or requirements (and in writing only), and these powers will not be delegated; that notice to or knowledge of the soliciting agent or the medical examiner, if any, is not notice to or knowledge of the company; and that neither the soliciting agent nor the medical examiner is authorized to accept risks or to pass upon insurability.

Unless prohibited by law, any rule or provision of law forbidding any physician, practitioner, nurse, hospital official or hospital employee, or other person who has attended, examined, or treated the Proposed Insured, or who may hereafter attend, treat, or examine the Proposed Insured, or any bureau, institution, or company which may have information concerning the Proposed Insured's health, from disclosing any such information or knowledge in court or elsewhere is expressly waived on behalf of the Proposed Insured and the Applicant and any person who shall have or claim any interest in any policy that may be issued on this application; and such physician or other person, institution, bureau, or company is expressly authorized to make such disclosures.

It is understood and agreed that the company shall incur no liability under this application until it has been received, approved, and a policy issued and delivered, and the initial premium specified in the policy has been paid during the lifetime and continued insurability of the Proposed Insured (and the Applicant, if WPP is being applied for), in which case such policy shall be deemed to have taken effect as of the Policy Date as recited on the first page thereof, except that if a Conditional Binding Receipt referring to this application has been duly signed and issued to the Applicant by an authorized agent of the company, on the date this application is signed, then the terms of such Conditional Binding Receipt shall be effective. In case of an apparent error or omission discovered by the company, the company is authorized to correct this application and make the notation "Corrected." The acceptance of any policy issued shall constitute a ratification by the Applicant of any such correction and of the beneficiary designation or settlement agreement in such policy.

1. (a) Proposed Insured (*Print name in full below*)

   (b) Mail Address

   (c) Birth — Month Day Year State or Province of Birth Insurance Age

   (d) Race   (f) Single, Married, Widowed, or Divorced

   (e) Sex

2. (a) Occupation of Proposed Insured (*If more than one, give all*)

   (b) Exact duties are

   (c) Length of present employment

   (d) Employer's name and address

3. Does Proposed Insured contemplate changing occupation or duties or residence?
   (*If so, explain fully on Page 3*) Yes or No

4. (a) How much personal and business Life Insurance, including war risk and group, is now in force on life of Proposed Insured? $_____
   (*If more than $5,000, give complete details on Page 3*)

   (b) Are other negotiations for insurance or an annuity on Proposed Insured's life now pending?
   (*If so, state companies and amounts on Page 3*) Yes or No

5. (a) Has Proposed Insured ever made any claim for sickness, accident, or pension benefits?
   (*If so, state dates, causes and from whom on Page 3*) Yes or No

   (b) Has Proposed Insured secured any Life Insurance without a medical examination?
   (*If so, give date and amount on Page 3*) Yes or No

   (c) Has insurance applied for on life of Proposed Insured ever been declined, postponed, or modified in amount, plan, or rate?
   (*If so, explain fully on Page 3*) Yes or No

6. If Purchaser's supplementary application for WPP, answer (a) only by inserting, "See Juv app on (name of child)."

   (a) Amount of Life Insurance $_____
   and additional Life Insurance consisting of
   _____ Units of Family Income for _____ years.
   NOTE: It is understood and agreed that any policy, other than a Single Premium policy, issued at Insurance Age 0 shall provide a death benefit not exceeding $250 during the first policy year for each $1,000 Amount of Life Insurance herein applied for.

   (b) Plan
   OFFICE USE ONLY

   (c) ☐ With AD   (d) ☐ With Dis   (e) ☐ With WPP

   (f) If Juv. app. print full name of Successor Purchaser.

   (g) How shall dividends be used?

   (h) If provided, is Automatic Premium Loan provision elected? Yes or No

7. Is Proposed Insured now free from disease, in sound health, and without deformity, loss, or impairment of limb, sight, hearing, and speech?
   (*If not, explain fully on Page 3*) Yes or No

8. Has Proposed Insured ever flown or does he contemplate flight in any kind of aircraft, as a pilot, crew member, or student pilot?
   (*If so, complete Aviation Section on Page 4*) Yes or No

9. Has Proposed Insured ever been exempted or discharged from service in the military, naval, or air forces of any country for physical or mental reasons? (*If so, explain fully on Page 3*) Yes or No

10. Is Proposed Insured now a member of the National Guard or of any other branch or reserve component of the armed forces of any country?
    (*If so, explain fully on Page 3*) Yes or No

    QUESTIONNAIRE FOR WOMAN

11. (a) Has Proposed Insured ever had any female disorder or tumor or disease of breast, womb, ovaries or pelvis?
    (b) Has Proposed Insured ever miscarried? If "yes" give dates, cause and stage of pregnancy when occurring.

    (c) Is Proposed Insured pregnant now?
    How far advanced? Date of last confinement?

    (d) If married, what was Proposed Insured's maiden name?

L-1110.4

FOR OFFICE USE ONLY

Name	Code No.	Name	Code No.
1. A.		M.	
2. A.		St.	

419

Regular Life Application Form (Continued)

MEDICAL HISTORY portion of REGULAR LIFE APPLICATION—Page Two | **AJAX LIFE INSURANCE COMPANY**

12. Exact Height _____ feet _____ inches; Exact Weight _____ pounds

13. (a) Has there been any change in Proposed Insured's weight within the past 3 years? (*If so, give details and explain loss or gain on Page 3*) _____ Yes or No

(b) Has Proposed Insured been under any restriction of diet for any cause? (*If so, explain fully on Page 3*) _____ Yes or No

14. Has Proposed Insured ever changed or been advised to change occupation or residence for the benefit of health? (*If so, explain fully on Page 3*) _____ Yes or No

15. (a) Family Record:

	IF LIVING			IF DEAD	
	Age	Health	Amount Now Insured For	Age	Year of Death	Cause of Death
Wife or Husband						
Father						
Mother						
Brothers						
Sisters						

(b) Have there ever been any cases of epilepsy, cancer, tuberculosis, insanity, or suicide in Proposed Insured's family? (*If so, explain fully on Page 3*) _____ Yes or No

16. (a) Has Proposed Insured ever been known to have abnormal blood pressure or sugar, casts, or pus in the urine? (*If so, explain fully on Page 3*) _____ Yes or No

(b) Has Proposed Insured ever taken insulin? (*If so, explain fully on Page 3*) _____ Yes or No

17. Does Proposed Insured contemplate a surgical operation for any cause? (*If so, explain fully on Page 3*) _____ Yes or No

18. (a) To what extent does Proposed Insured ★ use alcoholic beverages? _____

(b) Has Proposed Insured ever been treated for alcohol or drug habit? (*If so, explain fully on Page 3*) _____ Yes or No

(left margin, vertical) If the answer space for any question is insufficient, use Page Three of Application

19. Does Proposed Insured have or has Proposed Insured ever had any signs or symptoms of or suffered from any ailment or disease of: (*If so, explain fully on Page 3*)

(a) Brain or Nervous System? _____ Yes or No

(b) Heart, Blood Vessels or Lungs? _____ Yes or No

(c) Stomach, Intestines, Liver, Gall Bladder, Kidneys or Bladder? _____ Yes or No

(d) Enlarged Glands, Tumors, Goiter or Ulcers? _____ Yes or No

(e) Rheumatism or Gout? _____ Yes or No

(f) Any other disease or illness not mentioned above? _____ Yes or No

20. Has Proposed Insured, within the past 5 years, had ★ any unusual and recurrent pain or discomfort in region of chest or abdomen which caused Proposed Insured to take any home remedy, patent medicine, or drug, or to seek the advice of a physician, either formally or informally? (*If so, explain fully on Page 3*) _____ Yes or No

21. Has Proposed Insured been exposed to any contagious disease during the past month? (*If so, explain fully on Page 3*) _____ Yes or No

22. (a) Give names and addresses of the physicians the Proposed Insured usually consults:

(b) When and for *what* did Proposed Insured last arrange consultation?

Answer only if Proposed Insured is a child under 3 years of age.

23. (a) Was the Proposed Insured a premature or immature child at birth? (*If so, explain fully on Page 3*) _____ Yes or No

(b) What was the birth weight? _____

24. State below the particulars of ALL diseases, injuries, ailments, or surgical operations which the Proposed Insured has had or for which the Proposed Insured has been under treatment, observation, or diagnostic study in the past 5 years.

Disease, Injury, Ailment, or Surgical Operation	Date—Month and Year	Complications	Duration and Date of Recovery	Remaining Effects	Medical Attendant's Name and Address

25. Has a physician, specialist, or other practitioner been consulted by or for the Proposed Insured, or has the Proposed Insured been under medical care, in the past 5 years, for any reason not stated above? _____ Yes or No (*If so, explain fully on Page 3*)

★ *Ignore questions 11, 18 and 20 if the Proposed Insured is under insurance age 16.*

Regular Life Application Form (Continued)

REGULAR LIFE APPLICATION—Page Three | **AJAX LIFE INSURANCE COMPANY**

Show Question Number as Reference	Proposed Insured (*Print name in full below*)	Date of Application

(If space below is insufficient, use additional sheets—In giving details for answer to Question 4 on Page One, describe each policy by stating Company, Year Issued, Amount, Kind, and any extra benefits such as Waiver of Premium for Purchaser, Disability, Accidental Death, Family Income, and Family Maintenance.)

FACE AMOUNT SETTLEMENT SPECIFICATIONS

Do not use sections below with Change of Plan applications

Beneficiaries (*Give full name, age, and relationship*)	Method of Payment
PRIMARY: (Payee at death of Insured)	
SUCCESSOR: (Substitute payee if no Primary payee living)	(a) If Primary *survives* the Insured, the method for Successor shall be One Sum, except that any unpaid instalments under Option 2 or 4 or any unpaid certain instalments under Option 3 may be continued to Successor if requested by check mark here: ☐ (b) If Primary *does not survive* the Insured, specify method of settlement for Successor:
FINAL: (Substitute payee if no Primary or Successor payee living)	**ONE SUM** (only Method of Payment available to Final Beneficiary)

FAMILY INCOME SETTLEMENT SPECIFICATIONS (Check One Only)

Monthly Income ☐ If payees are to be the same as for Face Amount write "SAME" below. If different, designate payees below: Primary: Successor: Final, in one sum: Is any payee to have the right to withdraw all of any unpaid instalments...................? (Yes or No) If so, give full name of such payee:	**One Sum** ☐ If payees are to be the same as for Face Amount, write "SAME" below. If different, designate payees below: Primary: Successor: Final:	**Merge with Face Amount** ☐ Settlement will be made as specified above for the Face Amount.

(DO NOT WRITE IN THIS SPACE)

421

Regular Life Application Form (Continued)

AGENT'S STATEMENT

(On any Juvenile application this Agent's Statement refers in four places to the Purchaser who is the *Applicant*. When WPP is requested, leave Agent's Statement blank on Purchaser's supplementary application.)

1. (a) Exact Location of Applicant's residence

   (If outside town)............miles in..............direction from..............on..............road

   (If in town) Street address.. Town................

   COUNTY.. STATE.................

   (b) How long at this residence?   (c) What was exact previous residence address?

2. How long and how well have you known the Proposed Insured?

3. Are you related to the Proposed Insured?   *If so, how?*

4. Did you personally see the Proposed Insured?

5. What is your estimate of Applicant's annual income and net worth?
   Earned Income $ Investment Income $ Net Worth $

6. Is the Proposed Insured in the Medical Class?   *If so, when is the medical examination to be made, and by whom?*

7. What settlement was made for the initial premium?

8. Was a Conditional Binding Receipt issued?

9. What amount of premium was stated to the Applicant?

10. What shall be the regular mode of premium payment?

11. Who is to pay premiums? (*Full name and relationship required if this is a juvenile application*)

12. Is a pro rata premium to arrange due date desired?   *If so,* indicate here the month in which first regular premium is to be due.

13. For what purpose is the proposed insurance intended?

14. Have you ordered an inspection?

15. (a) Upon whom is the Proposed Insured dependent for support?

    (b) What amount of life insurance is carried by person designated in (a) above? $

16. Do you know of any insurance recently terminated or about to be terminated by the Proposed Insured or anything indicating that the proposed insurance would replace other insurance in this or any other company?   *If so, explain.*

17. What was previous exact business address of the Applicant and name of previous employer, if any?

18. (a) Is Proposed Insured now a _____ policyholder?

    Auto............Life............Fire............   Yes or No

    (b) Is Proposed Insured related to or associated with a State Farm policyholder?

    Auto............Life............Fire............   Yes or No

19. (a) If Proposed Insured is a farmer, does he own his farm?   Yes or No

    (b) If farming and Proposed Insured rents the farm, has he been a renter for 5 years or more, or less than 5 years? (*State which*)

20. If you used a Persistency Rater, state here the numerical rating.

REGULAR LIFE APPLICATION—Page Four

Proposed Insured   (*Print name in full below*)

AJAX LIFE INSURANCE COMPANY

Date of Application

AVIATION SECTION

PILOT—CREW MEMBER—STUDENT FLYING

1. Give particulars of all flights Proposed Insured has taken, giving data for each year separately and stating *"none"* where *none*: (Count each *take-off as a separate flight*)

History of Past Flights	Last 12 Months		1—2 Years Ago		Prior to 2 Years Ago	
	Flights	Hours	Flights	Hours	Flights	Hours
As a pilot or co-pilot, military aviation....						
As a pilot or co-pilot, civilian aviation....						
As a crew member, military aviation.....						
As a crew member, civilian aviation....						
As a student, military aviation..........						
As a student, civilian aviation..........						

2. Does Proposed Insured now hold or has Proposed Insured ever held a pilot's certificate for aircraft?   Yes or No

   Certificate No.................... Class........

   Date of issue.................... Date of last renewal....................

   Was such certificate granted subject to a physical waiver? (*If so, why?*)

   Does Proposed Insured hope to qualify for a higher classification?   Yes or No

3. How many solo hours has Proposed Insured flown?

4. Has Proposed Insured ever been disqualified for any type of certificate for medical reasons?   Yes or No

5. Does Proposed Insured now, or expect to, take off or land outside the continental limits of the United States? (*If so, explain fully*)   Yes or No

6. What types of planes has Proposed Insured been authorized to fly?

7. Is Proposed Insured required to or does Proposed Insured fly planes with untried or experimental features or designs? (*If so, explain fully*)   Yes or No

8. Has Proposed Insured ever been grounded or reprimanded for violation of regulations? (*If so, explain fully*)   Yes or No

9. Has Proposed Insured ever been in an aviation accident where there were physical injuries to persons, or serious damage to the aircraft, or both? (*If so, give dates and explain fully in a separate letter*)   Yes or No

10. Has Proposed Insured ever done exhibition, racing, stunt flying or parachute jumping, crop dusting or spraying, or made record trials or expeditions? (*If so, give dates and explain fully in a separate letter*)   Yes or No

422

CONDITIONAL BINDING RECEIPT

RECEIVED FROM _____

(Amount of cash) $ _____ in connection with the initial
(Settlement received)
premium on the proposed insurance for which an application is this day
made to the _____ Life Insurance Company ON THE LIFE OF

(Name of)
(Proposed Insured)

Life Insurance and any Accidental-Death Benefit (AD) in the amount
applied for (but not exceeding a maximum on the life of the Proposed
Insured of $50,000, including any Accidental-Death Benefit, if payable,
on all pending applications to the company combined) shall be deemed
to take effect as of the date of this receipt, subject to the terms and
conditions printed on the reverse side hereof.

The amount of settlement received shall be refunded to the Applicant
if the application is declined or if a policy is issued other than as applied
for and is not accepted by the Applicant.

_____   _____
Date of Receipt   Signature of Agent

This conditional binding receipt shall not apply to any Waiver of
Premium Disability Benefit (Dis) or Waiver of Premium for Purchaser
Benefit (WPP) applied for in the application. The term "Life In-
surance" as used herein includes the commuted value of any Family
Income Benefit applied for.

Subject to the limitations of this receipt and the terms and conditions of the policy that may be issued by the company on the basis of
the application, the Life Insurance (and Accidental-Death Benefit, if any)
shall not be deemed to take effect unless: (1) the company, after investigation and such medical examination, if any, as it may require,
shall be satisfied that the Proposed Insured on the date of this receipt
was insurable for the *amount* of Life Insurance and any Accidental-
Death Benefit applied for according to the company's rules and practice
of selection; and (2) the application is accepted and approved by the
company at its Home Office or at one of its Regional or Head Offices;
provided, however, that the approval by the company of the insurability
of the Proposed Insured for a plan of insurance other than that applied
for, or the denial of Accidental-Death Benefit, shall not invalidate the
terms and conditions of this receipt relating to Life Insurance.

(Not to be detached unless given to Applicant under the requirements for using
Conditional Binding Receipt)

PHYSICIAN'S AUTHORIZATION

You are hereby requested to give the Medical Director of the
_____ Life Insurance Company any information you may have regarding
my condition when under observation or treatment by you, including
history obtained, physical and laboratory findings, and your conclusions.

_____
Date Signed

_____
Personal Signature of Proposed Insured
(To be signed only on an Adult application or on Pur suppl for WPP)

AJAX LIFE INSURANCE COMPANY

AJAX Life
Insurance Company

under this Policy No.

000,000

hereby insures the life of the Insured

John Doe, Age 35,

and agrees to pay the Amount of Insurance

$10,000

as a death benefit when the insured dies.

The insurance provided by this policy, beginning on the Policy Date, is granted in consideration of the application and of the payment of premiums of

Two hundred forty and 40/100 Dollars on June 1st

in each policy year during the lifetime of the insured, the first such payment being due on the Policy Date.

This policy is issued and accepted subject to all the conditions, benefits, and privileges described on the following pages, which are hereby made a part of this contract.

In witness whereof, the _____ Life Insurance Company, at its Home Office
in   has caused this policy to be executed on the
Policy Date,
June 1, 1960.

Secretary   President

Registrar

Form L-4800–480101   Whole Life Policy. Premiums payable for life unless pre-   Annual Dividends
viously paid-up by Dividends or Premium Deposit Reserve.

Settlement Section

Payment of Benefits. Any sum payable upon maturity as an endowment or upon surrender for cash shall be payable to the insured, unless otherwise provided by endorsement hereon, and settlement of such sum shall be made by the company at its home office in _____ on receipt of due proof of the interest of the claimant and the legal surrender of this policy.

Settlement of any sum payable upon the death of the insured shall be made by the company, as hereinafter provided, at its home office in _____ on receipt of due proof of the death of the insured and of the interest of the claimant and the legal surrender of this policy.

See Settlement on Page Two A and Page Two B

Form L-4800-571202

Page Two

Specimen Policy Form (Continued)

Form L-4878A(N)—511217-for use with appropriate policy forms of 4800 series.

Settlement Section (Continued)
SETTLEMENT AGREEMENT

    The sum payable upon the death of the insured shall be applied for the benefit of the following beneficiaries in accordance with the following provisions.

Primary Beneficiary:................................ Mary Doe, wife of insured.

Option under which the sum payable is to be applied for Primary Beneficiary:........... ... ., Option 1.

Successor Beneficiary:............................... Children of insured by said wife.

Provision for Successor Beneficiary if last surviving Primary Beneficiary dies after the insured:......... One Sum.

Option under which the sum payable is to be applied for Successor Beneficiary if no Primary Beneficiary survives the insured:............................. .... One Sum.

Final Beneficiary to receive in One Sum:.............. None.

Special Provisions:................................. None.

Order of Payment to Classes of Beneficiaries. Any payments due will be made exclusively to the Primary Beneficiary, if living. If at any time there be no Primary Beneficiary living, any payments due will be made to the Successor Beneficiary, if living. If at any time there be no living Primary or Successor Beneficiary, the then present value of any guaranteed amounts unpaid will be paid in one sum to the Final Beneficiary, if any.

    If at any time there is no existing beneficiary (Primary, Successor, or Final), the then present value of any guaranteed amounts unpaid will be paid in one sum to the executors or administrators of the last survivor of the insured and all beneficiaries.

Specimen Policy Form (Continued)

Settlement Section (Continued)

Settlement if More Than One Primary or Successor Beneficiary. If at the death of the insured there be more than one Primary Beneficiary living, or if at the death of the last survivor of the insured and all Primary Beneficiaries there be more than one Successor Beneficiary living, the then present value of any guaranteed amounts unpaid will be first divided into equal shares among the Primary Beneficiaries then living or among the Successor Beneficiaries then living, as the case may be, and each person's share will be separately applied to the designated Option for his or her benefit. If any such beneficiary shall die after such division is made, the then present value of any guaranteed amounts unpaid on such beneficiary's share will be redivided into such number of equal shares as there shall be other beneficiaries of the same class then living. Each such additional share will be paid in one sum to the surviving beneficiary to whom such share was apportioned.

Agreement Covering More Than One Policy. If this settlement agreement covers more than one policy, any subsequent endorsement of a change of beneficiary or change of settlement agreement under any one or more of said policies shall not affect this present instrument in any way insofar as it may relate to the other or others of said policies.

Settlement Year. A settlement year shall begin on the date of the death of the insured and each successive settlement year shall begin on an anniversary of such date.

Limitations on Withdrawal. The right of commutation under Option 2 shall be exercised only on the basis of withdrawing the commuted value of all of any unpaid instalments. The right of withdrawal under Option 4 shall be exercised only as follows: Any withdrawal under Option 4 must be in the sum of $100 or a multiple thereof or must equal the unpaid balance of the fund.

Change of Option. Any payee who has the right of commutation or withdrawal may elect to substitute settlement under any other Option, subject to the conditions and limitations applicable thereto, provided that (i) any such election of Option 3 or Option 5 must be made at some time prior to the second anniversary of the death of the insured for settlement to begin either at the time of such election or on a specified future date if such payee is then living, and (ii) after a substitute settlement has been elected no change may be made in such election, except that on any instalment due date such payee shall have the right to make a single withdrawal of the commuted value of all of any unpaid instalments under Option 2 or of the balance of the fund under Option 4.

Lawful Children. If provision is made in this settlement agreement for the lawful children as a class of any person, the phrase shall include only lawful children born to or legally adopted by that person.

Reliance on Affidavit as to Beneficiaries. The company may rely upon an affidavit by any beneficiary relating to the date of birth, death, marriage or remarriage, names and addresses and other facts concerning all beneficiaries, and the company is hereby released from all liability in relying and acting upon the statements contained in such affidavit.

Settlement under Option 3. Anything hereinbefore to the contrary notwithstanding, it is agreed that if any beneficiary entitled to settlement in accordance with Option 3 at the death of the insured shall survive the insured but die prior to the thirtieth day after the death of the insured, settlement shall be made by payment to the same beneficiary or beneficiaries and in the same manner as hereinbefore provided for settlement had such beneficiary so dying not survived the insured.

Effect of Assignments. Any assignment of a policy payable under the provisions of this settlement agreement shall operate to the extent thereof to transfer the interests of any beneficiary whom the assignor has the right to change, and to render any part of the sum payable to which the assignee is entitled payable in one sum, notwithstanding any provisions of this settlement agreement to the contrary.

Option 4. Payments under Option 4 shall be made at the end of the payment intervals unless otherwise provided herein.

Other Provisions Incorporated. All the provisions on page three and page four of the policy are as much a part of this settlement agreement as though fully recited herein.

Settlement Section (Continued)

Change of Beneficiary or Settlement Agreement. The insured, subject to the rights of the assignee of record, if any, and subject to the limitations, if any, in the beneficiary designation or settlement agreement, may as often as desired change the beneficiary, or may change the settlement agreement to any other method of payment upon which the insured and the company may agree, by filing with the company written request therefor in such form as the company may require, such change to take effect only when endorsed hereon by the company in the lifetime of the insured. An assignee cannot change the beneficiary.

If any revocably or irrevocably designated beneficiary predeceases the insured, the interest of such beneficiary shall vest in the insured unless otherwise provided by endorsement hereon.

The endorsement of a change of beneficiary shall automatically revoke any existing settlement agreement, and the endorsement hereon of a settlement agreement shall automatically revoke any existing beneficiary designation or prior settlement agreement.

The insured, if there is no assignee of record, may designate irrevocably any beneficiary who is a natural person and to take in his or her own right, and the written consent of any irrevocably designated beneficiary will be required for the election of any right under this policy available to the insured.

One Sum Settlement. Settlement of the sum payable shall be made by payment in one sum, unless otherwise provided.

Optional Methods of Settlement. The insured, or a beneficiary for one sum settlement at the death of the insured, may elect to have settlement made in accordance with the following provisions concerning optional methods of settlement.

If an assignee of record, or a corporation, association, partnership, or estate is the payee, whether as trustee or otherwise, the optional methods of settlement shall be available only with the consent of the company.

Election by Insured. The insured may elect to have any sum payable upon the death of the insured, or upon maturity as an endowment, or upon surrender for cash, paid in accordance with one of the settlement options, or in any other manner upon which the insured and the company may agree, by filing with the company written request therefor in such form as the company may require, such election to take effect only when endorsed hereon by the company, as a settlement agreement, in the lifetime of the insured; provided, however, that no such election may be made for the sum payable upon maturity as an endowment or surrender for cash until this policy has been in force on the present plan of insurance for ten years.

No payee, other than the insured under option 1, 2, or 4, under a settlement agreement elected by the insured, shall have any right, in advance of actual receipt of payment from the company, to transfer, assign, alienate, encumber, anticipate, or commute any instalments or payments, or to make any change in the provisions elected; and, except as otherwise prescribed by law, no payment of interest or of principal shall, in advance of actual payment from the company to the payee, be subject to the debts, contracts, or engagements of any payee, nor to any judicial process to levy upon or attach the same for the payment thereof.

Election of Beneficiary. If no settlement agreement is in effect at the death of the insured, a beneficiary, after the death of the insured and before any settlement has been made, may elect to have the amount payable to such beneficiary paid in accordance with one of the settlement options, provided the amount of any stipulated payment would be not less than $10.

Under such an election by a beneficiary, such beneficiary shall have the right, as the case may be, to commute any unpaid certain instalments on the basis of compound interest at the rate of two per cent per annum or to withdraw any unpaid balance under the option, but such beneficiary shall not have the right to commute any instalments or make any withdrawal under option 3 or 5.

Except as otherwise prescribed by law, no payment of interest or of principal shall, in advance of actual payment from the company to the beneficiary, be subject to the debts, contracts, or engagements of any beneficiary, nor to any judicial process to levy upon or attach the same for the payment thereof.

Participation. Dividends or additional interest such as the company may apportion shall be payable under any settlement option.

Death of Payee. At the death of any payee under any settlement option the commuted value, on the basis of compound interest at the rate of two per cent per annum, of any unpaid certain instalments under option 2 or 3, or any unpaid balance under option 1 or 4, as the case may be, shall be paid in one sum to the executors or administrators of such deceased payee, unless otherwise provided.

Limitations. If, upon the death of the insured or upon the maturity of this policy as an endowment or upon its surrender for cash, the amount of any guaranteed payment provided for under a settlement agreement, other than the last payment, would be less than $10 per payee, immediate final settlement shall be made in one sum with the payee or payees who at the time of settlement would be entitled to the first such payment if living on the due date thereof. Similarly, if, at any time after payments or withdrawals have commenced under a settlement agreement, any future guaranteed payment provided for, other than the last payment, would be less than $10 per payee, immediate final settlement shall be made in one sum with the payee or payees who are then living and who would be entitled, if living, to the next succeeding payment.

Settlement Section (Continued)

Option 1—Interest. Retained by the company as a fund with payment of interest annually on the then balance of the fund at a rate not less than two per cent per annum, the amount so retained to be payable through withdrawal by the payee, unless otherwise provided, in sums of $100 or multiples thereof.

Option 2—Fixed Years Instalments. Payment in equal monthly instalments at the end of monthly payment intervals for a fixed number of years according to the Fixed Years Instalments Table.

FIXED YEARS INSTALMENTS TABLE

MONTHLY INSTALMENTS THAT $1,000 WILL OBTAIN FOR NUMBER OF YEARS ELECTED

No. of Years Elected	Monthly Instalments	No. of Years Elected	Monthly Instalments	No. of Years Elected	Monthly Instalments	No. of Years Elected	Monthly Instalments	No. of Years Elected	Monthly Instalments	No. of Years Elected	Monthly Instalments
1	$84.23	6	$14.74	11	$8.44	16	$6.08	21	$4.85	26	$4.10
2	42.53	7	12.76	12	7.81	17	5.78	22	4.68	27	3.99
3	28.63	8	11.27	13	7.28	18	5.51	23	4.51	28	3.88
4	21.69	9	10.12	14	6.82	19	5.27	24	4.37	29	3.78
5	17.52	10	9.19	15	6.43	20	5.05	25	4.23	30	3.69

Option 3—Life Income. Payment in equal monthly instalments at the end of monthly payment intervals continuously during the remaining lifetime of the payee, according to the Life Instalments Table for the sex and the age at nearest birthday of the payee on the date this option becomes effective. This option shall not be available for payment of the sum payable upon maturity as an endowment or upon surrender for cash unless the payee shall be the same person whose life is insured under this policy. The company reserves the right to require satisfactory evidence of age of the payee before making any payment under this option.

LIFE INSTALMENTS TABLE

This table illustrates instalments for specimen ages only. Instalments for ages not shown shall be determined on the same basis as those in this table.

Age at Nearest Birthday		MONTHLY INSTALMENTS FOR LIFE THAT $1,000 WILL OBTAIN					Age at Nearest Birthday		MONTHLY INSTALMENTS FOR LIFE THAT $1,000 WILL OBTAIN				
Man	Woman	Life	With 5 Years Certain	With 10 Years Certain	With 15 Years Certain	With 20 Years Certain	Man	Woman	Life	With 5 Years Certain	With 10 Years Certain	With 15 Years Certain	With 20 Years Certain
	15	$2.39	$2.39	$2.39	$2.39	$2.38	50	55	$4.24	$4.22	$4.15	$4.04	$3.87
15	20	2.49	2.49	2.49	2.49	2.48	55	60	4.81	4.77	4.64	4.44	4.17
20	25	2.62	2.62	2.61	2.61	2.60	60	65	5.54	5.46	5.23	4.88	4.46
25	30	2.77	2.76	2.76	2.75	2.74	65	70	6.50	6.34	5.92	5.34	4.71
30	35	2.95	2.95	2.94	2.93	2.90	70	75	7.78	7.47	6.69	5.75	4.89
35	40	3.18	3.17	3.16	3.14	3.10	75	80 and over	9.51	8.87	7.48	6.08	4.99
40	45	3.46	3.45	3.43	3.39	3.33	80 and over		11.88	10.55	8.19	6.29	5.04
45	50	3.80	3.79	3.75	3.69	3.59							

Option 4—Fixed Amounts Instalments. Retained by the company as a fund to be credited with interest annually on the then balance of the fund at a rate not less than two per cent per annum, from which shall be paid, until the fund is exhausted, instalments of fixed amounts, the final payment not to exceed the unpaid remainder. If the interest credited to the fund for any payment year exceeds the aggregate amount of the instalments paid during such year, the next succeeding instalment shall be increased by such excess.

Option 5—Joint Life Income. Payment in equal monthly instalments at the end of monthly payment intervals continuously while two payees live, according to the Joint Life Instalments Table for the sex and the age at nearest birthday of each of the two payees on the date this option becomes effective, and following the first death among the payees payment in equal monthly instalments at the end of monthly payment intervals of one-half the original amount continuously for the remaining lifetime of the surviving payee. This option shall not be available for payment of the sum payable upon maturity as an endowment or upon surrender for cash unless one of the payees shall be the same person whose life is insured under this policy. The company reserves the right to require satisfactory evidence of age of the payees before making any payment under this option.

JOINT LIFE INSTALMENTS TABLE

This table illustrates joint instalments for specimen age combinations only. Instalments for age combinations not shown shall be determined on the same basis as those in this table.

JOINT MONTHLY INSTALMENTS FOR BOTH LIVES THAT $1,000 WILL OBTAIN WITH ONE-HALF TO LAST SURVIVOR FOR LIFE

Age at Nearest Birthday	Man		40	45	50	55	60	65	70	75	80 and over
	Woman	40	45	50	55	60	65	70	75	80 and over	
Man	Woman										
	40	$3.18	$3.30	$3.46	$3.64	$3.82	$4.04	$4.26	$4.50	$4.76	$5.02
40	45	3.30	3.46	3.62	3.80	4.02	4.26	4.52	4.78	5.06	5.36
45	50	3.46	3.62	3.80	4.02	4.24	4.52	4.80	5.10	5.44	5.76
50	55	3.64	3.80	4.02	4.24	4.50	4.80	5.14	5.50	5.86	6.26
55	60	3.82	4.02	4.24	4.50	4.80	5.14	5.52	5.94	6.38	6.84
60	65	4.04	4.26	4.52	4.80	5.14	5.54	5.98	6.46	7.00	7.56
65	70	4.26	4.52	4.80	5.14	5.52	5.98	6.50	7.08	7.72	8.40
70	75	4.50	4.78	5.10	5.50	5.94	6.46	7.08	7.78	8.56	9.40
75	80 and over	4.76	5.06	5.44	5.86	6.38	7.00	7.72	8.56	9.50	10.56
80 and over		5.02	5.36	5.76	6.26	6.84	7.56	8.40	9.40	10.56	11.88

Form L-4800-480101 Page Four

General Section

Entire Contract. This policy and the application herefor, a copy of which is attached hereto and made a part hereof, constitute the entire contract. All statements made by or on behalf of the insured in applying for this policy shall, in the absence of fraud, be deemed representations and not warranties, and no statement shall avoid this policy or be used in defense of a claim hereunder unless it is contained in the application and a copy of the application is attached to this policy when issued.

Modification. No condition or provision of this policy can be waived or modified except by an endorsement hereon signed by the president, a vice-president, the secretary, or an assistant secretary of the company. No agent has power on behalf of the company to make or modify this contract, to extend the time for paying a premium, to waive any forfeiture, or to bind the company by making any promise or representation or by giving or receiving any information.

Control. The insured may, without the consent of any revocable beneficiary and in the absence of some special endorsement creating an exception hereto, assign or surrender this policy, amend or modify the same with the consent of the company, and exercise, receive, and enjoy every other right, benefit, and privilege contained in the policy.

Change of Plan. The plan, or Amount of Insurance, or both, may be changed by mutual agreement with the company.

Dividends. Annual dividends such as the company may apportion shall be payable while this policy is in force, other than as extended term insurance, without condition as to the payment of any subsequent premium. The insured shall have the option of electing in writing that each dividend payable be: (1) applied toward the payment of premiums hereon; or (2) used to purchase a participating paid-up dividend addition to this policy, the net value of which shall be not less than the dividend used to purchase such addition; or (3) left to accumulate at compound interest at a rate not less than two per cent per annum, any accumulated dividends not applied under Credits to Avoid Lapse to be added to, and be a part of, the sum payable upon the death of the insured, or upon maturity as an endowment, or upon surrender for cash, or to be withdrawable in cash at any time; or (4) paid in cash. If the insured does not elect one of the preceding methods in writing, method (3) shall automatically apply. The dividend method will be changed, as to any subsequent dividends, upon receipt by the company of the insured's written request for such change.

Election of Paid-Up Policy. This policy may be submitted to the company for endorsement as a participating paid-up policy whenever the sum of any accumulated dividends and any unapplied premium deposit reserve, if applied as a single premium, is sufficient to purchase paid-up insurance, payable under the same conditions as the insurance otherwise provided by this policy thereafter, in an amount equal to the difference between the amount of such insurance and the amount of paid-up insurance then available under the Non-Forfeiture Section. Such endorsement shall be made only upon written election by the insured and the surrender of any such accumulated dividends and unapplied premium deposit reserve.

Election of Matured Endowment. This policy may be matured as an endowment whenever the sum of any accumulated dividends and any unapplied premium deposit reserve, together with the cash surrender value of this policy, shall equal the amount of insurance then in force, but such endowment maturity shall be effective only upon written election by the insured and the surrender of this policy and of any such accumulated dividends and unapplied premium deposit reserve.

Premium Deposit Reserve. The insured may, while this policy is in force on a premium-paying basis, deposit sums of not less than five dollars each to be credited to the premium deposit reserve of this policy. On each anniversary of the Policy Date one year's interest shall be allowed on funds held under the premium deposit reserve not less than eleven months at a rate not less than two per cent per annum, the interest so allowed to be added to, and be a part of, the premium deposit reserve.

Any premium deposit reserve shall be added to, and be a part of, the sum payable upon the death of the insured, or upon maturity as an endowment, or upon surrender for cash, or shall be available for application as provided under Election of Paid-Up Policy, Election of Matured Endowment, Credits to Avoid Lapse, and Policy Loan. If the insured elects paid-up insurance as provided in the Non-Forfeiture Section, any unapplied premium deposit reserve shall be paid to the insured in cash.

Whenever the premium deposit reserve, if applied as a single premium, is sufficient to purchase paid-up insurance, payable under the same conditions as the insurance otherwise provided by this policy thereafter, in an amount equal to the difference between the amount of such insurance and the amount of paid-up insurance then available under the Non-Forfeiture Section, the premium deposit reserve shall be applied by the company as a single premium, without direction by the insured, and this policy shall become a participating paid-up policy.

Payment of Premiums. All premiums are payable in advance at the home office of the company, _____, or to a duly authorized agent of the company presenting the official receipt signed by the president, a vice-president, the secretary, or an assistant secretary, and countersigned by such agent. Subject to the minimum premium requirements of the company, premiums may be paid on an annual, semi-annual, quarterly, or monthly basis at the published rates in use by the company on the Policy Date. Change in the mode of premium payment may be made on any anniversary of the Policy Date upon written notice to the company.

General Section (Continued)

Grace Period. A grace period of thirty-one days shall be allowed, without interest, following the due date for the payment of any premium after the first. During such grace period this policy shall remain in force but if the premium due on such due date is not paid before the end of such grace period this policy shall lapse, except as provided under Credits to Avoid Lapse and Automatic Premium Loan. If death occurs within the grace period, the premium or any balance thereof, if unpaid, will be deducted from the death benefit.

Credits to Avoid Lapse. Without direction by the insured, any unapplied premium deposit reserve, any current dividends available under dividend methods (1), (2), or (3), and any accumulated dividends under dividend method (3) shall be applied successively toward the payment of any premium unpaid at the end of the grace period. If the total of such credits shall be less than such unpaid premium, such credits shall be applied as a pro rata premium as of the due date of such unpaid premium and on the day immediately following the last day of any pro rata premium payment period the unpaid balance of such premium shall be due and payable. A grace period shall be allowed for the payment of such unpaid balance as provided under Grace Period.

Reinstatement. If this policy lapses and a cash surrender value has not been paid, the company will reinstate it at any time within three years from the date of lapse, subject to any indebtedness to the company on this policy at the date of lapse, upon receipt of evidence of insurability, including good health, of the insured satisfactory to the company and payment of all arrears of premiums with interest at the rate of five per cent per annum on such premiums and on any such indebtedness.

Policy Loan. At any time while this policy is in force, other than as extended term insurance, the company, upon receipt of this policy and a loan agreement satisfactory to the company, will advance to the insured on the sole security of this policy any amount which shall be within the limit of the maximum loan value, if any, less any existing indebtedness to the company on this policy. The maximum loan value shall be that amount which, with interest at the rate of five per cent per annum to the date on which the next premium is due or, if no further premiums are payable, to the next anniversary of the Policy Date, equals, as of such date, the sum of the cash surrender value and any unapplied premium deposit reserve.

Interest on the loan shall accrue from day to day at the rate of five per cent per annum and shall constitute an indebtedness to the company against this policy as and when it accrues. Interest shall be payable on each anniversary of the Policy Date subsequent to the date of loan until such loan is repaid and if such interest is not paid when due it shall be added to and form a part of the loan, and bear interest at the same rate except that, if at any time the total indebtedness to the company on this policy, including accrued interest, is equal to the then maximum loan value, the accrued interest shall be then payable.

All or any part of the loan may be repaid, with accrued interest on the amount so repaid, at any time while this policy is in force other than as extended term insurance, provided this policy has not matured as an endowment or terminated by the death of the insured. Whenever the total indebtedness to the company on this policy is no longer within the limit of the then maximum loan value, this policy shall be void thirty-one days after the company has mailed notice to the last known address of the insured and the assignee of record, if any.

Automatic Premium Loan. If a written election by the insured for application of this automatic premium loan provision is on file with the company prior to the end of the grace period for payment of any unpaid premium or unpaid balance thereof which remains unpaid after application of Credits to Avoid Lapse, such unpaid premium or unpaid balance thereof shall be entered as paid and the amount thereof charged as an indebtedness against this policy, provided that the maximum loan value as defined under Policy Loan, less any existing indebtedness to the company on this policy, is equal to or in excess of such amount. Such indebtedness shall bear interest from the due date of such unpaid premium or unpaid balance thereof and shall be subject to the same terms and conditions as provided for other loans under Policy Loan. If the maximum loan value, less any existing indebtedness to the company on this policy, is not sufficient to pay such unpaid premium or unpaid balance thereof this provision shall not be effective. Any election of this provision by the insured will be revoked as to its subsequent application upon receipt by the company of written request for revocation by the insured.

Indebtedness. Any indebtedness to the company on this policy shall be deducted from any settlement.

Assignment. The company assumes no responsibility for the validity or effect of any assignment of this policy and no assignment will be recognized until it has been duly filed with the company. An assignment of this policy shall operate to the extent thereof to transfer the interest of any beneficiary whom the assignor has the right to change, and to render any part of the sum payable to which the assignee is entitled payable in one sum, notwithstanding any settlement agreement endorsed hereon at the time the assignment was executed. No assignment of this policy or any interest thereunder made after the death of the insured shall be valid unless the company consents thereto.

Age. This policy is issued at the age shown on page 1, which is the insured's age at nearest birthday on the Policy Date according to the date of birth as given in the application. If the age of the insured has been misstated, the amount payable and every benefit accruing hereunder shall be such as the premiums paid would have purchased at the correct age.

Incontestability. This policy shall be incontestable after it has been in force during the lifetime of the insured for a period of two years from the Policy Date, except for non-payment of premiums, and except as to provisions and conditions relating to benefits in the event of total and permanent disability, and those granting additional insurance specifically against death by accidental means, contained in any supplementary contract attached to, and made a part of, this policy.

Suicide. The suicide of the insured, while sane or insane, within two years from the Policy Date is a risk not assumed under this policy. In such event, however, there shall be a death benefit of an amount equal to the premiums received hereon, without interest.

Non-Forfeiture Section

Extended Term Insurance. If any premium or balance thereof remains unpaid at the end of the grace period after application of Credits to Avoid Lapse, and Automatic Premium Loan if elected by the insured, and if a cash surrender value is available, the amount of death benefit provided by this policy, increased by the amount of any paid-up dividend additions and less any indebtedness to the company on this policy, shall be continued in force automatically as non-participating extended term insurance from the due date of such unpaid premium or unpaid balance thereof. The term of the extended term insurance shall be such that the present value of the guaranteed benefits provided thereunder shall be equal to the cash surrender value, less any indebtedness to the company on this policy, on such due date.

Paid-Up Insurance. Upon receipt by the company of this policy for endorsement and written request by the insured prior to, or within ninety days after, the due date of any premium or balance thereof, if a cash surrender value is available, a reduced amount of insurance will be continued in force from such due date as participating paid-up life insurance. The reduced amount of insurance shall be such that the present value of the guaranteed benefits provided thereunder shall be equal to the cash surrender value, less any indebtedness to the company on this policy, on such due date.

Cash Surrender. Upon receipt by the company at any time of written request by the insured and the legal surrender of this policy, this policy shall terminate and the cash surrender value, if any, less any indebtedness to the company on this policy, shall be payable. The cash surrender value shall be determined as follows:

(a) If all premiums due to date have been paid, the cash surrender value for a policy providing $1,000 Amount of Insurance at the end of any policy year shall be the then present value of the future guaranteed life insurance benefits, exclusive of any additional benefits provided by any supplementary contract attached to this policy, which would have been provided if all future premiums were paid when due, including existing paid-up dividend additions, less the present value of the annual non-forfeiture factors specified in the Table of Values for subsequent policy years. If surrender shall occur at any time except at the end of a policy year, the cash surrender value shall be determined on a basis consistent with that described above, with due allowance for any premiums paid for the policy year then current. If the Amount of Insurance is more or less than $1,000, the cash surrender value shall be proportionately increased or decreased.

(b) If any premium or balance thereof due under this policy is unpaid, and less than ninety days have elapsed since the due date of such unpaid premium or unpaid balance thereof, the cash surrender value shall be the same as on such due date, and shall be determined as in (a) above.

(c) If this policy is being continued as extended term insurance or as paid-up insurance, and more than ninety days have elapsed since the effective date of such insurance, the cash surrender value shall be equal to the present value of the future guaranteed life insurance benefits which otherwise would have been provided if such form of insurance were continued in force, including any existing paid-up dividend additions.

TABLE OF VALUES
FOR A POLICY PROVIDING $1,000 AMOUNT OF INSURANCE

These values do not include allowance for any paid-up dividend additions and are subject to adjustment on account of any credits or indebtedness on this policy. Values not appearing in this table will be computed on the same basis and will be furnished on request.

Age 35
Annual Non-Forfeiture Factors:
First 10 Years $23.25050
Thereafter $21.24800

End of Policy Year	Cash Surrender or Maximum Loan Value	Extended Term Insurance Years	Extended Term Insurance Days	Paid-Up Insurance
2	$ 2.57	0	187	$ 6
3	21.43	3	307	45
4	40.56	6	188	83
5	59.94	8	244	120
6	79.58	10	150	156
7	99.47	11	303	191
8	119.60	12	361	225
9	139.96	13	341	259
10	160.54	14	258	292
11	179.27	15	74	320
12	198.13	15	216	347
13	217.10	15	326	374
14	236.18	16	42	400
15	255.34	16	98	425
16	274.57	16	133	449
17	293.84	16	149	472
18	313.14	16	148	495
19	332.45	16	133	517
20	351.75	16	104	539
Age 55	351.75	16	104	539
Age 60	447.29	15	173	635
Age 65	539.20	14	70	716

Specimen Policy Form (Continued)

Non-Forfeiture Section (Continued)

Deferment. At its option, the company may defer any payment under Cash Surrender or Policy Loan, other than to pay premiums on policies in this company, for a period not exceeding six months after request therefor and this policy have been received by the company.

Actuarial Basis. All present values referred to in the Non-Forfeiture Section of this policy shall be computed on the basis of the Commissioners 1941 Standard Ordinary Mortality Table and interest at the rate of two and one-half per cent per annum and assuming that deaths during any policy year occur at the end of that year.

All single premiums referred to in this policy shall be net single premiums, computed on the basis of the Commissioners 1941 Standard Ordinary Mortality Table and interest at the rate of two per cent per annum and assuming that deaths during any policy year occur at the end of that year, increased by three per cent.

The extended term insurance, paid-up insurance, cash surrender values, and loan values provided by this policy are not less than the minimum benefits and values which would result from use of the Standard Non-Forfeiture Value Method and interest at the rate of two and one-half per cent per annum and assuming that deaths during any policy year occur at the end of that year, nor are such benefits and values less than the minimum benefits and values required by the law of the State in which this policy is delivered.

Form L-4800–480101

Page Eight

Printed in U.S.A.

Accidental-Death Section

Supplementary Contract. This Accidental-Death Section constitutes a supplementary contract attached to and made a part of the life insurance policy herein designated. The Settlement Section of the policy and the provisions of the policy entitled Entire Contract, Modification, Control, Payment of Premiums *except as herein terminated*, Grace Period, Credits to Avoid Lapse, Reinstatement, Automatic Premium Loan (if included in the policy), Indebtedness, Assignment, and Age, are hereby referred to and by such reference made a part hereof. No other provision of the policy shall apply hereto or be a part hereof.

Benefit. The company agrees to pay, while the policy and this Accidental-Death Section are in force and subject to all the terms and conditions of this section, the Amount of Accidental-Death Insurance

$10,000

in addition to the death benefit under the policy, on receipt of due proof that the death of the insured resulted directly, and independently of all other causes, from bodily injury effected solely through external, violent, and accidental means as evidenced by a visible contusion or wound on the exterior of the body (except in case of drowning or internal injuries revealed by an autopsy) and that such death occurred within ninety days from the date of such injury.

The company shall have the right and opportunity to examine the body and to make an autopsy unless prohibited by law.

Consideration. The insurance provided by this Accidental-Death Section, beginning on the Supplementary Contract Date, is granted in consideration of the application, a copy of which is attached to the policy and made a part hereof, and of the payment of additional premiums of

Thirteen and 90/100 Dollars annually,

due and payable in the manner specified for premium payment in the policy and payable in each supplementary contract year, the first such payment being due on the Supplementary Contract Date; provided, however, that in no event shall any such additional premium be due or payable on or after the anniversary of the Supplementary Contract Date nearest the insured's attained age sixty-five.

Risks Not Assumed. This Accidental-Death Section does not cover nor insure against death resulting directly or indirectly from: (1) suicide or any attempt thereat or intentional self-inflicted injury of any kind, whether the insured be sane or insane; (2) the taking of any poison, drug, or sedative, or asphyxiation from or inhalation of gas, whether voluntary or involuntary; (3) committing or attempting to commit an assault or felony; (4) war or any act attributable to war, whether or not the insured is in military service; (5) military service for any country at war; (6) participating or engaging in riot or insurrection; (7) operating or riding in, or descending from or with while in flight, any kind of aircraft if the insured is a pilot, officer, or member of the crew of such aircraft or is giving or receiving any kind of training or instruction aboard such aircraft, or has any duties aboard such aircraft or requiring descent therefrom; (8) operating or riding in, or descending from or with while in flight, any kind of aircraft under the control or charter of, and while the insured is in the service of, the military, naval or air forces of any country; (9) bodily or mental infirmity or illness or disease of any kind; or (10) any bacterial infection not occurring simultaneously with and through a cut or wound caused by external, violent, and accidental means.

As used in this Accidental-Death Section the term "country" includes any government or any coalition of countries or governments through an international organization or otherwise; "war" means declared or undeclared war or any conflict between the armed forces of countries; "military service" means service in military, naval or air forces.

Execution. This Supplementary Contract is issued and accepted subject to all the conditions, benefits, and privileges hereinbefore described and described on the reverse side hereof, which are hereby made a part of this contract.

This Supplementary Contract is attached to and a part of Policy No.

000,000

issued on the life of the Insured

John Doe, Age 35.

In witness whereof, the _____ Life Insurance Company, at its Home Office in _____ _____ has caused this Supplementary Contract to be executed on the Supplementary Contract Date,

June 1, 1960.

Secretary

President

Registrar

Form L-4899-560901   Accidental-Death Insurance

Accidental-Death Section (Continued)

Termination. This Accidental-Death Section shall automatically terminate if the policy matures, expires, or becomes paid-up, or at the end of the supplementary contract year immediately preceding the anniversary of the Supplementary Contract Date nearest the insured's attained age sixty-five, whichever occurs first; or, if any of the provisions of the Non-Forfeiture Section, if any, of the policy become effective; or, on the due date of any unpaid premium payable under the policy or this Accidental-Death Section, except as provided under Grace Period.

Upon termination of this Accidental-Death Section the additional premium herefor shall no longer be payable. If for any reason any amount, not due before such termination, shall be received by the company under this Accidental-Death Section after such termination, the amount so received with compound interest thereon at the rate of five per cent per annum will be refunded and the company shall not incur any other or further obligation or liability under this section.

Upon receipt by the company at its home office, on any anniversary of the Supplementary Contract Date or within thirty-one days thereafter, of written request by the insured and the return of the policy for endorsement, the company will cancel this section as of such anniversary.

Termination of this Accidental-Death Section shall be without prejudice to claim for accidental-death on account of injury sustained prior to such termination.

Paid-Up. If the policy becomes a fully paid-up policy before the anniversary of the Supplementary Contract Date nearest the insured's attained age sixty-five the insured may, by written election and the payment of the required Single Premium on or before the date on which the policy becomes paid-up, continue this Accidental-Death Insurance as paid-up until otherwise terminated.

Disability Section

Supplementary Contract. This Disability Section constitutes a supplementary contract attached to and made a part of the life insurance policy herein designated. The provisions of the policy entitled Entire Contract, Modification, Control, Payment of Premiums *except as herein waived or terminated*, Grace Period, Credits to Avoid Lapse, Reinstatement, Automatic Premium Loan (if included in the policy), Indebtedness, Assignment, and Age, are hereby referred to and by such reference made a part hereof. No other provision of the policy shall apply hereto or be a part hereof.

Benefit. Upon receipt at its home office of due proof that the insured has become totally and permanently disabled as hereinafter defined, and subject to all the terms and conditions of this section, the company shall waive the payment of each premium becoming due during the continuance of such disability commencing with the premium due on or next following the date of commencement of such disability, provided, however, that no premium shall be waived, the due date of which is more than one year prior to the date of receipt by the company at its home office of written notice of claim hereunder on account of such disability.

Such waiver of premium shall apply to the entire premium under the policy, including the additional premium for every supplementary contract made a part thereof, and any premium credit payment provided for by the policy, and shall be in addition to all other benefits under the policy, including dividends, which benefits shall accrue as though the premiums so waived had been paid in cash.

The mode of premium payment shall not be changed during the continuance of disability.

Disability Defined. Total and permanent disability is disability as the result of bodily injury or disease originating after the insurance under the policy and this section took effect so that the insured is and will be thereby wholly prevented from performing any work, following any occupation, or engaging in any business for remuneration or profit, and which disability has continued uninterruptedly for a period of at least six months (disability of such duration being deemed to be permanent only for the purpose of determining the commencement of waiver of premiums hereunder).

Independently of any other cause, the total and irrecoverable loss of the sight of both eyes, or of the use of both hands, or of both feet, or of one hand and one foot, shall be considered total disability.

Waiver of premium shall be allowed only for total and permanent disability which commenced prior to the anniversary of the Supplementary Contract Date nearest the insured's attained age sixty.

Consideration. The insurance provided by this Disability Section, beginning on the Supplementary Contract Date, is granted in consideration of the application, a copy of which is attached to the policy and made a part hereof, and of the payment of additional premiums of

Eight and 40/100·Dollars annually for twelve years and thereafter Six and 90/100 Dollars annually,

due and payable in the manner specified for premium payment in the policy and payable in each supplementary contract year, the first such payment being due on the Supplementary Contract Date; provided, however, that in no event shall any such additional premium be due or payable on or after the anniversary of the Supplementary Contract Date nearest the insured's attained age sixty.

If any premium under the policy, or any additional premium under any supplementary contract made a part thereof, is due and unpaid before receipt by the company at its home office of written notice of claim hereunder, waiver of premium shall be allowed only if such notice is received within one year after the due date of the first such unpaid premium and the total disability as a result of which claim is made commenced either (a) before such due date; or, (b) subsequent to such due date but within the grace period allowed by the policy for the payment of such unpaid premium, in which case before waiver of premium is allowed the insured shall pay in cash such unpaid premium with compound interest at the rate of five per cent per annum from the end of the grace period following the due date of such unpaid premium.

Execution. This Supplementary Contract is issued and accepted subject to all the conditions, benefits, and privileges hereinbefore described and described on the reverse side hereof, which are hereby made a part of this contract.

This Supplementary Contract is attached to and a part of Policy No.

000,000

issued on the life of the Insured

John Doe, Age 35.

In witness whereof, the _____ Life Insurance Company, at its Home Office in _____ _____ has caused this Supplementary Contract to be executed on the Supplementary Contract Date,

June 1, 1960.

Secretary

President

Registrar

Disability Section (Continued)

Risks Not Assumed. This Disability Section does not cover nor insure against disability that results, directly or indirectly, from: (1) intentional self-inflicted injury of any kind; (2) war or any act attributable to war, whether or not the insured is in military service; or (3) military service for any country at war.

As used in this Disability Section the term "country" includes any government or any coalition of countries or governments through an international organization or otherwise; "war" means declared or undeclared war or any conflict between the armed forces of countries; "military service" means service in military, naval or air forces.

Notice of Claim. Written notice of claim hereunder must be received by the company at its home office during the lifetime and during the continuance of total disability of the insured. Failure to give such notice within such times shall not invalidate or diminish any claim if it shall be shown not to have been reasonably possible to give such notice within such times and that notice was given as soon as was reasonably possible.

Any premium under the policy, or any additional premium under any supplementary contract made a part thereof, falling due after notice of claim is received and prior to approval of claim shall be payable as though no notice of claim had been received, but will, if paid to the company, be refunded upon approval of such claim. Any premium paid to the company and later waived under this section but not refunded by the company prior to the insured's death shall be added to, and be a part of, the sum payable upon the death of the insured.

Proof of Continuance of Disability. Before waiving any premium, the company may demand due proof of the continuance of total disability, but such proof will not be required oftener than once a year after such disability has continued for two full years. If such proof shall not be furnished, or if at any time the insured shall become able to perform any work, follow any occupation, or engage in any business for remuneration or profit, no further premiums shall be waived. If, however, any such premiums shall have been waived they shall constitute an indebtedness against the policy bearing interest as provided for loans under loan provisions.

Termination. This Disability Section shall automatically terminate if the policy matures, expires, or becomes paid-up, or at the end of the supplementary contract year immediately preceding the anniversary of the Supplementary Contract Date nearest the insured's attained age sixty, whichever occurs first; or, if any of the provisions of the Non-Forfeiture Section, if any, of the policy become effective; or, on the due date of any unpaid premium payable under the policy or this Disability Section, except as provided under Grace Period.

Upon termination of this Disability Section the additional premium herefor shall no longer be payable. If for any reason any amount, not due before such termination, shall be received by the company under this Disability Section after such termination, the amount so received with compound interest thereon at the rate of five per cent per annum will be refunded and the company shall not incur any other or further obligation or liability under this section.

Upon receipt by the company at its home office, on any anniversary of the Supplementary Contract Date or within thirty-one days thereafter, of written request by the insured and the return of the policy for endorsement, the company will cancel this section as of such anniversary.

Termination of this Disability Section shall be without prejudice to claim for waiver of premium on account of total disability commencing prior to such termination.

C. Request for Settlement Agreement

REQUEST FOR SETTLEMENT AGREEMENT

To ——————— LIFE INSURANCE COMPANY:

    Request is hereby made, subject to the rights of present collateral assignees of record, if any, that the proceeds of Policy or Policies   0,000,000 on the life of **Ethan Allen** be applied upon the death of the Insured for the benefit of the following beneficiaries in accordance with the following provisions. Any and all previous provisions for payment of the proceeds at the death of the Insured are hereby revoked.

Primary Beneficiary:..........................   Mary Allen, wife of Insured.

Secondary Beneficiary:..........................   Lawful children of Insured.

Option under which proceeds are to be applied for each Primary Beneficiary:............   Option 1 for life.

Rights to withdraw or change reserved to each Primary Beneficiary:..........................   Right while Option 1 is operative (a) of withdrawal; (b) to elect settlement under Option 2 or Option 3 or Option 4, with such further withdrawal or commutation privilege as may then be agreed upon with the Company.

Option under which the value of any guaranteed amounts unpaid will be applied for each Secondary Beneficiary if at any time no Primary Beneficiary is living:..........................   Option 1 for life.

Rights to withdraw or change reserved to each Secondary Beneficiary (if at any time no Primary Beneficiary is living):....................   Right while Option 1 is operative (a) of withdrawal; (b) to elect settlement under Option 2 or Option 3 or Option 4, with such further withdrawal or commutation privilege as may then be agreed upon with the Company.

Frequency of payments to Primary and Secondary Beneficiary:..........................   Option 1: Monthly, commencing after one month.

Final Beneficiary to receive in one sum:.......   None.

Protection for Beneficiary: The Spendthrift Provision detailed in this settlement shall apply to.................................   Not requested.

    The right is reserved to change the beneficiary of any policy referred to herein. If the right to change the beneficiary is reserved a new beneficiary may be designated from time to time by filing at the Home Office of the Company written request therefor in such form as the Company may require. Any such designation shall be effective only when endorsed on the policy affected in accordance with the provisions of such policy and any such designation shall be subject to any collateral assignment of such policy duly filed with the Company prior to such designation.

Form 3712-59 Request and Agreement

Request for Settlement Agreement (Continued)

ORDER OF PAYMENT TO CLASSES OF BENEFICIARIES. Any payments due will be made exclusively to the Primary Beneficiary, if living. If at any time there be no Primary Beneficiary living, any payments due will be made to the Secondary Beneficiary, if living. If at any time there be no living Primary or Secondary Beneficiary, the proceeds at that time will be paid in one sum to the Final Beneficiary, if any.

If at any time there is no existing beneficiary, the proceeds at that time will be paid in one sum to the executors or administrators of the last survivor of the Insured and all beneficiaries, EXCEPT as may be otherwise provided in this agreement.

SETTLEMENT IF MORE THAN ONE BENEFICIARY IN A CLASS. If at the death of the Insured there be more than one Primary Beneficiary living, or if at the death of the last survivor of the Insured and all Primary Beneficiaries there be more than one Secondary Beneficiary living, the proceeds will be first divided into equal shares among the Primary Beneficiaries then living or among the Secondary Beneficiaries then living, as the case may be, and each person's share will be separately applied to the designated Option for his or her benefit. If any such beneficiary shall die after such division is made, the then present value of any guaranteed amounts unpaid on such beneficiary's share will be redivided into such number of equal shares as there shall be other beneficiaries of the same class then living. Each such additional share will be paid in one sum to the surviving beneficiary to whom such share was apportioned.

Except as may be otherwise provided in this agreement, any amount payable to the Final Beneficiary shall be paid only in equal shares to the persons included in that designation who are living at the time such amount becomes payable.

DEFINITION OF "PROCEEDS." The proceeds under a particular policy included in this settlement shall be:

1. As of the death of the Insured, the amount payable to the beneficiary under such policy, including (1) any dividends, dividend deposits or dividend additions standing to the credit of the policy, (2) the amount of any Accidental Death Benefit that may be payable, and (3) any premium refund; and decreased by any indebtedness and by any premium deduction provided by the policy. If the policy, by its terms, shall provide for instalments or deferred payments, in lieu of such instalments or deferred payments, the then present value thereof commuted on the basis provided in such policy shall be used in determining the amount of the proceeds of such policy.

2. As of any time subsequent to the death of the Insured, the then present value of any guaranteed amounts resulting from such policy and unpaid at such time.

If this agreement relates to a portion only of the proceeds, proportionate parts of the proceeds of all policies subject to this agreement shall be used in accordance with the terms of this agreement and the word "proceeds" wherever used in the distributive provisions of this agreement shall refer only to such portion of the proceeds.

Special Provisions: (Any provisions appearing under this heading shall supersede any conflicting provisions on the first page of this agreement or above on this second page.)

1. Common Disaster.
All provisions whatsoever of this agreement are to be so read that any beneficiary who survives the Insured but dies prior to noon of the tenth day after the death of the Insured will be considered as not having survived the Insured. (This provision may be deleted, if desired, or it may be altered by substituting for "tenth day" any number of days from one to ninety, inclusive. Any deletion or alteration must be initialed by the person or persons signing this request.)

2. Provision is hereby made, in accordance with the paragraph entitled "Payments to Issue" in this settlement, for the issue of any Secondary Beneficiary.

3. Anything to the contrary in this agreement (including paragraphs 1 and 2 of these Special Provisions) notwithstanding, said wife shall have the right, but only after the death of Insured, to revoke the designation of any and all beneficiaries hereunder and to appoint her executors or administrators to receive at her death the then present value of any guaranteed amounts unpaid. Any such revocation and appointment shall be effective only if made in writing and filed with the Company at its Home Office during the lifetime of said wife.

NO FURTHER SPECIAL PROVISIONS

Form 3712-59 Request and Agreement

Request for Settlement Agreement (Continued)

SETTLEMENT OPTIONS. The options referred to in this settlement shall have the following significance:

OPTION 1. The Company will retain the proceeds for the period agreed upon and pay interest on the proceeds of each policy at the rate specified for Option 1 in such policy and dispose of the proceeds at the end of such period of retention in such manner and to such persons as may be agreed upon. In addition, during retention at interest, on each anniversary of the date on which the option became effective, the Company will pay to the person or persons receiving interest such surplus interest, if any, as may be apportioned to the proceeds by the Board of Directors. Interest will accrue only to the date of death of the last survivor of all beneficiaries designated to receive under this option.

OPTION 2. The Company will pay the proceeds of each policy in instalments for a specified number of years, first payment immediate, in accordance with the table for Option 2 set forth in such policy. In addition, while instalments are being paid, on each anniversary of the date on which the option became effective, the Company will pay to the person or persons receiving instalments such surplus interest, if any, as may be apportioned to the proceeds by the Board of Directors.

OPTION 3. The Company will pay the proceeds of each policy in instalments, based on the age and the sex of the payee, for a specified number of years certain and will continue such instalments after the certain period for as long as such payee shall live, first payment immediate, in accordance with the table for Option 3 set forth in such policy, provided however that if Option 3 is elected by a beneficiary more than twelve months after the death of the Insured, the Option 3 table applicable shall be that in the policies the Company is issuing at the time the election is made. In addition, while instalments certain are being paid, on each anniversary of the date on which the option became effective, the Company will pay to the person or persons receiving instalments certain such surplus interest, if any, as may be apportioned to the proceeds by the Board of Directors.

OPTION 4. The Company will pay the proceeds in periodical instalments of such specified amount as may be agreed upon, first payment immediate, continuing such payments until the proceeds with interest on the proceeds of each policy at the rate specified in such policy for the held-at-interest optional mode of settlement (Option 1), and such share of surplus interest, if any, as may be apportioned thereto by the Board of Directors, compounded annually, are exhausted. Interest will accrue only to the date of death of the last survivor of all beneficiaries designated to receive under this option.

If at any time designated payments under Option 4 would not aggregate $60 per year for each $1000 of proceeds then retained under such Option 4, the Company shall have the right to make future payments under such Option 4 at the rate of $60 per year for each $1000 of proceeds then retained under such Option 4.

MINIMUM AMOUNT AND FREQUENCY OF PAYMENT. If the amount to be placed under an option for any payee is less than $1000, the Company will pay such amount in one sum to the payee who would then be entitled to receive payments thereunder in full discharge of all liability of the Company. If a periodical payment to a payee of less than $10 is called for, payments will instead be made at such less frequent intervals (quarterly, semi-annually, or annually) as will make the amount $10 or more, but if after instalment payments have once begun an instalment is divided among several payees so that the share of each is less than $10, the then present value of the guaranteed amounts unpaid will be paid to such payees as are then entitled to the instalments. If at any time a frequency of payments should be required different from that provided in the pertinent option of the policy, such payments will be the actuarial equivalent thereof.

SETTLEMENT COVERING MORE THAN ONE POLICY. If this settlement covers more than one policy, any withdrawal or other payment from principal or commutation of instalments will be made pro rata from the proceeds of all policies included in this settlement. Whenever it is necessary to divide the proceeds of policies settled under this settlement into shares, a proportionate amount of the proceeds of each policy subject to the settlement shall be included in each share.

SETTLEMENT YEAR. A settlement year shall begin on the date of the death of the Insured and each successive settlement year shall begin on an anniversary of such date.

CHANGE OF OPTION. The Company shall not be required to permit a change of option except upon the death of the insured or on any anniversary thereof.

COMMUTATION. If under this settlement the Company at any time becomes obligated to determine the then present value of instalments, such value shall be determined by commuting the instalments at the rate of interest used in computing the amount of such instalments, compounded annually. Any payment of such commuted value shall be in full discharge of all liability of the Company with respect thereto, and shall be in lieu of such portion of the payments.

LIMITATIONS ON WITHDRAWAL. Any rights of withdrawal reserved in this settlement are subject to the following provisions:

Withdrawals will not be allowed in sums of less than $200 and will be restricted to a maximum of three per settlement year.

If by any withdrawal (except those resulting from the periodical payments under an Option 4 settlement) the balance retained for the payee would be reduced to less than $1000, the Company will pay such balance in one sum to the payee in full discharge of all liability of the Company with respect thereto even though such act results in a payment to the then payee of an amount in excess of any limitation on such payee's right of withdrawal.

If withdrawal occurs off an interest payment date, guaranteed interest shall be paid on the funds withdrawn only for whole months from the last interest payment date.

LAWFUL CHILDREN. If provision is made in this settlement for the lawful children as a class of any person, the phrase shall include only lawful children born to or legally adopted by that person.

PAYMENTS TO "ISSUE." If this settlement shall make any provision for the issue, as a class, of a person and if the person shall not be living on any date on which he or she would become a payee, if living, or if the person shall become a payee and subsequently shall die while any provision hereof is operative, the then living issue of such person shall be entitled to the then present value of the portion of any guaranteed amounts unpaid determined by the interest which such person, living would have had as a payee. Such amount shall be paid in one sum to the then living issue of such person, in equal shares per stirpes. Such payment shall be in full discharge of all liability of the Company with respect thereto, and shall be in lieu of such portion of the payments. Issue shall include only lawful children born to or legally adopted by a person and lawful children born to or legally adopted by such children.

BENEFICIARIES NOT SPECIFIED BY NAME. If this settlement shall provide for any beneficiaries or payees not specified by name, the Company in determining at any time such beneficiaries or payees is hereby authorized to rely on an affidavit or affidavits by such person or persons as the Company considers likely to be familiar with the facts, and the Company shall be discharged from all liability upon making settlement in accordance with such affidavit or affidavits.

SPENDTHRIFT PROVISION. Except as otherwise specifically provided in this settlement the benefits accruing under this settlement for any beneficiary shall not be subject to withdrawal, anticipation or commutation by such beneficiary, and, to the extent permitted by law, the benefits accruing under this settlement for any beneficiary to whom the spendthrift provision is made applicable, shall not be subject to transfer or encumbrance by such beneficiary and shall not be subject to the claims of creditors of such beneficiary nor to any judicial process against such beneficiary.

EFFECT OF ASSIGNMENTS. Any assignment of a policy payable under the provisions of this settlement shall operate to the extent thereof to transfer the interests of any beneficiary whom the assignor has the right to change and to render proceeds to which the assignee is entitled payable in one sum, notwithstanding any provisions of this settlement to the contrary.

Form 3711-59 and 3712-59
Request and Agreement

EXECUTION PAGE

This request is executed at--

(Include place and date)

Owner--

    Ethan Allen

——————— LIFE INSURANCE COMPANY agrees that the policy or policies described in this request, or copy of request, for settlement agreement shall be payable upon the death of the Insured in accordance with the foregoing provisions and conditions.

Executed at Montpelier, Vermont,

AJAX LIFE INSURANCE COMPANY

By   *Secretary*

Countersigned:

Registrar

(Not valid until countersigned by a Registrar of the Company and incorporated by the Company into the policy or policies involved.)

D. Assignment of Life Insurance Policy as Collateral Form

FORM DESIGNED, PRINTED, AND DISTRIBUTED BY
AMERICAN BANKERS ASSOCIATION
BANK MANAGEMENT COMMISSION

FORM No. 10—LIFE INSURANCE ASSIGNMENT (REVIEWED AND APPROVED 1950)

ASSIGNMENT OF LIFE INSURANCE POLICY AS COLLATERAL

A.　**For Value Received** the undersigned hereby assign, transfer and set over to _____

_____ of _____

its successors and assigns, (herein called the "Assignee") Policy No. _____ issued by the

_____

(herein called the "Insurer") and any supplementary contracts issued in connection therewith (said policy and contracts being

herein called the "Policy"), upon the life of _____

of _____ and all claims, options, privileges, rights, title and interest therein and thereunder (except as provided in Paragraph C hereof), subject to all the terms and conditions of the Policy and to all superior liens, if any, which the Insurer may have against the Policy. The undersigned by this instrument jointly and severally agree and the Assignee by the acceptance of this assignment agrees to the conditions and provisions herein set forth.

B.　It is expressly agreed that, without detracting from the generality of the foregoing, the following specific rights are included in this assignment and pass by virtue hereof:
1. The sole right to collect from the Insurer the net proceeds of the Policy when it becomes a claim by death or maturity;
2. The sole right to surrender the Policy and receive the surrender value thereof at any time provided by the terms of the Policy and at such other times as the Insurer may allow;
3. The sole right to obtain one or more loans or advances on the Policy, either from the Insurer or, at any time, from other persons, and to pledge or assign the Policy as security for such loans or advances;
4. The sole right to collect and receive all distributions or shares of surplus, dividend deposits or additions to the Policy now or hereafter made or apportioned thereto, and to exercise any and all options contained in the Policy with respect thereto; provided, that unless and until the Assignee shall notify the Insurer in writing to the contrary, the distributions or shares of surplus, dividend deposits and additions shall continue on the plan in force at the time of this assignment; and
5. The sole right to exercise all nonforfeiture rights permitted by the terms of the Policy or allowed by the Insurer and to receive all benefits and advantages derived therefrom.

C.　It is expressly agreed that the following specific rights, so long as the Policy has not been surrendered, are reserved and excluded from this assignment and do not pass by virtue hereof:
1. The right to collect from the Insurer any disability benefit payable in cash that does not reduce the amount of insurance;
2. The right to designate and change the beneficiary;
3. The right to elect any optional mode of settlement permitted by the Policy or allowed by the Insurer;
but the reservation of these rights shall in no way impair the right of the Assignee to surrender the Policy completely with all its incidents or impair any other right of the Assignee hereunder, and any designation or change of beneficiary or election of a mode of settlement shall be made subject to this assignment and to the rights of the Assignee hereunder.

D.　This assignment is made and the Policy is to be held as collateral security for any and all liabilities of the undersigned, or any of them, to the Assignee, either now existing or that may hereafter arise in the ordinary course of business between any of the undersigned and the Assignee (all of which liabilities secured or to become secured are herein called "Liabilities").

E.　The Assignee covenants and agrees with the undersigned as follows:
1. That any balance of sums received hereunder from the Insurer remaining after payment of the then existing Liabilities, matured or unmatured, shall be paid by the Assignee to the persons entitled thereto under the terms of the Policy had this assignment not been executed;
2. That the Assignee will not exercise either the right to surrender the Policy or (except for the purpose of paying premiums) the right to obtain policy loans from the Insurer, until there has been default in any of the Liabilities or a failure to pay any premium when due, nor until twenty days after the Assignee shall have mailed, by first-class mail, to the undersigned at the addresses last supplied in writing to the Assignee specifically referring to this assignment, notice of intention to exercise such right; and
3. That the Assignee will upon request forward without unreasonable delay to the Insurer the Policy for endorsement of any designation or change of beneficiary or any election of an optional mode of settlement.

F.　The Insurer is hereby authorized to recognize the Assignee's claims to rights hereunder without investigating the reason for any action taken by the Assignee, or the validity or the amount of the Liabilities or the existence of any default therein, or the giving of any notice under Paragraph E (2) above or otherwise, or the application to be made by the Assignee of any amounts to be paid to the Assignee. The sole signature of the Assignee shall be sufficient for the exercise of any rights under the Policy assigned hereby and the sole receipt of the Assignee for any sums received shall be a full discharge and release therefor to the Insurer. Checks for all or any part of the sums payable under the Policy and assigned herein, shall be drawn to the exclusive order of the Assignee if, when, and in such amounts as may be, requested by the Assignee.

G.　The Assignee shall be under no obligation to pay any premium, or the principal of or interest on any loans or advances on the Policy whether or not obtained by the Assignee, or any other charges on the Policy, but any such amounts so paid by the Assignee from its own funds, shall become a part of the Liabilities hereby secured, shall be due immediately, and shall draw interest at a rate fixed by the Assignee from time to time not exceeding 6% per annum.

H.　The exercise of any right, option, privilege or power given herein to the Assignee shall be at the option of the Assignee, but (except as restricted by Paragraph E (2) above) the Assignee may exercise any such right, option, privilege or power without notice to, or assent by, or affecting the liability of, or releasing any interest hereby assigned by the undersigned, or any of them.

I.　The Assignee may take or release other security, may release any party primarily or secondarily liable for any of the Liabilities, may grant extensions, renewals or indulgences with respect to the Liabilities, or may apply to the Liabilities in such order as the Assignee shall determine, the proceeds of the Policy hereby assigned or any amount received on account of the Policy by the exercise of any right permitted under this assignment, without resorting or regard to other security.

J.　In the event of any conflict between the provisions of this assignment and provisions of the note or other evidence of any Liability, with respect to the Policy or rights of collateral security therein, the provisions of this assignment shall prevail.

K.　Each of the undersigned declares that no proceedings in bankruptcy are pending against him and that his property is not subject to any assignment for the benefit of creditors.

Signed and sealed this _____ day of _____, 19_____

_____	_____(L.S.)
Witness	*Insured or Owner*
_____	_____
	Address
_____	_____(L.S.)
Witness	*Beneficiary*
	_____
	Address

Assignment of Life Insurance Policy as Collateral Form (Continued)

INDIVIDUAL ACKNOWLEDGMENT

STATE OF _____⎫
                          ⎬ss:
COUNTY OF_____⎭

On the _____day of _____ 19 _____, before me personally came

_____, to me known to be the individual _____ described in and who

executed the assignment on the reverse side hereof and acknowledged to me that _____ he _____ executed the same.

_____
Notary Public

My commission expires_____

CORPORATE ACKNOWLEDGMENT

STATE OF _____⎫
                          ⎬ss:
COUNTY OF_____⎭

On the _____ day of _____19____, before me personally came _____

_____, who being by me duly sworn, did depose and say that he resides in _____

that he is the _____ of _____, the corporation described in and which executed the assignment on the

reverse side hereof; that he knows the seal of said corporation; that the seal affixed to said assignment is such corporate seal; that

it was so affixed by order of the Board of Directors of said corporation, and that he signed his name thereto by like order.

_____
Notary Public

My commission expires_____

• • • • •

Duplicate received and filed at the home office of the Insurer in _____, this_____ day of _____ 19____

_____

By_____
Authorized Officer

NOTE: When executed by a corporation, the corporate seal should be affixed and there should be attached to the assignment a certified copy of the resolution of the Board of Directors authorizing the signing officer to execute and deliver the assignment in the name and on behalf of the corporation.

AJAX LIFE INSURANCE COMPANY

NOTICE OF LIFE INSURANCE LAPSE
AND LATE REMITTANCE OFFER

POLICY NUMBER

DATE PAYMENT DUE

TOTAL AMOUNT TO REMIT $_____

To restore full protection
mail remittance before this late remittance offer expires _____

CONDITIONS FOR ACCEPTING LATE REMITTANCE WITHOUT PROOF OF INSURABILITY

The policy referred to above having terminated at expiration of the 31-day grace period, except as any Automatic Premium Loan or nonforfeiture provision may apply, this offer to accept a late remittance without requiring evidence of insurability is made subject to each of the following conditions:

1—OFFER IS FOR LIMITED PERIOD

The remittance must be post-marked on or before the date this Late Remittance offer expires. Checks and drafts will be accepted subject to collection only.

2—INSURED MUST BE ALIVE

Payment must be tendered BEFORE death of the Insured.

3—NOT A PRECEDENT

The voluntary offer to waive evidence of insurability is a special offer and is NOT to be considered a precedent.

4—GRACE PERIOD IS NOT EXTENDED

This offer is NOT an extension of the regular 31-day grace period, and does NOT continue the protection in force. If the payment is not made before death of the Insured occurs, the situation is the same as though the offer had not been made.

If advantage of this Late Remittance Offer cannot be taken before it expires, application for reinstatement may still be made thereafter by using the form on the other side of this Notice of Life Insurance Lapse.

Please
MAKE A QUICK CHECK
BEFORE LATE REMITTANCE OFFER EXPIRES

L-1157-3
(ADULT)

ADULT REINSTATEMENT APPLICATION
SUBMITTED IN CONNECTION WITH POLICY No._____
A written answer to each question is necessary—do not use check marks.

1. Are you now free from disease, in sound health, and without deformity, loss, or impairment of limb, sight, hearing, and speech? (*If not, explain fully*) ___ Yes or No

2. What is your present exact height and weight?

   _____feet_____inches_____pounds.

3. Since the date of original application applying for this policy:

   (a) Has there been any change in your weight? (*If so, give details and explain loss or gain*) ___ Yes or No

   (b) Are you now or have you been under any kind of treatment or on a restricted diet for any complaint or cause? (*If so, explain fully*) ___ Yes or No

   (c) Have you had any unusual and recurrent pain or discomfort in region of chest or abdomen which caused you to take any home remedy, patent medicine, or drug, or to seek the advice of a physician, either formally or informally? (*If so, explain fully*) ___ Yes or No

   (d) Has any medical examiner or physician expressed an unfavorable opinion as to your insurability or health? (*If so, explain fully*) ___ Yes or No

   (e) Has insurance applied for on your life been declined, postponed or modified in amount, plan or rate? (*If so, explain fully*) ___ Yes or No

   (f) Have you made any claim for sickness, accident, or pension benefits? (*If so, explain fully*) ___ Yes or No

4. To what extent do you use alcoholic beverages?

5. (a) What is your present occupation and what are the exact duties?

   (b) What is your employer's name and address?

6. Have you ever flown or do you contemplate flight in any kind of aircraft, as a pilot, crew member, or student pilot? (*If so, explain fully*) ___ Yes or No

7. Have you ever been exempted or discharged from service in the military, naval, or air forces of any country for physical or mental reasons? (*If so, explain fully*) ___ Yes or No

8. Are you now a member of the National Guard or of any other branch or reserve component of the armed forces of any country? (*If so, explain fully*) ___ Yes or No

9. Give names and addresses of the physicians you usually consult:

10. *To explain your answer to any question herein, give details in this space or in a separate letter.*

11. State below the particulars of **ALL** diseases, injuries, ailments, or surgical operations which you have had or for which you have been under treatment, observation, or diagnostic study since the date of original application applying for this policy.

Disease, Injury, Ailment, or Surgical Operation	Date—Month and Year	Complications	Duration and Date of Recovery	Remaining Effects	Medical Attendant's Name and Address

12. Has a physician, specialist or other practitioner been consulted by or for you, or have you been under medical care, since the date of original application applying for this policy, for any reason not stated above? ___ Yes or No (*If so, explain fully*)

All statements, answers, representations and agreements in this reinstatement application, and in the original application for the policy, are represented by me to be true and complete, and correctly recorded; and I further represent that no material circumstance or information has been withheld or omitted concerning my past and present state of health, habits of life and occupation; and on behalf of myself and any person who shall have or claim any interest in any and every policy which may be reinstated pursuant hereto, I understand and agree: (1) That this reinstatement application, any action hereon, or any lapse of time, shall not be considered to effect a reinstatement by waiver or estoppel, and that the company shall not be deemed to have approved reinstatement unless an official proper notice Notice of Reinstatement is issued; (2) and that no one except the president, a vice-president, the secretary, or an assistant secretary has the power on behalf of the company to make, modify, or discharge contracts or to waive any of the company's rights or requirements (and in writing only), and these powers will not be delegated.

Unless prohibited by law, I hereby expressly waive, on behalf of myself and any person who shall have or claim any interest in any and every policy which may be reinstated pursuant hereto, any rule or provision of law forbidding any physician, practitioner, nurse, hospital official or hospital employee, or other person who has attended, examined, or treated me, or who may hereafter attend, treat, or examine me, or any bureau, institution, or company which may have information concerning my health, from disclosing any such information or knowledge in court or elsewhere; and such physician or other person, institution, bureau, or company is expressly authorized to make such disclosures.

Dated this_____day of_____ 19____ at_____

_____   _____
Signature of Witness   Personal Signature of Applicant

Indexes

Index of Cases

Index

This book has been set on the Linotype in 10 point Caledonia, leaded 2 points. Chapter numbers are in 18 point Bulmer caps and 36 point Onyx roman numerals. Chapter titles are in 30 point Bulmer italic cap and lower case. The size of the type page is 27 by 45 picas.

Date Due